EIGHTH EDITION

Building a Dream

A Canadian Guide to Starting Your Own Business

Walter S. Good

University of Manitoba

McGraw-Hill Ryerson

Connect. Learn. Succeed.

The McGraw·Hill Companies

BUILDING A DREAM
A Canadian Guide to Starting Your Own Business
Eighth Edition

ISBN-13: 978-0-07-000019-3
ISBN-10: 0-07-000019-0

1 2 3 4 5 6 7 8 9 10 QDB 1 9 8 7 6 5 4 3 2 1

Printed and bound in the United States of America.

Vice president, Editor-in-Chief: Joanna Cotton
Executive Sponsoring Editor: Kim Brewster
Marketing Manager: Cathie Lefebvre
Developmental Editor: Lori McLellan
Senior Editorial Associate: Christine Lomas
Supervising Editor: Graeme Powell
Proofreader: Elaine Melnick
Production Coordinator: Emily Hickey
Cover Design: Katherine Strain
Cover Image: Fotosearch
Interior Design: Katherine Strain
Page Layout: Aptara®, Inc.
Printer: Quad Graphics

Library and Archives Canada Cataloguing in Publication
Good, Walter S.
    Building a dream: a Canadian guide to starting your own business / Walter S. Good. — 8th ed.

Includes bibliographical references and index.
ISBN 978-0-07-000019-3

1. New business enterprises — Textbooks.   2. Entrepreneurship — Textbooks.   3. New business enterprises — Canada — Textbooks.   4. Entrepreneurship — Canada — Textbooks. — I. Title.

HD62.5.G66 2011   658.1'1   C2010-905568-3

Brief Contents

PREFACE   vi

STAGE ONE: What Is Entrepreneurship?   2

STAGE TWO: Assessing Your Potential for an Entrepreneurial Career   14

STAGE THREE: Exploring New Business Ideas and Opportunities   50

STAGE FOUR: Buying a Business   90

STAGE FIVE: Considering a Franchise   126

STAGE SIX: Organizing Your Business   158

STAGE SEVEN: Conducting a Feasibility Study   180
    Part 1: Technical and Market Assessment

STAGE EIGHT: Conducting a Feasibility Study   242
    Part 2: Cost and Profitability Assessment

STAGE NINE: Protecting Your Idea   272

STAGE TEN: Arranging Financing   288

STAGE ELEVEN: Preparing Your Business Plan   318

CLEANAIR TECHNOLOGIES INC. BUSINESS PLAN   345

LITE BITES GRILL BUSINESS PLAN   369

LIST OF WEB SITES REFERENCED IN *BUILDING A DREAM*   403

GLOSSARY OF FINANCIAL TERMS   410

INDEX   413

Contents

PREFACE   vi

STAGE ONE: What Is Entrepreneurship?   2

What Is Entrepreneurship?   4
The Entrepreneurial Process   7
Myths and Realities Concerning Entrepreneurship   10

STAGE TWO: Assessing Your Potential for an Entrepreneurial Career   14

The Entrepreneurial Personality   14
  Entrepreneurial Quiz   14
  Personal Self-Assessment   21
  What Kind of Entrepreneur Are You Likely to Be?   22
Evaluating Your Business Skills   23
  What Skills Are Needed by Small Business Owners?   25
Inventory of Your Managerial and Administrative Skills   25
  Where Can You Acquire the Necessary Skills?   26
Assessing Your Personal Financial Situation   27
  Your Personal Balance Sheet   27
  Developing a Personal Budget   28
  Check Your Credit Rating   28
Are You Ready for an Entrepreneurial Career?   28
  External Role Demands   28
The Concept of Social Entrepreneurship   29
Dealing with the Ethical Challenge   31
Being Socially Responsible   35
  A Final Analysis   35

STAGE THREE: Exploring New Business Ideas and Opportunities   50

Long-Term Expectations for Your Business   55
  Lifestyle Ventures   55
  Small, Profitable Ventures   55
  High-Growth Ventures   56
Sources of Ideas for a New Business   56
  Previous Employment   56
  Your Hobbies   59
  Personal Observation   60
  Magazines and Other Publications   64
  Trade Shows and Conventions   65
  Product Licensing Information Services   65
  Friends, Acquaintances, and Other Social Contacts   66
  Government Agencies and Departments   66
  Use Creative Thinking   66
  Where do New Venture Ideas Actually Come From?   69
Areas of Future Opportunity   70
Some Specific Ideas and Concepts for the Future   72
Evaluating Your Ideas   77
The Venture Opportunity Screening Model   82
Deciding How to Proceed   86
  Buy a Business   86
  Acquire a Franchise   87
  Start a Business of Your Own   87

STAGE FOUR: Buying a Business   90

Advantages and Disadvantages of Buying an Existing Business   90
  Reasons for Buying an Established Business   90
  Disadvantages of Buying an Established Business   90
How to Find the Right Business to Buy   92
Important Factors to Consider   94
  Why Is the Business for Sale?   94
  Financial Factors   94
  Marketing Considerations   102
  Human Factors   102
  Other Concerns   103
How to Determine an Appropriate Price to Pay for a Business   104
  Balance Sheet Methods   105
  Income Statement Methods   106
  Rule-of-Thumb Approaches   109
What to Buy — Assets or Shares?   111
Financing the Purchase   113
A Word of Warning   113
Striking a Deal   114
Taking Over a Family Business   115
  The Question of Succession   116
  Grooming an Heir   118
  Family Acceptance of the Plan   118
  The Use of Outside Assistance   118
  How Can You Prepare for Running the Family Business?   118
Checklist for a Business Acquisition   121

STAGE FIVE: Considering a Franchise   126

An Introduction to Franchising   126
  What Is Franchising?   126
  Advantages of Franchising   128
  Disadvantages of Franchising   128
Types of Franchises   132
  Franchise Formats   132
  Range of Available Franchises   132
  Canadian Legislation and Disclosure Requirements   133
  The Franchise Agreement   134
Buying a Franchise   141
  Finding a Franchise Business   141
  Checking Out the Franchise Oportunity   141
  Franchise Financing   143
  Franchise Your Business   144
Future Trends in Franchising   149
Evaluating a Franchise — A Checklist   150

STAGE SIX: Organizing Your Business   158

Individual or Sole Proprietorship   158
  Advantages of Sole Proprietorship   158
  Disadvantages of Sole Proprietorship   159
Partnership   160

General Partnership   160
Limited Partnership   162
Limited Liability Partnership   163
Corporation   163
Advantages of a Corporation   164
Disadvantages of a Corporation   164
Co-operatives   165
Advantages of a Co-operative   167
Disadvantages of a Co-operative   167
Getting into Business   167
Registration and Incorporation — Making
It Legal   167
Choosing a Name   169
Obtaining a Business Licence   172
Mandatory Deductions and Taxes   174
Employment Standards   175
Risk Management   175
Conclusion   178

STAGE SEVEN: Conducting a Feasibility Study   180

Part 1: Technical and Market Assessment

Your Venture Concept   180
Technical Feasibility   182
Market Assessment   184
Who Is Your Customer?   185
Estimating Total Market Size and Trends   198
Your Competitive Strategy   200
Developing a Sales Forecast   201
Fleshing Out Your Marketing Program   209
Developing a Preliminary Marketing Plan   216
Managing the Supply Situation   218

STAGE EIGHT: Conducting a Feasibility Study   242

Part 2: Cost and Profitablility Assessment

Determine Your Start-Up Financial
Requirements   242
Develop Short-Term Financial Projections   245
Pro Forma Income Statement   245
Forecast Your Cash Flow   248
Developing Your Cash Flow Statement   253
Pro Forma Balance Sheet   254
Determine Your Break-Even Point   256
Conduct a Comprehensive Feasibility Study   261

STAGE NINE: Protecting Your Idea   272

Applying for a Patent   272
How to Apply   272
Protection Provided by Your Patent   274
Registering Your Trademark   281
How to Register Your Trademark   281
Maintaining and Policing Your Trademark   282
Obtaining Copyright   283
How to Obtain a Copyright   284
Protection Provided by Copyright   284
Registering Your Industrial Design   284
How to Register Your Industrial Design   284

Protection Provided by Industrial Design
Registration   285
Protecting Integrated Circuit Topographies   285
What Protection Does the Act Provide?   285
How to Protect an IC Topography   285
Use of a Nondisclosure Agreement (NDA)   286
Trade Secrets   286
For More Information on Intellectual Property   286
Conclusion   287

STAGE TEN: Arranging Financing   288

Debt Financing   288
Equity Financing   289
Major Sources of Funds   290
Personal Funds   291
Bootstrapping   291
"Love Money"   293
Banks, Trust Companies, Credit Unions, and Similar
Institutions   297
Federal Government Financial Assistance
Programs   297
Provincial Government Financial Assistance
Programs   300
Venture Capital   302
Angel Investors   305
What's on the Table?   307
Additional Sources of Financing   308
Evaluating Your Ability to Secure Financing   312

STAGE ELEVEN: Preparing Your Business Plan   318

Business Planning — The "Big Picture"   318
Why Consider the "Big Picture"?   318
The Steps in the Business Planning Process   318
Why Develop a Business Plan?   321
How Long Should Your Business Plan Be?   323
Who Should Write Your Business Plan?   325
How Long Does It Take?   325
What Should Your Plan Contain?   326
1. Letter of Transmittal   326
2. Title Page   326
3. Table of Contents   326
4. Executive Summary and Fact Sheet   326
5. Body of the Plan   329
6. Appendices   335
Conclusion   337

CLEANAIR TECHNOLOGIES INC. BUSINESS PLAN   345

LITE BITES GRILL BUSINESS PLAN   369

LIST OF WEB SITES REFERENCED IN *BUILDING A DREAM*   403

GLOSSARY OF FINANCIAL TERMS   410

INDEX   413

Preface

ABOUT THIS BOOK

This self-help guide and workbook is intended to provide a vehicle to lead prospective small-business owners and potential entrepreneurs through the conceptual stages involved in setting up a business of their own in a logical and sequential way.

Many people fantasize about being self-employed and having a business of their own at some stage in their lives. For most, this dream never becomes a reality. They don't really know the risks involved and feel very uncomfortable with the uncertainty associated with taking the initial step. In addition, they don't entirely understand the tasks required to get a new business venture off the ground successfully.

For the past decade or so, the number of people who have started their own business has increased dramatically across North America. People's level of interest in and awareness of the entrepreneurial option has virtually exploded. This has been fostered and reinforced by governments at all levels, who have come to recognize the positive impact small-business start-ups have on job creation and regional economic development. Business magazines, the popular press, and radio and television have also fuelled this interest with numerous items on the emotional and financial rewards of having a business of your own. They have glamorized the role of entrepreneurs in our society, and established many of them, such as Ted Rogers of Rogers Communications Inc.; Christine Magee of Sleep Country Canada; Jim Balsillie and Mike Lazaridis of Research in Motion; Heather Reisman of Indigo Books & Music Inc.; Peter Nygard of Nygard International Ltd.; Bobby Julien of Kolter Property Co.; and Ron Joyce of Tim Hortons as attractive role models. This has been accentuated over the past few years with the phenomenal success and, in some cases, subsequent failure of many Internet-based companies. However, some businesses like Google, Yahoo! and eBay have made a number of young entrepreneurs such as Jerry Yang, Jeff Skoll, Dave Filo, and Pierre Omidyar as well as many of their employees multi-millionaires or even billionaires within a very short period of time.

STRUCTURE

Building a Dream has been written for individuals who wish to start a business of their own or want to assess their own potential for such an option. This includes all men and women who dream of some type of self-employment, on either a full-time or a part-time basis. This book contains a comprehensive overall framework outlining the entrepreneurial process, descriptive information, practical outlines, checklists, screening questionnaires, and various other tools that will enable you to evaluate your own potential for this type of career and guide you through the early stages of launching a successful business of your own.

This book covers a range of topics that will increase your understanding of what it takes to succeed in an entrepreneurial career. From an overview of entrepreneurship and the entrepreneurial process, the book spreads outward to consider the skills, personality, and character traits possessed by many successful entrepreneurs, how to find and evaluate a possible idea for a business, buy an existing firm, or acquire a franchise. It provides a comprehensive outline for conducting a feasibility study to evaluate the potential of your concept and discusses the ways you can carry on your business, protect your product or service concept or idea, and find the financing necessary to get your new business off the ground. It concludes with a comprehensive framework for preparing a detailed and professional business plan.

PEDAGOGICAL DEVICES TO AID LEARNING

Building a Dream is divided into "Stages," each of which provides a descriptive overview of a topic, some conceptual material indicating the principal areas to be considered or evaluated, and a series of outlines, worksheets, checklists, and other forms that can be completed in conducting a comprehensive assessment of that stage in the new venture development process.

The **"Other Considerations"** boxes highlight some additional material that is directly related to that stage.

Other considerations — **WHY BECOME AN ENTREPRENEUR?**

PROFIT magazine asked a number of successful entrepreneurs, "What do you love about being an entrepreneur?" Here are a few of their responses.

The **"FYI"** (For Your Information) boxes refer you to a number of Web sites that have supplementary material specifically related to the topics discussed in that Stage. This enables you to readily obtain further information on subjects that may be of particular interest.

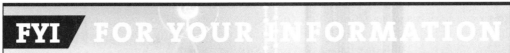

FYI / FOR YOUR INFORMATION

With the ever-increasing popularity of e-business, here are a few Web sites you might want to check out for more information on doing business on the Internet:

E-Business Info-Guide A document designed to help you navigate through the different government programs, services, and regulations that deal with electronic commerce, and identify those of interest.

This eighth edition also contains an increased number of **"Entrepreneurs in Action"** examples illustrating how people are actually going about building their businesses and trying to make things work for them on a day-to-day basis.

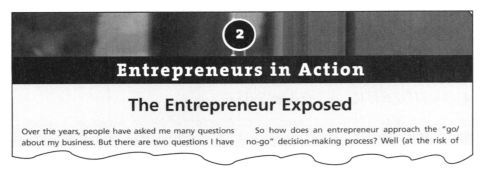

2

Entrepreneurs in Action

The Entrepreneur Exposed

Over the years, people have asked me many questions about my business. But there are two questions I have

So how does an entrepreneur approach the "go/no-go" decision-making process? Well (at the risk of

Figures and tables are included to illustrate relevant ideas and concepts.

FIGURE 2.1	**ENTREPRENEURIAL QUIZ**

Below are a number of questions dealing with your personal background, behavioural characteristics, and lifestyle patterns. Psychologists, venture capitalists, and others believe these to be related to entrepreneurial success. Answer each question by placing an "X" in the space that best reflects your personal views and attitudes. The most important result of this exercise will be an honest, accurate self-assessment of how you relate to each of these dimensions.

Rarely or no   Mostly or yes

Overall the book will provide a practical opportunity for you to realistically assess the potential opportunity for your concept or idea and enable you to develop a detailed program or plan for your own new venture.

ORGANIZATION

STAGE ONE: WHAT IS ENTREPRENEURSHIP?

This Stage introduces you to the concept of entrepreneurship and provides an overview of the other elements that are required to launch a successful new business venture: a viable business idea or opportunity, an organization, resources, a strategy, and a business plan. It also discusses some of the myths and stereotypes that have evolved over time about entrepreneurs and entrepreneurship.

STAGE TWO: ASSESSING YOUR POTENTIAL FOR AN ENTREPRENEURIAL CAREER

This Stage provides you with an opportunity to assess your personal attitudes and attributes and to see how they compare with those of "practicing" entrepreneurs. It will also enable you to evaluate your managerial and administrative skills and experience and determine your financial capacity for starting a business. The importance of conducting your business affairs in an ethical manner is also emphasized, and an example of a code of ethics developed by a small organization is provided for your information and guidance.

STAGE THREE: EXPLORING NEW BUSINESS IDEAS AND OPPORTUNITIES

This Stage describes several sources from which you might obtain ideas for your prospective new venture and identifies a number of areas of opportunity for the future on the basis of dynamic changes now taking place within Canadian society. It also outlines a six-step opportunity selection process, describes the characteristics of an "ideal" or "model" business, and presents a framework for assessing the attributes of your product or service idea in comparison to this ideal. Stage Three also discusses the Venture Opportunity Screening Model (VOSM) for identifying entrepreneurial opportunities on the basis of a series of criteria identified by actual entrepreneurs as being important in their venture selection process. A number of entry strategies are outlined as well that can help you decide on the best way to proceed.

STAGE FOUR: BUYING A BUSINESS

The obvious route to self-employment is to start a business of your own based on a new or distinctive idea. Another route to explore is the possibility of buying an existing firm. This Stage deals with such issues as finding a business to buy and the factors to consider in making the acquisition. It also discusses a number of ways to determine an appropriate price to pay for a business and the pros and cons of buying versus starting one. A comprehensive checklist is provided for considering a number of potential business acquisitions.

We also discuss some of the issues involved in working in a family business — a situation that has some unique opportunities and risks, and can become very complicated. Planning for succession is typically the most important issue, so it is critical that the business have a viable succession plan in place.

STAGE FIVE: CONSIDERING A FRANCHISE

In recent years franchising has been one of the fastest-growing sectors of North American business. More and more people are considering the franchise alternative as a means of getting into business for themselves. This Stage explores the concept of franchising in some detail. It defines franchising so that you know exactly what the concept means. The broad range of types of franchises available is presented, along with an overview of the legal requirements associated with franchising and the terms and conditions contained in a typical franchise agreement. This Stage also discusses how to find and apply for a franchise as well as some guidance on franchising your own business. It presents an extensive checklist for evaluating potential franchise opportunities.

STAGE SIX: ORGANIZING YOUR BUSINESS

One of the principal issues to be resolved when starting a new business is the legal form of organization the business should adopt. The most prevalent forms a business might assume include individual or sole proprietorship, general or limited partnership, and incorporation. This Stage reviews each of these forms and discusses the advantages and disadvantages of each from the standpoint of the prospective entrepreneur. It discusses how to select and register a name for your business and presents an overview of such issues as the types of licences and permits your business might require, your responsibilities for collecting and remitting a variety of employee contributions and taxes, the impact of provincial employment standards on your business, and protecting your investment.

STAGES SEVEN AND EIGHT: CONDUCTING A FEASIBILITY STUDY — PARTS 1 AND 2

Stages Seven and Eight provide a step-by-step process for transforming your chosen new venture concept from the idea stage to the marketplace. This is accomplished by means of a feasibility study. A typical feasibility study considers the following areas:

- The concept of your proposed venture
- The technical feasibility of your idea
- A detailed assessment of your market potential
- Managing the supply situation
- Conducting a cost and profitability assessment
- Your plans for future action

Comprehensive outlines are provided to enable you to assess each of these areas in a preliminary way and to put your thoughts and ideas down on paper. Much of this material can be incorporated into your subsequent business plan.

STAGE NINE: PROTECTING YOUR IDEA

Many entrepreneurs are also innovators and inventors, and are faced with the problem of how to protect the idea, invention, concept, system, name, or design that they feel will be the key to their business success. This

Stage discusses the various forms of intellectual property such as patents, copyrights, trademarks, and industrial design, and what is required to protect your interest in their development. It is also suggested that you be wary of organizations that offer to help you patent your idea and market it for you. Many of these offers are outright scams and should be avoided.

STAGE TEN: ARRANGING FINANCING

The principal question relating to any new venture is where the money is going to come from to get the new business off the ground. This Stage examines the major sources of funds for new business start-ups — personal funds, "love money," boot-strapping, bank loans, government agencies and programs, and venture capital. It also discusses the main issues that need to be addressed when looking to raise capital from private sources. A framework for you to determine just how much money you think you will need to launch your business and where that financing might possibly come from is provided as well.

STAGE ELEVEN: PREPARING YOUR BUSINESS PLAN

This Stage, which serves as a capstone for the book, provides a framework for the development of a comprehensive business plan for your proposed new business venture, whether it is a retail or service business or a manufacturing company. It lays out the necessary steps in the business planning process such as:

- Developing a vision statement
- Formulating a mission statement
- Defining the fundamental values by which you will run your business
- Setting clear and specific objectives
- Developing a realistic business plan

It also explains what a business plan is, how long it should be, and why it is important that you develop such a plan for your proposed venture and actually write it yourself. It lays out the contents of a typical business plan and provides an outline to follow for developing your plan.

This Stage also contains two examples of completed business plans. Lite Bites Grill is an example of a relatively simple business plan for an exciting new restaurant concept to provide healthy and nutritional meals in a fast-food-type environment. CleanAir Technologies Inc. is a more technical plan to manufacture and market specially grooved wall panels and an active dehumidification system designed to remove moisture from interior basement walls and prevent mould.

This section is followed by a glossary of financial terms as well as a summary listing of all the Web sites referenced in the book so that you can readily access the source of much of the material referred to in the book without having to flip through all the pages to find it.

Following the framework outlined in *Building a Dream* will give you hands-on, practical experience with the entire new venture development process and enable you to come up with a comprehensive plan for a proposed venture of your own selection. This plan will not only give you a better understanding of the potential opportunity and success requirements of your new venture idea, but also put you in a much stronger position to attract the necessary external resources and support to get your proposed business off the ground.

Good luck in successfully building your dream.

INSTRUCTOR AND STUDENT SUPPORT

INTEGRATED LEARNING SYSTEM

Great care was used in the creation of the supplemental materials to accompany *Building a Dream*, Eighth Edition. Whether you are a seasoned faculty member or a newly minted instructor, you will find the support materials to be comprehensive and practical.

CBC VIDEOS

CBC video segments are available from the Online Learning Centre. They are an excellent supplement to lectures and useful for generating in-class discussion.

INSTRUCTOR AND STUDENT SUPPORT

Great care was used in the creation of the supplemental materials to accompany *Building a Dream,* Eighth Edition. Whether you are a seasoned faculty member or a newly minted instructor, you will find the support materials to be comprehensive and practical. This online learning centre, found at **www.mcgrawhill.ca/olc/good**, is a text Web site that follows the text material chapter by chapter. Students will find supplementary material for chapter content. Instructors will find downloadable supplements.

The Building a Dream student Online Learning Centre (OLC) Web site provides a number of additional resources to enhance the textbook and the classroom experience for students:

FINANCIAL TEMPLATES Students have access to Microsoft® Excel® financial templates to help them analyze the financial aspects of their new business ideas. These templates also facilitate preparation of financial statements required for their feasibility study in Stage Eight and their overall business plan preparation in Stage Eleven. Accompanying the spreadsheets is a step-by-step guide to using the financial schedules.

ONLINE VERSION OF WORKSHEETS The OLC contains online versions of most of the worksheets found at the end of each Stage. The student can complete each of these worksheets on the computer rather than having to make copies and complete them by hand.

SAMPLE BUSINESS PLANS In addition to the two sample business plans provided in the textbook, the students will find examples of two other business plans on the OLC to further assist them in preparing a business plan for a venture.

VENTURE CHALLENGE EXERCISES The Student OLC also contains copies of the Venture Challenge Exercises found on the Instructor's OLC.

GUIDE TO EFFECTIVE BUSINESS PLAN PRESENTATIONS The OLC provides a guide on how to structure, prepare, and deliver effective business plan presentations.

INSTRUCTOR'S MANUAL The Instructor's Manual, prepared by the author, includes a wealth of information to assist instructors in presenting this text and their course to its best advantage. It includes:

- An additional presentation that focuses on the preparation of a business plan
- Typical outlines for a course in New Venture Development
- Venture Challenges Exercises that can be incorporated into a New Venture course
- Discussion questions and corresponding answers for each of the CBC videos
- Details of Web sites where further information can be obtained

MICROSOFT® POWERPOINT® PRESENTATIONS A complete set of PowerPoint® Presentation slides is provided for each chapter. The presentations are based around the learning goals and include many of the figures and tables from the textbook as well as some additional slides that support and expand the text discussions. Slides can be modified by instructors.

NEW BUSINESS MENTOR

For instructors who incorporate a business plan project into their class, the New Business Mentor software can be bundled with student textbooks and includes sample business plans, resources to help you as you start your business, a business planning and feasibility planning software, and the "mentor" who will walk you through each step of the business plan. Teaching notes are available.

WebCT/BLACKBOARD

This text is available in two of the most popular course-delivery platforms — WebCT and BlackBoard — for more user-friendly and enhanced features. Contact your local McGraw-Hill Ryerson *i*Learning Specialist for more information.

*i*LEARNING SALES SPECIALIST

Your Integrated Learning Sales Specialist is a McGraw-Hill Ryerson representative who has the experience, product knowledge, training, and support to help you assess and integrate any of the above-noted products, technology, and services into your course for optimum teaching and learning performance. Whether it's how to use our test bank software, helping your students improve their grades, or how to put your entire course online, your *i*Learning Sales Specialist is there to help. Contact your local iLearning Sales Specialist today to learn how to maximize all of McGraw-Hill Ryerson's resources!

*i*LEARNING SERVICES PROGRAM

McGraw-Hill Ryerson offers a unique *i*Services package designed for Canadian faculty. Our mission is to equip providers of higher education with superior tools and resources required for excellence in teaching. For additional information, visit www.mcgrawhill.ca/highereducation/iservices.

McGRAW-HILL RYERSON'S NATIONAL TEACHING AND LEARNING CONFERENCE SERIES

The educational environment has changed tremendously in recent years, and McGraw-Hill Ryerson continues to be committed to helping you acquire the skills you need to succeed in this new milieu. Our innovative Teaching and Learning Conferences Series brings faculty from across Canada together with 3M Teaching Excellence award winners to share teaching and learning best practices in a collaborative and stimulating environment. Pre-conference workshops on general topics, such as teaching large classes and technology integration, will also be offered. We will also work with you at your own institution to customize workshops that best suit the needs of your faculty at your institution.

ACKNOWLEDGEMENTS

Developing a workbook of this type can be accomplished only with the co-operation and support of a great many people. Much of the material would not have been developed without the assistance of Steve Tax of the University of Victoria, who was largely responsible for many of the ideas that were incorporated into the first edition and have been carried forward to the current one. I am also indebted to David Milstein of David Milstein & Associates of Brisbane, Australia, for contributing the material on the "Big Picture" of strategic planning and to Vance Gough of Mount Royal College for the exercise on creative thinking. My appreciation also goes to Carole Babiak whose organizational and word processing skills enabled me to keep the material moving during the revision process.

Very comprehensive suggestions for changes and improvements based on the previous edition and drafts of this edition were received from numerous professors across the country, including:

- Bob Walpole, Canadore College
- Larry Drew, Conestoga College
- Vic De Witt, Red River College
- Alan Andron, Lethbridge College
- Ike Hall, British Columbia Institute of Technology
- Bryan Mackay, Confederation College
- Don Haidey, Mount Royal College
- Jeff Zakoor, Durham College
- Barbara Rice, Conestoga College
- Reid MacWilliam, Mohawk College

Their comments were very helpful in improving and refining the concept of the book to make it even more useful to students and prospective entrrepreneurs.

My appreciation also goes to Kim Brewster, executive sponsoring editor; Lori McLellan, developmental editor; and my proofreader, Elaine Melnick, for keeping me on track.

I would also like to thank Moe Levy of the Asper Foundation and Shannon Coughlan of the Canada/Manitoba Business Service Centre for their comments on several components of the book and their encouragement during the early stages of the development of the concept behind the workbook. Special thanks go to Dean Beleyowski for his assistance in compiling many of the Web sites and much of the other supplementary material included in this book. The belief of these individuals in entrepreneurship as a vehicle for successful economic development in Canada and their faith in the premise of the self-help concept may finally pay off.

Finally, I would like to thank the college and university students and others who have used the earlier editions of this book over the years and have gone on to start new business ventures of their own. Their insatiable desire to explore their personal capacity for an entrepreneurial career and their drive to explore the mysteries of franchising, venture capital, and similar topics associated with the formation of a successful new business has enabled many of them to build their dream. I hope all of us have been able to play a small part in that process.

What Is Entrepreneurship?

In 2007 Murray Hugel left a secure job with a Regina-based manufacturing company to start his own business making gasoline and diesel fuel storage tanks for agricultural and commercial purposes. This was not a decision he made lightly, but represented a dream he had held for the past 20 years. He had felt he was ready to make this jump for a number of years, but just didn't know what kind of product or service he could build his business around. However, he was committed in his own mind that somehow he was going to make the decision in 2006, and when he recognized the need in the rapidly growing oil and gas industry for metal fuel storage tanks, that provided the opportunity for him to make the move. Hugel had done his homework. He had found a business idea that built upon his background as an industrial engineer. He researched business strategy and practices on the Internet. He prepared a business plan so that when he approached the local bank to fund his dream they would be impressed. That foresight and his commitment to the role enabled him to go from having nothing to shipping his first product to market in only three weeks.

Murray Hugel and other Canadians like him are starting businesses of their own more frequently than ever before. Of the more than 2.3 million businesses in Canada, almost 98% are considered "small".[1] Every year more than 130,000 other Canadians join this number by initiating new start-ups, principally in the construction, retail, and business services sectors. This has led to a major entrepreneurial revolution across the country and caused the small business sector of the economy to become more widely acknowledged by all levels of government, the chartered banks and other financial institutions, and secondary and post-secondary educational institutions.

While the Canadian business start-up numbers are impressive, they do not put Canada at the top in terms of the most entrepreneurial countries in the world. A recent report from an ongoing study titled the *Global Entrepreneurship Monitor (GEM)* ranked Canada 22nd in the world in terms of the percentage of the population between 18–64 involved in early-stage entrepreneurial activity, behind such other developed countries as Australia, Norway, the USA, Argentina, and Spain but ahead of Sweden, Germany, France, and Finland.[2]

The overall economic impact of this revolution on Canada is difficult to determine precisely, but it is substantial and suspected to drive longer-term growth. It is being fuelled by such factors as:

- Structural changes in the economy, such as organizational downsizing or "rightsizing," with the consequent loss of middle-management positions in many larger companies and government departments; this has led to considerable outsourcing of services previously performed in-house and the growth of self-employment to meet this need

- Younger Canadians wanting more independence and so becoming more interested in self-employment

- A growing number of immigrants who have difficulty with conventional employment because of their limited skills and/or language issues or whose academic credentials are not recognized in Canada

- An aging population and a large number of baby boomers reaching their fifties, an age when people often tend to look toward self-employment

- Increasing consumer demand for more personalized products and services that smaller companies are often better positioned to provide

1. Industry Canada, Small Business and Tourism Branch, *Key Small Business Statistics,* July 2009, p. 9-10.
2. Global Entrepreneurship Monitor, *GEM 2006 Summary Results*, p. 7 (www.gemconsortium.org/about.aspx?page=global_reports_2006), accessed April 26, 2010.

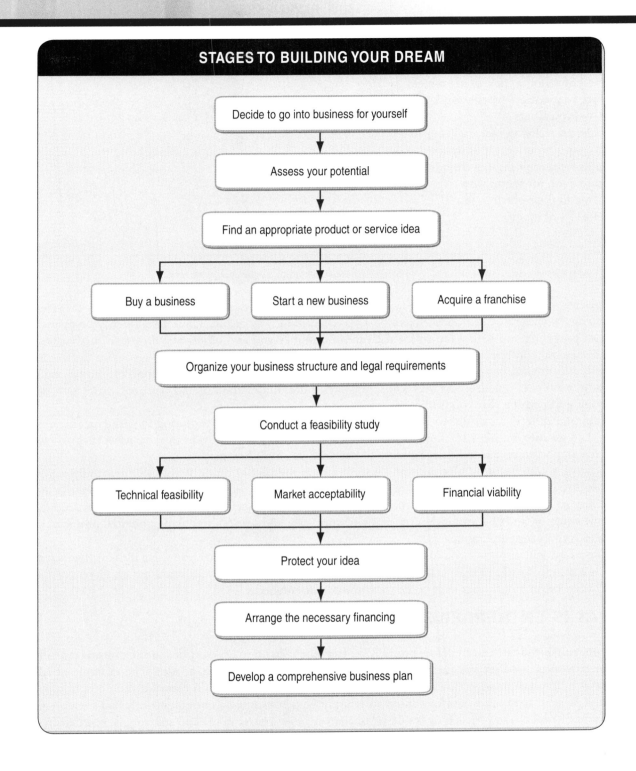

STAGES TO BUILDING YOUR DREAM

Decide to go into business for yourself

↓

Assess your potential

↓

Find an appropriate product or service idea

↓

Buy a business   Start a new business   Acquire a franchise

↓

Organize your business structure and legal requirements

↓

Conduct a feasibility study

↓

Technical feasibility   Market acceptability   Financial viability

↓

Protect your idea

↓

Arrange the necessary financing

↓

Develop a comprehensive business plan

The entrepreneurial revolution has also been propelled by the explosion of the Internet and technology-based companies and the publicity surrounding the creation of many so-called "dot-com millionaires," although this bubble has largely burst. One thing that is clear, however, is that the proportion of total employment in the country accounted for by these smaller firms has increased dramatically. They have created the lion's share of new jobs, while employment levels in large businesses have remained constant or decreased.

This book has been developed for people who may be aspiring entrepreneurs and are giving some thought to the possibility of joining the many others who have started some kind of business of their own. Most of us

TABLE 1.1	WHY CANADIANS START BUSINESSES	
To seize an opportunity		17%
To achieve a sense of personal accomplishment		13%
Dreamed of running their own business		9%
A chance to use their experience/skills		9%
To be their own boss		8%
Economic necessity; to make a living		7%
Had previous experience they wished to use		7%
To supplement their income from other employment		5%
To create a job for themselves		4%
Frustrated in their previous job		3%
To make lots of money		3%
Other reasons		15%

Source: Canada Business Service Centre (www.cbsc.org/alberta/tbl.cfm?fn=cutout&pf=1), accessed August 18, 2004.

have given some thought to owning and managing our own business at some point in our lives. Provided you know what it takes to be successful, it can be a very rewarding way of life. These rewards may be financial, in terms of providing you with a return for the time and money you and others may invest in the business and the risks you take in operating your own firm. Having an independent business also gives you the freedom to act independently, make your own decisions, and be your own boss. This is a very important motivating factor for many people. It can also be a very satisfying way of life, full of the fun and personal satisfaction derived from doing something that you genuinely love to do.

Table 1.1 reflects the results of a survey of Canadian business owners, exploring the principal reasons they decided to go into business for themselves. The primary considerations were to seize what they felt was an attractive opportunity and to achieve a sense of personal accomplishment.

Starting a new business, however, can be very risky at the best of times. It typically demands long hours, hard work, a high level of emotional involvement and commitment, as well as significant financial risk and the possibility of failure. Your chances of succeeding will rise if you spend some time carefully evaluating your personal situation and circumstances and trying to anticipate and work out as many potential problems as you can before you invest any money.

Stage One will introduce you to the concept of entrepreneurship and give you some idea of what is required to be successful. It will also discuss some of the folklore and stereotypes that exist around entrepreneurship and dispel a few of the myths that have come to surround entrepreneurs.

WHAT IS ENTREPRENEURSHIP?

Entrepreneurship is difficult to define precisely. Entrepreneurs tend to be identified, not by formal rank or title, but in retrospect — after the successful implementation of an innovation or idea. The example of Murray Hugel in Entrepreneurs in Action #1 may help to illustrate this definition problem for you.

It is difficult to say at what exact moment Murray Hugel became an entrepreneur. It had been a personal dream for 20 years largely fuelled by his desire to chart his own course in life and control his own destiny. Why it took him so long to realize his dream is hard to say, other than he didn't feel he had found the right business concept or idea for him. He hadn't felt that other notions he had considered represented a real entrepreneurial opportunity *for him*. But once the decision to go ahead with his own business was made, things came together in a hurry. Now Murray appears to be well on his way to building a very successful venture.

For some people, like Murray Hugel, giving up a secure job to start a business of their own is a conscious and deliberate career choice. For others, there may be some kind of significant *triggering* event. Perhaps these individuals had no better career prospects than starting businesses of their own. Sometimes the individual has received an inheritance or otherwise come into some money, moved to a new geographic location, been passed over for a promotion, taken an early retirement, or been laid off or fired from a regular job. Any of these factors can give birth to a new business.

Entrepreneurs in Action

Entrepreneur has drive, goals

If starting your own business is your dream, you need to follow Murray Hugel's lead.

Hugel's drive to be a small business owner has made him a success in just four short months in operation.

"The idea of doing something on my own has been something that has been in my mind for a long time," Hugel said of his 20-year-old goal of becoming a business owner. "I use the old adage, 'If you control your own destiny, somebody else can't control it for you.'

"I wanted to be able to chart my own course without any boundaries and limits," he continued.

"And a lot of times when you're working for somebody else, there's always limits. With this enterprise I've got, there's no limits and I'm working from that point and that's a lot more exciting."

Hugel started Huge L Steel roughly four months ago. He went from nothing — no building, no equipment, no employees — to shipping his first product in just 21 days and he hasn't looked back.

"That's what really impressed a lot of people," he said. "So we really had our (stuff) together and we knew what we were doing. I'd like to see somebody else do it that quickly. I'm very proud of that."

Huge L Steel manufactures gasoline and diesel fuel storage tanks for agricultural and commercial use. ...

Hugel, who was trained as an industrial systems engineer, has been ready to be a businessman for some time, but he wasn't sure what product he would build his business around until recently when he recognized a need in the oil and gas industry for the product.

"While I didn't really know what product I was going to work with, I knew I was going into business in 2006," he said.

"I didn't really know how I was going to do it, but that was driving me, 'I'm just going to do it.'"

Hugel researched business practices and strategies on the Internet so he would be ready when he found the right product.

"The Internet is just an amazing tool for that because I would even just click in 'entrepreneur' and I would read stories about how other people took the plunge and stuff," he said.

And that research paid off. After 20 years working in the local manufacturing industry, he easily convinced his bank to finance his dream company.

"Murray is very driven. We believed in him the second he walked through the door," said Catherine Vanderzwan, an account manager for small business for a Regina branch of Scotiabank. . . .

"It's not like he's a florist deciding to be a manufacturer. It was in keeping with what he's done, what his experience is," said Vanderzwan of Hugel's successful start. "I think someone might have a hard time if they were trying to develop those experiences at the same time."

Source: David Freeman, *The Leader-Post* (Regina), October 23, 2006. Used with permission.

The word "entrepreneur" is of French origin, derived from the term "entreprendre," literally translated as "between-taking." This term describes the activities by which an individual takes a position between available resources and perceived opportunities and, because of some unique behaviour, makes something positive happen. One of the first uses of the word was in the late 1700s by economist Jean-Baptiste Say, who is credited with developing the concept of "entrepreneurship."

Over time many other formal definitions of the term "entrepreneur" have emerged. Many of these modern definitions incorporate the notions of "risk taking" and "innovation," as well as the elements put forward by Say. For example, the *Fast Times Political Dictionary* defines an entrepreneur as *someone who sets up a new business undertaking, raises the money necessary, and organizes production and appoints the management. The entrepreneur bears the financial risk involved, in the hope that the business will succeed and make a profit.*[3]

Other definitions are quite simple, such as *an individual who starts his/her own business.*[4]

Perhaps one of the most straightforward definitions is that an entrepreneur is *someone who perceives an opportunity and creates an organization to pursue it.*[5]

Many people have said that entrepreneurship is really a "state of mind." Though you may be extremely innovative and creative, prepared to work hard, and willing to rely on a great deal of luck, these qualities may still be insufficient to guarantee business success. The missing element may be a necessary entrepreneurial mindset: a single-mindedness and dedication to the achievement of a set of personal goals and objectives; confidence in your intuitive and rational capabilities; a capacity to think and plan in both tactical and strategic terms; and an attitude that reflects a penchant for action, frequently in situations in which information is inadequate.

Hugel, for example, associates entrepreneurship with "freedom," the capacity to act and control your own destiny without any boundaries or limits, unlike working for someone else. He feels being on his own gives him this freedom to achieve whatever *he* is able to accomplish with his own capabilities.

Entrepreneurship is not the same as management. The principal job of professional managers is to make a business perform well. They take a given set of resources — such as money, employees, machines, and materials — and orchestrate and organize them into an efficient and effective production operation. Managers tend to delegate much of their authority and to rely on the use of formal control systems, and are usually evaluated on the basis of organizationally determined objectives. In contrast, entrepreneurs typically rely more on an informal, hands-on management style and are driven by their personal goals. Their principal job is to bring about purposeful change within an organizational context. They break new ground and, in many cases, each step is guided by some larger plan.

As agents of change, entrepreneurs play, or can play, a number of roles or perform a variety of different functions in the economy. They can, for example:

1. Create new product and/or service businesses

2. Bring creative and innovative methods to developing or producing new products or services

3. Provide employment opportunities and create new jobs as a result of growing their business consistently and rapidly

4. Help contribute to regional and national economic growth

5. Encourage greater industrial efficiency/productivity to enhance our international competitiveness

You should keep in mind, however, that other people also play a significant role in determining who will succeed or fail in our society. For example, entrepreneurs will succeed only when there are customers for the goods and services they provide. But, in most circumstances, it is the entrepreneurs themselves who play the principal role in determining their success or failure. Many still manage to succeed in spite of poor timing, inferior marketing, or low-quality production by combining a variety of talents, skills, and energies with imagination, good planning, and common sense. The entrepreneurial or self-employed option has many attractions, but along with these come risks and challenges and the possibility of failure.

---

3. American Spirit (www.fast-times.com/political/dictionary.html), accessed August 18, 2004.

4. Investor Words (investorwords.com/e2.htm#entrepreneur), accessed August 18, 2004.

5. William D. Bygrave, "The Entrepreneurial Process" in William D. Bygrave, Ed., *The Portable MBA in Entrepreneurship*, 3rd. ed. (Hoboken, NJ: John Wiley & Sons, Inc., 2004), p. 2.

Other considerations ▶ WHY BECOME AN ENTREPRENEUR?

PROFIT magazine asked a number of successful entrepreneurs, "What do you love about being an entrepreneur?" Here are a few of their responses.

JOHN BREAKEY

CEO
Unis Lumin Inc.
Oakville, Ont.

"You get to see your dreams come true. I think that you start off with a passion and a vision that you think you can do something better and different than what's already being done in the marketplace, and your ability to execute that and realize it is phenomenal."

LINDA LUNDSTRÖM

President & Chief Creative Officer
Linda Lundström Inc.
Toronto, Ont.

"Building a company from zero is like creating a living, breathing piece of art. It requires creativity and resource-fulness; it involves insecurity, public acclaim, and private doubt. I don't think there's an entrepreneur that doesn't have some of the same doubts, fears, and insecurities that an artist does. The only difference is that we're expressing that through the companies that we build."

EREZ ZEVULUNOV

Director
MIT Consulting
Toronto, Ont.

"There's nothing more empowering than walking into a boardroom of executives, doing your sales pitch, closing the deal, walking out of there and just feeling the rush of making that next business deal. Being an entrepreneur is the best job you can have."

Source: *PROFIT*, May 2007, p. 19.

THE ENTREPRENEURIAL PROCESS

The successful launch of new business ventures requires a number of other components in addition to an entrepreneur. For example, while there may be any number of specific parts, virtually every new start-up also requires:

- A viable business idea or opportunity for which there is a receptive market
- An organizational structure for the business
- Access to financial and other resources
- A distinctive strategy that, if effectively implemented, will set the business apart from its competitors and enable it to become established

As illustrated in Figure 1.1, all of these elements are outlined and captured in the business plan.

THE ENTREPRENEUR It all begins with the entrepreneur, the driving force behind the business and the coordinator of all the activities, resources, and people that are needed to get it off the ground. This individual will have conducted some assessment of his or her own resources and capabilities and made a conscious decision to launch the business.

FIGURE 1.1 ## THE COMPONENTS OF SUCCESSFUL ENTREPRENEURIAL VENTURES

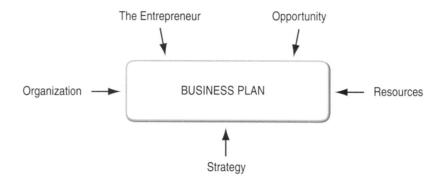

THE OPPORTUNITY The entrepreneur must then find a concept or idea that he or she feels has the potential to develop into a successful enterprise. The concept behind the business must be carefully evaluated to determine whether there is likely to be a market, and if it might represent a viable opportunity. The object is to determine the magnitude of the returns that might be expected with successful implementation.

ORGANIZATION To capitalize on any business opportunity, an organizational structure must be established, with a manager or management team and a form of ownership.

RESOURCES Some essential financial and other resources must be obtained. The key usually is money. Money is the "enabler" that makes everything else happen. Other key resources typically include physical plant and equipment, technical capability, and human resources.

STRATEGY Once a start-up appears likely, a specific strategy must be developed and a feasibility study conducted. The feasibility study is a way to test your business concept to see whether it actually does have market potential. It is a series of tests you should conduct to discover more and more about the nature and size of your business opportunity. After each test you should ask yourself whether the opportunity still appears to be attractive and if you still want to proceed. Has anything come up that would make the business unattractive or prevent you from going forward with its implementation? Throughout this process you probably will modify your concept and business strategy several times until you feel that you have it right.

THE BUSINESS PLAN The business plan not only describes your business concept, but outlines the structure that needs to be in place to successfully implement the concept. The plan can be used to assist in obtaining the additional resources that may be needed to actually launch the business and guide the implementation of the strategy. It assumes you have a feasible business concept and have now included the operational components needed to execute the strategy. It describes in some detail the company you are going to create.

Figure 1.2 illustrates how these components interrelate, the action required at each phase of the implementation of the process, and where these issues are addressed in the book.

This process proceeds in one manner or another to a conclusion, resulting in the implementation of the business. While the model gives the appearance that this is a linear process and that the flow is sequential from one stage to another, this has been done to provide a logical structure for the book and is not necessarily the case. For example, the entrepreneur may pursue two or three different elements at the same time, such as finalizing an organizational structure while also trying to compile the resources necessary to get the business off the ground.

FIGURE 1.2 OUTLINE OF THE ENTREPRENEURIAL PROCESS

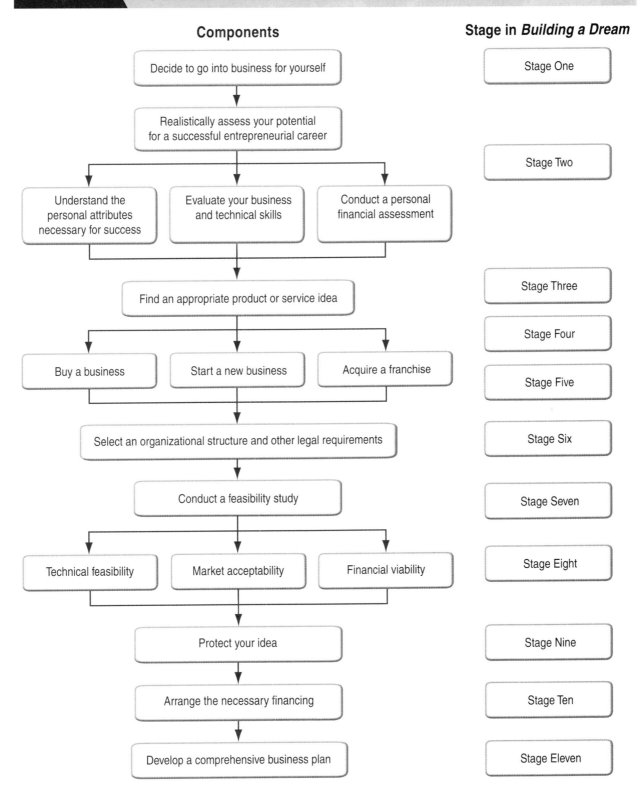

Components   Stage in *Building a Dream*

MYTHS AND REALITIES CONCERNING ENTREPRENEURSHIP

According to noted author-lecturer-consultant Peter Drucker, entrepreneurs defy stereotyping. He states, "I have seen people of the most diverse personalities and temperaments perform well in entrepreneurial challenges."[6] This suggests that some entrepreneurs may be true eccentrics while others are rigid conformists; some are short and fat while others are tall and thin; some are real worriers while others are very laid-back and relaxed; some drink and smoke very heavily while others abstain completely; some are people of great wit and charm while others have no more personality than a frozen fish.

Despite all that is known about entrepreneurs and entrepreneurship, a good deal of folklore and many stereotypes remain. Part of the problem is that while some generalities may apply to certain types of entrepreneurs and certain situations, most entrepreneurial types tend to defy generalization. The following are examples of long-standing myths about entrepreneurs and entrepreneurship:[7]

- **Myth 1   Entrepreneurs are born, not made.**

  Reality   While entrepreneurs may be born with a certain native intelligence, a flair for innovation, a high level of energy, and a core of other inborn attributes that you either have or you don't, it is apparent that merely possessing these characteristics does not necessarily make you an entrepreneur. The making of an entrepreneur occurs through a combination of work experience, know-how, personal contacts, and the development of business skills acquired over time. In fact, other attributes of equal importance can also be acquired through understanding, hard work, and patience.

- **Myth 2   Anyone can start a business. It's just a matter of luck and guts.**

  Reality   Entrepreneurs need to recognize the difference between an idea and a real opportunity to significantly improve their chances of success. If you want to launch and grow a high-potential new venture, you must understand the many things that you have to do to get the odds in your favour. You cannot think and act like a typical bureaucrat, or even a manager; you must think and act like an entrepreneur. That often means initiating action even if conditions are uncertain and existing rules have to be pushed to the limit.

- **Myth 3   Entrepreneurs are gamblers.**

  Reality   Successful entrepreneurs only take what they perceive to be very carefully calculated risks. They often try to influence the odds by getting others to share the risk with them or by avoiding or minimizing the risk if they have the choice. They do not deliberately seek to take more risk or to take unnecessary risks, but they will not shy away from taking the risks that may be necessary to succeed.

- **Myth 4   Entrepreneurs want to run the whole show themselves.**

  Reality   Owning and running the whole show effectively limits the potential for the business to grow. Single entrepreneurs can make a living, perhaps even a good one, but it is extremely difficult to grow a business by working single-handedly. Most successful ventures typically evolve to require a formal organization, a management team, and a corporate structure.

- **Myth 5   Entrepreneurs are their own bosses and completely independent.**

  Reality   Most entrepreneurs are far from independent and have to serve a number of constituencies and a variety of masters, including partners, investors, customers, employees, suppliers, creditors, their families, and pressures from social and community obligations. They do have the choice, however, to decide whether and when to respond to these pressures.

- **Myth 6   Entrepreneurs work longer and harder than corporate managers.**

  Reality   There is no evidence at all that entrepreneurs work harder than their corporate counterparts. Some do, some don't. Both are demanding situations that require long hours and hard work. However, as owners they are tied to the business and responsible in ways that are different from employees' roles.

---

6. Peter Drucker, *Innovation and Entrepreneurship: Practice and Principles* (New York: Harper and Row, 1985), p. 25.

7. Adapted from Jeffrey A. Timmons, *New Venture Creation: Entrepreneurship for the 21st Century,* 4th ed. (Homewood, IL: Richard D. Irwin, 1994), p. 23.

Other Considerations — WHY SMALL BUSINESSES FAIL

1. Poor cash flow management
2. The absence of adequate performance monitoring
3. A lack of understanding or use of performance monitoring information
4. Poor debt management. A combination of not paying their debts on time and not coordinating payments with incoming cash flows
5. Over borrowing. The company is excessively leveraged and debt is not being reduced
6. Excessive reliance on a few key customers
7. Poor market research leading to an inaccurate understanding of the market's wants and needs
8. Lack of financial skills and insufficient planning
9. Failure to innovate
10. Poor inventory management
11. Poor communications throughout the business
12. Failure to recognize their own strengths and weaknesses
13. Trying to go it alone. Attempting to do everything themselves and not seeking external help

Source: Deborah Barrie, *Failure Factors – Thirteen Common Causes of Business Failure,* (www.canadabusiness.ab.ca/index.php/operations/160-failure-factors-thirteen-common-causes-of-business-failure-), accessed April 23, 2010.

- **Myth 7 Entrepreneurs face greater stress and more pressures, and thus pay a higher personal price in their jobs than other managers.**

  Reality Being an entrepreneur is undoubtedly stressful and demanding. But there is no evidence it is any more stressful than numerous other highly demanding professional roles, such as being the principal partner in a legal or accounting practice or the head of a division of a major corporation or government agency. Most entrepreneurs enjoy what they do. They have a high sense of accomplishment. For them it is fun rather than drudgery. They thrive on the flexibility and innovative aspects of their job and are much less likely to retire than those who work for someone else.

Used by permission of Johnny Hart and Creators Syndicate, Inc.

- **Myth 8 Starting a business is risky and often ends in failure.**

    Reality This statement is undoubtedly true in many instances. Some studies have indicated that upward of 80 per cent of new business start-ups fail within their first five years. However, success tends to be more common than failure for higher-potential ventures because they typically are directed by talented and experienced people able to attract the right personnel and the necessary financial and other resources.

    Vince Lombardi, the well-known former coach of the Green Bay Packers, is famous for the quotation, "Winning isn't everything — it's the *only* thing." But a lesser-known quote of his is closer to the true entrepreneur's personal philosophy. Looking back on a season, Lombardi was once heard to remark, "We didn't lose any games last season, we just ran out of time twice." Entrepreneurs learn from experience and are inclined to believe they have failed if they quit.

    Owning your own business is a competitive game, and entrepreneurs have to be prepared to run out of time occasionally. Businesses fail but entrepreneurs do not. Many well-known entrepreneurs experience business failure, sometimes several times, before achieving success.

- **Myth 9 Money is the most important ingredient for success.**

    Reality If the other important elements and the people are there, the money tends to follow. But it is not true that entrepreneurs are assured of success if they have enough money. Money is one of the least important ingredients of new venture success.

- **Myth 10 New business start-ups are for the young and energetic.**

    Reality While youth and energy may help, age is absolutely no barrier to starting a business of your own. However, many people feel there is some threshold for an individual's perceived capacity for starting a new venture. Over time you gain experience, competence, and self-confidence: These factors increase your capacity and readiness to embark on an entrepreneurial career. At the same time, constraints such as increases in your financial and other obligations grow and negatively affect your freedom to choose. The trade-offs between individual readiness and these restraints typically result in most high-potential new businesses being started by entrepreneurs between the ages of 25 and 40.

- **Myth 11 Entrepreneurs are motivated solely by their quest for the almighty dollar.**

    Reality Growth-minded entrepreneurs are more driven by the challenge of building their enterprise and long-term capital appreciation than by the instant gratification of a high salary and other rewards. Having a sense of personal accomplishment and achievement, feeling in control of their own destiny, and realizing their vision and dreams are also powerful motivators. Money is viewed principally as a tool and a way of "keeping score."

- **Myth 12 Entrepreneurs seek power and control over other people so that they can feel "in charge."**

    Reality Successful entrepreneurs are driven by the quest for responsibility, achievement, and results rather than for power for its own sake. They thrive on a sense of accomplishment and of outperforming the competition, rather than a personal need for power expressed by dominating and controlling other people. They gain control by the results they achieve.

FYI FOR YOUR INFORMATION

***About:* Small Business: Canada** An extensive source of information and links for Canadians running their own small business or thinking of starting one. This site will give you all the business resources, contacts, financial sources, and tools that you need to be a successful entrepreneur. (sbinfocanada.about.com)

Canada Business Service for Entrepreneurs A key network of business information and services and your link to the particular Canada Business Service Centre in your province or territory. (canadabusiness.gc.ca/eng)

Industry Canada Canada's principal business and consumer site, containing a wealth of information useful to small business and access to the range of services provided by Industry Canada. (www.ic.gc.ca/ic_wp-pa.htm)

CanadaOne An online publication for Canadian businesses with articles, resources, promotional tools, a free directory for Canadian companies, and more. (www.canadaone.ca)

PROFIT Magazine A site with articles, links, and quizzes of interest to Canadian entrepreneurs. (www.canadianbusiness.com/profit_magazine/index.jsp)

Enterprise Magazine This Web site includes selected articles from the magazine of the same name. Some additional features are available online. (www.enterprisemag.com)

Entrepreneur Magazine The Web site of Entrepreneur magazine with articles about starting a business, money and finance, management and human resources, franchising and a number of other related topics. (www.entrepreneur.com)

Inc.com The website for Inc magazine which provides advice, tools, and services, to help business owners start, run, and grow their businesses more successfully. Contains information and advice covering virtually every business and management topic, including marketing, sales, finding capital, managing people, and much more. (www.inc.com)

Assessing Your Potential for an Entrepreneurial Career

The discussion in Stage One should have served to dispel many of the popular myths concerning entrepreneurship. This section will expand on the theme of entrepreneurial characteristics by proposing and discussing two important questions that are vital to you if you are interested in an entrepreneurial career:

1. Are there certain common attributes, attitudes, and experiences among entrepreneurs that appear to lead to success?

2. If such attributes, attitudes, and experiences exist, can they be learned or are they inborn and thus available only to those with a "fortunate" heritage?

Research into these questions suggests that the answer to question 1 is yes, while the answer to question 2 is both yes and no. These answers, of course, are of little value to you on their own without some further explanation.

THE ENTREPRENEURIAL PERSONALITY

In 1980, Tom Wolfe wrote a perceptive bestseller that examined the lives of America's leading test pilots and astronauts. According to Wolfe, becoming a member of this select club meant possessing "The Right Stuff," that is, the proper mix of courage, coolness under stressful conditions, a strong need for achievement, technical expertise, creativity, and so on. While Wolfe was not talking about entrepreneurs, his viewpoint is similar to the basic thesis held by many members of the "people school" of entrepreneurship: A person has to have the "right stuff" to become a successful entrepreneur.

There is considerable evidence, however, that a great deal of the ability and "right stuff" needed to become a successful entrepreneur can be learned (though probably not by everyone).

ENTREPRENEURIAL QUIZ

While most writers in the field of entrepreneurship agree that there is no single profile, no specific set of characteristics, that defines a successful entrepreneur, there do appear to be some common attributes, abilities, and attitudes. Prior to proceeding any further with our discussion of these entrepreneurial characteristics, it is suggested that you take the Entrepreneurial Quiz that appears as Figure 2.1, starting on page 37. This will enable you to compare your personal attitudes and attributes with those of "practising" entrepreneurs.

What Attributes are Desirable and Acquirable?

In a study of the 21 inductees into the Babson University Academy of Distinguished Entrepreneurs, only three attributes and behaviours were mentioned by all 21 as the principal reasons for their success, and they were all learnable:

1. Responding positively to all challenges and learning from mistakes

2. Taking personal initiative

3. Having great perseverance

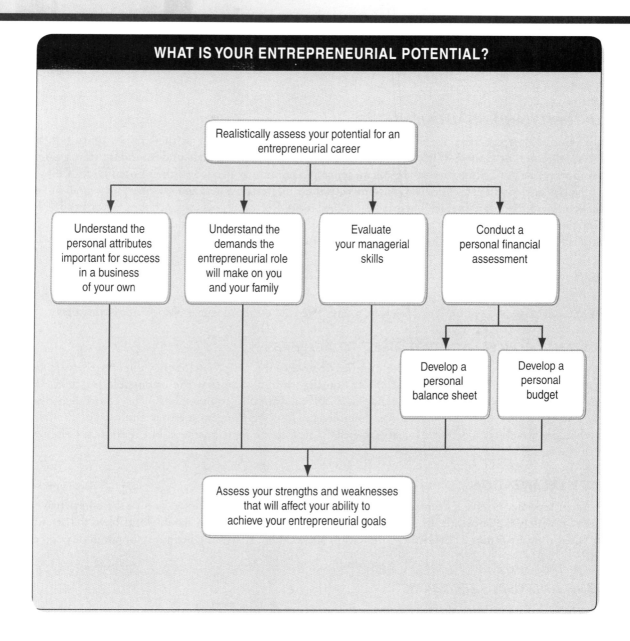

WHAT IS YOUR ENTREPRENEURIAL POTENTIAL?

Realistically assess your potential for an entrepreneurial career

- Understand the personal attributes important for success in a business of your own
- Understand the demands the entrepreneurial role will make on you and your family
- Evaluate your managerial skills
- Conduct a personal financial assessment
  - Develop a personal balance sheet
  - Develop a personal budget

Assess your strengths and weaknesses that will affect your ability to achieve your entrepreneurial goals

Other research has uncovered different lists of common learnable attributes. These qualities are also very desirable in the people entrepreneurs want to surround themselves with in building a high-potential business.

Following is a summary of the attitudes and behaviours that can be valuable in turning a business dream into reality. The proposed characteristics represent the conclusions of over 50 separate research studies into the essential nature of the entrepreneur.

COMMITMENT, DETERMINATION, AND PERSEVERANCE

More than any other single factor, a combination of perseverance and total dedication is critical. In many cases these qualities have won out against odds considered impossible to overcome.

Determination and commitment can compensate for other weaknesses you may have. It requires substantial commitment to give up a well-paid job, with its regular paycheques, medical insurance, and pension and profit-sharing plans, and start out on your own.

SUCCESS ORIENTATION

Entrepreneurs are driven by an immense desire to achieve the goals they initially set for themselves and then to aim for even more challenging standards. The competitive needs of growth-minded entrepreneurs are to outperform their own previous best results, rather than just to outperform another person. Unlike most people, entrepreneurs do not allow themselves to be concerned with failure. What they think about is not what they are going to do if they don't make it, but what they have to do to succeed.

OPPORTUNITY AND GOAL ORIENTATION

Growth-minded entrepreneurs are more focused on the nature and extent of their opportunity rather than resources, structure, or strategy. They start with the opportunity and let their understanding of it guide these other important issues. Entrepreneurs are able to sense areas of unmet needs and their potential for filling these gaps. Effective entrepreneurs set goals consistent with their interests, values, and talents. These goals are generally challenging but still attainable. Their belief in the "reality" of their goals is a primary factor in their fulfillment of them. Having goals and a clear sense of direction also helps these individuals define priorities and provides them with a measure of how well they are performing.

ACTION ORIENTATION AND PERSONAL RESPONSIBILITY

Successful entrepreneurs are action-oriented people; they want to start producing results immediately. They like to take the initiative and get on with doing it, today. The true entrepreneur is a doer, not a dreamer.

PERSISTENT PROBLEM-SOLVING, NEED TO ACHIEVE

Entrepreneurs are not intimidated by the number or severity of the problems they encounter. In fact, their self-confidence and general optimism seems to translate into a view that the impossible just takes a little longer. They will work with a stubborn tenacity to solve a difficult problem. This is based on their desire to achieve the goals they have established for themselves. However, they are neither aimless nor foolhardy in their relentless attack on a problem or obstacle that can impede their business, but tend to get right to the heart of the issue.

REALITY ORIENTATION

The best entrepreneurs have a keen sense of their own strengths and weaknesses and of the competitive environment in which they operate. In addition, they know when they are in trouble and have the strength to admit when they are wrong. This reality orientation allows them to avoid continuing on an ill-advised course of action.

SEEKING AND USING FEEDBACK

Entrepreneurs have a burning desire to know how they are performing. They understand that to keep score and improve their performance they must get feedback, digest the results, and use the information they receive to do a better job. In that way they can learn from their mistakes and setbacks and respond quickly to unexpected events. For the same reason, most entrepreneurs are found to be good listeners and quick learners.

SELF-RELIANCE

Successful entrepreneurs trust the fate of their ventures to their own abilities. They do not believe that external forces or plain luck determine their success or failure. This attribute is consistent with their achievement and motivational drive and desire to achieve established goals.

In a similar vein, entrepreneurs are not joiners. Studies have shown that the need for affiliation, or a high need for friendship, often acts as a deterrent to entrepreneurial behaviour.

SELF-CONFIDENCE

The self-confidence displayed by entrepreneurs is based on their feeling that they can overcome all the necessary challenges and attain their desired goal. They almost never consider failure a real possibility. While this self-confidence implies a strong ego, it is a different kind of ego — an "I know I'm going to do well" type of attitude.

TOLERANCE OF AMBIGUITY AND UNCERTAINTY

Entrepreneurs tolerate ambiguous situations well and make effective decisions under conditions of uncertainty. They are able to work well despite constant changes in their business that produce considerable ambiguity in every part of their operation.

Entrepreneurs take change and challenge in stride and actually seem to thrive on the fluidity and excitement of such undefined situations. Job security and retirement are generally not of great concern to them.

MODERATE RISK-TAKING AND RISK-SHARING

Despite the myth that suggests entrepreneurs are gamblers, quite the opposite is true. Effective entrepreneurs have been found, in general, to prefer taking moderate, calculated risks, where the chances of losing are neither so small as to be a sure thing nor so large as to be a considerable gamble. Like a parachutist, they are willing to take some measurable and predetermined risk.

The strategy of most entrepreneurs also includes involving other parties in their venture to share the burden of risk: Partners put money and reputations on the line; investors do likewise; and creditors and customers who advance payments, and suppliers who advance credit all share in the financial risk of the business.

© Jim Toomey, King Features Syndicate.

RESPONSE TO FAILURE

Another important attribute of high-performance entrepreneurs is their ability to treat mistakes and failures as temporary setbacks on the way to accomplishing their goals. Unlike most people, the bruises of their defeats heal quickly. This allows them to return to the business world again soon after their failure.

Rather than hide from or dismiss their mistakes, entrepreneurs concede their errors and analyze the causes. They have the ability to come to terms with their mistakes, learn from them, correct them, and use them to prevent their recurrence. Successful entrepreneurs know that they have to take personal responsibility for either the success or the failure of their venture and not look for scapegoats when things do not work out. They know how to build on their successes and learn from their failures.

LOW NEED FOR STATUS AND POWER

Entrepreneurs derive great personal satisfaction from the challenge and excitement of creating and building their own business. They are driven by a high need for achievement rather than a desire for status and power. It is important, therefore, to recognize that power and status are a result of their activities and not the need that propels them.

In addition, when a strong need to control, influence, and gain power over other people characterizes the lead entrepreneur, more often than not the venture gets into trouble. A dictatorial and domineering management style makes it very difficult to attract and keep people in the business who are oriented toward achievement, responsibility, and results. Conflicts often erupt over who has the final say, and whose prerogatives are being infringed upon. Reserved parking spaces, the big corner office, and fancy automobiles become symbols of power and status that foster a value system and an organizational culture not usually conducive to growth. In such cases, the business's orientation toward its customers, its market, or its competitors is typically lost.

Other considerations
TOP 10 CHARACTERISTICS OF SUCCESSFUL ENTREPRENEURS

1. Independence — a desire to seize control of their future and become their own boss
2. Persistence and Determination — the doggedness to continue pursuing a goal despite some setbacks and obstacles
3. Self Confidence — a strong belief in their own capabilities
4. Creativity — a natural curiosity, inquisitiveness and the ability to "think outside the box"
5. Organized and Goal-oriented — the ability to consolidate resources
6. Visionary — has a vision for his/her future
7. Risk-taking and Tolerance for Failure — ready to take calculated risks and face whatever consequences accompany those risks
8. Perseverance and Hard work — keep working at a problem until they solve it or find an alternative
9. Commitment — remain focused on an idea or task and not give up at the first sign of trouble
10. Honesty and Honour — being honest and honourable in all business dealings and interpersonal relationships

Source: Adapted from Hilary Basile, *Entrepreneurs — Top 10 Essential Entrepreneurial Traits,* (ezinearticles.com/?Entrepreneurs — Top-10-Essential-Entrepreneurial-Traits&idid=531367), accessed April 27, 2010

Successful entrepreneurs appear to have a capacity to exert influence on other people without formal power. They are skilled at "conflict resolution." They know when to use logic and when to persuade, when to make a concession and when to win one. In order to run a successful venture, entrepreneurs must learn to get along with many different constituencies, who often have conflicting aims — customers, suppliers, financial backers, and creditors, as well as partners and others inside the company.

INTEGRITY AND RELIABILITY

Long-term personal and business relationships are built on honesty and reliability. To survive in the long run, an approach of "Do what you say you are going to do!" is essential. With it the possibilities are unlimited. Investors, partners, customers, suppliers, and creditors all place a high value on these attributes. "Success" resulting from dishonest practices is really long-term failure. After all, anyone can lie, cheat, or steal and maybe get away with it once, but that is no way to build a successful entrepreneurial career.

TEAM BUILDER

Entrepreneurs who create and build successful businesses are not isolated, super-independent types of individuals. They do not feel they have to receive all of the credit for their success, nor do they feel they have to prove they did it all by themselves. Just the opposite situation actually tends to be true. Not only do they recognize that it is virtually impossible to build a substantial business by working alone, but they also actively build a team. They have an ability to inspire the people they attract to their venture by giving them responsibility and by sharing the credit for their accomplishments. This hero-making ability has been identified as a key attribute of many successful corporate managers as well.

In addition to these characteristics, other attributes that have been associated with successful entrepreneurs are the following:

1. They are determined to finish a project once it has been undertaken, even under difficult conditions.
2. They are dynamic individuals who do not accept the status quo and refuse to be restricted by habit and environment.
3. They are able to examine themselves and their ideas impartially.
4. They are not self-satisfied or complacent.

5. They are independent in making decisions while willing to listen to suggestions and advice from others.

6. They do not blame others or make excuses for their own errors or failures.

7. They have a rising level of aspirations and expectations.

8. They have a good grasp of general economic concepts.

9. They are mature, self-assured individuals who are able to interact well with people of varying personalities and values.

10. They are able to exercise control over their impulses and feelings.

11. They have the ability to make the very best of the resources at hand.

The consensus among most experts is that all of these personal characteristics can be worked on and improved through concerted practice and refinement. Some require greater effort than others, and much depends on an individual's strength of motivation and commitment to grow. Developing these attributes should not be very different from personal growth and learning in many other areas of your life.

The Not-So-Learnable Characteristics

The attributes listed next are those that many experts consider to be innate, and thus not acquirable to any great degree. Fortunately the list is quite short. It is from these not-so-learnable characteristics that the conclusion that entrepreneurs are "born, not made" is principally derived. However, while possessing all these attributes would be beneficial, there are many examples of successful business pioneers who lacked some of these characteristics or who possessed them to only a modest degree:

1. High energy, good health, and emotional stability

2. Creativity and an innovative nature

3. High intelligence and conceptual ability

4. The ability to see a better future and a capacity to inspire others to see it

It is apparent from this discussion that entrepreneurs work from a different set of assumptions than most "ordinary" people. They also tend to rely more on mental attitudes and philosophies based on these entrepreneurial attributes than on specific skills or organizational concepts.

Many of these points are summed up in "An Entrepreneur's Creed" in the Other considerations feature below, a general philosophy outlining the entrepreneurial approach to doing business.

A Different Approach

Some people feel this personality approach to identifying entrepreneurial tendencies in individuals is fraught with methodological problems and validity issues. For example, much of the research the questionnaire in Figure 2.1 is based upon was not specifically intended to be used in measuring entrepreneurship. The results were borrowed from psychology and applied to the area of entrepreneurship. Critics also claim these theories were intended for use across a broad range of situations and to measure general personal tendencies and do not have the level of situational specificity necessary to be any useful predictor of entrepreneurial success. They also feel the traditional assumption in much of this research that personality is formed in an individual's earliest years and essentially remains stable thereafter ignores the fact that entrepreneurship involves an individual operating *in an environment,* so theoretical models to predict entrepreneurial success need to be more interactive. Attributes are susceptible to change over time and circumstances. They are dependent upon the situational context.

To overcome these issues, some authors feel that "attitude" is a better approach to the description of entrepreneurs than personality and personal characteristics. Robinson *et al.* developed and tested an Entrepreneurial Attitude Orientation (EAO) scale intended to overcome some of the issues related to the personality approach.[1] They defined "attitude" as the predisposition of the individual to respond in a generally favourable or unfavourable manner with respect to the object of the attitude (in this case organizational creation and innovation).

---

1. P. Robinson, D.V. Stimpson, J.C. Huefner, and H.K. Hunt, "An Attitude Approach to the Predictions of Entrepreneurship," *Entrepreneurship Theory & Practice,* Summer 1991, Vol. 15, Issue 4.

Other considerations   AN ENTREPRENEUR'S CREED

1. Do what gives you energy — have fun.
2. Figure out how to make it work.
3. Anything is possible if you believe you can do it.
4. If you don't know it can't be done, then you'll go ahead and do it.
5. Be dissatisfied with the way things are — and look for ways to improve them.
6. Do things differently.
7. Businesses can fail. Successful entrepreneurs learn from failure — but keep the tuition low.
8. It's easier to beg for forgiveness than to ask for permission in the first place.
9. Make opportunity and results your obsession — not money.
10. Making money is even more fun than spending it.
11. Take pride in your accomplishments — it's contagious.
12. Sweat the details that are critical to success.
13. Make the pie bigger — don't waste time trying to cut smaller pieces.
14. Play for the long haul. It's rarely possible to get rich quickly.
15. Remember: Only the lead dog gets a change in scenery.

Attitudes, therefore, represent the way we interact with the world around us. Their research also recognized that people relate to the world through three types of reaction:

- Cognition: this includes mental activities such as knowledge, thoughts, beliefs, and opinions.
- Affect: that is, emotions associated with thoughts, actions, or objects in our environment.
- Behaviour: the way we respond to conditions in our environment, including habits and intentions.

"Attitude" is a combination of all three. The EAO focuses specifically on "business" activities and considers what you think or believe about those activities (cognition), how you feel about those activities (affect), and how you might tend to behave regarding business activities (behaviour). Their EAO model is based on this tripartite notion of attitude. It contains four subscales that measure:

1. Achievement in business, referring to the extent of your desire to achieve concrete results in business.
2. Innovation in business, relating to how you perceive you might act upon business activities in new and unique ways.
3. The extent of your desire for personal control over business outcomes.
4. Your sense of self-worth or self-esteem relative to business affairs.

Robinson *et al.* were able to show that EAO successfully discriminated between existing entrepreneurs and non-entrepreneurs. Other research has further demonstrated that individuals who indicated that they had intentions of starting a business also demonstrated high levels of EAO.[2]

A condensed version of the EAO Business Attitudes Survey is contained in Figure 2.2 (page 41). It largely focuses on the four basic subscales. Consistency across these scales is an indicator of your personal, internal focus. You want to determine the extent to which your thoughts, feelings and behaviour are consistent with each other. When all three are aligned there is a synergy that enables you to stay on track and continue to perform at a high level. That is very positive from the standpoint of becoming a successful entrepreneur. Try it and get some idea of the extent to which you have an "Entrepreneurial Mindset" as well as a comparison to entrepreneurs who have already started and operate their own businesses. A much more comprehensive and

---

2. N.J. Lindsay, A. Jordaan and W.A. Lindsay, "Values and Entrepreneurial Attitude as Predictors of Nascent Entrepreneur Intentions," Working Paper, Centre for the Development of Entrepreneurs, School of Management, University of South Australia, Adelaide.

detailed version of the EAO business attitudes survey is available at www.entleap.com. It provides a more extensive evaluation of your overall attitude toward business and entrepreneurship.

PERSONAL SELF-ASSESSMENT

The purpose of this discussion has been to have you evaluate your personal attitudes, behaviour tendencies, and views to determine the extent to which you seem to fit the typical entrepreneurial profile. Now you should complete Figure 2.6 on page 48, the Personal Self-Assessment Questionnaire, which will help you summarize your feelings regarding your potential for self-employment.

Many of these attitudes are illustrated by the comments made by Tom Poole in Entrepreneurs in Action #2. Poole, for example, feels the principal character trait common to himself and other entrepreneurs is the "act of faith" — their strong belief that their concept or idea is "fantastic," and their readiness to jump in with both feet. Is this approach always successful? Of course not. But by being flexible and driven by a strong desire to "make it," he feels these individuals succeed more often than they should.

Entrepreneurs in Action

The Entrepreneur Exposed

Over the years, people have asked me many questions about my business. But there are two questions I have found myself answering most often: "Why did you give up a promising career to leap into the world of the entrepreneur?" (which my father-in-law continues to ask me weekly) and, "Would you do it again?" For the longest time I was unable to provide good answers, and quite frankly, I never gave them much thought. However, as I grow older and perhaps more philosophical, I have pondered these questions. The answers are slowly beginning to take shape, and I believe my conclusions might shed some light on entrepreneurs in general.

I think the answers lie in a character trait common to most, if not all, entrepreneurs. By "entrepreneur," I do not mean the corporate executive who takes an early retirement package to start a home-based consulting business (not that there's anything wrong with that). I am talking about that crazy s.o.b. who quits his job as a C.A. and sells his mother to secure the capital needed to start a rubbish-collection company. Take a look around you at the entrepreneurs that you know. What do these people have in common? Are they all a little wacky? Eccentric? Unorthodox? Most likely; it goes with the territory.

If the prospective entrepreneur were reasonable and orthodox, he or she would use conventional methods of measuring the risk associated with giving up everything for a leap into the unknown. The consequence of conducting a proper "decision-tree" analysis would be that no one would ever take the step.

So how does an entrepreneur approach the "go/no-go" decision-making process? Well (at the risk of revealing that I never really had a master plan), I think the typical entrepreneur does some initial research, becomes absolutely convinced that his or her idea is fantastic, and jumps. This act of faith is the litmus test for entrepreneurs. Some people may decide that an idea is great but requires more research, and some spend years explaining to their friends how they had developed the concept long before Ms. X (who went on to make a fortune with the idea). But true entrepreneurs leap in with both feet.

I decided to jump in February 1989. I quit my high-paying, secure job with a multinational company, moved my wife and two and one-half children into a camper van, and set out to find a business to run. My gamble paid off — the company I eventually bought has grown from three employees, a 1,800-square-foot "factory" and $350,000 in annual sales to the current 800 employees, five production facilities and $80 million plus in revenue.

Do entrepreneurs always succeed? Of course not. We simply don't hear as much about the failures. But entrepreneurs do succeed more often than circumstances suggest they should. Why? Often for what business schools call the "wrong" reasons: the speed of their decision-making, the dearth of analysis and the fact that they hold nothing back, financially, physically or emotionally. How do these seemingly irrational actions improve the chances of success? By acting quickly, the entrepreneur reduces the likelihood of having the idea

continued

Entrepreneurs in Action #2 — continued

"stolen"; the cursory analysis allows the entrepreneur to avoid an analysis-paralysis affliction; and by investing everything, the consequences of failure are so dire that . . . well, they just cannot afford to fail! . . .

Now back to the questions that I have been asked so many times over the years. First, why did I do it? Well, it was a "mix" of about one part crazy and two parts ignorance. And once I had taken the plunge, it was about 100 percent fear. Most entrepreneurs, if pressed for an honest response, would likely acknowledge that their early days were not unlike mine.

Would I do it again? The answer is complicated. In this hypothetical situation, assuming I had the knowledge I have now, the answer is a categorical "No." Of course not. I would know that what I was undertaking was probably close to impossible. Equipped with this information, my analysis would result in a "no-go" decision. I may be crazy, but I'm not stupid!

But if you re-phrase the question and ask whether I would take another entrepreneurial plunge, the answer

is "Yes, of course." Why? I think the Steve Martin film *Parenthood* contains the best answer to that question. Toward the end of the movie, a mother explains life to her risk-averse son (Martin). She tells of being young and going to the fair with his father. He always wanted to ride on the merry-go-round, while she preferred the roller coaster. On the merry-go-round, she explained, you saw the same things go by again and again. It became rather boring. The roller coaster, on the other hand, was exhilarating, sometimes even frightening. But once she had ridden the roller coaster, she could never go back to the merry-go-round.

So, having taken the plunge and ridden the roller coaster, I can never return to the merry-go-round. And to those of you who are riding the merry-go-round, mix yourself a cocktail consisting of one part crazy and two parts ignorance. Drink it in one gulp and go for the ride of your life. (www.seppsfoods.com)

Source: Tom Poole, "The Entrepreneur Exposed," PROFIT (PROFITguide.com), July 12, 2001. Used with permission.

Others may think of business as a "gritty reality" involving constant responsibility and considerable stress rather than the glamourous lifestyle commonly perceived by the general public. Yet they are still prepared to undertake such burdens. Why? Perhaps it's a personal need to challenge themselves, to test their potential, reach goals and fulfill a mission.

WHAT KIND OF ENTREPRENEUR ARE YOU LIKELY TO BE?

Many references to the term "entrepreneur" seem to presume there is only one kind of individual who fits the definition. As you can see from the Entrepreneurs in Action examples, however, not all entrepreneurs are the same. John Warrillow, a Toronto-based marketing consultant, spent three years interviewing more than 500 small-business owners. He used that research to develop attitudinal profiles for three entrepreneurial archetypes:

CRAFTSPEOPLE They comprise 60 per cent of small business owners and derive their sense of self-worth from their mastery of a craft or trade. While they don't think of themselves as entrepreneurs, they still have the resources and confidence to operate independently. They are more interested in developing their skills than growing their revenue and generally work alone or employ one other person, often a spouse.

FREEDOM FIGHTERS They work hard to control their own destiny. That's because their prime motivator isn't growth, but simply being in business for themselves. They comprise 30 per cent of all small businesses and typically employ 3 to 50 staff and grow less than 30 per cent a year. More than half the freedom fighters are college educated, and 30 per cent are women. They are more likely to hire family and tend to treat their staff as family members.

MOUNTAIN CLIMBERS They are the 10 per cent of growth-oriented business owners who are motivated almost solely by achievement, usually measured in terms of company growth. You can usually identify mountain climbers by the fact that their companies grow by more than 30 per cent annually. As a result, they are the most high-profile and high-profit group. More than 75 per cent have college or university degrees. These go-getters work long hours, and expect a lot from themselves and their staff. Eighty-three per cent claim to be married.[3]

If you are planning to go into a business of your own, into which of these three groups do you think you would fall? Mountain climbers are the people we tend to read about in the newspapers and financial magazines and are likely to be the kind of individuals profiled throughout this book. It is important to recognize, however,

3. Kara Kuryllowicz, "What Kind of Entrepreneur are You?," *PROFIT* (2000).

that not everyone can be or wants to be a mountain climber and there are many other opportunities for you to start a business and still be quite happy and do very well.

Similarly, Vesper identified a considerable number of entrepreneurial types.[4] His typology includes:

1. **Solo, self-employed individuals.** These include most independent small business operators, tradespeople such as agents, repairmen, and brokers, and many hourly-rate professionals such as accountants, dentists, doctors, and lawyers.

2. **Deal-to-dealers.** These small business owners have had more than one venture, often in quite different lines of business.

3. **Team builders.** These entrepreneurs go on to build larger companies through hiring and delegation of authority.

4. **Independent innovators.** These are traditional inventors who hit upon ideas for better products and then create companies to develop, produce, and sell them in the marketplace.

5. **Pattern multipliers.** This group includes entrepreneurs who spot an effective business pattern and multiply it to realize profits on the multiple units. Becoming a franchisor is one effective way of multiplying business patterns for a profit.

6. **Economy-of-scale exploiters.** These entrepreneurs exploit the fact that unit costs tend to shrink as volume expands. This has been practiced principally by entrepreneurs in the discount retail merchandising business.

7. **Capital aggregators.** These entrepreneurs are able to pull together a substantial financial stake that enables them to initiate ventures that require large front-end capital, including banks, insurance companies, and mutual funds.

8. **Acquirers.** These entrepreneurs buy a going concern. They will often take over businesses that are in trouble and try to straighten them out or buy businesses that they can *add value* to in some way, perhaps before selling them off again.

It has been said that entrepreneurship is really a state of mind. An individual may be extremely innovative and creative, be prepared to work long hours, and feel luck is on his/her side, but this is not sufficient to guarantee business success. What is missing is the necessary entrepreneurial mindset: a single-mindedness and dedication to the achievement of a set of personal goals and objectives, a confidence in their intuitive and rational capabilities, a capacity to think and plan in both strategic and tactical terms, and an attitude that reflects a penchant for action. The individuals in the Entrepreneurs in Action examples definitely seem to possess this mindset.

EVALUATING YOUR BUSINESS SKILLS

There is a lot more to succeeding as an entrepreneur than just having the proper background, attitudes, and lifestyle. This next section discusses another factor you should consider in assessing your potential for becoming a successful entrepreneur: Do you have the requisite managerial and administrative skills needed to manage and operate a business?

Possessing the necessary managerial skills is an essential ingredient to succeeding in any small venture. It is estimated that the principal reason for the failure of small firms is poor management. Witness the experience of restaurateurs Richard Jaffray and Scott Morison (Entrepreneurs in Action #3). They thought they had learned a lot in building up their chain of Cactus Club Cafes in the lower mainland of British Columbia. They figured they "could do no wrong," decided to branch out, and opened four additional Clubs, two each in Calgary and Edmonton. Within six months, they knew they had a problem, and six months later it all fell apart.

What could have gone wrong for these relatively seasoned entrepreneurs? "Everything," says Jaffray. Restaurant locations were selected by price rather than by location as they had been in British Columbia. They changed the original concept of the restaurants and abandoned their long-time practice of grooming existing employees to take over the management of new restaurants. They neglected to take local culture into account and charged British Columbia prices, which were 10 per cent to 20 per cent higher than comparable price levels in Alberta. In the end, three of the four Alberta locations were closed and the whole experience ended up costing them about $3 million.

Having learned their lesson and rebuilt the business in British Columbia, the pair are now looking to take their concept back into Alberta. This time they are not too worried. They feel they have been through it before and can be successful now. "Had we not gone right to the very bottom, I don't think we'd be as successful as we are today," says Jaffray. Cactus Club has now grown to 16 restaurants throughout British Columbia and Alberta.

---

4.   K. Vesper, *New Venture Strategies,* Rev. Ed., (Prentice-Hall, Englewood Cliffs, NJ, 1990), pp. 3–9.

Entrepreneurs in Action

Rock Bottom and Back

It's 4:00 p.m. on a Monday, and business is booming in the newest uptown Vancouver location of Cactus Club Cafe. Hip young 20-somethings lounge in leather armchairs at tables surrounding a massive centrepiece mahogany bar, drinking Cactus Bellinis, a peach/rum/champagne/sangria slurpie billed as "better than sex." Others relax in plush leather booths next to massive windows framed with crushed velvet drapes. Still others gather around glowing-eyed gargoyle fountains, kibitzing with service staff as they sample diverse cuisine, ranging from jerk chicken and sea-salted fries to the Millionaire's Cut filet mignon.

It's an opulent yet informal, eclectic atmosphere that's become the tongue-in-cheek trademark of restaurateurs Richard Jaffray and Scott Morison. The new $1.8-million restaurant is fanciful and fun. And that's a key component in Cactus Club's recipe for success, says Jaffray. It's a formula that's proving popular with West Coast consumers, fuelling Cactus Club's growth into a 16-chain restaurant.

But that success hasn't come without challenges. An overzealous expansion into Alberta brought the company to the brink of ruin. Opening four restaurants in less than 15 months without adequate research and preparation proved nearly fatal, says Jaffray. Undaunted by the near-disaster, the ambitious partners rolled up their sleeves to retrench and reorganize. "Our objective," says Jaffray, "is to be the best upscale, casual, fun restaurant in North America." A lofty ambition, perhaps, but one the partners are confident they can meet by learning from their past mistakes and adhering to the first rule of business: know thy customers.

Jaffray began waiting tables for Earl's Restaurants Ltd., a popular family-restaurant chain. It was there he met Morison, a fellow waiter and would-be entrepreneur. Eager to strike out on their own, two years later the then 21-year-olds launched an ice cream and cappuccino bar called Café Cucamongas.

Revenues reached $250,000 in the first year, enough to attract the attention of the pair's former boss at Earl's, Stan Fuller. Fuller approached them about a potential partnership in a new restaurant geared to a younger clientele. His timing was perfect, since Jaffray and Morison were already looking beyond Cucamongas. The partnership provided them with the capital they needed to develop a full-scale restaurant chain, plus access to Fuller's

expertise and experience. In return, Earl's got an investment in a new market without having to manage it. . . .

Morison and Jaffray sold Cucamongas and wrangled a $225,000 bank loan, giving them enough cash to finance their half-share in the new venture. The concept was simple: to combine the best attributes of a pub, restaurant and nightclub in a single nightspot. The vision, says Jaffray, was to establish a restaurant that would become a local neighbourhood hangout, with its own character and vitality.

Cactus Club seemed to fit the bill. Its quirky decor, music, party atmosphere and progressive menu proved popular with hip consumers. Cactus Club grew to include five restaurants in the lower mainland. "We could do no wrong," says Jaffray.

Emboldened, Jaffray and Morison decided to branch out, opening four Cactus Clubs, two each in Calgary and Edmonton. "Within six months, we knew we were headed for trouble big time," says Jaffray. "Six months later, it all fell apart."

What went wrong? "Everything," says Jaffray. For starters, restaurant locations were chosen not by market research as they were in B.C., says Jaffray, but by price. They tweaked their original concept and ended up with more of a bar than a fun eatery. They neglected to take into account local cultures such as Edmonton's tradition of "happy hour" discount drinks. Plus, they

PERRY ZAVITZ

charged B.C. prices — 10% to 20% above local price point — despite the fact that Alberta costs were lower. Unimpressed by the West Coast whiz kids, customers stayed away.

Within a year of opening in Alberta, they realized they would have to cut their losses or lose everything.

In the end, three of the four Alberta locations were closed. "The whole exercise cost about $3 million." says Jaffray.

While Jaffray and Morison remain cautious about again expanding into a new market, they aren't -overly worried. They've been through this before. "Had we not gone right to the very bottom, I don't think we'd be as successful as we are today," says Jaffray. "We now know all the things that can go wrong." (www.cactusclubcafe.com)

Source: Diane Luckow, "Rock bottom and back," PROFIT, April 1999, pp. 53–55. Reprinted with permission.

WHAT SKILLS ARE NEEDED BY SMALL-BUSINESS OWNERS?

Businesses, whether large or small, have to perform a number of diverse functions to operate successfully. An entrepreneur, because of the limited amount of resources (human and financial) at his or her disposal, faces a particularly difficult time.

The business skills required by an entrepreneur (or some other member of the organization) can be broken down by function, as shown in Table 2.1.

INVENTORY OF YOUR MANAGERIAL AND ADMINISTRATIVE SKILLS

Now that you understand the range of skills necessary to enable your new business to succeed, the Managerial Skills Inventory in Figure 2.3 on page 44 can be used to develop an inventory of your skills and capabilities in several aspects of management. Your present level of expertise may be anything from minimal to having a great deal of skill. The goal of the inventory is to assess your present skills, with the purpose of identifying areas that may need improvement. Since each of these management skills is not required at an equivalent level in all new business situations, completing this inventory might also provide you with some insight into the type of business opportunities for which you are best suited.

TABLE 2.1 BREAKDOWN OF ENTREPRENEURIAL BUSINESS SKILLS

1. **Managing money**
   a. Borrowing money and arranging financing
   b. Keeping financial records
   c. Managing cash flow
   d. Handling credit
   e. Buying insurance
   f. Reporting and paying taxes
   g. Budgeting

2. **Managing people**
   a. Hiring employees
   b. Supervising employees
   c. Training employees
   d. Evaluating employees
   e. Motivating people
   f. Scheduling workers

3. **Directing business operations**
   a. Purchasing supplies and raw materials
   b. Purchasing machinery and equipment
   c. Managing inventory
   d. Filling orders
   e. Managing facilities

4. **Directing sales and marketing operations**
   a. Identifying different customer needs
   b. Developing new product and service ideas
   c. Deciding appropriate prices
   d. Developing promotional strategies
   e. Contacting customers and making sales
   f. Developing promotional material and media programs

5. **Setting up a business**
   a. Choosing a location
   b. Obtaining licences and permits
   c. Choosing a form of organization and type of ownership
   d. Arranging initial financing
   e. Determining initial inventory requirements

WHERE CAN YOU ACQUIRE THE NECESSARY SKILLS?

It should be apparent from the lengthy list in Table 2.1 that few people can expect to have a strong grasp of all of these skills prior to considering an entrepreneurial career. The key question then becomes where and how you can acquire these skills. The available means for developing these business skills are outlined below.

Job Experience

Every job you have had should have contributed to the development of some business skills. For example, working as an accountant might teach you:

1. How to prepare financial statements
2. How to make financial projections and manage money
3. How to determine the business's cash requirements, among other things

Working as a sales clerk might teach you:

1. How to sell
2. How to deal with the public
3. How to operate a cash register

In fact many aspiring entrepreneurs consciously follow a pattern of "apprenticeship," during which they prepare themselves for becoming entrepreneurs by working in a family business or obtaining job experience directly related to their particular interests.

Perhaps the best experience, however, is working for another entrepreneur. In that case you will learn to understand the overall process and skills required to operate your own business.

Club Activities

Many of the functions that service clubs and similar organizations perform in planning and developing programs are similar to those performed by small businesses. Some examples of what can be learned from volunteer activities are:

1. How to organize and conduct fund-raising activities
2. How to promote the organization through public service announcements and free advertising
3. How to manage and coordinate the activities of other members of the organization

Education

Universities, community colleges, high schools, and government agencies such as local business development organizations and the Business Development Bank of Canada provide many programs and individual courses in which essential business-related skills can be acquired. Some examples of applicable skills that can be learned from these programs include:

1. Business skills (from particular business classes)
2. Socialization and communication skills (from all school activities)
3. Bookkeeping and record-keeping skills (from accounting classes)

Your Friends

Most of us have friends who through their job experience and education can teach us valuable business skills. Some examples of useful information we may acquire from this source are:

1. Possible sources of financing
2. Assistance in selecting an appropriate distribution channel for your products
3. Information on the availability of appropriate sites or locations for your business
4. Sources for finding suitable employees

Your Family

Growing up with an entrepreneur in the family is perhaps the best learning experience of all, even though you may not be aware of the value of this experience at the time. Some examples of what you might learn from other members of your family are:

1. How to deal with challenges and problems
2. How to make personal sacrifices and why
3. How to keep your personal life and business life separate
4. How to be responsible with money

Home Experiences

Our everyday home experiences help us develop many business skills. Some examples of such skills are:

1. Budgeting income
2. Planning finances
3. Organizing activities and events
4. Buying wisely
5. Managing and dealing with people
6. Selling an idea

It can be hard for a single individual to wear all these "hats" at once. Partnerships or the use of outside technical or general business assistance can be an excellent supplement for any deficiencies in characteristics and skills a small-business owner may have. Thus, it often becomes essential to identify an individual, or individuals, who can help you when needed. This outside assistance might come from one of the following sources:

1. A spouse or family member
2. A formal partnership arrangement
3. Hired staff and employees
4. External professional consultants
5. A formal course or training program
6. Regular idea exchange meetings or networking with other entrepreneurs

ASSESSING YOUR PERSONAL FINANCIAL SITUATION

In addition to your managerial capabilities, your financial capacity will be a very important consideration in your decision as to whether an entrepreneurial career is right for you. It will certainly be a critical factor to those you may approach for a loan to provide investment capital for your venture.

YOUR PERSONAL BALANCE SHEET

Your personal balance sheet provides potential lenders with a view of your overall financial situation so they can assess the risk they will be assuming. Generally, if you are in a strong financial position, as indicated by a considerable net worth, you will be considered a desirable prospect. On the other hand, an entrepreneur with a weak financial position and a large number of outstanding debts may not meet the standards of most lenders.

From a personal standpoint, you might also want to reconsider becoming a small-business owner if you cannot afford a temporary or perhaps even a prolonged reduction in your personal income.

Your personal balance sheet includes a summary of all your assets — what you own that has some cash value — and your liabilities or debts. Preparing a personal balance sheet is a relatively simple process:

- **Step 1** Estimate the current market value of all your "assets" — the items you own that have cash value — and list them.
- **Step 2** Add up the value of these assets.

- **Step 3**   List all your debts, also known as "liabilities."
- **Step 4**   Add up your liabilities.
- **Step 5**   Deduct your total liabilities from your total assets to find your "net worth."

Figure 2.4 on page 46 shows a Sample Balance Sheet Form that you can use to help organize your assets and liabilities. The items listed are not exhaustive; the form is provided only as a guide for thinking about your present position. Since every business opportunity has its own unique capital (money) requirements, there is no specific dollar value for the personal net worth necessary to start a business. However, you should keep in mind that most private lenders or lending institutions typically expect a new small-business owner to provide at least 40 to 50 per cent of the capital required for start-up. In addition, lenders consider the net worth position of prospective borrowers to determine their ability to repay the loan should the new business fail.

DEVELOPING A PERSONAL BUDGET

As well as determining your present net worth, you must also consider your personal living expenses when assessing your ability to provide the total financing needed to start a new business. In fact, you should evaluate your personal financial needs while in the process of determining whether an entrepreneurial career is right for you.

In some situations you will need to take money from the business each month to pay part or all of your personal living expenses. If such is the case, it is crucial that this amount be known and that at least that much be set aside to be paid out to you each month as a salary.

If your new business is starting off on a limited scale, you might wish to continue holding a regular job to cover your basic living expenses and provide some additional capital to your fledgling operation. In some cases, your spouse's income may be sufficient to cover the family's basic living expenses and it may not be necessary to consider your personal financial needs in making a go/no-go decision.

The Personal Living Expenses Worksheet shown in Figure 2.5 on page 47 is an effective means of estimating your present cost of living. From the totals on the worksheet, you can calculate the minimum amount of money you and your family will require on a regular monthly basis and determine from what sources this regular income will be obtained.

CHECK YOUR CREDIT RATING

One thing that may significantly impact your ability to obtain a loan or other financing for your venture is your *credit rating*. Your rating is based on your prior history in borrowing and repaying money. By regularly paying your bills, including credit cards, telephone bills, mortgages, lines of credit and similar debts, on time you are building your credit rating. Without a good credit rating few institutions will lend you money.

Your credit rating is maintained by two consumer reporting agencies in Canada including Equifax Canada Inc. (www.Equifax.ca), and TransUnion Canada (www.transunion.ca). Lenders such as retailers and financial institutions provide these agencies with information about how you pay your bills. The agencies then assemble this information into your credit file indicating whether your bills are being paid on time (R1), late (R4) or have not been paid and been placed with an agency for collection (R9). This information can dramatically affect your ability to obtain a personal loan or any other credit for personal or business purposes.

The information in the files of these reporting agencies is not always entirely accurate. You have a right to know what's in your file, so you should check the file periodically. Contact either of the above agencies and they will tell you how you can obtain a copy of your personal report. If you notice any errors, report them back to the agency right away and they will investigate the situation with the lender who reported the item. If the file is inaccurate it will be changed right away.

ARE YOU READY FOR AN ENTREPRENEURIAL CAREER?

EXTERNAL ROLE DEMANDS

It is not enough simply to possess a large number and high level of the characteristics previously discussed as prerequisites for a successful entrepreneurial career. There are also certain external conditions, pressures, and demands inherent in the small-business ownership role itself.

While successful entrepreneurs may share several characteristics with successful people in other careers, entrepreneurs' preference for and tolerance of the combination of requirements unique to their role is a major distinguishing feature.

Many of these requirements were mentioned earlier. What follows is a discussion of a few of the most relevant issues you should consider concerning your degree of readiness and preparedness for such a career.

Need for Total Commitment

As an entrepreneur you must live with the challenge of trying first to survive in the business world, then to stay alive, and always to grow and withstand the competitive pressures of the marketplace. Almost any venture worth considering requires top priority on your time, emotions, and loyalty. As an entrepreneur you must be prepared to give "all you've got" to the building of your business, particularly during the initial stages of its development. Anything less than total commitment will likely result in failure.

Management of Stress

Stress, the emotional and physiological reaction to external events or circumstances, is an inevitable result of pursuing an entrepreneurial career option. Depending on how it is handled, stress can be either good or bad for an entrepreneur. The better you understand how you react to stressful situations, the better you will be able to maximize the positive aspects of these situations and minimize the negative aspects, such as exhaustion and frustration, before they lead to a serious problem.

Stress, in the short term, can produce excellent results, because of its relationship to the type of behaviour associated with entrepreneurial activities, especially during the start-up stage of a new business. There is some evidence that once individuals become accustomed to producing under stressful conditions, they seem to continue to respond in a positive manner; entrepreneurs tend to create new challenges to replace the ones they have already met, and to continue to respond to those challenges with a high level of effectiveness.

Economic and Personal Values

Entrepreneurs engaged in "for-profit" as opposed to social or "not-for-profit" organizations must share the basic values of the free enterprise system: private ownership, profits, capital gains, and growth. These dominant economic values need not exclude social or other values. However, the nature of the competitive market economy requires belief in, or at least respect for, these values.

THE CONCEPT OF SOCIAL ENTREPRENEURSHIP

Up to now our focus has been on "economic" entrepreneurship; the discovery, evaluation and exploitation of opportunities for financial profit. However, we are hearing more and more about the concept of "social" entrepreneurship. This can be thought of as the discovery, evaluation and pursuit of opportunities for social change. While both types of entrepreneurs are visionary, tend to be opportunistic, and pay a lot of attention to building networks of contacts, social entrepreneurs tend to communicate their visions in moral terms, driven by a desire to achieve some form of social justice rather than make a dollar.[5]

Jeff Skoll, eBay's first president, has established a foundation specifically to support the efforts of social entrepreneurs. Since its founding in 2002 his foundation has given away millions of dollars to support the efforts of social entrepreneurs including Craig and Mark Kielburger of Toronto and their Free the Children organization. As a 12-year-old Craig was inspired by an article in the newspaper about a South Asian boy who was sold into slavery at the age of four and chained to a carpet weaving loom but still had the courage to speak out for children's rights. Craig gathered together a group of his classmates in Grade 7 and Save the Children was born with a mission to free children of the world from poverty and exploitation. To date, Free the Children has worked with more than one million youth involved in 45 countries to educate and empower young people to act locally and globally as agents of change for their peers around the world. It is the world's largest network of children helping children through education.[6]

5. D. Roberts, and C. Woods, "Changing the World on a Shoestring: The Concept of Social Entrepreneurship," *University of Auckland Business Review*, Autumn 2005, pp. 45–51.

6. (www.freethechildren.com/aboutus/history.php), accessed June 8, 2010.

An excellent example of a successful social entrepreneur is little Hannah Taylor. At the age of five she happened to see a homeless man eating from a garbage can and was deeply impacted by the notion that there was such a thing as people who didn't have a home. She began to learn about homelessness and in conjunction with the manager of a local mission was inspired to start some innovative fundraising ventures to do all she could to help put an end to homelessness. Soon afterward, she started the Ladybug Foundation. To date, the foundation has helped to raise over two million dollars, largely through the distribution of Ladybug jars — red jars painted with pictures of ladybugs that are given to businesses and schools to collect people's spare change during their "Make Change" month. Now thirteen, Hannah has had an emergency shelter named after her, been named the recipient of an international award for community building and has embarked on a new program, the National Red Scarf Campaign, to raise more funds to help curb hunger and homelessness in the local community. (Entrepreneurs in Action #4)

Social entrepreneurs are not necessarily just involved with not-for-profit ventures. They can also work on behalf of for-profit community development banks and similar initiatives, and hybrid organizations mixing not-for-profit elements, such as homeless shelters that start small businesses of various kinds to train and employ their clients, or sheltered workshops working with the disabled. These individuals also have to have a vision, be ambitious, mission driven, resourceful, and results-oriented, just like conventional entrepreneurs.

Entrepreneurs in Action

Hannah gets a helping hand

WORKING WITH THE PERSON WHO INSPIRED THE FOUNDATION

Rick Adams and Hannah Taylor are working together on the National Red Scarf Campaign.

For the first time, Hannah Taylor is getting a chance to work with the man who inspired her to set up a charitable foundation for the homeless.

Taylor was only eight years old when she met Rick Adams while volunteering with her family at a soup kitchen.

She remembers seeing Adams and immediately feeling his eyes had a wealth of kindness and knowledge. The two were introduced and Taylor gave Adams a big hug.

Taylor, now 13 years old, and Adams are working together on the National Red Scarf Campaign, a project supported by Taylor's Ladybug Foundation — which has raised over $2 million to help charitable organizations which provide food, shelter and other needs of the homeless in Canada.

The campaign involves the sale of scarves for $20, with proceeds to help curb hunger and homelessness. Taylor thought of the idea a few winters back when her neck got cold, and she imagined all Canadians wearing scarves and thinking about the plight of the homeless.

"A scarf is like a hug, and we need to wrap our hearts around the homeless," she said.

Since their first meeting, Adams went back to school and then got a place of his own. He now holds an advisory position on the Ladybug Foundation and is working on the Red Scarf Campaign.

Adams said Taylor's one simple act of kindness was instrumental in turning his life around, after living without a home for 20 years.

"(Hannah) showed me that there are people who do care. She treated me like a human being. She treated me respectfully," said Adams. "For a long time I had lost all of that. I didn't really care what life had to offer, I was foolish, I slipped through the cracks. What happened is that I realized before it was too late."

Taylor said she's overjoyed to be working with her great friend on this year's project.

"When I first met him, his heart shone through his eyes. We just became friends and stayed in touch," said Taylor. "I love him so much and he has an amazing story. Because he's been to different shelters — because he had to get his love and food there — he gives great input on what we should look for when we are finding a shelter to support."

Gail Asper, a member of the Ladybug Foundation board of advisers, said she continues to stay involved with Taylor's projects because she's always learning from the inspirational teen. "She is one of the people that I most admire and respect in this world," said Asper. "Her energy is phenomenal and her heart is huge." (www.ladybugfoundation.ca)

Source: (www.winnipegfreepress.com/local/hannah-gets-a-helping-hand-69948307.html), accessed June 8, 2010.

DEALING WITH THE ETHICAL CHALLENGE

With the collapse of Enron, WorldCom, the coming to light of Ponzi schemes by Bernie Madoff and others and similar incidents in the world of big business in recent years, there has been a dramatic increase in the ethical expectations of all businesses and professionals. Increasingly, consumers, clients, employees, and others are seeking out those who define the basic ground rules of their businesses on a day-to-day basis.

Entrepreneurs are typically faced with many ethical decisions. These may relate to such issues as potential conflicts of interest between your personal situation and the interests of your business; temptations to provide gifts, expensive entertainment, or even bribes or kickbacks to certain people or organizations in order to attract or influence their business activity; or the use of proprietary or confidential information in order to influence the outcome of a deal or a sale. To be successful as an entrepreneur, it is important that you act and conduct your business in an ethical manner, and the significance of ethics when initiating a new venture must be emphasized.

What specifically do we mean by "ethics"? One dictionary defines it as *the moral quality of a course of action; fitness; propriety.*[7] One could think of ethics as a set of principles outlining a behavioural code that lays out what is good and right or bad and wrong. Ethics may also outline obligations and appropriate moral actions for both the individual and the organization.[8] The problem with these kinds of definitions, however, is that they think of ethics as a static description, implying that society universally agrees on certain fundamental principles that everyone regards as being "ethical." With society being a dynamic and rapidly changing environment, however, such a consensus clearly does not exist. In fact, considerable conflict and general disagreement over what would be considered "ethical" in most decision situations is probably more typical.

© Jim Toomey, King Features Syndicate.

---

7. *The American Heritage Dictionary of the English Language*, 4th ed., William Morris, Ed. (Boston: Houghton Mifflin Company, 2000).

8. V.E. Henderson, "The Ethical Side of Enterprise," *Sloan Management Review*, Spring 1982, p. 38.

Another dilemma for the entrepreneur is the issue of legal versus ethical considerations. Survival of their business is a strong motivating factor for most entrepreneurs and the question arises as to how far they can go in order to help their business become established and successful. The law provides the boundaries defining just what activities are illegal (although they are often subject to some interpretation) but it does not provide any specific guidance for ethical considerations. So what is legal and illegal is usually very clear but what is ethical and unethical is frequently not obvious. Rather, situations involving ethical issues are often very ambiguous.

Because the system is so unclear and filled with situations involving potential conflicts, entrepreneurs need to commit to a general strategy for ethical responsibility. Most professional organizations and business associations have a code of ethics that members are expected to follow. Failure to do so can result in expulsion from the organizations. AIM Personnel Services Inc., a full service employee recruiting and staffing organization in Ottawa, for example, is a member of the Association of Canadian Search, Employment & Staffing Services and prominently displays the association's code of ethics on its Web site (www.aimpersonnel.ca/ottawa/who-we-are/code-of-ethics). This code is reproduced in the Other considerations box on the next page.

Many organizations, on the other hand, prefer to develop their own codes of ethics or conduct. These documents often lay out in considerable detail just how the company's management and employees are expected to behave in particular situations and what the company feels is the right thing to do in such circumstances.

Having a code of ethics can be a great start but it may not be sufficient to take the greyness out of an ethical situation and help you to determine a solution. It is easy to charge ahead without thinking and then rationalize your decision after the fact. Kenneth Blanchard and Norman Vincent Peale suggest using an *Ethics Check* that helps you to sort out dilemmas by examining the situation at several different levels. Their Ethics Check is intended to help you clarify issues by addressing three questions when confronted with an ethical problem:

1. *Is it legal?*

   Will you be violating either civil law or your organization's code of ethics?

2. *Is it balanced?*

   Is it fair to all concerned in the short term as well as the long term? Does it promote win–win relationships?

3. *How will it make you feel about yourself?*

   Will it make you proud?

   Would you feel good if your decision was published in the newspaper?

   Would you feel good if your family knew about it?[9]

Other considerations — OUTLINE FOR A CODE OF ETHICS

Over all, a code of ethics should be a formal statement of a business's values concerning ethics and social issues. It commonly speaks to acceptable norms of behaviour, guided by six areas of concern:

1. Honesty: to be truthful in all your endeavours; to be honest and forthright with one another and with customers, communities, suppliers, and other stakeholders.
2. Integrity: to say what you mean, to deliver what you promise, and to stand up for what is right.
3. Respect: to treat others with dignity and fairness, appreciating the diversity of the people you deal with and their uniqueness.
4. Trust: to build confidence through teamwork and open, candid communication.
5. Responsibility: to speak up — without fear of retribution — and report concerns in the workplace and elsewhere, including violations of laws, regulations, and company policies.
6. Citizenship: to obey all laws of the countries where you do business and to improve the communities where you live and work.[10]

---

9. K. Blanchard and N.V. Peale, *The Power of Ethical Management* (New York: William Morrow and Co. Inc., 1988), p. 27.
10. Alford, J.M., "Finding Competitive Advantage in Managing Workplace Ethics," paper presented at the 19th National Conference of the United States Association for Small Business and Entrepreneurship (USASBE), Dallas, Texas, 2005.

Other considerations

THE AIM GROUP CODE OF ETHICS & STANDARDS

As members of the Association of Canadian Search, Employment & Staffing Services we commit to uphold this Code of Ethics & Standards and to display it prominently in our place of business. We support the principles set forth below and acknowledge that compliance with these principles is in the best interests of ACSESS member companies, their candidates, employees, client organizations, and the reputation of the search, employment and staffing services profession in Canada.

- We will observe the highest principles of integrity, professionalism and fair practice in dealing with clients, candidates, employees and all regulatory authorities; and will respect the confidentiality of records in accordance with law and good business practices.

- We will provide leadership in the adherence to both the spirit and letter of all applicable human rights, employment laws and regulations. We will treat all candidates and employees without prejudice and will not accept an order from any client that is discriminatory in any way.

- We will take all reasonable steps to provide clients with accurate information on each candidate's employment qualifications and experience; and will only present those candidates who have given us authorization to represent their application for employment.

- We will supply candidates and employees with complete and accurate information as provided by the client, regarding terms of employment, job descriptions and workplace conditions.

- We will not recruit, encourage or entice a candidate whom we have previously placed to leave the employ of our client, nor will we encourage or coerce an individual to leave any temporary assignment before the stated completion date.

- We will not restrict the right of a candidate or employee to accept employment of their choice.

- We will not misuse membership privileges for the purpose of recruiting a member's staff, or in any way that may otherwise injure our candidates, employees or competitors.

- We will derive income only from clients and make no direct or indirect charges to candidates or employees unless specified by a license.

- We will maintain the highest standards of integrity in all forms of advertising, communications and solicitations; and will conduct our business in a manner designed to enhance the operation, image and reputation of the employment, recruitment and staffing services industry.

- We will recognize and respect the rights and privileges of competitors in the true fashion of individual initiative and free enterprise, and will refrain from engaging in acts of unfair competition.

- We will ensure that our clients, candidates and employees are aware of our duty to abide by this Code of Ethics & Standards and such supporting policies and guidelines as may from time to time be adopted by the Association; and will undertake to bring any potential infringements before the appropriate Association body.

Source: AIM Personnel Services Inc. (www.aimpersonnel.ca/ottawa/who-we-are/code-of-ethics), accessed June 8, 2010.

Regardless of the approach, having a code of ethics can be the foundation for the success of your business. By being honest and truthful and adhering to a clearly defined set of principles, not only will you feel good about yourself but you will also gain the respect of your customers, suppliers, bankers, and other business associates.

Consider the views of Elias Vamvakas of TLC Laser Eye Centres described in Entrepreneurs in Action #5. TLC clinics became the largest provider of laser eye surgery in the world, and Vamvakas attributes much of this success to the "goodwill cycle" the company created for the business and to a very conscious effort on its part to follow a specific set of ethical business practices. It is clear that integrity and ethical conduct can have a powerful impact on your success in creating a successful and growing business.

Entrepreneurs in Action

Goodwill Hunting

Right from the beginning, we knew we had found a great business idea that we truly believed in, but the challenges of tackling a new, emerging industry were daunting. Looking back, we have learned that our success began with a "goodwill cycle" that started with ethical business practices. Doing the right thing, along with hard work, has sustained us from startup through the challenge of presenting public offerings, and still forms the basis of each decision to this day. It all started on the day I received a call from my best friend, Dr. Nick Nianiaris. He was completely exasperated with his friend and colleague, Dr. Jeff Machat, who was about to "throw away" his career. Dr. Machat, an award-winning ophthalmology graduate, had a potentially incredible future ahead of him, but he wanted to risk it all to perform a revolutionary new procedure called PRK (a procedure using a highly accurate laser to reshape the front part of a person's eye, eliminating the need for contacts or glasses).

My job, as the only senior business person that these young doctors knew, was to convince the wayward Dr. Machat that he should get back to practicing medicine as a "real" doctor. But I couldn't do it. He had travelled the world to study this new laser, and was extremely excited about the results. I was so impressed with his personality and drive that I became hooked on the same dream — we believed PRK would change the world as we knew it. TLC Laser Eye Centres was born.

We spent two years doing research on the procedure, the outcomes and other surgical business models throughout the world before raising the initial funds ($1.5 million from three investors and mortgages on both Dr. Machat's house and my own). It was difficult to decide upon an approach to entering this emerging industry. We considered setting up hospital associates, stand-alone clinics, and private clinics that simply rented equipment to doctors. We considered direct consumer marketing models as well as mobile systems. But as new partners, we made one key agreement: I would not be involved in clinical decisions and he would not be involved in business decisions.

We felt that the ultimate winner in this emerging industry would be the organization that provided the

highest level of clinical care while maintaining a business environment founded on integrity and the desire to always do the right thing. We decided to never take short cuts or jeopardize clinical care to satisfy business or financial needs.

Following these principles set in motion what I call a "goodwill cycle." Our company, with only one clinic in Windsor, Ontario, started to get a reputation for providing incredible results. It soon became one of the busiest clinics in the world, attracting worldwide attention. Dr. Machat was open to sharing his knowledge and experience. This openness and focus on positive clinical results attracted excellent doctors to TLC. Having the best doctors provided more referrals, leading to the opening of more clinics, which attracted more of the best doctors, and so on.

This goodwill cycle also extended to the staff, whose work involved helping people to see better. Positive affirmation (including hugs, chocolates, flowers and thank-yous) from delighted patients became a tremendous motivator. The staff loved their jobs and it began to show.

I have learned one very important lesson in business: Ethical business practices always work out for the best and unethical practices always result in disaster. Decisions about right and wrong need to be made every day. Will you strive to honour the intent of an agreement rather than the words that may be translated in your favour? Pay individuals what they deserve, not just what they will accept? Promote based on merit, not friendship? Try to preserve the reputation of competitors? We try to do the right thing, because although it may take a while before actions produce the appropriate reaction, they always do.

Source: By Elias Vamvakas, Chairman and CEO, TLC Vision Corporation, "Goodwill Hunting," *PROFITguide.com* (www.canadianbusiness.com/profit_magazine/article.jsp?content=20031103_152750_35 88&page=2), accessed June 8, 2010.

BEING SOCIALLY RESPONSIBLE

Companies today are expected to go beyond just being "ethical" in their dealing with customers, employees and other stakeholders. They are expected to generally act in a *socially responsible* manner. That means their behaviour should reflect not only their efforts to make money and achieve a high level of financial performance, but that they need to be good citizens as well and give something back to the societies in which they exist.

What's the basis for this argument that companies should "give back"? First, all firms make use of society's basic infrastructure — land, plants, animals, and so on — in order to earn a profit. Second, companies should reimburse society for the negative consequences their activities might create — noise, smell, traffic congestion, toxic emissions. Just as individuals have a "moral duty" to contribute to the community they live in, companies are also obliged to contribute to their community through corporate volunteering, charitable donations, sponsoring community and cultural events, providing school equipment, funding university buildings and libraries, and so forth.[11] This is based on the belief there is an integral link between the strength of the community and the strength of the company.

Why should businesses be concerned about being more socially responsible? The argument is that activities in this area can have positive financial benefits to the organization as well, resulting in better long-term, more stable profits, and a higher level of employee, stakeholder and company well-being. This can result from:

- cost savings due to more efficient operations
- development of a more positive organizational image and reputation
- creation of a clearly identifiable market niche with consumers who are interested in health and the environment, social justice, and sustainable living
- being forced to become more innovative to accommodate these values within the company's organizational strategy.

Rather than just focusing on the company's financial performance as reflected in its Income Statement, the success of organizations in being socially responsible is commonly measured against a *triple bottom line* assessment of financial performance, environmental impact, and social well-being. The idea is to make a positive contribution to the environment and society in a financially responsible manner. Even though the assessment of social and environmental performance is largely subjective, many large companies are reporting their performance in this area in a Corporate Social Responsibility (CSR) report, or a non-financial report, although smaller firms are jumping on this bandwagon as well and this number is likely to increase substantially over time. Starbucks, for example, has established a number of key guiding principles relating to the ethical sourcing of their coffee and other raw materials, their level of involvement in the community and stewardship of the environment and their efforts to reduce their environmental impact. Every year they set targets for their performance in each of those areas and publish a comprehensive Global Responsibility Report and scorecard showing their achievement level on a number of factors related to each of these dimensions and how they compared with the previous year and their targets. A summary of part of their scorecard for 2009 and how their performance compared with the previous couple of years is illustrated in the following Other Considerations box.

A FINAL ANALYSIS

The Personal Self-Assessment Questionnaire in Figure 2.6 is designed to help you summarize your thinking concerning what you need to do to become a successful entrepreneur. The questions get you to focus on areas of strength and weakness you have identified from the previous questionnaires and to think about how compatible you seem to be with the typical requirements of an entrepreneurial life style. If you have answered all the questions carefully, you have done some hard work and careful thinking. Try to do as much of this as you can for yourself but don't hesitate to also ask for help from other family and friends who may know you very well to get their perspective too.

This assessment of your entrepreneurial potential is based on a series of self-evaluations, and for it to reveal anything meaningful, an absolute requirement is for you to be completely honest with yourself. This, however, is

11. Earl, M. "Note on Individuals, Corporations and Society," Note 9B04M072, Richard Ivey School of Business, University of Western Ontario, 2004.

Other considerations

STARBUCK™ SHARED PLANET™ GLOBAL RESPONSIBILITY SCORECARD 2009

GOALS	PROGRESS				
Increase our annual purchases of coffee verified through C.A.F.E. Practices	*Our purchases of C.A.F.E. Practices verified coffee increased from 77% of total coffee purchases in 2008 to 81% of total coffee purchases in 2009* **ACHIEVED**	Total coffee purchases (Millions)	352 / 160	385 / 174	367 / 167 (lb) / (kg)
		Total C.A.F.E. Practices purchases (Millions)	228 / 103	295 / 134	299 / 136 (lb) / (kg)

2007   2008   2009

Double our purchases of Fairtrade certified coffee in 2009	*Our purchases of Fairtrade certified coffee increased from 19 million pounds in 2008 to 39 million pounds in 2009* **ACHIEVED**	19 Million lb* / 9 Million kg 39 Million lb** / 18 Million kg 2008 2009

* Coffee purchased October 2007 through September 2008 (baseline year)
** Coffee purchased (including on-hand inventory) January through December 2009

Invest in farmers and their communities by nearly doubling farmer loans to $20 million by 2015	*Our farmer loan commitments increased by $2 million in 2009* **ON TRACK**	$20 Million — 2015 $14.5 Million — 2009 $12.5 Million 2000 – 2008 Baseline year: 2008

Mobilize our partners (employees) and customers to contribute more than 1 million hours of community service per year by 2015	*Our service hours decreased by 24% in 2009* **NEEDS IMPROVEMENT**	245,974 Hours* 186,011 Hours** 1 Million Hours 2008 2009 2015

* U.S. and Canada only
** Global representation. The 2009 community service hours total does not reflect Youth Action Grant activities.

Engage 50,000 young people to innovate and take action in their communities by 2015	*Through grants awarded in 2009, we engaged 20,868 young people in community activities, reaching 42% of our 2015 goal* **ON TRACK**	50,000 — 2015 20,868 — 2009 Global representation. Baseline year: 2008

Source: (assets. starbucks.com/assets/ssp-g-p-scorecard.pdf), accessed Oct. 18, 2010.

only the first step. The road to entrepreneurship is strewn with hazards and pitfalls and many who start on it fall by the wayside for one reason or another. However, those who persevere and reach the end by building a successful venture may realize considerable financial and psychological rewards as well as a lot of personal satisfaction.

The remainder of this book can help you evaluate other important parts of this process and improve your chances for success. It will help you decide what else you need to consider and enable you to go after it. Good luck!

FIGURE 2.1	ENTREPRENEURIAL QUIZ

Below are a number of questions dealing with your personal background, behavioural characteristics, and lifestyle patterns. Psychologists, venture capitalists, and others believe these to be related to entrepreneurial success. Answer each question by placing an "X" in the space that best reflects your personal views and attitudes. The most important result of this exercise will be an honest, accurate self-assessment of how you relate to each of these dimensions.

	Rarely or no	Mostly or yes
1. Are you prepared to make sacrifices in your family life and take a cut in pay to succeed in business?	_____	_____
2. Are you the kind of individual that once you decide to do something you'll do it and nothing can stop you?	_____	_____
3. When you begin a task, do you set clear goals and objectives for yourself?	_____	_____
4. When faced with a stalemated situation in a group setting, are you usually the one who breaks the logjam and gets the ball rolling again?	_____	_____
5. Do you commonly seek the advice of people who are older and more experienced than you are?	_____	_____
6. Even though people tell you "It can't be done" do you still have to find out for yourself?	_____	_____
7. When you do a good job, are you satisfied in knowing personally that the job has been well done?	_____	_____
8. Do you often feel, "That's just the way things are and there's nothing I can do about it"?	_____	_____
9. Do you need to know that something has been done successfully before, prior to trying it yourself?	_____	_____
10. Do you intentionally try to avoid situations where you have to converse with strangers?	_____	_____
11. Do you need a clear explanation of a task before proceeding with it?	_____	_____
12. Are you a good loser in competitive activities?	_____	_____
13. After a severe setback in a project, are you able to pick up the pieces and start over again?	_____	_____
14. Do you like the feeling of being in charge of other people?	_____	_____
15. Do you enjoy working on projects that you know will take a long time to complete successfully?	_____	_____
16. Do you consider ethics and honesty to be important ingredients for a successful career in business?	_____	_____
17. Have you previously been involved in starting things like service clubs, community organizations, charitable fund-raising projects, etc.?	_____	_____
18. Did your parents or grandparents ever own their own business?	_____	_____
19. When you think of your future do you ever envision yourself running your own business?	_____	_____

continued

Entrepreneurial Quiz — continued

	Rarely or no	Mostly or yes
20. Do you try to do a job better than is expected of you?	___	___
21. Do you make suggestions about how things might be improved on your job?	___	___
22. Are you usually able to come up with more than one way to solve a problem?	___	___
23. Are you between 25 and 40 years of age?	___	___
24. Do you worry about what others think of you?	___	___
25. Do you read a lot of books, particularly fiction?	___	___
26. Do you take risks for the thrill of it?	___	___
27. Do you find it easy to get others to do something for you?	___	___
28. Has someone in your family shared with you his or her experience in starting a business?	___	___
29. Do you believe in organizing your tasks before getting started?	___	___
30. Do you get sick often?	___	___
31. Do you enjoy doing something just to prove you can?	___	___
32. Have you ever been fired from a job?	___	___
33. Do you find yourself constantly thinking up new ideas?	___	___
34. Do you prefer to let a friend decide on your social activities?	___	___
35. Did you like school?	___	___
36. Were you a very good student?	___	___
37. Did you "hang out" with a group in high school?	___	___
38. Did you actively participate in school activities or sports?	___	___
39. Do you like to take care of details?	___	___
40. Do you believe there should be security in a job?	___	___
41. Will you deliberately seek a direct confrontation to get needed results?	___	___
42. Were you the firstborn child?	___	___
43. Was your father or another older male generally present during your early life at home?	___	___
44. Were you expected to do odd jobs at home before 10 years of age?	___	___
45. Do you get bored easily?	___	___
46. Are you sometimes boastful about your accomplishments?	___	___
47. Can you concentrate on one subject for extended periods of time?	___	___
48. Do you, on occasion, need pep talks from others to keep you going?	___	___
49. Do you find unexpected energy resources as you tackle things you like?	___	___

	Rarely or no	Mostly or yes
50. Does personal satisfaction mean more to you than having money to spend on yourself?	_____	_____
51. Do you enjoy socializing regularly?	_____	_____
52. Have you ever deliberately exceeded your authority at work?	_____	_____
53. Do you try to find the benefits in a bad situation?	_____	_____
54. Do you blame others when something goes wrong?	_____	_____
55. Do you enjoy tackling a task without knowing all the potential problems?	_____	_____
56. Do you persist when others tell you it can't be done?	_____	_____
57. Do you take rejection personally?	_____	_____
58. Do you believe you generally have a lot of good luck that explains your successes?	_____	_____
59. Are you likely to work long hours to accomplish a goal?	_____	_____
60. Do you enjoy being able to make your own decisions on the job?	_____	_____
61. Do you wake up happy most of the time?	_____	_____
62. Can you accept failure without admitting defeat?	_____	_____
63. Do you have a savings account and other personal investments?	_____	_____
64. Do you believe that entrepreneurs take a huge risk?	_____	_____
65. Do you feel that successful entrepreneurs must have advanced college degrees?	_____	_____
66. Do you strive to use past mistakes as a learning process?	_____	_____
67. Are you more people-oriented than goal-oriented?	_____	_____
68. Do you find that answers to problems come to you out of nowhere?	_____	_____
69. Do you enjoy finding an answer to a frustrating problem?	_____	_____
70. Do you prefer to be a loner when making a final decision?	_____	_____
71. Do your conversations discuss people more than events or ideas?	_____	_____
72. Do you feel good about yourself in spite of criticism by others?	_____	_____
73. Do you sleep as little as possible?	_____	_____
74. Did you ever have a small business of your own while in school?	_____	_____

Adapted from Judy Balogh et al., *Beyond a Dream: An Instructor's Guide for Small Business Explorations* (Columbus: Ohio State University, 1985), pp. 26–28.

Answers to the Entrepreneurial Quiz

The answers provided in Table 2.2 for the Entrepreneurial Quiz represent the responses that best exemplify the spirit, attitudes, and personal views of proven, successful entrepreneurs. Here they are *not* arranged in numerical order (1–74) but by the characteristic that they are measuring (personal background, behaviour patterns, and lifestyle factors).

TABLE 2.2   ANSWERS TO ENTREPRENEURIAL QUIZ

Personal Background

Most Desirable Response	Question Number
Rarely or No	30, 36, 37, 43
Mostly or Yes	17, 18, 23, 28, 32, 35, 38, 42, 44, 74

Behaviour Patterns

Most Desirable Response	Question Number
Rarely or No	8, 9, 10, 11, 12, 14, 24, 39, 40, 48, 54, 57, 64, 65
Mostly or Yes	2, 4, 5, 6, 7, 13, 16, 20, 21, 22, 26, 27, 29, 31, 33, 41, 45, 46, 47, 49, 50, 52, 53, 55, 56, 58, 60, 61, 62, 66, 68, 69

Lifestyle Factors

Most Desirable Response	Question Number
Rarely or No	25, 34, 51, 67, 71
Mostly or Yes	1, 3, 15, 19, 59, 63, 70, 72, 73

What Is Your Score?

Answering this questionnaire will let you determine the extent to which your responses match those that best exemplify the spirit, attitudes, and personal views of proven, successful entrepreneurs. To determine your score, count the number of your responses that appear to be correct in Table 2.2 and mark it in Table 2.3. Your responses in Table 2.3 have also been arranged by the characteristic they are measuring (your personal background, behaviour patterns, and lifestyle factors).

TABLE 2.3   SELF-ASSESSMENT: RESULTS

	Number of Most Desirable Responses
Your Personal Background	/14
Your Behaviour Patterns	/46
Your Lifestyle Factors	/14
Total Number of Most Desirable Responses	/74

What Does Your Score Mean?

The Entrepreneurial Quiz is *not* intended to predict or determine your likely success or failure. However, if you answer and score the questionnaire honestly, it will provide considerable insight into whether you have the attitudes, lifestyle, and behaviour patterns consistent with successful entrepreneurship.

The higher your number of most desirable responses, the more your responses agree with those of successful entrepreneurs. High levels of agreement indicate that you *may* have the "right stuff" to succeed in an entrepreneurial career. You should make certain, however, that your responses reflect your real opinions and attitudes.

The word *may* is highlighted above because of the overwhelming importance of one particular set of attributes/characteristics: commitment, determination, and perseverance. Scoring well on the test is not necessarily a guarantee of entrepreneurial success. Anything less than total commitment to your venture, and considerable determination and perseverance, will likely result in failure, regardless of the degree to which you may possess other important attributes. Your total commitment and determination to succeed helps convince others to "come along for the ride." If you are not totally committed, both financially and philosophically, to the venture, it is unlikely that potential partners, your employees, bankers, suppliers, and other creditors will have the confidence in you to provide the level of support your business will require.

FYI FOR YOUR INFORMATION

Several other instruments are available that will also enable you to assess your potential for an entrepreneurial career. You might check out:

Business Start-up Quiz An interactive entrepreneurship quiz hosted by Youth Employment Services (YES) Montreal to help determine if you are ready for self-employment. (www.yesmontreal.ca/yes.php?section-entrepreneurship/quiz)

Entrepreneurial Self-Assessment A questionnaire from the Business Development Bank of Canada on attitude and lifestyle that will enable you to assess how consistent your character is with that of proven successful entrepreneurs. (www.bdc.ca/en/business_tools/entrepreneurial_self-Assessment/Entrepreneurial_self_assessment.htm?cookie%5Ftest=1)

The Entrepreneur Test Do you have what it takes to succeed as an entrepreneur? This interactive quiz will help you assess your entrepreneurial skills and indicate to what extent you have the personal traits important to a business owner. (www.bizmove.com/other/quiz.htm)

FIGURE 2.2 ENTREPRENEURIAL ATTITUDE ORIENTATION (EAO) SURVEY

This Entrepreneurial Attitude Orientation (EAO) questionnaire consists of 21 items, each consisting of a statement followed by a 10-point scale asking how much you agree or disagree with the statement. Move through the survey as quickly as you can, without thinking too much about each item. Your initial response is usually the best one.

Indicate how much you agree or disagree with each statement by circling a number between **"1"** to indicate you **Strongly Disagree** with the statement and **"10"** to say you **Strongly Agree** with the statement. A "5" indicates you only slightly disagree, while a "6" shows only slight agreement. Work as quickly as you can and indicate your first thought about the issue. **Please answer all the questions.**

1. I often approach business tasks in unique ways.
Strongly Disagree   Strongly Agree
  1   2   3   4   5   6   7   8   9   10

2. I enjoy being the catalyst for change in business affairs.
Strongly Disagree   Strongly Agree
  1   2   3   4   5   6   7   8   9   10

3. I believe that when pursuing business goals or objectives, the final result is far more important than following accepted procedures.
Strongly Disagree   Strongly Agree
  1   2   3   4   5   6   7   8   9   10

4. I don't hesitate to take control in unstructured situations.
Strongly Disagree   Strongly Agree
  1   2   3   4   5   6   7   8   9   10

5. I enjoy being able to use old business concepts in new ways.
Strongly Disagree   Strongly Agree
  1   2   3   4   5   6   7   8   9   10

6. I believe it is important to continually look for new ways to do things in business.
Strongly Disagree   Strongly Agree
  1   2   3   4   5   6   7   8   9   10

continued

Entrepreneurial attitude orientation (EAO) Survey — continued

7. I believe that in order to succeed, one must conform in accepted business practices.
Strongly Disagree   Strongly Agree
  1   2   3   4   5   6   7   8   9   10

8. I create the business opportunities I take advantage of.
Strongly Disagree   Strongly Agree
  1   2   3   4   5   6   7   8   9   10

9. I feel very good because I am ultimately responsible for my own business success.
Strongly Disagree   Strongly Agree
  1   2   3   4   5   6   7   8   9   10

10. My knack for dealing with people has enabled me to create many of my business opportunities.
Strongly Disagree   Strongly Agree
  1   2   3   4   5   6   7   8   9   10

11. I get excited creating my own business opportunities.
Strongly Disagree   Strongly Agree
  1   2   3   4   5   6   7   8   9   10

12. I get a sense of accomplishment from the pursuit of my business opportunities.
Strongly Disagree   Strongly Agree
  1   2   3   4   5   6   7   8   9   10

13. I believe it is more important to think about future possibilities than past accomplishments.
Strongly Disagree   Strongly Agree
  1   2   3   4   5   6   7   8   9   10

14. I get my biggest thrills when my work is among the best there is.
Strongly Disagree   Strongly Agree
  1   2   3   4   5   6   7   8   9   10

15. I often sacrifice personal comfort in order to take advantage of business opportunities.
Strongly Disagree   Strongly Agree
  1   2   3   4   5   6   7   8   9   10

16. I never put important matters off until a more convenient time.
Strongly Disagree   Strongly Agree
  1   2   3   4   5   6   7   8   9   10

17. I feel very self-conscious when making business proposals.
Strongly Disagree   Strongly Agree
  1   2   3   4   5   6   7   8   9   10

18. I feel uncomfortable when I'm unsure of what my business associates think of me.
Strongly Disagree   Strongly Agree
  1   2   3   4   5   6   7   8   9   10

19. I spend a lot of time looking for someone who can tell me how to solve all my business problems.
Strongly Disagree   Strongly Agree
  1   2   3   4   5   6   7   8   9   10

20. I always try to make friends with people who may be useful in my business.
Strongly Disagree   Strongly Agree
  1   2   3   4   5   6   7   8   9   10

21. I feel self-conscious when I am with very successful business people.
Strongly Disagree   Strongly Agree
  1   2   3   4   5   6   7   8   9   10

Interpreting Your Results On The Entrepreneurial Attitude (EAO) Survey

To determine your assessment of the EAO survey follow the following steps:

1. Sum your score on Items 1, 2, 3, 5, 6 and 7. Divide by 6. That is your score on the ***Innovation*** dimension.

2. Sum your score on Items 12, 13, 14, 15 and 16. Divide by 5. That is your score on the ***Achievement*** dimension.

3. Sum your score on Items 4, 8, 9, 10 and 11. Divide by 5. That is your score on the ***Personal Control*** dimension.

4. Sum you score on Items 17, 18, 19, 20 and 21. Divide by 5. That is your score on the ***Self-esteem*** dimension.

Only about 15 per cent of the people in North America can be categorized as entrepreneurs, that is, they own and operate their own business entity, usually for profit. This puts them in a unique class both as individuals and collectively. Entrepreneurs are different. They may not look or act different in everyday situations, but they are different:

- In the way they react to the world and their own situation, and
- In the strength of their passion that compels them to action.

Entrepreneurship, however, is not some exclusive club that admits only certain people. Entrepreneurs were not born as business owners. For the most part they did not go to special schools or have special privileges as they were growing up. Yet somehow through their experiences they have acquired the mindset and the passion to make it as an entrepreneur. If you haven't already acquired this attitude toward the world, you can do so through your experience, your desire, and your commitment.

The analysis you just completed was designed and tested to measure the entrepreneur's mindset. You now have some insight and feedback on your own "Entrepreneurial Mindset" and can now compare it to entrepreneurs who have already started and operate their own businesses.

The EAO measures your attitude or mindset that influences your behaviour with regard to business activities. The mindset of entrepreneurs consists of a set of attitudes that help the entrepreneur see and react to the world differently than most other people. This set of attitudes includes:

- ***Innovation*** or creativity in business activities.
- ***Achievement*** or a desire to achieve concrete results in business.
- ***Personal Control*** or a desire to have personal control over your business activities.
- ***Self-esteem*** or a strong sense of self-worth.

You have determined your score from the survey on each of these dimensions. You can now compare your scores with those of a group of practicing entrepreneurs. Remember that it is not the absolute level of your scores that is important, but the consistency of your scores across all these dimensions. The shaded areas on the following bars represent the typical scores on previous tests from samples of successful student and non-student entrepreneurs. Plot your scores and see how they compare.

INDIVIDUAL RESULTS

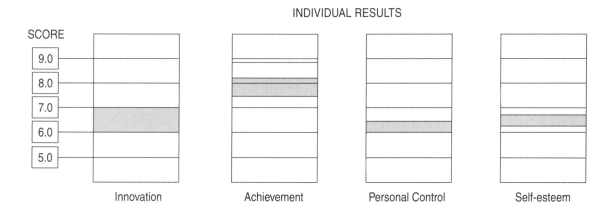

DESCRIPTION OF RESULTS

If your results are within the normal range for people who have started and managed their own businesses, this is what they tend to imply about your attitudinal profile:

INNOVATION IN BUSINESS This indicates you are capable of seeking out new ways of solving problems and working in unique ways to achieve your business objectives.

ACHIEVEMENT This indicates a reasonable emphasis and commitment to making your business activities lead to successful outcomes. You have realistic expectations in terms of your business objectives and the effort necessary to accomplish these goals.

PERSONAL CONTROL This indicates you have a desire to control your business affairs that is typical of others who manage their own business. This means you will likely exercise appropriate levels of control of information, resources, and authority in the start-up of a new business.

SELF-ESTEEM This indicates you generally have a level of self worth consistent with what others who have started and managed their own business normally score.

FIGURE 2.3   **MANAGERIAL SKILLS INVENTORY**

The following questionnaire can be used to develop an inventory of your skills and capabilities in each of the five areas of management outlined in this Stage. For each management area, the questionnaire lists some corresponding skills. Rate your present level of expertise for each skill listed by placing an "X" under the appropriate number in the charts below (1 indicates minimal skill, while 5 indicates a great deal of skill). Beneath each section, in the space provided, briefly describe where and when you obtained this experience.

The goal of this inventory is to assess the level of your present skills, with the purpose of identifying areas that may need improvement.

MONEY MANAGEMENT	1	2	3	4	5
Borrowing money and arranging financing	❏	❏	❏	❏	❏
Keeping financial records	❏	❏	❏	❏	❏
Cash flow management	❏	❏	❏	❏	❏
Handling credit	❏	❏	❏	❏	❏
Buying insurance	❏	❏	❏	❏	❏
Reporting and paying taxes	❏	❏	❏	❏	❏
Budgeting	❏	❏	❏	❏	❏

Describe where and when you obtained this expertise.

_____

_____

_____

_____

MANAGING PEOPLE	1	2	3	4	5
Hiring employees	❏	❏	❏	❏	❏
Supervising employees	❏	❏	❏	❏	❏
Training employees	❏	❏	❏	❏	❏
Evaluating employees	❏	❏	❏	❏	❏
Motivating people	❏	❏	❏	❏	❏
Scheduling workers	❏	❏	❏	❏	❏

Describe where and when you obtained this expertise.

_____

_____

_____

_____

DIRECTING BUSINESS OPERATIONS

	1	2	3	4	5
Purchasing supplies and raw materials	❑	❑	❑	❑	❑
Purchasing machinery and equipment	❑	❑	❑	❑	❑
Managing inventory	❑	❑	❑	❑	❑
Filling orders	❑	❑	❑	❑	❑
Managing facilities	❑	❑	❑	❑	❑

Describe where and when you obtained this expertise.

_____

_____

_____

_____

DIRECTING SALES AND MARKETING OPERATIONS

	1	2	3	4	5
Identifying different customer needs	❑	❑	❑	❑	❑
Developing new product and service ideas	❑	❑	❑	❑	❑
Deciding appropriate prices	❑	❑	❑	❑	❑
Developing promotional strategies	❑	❑	❑	❑	❑
Contacting customers and making sales	❑	❑	❑	❑	❑
Developing promotional material and a media program	❑	❑	❑	❑	❑

Describe where and when you obtained this expertise.

_____

_____

_____

_____

SETTING UP A BUSINESS

	1	2	3	4	5
Choosing a location	❑	❑	❑	❑	❑
Obtaining licences and permits	❑	❑	❑	❑	❑
Choosing a form of organization and type of ownership	❑	❑	❑	❑	❑
Arranging initial financing	❑	❑	❑	❑	❑
Determining initial inventory requirements	❑	❑	❑	❑	❑

Describe where and when you obtained this expertise.

_____

_____

_____

FIGURE 2.4   SAMPLE BALANCE SHEET FORM

Name: _____

BALANCE SHEET
as of

_____   _____   _____
(Month)   (Day)   (Year)

ASSETS

Cash & cash equivalents

Cash	_____
Chequing/savings	_____
Canada Savings Bonds	_____
Treasury bills	_____
Short-term deposits	_____
Money market funds	_____
Other	_____
Subtotal	

Subtotal _____

Business/property

Investment property	_____
Business Interests	_____
Subtotal	

Subtotal _____

Registered assets

Registered Retirement Saving Plan (RRSP)	_____
Employer's pension plan (Registered Pension Plan: RPP)	_____
Registered Retirement Income Fund (RRIF)	_____
Deferred Profit Sharing Plan (DPSP)	_____
Other	_____
Subtotal	

Subtotal _____

Personal Property

Home	_____
Seasonal home	_____
Cars and/or other vehicles	_____
Equipment	_____
Collectibles (art)	_____
Jewellery	_____
Household furnishings	_____
Subtotal	

Subtotal _____

Investments

Guaranteed Income Certificate (GIC) and term deposits	_____
Mutual funds	_____
Stocks	_____
Bonds	_____
Life insurance (cash surrender value)	_____
Provincial stock savings plan	_____
Subtotal	_____
TOTAL	_____ **(A)**

LIABILITIES

Short-term
Credit card debt _____

Personal line of credit, margin account _____

Instalment loans (e.g., car, furniture, personal loans) _____

Demand loans _____

Loans for investment purposes _____

Tax owing (income and property) _____

Other _____

Subtotal _____

Long-term
Mortgage — home _____

Mortgage — seasonal home _____

Mortgage — investment property _____

Other _____

Subtotal _____

TOTAL _____ **(B)**

NET WORTH ANALYSIS

Liquid assets vs. short-term debt
Total assets _____ (A)

Total liabilities _____ (B)

Assets exceed debt by _____

(Debt exceeds assets by) _____

Net worth (assets less total liabilities) _____ **(A – B)**

FIGURE 2.5	PERSONAL LIVING EXPENSES WORKSHEET — DETAILED BUDGET*

1. REGULAR MONTHLY PAYMENTS
Rent or house payments (including taxes) $ _____

Car payments (including insurance) _____

Appliances/TV payments _____

Home improvement loan payments _____

Personal loan payments _____

Health plan payments _____

Life insurance premiums _____

Other insurance premiums _____

Miscellaneous payments _____

Total $ _____

2. FOOD EXPENSE
Food at home $ _____

Food away from home _____

Total $ _____

3. PERSONAL EXPENSES
Clothing, cleaning, laundry, shoe repair $ _____

Drugs _____

Doctors and dentists _____

Education _____

continued

Personal living expenses worksheet — detailed budget* — continued

Union and/or professional dues   _____
Gifts and charitable contributions   _____
Travel   _____
Newspapers, magazines, books   _____
Auto upkeep, gas, and parking   _____
Spending money, allowances   _____
    Total $ _____

4. HOUSEHOLD OPERATING EXPENSES

Telephone $ _____
Gas and electricity   _____
Water   _____
Other household expenses, repairs, maintenance   _____
    Total $ _____

GRAND TOTAL

1. Regular monthly payments $ _____
2. Food expense   _____
3. Personal expenses   _____
4. Household operating expenses   _____
    Total Monthly Expenses $ _____

---

*This budget should be based on an estimate of your financial requirements for an average month based on a recent 3- to 6-month period, and should not include purchases of any new items except emergency replacements.

FIGURE 2.6   **PERSONAL SELF-ASSESSMENT QUESTIONNAIRE**

1. What personal weaknesses did you discover from analyzing your responses to the questionnaire?

_____

_____

_____

_____

2. Do you feel you can be an entrepreneur in spite of these weaknesses?

_____

_____

_____

_____

_____

3. What can you do to improve your areas of weakness?

_____

_____

_____

_____

_____

4. What did the questionnaire indicate as your strengths?

_____
_____
_____
_____
_____

5. Do your strengths compensate for your weaknesses?

_____
_____
_____
_____
_____

6. Does your lifestyle appear to be compatible with the demands of an entrepreneurial career?

_____
_____
_____
_____
_____

Exploring New Business Ideas and Opportunities

In Stage Two you had an opportunity to evaluate your own potential for an entrepreneurial career from the standpoint of your personal fit with the requirements for success, the business skills required to start and run a business of your own, and the adequacy of your financial resources. Assuming that you feel you have the "right stuff" to continue to explore this career option, you will need an idea — the seed that will germinate and, hopefully, grow and develop into a profitable enterprise. This is the topic of Stage Three.

Before getting into that, however, it is important that you have some understanding of the relationship between the entrepreneur and the actual start-up of a business. One of the major steps in this process is the recognition of an appropriate opportunity by the entrepreneur. This "opportunity recognition" has been described as perceiving a possibility for new profit potential through a) the founding of a new business, or b) the significant improvement of an existing business.[1]

Figure 3.1 illustrates a conceptual model of the relationship between an entrepreneur, their environment, and an opportunity to potentially start a new business.

An entrepreneur's personal characteristics and environment influence the process of proceeding from a new venture idea to an entrepreneurial opportunity. An important issue that relates to this process is timing; specifically

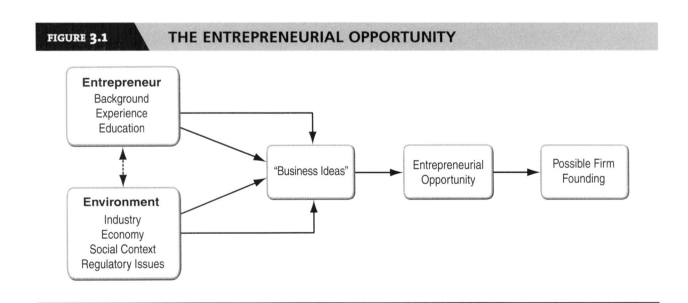

| FIGURE 3.1 | THE ENTREPRENEURIAL OPPORTUNITY |

---

1. R.P. Singh, G.E. Hills, and G.T. Lumpkin, "New Venture Ideas and Entrepreneurial Opportunities: Understanding the Process of Opportunity Recognition." Paper presented at the United States Association for Small Business and Entrepreneurship Annual Conference, 1999 (www.sbaer.uca.edu/Research/1999/USASBE/99usa657.htm).

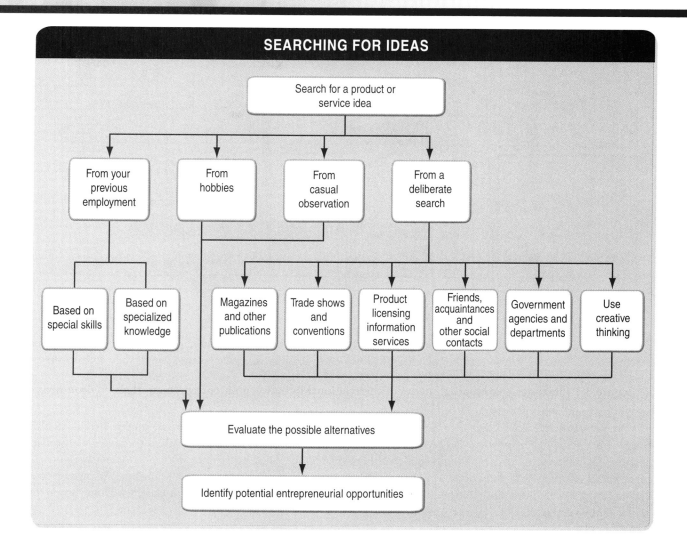

SEARCHING FOR IDEAS

Search for a product or service idea

- From your previous employment
- From hobbies
- From casual observation
- From a deliberate search

From your previous employment:
- Based on special skills
- Based on specialized knowledge

From a deliberate search:
- Magazines and other publications
- Trade shows and conventions
- Product licensing information services
- Friends, acquaintances and other social contacts
- Government agencies and departments
- Use creative thinking

Evaluate the possible alternatives

Identify potential entrepreneurial opportunities

when does an idea become an opportunity and how long after the opportunity is recognized are the necessary resources acquired and a business actually founded.[2]

As you can see from Figure 3.1, an idea is the first thing you will require to start a business. Ideas that succeed are difficult to find and evaluate but they are critical to the entire process. So while an idea is at the centre of every opportunity, not every idea represents an opportunity to start a viable business.

How entrepreneurs recognize opportunities has been a matter of considerable academic debate. Perhaps this can best be summarized by thinking in terms of two basic approaches; economic events and process models. The economic approach assumes that events occur in the economy that give rise to new opportunities. These may be conditions like demographic changes such as aging baby boomers, sociopolitical trends like the increasing recognition and acceptance of gay consumers, or the explosive growth currently taking place in certain market areas, or changes in government regulations. Changes of this nature create situations of disequilibrium in the economy that may be first recognized by certain people who have unique knowledge of marketplace conditions. This knowledge enables them to find and exploit opportunities to capitalize on these changing circumstances.

2. Singh *et al., ibid.*

© Jim Toomey, King Features Syndicate.

The second major approach to opportunity recognition views it as a multi-stage and often very complex process. There have been any number of models proposed to explain this process but one of the more comprehensive was developed by Lumpkin, Hills, and Shrader.[3] They viewed the opportunity recognition process as a type of creativity consisting of five basic elements — preparation, incubation, insight, evaluation, and elaboration. This framework is illustrated in Figure 3.2.

Preparation refers to the background, experience and prior knowledge the entrepreneur brings to the opportunity recognition process. Such preparation is typically an effort by the individual to develop expertise in some particular area. This may include such things as previous work experience, technical or market knowledge, social contacts and networks, and conscious research or general information scanning for prospective ideas. It may also include knowledge and experience that has been gathered unintentionally without any particular aim to discover some business opportunity.

FIGURE 3.2   MODEL OF ENTREPRENEURIAL OPPORTUNITY RECOGNITION

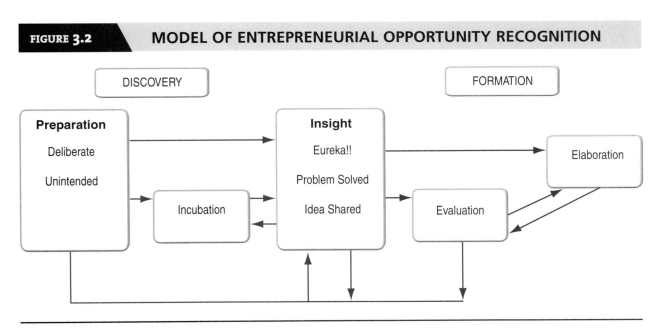

---

3. Lumpkin, G.T., G.E. Hills, and R.C. Shrader, "Opportunity Recognition," in H.P. Welsch (ed.) *Entrepreneurship: The Way Ahead*, (London, Routledge, 2004) pp. 73–90.

Incubation refers to that part of the process where the individual contemplates an idea or a specific problem. This is typically the time when the individual is mulling over the general concept or idea unconsciously in their mind.

Insight may refer to what is commonly called the "eureka" moment or the "aha" experience. This is the moment of insight or conscious awareness that the idea may, in fact, represent an entrepreneurial opportunity for them. This may be reflected in a sudden confidence that an idea will actually work or will actually solve a problem the individual has been contemplating.

Evaluation is when these insights are analyzed for their viability. This is when the entrepreneur investigates whether a concept is actually workable, whether they have the skills and capabilities to implement it, and whether it is really worthwhile for them to pursue. This evaluation often involves a feasibility study where the ideas are "put to the test" by means of concept testing, a preliminary market analysis, an initial financial assessment, and preliminary discussion of the merits of the idea with professionals and other people.

Elaboration involves moving the concept forward if it survives the Evaluation stage. This means continuing the process of business planning, finalizing choices regarding business strategy and structure, organizing resources, and all other activity that may be required to actually start up the venture.

The process in this model appears linear; it isn't. There is constant iteration and feedback during the process. At any time the entrepreneur may decide the opportunity is not a good one, that there aren't the resources available, or that the time isn't right, and bail out.

So, as you can see, an idea is the first thing you will require to start a business. However, while an idea is at the centre of every opportunity, not every idea represents a "viable entrepreneurial opportunity." This relationship is illustrated below.

Some people may come up with any number of initial new venture ideas. After some additional thought and evaluation, they may recognize that some of their ideas are potential entrepreneurial opportunities. With even further thought and consideration they may then decide to start a new venture. Perhaps only one idea in a hundred will possess the elements required to make it a success. But how do you tell an idea from an entrepreneurial opportunity? Harvard professor J.A. Timmons says *an opportunity has the qualities of being attractive, durable, and timely and is anchored in a product or service that creates or adds value for its buyer or end user.*[4] Many ideas for a prospective new business do not add much value for customers or users. To help you distinguish between a list of ideas and real opportunities you might start by asking yourself the following questions:

- Does the idea solve some fundamental consumer or business want or need?
- Is there a demand? Are there enough people who will buy the product to support a business and how much competition exists for that demand?
- Can the idea be turned into a business that will be *profitable*?
- Do you have the skills needed to take advantage of the opportunity? Why hasn't anyone else tried this concept? If anyone has, what happened to them?

In some instances what was felt to be a good idea was the key element stimulating an individual to think of going into business. In others it was the lack of an acceptable concept that was the principal factor holding back an aspiring entrepreneur. Perhaps you fall into this category. If so, it is important not to be impatient. It may take several years to fully develop and evaluate an idea that is suited to your particular circumstances and that you feel represents a real opportunity. Don't try to force the issue. Actively pursue a range of possible options, but wait until the right situation presents itself before investing your time and money.

---

4. J.A. Timmons, *New Venture Creation*, 4th ed. (Burr Ridge, IL: Irwin, 1994), p. 87.

There is no shortage of real opportunities. For example, the recipients of the 2009 Canadian Youth Business Foundation Best Business Awards were involved in a wide range of different businesses, including a retail store selling affordable activewear at reasonable prices, a physiotherapy clinic, a casual, fine dining restaurant and a number of other diverse businesses. To illustrate:

- **Shanda Jerrett** owns a retail and Internet-based wet weather boutique in Vancouver. It is a one-stop shop for wet weather products for men, women, children, and dogs from top to toe. (www.gumdropsonline.com)

- **Bryan Shopka** operates a physiotherapy clinic providing a range of treatments to treat and aid musculoskeletal conditions as well as selling orthotics and bracing products and offering Pilates and massage therapy services. (www.youtube.com/watch?v=zy6cHuXa8Hs)

- **Jessica Williamson** owns Hoopla Clothing which offers high quality, Canadian-made activewear clothing to consumers in southern Saskatchewan. (www.hooplaclothing.ca)

- **Crystal Kaufman** owns and operates a franchise of Bioped in North Bay, Ontario. As a Certified Pedorthist she specializes in assessing and providing non-surgical treatment to alleviate painful or debilitating conditions related to the feet and lower limbs. (www.bioped.com)

- **Yan** and **Sebastian Gagnon** design and manufacture motion detector digital cameras and pocket-size wireless motion detectors and receivers that are sold nation-wide. (www.ggtelecom.ca)

- **George Christakos** owns and operates The Brooklyn Warehouse, a casual, fine dining restaurant located in a historic area of Halifax. (www.brooklynwarehouse.ca)[5]

Other considerations   START-UP MYTHS AND REALITIES

Myth 1: I'm smart — I can just wing it.

Reality: Face it — you need a plan. One of the few things that small-business lenders, advisors, and consultants agree on is the need for a business plan.

Myth 2: I can do it on a shoestring.

Reality: While no one ever has enough money, having too little can spell doom. You have to have enough money for you and the company to survive until it can support itself.

Myth 3: No sweat. I have a great idea.

Reality: Great ideas are an important start for businesses but ideas alone won't get you far. You also need the resources, skills, and products to make a business grow. About 5 per cent of the success equation is having a good idea.

Myth 4: I've got nothing better to do.

Reality: You cannot start a successful small business half-heartedly. The level of commitment associated with making a quick buck is a long way from the reality needed for success in starting a new business.

Myth 5: Maybe starting a business will help our marriage.

Reality: A risky bet. The stress involved in starting a business can amplify marital weaknesses.

Myth 6: A bad economy will mean fewer competitors.

Reality: Maybe. But it can also make the survivors more fierce competitors.

Myth 7: I'm mad as hell and I'm not going to take it anymore.

Reality: The frustration that you may feel with your current job can be a good rationale for starting your own business, but only if your anger is focused on finding a positive outcome.

Myth 8: If I can't think of anything else, I'll open a bar.

Reality: Despite common opinion, restaurants and bars are not easy businesses to start or run.

Source: Dave Kansas, "Don't Believe It," *The Wall Street Journal—Small Business*, October 15, 1993, p. R8.

---

5. 2009 CYBF Best Business Award Winners (www.cybf.ca/awards/2009/entrepreneur.htm), accessed April 28, 2010.

In Stage Three we will describe a number of sources from which you might obtain ideas for a prospective new venture and present a variety of techniques you can use to evaluate the conceptual, technical, and financial aspects of your idea to determine whether it might represent a real opportunity.

These ideas will not all be equal and will originate from a number of different sources. There are three basic categories into which most of these concepts fall. They either:

- Cater to consumers in new markets (Type A)

- Introduce new technologies to the marketplace (Type B)

- Provide consumers with new or more benefits than competitive offerings currently available in the marketplace (Type C)[6]

Type A ideas typically provide customers with a product or service that does not exist in their market but already exists somewhere else. This could be something as simple as a bar or restaurant concept that you observed while on a trip and thought would be well received in your home market area.

Type B ideas involve a technically new product or process. Software you have developed to solve some business problem or a new invention or innovation that provides a better way of performing certain functions.

Type C ideas are concepts for performing old functions in new and/or better ways. They probably account for the largest number of new start-ups. These are often "me too" kind of ideas that try to differentiate themselves from other businesses by offering better service, higher quality, better performance, or lower cost.[6]

LONG-TERM EXPECTATIONS FOR YOUR BUSINESS

Whether your plans are to own and operate a business for a number of years or sell it shortly after it becomes operational, you will want to consider the long-term prospects of your venture. If you plan to keep the business, you are bound to have an interest in how it is expected to prosper; if you plan to sell the business, the prospective buyer will consider the long-term viability of the business in his or her purchase offer. So, either way, the long-term performance — the kind of firm your business may become — is important in evaluating alternatives. Opportunities with higher growth potential generally offer greater economic payoffs. However, those are not the only kind of payoffs that are important. Some small but stable ventures provide very enjoyable situations and lucrative benefits to their owners.

For purposes of assessing the expected long-term prospects of your venture, three types of possibilities should be considered:

1. Lifestyle ventures
2. Small, profitable ventures
3. High-growth ventures

LIFESTYLE VENTURES

These include most "one-man shows," mom-and-pop stores, and other lifestyle businesses such as gas stations, restaurants, dry cleaning shops, and small independent retail stores. Typically, their owners make modest investments in fixed assets and inventory, put in long hours, and earn considerably less income than the average unskilled auto worker or union craftsperson. The profit in reselling these businesses tends to be quite low.

The operator of a lifestyle business often risks his or her savings to capitalize the enterprise, and works longer hours with less job security than the average employee. Most lifestyle businesses have a high risk of failure. Unless you are willing to put up with these inherent conditions, such types of businesses should probably be avoided in favour of staying with your job until a more attractive opportunity can be identified.

SMALL, PROFITABLE VENTURES

Small manufacturing firms, larger restaurants and retail firms, small chains of gas stations, and other multi-establishment enterprises commonly fall into this category. Usually they involve a substantial capital investment — $500,000 or more. Some owners put in long hours, others do not. Once established, many owners enjoy a

---

6. Longnecker, J.G., L.B. Donlevy, V.A.C. Calvert, C.W. Moore, J.W. Petty and L.E. Palich, *Small Business Management*, fourth Canadian edition, Nelson Education, 2010, p. 30.

comfortable living. The profit in reselling the business can be high to a buyer who sees both an attractive job and a profitable investment.

You might be surprised at how many small, virtually unnoticed businesses around your city or town have managed to provide a very comfortable living for their founders. Almost always there is a very particular reason that they are able to do so: a contract the entrepreneur was able to land at favourable terms; or a market that was unknown to others or too small to attract competitors, which therefore permitted a high profit margin; or special skills or knowledge on the part of the proprietor that enabled him or her to charge high rates for his or her time. The business's advantage may be its location, perhaps purchased for a low price many years earlier, or a patented process others are not able to copy. It may even be simply a brand that is protected by trademark and has become well known over time or through successful advertising.

HIGH-GROWTH VENTURES

Much rarer than lifestyle ventures or small, profitable ventures, but typically more highly publicized, are small firms that have the capability of becoming large ones. They include many high-technology companies formed around new products with large potential markets, and also some of the small, profitable firms that, due to such factors as having amassed substantial capital or having hit on a successful formula for operating, can be expanded many times. Ventures of this type are often bought and absorbed by larger companies. The potential for significant capital gain on resale of such a business can be substantial.

A key factor in starting a high-growth venture is choosing the right industry to enter. The rate of growth of the industry as a whole often plays a large role in determining the growth patterns of start-ups within it. In addition, however, there has to be some property of the business that can readily be multiplied by that company but cannot easily be duplicated by others for there to be significant growth potential. In franchising, for example, it can be a format for doing business that has proven exceptionally effective and can be taught. In high-technology firms, it is specialized know-how in creating something at a hard-to-reach frontier of engineering for which there is a demand. If a technology is common knowledge and not too capital-intensive, then companies providing it generally do not grow very rapidly.

SOURCES OF IDEAS FOR A NEW BUSINESS

In Stage Two it was suggested that your previous jobs, hobbies, personal experiences, and the like could provide you with some of the requisite business and technical skills needed to operate your own business. Similarly, your past work experience, hobbies, and acquaintances can provide a starting point for developing a list of business ventures you might wish to consider for further investigation. The following is a brief description of some of the sources most often used by entrepreneurs in search of new business opportunities.

PREVIOUS EMPLOYMENT

Prior work experience is the most common source of new business ideas. It has been estimated that as many as 85 per cent of new businesses started are based on product ideas similar to those of prior employers of the founders. When you think about it, the attractions of starting a business in a field in which you have experience and expertise are obvious. You are already familiar with the products and services you will provide, you understand the competitive environment, you have some knowledge and understanding of customer requirements, you may already know several prospective clients, and so on.

Ideas from your previous employment can take several forms. For example, you might set yourself up as a consultant in some technical area using the background and experience you acquired in a previous job. You might develop a product or service for which your prior employer might be a prospective customer. You might even be interested in providing a product or service similar or related to that provided by your previous employer. In this last case you should check with a lawyer to ensure your plans do not violate the legal rights of that employer. You must be certain your actions do not infringe on any patent, trademark, or other proprietary rights, break any non-competition clause or other agreements you may have signed, involve the direct solicitation of your former employer's customers, or raise similar legal or ethical problems.

Jacques Lamontagne, for example, worked as a journalist and a cameraman-reporter before getting involved in the video equipment rental business. When the owner of the company he was working for decided to make some structural changes to the business that Jacques felt would negatively impact the quality of their services, he offered to buy him out. When the owner refused his offer Jacques resigned and set up a similar business of his own. Because he already had a number of contacts and several contracts from his previous position, the company appears to be heading in the right direction (Entrepreneurs in Action #6).

In another instance Mandy Kan (Entrepreneurs in Action #7) had always wanted to start her own business involving something to do with food. After graduating with a Commerce degree, she worked in a number of professional kitchens to gain some experience and attended the French Culinary Institute of New York to become a pastry chef. With more experience under her belt, gained at a number of Toronto restaurants and a stint at the Ritz Carlton hotel in Florida, she returned to Toronto to take a job as a pastry chef at an upscale grocery store and put together her business plan to open her own shop. Her plan was to sell high-quality ice cream, truffles, homemade cookies, and similar items. A year later she finally found a location in Toronto's

(6) Entrepreneurs in Action

Carving out a niche — and keeping it!

"You have to believe in what you're doing, never give up and always be honest." This could be described as the motto of Jacques Lamontagne, 34, who runs Dèpartement Camèra, a business specializing in video equipment rentals that he set up last March.

For as long as he can remember, this young businessman has had an entrepreneurial approach. "I've always worked for myself," he explains. "To start with, I installed bathroom tiles to pay for my education. After trying out the world of journalism as a presenter and cameraman-reporter for the TVA network, I switched to video equipment rentals. Now, I'm living this new adventure to the full, while completing my MBA at the same time."

To get to this point, he has had to show a lot of courage and determination. "Until the beginning of this year, I worked as a consultant for a company offering video services and equipment rentals. I put a lot into it, and when the owner decided to make a drastic change to the structure of the company which I felt would reduce the quality of the services provided, I decided to make an offer to buy him out. It was rejected. I saw it as an opportunity to set up my own business." Jacques resigned and, overnight, had to create his own enterprise.

This was a major challenge in a particularly difficult market. He was joined by six of his former colleagues, and had only a few days to get organized and obtain financing, besides convincing potential clients to trust their new venture. "Even with all the experience in the world, we were still a new business and had to prove ourselves like any other start-up — as we still do." He found this situation particularly challenging. "We are operating in a field where each piece of equipment costs several hundred thousands of dollars. We had to pay almost $350,000 for our first camera. It was no easy task to find financial backers who were willing to take up the challenge."

No doubt because he already had several contracts (Dèpartement Camèra rents out the equipment used to shoot the TV series Rumeurs and Au Nom de la Loi, among others), but also because Lamontagne is extremely persuasive and at the head of a serious, well-prepared project, he managed to convince his partners that this was a serious proposition, despite several obstacles. "It wasn't easy, our competitors put up a ferocious fight to stop us," he says. "But we had decided not to give up and we managed to persuade our suppliers to help us and work alongside us in this new adventure."

The challenge has paid off. Although the company is still in its infancy and he is putting in countless hours at the office, the entrepreneur is satisfied with what he has achieved. "It's hard to build up a company and provide customer service at the same time," he points out. "But we stuck to our plan and, even though we have to work over 80 hours a week, we are heading in the right direction."

Jacques Lamontagne believes that many entrepreneurs get discouraged early on in their project when they have to deal with financial stresses. Even though his own battle is not yet won, and probably never will be completely, he feels that he is on the right track.

Source: Yasmine Berthou, Bulletin of the Centre de Vigiesur la Culture Entrepreneuriale, Number 43, October 2005. (www.departementcamera.com)

Entrepreneurs in Action

The Dessert Lady

Choosing a name for her new Toronto bakery was a no-brainer for Mandy Kan. The 28-year-old had spent two years working as the pastry chef at the Ritz Carlton in Florida, where her loyal customers nicknamed her "the Dessert Lady."

When Ms. Kan graduated from university, she knew she wanted to open her own business — and she knew that business would involve food. She'd already worked in a couple of professional kitchens, but to give herself a real edge, she decided to attend the French Culinary Institute of New York. Six months and $26,000 later, Ms. Kan was a professional pastry chef.

She returned to Toronto, her hometown, in 2002 and, while working as a pastry chef at a high-end grocer, she began to put together a business plan for her own shop. In February 2004, she started shopping for a location.

Her plan was to sell high-quality products at her bakery, so she had to find a space in a neighbourhood that could support her business. It took an entire year to find the right spot. "I got 22 rejections before I found my location," says Mandy, who says her lack of experience as a retailer put landlords off. "I kept getting no, no, no."

One year later, Ms. Kan saw a space in Toronto's trendy Yorkville neighbourhood. She instantly knew it was right for her. "It was love at first sight," she says. And the landlord liked her idea of selling homemade cookies, cakes, truffles and ice cream.

She quit her job at the grocer. Then she researched and ordered her equipment — an oven, mixers, a fridge and freezer, and an Italian ice cream machine — all of which took nearly two months to arrive. While she waited, she began designing and renovating the 800-square-foot space, which was a blank canvas. Luckily, she had lots of friends (among them an interior designer) willing to lend a hand. They did everything themselves, except the electrical work. A graphic designer pal helped her design a logo. Doing the work herself not only saved lots of cash, but it also gave her a sense of ownership, as well. "It made me love my shop even more," she says.

With construction under way, Ms. Kan took care of the details: She bought a used cash register, and ordered her sign and packaging. She also tracked down suppliers and hired two employees.

Two months after taking over the space, Mandy was ready to open her doors. There was just one problem: She hadn't done any marketing, and money was tight. "When you open a small business, it's all about money," she says. Instead of buying ads, she launched her own word-of-mouth campaign by hosting a grand-opening party. "I printed 500 invitation cards. I went door-to-door in the neighbourhood, and passed them out to anyone who walked by," she says. Hundreds of guests showed up.

Two days before opening day, Ms. Kan and three friends began preparing inventory. In just 48 hours, they whipped up 14 flavours of ice cream, 15 kinds of truffles, and 20 varieties of cookies and biscotti, plus half a dozen cakes.

The Dessert Lady was a hit. Ms. Kan still hasn't spent a cent on marketing — instead, she relies on her repeat customers to spread the word. To lure passers-by into the shop, a staff member often stands outside handing out samples.

Now the reality of running a business has finally sunk in. "I go for a month without a single day off sometimes," says Ms. Kan. And meeting sales targets can be tricky. She quickly realized that the bakery business is seasonal — holidays like Christmas and Valentine's Day are crucial. "So when you have a chance to make money, you have to work hard and plan for those times."

Her favourite part of owning a pastry shop is coming up with original creations. It makes good business sense, too. "You can't offer the same things everyone else has," she says. "I come up with a new product at least once a month."

Ms. Kan wasn't sure how customers would take to her smoked chili chocolate cookies or her cappuccino cinnamon biscotti, but those are the products that keep regulars coming back again and again.

What really takes the cake for Ms. Kan is the pleasure she brings to her customers. "I'm a real people person," she says. "I love making each customer's day, and seeing them smile after they've tried my products." (www.dessertlady.ca)

Source: Rasha Mourtada, *The Globe and Mail*, *Globe and Mail Update*, March 13, 2007.

trendy Yorkville area that fit her concept of her business, quit her job, and started to implement her dream. The Dessert Lady was an instant hit and sales took off, even though the only marketing she did was distributing invitations in the local neighbourhood for the grand opening to generate some word-of-mouth and offering samples to passers-by on the street. Undoubtedly her prior experience in the food service field stood her in good stead in coping with the challenges of getting The Dessert Lady successfully off the ground.

YOUR HOBBIES

Some people are deeply involved with their hobbies, often devoting more time to them than to their regular job. There are many instances of such secondary interests leading to new business ventures. For example, serious athletes may open sporting goods stores, amateur photographers open portrait studios, hunters offer guiding services and run hunting lodges and game farms, pilots start fly-in fishing camps, philatelists open coin and stamp stores, and so forth.

Witness the case of Steve Sullivan in Entrepreneurs in Action #8. Steve began skateboarding at the age of 12 in his home town of Sault Ste. Marie and was instantly hooked on the sport. After attending college for a year in southern Ontario he decided to drop out and return home to attend college there. On returning to the Sault he realized just how badly the city needed a real skateboard facility and spent the next eight months

Entrepreneurs in Action

The Skateboard Specialists

24-year-old Steve Sullivan is the young owner and operator of Illenium Board Shop. It is one of the only skate shops in the area that sells skateboards, snowboards and wakeboards as well as the many accessories and paraphernalia that accompany the skateboarding lifestyle. On top of all that, Illenium also offers the use of a half pipe ramp. Steve's story is quite simple really; he merely wanted to open a business that would accommodate the growing number of people getting involved in the sport of skateboarding, and provide them with a place in town to do what they love to do best.

When Steve finished high school in Sault Ste. Marie, he moved to Barrie in order to pursue a post secondary education. After attending college for a year, he realized that he didn't enjoy the program, and didn't want to waste any more money on it. He decided that it would be more economically feasible to move back to Sault Ste. Marie to attend Sault College. With this arrangement, he could save money by living with his parents. It wasn't until Steve returned home from Southern Ontario that he realized just how badly Sault Ste. Marie needed a skateboard facility. For the next 8 months, Steve devoted himself entirely to researching everything involved in opening a skateboard park or shop/facility.

Steve's research indicated a huge need for services and opportunities targeted toward youth skateboarders in the Sault Ste. Marie area. He believed that opening a skate shop with a ramp would be a step toward a positive community development strategy. Steve and his business partner at the time went ahead and created Illenium Board Shop. It is clearly one of the best shops around, for not only does Illenium carry a huge selection of skateboards, accessories, footwear and clothing, but Steve also special orders products for his customers. He has even gone as far as building a half pipe ramp for customers to use at their own discretion, and has provided little extra services such as having a foosball table and tons of comfortable space to just hang out.

Steve began skateboarding at the age of 12 and was instantly hooked on the sport from day one. It has become a very significant part of his life ever since. Skateboarding has created an outlet for self-expression and developed an individual competitiveness within Steve that he never really knew he had. By opening Illenium, Steve has not only been able to provide many individuals with the opportunity to get more involved in skateboarding, but he has also become an important role model to many young customers, where his opinion is of the utmost importance and his advice is always taken to heart. This is what distiniguishes Steve from other local competitors: He lives the lifestyle, is part of the culture, and shares the same passion as his customers for the sport.

Source: (www.sault-canada.com/ecssm/index. aspx?1=0,2,33,65,139), accessed April 28, 2010.

researching everything involved in opening a skateboard park or shop. Steve and a business partner created Illenium Board Shop. Not only does Illenium carry a selection of skateboards, footwear, clothing and accessories but they also built a half pipe ramp that boarders can use at their discretion and provide a comfortable place where they can just hang out. Steve, himself, lives the lifestyle, is part of the culture and shares the same passion for the sport as his customers.

Many such ventures do very well, but there can be considerable conflict. Hobbies are typically activities that you and others are prepared to do at your own expense. This can exert downward pressure on the likely profitability of your business. As a result, margins are quite low in such areas as the production of arts and crafts; small-scale farming; trading in stamps, coins, and other collectibles; antique automobile restorations; and similar hobby-based operations.

PERSONAL OBSERVATION

For many people personal observation is the most practical way of identifying a business idea. Personal observations may arise from either casual observation or deliberate search.

Casual Observation

Often, ideas for a new product or service result from chance observation of daily living situations. This commonly occurs when people travel and observe product or service concepts being provided that are not yet available in the United States, Canada, or, perhaps, the person's local market area.

Restaurant themes and concepts, such as Thai, Mexican, health food, and salads, typically are established in most cities only after they have proven successful somewhere else. Sporting trends, such as wakeboarding and rollerblading, and fashion colours and styles are also usually imported from outside the country.

For this type of observation to yield results, you have to recognize the need for a new type of product or service offering and then work out some kind of solution.

For example, studies have shown that in Chicago alone, more than 80,000 cell phones are left in taxicabs over a six-month period and most are never reunited with their owners because the owners often have no idea where they lost their items. Like many other people, Jason Wagner had lost his wallet a couple of times, as well as two cell phones, his PDA, his keys, and a number of similar items. Determined to find a solution to the problem, he developed the relatively simple Trackitback system so these types of items can find their way back to their proper owner (Entrepreneurs in Action #9). Trackitback is an adhesive identification tag that can be placed on these and similar items. If someone finds a lost item, the finder can report it to Wagner's company 24/7 via its Web site or toll-free number, and Trackitback will make all the necessary arrangements to return the item to its owner. Wagner appeared on the Dragon's Den television show on CBC in early 2010 and was offered $200,000 for 25 percent of his business plus a small royalty by one of the dragons.

Entrepreneurs in Action

A Golden Retriever

To make do without some of the things you want is an indispensable part of happiness. Try espousing that bit of Bertrand Russell's philosophy to someone who's just lost his cellphone or PDA, however, and you're likely to get a withering look, if not something more physical. Gadgets often hold a career's worth of contacts and info — not to mention some pretty cool games. But they're getting smaller all the time, and a lot easier to misplace. Taxis, in particular, have become digital black holes: one study reports that nearly seven cellphones and two PDAs are left in every Chicago cab on average each year. Some claim only 5% of lost devices are ever reunited with their owners. That's partly because of a pervasive "finders keepers, losers weepers" mentality;

but, more importantly, there's typically no sure way of returning items to their rightful owners, who often have no idea where they left the stuff behind.

Winnipeg businessman Jason Wagner has lost plenty of stuff — his wallet once or twice, two cellphones, a PDA, his keys. But he's more likely to recover his belongings since his family put Trackitback labels on just about everything valuable. Trackitback is Wagner's solution to recovering lost goods. It's a simple adhesive identification tag available from most major electronics retailers for $9.99. Find something with a label on it, report it to the company 24/7 via its Web site or toll-free number, and Trackitback makes all the arrangements to return it. Finders even get a reward: $30 worth of labels.

Wagner started his recovery service three years ago (although the brand name has been in use only for the past year). He has sold 250,000 identification labels that help finders do the right thing without a whole lot of hassle. So far, he says, Trackitback has returned "hundred of items."

It's a simple concept, one similar to the key chain ID tags the War Amps charity has used for more than half a century to solicit donations. The idea is so simple, in fact, that Wagner can't patent Trackitback's technology. That's leaving him open to potential competition. There are already two competitors in the United States, although neither operates 24/7 and both charge a recovery fee on top of the cost of their labels. Wagner thinks he has a better service, and he's managed to get such Canadian retailers as London Drugs, Future Shop, Best Buy and Staples Business Depot on board. Now, the 33-year-old entrepreneur has to expand outside Canada — fast — to ward off competition. "Truth be told, the only tangible thing a customer is buying is an ID label," says Wagner. "We need to blanket this out there to prevent others from deciding they can do it, or do it better." . . .

Wagner was involved with a company that essentially tried to do the same thing nine years ago, but failed miserably. That firm, called Total Recall International, was owned by two young entrepreneurs. It marketed itself to the travel industry and relied mostly on a toll-free number. After three months on the job, Wagner was paid in company stock because the owners ran out of money. Within a year, the business was dead. "Back then it didn't work out because cellphones were the size of your shoe, PDAs didn't even exist, and the Internet was relatively in its infancy stage," Wagner says. But the idea stuck with him, even as he went on to a couple of more sales jobs. "I formulated different scenarios every night at bedtime for years and years."

Just over three years ago, Wagner finally put his thoughts into practice, testing the concept on the Web

WAYNE GLOWACKI © FREEPRESS.MB.CA

as Elissano Identification and Recovery Services. Six months in, Wagner was getting a couple of sales a week by advertising through different search engines. But it wasn't until January 2004 that he officially launched Trackitback into the retail marketplace and quit his day job as a vice-president of sales for a lighting technology company.

For the first four months after striking out on his own, Wagner worked out of his basement. But the tipping point came in February 2004, when he flew to Vancouver to meet Future Shop, London Drugs, a cellphone distribution company and Best Buy Canada. By the end of the day, the first three had agreed to carry Trackitback, and Wagner has since convinced Staples Business Depot and A&B Sound, as well as some smaller outlets, to come on board. Today, Trackitback is available in roughly 1,200 cellphone stores and more than 500 other retailers across the country. "It gives peace of mind for customers who have a product they might leave somewhere," says Nicole Spencer, a merchandise manager at Future Shop and Best Buy Canada. "It's a fairly simple service. It does take some selling at the store level, but that's the same as with any new product or service on the market." . . .

Of course, there nothing to stop U.S. competitors from changing their models to match Trackitback's offering. The idea of using ID tags to track items can't be patented, because it's not new. Still, Wagner hopes he can patent the business method behind his product as a way of fending off competition. "Really what we're selling is a service," he says. "We've just packaged it in the form of a product." (www.trackitback.com/portal)

Source: Andy Holloway, *Canadian Business*, April 11–24, 2005, pp. 75–77.

Tyler Gompf had a bad customer service experience while purchasing a home-electronics product, which gave him and his brother the idea to start a business when they graduated from university, one that could provide companies with a better way of communicating with their customers and collecting customer feedback data. Tell Us About Us (TUAU) started by developing a software application for the restaurant industry that enabled customers to answer a short questionnaire about the business using their telephone rather than by filling out the traditional comment card found on the table. The company has since expanded its service to include customer surveys, employee surveys, dial-in-and-win promotional campaigns, and mystery-shopper services for clients such as Dunkin Donuts, Dairy Queen, Arby's, and Baskin-Robbins. Revenues have doubled every year since they established the business (Entrepreneurs in Action #10).

The observation may emerge from your own experience in the marketplace, be expressed by someone else who has recognized some opportunity or problem, or be the result of observing the behaviour of other people. Regardless of its source, this type of simple observation can be the source of numerous excellent new business ideas.

Deliberate Search

While deliberate search may seem to be the most rational way of finding viable business ideas, in fact most new ventures do not start in this manner. The majority of business start-ups arise almost incidentally from events relating to work or everyday life. However, this approach should not be completely ignored, as it can be fruitful if you are committed to investigating the possibilities of starting a new business but lack the seed of any real, likely idea. For example, while studying commerce in university Chad Fischl and Dan Robinson decided to research a natural and safe product that could kill bacteria and bad odours arising from intensive sports-related activities. They found a Korean manufacturer with a patent for nano silver technology. Nano silver is an antibacterial technology which uses silver nanoparticles in water as a sterilizing agent. After visiting the facility and further investigation the pair commissioned a nano silver body wash, a deodorant, a sports equipment spray and a detergent to be marketed under the brand name of Shutout Solutions. Initial response has been very positive as they have already received endorsements from a couple of professional athletes as well as strong expressions of interest from a number of sporting goods outlets. (Entrepreneurs in Action #11)

Entrepreneurs in Action

Tell Us About Us

THE INDUSTRY

Tyler Gompf said there's a growing demand in North America for the kinds of products and services that Tell Us About Us offers.

The firm got its start by developing a software application for the restaurant industry that enabled restaurant customers to answer a short questionnaire about the establishment using their telephones, rather than by filling out a traditional comment card.

Since then, TUAU has expanded its product offering to include customer surveys, employee surveys, 1-800 customer-support services, dial-in-and-win promotional campaigns and mystery-shopper services.

"We're now a multi-tiered resource company," Gompf said.

While restaurant chains like Dunkin Donuts, Dairy Queen, Arby's and Baskin-Robbins have been a big part of TUAU's business, its customer base has since expanded to include large corporations in the telecommunications, entertainment, retailing and financial-services sectors.

And while Tell Us About Us got its start in Canada, that market now accounts for only about 10 per cent of its yearly revenues. The rest comes from the United States, which Tell Us entered into within its first year in business after a Montana casino operator stumbled upon its Web site, liked what it saw, and hired the firm to do market research.

"Up until then, we had no thought of working in the States," Gompf said. "But after that, we just never looked back." He said the company's main focus now is south of the border.

THE ENTREPRENEURS

Tyler and Kirby Gompf were fresh out of university — Tyler was 23 years old and had a sociology degree and Kirby was 22 and had a degree in information systems management — when they launched Tell Us About Us.

Tyler sounded like he wasn't quite sure how to answer when asked recently why they opted to become entrepreneurs, rather than go to work for someone else.

"It's just the way it was," he said after a brief hesitation. "Right out of school, I just knew it was something I wanted to do."

He admitted that because of their young age, they sometimes had trouble persuading prospective clients that they knew what they were doing.

"But being a technology-driven business helped," he said, because those kinds of businesses tend to be dominated by younger people who have grown up using technology and are comfortable with it.

Gompf said a bad experience while purchasing a home-electronics product gave him the idea to start a business that could provide companies with a better way of communicating with their customers and collecting customer feedback data.

KIRBY GOMPF (LEFT) AND BROTHER TYLER.
PHOTO: MIKE DEAL, *WINNIPEG FREE PRESS.*

He said there seemed to be a need for such a service, and not a whole lot of firms providing it.

Gompf said the company has managed to double its revenues every year since it was launched, and he and Kirby expect that to continue.

He added that when people ask him if he's surprised at how successful TUAU has become, "I tell them we're not there yet. There is still lots of room for growth." (www.tellusaboutus.com)

Source: Murray McNeill, "A Plan for Making a Happy Workplace," *Winnipeg Free Press*, February 6, 2007, p. B3. Reprinted with permission.

11

Entrepreneurs in Action

Rising stars help duo clean up in sports market

Two Saskatchewan entrepreneurs have managed to leverage a little stardust to help launch their product. Chad Fischl and Dan Robinson, who've yet to host the official grand opening of their business, Shutout Solutions Inc., have already enlisted endorsements from Ultimate Fighting Championship contender, Jason MacDonald, along with Joe Schuster, an internationally ranked freestyle skier from British Columbia.

If those names don't ring any bells right now, the entrepreneurs suggest they will very soon: The hope is as the athletes rise to prominence, so will Shutout Solutions product line, a suite of branded products developed to combat sports-related bacteria that cause skin irritations and bad odours from intense sweating.

While studying commerce in university, Mr. Fischl and Mr. Robinson, both recreational athletes, decide to research a natural and safe product that could kill bacteria and related athletic odours.

They found a Korean manufacturer with a patent for nano silver technology and, after graduating, visited the facility. After further extensive research, the pair commissioned a nano silver body wash, deodorant and odour-fighting sports equipment spray that is free of chemicals and irritants.

However, when their first shipment arrived, they became bogged down in import issues and border delays that held up their business for months.

"It took several months to get product through the port in Vancouver," Mr. Robinson says. "We were

continued

Entrepreneurs in Action #11 — continued

expecting it to get through in about a week but that didn't happen."

The focus and time spent simply getting the product into the country took away from other important aspects of launching a business, such as marketing and promotion.

A spontaneous decision to send product samples to athletes last April, just as the Ultimate Fighting Championship was getting underway in Montreal, paid off for the pair. "We were just kind of looking at the good guys who could maybe bring our brand up," Mr. Fischl says. "Jason MacDonald, he's the second best in Canada and trains out of Red Deer, so we thought maybe he's a little more attainable for us."

Mr. MacDonald was sent a package of Shutout Solutions samples. "He tried out our body wash and our spray on his mats and gear and then our detergent on his undergarments, which were pretty stinky," Mr. Fischl says. "About a week later he got back to his promoter and said 'Who are these Shutout guys? I really like their product and I want to get a hold of them.'"

Mr. MacDonald has since introduced the bacteria and odour-fighting products as a requisite cleaning regimen at his martial arts gym in Red Deer, Alta., and provided the entrepreneurs with a testimonial and endorsement in exchange for free product.

RICHARD MARJAN/CANWEST NEWS SERVICE

The pair received the same response from Mr. Schuster.

They've also received a tremendous reception from sporting goods outlets, including Al Anderson's Source for Sports store in Saskatoon and retail sports guru, Joe Forzani, enabling them to grow their distribution to 50 stores within months. (www.shutoutsolutions.com)

Source: Daryl-Lynn Carlson, *Financial Post*, Published: Friday, September 12,2008

A deliberate search process can be initiated by consulting the following sources.

MAGAZINES AND OTHER PUBLICATIONS

Reading business publications and other printed sources such as newspapers, specialty magazines, newsletters, and trade publications can provide ideas that might stimulate your entrepreneurial thinking. Some of the more important of these sources are listed below.

NEWSPAPERS AND MAGAZINES *The Globe and Mail* (www.theglobeandmail.com), the *National Post* (www.nationalpost.com), and *The Wall Street Journal* (www.wsj.com) offer business and classified sections that provide a listing or make other reference to available small-business opportunities. A number of Canadian magazines such as *Canadian Business* (www.canadianbusiness.com), *PROFIT* (www.canadianbusiness.com/profit_magazine/index.jsp), the Globe and Mail Report on Business Magazine (www.theglobeandmail.com/report-on-business/rob-magazine) and the Financial Post Magazine (www.financialpost.com/magazine/index.html), and U.S. publications such as *Inc.* (www.inc.com), *Entrepreneur* (www.entrepreneur.com), and *Fortune* (www.money.cnn.com/magazines/fortune/) provide further descriptions of a range of business possibilities.

NEWSLETTERS Thousands of newsletters are available, covering almost every conceivable subject. The information they contain is current and specialized, and can provide valuable access to opportunities in any field. For further information, contact the reference librarian at your public library and ask for *Newsletters in Print* (Gale Research Company, www.gale.com). It lists every major publication.

TRADE PUBLICATIONS A list of available trade publications can be obtained from *Standard Rate and Data Service* (www.srds.com), *Canadian Advertising Rates and Data* (cardonline.ca/), or similar publications available in most libraries. Trade magazines are usually the first to publicize a new product. In many cases the manufacturer is looking for help in distributing a new line. The ads will also provide information about potential competitors and their products. These trade publications are some of the best sources of data about a specific industry, and frequently print market surveys, forecasts, and articles on needs the industry may have. All this information can serve as a stimulating source of ideas.

TRADE SHOWS AND CONVENTIONS

INVENTORS' SHOWS These shows provide inventors and manufacturers with a place to meet to discuss potential products for the marketplace. Major inventors' shows are held annually in the larger cities throughout Canada and the United States. Information on upcoming shows may be available from online sources like InventNET, the Inventor's Network (www.inventnet.com/tradeshows.html), which provides a list of the major shows held throughout the United States.

TRADE SHOWS Shows covering the industry you want to enter can also be an excellent way to examine the products and services of many of your potential competitors. It can also be a way for you to meet distributors and sales representatives, learn of product and market trends, and identify potential products or services for your venture. Trade shows usually take place several times a year, in various locations. You will find trade show information in the trade magazines servicing your particular field or industry, or you could refer to the following sources:

- *Trade Shows Worldwide*, in print or online versions, Gale Research Company (www.gale.com).
- Global Sources Trade Show Centre (tradeshowcalendar.globalsources.com/TRADE-SHOW/ALL-TRADE-SHOWS.HTM) provides a detailed listing of trade shows all over the world by industry.
- EventsEye (www.eventseye.com) provides a friendly, searchable database of almost 7,000 Trade Shows, Exhibitions and Conferences scheduled to be held all over the planet.

CONVENTIONS Fairs or conventions are also an excellent place to stimulate your creative thinking. At a convention you are exposed to panels, speakers, films, and exhibitions. You also have an opportunity to exchange ideas with other people attending. Information on conventions and meetings scheduled to take place around the world can be obtained from:

- AllConferences.com (www.allconferences.com) is a directory focusing on conferences, conventions, trade shows, and workshops. The information ranges from specialized scientific, medical, and academic conferences to all kinds of general events.

PRODUCT LICENSING INFORMATION SERVICES

An excellent way to obtain information about the vast number of new product ideas available from inventors, corporations, or universities is to subscribe to a service that periodically publishes data on products offered for licensing. Licensing means renting the right to manufacture or distribute a product within agreed rules or guidelines. For example, you might purchase the right to manufacture T-shirts and sweaters with the logo of Batman, Dilbert, or other popular fictional characters, or use the trademark of a popular product such as Labatt's or Coca-Cola or sports teams from the NFL, NHL, Major League Baseball, or other organizations on similar apparel. The owner of the licence retains ownership and receives a royalty or fixed fee from you as the licensee. Here are some of the information services you can contact to locate product or service licensing opportunities:

- Flintbox (www.flintbox.com/) an intellectual property matchmaking system started by UBC Research Enterprises and now managed by Wellspring Worldwide LLC linking industry, researchers and others from over 100 countries around the world.
- Canadian Patents Database (patents1.ic.gc.ca/) administered by the Canadian Intellectual Property Office as a vehicle for inventors and entrepreneurs to get together. This database includes the full content of all patent files including an indication of which patent-holders wish to make patents available for sale or licensing. The site includes access to similar databases for trademarks, copyrights, and industrial designs as well.

FRIENDS, ACQUAINTANCES, AND OTHER SOCIAL CONTACTS

Discussions with those you know should not be overlooked as a source of insight into needs that might be fulfilled by a new venture. Comments such as "wouldn't it be nice if someone came up with something to do away with . . . " or "what this place needs is . . . " and other complaints and observations can provide a number of potential ideas.

Social networks are becoming recognized as one of the key factors in assisting many entrepreneurs in determining whether their idea may represent a real opportunity for them.

Julian Brass developed his concept for Notable TV after returning to Toronto from San Francisco where he had worked at Engage.com, a social networking site for singles. He was impressed with the number of activities and events that targeted young professionals like him and the ease with which information about those events was disseminated through his peer group. On his return to Toronto he wanted to develop some means of promoting similar events there. Initially that involved setting up a Facebook page to publish a calendar of events for his friends and colleagues and anyone else who wanted to join. When that proved successful he launched Notable TV financing it with savings and a loan from the Canadian Youth Business Foundation. After only five months the Web site seems to be doing well and is revenue positive with a growing number of businesses coming on board as content partners. (Entrepreneur's in Action #12)

GOVERNMENT AGENCIES AND DEPARTMENTS

Industry Canada, the provincial departments of economic development, the Business Development Bank (BDC), university entrepreneurship centres, small-business development centres, community colleges, and various other federal and provincial government agencies are all in the business of helping entrepreneurs by means of business management seminars and courses, advice, information, and other assistance. You can also get feedback on the viability of your business idea, or even suggestions. The Canadian Innovation Centre (www.innovationcentre.ca), for example, has a program to help inventors and entrepreneurs crystallize their ideas and commercialize and market the resulting products. The cost in most cases is nominal.

Numerous other government agencies, such as the Canada Business Services Centres of Industry Canada (www.canadabusiness.ca/eng/) also have publications and resources available to stimulate ideas for new business opportunities. Your public library can provide you with further information on all the government departments relevant to your area of interest. It is possible to get your name on mailing lists for free material, or even a government source list so that others can find out about goods or services that you may want to provide.

USE CREATIVE THINKING

Tremendous opportunities can materialize from the simple exchange of ideas among a number of people. A variety of analytical techniques and creative thinking concepts can be used to facilitate this exchange. They help to generate and subjectively evaluate a number of prospective new business opportunities. These include such approaches as the use of decision trees, force field analysis, Plus/Minus/Interesting (PMI) assessment, the Simplex Problem Solving Process — and similar concepts (see www.mindtools.com/page2.html). Perhaps the most popular approach used for this purpose is "brainstorming."

Brainstorming is a method for developing creative solutions to problems. It works by having a group of people focus on a single problem and come up with as many deliberately unusual solutions as possible. The idea is to push the ideas as far as possible to come up with distinctly creative solutions. During a brainstorming session there is no criticism of the ideas that are being put forward — the concept is to open up as many ideas as possible, and to break down any previously held preconceptions about the limits of the problem. Once this has been done the results of the brainstorming session can be explored and evaluated using further brainstorming or other analytical techniques.

Group brainstorming requires a leader to take control of the session, encourage participation by all members, and keep the dialogue focused on the problem to be resolved. It is helpful if participants come from diverse backgrounds and experiences, as this tends to stimulate many more creative ideas. A brainstorming session should be fun as the group comes up with as many ideas as possible from the very practical to the wildly impossible, without criticism or evaluation during the actual session.

Ross McGowan and his friends used a brainstorming session to generate ideas for a prospective golf-related business they might start. Eventually someone hit on the idea of establishing a golf-training centre devoted

Entrepreneurs in Action

Hey, the party's over here

Julian Brass breezes in to a stylish downtown Toronto coffee shop looking for all the world like the model of a mid-20s entrepreneur convinced that the road in front of him is wide open, and understandably so. Smartly dressed and energetic, he's just returned from Banff and the next MEDIA digital media conference where his start-up firm, NotableTV, was honoured as one of Canada's top five emerging interactive brands. "It was fantastic," Brass gushes. "I was meeting a lot of interesting people."

People who've been introduced to Brass will know that it's the second half of his statement that's the more important. Public honours are great, but it's the networking that really counts. That has been the theme that's guided his career to date and, more importantly, is now the centre of the business model for his 10-month-old Internet hub. Targeting Toronto's community of young professionals and scenesters, NotableTV is a turbo-charged take on an entertainment and lifestyle Web site, rich with video reports, blogs, photos, email alerts and commentaries from glamorous professional and lifestyle events.

The goal, Brass says, is to build his brand as the premier destination for hip Torontonians to find out what's going on around town, and where they should be heading to rub shoulders with each other. That — audience or network — can then be leveraged to generate revenue through advertising, sponsored content, event sponsorships and, eventually, licensing NotableTV content to other media, both online and traditional.

A commerce graduate from the University of Guelph, Brass developed the concept for NotableTV after returning to Toronto from San Francisco, where he'd spent 18 months working for Engage.com, a social-networking Web site for singles. Brass had been impressed in California by the sheer volume of networking events that targeted young professionals like himself, as well the ease with which information about the events moved through his peer group. When he got back to Toronto, he wanted to promote similar events in the city.

Initially, that involved setting up a Facebook group so that he could publish a calendar of events for friends

COOPER LANGFORD, FP MAGAZINE
PHOTO JAMIE HOGGE

and colleagues — or anyone else who wanted to join — and send them messages about anything that looked interesting. The group started with 75 members. Before long, it had grown to 700. Brass realized he had the makings of a business.

Brass launched NotableTV in November of 2008, financing it with savings and a loan from the Canadian Youth Business Foundation. Determining that online video would be the centrepiece of his Web site, he spent the next five months bringing together his company's core freelance team and creating content, finally going live in March.

Today, in addition to running the company, Brass serves as its public face, hosting videos, conducting interviews and figuring prominently in all aspects of the Web site, developing a personal brand to focus the company brand.

After five months, he says the company is doing well. He won't discuss financials, but he will say that NotableTV is revenue positive. He adds that he is negotiating a syndication deal with a major online portal. And with a growing number of brands, such as Bombay Sapphire, Escada, Questrade.com and New York Fries, coming on board as content partners, you may be seeing a lot more of Brass around. (notabletv.com)

entirely to the short game (Entrepreneurs in Action #13). From there they were able to go out and do a market analysis to see if the concept had any potential and the nature and extent of the competition. That analysis revealed that outside of one school in Florida, no one had thought to open a short game facility anywhere in North America and there seemed to be a tremendous need for such a centre. That was the motivation

Entrepreneurs in Action

Short Game, Big Ideas

Helping players get up and down appears to be on the upswing these days. That's what a group of golf-minded Winnipeggers guessed would be the case a little over four years ago.

Intent on starting a golf-related business but unsure about what that enterprise might be, the group convened a brainstorming session to determine what form their prospective business should take. Eventually, someone finally hit on an idea — why not open a golf training centre devoted entirely to the short game?

"The concept evolved from an idea put forth by one of our Toronto-based partners, Richard Donnelly," explained Ross McGowan, president of Winnipeg-based Short Game Golf Corporation. "The next step was to go out and do a market analysis to see if it had any potential."

What that analysis revealed was that outside of Dave Pelz's short game school in Boca Raton, Fla., no one had thought to open a short game-only practice facility anywhere in North America. Furthermore, the research showed that an untapped continental market of over 30 million golfers was there for the taking. And there was more, said McGowan.

"Our research also uncovered some other facts that underscored the need for a short game facility. First, 80 per cent of a golfer's handicap is created from 60 yards and in. Second, 65 per cent of the strokes taken in an average round occur from 60 yards and in. We also found that putting makes up 43 per cent of the strokes in an average round of golf."

Elated by its discovery, the group knew that it had to move fast to take advantage of the niche opportunity it had unearthed.

Although it took 14 months to refine the concept and find a suitable location, the wait proved to be worthwhile. A 3.8-acre parcel of land was purchased in South Winnipeg, and by May, the first PGX Short Game and Golf Training Centre was open for business.

"Winnipeg is a representative example of a mid-sized city, and the originating partners are from Winnipeg, as well. Plus there's the saying: 'If it works in Winnipeg, it will work anywhere,'" said McGowan.

Apparently, Winnipeggers have liked what they've seen.

"The reception has been excellent and is continuing to build in a positive way," McGowan said. "Membership has increased in each of the three years, and we expect to keep building on that."

Unlike other practice facilities that leave customers to their own devices, there is plenty of expert advice readily available at the Short Game Centre. Each of the six major hitting stations features a video kiosk, where instruction on any facet of the short game is only a touch of a video screen away.

While the short game concept provides the average public player an opportunity to refine what is traditionally the worst part of his or her game, McGowan is also cognizant of the fact that the facility makes a great venue to stage corporate golf outings.

"Corporate events are a huge part of our business in Winnipeg, and we see it being no different elsewhere," he said. "Staging an event at a centre is an excellent alternative to a golf tournament. It's less costly and everyone is in one place. Our goal is to have 40 corporate outings this year. We already had 25 booked by May."

The Short Game Centres [will also] get into the retail side of the game, something McGowan sees as a natural progression.

While McGowan and his cohorts want to take the concept worldwide, their main goal remains a simple one.

"Where Dave Pelz is the Rolls Royce of the short game business, we want to be the Henry Ford of the short game. We want to give the average golfer access to the finest golf and training facility in the world."

Source: Todd Lewys, "Short Game, Big Ideas," *Score*, August/ September 2001, p. 29. Reprinted with permission of *SCOREGolf* Magazine.

McGowan and his group needed to move forward with the implementation of their plan and the opening of their first centre.

However, not all ideas, even good ones, necessarily succeed. The Short Game facility in Winnipeg closed for good early in the summer of 2002. The concept definitely seemed to work but the owners miscalculated the length of the season. Rather than an April-to-October season as they expected, they discovered their season was really from May to the end of July. Manitoba golfers were just not interested in practising in August and

September. They were principally interested in getting their real games in. All was not lost, however. The U.S. Short Game rights were sold to a group looking to open a facility in Las Vegas, which has a much longer season.

The following is an example of a modified brainstorming exercise that you could use to help identify opportunities you might choose to develop for a new business.

A Four-Step Process

1. Meet with someone you trust (a close friend, relation, or other person) for one hour. With this individual discuss your strengths, weaknesses, personal beliefs, values, and similar topics. In other words, focus on what you enjoy doing because you do it well (jobs, hobbies, sports, pastimes, etc.) and where your limits are in terms of interests, ethics, capabilities.

2. After considering your strengths and weaknesses, pick the activity (job, hobby, etc.) that you enjoy the most. Think of a number of problem areas that affect you when you engage in that activity. Then meet with a group of personal acquaintances (3–5) and actively brainstorm a number of potential products or services that could solve those problems (no criticism or negative comments). In an hour you should be able to come up with 80–100 potential product/service ideas.

3. Take this list of potential ideas back to the same person you met with in (1). Reflect back on what you previously identified as your strengths and weaknesses and use that information to develop a framework to narrow the 80–100 ideas down to what you think are the five best new business ideas for you.

4. By yourself, take the five ideas and refine them down to the *one* that you feel relates most closely to your individual interests. Answer the following questions about that top idea:

   - Why did you select it?
   - Where did the idea come from?
   - What are the principal characteristics or attributes of the idea?
   - In what context did it come up during the brainstorming session?
   - What is your ability to carry out the idea?
   - What resources would you need to capitalize on the idea?
   - How profitable is a business venture based on the idea likely to be?
   - Who else might you need to involve?
   - What do you feel is the success potential of the idea you have proposed on a scale of 1 to 5 (with 5 being a very profitable venture)?[7]

The range of sources discussed here is certainly not exhaustive. Through careful observation, enthusiastic inquiry, and systematic searching, it is possible to uncover a number of areas of opportunity.

As you go about this kind of search it is important to write down your ideas as they come to mind. If you don't, a thought that might have changed your life may be lost forever.

WHERE DO NEW VENTURE IDEAS ACTUALLY COME FROM?

A survey of over 300 entrepreneurs asked them to provide the sources of the initial ideas for their business. The results are shown in Table 3.1.

Prior experience was by far the most important source of new venture ideas that led to the founding of these firms (73 per cent). However, social contacts were also very important in identifying the ideas on which their businesses were based. A large percentage of entrepreneurs identified business associates (32.8 per cent) and friends and family (19.1 per cent) as important sources of the ideas for their business.

A substantial percentage also reported that they had seen a similar business somewhere else and used that as the basis for their firm (25.8 per cent). Most of those who reported that they had seen a similar business somewhere else also based their business on their prior personal experience. This indicates that that by far the majority of entrepreneurs model their firms in some way on companies where they have previously worked; for

---

7. I would like to thank Vance Gough of Mount Royal College for permission to include this exercise.

TABLE 3.1	WHERE ENTREPRENEURS GET THE IDEAS FOR THEIR NEW VENTURES[8]

SOURCE OF IDEA	PER CENT OF RESPONDENTS*
Prior business experience	73.0%
Business associates	32.8%
Saw a similar business somewhere else	25.8%
Suggestion by friends or relatives	19.1%
Hobby/personal interest	17.2%
Personal research	11.3%
It just came to mind	10.9%
Saw something in a magazine/newspaper	2.3%
Saw or heard something on radio/television	0.4%
Other sources	4.7%

*Sums to more than 100% since respondents could indicate more than one source.

example, after working for some information technology company, these individuals may have realized they could provide some aspect of that or a similar service to clients themselves or provide a service to their employer and similar companies on a contract basis. Working in an industry provides individuals with information and access to professionals within that industry that can help them identify new venture opportunities.

AREAS OF FUTURE OPPORTUNITY

In searching for a unique business idea the best thing to keep in mind is the dynamic changes taking place within our society, our economy, and our everyday way of doing things. These changes are usually difficult to get a handle on and it is hard to understand their implications for new business possibilities, but they represent the principal areas of opportunity available today. If you think about it for a minute, most of the major growth areas in business — such as computers and information technology; satellite television systems; fast food; a wide range of personal services; smart phones and the Internet — did not even exist just a few years ago. But now they are so commonplace we take them for granted. Getting information on emerging trends and assessing their implications for various business situations can be a major road to significant business success.

What can we expect in the future? No one has a crystal ball that can predict these changes with 100 per cent accuracy, but many books and business publications provide projections of future trends and changes that could be useful to the insightful observer. For example, over 10 years ago Faith Popcorn, the consumer trend diva, first prophetically envisioned a number of evolving social trends she felt would have a major impact in North American society. These included:

- **99 Lives** Too fast a pace and too little time causes societal schizophrenia and forces us to assume multiple roles. Popcorn says that time is the new money — people would rather spend money than time — and predicted that 90 per cent of all consumer goods will soon be home-delivered.

- **Anchoring** A reaching back to our spiritual roots, taking what was secure from the past to be ready for the future. Popcorn noted that more and more people are returning to traditional Western religions, feeling that religion is an important part of their lives, or are exploring non-western alternatives in their search for spirituality and healing.

- **AtmosFEAR** Polluted air, contaminated water, and tainted food stir up a storm of consumer doubt and uncertainty. Headlines scream about E. coli, mad cow disease, anthrax threats, and other environmental problems. Bottled water has become a billion-dollar business in North America alone.

- **Being Alive** Awareness that good health extends longevity and leads to a new way of life. Look at the tremendous surge in the sales of organic products and herbal additives and remedies, and the popularity of fitness clubs and gyms, acupuncture, magnets, meditation, and other forms of alternative medicine.

---

8. Singh, Hills, and Lumpkin (1999).

- **Cashing Out** Working women and men, questioning personal/career satisfaction and goals, opt for simpler living. Stressed consumers, she says, are searching for fulfillment and simplicity but going back to basics in their lifestyles, consciously opting for more leisure time or getting out of the rat race by starting a home-based or other small business.

- **Clanning** Belonging to a group that represents common feelings, causes, or ideals; validating one's own belief system. People are banding together to form common-interest clubs, groups, and other organizations where they can share opinions, beliefs, complaints, or whatever else they are feeling with other like-minded individuals.

- **Down-Aging** Nostalgic for their carefree childhood, baby boomers find comfort in familiar pursuits and products from their youth. Music, automobile brands, movies, and a variety of other names and products from the 1960s and 1970s are all being resurrected in response to this demand.

- **Egonomics** To offset a depersonalized society, consumers crave recognition of their individuality. This has created opportunities for improved customer service by increasingly recognizing the specific needs of individuals or for the "ultracustomization" of products and services to the specific requirements of particular customers.

- **EVEolution** The way women think and behave is impacting business, causing a marketing shift away from a traditional, hierarchical model to a relationship model. As Popcorn notes, women have far more financial influence then has traditionally been recognized. They own one-third of all North American businesses and control 80 per cent of all household spending in the country. As a consequence, marketing to them in an appropriate manner can mean a significant business opportunity.

- **Fantasy Adventure** The modern age whets our desire for roads untaken. Exotic theme hotels in Las Vegas are exploding, theme parks are booming, cruise lines are expanding, adventure and eco-tourism are growing, and theme rooms and suites in hotels are becoming increasingly popular as people strive to satisfy their exotic fantasies.

FYI / FOR YOUR INFORMATION

The Best Business Opportunities for 2010

1. **E-Learning:** Learning electronically over the Internet by specializing in delivering highly focused content.
2. **Contractor Referral Service:** Helping homeowners find a reliable and trusted service for home repairs.
3. **On-Site Computer Service:** Serving business and consumer clients on-site with computer repair, upgrades and networking services.
4. **Direct Selling:** Direct selling and network marketing are hot in times of economic uncertainty like now with the increasing need for supplementary income.
5. **Online Gaming:** The online gaming industry is exploding and while competition is tough for online gaming developers, opportunities exist to serve the companies that are developing all these games.
6. **Management Consulting:** Prospects look strong because consulting is driven by factors like globalization, deregulation, rapid technological change and outsourcing.
7. **Search Engine Optimization:** For large and small companies optimizing their Web pages to provide top listing on search engines such as Google is a task to be outsourced to professionals
8. **Public Relations Consulting:** Freelance PR consulting offers varied projects and the opportunity for a high level of creativity.
9. **Home Inspection:** The housing market is hot and buying a home is a large investment creating a need for due diligence which can be provided by a certified home inspector.
10. **Information Professional:** Information professionals or researchers can search the Internet for information using advanced search techniques beyond the scope of most average Internet users.

Source: Darrell Zahorsky, About: Small Business: Canada (sbinfocanada.about.com/cs/bestpractices/a/aa122902a_htm).

- **Icon Toppling** A new socioquake transforms mainstream North America and the world as the pillars of society are questioned and rejected. Increasingly sceptical consumers are ready to bring down the long-accepted monuments of business, government, and society. Large companies no longer hold our trust. Loyalty to a single employer has gone the way of the dinosaur. Governments are now a reminder of cynicism and distrust. And the views of doctors, lawyers, and other professionals are no longer accepted without question.

- **Pleasure Revenge** Consumers are having a secret bacchanal. They're mad as hell and want to cut loose again. They are tired of being told what's good for them, so are indifferent to rules and regulations and want to enjoy some of the more "forbidden" aspects of life. Steakhouses, martini bars, and similar diversions are all popular reflections of this trend.

- **Small Indulgences** Stressed-out consumers want to indulge in affordable luxuries and seek ways to reward themselves. Premium-priced products such as ice cream, sunglasses, chocolate, liqueur, and similar items have become one way for consumers to reward themselves at moderate expense at the end of a hard day or week.

- **SOS (Save Our Society)** The country has rediscovered a social conscience of ethics, passion, and compassion. We are seeing more corporations make a commitment to return some proportion of their profits to the community; consumers are becoming more responsive to companies that exhibit a social conscience attuned to ethical concerns, education, or the environment; and there has been a increase in the popularity of "ethical" and "socially responsible" mutual funds.

- **Vigilante Consumer** Frustrated, often-angry consumers are manipulating the marketplace through pressure, protest, and politics. Consumers seek real products, benefits, and value. When they are disappointed, they can be formidable enemies. At any one time there are typically a number of boycotts in progress against some company. This has really been facilitated by the growth of the Internet, where consumers can set up chat rooms, news groups, and Web sites to carry on their complaint against some particular company or brand.[9]

The kind of social changes mentioned by Popcorn have largely materialized and evolved over the past few years and will help define the future orientation of our society. And while being aware of such changes is interesting, how does it translate into an entrepreneurial opportunity? Keeping on top of such trends can provide the inspiration for many significant new businesses for an observant entrepreneur. As the futurist John Naisbitt said, "trends, like horses, are easier to ride in the direction they are going".

SOME SPECIFIC IDEAS AND CONCEPTS FOR THE FUTURE

In view of all these evident trends, a number of specific business ideas might be expected to do well in the marketplace of the future.

The list that follows will expand on some of the possible implications of these trends and give you some idea of specific businesses they indicate should be potential opportunities. The list is by no means complete, but it will give you a few things to think about.

MAINTAINING "WELLNESS" is an emerging theme that will create a growing demand for a variety of fitness and health-related products. People are focusing on experiencing a better quality of life by shaping up and healing their minds and bodies. New venture opportunities exist in the following areas:

- Healthier and organically-grown food products
- Alternative medicine and homeopathic remedies
- Spas and cosmetic surgery centres
- Holistic health clubs and fitness centres
- Holistic healing and the use of ancient remedies
- Restaurants emphasizing low-fat and other types of "healthy" foods

PERSONAL INDULGENCE is almost the opposite of the "wellness" trend, with people wanting to reward themselves periodically with small, affordable luxuries. New venture opportunities here could include:

- Individual portions of gourmet foods
- Specialty ice cream and other exotic desserts

---

9. F. Popcorn and L. Marigold, *Clicking: 17 Trends That Drive Your Business — and Your Life* (New York: HarperBusiness, 1998).

- Specialty coffee, tea, and wine shops
- Exotic meats such as elk, wild boar, bison, ostrich, and venison
- Bed-and-breakfast places or small hotels with specialty services
- Aromatherapy

HOME HEALTH SERVICE AND ELDERCARE will continue to be a rapidly growing market with the aging of the baby boomers and the ever-increasing costs and declining quality of health care. Opportunities for businesses in this area include:

- Home health care providers such as physiotherapists, occupational therapists, and nursing assistants
- Door-to-door transportation services for the elderly
- Homemaking services
- Daycare centres for the elderly
- Seniors' travel clubs
- Independent, residential, and assisted-living centres
- Products and services for the physically challenged

PET CARE AND PAMPERING represents a significant market opportunity as well for specialized care products and services. Some opportunities for businesses here include:

- Pet daycare centres and hotels
- Pet snacks and treats
- Home grooming services for pets
- 24-hour veterinary care
- Baked products for dogs
- Pet furniture and clothing stores

RETAIL BOUTIQUES with narrow sales niches will increase in number as the category-killer box stores and discount department stores expand across the country and come to dominate most conventional retail markets like building materials, lawn and garden supplies, books, computers and office supplies, consumer electronics, food products, and other categories. Opportunities for one-of-a-kind stores include:

- Second-hand goods
- Bakery cafés
- Specialty shoe stores
- Home decorating
- Birding
- Gardening centres
- Stress relief
- Craft stores
- Travel-related products and services
- Homeopathic remedies
- Microbreweries

PERSONAL SERVICES OF ALL TYPES will grow in popularity as people spend more time at work and have fewer leisure hours. As a result they will be willing to pay others to run their errands and handle many time-consuming home and family-related matters. Providers of these personal errand services could perform a variety of tasks such as grocery shopping, picking up laundry, buying theatre tickets, having shoes repaired, and other

Other considerations   WHY AN E-BUSINESS TODAY?

1. The Internet is the fastest-growing market opportunity today, promising a remarkable growth curve for entrepreneurs who like to think big.
2. The Net can make things better, faster, and cheaper, all in one place.
3. The number of Canadians with access to the Internet is soaring and they represent an affluent group.
4. The Web loves entrepreneurs, particularly women, because it's an ideal equalizer. It allows the breakdown of gender, geographic, and other barriers and enables small businesses to compete against big firms.
5. E-commerce makes your domestic market everyone's export market. It blurs the distinction between domestic and international markets.

Source: Based on Royal Bank, *Champions: Breakthroughs and Resources for Women Entrepreneurs*, Summer 2000.

jobs. They could also arrange for the repair and servicing of cars, take care of pets, choose gifts, consult on the selection of clothes, and handle similar personal matters. Other opportunities in this area include:

- Personal concierge service
- Gift services
- Pickup and delivery service for guests and clients
- Rent-a-driver
- Rent-a-chef
- Personal escort service

E-BUSINESS is growing explosively and interest is likely to continue to be strong despite the problems and failures of a number of business-to-consumer (B2C) Web-based companies. These were largely situations where the business model had not been well defined and developed, where the business operators had underestimated the financial and technical resources required to get their business to the break-even point, or that were simply poorly managed and the financial reserves that were available for them to get the business off the ground were squandered. Despite this shakeout, use of the Internet continues to grow rapidly and e-commerce still presents a large number of potential opportunities for either new or existing businesses. Many forecasters predict that business-to-business (B2B) e-commerce will grow more than 10 times faster then B2C commerce, so most of the attractive opportunities are likely to be found in this arena.

There is no doubt the Internet will continue to change the way we communicate and conduct business. Regardless of whether your venture is Web-based or not, you will still likely have a Web page for customer support and communication, to complement your advertising and marketing program, to offer product information, to conduct research and obtain competitive intelligence, or to network with other business owners. New venture opportunities using the Internet could include:

- Designing, hosting, and maintaining Web sites
- Internet marketing consulting services
- Software development for very specific applications
- Selling specialty products such as small-business equipment, health-related equipment and supplements, cosmetics and anti-aging products, home-delivered meals and specialty foods, gaming services and related products, travel and leisure products and services, multimedia packages and programs, and a wide range of other products that serve narrow markets around the globe, 24 hours a day, 7 days a week.

Register a Domain Name

If you decide you want to do business online, the first thing you will need is a *domain name*. A domain name gives your Web site an Internet address. It consists of three components — a server prefix (www), a domain name (blueskycorp) and a domain extension (dot-com or dot-ca). Your domain name should be something that not only identifies your business but is easy to remember. The name of your business is probably the best choice for you if it hasn't already been taken.

In most cases you will probably want to register both the generic top level domain extension (dot-com) as well as the country code domain extension (dot-ca) if only to prevent someone else from registering that domain. You may choose to use either one depending upon whether you wish your business to have a distinctively Canadian identity for some reason or if you hope to be able to do business in more than this country. You could choose to register other similar variations of your preferred domain name as well to make certain no one else is able to register them.

Once you have decided on the domain name you might like, it needs to be registered with an accredited registrar. Log onto the Web site of the Canadian Internet Registration Authority (CIRA) at www.cira.ca. They maintain an extensive list of Accredited Registrars and you must use one of them to register a dot-ca domain name. You can also register generic domain names like dot-com or dot-org there as well. The CIRA's Web site and the registrar's Web sites also have a link where you can search the availability of the domain name(s) you have selected. Once you have found a domain name that is available it's just a matter of following the directions on the Web site to register the name.

Domain names can typically be registered for one year or for up to five years. Registrars set their own fee schedules but averages between $30 and $50 per name per year. Many registrars will host the Web site you set up for your domain name for a fee as well.

Choose an Online Business Model

The next step if you intend to set up an Internet-based business is to figure out how you are going to make any money. Numerous Web sites generate lots of traffic but never make any money because they don't have a well developed business model. Susan Ward identified seven different online models that can get you started on the right financial path.

1. **Set up an E-Commerce Site** The classic, conventional site is designed to make money online by selling products. Today most bricks and mortar retailers also have an e-commerce site although more and more we are seeing businesses that only sell over the Internet. You can set up your own online store from scratch or choose one of the many complete 'business in a box' solutions such as eBay's ProStores or osCommerce Online Merchant.

2. **Set up a Sales Letter E-Commerce Web site** These Web sites are like infomercials on TV and make the pitch focusing on educating potential customers on the merits or benefits of the products or services being promoted and sold. These Web sites tend to be long on copy and short on pictures generally focused around some theme such as losing weight, getting into better shape, curing some medical problem like arthritis or migraines, increasing sales in your business, etc. Special 'buy-now' offers are common to encourage customers to act right away.

3. **The eBay Auction Model** The eBay auction model can be especially attractive to people just starting an online business. It's a cheap and easy way to get started and test the demand for the products you want to sell. Then, if things go well, you can move on to your own online store in conjunction with eBay or on your own. All you have to do is register with eBay or eBay Canada, sign up for Paypal if you wish and fill out a "Sell Your Item" form.

4. **Establish a Stand-Alone Blog** Blogs are popping up all over the Net in many cases just to get someone's thoughts and ideas 'out there' but anyone can self-publish their work online very easily or find other ways to make money from their blog. The standard business model to make money is to run ads on the blog but there are also other methods such as joining affiliate programs like Amazon and others, getting yourself hired or sponsored by a company, creating a blog to advertise a specific product or service or selling your own intellectual property like books, educational courses or consulting services over the Net.

5. **Set up a Service Business Web site** A service business Web site is typically designed to sell the services and skills of the individual or group of individuals behind the site. These are difficult to

show online so sites focused on biographies of the people and testimonials from previous users of their service. Such sites are usually supported by some sort of free service such as a newsletter to which viewers can subscribe or tips that may be helpful to people who are interested in the service area. These sites can also be used for selling books and/or CD's and tapes prepared by the owner of the site.

6. **Create an Info-Site** An info-site is a Web site that focuses on presenting information usually on a specific topic such as small business, gardening, video gaming or similar areas of interest to many people. They are developed on the theory that enough people will be interested in the information to seek it out, visit the site and support it by clicking on or buying something. NotableTV developed by Julian Brass (Entrepreneurs in Action #10) is a social networking and info-site letting Toronto's young professionals know what's happening around town that may be of interest to them. Info-sites can make money by selling their content through subscription or syndication, or through advertising and affiliate programs. Some may sell products directly related to the information they provide as well.

7. **Establish a Brochure Site** A brochure site is really an adjunct to a business that already has a strong offline presence. It is essentially an online business card presenting the name of the business, some information about the products and services the business provides and how to contact the business for further information. A brochure site is not likely to make money online in and of itself. It is essentially an Internet billboard providing people with a way to quickly obtain basic information about the business such as phone numbers and directions to the offline location. As a business model it can be useful for purposes like a registration site for conferences, conventions and special events.[10]

Any of these business models have the potential to be successful. While presented as being distinct situations that doesn't have to be the case. You might decide to combine more than one of these models into a single site. For example, to add a blog to your conventional e-commerce business site or to have more than one site each based on a different model to reach different markets or to drive more business to your primary site.

FYI FOR YOUR INFORMATION

With the ever increasing popularity of e-business, here are a few Web sites you might want to check out for more information on doing business on the Internet:

E-Business A series of Web sites discussing what you need to know to set up an E-Business (/www.canadabusiness.ca/eng/145/148/)

Ebiz.enable A comprehensive online resource that allows you to explore e-business problems and solutions relevant to your company and its success (/www.ic.gc.ca/eic/site/ee-ef.nsf/eng/home)

E-Business Info-Guide A Web site designed to help you navigate through the different government programs, services and regulations that deal with electronic commerce, and identify those of interest. (www.ontario.ca/en/business/STEL02_039938)

E-Business Overview A guide to help you understand the concept of e-business and how e-business can improve your business operations. (*www.canadabusiness.ab.ca/docs/E-Business_Overview%5B1%5D.doc*)

About.com: Small Business: Canada A link to a series of Web sites about starting an online business (sbinfocanada.about.com/lr/starting_an_online_business/201275/4/)

---

10. Susan Ward, *7 Online Business Models, Part 1: How to Make Money Online,* About.com Small Business: Canada (sbinfocanada.about.com/od/onlinebusiness/a/onlinebizmodels.htm) accessed May 2, 2010.

EVALUATING YOUR IDEAS

As you have seen, generating ideas for a prospective new business is a relatively simple procedure — the end result of which is a number of potential business opportunities that may, or may not, have a chance of becoming successful ventures.

Discovering ideas is only part of the process involved in starting a business. The ideas must be screened and evaluated, and a selection made of those that warrant further investigation. It is essential that you subject your ideas to this analysis to find the "fatal flaws" if any exist (and they often do). Otherwise, the marketplace will find them when it is too late and you have spent a great deal of time and money.

But how can you determine which ideas you should evaluate? Of the multitude of possible alternatives, which are likely to be best for you? Knowles and Bilyea suggest that you think of the process of selecting the right opportunity for you as a huge funnel equipped with a series of filters. You pour everything into this funnel — your vision, values, long-term goals, short-term objectives, personality, problems, etc. — and a valuable business idea drains out the bottom.[11] This opportunity selection process contains six steps:

1. Identify your business and personal objectives.
2. Learn more about your favourite industries.
3. Identify promising industry segments.
4. Identify problem areas and brainstorm solutions.
5. Compare possible solutions with your objectives and opportunities in the marketplace.
6. Focus on the most promising opportunities.

Step 1: Identify Your Business and Personal Goals

List your personal and business goals. What do you want from your business? Money? Personal fulfillment? Independence? To be your own boss? Freedom? Control over your own destiny? Think back to what stimulated your interest in thinking about going into a business of your own in the first place. List everything you would like to accomplish and what you expect your business to be able to provide.

At this stage it might help to meet with someone whom you trust — a close friend, relation, or other person — for an hour or so. With this individual you can discuss your strengths and weaknesses, goals, values, ethical standards, and similar personal issues. She or he can help you focus your goals and refine your thinking in relation to what you enjoy doing, what you are good at, and where your limits are in terms of interests and capabilities.

Step 2: Research Your Favourite Industries

As you considered the variety of trends we discussed earlier in this Stage, there were undoubtedly a number of possibilities that captured your interest. Now you should explore a couple of these situations in more detail. These industries should be ones that interest you and about which you have some first-hand knowledge. They could be food service, travel, manufacturing, retailing, construction, or whatever.

After you have picked your industries, investigate all the information you can find about them from business publications, government agencies and departments, trade magazines, the Internet, and similar sources. The Industry Canada Web site (www.ic.gc.ca) and online databases such as ABI/Inform and Canadian Business and Current Affairs (CBCA) available at your local university library can point you to hundreds of articles related to almost any field. Focus on such areas as the history of the business, the nature and degree of competition, recent industry trends and breakthroughs, number and distribution of customers, and similar topics. It will help to write a brief industry overview of each situation after you have completed your investigation.

Step 3: Identify Promising Industry Segments

With a thorough understanding of one or more industry situations you are now in a position to identify possible market segments where you think you could survive and prosper. Profile your typical target customer — a person or business who needs a particular product or service you could provide.

11. Ronald A. Knowles and Cliff G. Bilyea, *Small Business: An Entrepreneur's Plan*, 3rd Canadian ed. (Toronto: Harcourt Brace & Company, 1999), p. 55.

If you are looking at the consumer market, identify what this prospect will look like in terms of demographic factors such as age, gender, location, income, family size, education, and so on, and in terms of psychographic and other factors such as interests, values, lifestyle, leisure activities, and buying patterns. If you are looking at a commercial/industrial market, use company size, industry, geographic location, number of employees, and so on.

Step 4: Identify Problem Areas and Brainstorm Solutions

Identify the problem areas for some of these groups of customers that you feel are currently being met ineffectively. What "gaps" are there in terms of the needs of these customers that you feel you can address? Get together with a group of people who know something about business and the industry. Try to actively brainstorm a list of products and services that could represent potential ways to solve these problems. Keep your discussion positive. Let your imagination roam. Don't be concerned with the merits or demerits of an idea at this stage. Just try to make note of as many potential ideas as you can. You should be able to come up with 80 – 100 or more prospective ideas in an hour.

Refine your list. Try to narrow it down to the five or ten best ideas for you based on your interests, goals and objectives, strengths and weaknesses, and available resources.

Step 5: Compare Possible Solutions with Your Objectives and Opportunities in the Marketplace

THE "IDEAL" OR "MODEL" BUSINESS MODEL

Richard Buskirk of the University of Southern California designed a framework you can use to evaluate the pros and cons of your potential business ideas.[12] It is built around what he calls the "Ideal" or "Model" business. The framework contains 19 distinct factors that affect the chances of success for any new business. Very few ideas will conform precisely to the specifications of the model, but the more a business idea deviates from the "ideal," the more difficulties and greater risks you will encounter with that venture. Testing your concepts against the model will also help identify the areas in which you might expect to have difficulties with your business.

The model is presented in Table 3.2. Let us briefly discuss each of the factors listed.

TABLE **3.2**	CHARACTERISTICS OF THE "IDEAL" BUSINESS

- Requires no investment
- Has a recognized, measurable market
- A perceived need for the product or service
- A dependable source of supply for required inputs
- No government regulation
- Requires no labour force
- Provides 100 per cent gross margin
- Buyers purchase frequently
- Receives favourable tax treatment
- Has a receptive, established distribution system
- Has great publicity value
- Customers pay in advance
- No risk of product liability
- No technical obsolescence
- No competition
- No fashion obsolescence
- No physical perishability
- Impervious to weather conditions
- Possesses some proprietary rights

12. Richard Buskirk, *The Entrepreneur's Handbook* (Los Angeles: Robert Brian, Inc., 1985), pp. 41–45.

REQUIRES NO INVESTMENT If you don't have to put any money into your business, then you can't lose any if it fails. You lose only the time you have invested. The more money that must be committed to the venture, the larger the risk and the less attractive the business becomes. Some new businesses, such as fancy theme restaurants, may require so much initial capital there is really no way they can be financially profitable. Smart businesspeople tend to avoid businesses that require a large investment of their own money.

HAS A RECOGNIZED, MEASURABLE MARKET The ideal situation is to sell a product or service to a clearly recognized market that can be relied on to buy it. This may require doing a preliminary investigation of the market acceptance of your idea or concept. Look for some market confirmation of what you propose to offer before proceeding any further.

A PERCEIVED NEED FOR THE PRODUCT OR SERVICE Ideally, your intended customers should already perceive a need for what you intend to sell them. They should know they need your product or service now, thus simplifying your marketing efforts. If they don't recognize their need, you have to first persuade them they need the product and then convince them to buy it from you. Try to avoid products or services that require you to educate the market before you can make a sale.

A DEPENDABLE SOURCE OF SUPPLY FOR REQUIRED INPUTS Make certain you can make or provide what it is you plan to sell. Many businesses have failed because they were unable to obtain essential raw materials or components under the terms they had originally planned. Sudden changes in price or availability of these key inputs can threaten the viability of your entire venture. Large corporations commonly try to directly control or negotiate long-term contracts to assure reliable and consistent supplies. You have to be just as concerned if there are only one or two sources for the materials you require.

NO GOVERNMENT REGULATION The ideal business would not be impacted at all by government regulation. This is impossible in today's world, but some industries are more subject to government involvement than others. Food, drugs, financial services, transportation, communications, etc., are all examples of businesses that require extensive government approval. If your business falls into this category, make sure you understand how government regulations will affect you in terms of time and money.

REQUIRES NO LABOUR FORCE The ideal business would require no labour force. This is possible in one-person operations — the "one-man show." Once you hire an employee you have a lot of government paperwork to deal with relating to Employment Insurance, Canada Pension, and other legal requirements. You are also subject to a broad range of regulations concerning such things as occupational health and safety, human rights, and pay equity. Few small-business operators enjoy dealing with these requirements, and they can be quite time-consuming. If your business demands the hiring of additional employees you must be prepared to take on the responsibility for managing these people effectively.

PROVIDES 100 PER CENT GROSS MARGIN While virtually no businesses provide a 100 per cent gross margin, the idea is that the larger the gross margin, the better the business. Gross margin is what you have left after paying the *direct* material and labour costs for whatever it is you are selling. For example, say you are running an appliance repair business. A typical service call takes one hour, for which you charge the customer $50. However, this call costs you $15 in direct labour and $5 in parts and materials; therefore, your gross margin is $30, or 60 per cent. Service industries like this generally have larger gross margins than manufacturing businesses.

In businesses with low gross margins, small errors in estimating costs or sales can quickly lead to losses. These businesses also tend to have a high break-even point, making it very difficult to make a lot of money. High-margin businesses, on the other hand, can break even with very small sales volumes and generate profits very quickly once this volume of business is exceeded.

BUYERS PURCHASE FREQUENTLY The ideal business would provide a product or service that customers purchase very frequently. This gives you more opportunities to sell to them. Frequent purchasing also reduces their risk in case your offering doesn't live up to their expectations. You are much more likely to try a new fast-food restaurant that has opened in town than you are to purchase a new brand or type of washing machine, fax machine, home theatre system, or other such item.

RECEIVES FAVOURABLE TAX TREATMENT Firms in certain industries may receive tax incentives such as accelerated depreciation on capital assets, differential capital cost allowances, investment tax credits, or various other tax breaks. The ideal business will receive some sort of favourable or differential tax treatment. This sort of advantage can make your business more profitable and attractive to other investors should you require outside capital.

HAS A RECEPTIVE, ESTABLISHED DISTRIBUTION SYSTEM Ideally, your business would sell to established middlemen and distributors who are eager to handle your product. If you have to develop a new method of distribution or are unable to obtain access to an existing one, getting your product to market can be a long and costly process. If traditional wholesalers and retailers are not prepared to carry your line, achieving any reasonable level of market coverage can be extremely difficult.

HAS GREAT PUBLICITY VALUE Publicity in magazines, in newspapers, and on television has great promotional value, and what's more, it's free. If your offering is sufficiently exciting and newsworthy, the resulting publicity may be sufficient to ensure a successful launch for your business. The publicity given to restaurant concepts like the Cactus Club, the initial radio and television coverage of Al Pooper Scoopin', a business to clean up the "doggie doo" in one's backyard, and favourable reviews of local restaurants by newspaper food critics are all examples of tremendously helpful public notice of new products.

CUSTOMERS PAY IN ADVANCE A major problem facing most new businesses is that of maintaining an adequate cash flow. Typically, small firms are chronically short of cash, the lifeblood they require to pay their employees, their suppliers, and the government on an ongoing basis. The ideal business would have customers who pay in advance. This is in fact the case for many small retail service firms, the direct-mail industry, and manufacturers of some custom-made products. Businesses where customers pay in advance are usually easier to start, have smaller start-up capital requirements, and don't suffer the losses due to bad debts incurred on credit sales.

NO RISK OF PRODUCT LIABILITY Some products and services are automatically subject to high risk from product liability. Anything ingested by the customer, amusement facilities such as go-cart tracks and water slides, and many manufactured products that possibly could cause injury to the user — all are loaded with potential liability. Liability can occur in unexpected situations, such as the serious injury recently sustained by a golfer whose golf club shattered and impaled him in the chest.

Try to avoid such high-risk businesses, or take every precaution to reduce risk, and carry lots of insurance.

NO TECHNICAL OBSOLESCENCE The ideal product or service would not suffer from technical obsolescence. The shorter the product's expected technical life expectancy, the less desirable it is as an investment. Products like popcorn, shampoo, garden tools, and electric drills seem to have been with us for as long as most of us can remember. On the other hand, the Blue-ray player, MP3 player, and smart phone are of recent origin and are undergoing rapid technological transformation. Businesses built around these products are extremely risky for smaller firms and have a very high probability of failure.

NO COMPETITION Too much competition can be a problem, since aggressive price competitors can make it very difficult for you to turn a profit. Not having any competition can certainly make life much easier for a new small business. But if you ever find yourself in this happy situation, you should ask yourself why. True, your offering may be so new to the marketplace that no other firms have had a chance to get established. But maybe it is just that other firms have already determined there really is no market for what you are planning to provide.

NO FASHION OBSOLESCENCE Fashion products usually have extremely short life cycles. You must be sure you can make your money before the cycle ends, or be prepared to offer an ongoing series of acceptable products season after season, if you hope to build your business into a sizeable enterprise. Fashion cycles exist not only for clothing and similar products but also for items like toys — witness what happened with the hula hoop, Wacky Wall Walker, Rubik's Cube, and Cabbage Patch dolls.

NO PHYSICAL PERISHABILITY Products with a short physical life have only a limited window available for their disposition. This applies not only to most food items but also to a wide variety of other goods such as photographic film. If your product is perishable, your business concept must include some method of selling your inventory quickly or a contingency plan to dispose of aged merchandise before it spoils.

IMPERVIOUS TO WEATHER CONDITIONS Some businesses are, by their very nature, at the mercy of the weather. If the weather is right for them, they prosper; if not, they may go broke. Pity the ski resort owner without any snow, the waterslide operator with a year of unseasonably cold weather, the beach concession during a summer of constant rain, the market gardener in the midst of an unexpected drought. The ideal business would not be impacted by these unpredictable changes in the weather.

POSSESSES SOME PROPRIETARY RIGHTS The ideal business would possess significant proprietary rights that give it some unique characteristic and protection against competition. These rights can be in the form of registered patents, trademarks, copyrighted material, protected trade secrets, licensing agreements that provide some sort of exclusive manufacturing arrangements, or perhaps rights for exclusive distribution of certain products in particular markets. Gendis Corporation, for example, was largely built on the rights to distribute first Papermate pens and then Sony products in Canada on an exclusive basis.

Of the ideas that you have generated you might want to pick three and evaluate each of them against the factors described in the Buskirk model in Figure 3.3. This evaluation will illustrate how well these ideas fit with all the characteristics of the "ideal" business. How would you rate each idea on each of Buskirk's 19 factors? On the basis of this evaluation, which of these ideas do you feel represents the most significant new venture opportunity for you? Can you justify your response? Did the idea you picked score less than five on any of Buskirk's factors? If so, can you think of any way to overcome the situation or find other solutions to the problem?

For a more formal evaluation of an invention, software concept, or other innovative idea, the Canadian Innovation Centre will conduct a comprehensive assessment to assist you in the decisions you must make

---

FIGURE 3.3   **COMPARE YOUR IDEAS TO THE "IDEAL" BUSINESS**

Directions: Evaluate your concept in comparison with a model business by indicating how well each of the ideal characteristics below applies to your concept. Use a scale from 1 to 10, where 1 means the ideal trait is not at all true for your concept, and 10 means it is perfectly true.

FIT WITH MODEL BUSINESS

Requires no investment	1 2 3 4 5 6 7 8 9 10
Has a recognized, measurable market	1 2 3 4 5 6 7 8 9 10
A perceived need for the product or service	1 2 3 4 5 6 7 8 9 10
A dependable source of supply for required inputs	1 2 3 4 5 6 7 8 9 10
No government regulation	1 2 3 4 5 6 7 8 9 10
Requires no labour	1 2 3 4 5 6 7 8 9 10
Provides 100 per cent gross margin	1 2 3 4 5 6 7 8 9 10
Buyers purchase frequently	1 2 3 4 5 6 7 8 9 10
Receives favourable tax treatment	1 2 3 4 5 6 7 8 9 10
Has a receptive, established distribution system	1 2 3 4 5 6 7 8 9 10
Has great publicity value	1 2 3 4 5 6 7 8 9 10
Customers pay in advance	1 2 3 4 5 6 7 8 9 10
No risk of product liability	1 2 3 4 5 6 7 8 9 10
No technical obsolescence	1 2 3 4 5 6 7 8 9 10
No competition	1 2 3 4 5 6 7 8 9 10
No fashion obsolescence	1 2 3 4 5 6 7 8 9 10
No physical perishability	1 2 3 4 5 6 7 8 9 10
Impervious to weather conditions	1 2 3 4 5 6 7 8 9 10
Possesses some proprietary rights	1 2 3 4 5 6 7 8 9 10

Total points =

160–190 = A concept; 130–159 = B; 110–129 = C; 80–109 = D; Below 80, drop concept.

After completing this evaluation, does it make sense to proceed with the venture? Explain your answer.

regarding your idea. For more information, contact Canadian Innovation Centre, 1A-490 Dutton Dr., Waterloo, Ontario N2L 6H7 (www.innovationcentre.ca).

Step 6: Focus on the Most Promising Opportunities

Which of the ideas you have evaluated seems to be the best fit with the "ideal" business and is most consistent with your goals and values? This is probably the one you should be looking to pursue. However, no matter how exhaustive your evaluation, there is no guarantee of success. The challenge is to do the best you can in conducting an assessment of each of your principal ideas, knowing that at some point you will have to make a decision with incomplete information and less than scientific accuracy. As a good friend of mine commented during a dinner speech not long ago, "Entrepreneurship is like bungee jumping. Both require an act of faith."

THE VENTURE OPPORTUNITY SCREENING MODEL

While the Buskirk model can be very useful for doing a "quick and dirty" evaluation of any prospective business idea and understanding how it might deviate from your notion of the "Ideal" or "Model" business, it is a simplification of the process. It gives you some insight into the issues you may have to wrestle with or overcome in implementing a particular business idea, but does not tell you how it stacks up on such strategic issues as:

- Market size and growth potential
- Current relationship with any customer base
- The degree of innovation and how related the concept is to customer needs
- The expected speed to market and difficulty with actual implementation
- The overall business strategy and strength of the business model
- The capabilities of the CEO and strength of the management team
- Anticipated risks and expected return on the investment
  as well as a number of other important factors.

To overcome these issues and provide a more comprehensive process for identifying entrepreneurial opportunities, you might also consider using the following **Venture Opportunity Screening Model (VOSM)**. It is based on Rae's work in the realm of opportunity recognition and his proposed Opportunity Recognition Model.[13] The VOSM is intended to give you a clearer idea of the relative attractiveness of a number of new venture opportunities you may be considering. This is not a cut-and-dried process. Most of the time there will be considerable uncertainty and numerous unknowns and risks. Going through this exercise, however, will help you understand some of the uncertainties and risks as you make a decision about an idea. It may even help you devise ways to overcome some of these uncertainties and risks and make them more acceptable to you. Every potential venture is unique. As a result, you may find that certain issues are more pertinent in some situations than in others. Or you may need to tailor some questions and issues to your particular circumstances. Don't be afraid to do so. The idea is to determine if your opportunity is attractive enough, according to the various criteria in the model, to go ahead and conduct a comprehensive feasibility study or develop a business plan.

The model is based on a series of constructs identified by entrepreneurs as being important in their venture selection process. It aims to distinguish between high value opportunities that are worthy of exploration and low value opportunities less likely to be worth pursuing. These constructs have been clustered into a number of categories to facilitate their assessment. These include:

- The assessment of the market opportunity
- The role of innovation
- Strategic potential
- The investment, risk, and return situation
- The effectiveness of the people involved in the venture

An outline for the VOSM is contained in Figure 3.4. You can make as many copies as you need to assess the variety of potential opportunities you have in mind. Indicate for each of the criteria just where you feel the

continued on page 86

13. David Rae, "How Does Opportunity Recognition Connect With Entrepreneurial Learning?" Working Paper, Centre for Entrepreneurial Management, University of Derby, U.K.

FIGURE 3.4 · VENTURE OPPORTUNITY SCREENING MODEL

Make as many copies of the Venture Opportunity Assessment Worksheets as you need to assess the variety of opportunities you have in mind.

THE VENTURE OPPORTUNITY ASSESSMENT

Fill in this profile for each of the new venture opportunities you plan to assess. Indicate for each criterion where the venture is located on the **Value** continuum from Low to High. Give your best estimate of just where you think that idea stacks up. Try to be as specific as possible.

OPPORTUNITY DESCRIPTION AND STRATEGY

Briefly describe the concept or idea behind your potential opportunity and the strategy you would pursue to implement it. Limit your description to a maximum of 25 words.

_____

_____

_____

_____

_____

_____

VENTURE OPPORTUNITY ASSESSMENT CONSTRUCTS

Criterion	Low Value Opportunity	High Value Opportunity
Market Opportunities		
Market growth rate	1 2 3 4 5 6 7 8 9 10 Limited growth potential in smaller markets	Able to access a market of growing size & value
Customer base	1 2 3 4 5 6 7 8 9 10 Limited or non-specific customer base	Known, identifiable customers in defined market sector
Customer reliance & convergence	1 2 3 4 5 6 7 8 9 10 Customers not reliant on product, divergent from their needs	Customer reliance on product increasing over time
Customer interaction	1 2 3 4 5 6 7 8 9 10 Adversarial customer relationships; lack of fit	Trust & open relationships with clients; compatible practices
Partnering & networks	1 2 3 4 5 6 7 8 9 10 One-off relationships within weak networks	Long-term partnerships within strong supplier & technology networks
Competition	1 2 3 4 5 6 7 8 9 10 Undifferentiated from competitors, forced to compete on price	Unique advantages & strengths apparent in relation to competition
	TOTAL SCORE /60	

continued

Venture Opportunity Screening Model — continued

Criterion	Low Value Opportunity								High Value Opportunity		

The Role of Innovation

Criterion	Low Value Opportunity									High Value Opportunity
Innovation leadership	1　2　3	4	5	6	7	8	9	10		
	Learn as you go along to catch up									Able to lead the market using prior experience
Innovation related to customer needs	1　2　3	4	5	6	7	8	9	10		
	Application does not solve customers' real problem									Application solves a problem informed by customers' needs
Technology differentiation	1　2　3　4		5	6	7	8	9	10		
	Undifferentiated technology, marginal performance & cost improvement									Differentiated technology — optimal performance & cost benefits
Intellectual property	1　2　3　4		5	6	7	8	9	10		
	Weak or no IP protection — can be copied									Strong IP protection with clear ownership & control, hard to copy
Speed to market	1　2　3	4	5	6	7	8	9	10		
	Unlikely to be first to market									Opportunity to be first to market
Feasibility of implementation	1　2　3	4	5	6	7	8	9	10		
	Difficult to implement, with many obstacles									Implementation feasible; challenges can be overcome
	TOTAL SCORE						**/60**			

Criterion	Low Value Opportunity									High Value Opportunity

Strategic Potential

Criterion	Low Value Opportunity									High Value Opportunity
Business growth	1　2　3　4		5	6	7	8	9	10		
	Limited purpose and scope to build a business									Have a strategy to create & grow a business
Strategic options	1　2　3	4	5	6	7	8	9	10		
	Single or limited exploitation options									Create multiple options for strategy & exit
Value creation	1　2　3	4	5	6	7	8	9	10		
	Low perceived value & profit margin									High value creation from high profit margin & cash generation
Innovative business model	1　2　3	4	5	6	7	8	9	10		
	Similar to existing business models									Superior business model
	TOTAL SCORE						**/40**			

Criterion	Low Value Opportunity							High Value Opportunity		

Investment, Risk and Return

Criterion	Low Value Opportunity	1	2	3	4	5	6	7	8	9	10	High Value Opportunity
Investment reward	Low financial return for investment	1	2	3	4	5	6	7	8	9	10	High return & profitability in relation to investment
Investor attraction	Unattractive to investors, offering limited increase in equity value	1	2	3	4	5	6	7	8	9	10	Attractive to potential investors, with growing equity value
Risk	Unacceptably high downside risk	1	2	3	4	5	6	7	8	9	10	Acceptable risk of loss in worst-case scenario
Viability & cash flow	Unpredictable cash flow, unable to achieve viability	1	2	3	4	5	6	7	8	9	10	Commercially viable with predictable break-even & cash flow
Timescale	Short-term timeframe & rapid exit strategy	1	2	3	4	5	6	7	8	9	10	Long-term opportunity & income stream

TOTAL SCORE /50

Criterion	Low Value Opportunity							High Value Opportunity		

People Resources

Criterion	Low Value Opportunity	1	2	3	4	5	6	7	8	9	10	High Value Opportunity
CEO Leadership	CEO not an innovative leader	1	2	3	4	5	6	7	8	9	10	CEO able to show leadership & innovation
Management Team Effectiveness	Team lacks management skills, fit & motivation	1	2	3	4	5	6	7	8	9	10	Management team skilled, compatible & motivated to achieve
Contextual Experience	No pre-knowledge of industries or technology	1	2	3	4	5	6	7	8	9	10	Able to use prior experience & knowledge of industry
Staff Capability	Suitably experienced & capable staff not available	1	2	3	4	5	6	7	8	9	10	Able to recruit experienced people from within industry

TOTAL SCORE /40

Overall Score

Once you have evaluated your idea on each of the criteria, you add up the total raw score (1) for each of the five constructs. Convert this raw score into a percentage (2) expressed in decimal terms to standardize the scores for each construct. Since some of these constructs may be more relevant to your idea than others, or may be more important to you from a personal standpoint, it would be helpful to weight each of the constructs to reflect your preferences. Distribute 100 points (3) across the six constructs according to your assessment of their

continued

Venture Opportunity Screening Model — continued

relative importance or significance to your assessment. You can then determine the weighted score and **Total Aggregate Score (4)** for that concept, as indicated below:

	(1) Construct Raw Score	(2) % Score	(3) Weight	(4) Weighted Score
Marketing Opportunities	/60	×	=	
The Role of Innovation	/60	×	=	
Strategic Potential	/40	×	=	
Investment, Risk & Return	/50	×	=	
People Resources	/60	×	=	
	/250	1.00	100	
TOTAL AGGREGATE SCORE				**/100**

Conclusions

- What is your overall assessment of this opportunity? Articulate your reasons for believing it may have some attractive possibilities.
- If positive, why does this opportunity exist now?
- What major problems or difficulties are you likely to encounter in moving the venture forward?
- What market entry strategy appears to best suit the opportunity? Why?
- What indications do you have that there is a fit between the current external environment and the factors assessed above that seem to create your opportunity?

Adapted from: D. Rae, *How Does Opportunity Recognition Connect with Entrepreneurial Learning?*, Unpublished working paper, Centre for Entrepreneurial Management, The Derbyshire Business School, University of Derby, Derby, U.K.

continued from page 82

venture is located on the **Value** scale from Low (1) to High (10). Once you have evaluated the idea according to each of the criteria, you can determine its total raw score for each of the five major constructs. Since some of these constructs may be more relevant to your idea than others, or may be more important to you from a personal standpoint, you can weight each of them to reflect your preferences. You can then determine the weighted score and the **Total Aggregate Score** for that concept. This will be helpful in forming your overall assessment of the venture idea and determining whether you believe it may or may not hold attractive possibilities as a real entrepreneurial opportunity for you.

DECIDING HOW TO PROCEED

Once satisfied you have identified an idea that represents a significant business opportunity, you must determine the best way to proceed. There are all sorts of *entry strategies* — ways people start new enterprises.

Reflecting on these alternatives and judging how they fit with your specific idea and your particular abilities and circumstances will enable you to turn them into real opportunities. No general rules have been developed to guarantee success, or even to indicate which concepts and strategies will work best in different situations, but being aware of the possibilities will give you a clearer picture of the job you need to do to succeed.

BUY A BUSINESS

One possibility is to find a business presently operating in your area of interest, buy it, and take over its operations. You may want to buy the business either because it is already quite successful but the current owners want to get out for some reason, or because the business is not doing very well under the current owners and you feel you can turn it around.

This can be a good entry strategy. A good deal of time and effort is involved in the start-up phase of any business. This stage can be bypassed when you buy a going concern. You also acquire a location, customers, established trade relationships, and a number of other positive elements.

These advantages don't come for free, however. Buying an existing business may cost you more than getting into a similar business on your own. The current owner may expect to receive "goodwill" for certain assets already acquired or the effort devoted to the business so far. You may also inherit some problem, such as obsolete equipment, the bad image and reputation of the previous owners, or labour difficulties.

For a more complete discussion of this entry strategy, refer to Stage Four of this book.

ACQUIRE A FRANCHISE

Another alternative is to buy the rights to operate a business that has been designed and developed by someone else, i.e., to acquire a *franchise*. Under a franchise agreement, an established company, the *franchisor*, with one or more successful businesses operating in other locations, provides assistance to a new firm in breaking into the marketplace. In return, the new owner, or *franchisee*, pays a fee for the assistance, invests money to set up and operate the business, pays a percentage of sales as a royalty to the franchisor, and agrees to operate the business within the terms and conditions laid out in the franchise agreement.

The assistance provided by the franchisor can take many forms, such as:

- The right to use the franchisor's brand names and registered trademarks
- The right to sell products and services developed by the franchisor
- The right to use operating systems and procedures developed by the franchisor
- Training in how to run the business
- Plans for the layout of the business facilities and the provision of specialized equipment
- A regional or national advertising program
- Centralized purchasing and volume discounts
- Research and development support

While the failure rate of franchised businesses is reported to be lower than that for independently established firms, there are a number of disadvantages associated with the concept.

For more detailed information, refer to Stage Five of this book.

START A BUSINESS OF YOUR OWN

The third and probably most common means of getting into business for yourself is to start a business of your own from scratch. This is the route most frequently travelled by the true entrepreneur who wants a business that is really his or her own creation. Starting your own business can take many forms and involve a variety of entry strategies. While we are unable to discuss all the possibilities here in any detail, a few alternatives will be mentioned to get you thinking about their fit with your particular situation. Some of the possibilities available for you are:

1. Develop an entirely new product or service unlike anything else available in the market.
2. Acquire the rights to manufacture or sell someone else's product or use someone else's name or logo under licence. These rights could be exclusive to a product category, a geographic area, or a specific market.
3. Find a customer who wants to buy something. Then create a business to make that sale or serve that need.
4. Take a hobby and develop it into a business.
5. Develop a product or service similar to those currently on the market but that is more convenient, less expensive, safer, cleaner, faster, easier to use, lighter, stronger, more compact, or has some other important distinguishing attribute.
6. Add incremental value to a product or service already available by putting it through another production process, combining it with other products and services, or providing it as one element in a larger package.

7. Become an agent or distributor for products or services produced by someone else. These may be domestically produced or imported from other countries.

8. Open a trading house or become a selling agent for Canadian firms who may be interested in selling their products or services abroad.

9. Develop a consulting service or provide information to other people in a subject area you know very well.

10. Become a supplier to another producer or large institutional customer. Large organizations require an extensive range of raw materials, supplies, and components to run their business. A small portion of their requirements could represent a significant volume of sales for you. This type of "outsourcing" is an excellent opportunity to pursue either through a contract or a strategic alliance with a larger organization.

11. Identify a situation where another firm has dropped what may be profitable products or product lines. They may have abandoned customer groups or market segments that are uneconomic for them to serve effectively but that may still be quite lucrative for a smaller company.

12. Borrow an idea from one industry or market and transfer it to another. A product or service that has been well accepted in one situation may well represent a substantial opportunity in other circumstances as well.

13. Look for opportunities to capitalize on special events and situations or unusual occurrences. You may be able to "piggyback" your business onto these situations.

Buying a Business

Stages Two and Three of this book have provided you with a means of evaluating your personal potential for an entrepreneurial career and a procedure for generating and evaluating the basic attractiveness of an idea on which to base your own business. The obvious route to self-employment is to start a business of your own based on this idea. Another route that should be explored is that of buying an existing firm. For many people this may even be their preferred course of action. How do you decide which route to take?

Stage Four discusses the various aspects that should be evaluated in considering whether you should start a new business or buy an existing one.

ADVANTAGES AND DISADVANTAGES OF BUYING AN EXISTING BUSINESS

The case for buying an existing firm, as against setting up a new one of your own, is not clear-cut either way. Each situation must be decided on its merits. There are distinct advantages and disadvantages to each course of action. You must consider how well your personal preferences fit into each of these options.

REASONS FOR BUYING AN ESTABLISHED BUSINESS

Here are some reasons why one *should* consider buying an established business:

1. Buying an existing business can reduce the risk. The existing business is already a proven entity. And it is often easier to obtain financing for an established operation than for a new one.
2. Acquiring a "going concern" with a good past history increases the likelihood of a successful operation for the new owner.
3. The established business has a proven location for successful operation.
4. The established firm already has a product or service that is presently being produced, distributed, and sold.
5. A clientele has already been developed for the product or service of the existing company.
6. Financial relationships have already been established with banks, trade creditors, and other sources of financial support.
7. The equipment needed for production is already available and its limitations and capabilities are known in advance.
8. An existing firm can often be acquired at a good price. The owner may be forced to sell the operation at a low price relative to the value of the assets in the business.

DISADVANTAGES OF BUYING AN ESTABLISHED BUSINESS

Here are some reasons why one may decide not to buy an existing business:

1. The physical facilities (the building and equipment) and product line may be old and obsolete.
2. Union/management relationships may be poor.

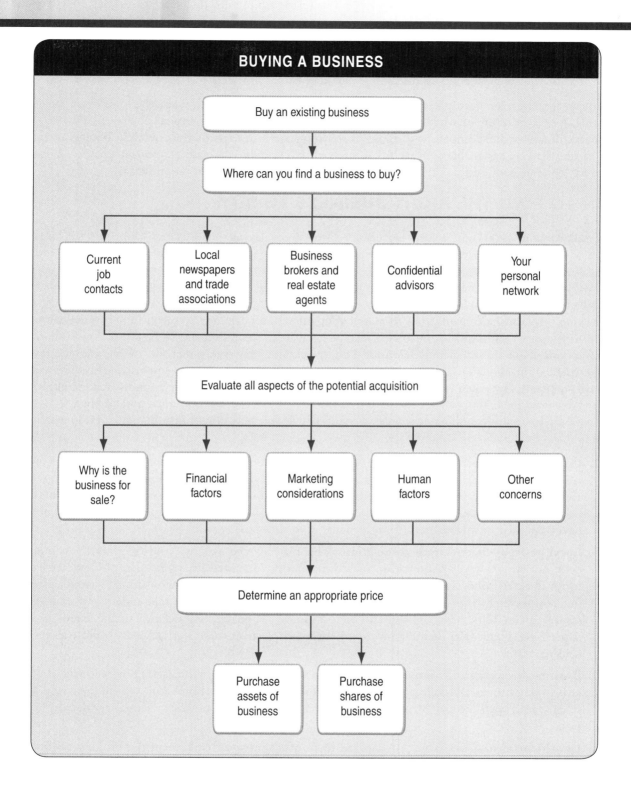

BUYING A BUSINESS

Buy an existing business

Where can you find a business to buy?

- Current job contacts
- Local newspapers and trade associations
- Business brokers and real estate agents
- Confidential advisors
- Your personal network

Evaluate all aspects of the potential acquisition

- Why is the business for sale?
- Financial factors
- Marketing considerations
- Human factors
- Other concerns

Determine an appropriate price

- Purchase assets of business
- Purchase shares of business

3. Present personnel may be unproductive and have a poor track record.
4. The inventory may contain a large amount of "dead" stock.
5. A high percentage of the assets may be in poor-quality accounts receivable.
6. The location of the business may be bad.

7. The financial condition of the business, and its relationships with financial institutions, may be poor.

8. As a buyer, you inherit any ill will that may exist toward the established firm among customers or suppliers.

9. As an entrepreneur, you have more freedom of choice in defining the nature of the business if you start one of your own than if you purchase an existing firm.

As you can see, there are both pluses and minuses in choosing to acquire an established business. You should view this option in terms of whether it will enable you to achieve your personal objectives. How do these advantages/disadvantages compare with those of starting a new business of your own? In buying an existing business do you see a reasonable opportunity to succeed? No one else can really advise you what to do. Instead, you must "do your own thing" and match the alternatives with your abilities and interests.

HOW TO FIND THE RIGHT BUSINESS TO BUY

Just finding a business to buy is easy. Dozens are listed every day in the "Business Opportunities" classified section of your local newspaper as well as the major business newspapers. However, what tends to be found in these classified sections are mostly hotel, motel, restaurant, and franchise propositions, which are largely high-risk, low-profit ventures generally unattractive to investors. Many of these are failing businesses that their current owners are trying to unload.

Seeking out a business acquisition to match your desires and experiences can be a very time-consuming and difficult process. Hundreds of businesses change hands every year, so it should be possible to find one that appeals to you if you are sufficiently determined and persistent. However, rather than being sold as a result of an advertisement in some newspaper, most businesses are sold to people who had some active business relationship with the company when it became available. It is usually not sufficient for an individual determined to acquire a business to sit and wait for the right opportunity to come along. You must go looking.

There are basically five different sources through which you may obtain information regarding attractive companies to buy:

1. **Current job contacts** Acquisition candidates may include present or potential competitors of your current employer, suppliers, customers, and perhaps even your present employer. These situations probably provide the best match between your experience and strengths and the unique requirements of the business. This was how Sherrie Versluis came to buy The Preferred Perch from its previous owner after having worked in the business (Entrepreneurs in Action #14).

2. **Local newspapers and trade associations** This may involve making "cold calls" on firms that look good or that you have an interest in; such firms may be identified from Chamber of Commerce directories and trade association membership lists. Another way is to place "Acquisition Wanted" advertisements in several major newspapers. In addition, despite what has been said earlier, you may wish to follow up on some advertisements in the "Business Opportunities" section of the major financial papers. Every now and then an advertisement may appear in these sections that would warrant your consideration.

3. **Business brokers and commercial real estate agents** These individuals are professionals who work at bringing buyers and sellers together for a commission. The commission, typically payable by the seller, varies with the size of the deal but may be as high as 10 per cent of the negotiated purchase price.

4. **Confidential advisors** These include the loans officer at your bank, securities brokers, professional accountants, and lawyers. These advisors are often aware of what businesses are or may soon be available for sale. These sources may be difficult to use, however, because their information is shared mostly with other clients with whom they have developed some relationship over time. In many cases it may be necessary for you to have gained the confidence of the source over an extended period.

5. **Your personal network** These include venture capital firms, personal friends and acquaintances, and insurance brokers and agents. Essentially you should consider all individuals within your personal network of business contacts who may have access to information on attractive businesses for sale. This

14

Entrepreneurs in Action

Wild On Wild Birds

When Sherrie Versluis saw a blue jay for the first time her eyes lit up like a 10-year-old's.

Now, 34, but no less enthusiastic about wild birds of all kinds, Versluis owns The Preferred Perch, a small business celebrating its 10th anniversary.

Supplying people with proper bird feed and feeding systems for the song bird population in their area is a key element of the store's core consulting business.

Versluis, 34, has a background in grains and seeds, having worked in the business, so she is savvy when it comes to choosing suppliers. She worked in the current store for 10 years as an employee. She bought the store from the previous owner five years ago and has expanded its expertise.

She knows the natural foods of birds, which can make all the difference when people plant flowers in their yards. . . .

There are a variety of feeding systems, from platform to tube feeders and houses for specific species. Wild birds bring a back yard alive, not only in song, but in their activities.

Versluis says "birders" come to Manitoba for its huge population of summer song birds like warblers, Indigo bunting, blue birds, or red tanager, red and white breasted nuthatches, evening grosbeaks and song sparrows, to name only a few. They are enticed to bird feeders. . . .

An avid birder, she set up shop to offer a proper selection of feeds, such as black oil seeds and a range of millet ground feed.

Her almost cottage-like store offers a selection of bird feeders and specialized bird houses, as well as a "bulk bird food" section. . . .

Like the birds, sales vary with the seasons and the weather.

"Low bird population can mean low sales," Versluis says.

Storms in the southern states have greatly reduced the migratory population from making it to their summer nesting grounds. That meant not only fewer birds but also less food was consumed.

Knowing such things can affect the bird populations, Versluis expanded her inventory into a 'nature lover's' line of giftware which has done very well.

"But there's no business like the bird business," says Versluis, whose passion for winged creatures is obvious. In addition to running the store, she delivers seminars and speeches about wild birds, is a guest on radio and television programs to push the cause. She is a Board member of the Manitoba Wildlife Rehabilitation Organization, which rescues wounded or sick raptors such as eagles, owls.

"People get attached to birds," she adds. "Few things match the sight of an eagle soaring . . . or a guy on a Harley with a 50-pound bag of bird seed on the back of his bike."

Source: Barbara Edie, "Wild on Wild Birds," © Manitoba Business Magazine, October 2005, page 13. Reprinted with permission.

requires letting many of these people know about your search and the kind of business for which you are looking. You will need to keep reminding them about your interest, so that when the information comes along there is a good probability that it will make its way back to you.

Which of these sources you should utilize depends on many factors, such as the time you have available, whom you know within the business community, and the kind of company you are looking for. You should experiment with each of these sources and decide on the one or two that work best for you.

IMPORTANT FACTORS TO CONSIDER

An essential requirement for the successful purchase of an existing firm is knowing how to assess and evaluate the operation. This is a complicated process, so you are well advised to have professionals such as an accountant, lawyer, or business evaluator assist you in negotiations when considering buying a business. As a potential buyer, you should also have a good understanding of the nature of the target business and the industry in which it competes to be able to assess its future performance, strengths, weaknesses, unexploited market opportunities, and other factors. Learning about a business after the fact can be a recipe for failure. A number of basic factors must be considered in determining the value of the business to you. Some of these are more complex and involved than others, but each one must be carefully investigated and studied. The most important of these concerns are:

WHY IS THE BUSINESS FOR SALE?

You should have this question in mind at all times during the evaluation of a possible acquisition. When the owner of a business decides to dispose of it, the reason presented to the public may be somewhat different from the facts of the situation. Owners may be quite willing to express some reasons for wanting to sell their businesses. They wish to retire, or they want to move to another city, or illness is pressuring the owner to leave the business. But there are a number of others that the current owner may not be quite so likely to volunteer. For example, the owner may be experiencing family pressures or marital problems, or perhaps the owner sees a better business opportunity somewhere else. None of these reasons is cause for concern. But what if the company needs more financing than the owner can raise, or the current market for the firm's products is depressed? What if competitors are moving in with more effective products or methods, or the current plant and equipment is worn out or obsolete, and the firm is no longer able to compete successfully? And what if the firm is having to contend with new government regulations that are creating some difficulties, or certain key employees are leaving the firm to set up a similar business of their own?

As you can see, there are many possible reasons why a business may be up for sale. It is important that you retain a sceptical attitude, because behind each of the offered explanations may be a number of hidden ones. A sceptical attitude forces you to examine the situation from all angles and not necessarily accept at face value everything you are told. When the real reasons for selling are factors that may lead to the eventual collapse of the company, the present owner may be hard-pressed to justify your purchase of the enterprise.

This is not to say that all businesses for sale are bad buys. Many companies are sold for very plausible and honest reasons. However, to keep from losing your shirt as well as your savings, a detailed evaluation should be conducted to determine the true character of the business.

FINANCIAL FACTORS

An analysis of the financial statements of the firm being sold, preferably with the help of a professional accountant, can help you assess its current health. You should not fall into the trap, however, of accepting these statements as the absolute truth. Even in those situations where the statements have been audited, many accounting techniques allow business owners to present a less than accurate picture of the financial situation of their company. You must be careful to ensure that the statements have not been biased in favour of the seller.

The most important financial factors are: (1) the trend in profits, (2) ratio analysis, (3) the value of the business's tangible assets, (4) the value of the business's intangible assets, and (5) cash flow. Let us discuss each in turn.

The Trend in Profits

A study of the records of the business will indicate whether sales volume and profits have been increasing or decreasing. If they have been going up, it is useful to know which departments within the business, or products within the firm's product line, have accounted for this increased sales and/or profitability.

If sales and profits are declining, the question may arise as to whether this is due to a failure by the firm to keep up with the competition, to its inability to adjust to changing circumstances, or perhaps to a lack of selling effort. Some experience with this type of business situation, plus a few questions directed to appropriate sources, may elicit an explanation.

Ratio Analysis

For every size and type of business there are certain financial ratios that have become generally accepted as reasonable for that kind of operation. Some information on these ratios is collected and published by trade organizations and associations such as the National Retail Hardware Association or the National Association of Retail Grocers. Ratios have also been developed by various manufacturers for use by retailers that handle their product lines. Ratios for firms in a wide variety of retail, service, and manufacturing sectors are published by Dun & Bradstreet (www.dnb.com), the Risk Management Association (formerly Robert Morris Associates) (www.rmahq.org), and other companies. Industry Canada, as part of its SME Benchmarking Tool Web site (sme.ic.gc.ca), can provide information as well. A study of the ratios of any business offered for sale, compared with standard ratios for that industry and size of company, will quickly indicate any discrepancies. These discrepancies may be due to mismanagement, neglect, carelessness, or perhaps even the lack of appropriate financing. The most frequently considered ratios are:

1. **Current ratio** The current ratio is defined as current assets divided by current liabilities. It is a measure of short-term solvency. Current assets normally include cash, marketable securities, accounts receivable, and inventories. Current liabilities consist of accounts payable, short-term notes payable, income taxes payable, and accrued expenses. A general rule of thumb is that a current ratio of 2:1 could be considered satisfactory for a typical manufacturing business. Service firms typically have a lower ratio, since they tend to have less inventory. However, as with any rule of thumb, extreme care should be exercised in evaluating this ratio. A cash-poor firm may be unable to pay its bills even though its ratio appears to be acceptable. On the other hand, many businesses with a current ratio less than the rule of thumb are quite solvent.

   Too high a ratio can indicate the business is not utilizing its cash and other liquid assets very efficiently; too low a ratio may raise questions about the firm's ability to meet its short-term obligations. In practice, however, what is more important than the absolute level of the current ratio is how the ratio is changing over time. An improving current ratio would tend to indicate improved short-term financial solvency unless the business is building up excessive or obsolete inventories.

   $$\text{Current Ratio} = \frac{\text{Current Assets}}{\text{Current Liabilities}}$$

2. **Quick ratio** The quick ratio is obtained by dividing current liabilities into current assets minus inventories. The quick ratio can be used to estimate the ability of a firm to pay off its short-term obligations without having to sell its inventory. Inventories tend to lose their value faster than other assets if disposed of in a hurry. The quick ratio is probably a more valid test of the firm's ability to meet its current liabilities and pay its bills than the current ratio.

   $$\text{Quick Ratio} = \frac{\text{Current Assets} - \text{Inventories}}{\text{Current Liabilities}}$$

3. **Debt to net worth** The debt-to-net-worth ratio indicates the firm's obligations to its creditors relative to the owner's level of investment in the business. Debt includes current liabilities, long-term loans, bonds, and deferred payments; the owner's net worth includes the value of common stock, preferred stock, any capital surplus, and retained earnings. Any outstanding shareholders' loans to the business should be considered part of the owner's net worth rather than as part of the business's present debt. This ratio is commonly used by creditors to assess the risk involved in lending to the firm. For example, if the debt-to-net-worth ratio is too high, say about 2:1 or 3:1, you may find it difficult to borrow additional funds for the business. Too low a ratio, on the other hand, may indicate the business is not being operated very efficiently and some profits are being sacrificed.

   $$\text{Debt-to-Net-Worth Ratio} = \frac{\text{Total Outstanding Current and Long-Term Debt}}{\text{Net Worth}}$$

4. **Gross profit to sales** This ratio is determined by dividing gross profit or gross margin by net sales. Gross profit is determined by deducting costs of goods sold from net sales. No general guidelines exist for this ratio, or even among companies within an industry, as it can vary substantially.

$$\text{Gross-Profit-to-Sales Ratio} = \frac{\text{Gross Profit}}{\text{Net Sales}}$$

5. **Net profit to sales** This ratio is calculated by dividing net profit by net sales. You may use net profit either before or after taxes. As with the previous ratio, no general guidelines exist because of the variability among companies and industries. This figure can be as low as 1 per cent or less for retail food stores and supermarkets, and as high as 8 or 9 per cent in some service sectors.

However, you might evaluate how these ratios compare with those of other, similar companies or how they have been changing over time. If the ratio has recently been declining, why? This may indicate that the firm's costs have been increasing without a commensurate increase in prices, or perhaps competition may have increased and the company is forced to keep its prices low in order to compete.

$$\text{Net-Profit-to-Sales Ratio} = \frac{\text{Net Profit (Before or After Taxes)}}{\text{Net Sales}}$$

6. **Return on assets** This ratio is determined by dividing net profit (before or after taxes) by total assets. It is an excellent indicator of whether all the firm's assets are contributing to its profits and how effectively the assets are being employed — the real test of economic success or failure. Unfortunately, this is not an easy ratio to apply, because it is a measure of the movement of assets in relation to sales and profits during a particular period of time. The methods used by accountants to determine the level of total assets in the business can have a great effect on this ratio, and there are no real general or convenient rules of thumb for finding out whether the current return on assets is acceptable.

$$\text{Return on Assets} = \frac{\text{Net Profit (Before or After Taxes)}}{\text{Total Assets}}$$

7. **Sales to inventory** This ratio is determined by dividing annual net sales by the average value of inventories. This does not indicate actual physical turnover since inventories are usually valued at cost while sales are based on selling prices, including markups, but this ratio does provide a reasonable yardstick for comparing stock-to-sales ratios of one business with another or with the average values for the industry.

$$\text{Sales-to-Inventory Ratio} = \frac{\text{Net Sales}}{(\text{Beginning Inventory} + \text{Ending Inventory})/2}$$

8. **Collection period** To determine the average collection period for the business's outstanding accounts receivable, annual net sales are divided by 365 days to determine the business's average daily credit sales. These average daily credit sales are then divided into accounts receivable to obtain the average collection period. This ratio is helpful in assessing the collectability of any outstanding receivables.

$$\text{Average Collection Period} = \frac{\text{Accounts Receivable}}{\text{Net Sales}/365}$$

All these ratios are calculated from information on the firm's income statement or balance sheet. Figures 4.1 and 4.2 illustrate simplified financial statements for a hypothetical firm called The Campbell Co. The value of each of these ratios for that company would be as follows:

1. Current ratio $= \dfrac{\$158{,}000}{\$95{,}000} = 1.66$

2. Quick ratio $= \dfrac{\$78{,}000}{\$95{,}000} = 0.82$

3. Debt to net worth $= \dfrac{\$135,000}{\$50,000} = 2.70$

4. Gross profit to sales $= \dfrac{\$133,000}{\$425,000} = 0.31$ or 31%

5. Net profit to sales $= \dfrac{\$13,500}{\$425,000} = 0.03$ or 3%

6. Return on assets $= \dfrac{\$13,500}{\$185,000} = 0.07$ or 7%

7. Sales-to-inventory ratio $= \dfrac{\$425,000}{\$75,000 + 80,000/2} = 5.48$

8. Average collection period $= \dfrac{\$53,000}{\$425,000/365} = 45$ days

It would appear from these ratios that The Campbell Co. is in reasonably sound shape financially. Its debt-to-net-worth ratio is within acceptable limits and the business is quite solvent, as indicated by the current and

FIGURE 4.1 EXAMPLE OF SIMPLIFIED BALANCE SHEET

THE CAMPBELL CO. BALANCE SHEET
AS OF DECEMBER 31, 201Y

ASSETS			(000s)
Current Assets			
Cash		$ 25	
Accounts receivable		53	
Inventory		80	
Total current assets			$ 158 **(A)**
Fixed Assets			
Machinery	$ 40		
Less: Accumulated depreciation	25	15	
Equipment and fixtures	30		
Less: Accumulated depreciation	18	12	
Total fixed assets			27 **(B)**
Total Assets (C = A + B)			$ 185 **(C)**

LIABILITIES AND OWNER'S EQUITY			
Current Liabilities*			
Accounts payable	$ 60		
Notes payable	35		
Total current liabilities		95	
Long-Term Liabilities			
Notes payable†	$ 40		
Total long-term liabilities		40	
Total liabilities			$ 135 **(D)**

OWNER'S EQUITY			
Capital investment		20	
Retained earnings		30	
Total owner's equity			50 **(E)**
Total Liabilities and Owner's Equity (F = D + E)			$ 185 **(F)**

*Debt is due within 12 months.
†Debt is due after 1 year.

FIGURE 4.2   **EXAMPLE OF SIMPLIFIED INCOME STATEMENT**

THE CAMPBELL CO.
INCOME STATEMENT
FOR YEAR ENDING DECEMBER 31, 201Y

	(000s)		
Gross sales	$428		
Less: Returns	3		
Net Sales		$ 425	(A)
Cost of goods sold:			
Beginning inventory	$ 75		
Plus: Net purchases	297		
Cost of goods available	372		
Less: Ending inventory	80		
Cost of Goods Sold		292	(B)
Gross Profit (C = A − B)		$ 133	(C)
Selling Expenses		$ 29	(D)
Administrative expenses:			
Office salaries	$ 60		
Interest	9		
Depreciation	10		
Other administrative expenses	7		
Total Administrative Expenses		86	(E)
Profit Before Income Tax (F = C − D − E)		$ 18	(F)
Income Tax (G = 25% of F)		4.5	(G)
Net Profit (G = F − G)		$ 13.5	(H)

quick ratios. The other ratios are more difficult to evaluate, but they would be quite acceptable for firms in many lines of business.

To illustrate the range of possible values for each of these ratios, some typical examples for Canadian companies in a number of industries are shown in Table 4.1. Notice that there can be considerable variation in the value of each ratio within economic sectors as well as between sectors. Within a sector these ratios represent an average for each industry code and, therefore, may be somewhat misleading. These figures include a range of firms, some of which may be doing extremely well and others that may be on the verge of bankruptcy. The variations from sector to sector are largely due to structural differences that impact the financial profile of firms in each line of business in quite different ways.

This data as well as other detailed financial and employment data on small businesses by industry in Canada is available from the SME Benchmarking Tool database of Industry Canada at sme.ic.gc.ca. These profiles are usually produced every two years, with 2006 being the most current available. These data can provide performance benchmarks for the financial planning of both start-up and established businesses.

Keep in mind that financial ratios are open to wide interpretation and should be relied on only to get a general perspective of the relative financial health of the business, to measure the financial progress of the business from one time period to another, or to flag major deviations from an industry or sector norm.

Value of Tangible Assets

In assessing the balance sheet of the prospective acquisition, you must determine the actual or real value of the tangible assets. A physical count of the inventory must be taken to determine if the actual level corresponds to the level stated on the balance sheet. This inventory must also be appraised in terms of its age, quality, saleability, style, condition, balance, freshness, and so on. Most large inventories will have some obsolescence. You

| | | **TABLE 4.1** | | KEY BUSINESS RATIOS IN CANADA — CORPORATIONS |

NAICS Category	Line of Business	I Current Ratio (Times)	II Debt/ Net Worth (Times)	III Gross Profit/ Sales (%)	IV Net Profit/ Sales (%)	V Return on Assets (%)	VI Sales to Inventory (Times)	VII Collection Period (Days)
44	**Retail Trade**	**1.6**	**2.2**	**29.6%**	**1.9%**	**7.0**	**6.9**	**14.2**
45121	Book Stores and News Dealers	1.6	2.3	35.3%	1.6%	5.5	5.6	12.4
44812	Women's Clothing Stores	1.4	4.3	42.4%	1.4%	6.0	4.5	9.1
44422	Nurseries and Garden Centres	1.5	2.2	41.2%	2.3%	6.5	6.8	19.0
4422	Home Furnishings	1.5	2.4	36.8%	2.8%	8.8	6.2	26.5
4482	Shoe Stores	1.7	2.5	43.1%	3.0%	8.3	3.3	6.8
722	**Food Services and Drinking Places**	**0.8**	**6.1**	**54.3%**	**1.9%**	**8.0**	**49.0**	**4.0**
7224	Drinking Places (Alcoholic Beverages)	1.0	2.9	52.0%	2.6%	8.2	35.0	4.8
7221	Full-Service Restaurants	0.8	10.1	55.0%	1.2%	6.8	46.2	3.8
7222	Limited-Service Eating Places	0.8	4.9	54.5%	2.8%	10.2	63.0	2.9
41	**Wholesale Trade**	**1.7**	**1.8**	**34.7%**	**2.6%**	**6.5**	**7.1**	**45.3**
4131	Food Wholesaler-Distributor	1.4	2.6	26.5%	1.3%	5.2	15.3	29.8
4162	Metal Service Centre	1.8	1.6	30.8%	3.8%	8.7	7.9	52.6
31–33	**Manufacturing**	**1.5**	**1.9**	**37.6%**	**0.9%**	**4.2**	**8.6**	**53.0**
311814	Commercial Bakeries and Frozen Bakery Product Manufacturing	1.3	2.2	39.6%	2.5%	7.9	23.2	24.0
31523	Women's and Girls' Cut and Sew Clothing Manufacturing	1.7	2.5	30.9%	−3.5%	−3.6	6.1	60.6
31142	Fruit and Vegetable Canning, Pickling and Drying	0.9	30.8	35.3%	−3.4%	−3.3	8.6	40.7
3212	Veneer, Plywood and Engineered Wood Product Manufacturing	1.6	1.6	33.3%	−29.7%	−19.0	8.0	45.7
31212	Breweries	0.8	18.8	50.8%	−11.2%	−9.3	9.3	33.5
3343	Audio Video Equipment Manufacturing	1.7	3.9	46.5%	−13.3%	−10.5	5.3	65.1
33712	Household and Institutional Furniture Manufacturing	1.5	2.4	32.4%	1.4%	4.8	7.5	42.8
23	**Construction**	**1.5**	**2.1**	**40.9%**	**5.9%**	**4.8**	**8.3**	**47.8**
2361	Residential Building Construction	1.5	2.8	31.9%	4.5%	6.9	4.6	35.0
54	**Professional, Scientific and Technical Services**	**1.8**	**1.2**	**79.1%**	**7.7%**	**9.1**	**37.6**	**56.6**
5412	Accounting, Tax Preparation, Bookkeeping and Payroll Services	1.6	1.2	92.4%	14.8%	14.4	32.7	52.3
71311	Amusement and Theme Parks	0.9	3.4	76.2%	−7.2%	−2.5	28.2	21.4
51511	Radio Broadcasting	1.4	1.7	84.7%	99.7%	4.3	120.6	57.2
48–49	**Transportation and Warehousing**	**1.1**	**2.2**	**73.2%**	**3.3%**	**8.4**	**97.9**	**38.3**
484	Truck Transportation	1.1	2.3	77.3%	3.6%	9.7	158.8	34.3
4871	Scenic and Sightseeing Transportation, Land	0.7	9.6	70.3%	0.6%	4.1	60.0	25.6
493	Warehousing and Storage	0.9	2.8	72.8%	4.4%	6.0	40.2	45.2

Source: Industry Canada SME Benchmarking Tool, 2006 (www.ic.gc.ca/eic/site/pp-pp.nsf/eng/home), accessed May 19, 2010.

must determine whether the present inventory is consistent with current market conditions. Also, take care that the seller does not sell this inventory after you have checked it. Any consignment goods in inventory should be clearly identified as well. This evaluation is best performed by someone with considerable experience in the industry involved. Perhaps you can hire the services of the owner of a similar but non-competing firm to assist you in this appraisal.

You must also check the age of any outstanding accounts receivable. Some businesses continue to carry accounts receivable on their books that should have been charged off as bad debts, resulting in an overstatement of the firm's profit and value. Generally, the older the receivables, the lower their value. Old outstanding accounts may reveal a slack credit policy by the present owner. These old accounts will have to be discounted in determining the present value of the business.

The fixed assets of the business must also be scrutinized. You should determine if the furniture, fixtures, equipment, and building are stated at their market or depreciated value. Some questions you should ask include: How modern are these assets? Are they in operating condition? How much will it cost to keep these assets in operation? Are the assets all paid for? You must be aware of any liens or chattel mortgages that may have been placed against these assets. This pledging of assets to secure a debt is a normal business practice; however, you should know about any such mortgages. Other liabilities such as unpaid bills, back taxes, back pay to employees, and so on, may be hidden; you must be aware of the possibility of their existence, and contract with the seller that all claims not shown on the balance sheet will be assumed by him or her.

Value of Intangible Assets

In addition to the more obvious physical goods and equipment, certain intangible assets may also have a real value to a prospective purchaser. Among the most important of these are goodwill; franchise and licensing rights; and patents, trademarks, and copyrights.

You must be very realistic in determining what you can afford or are prepared to pay for goodwill. Is the public's present attitude toward the business a valuable asset that is worth money, or is it a liability? Typically, few businesses that are for sale have much goodwill value. Is any goodwill associated with the business personal to the owner or largely commercial due to the location, reputation, and other characteristics of the business? If largely personal, this goodwill may not be transferable to a new owner, so you should not pay very much for it. Many business owners, however, often have very unrealistic and inflated ideas of the goodwill associated with their business because they have built it up over the years with their own "sweat equity" and, therefore, are not very objective. So you should be careful, and talk to customers, suppliers, neighbours, employees, and perhaps even competitors, to determine if this level of goodwill does actually exist.

In fact, quite often things are not always as they appear. When Jeanne Lawrence bought what she thought was a reputable and thriving fashion design business and retail store, she expected business to carry on as usual. It was only after she had taken over the firm that she discovered the company's once reputable name had become tarnished in the past year. She was bombarded with a litany of customer-service complaints ranging from poor workmanship to ill-fitting clothing, to people who had paid in full for work that hadn't been done. The situation was so bad that she was spending all the money she was taking in on new business repairing the damage that had been done before she took over the company. Eventually Lawrence realized that she could repair the merchandise that had been sold before she took over but she couldn't repair the reputation of the business, so she changed the name (Entrepreneurs in Action #15).

If franchise, licensing, or other rights are involved in the business, you should make certain that you understand the terms and conditions associated with such rights, and that these rights will be transferred to you on acquisition of the company. An effort should also be made to determine the market value of any patents, trademarks, or copyrights the company may hold, and make sure these are part of the sale — i.e., do not remain with the current owner on completion of the transaction.

Cash Flow

You must also observe the cash flows generated by the operation. A business can be very profitable but chronically low in cash due to overly generous credit terms, excessive inventory levels, or heavy fixed-interest payments. You must assure yourself that on your entry into the business you will have sufficient inflows of cash to meet your cash outflow requirements. Constant cash problems can indicate that the business is possibly being run by ineffective management or that the firm's resources have generally been badly allocated. You must ask

Entrepreneurs in Action

Buyer Beware Doesn't Apply Only to Customers

CLOTHING STORE OWNER BOUGHT BAD REPUTATION

When Jeanne Lawrence bought a reputable and thriving company this year, she expected business would carry on as usual.

Lawrence bought a fashion design and retail store earlier this fall that specializes in made-to-order evening wear, bridal gowns and daytime apparel. Clothing ranges from $100 lingerie sets to $2,000 evening gowns. Lawrence is a designer with 25 years' experience and has also operated a store before.

SERVICE COMPLAINTS

But when she took over from the previous owner she was bombarded with a litany of customer service complaints. So many in fact that she says she's spending all the money she's taking in on new business repairing damage done before she took control.

"I've been trying to repair the reputation this place had at one time," says Lawrence.

Lawrence says customer complaints range from poor workmanship to poor-fitting clothing, to people who paid in full for work that hadn't been done. Since she has taken over, Lawrence discovered the business's once reputable name has fallen in the last year.

Lawrence estimates about 75 per cent of the clientele was lost in the last year or two.

"Complaints were never redressed. I've been contacted by the Better Business Bureau with horror stories."

Lawrence wouldn't reveal the purchase price of the business but said it was considerable. She said she thought she was also buying the goodwill that went with the company's name.

"To buy a name that's reputable — that doesn't come cheap," she comments.

Marty Eakins is a partner with the Winnipeg office of KPMG. Eakins says when buying a business, it's very much caveat emptor.

"The whole notion of due diligence is critical."

He says that means hiring an experienced financial

WAYNE GLOWACKI/WINNIPEG FREE PRESS. REPRINTED WITH PERMISSION.

person to review financial statements both current and past. But Eakins says even at that, no firm can give 100 per cent assurance that what you're buying is solid gold.

Lawrence says she had her accountant look at the books (her accountant recommended she buy the company). And financially, the business was solid. It was the company's reputation that wasn't what she expected.

Lawrence is sticking with the business, but she's already made changes. Along with her associate, designer Karen Dolan, she's bringing in more seasonal wear and gift items. Lawrence says they've even started selling ready-to-wear that's 80 per cent completed and then can be altered to the individual.

CHANGED THE NAME

Most importantly, Lawrence realizes that she can repair merchandise sold previously, but she can't repair the reputation associated with the name. So the store name has been changed to Loiselle.

Source: Paul McKie, "Clothing Store Owner Bought Bad Reputation," © *Winnipeg Free Press*, December 1, 1997, p. B5. Reprinted with permission.

yourself if you have the know-how to overcome this misallocation of resources. If the firm's cash flow is very low and the long-term debt is quite high, the business may be eating up its capital to pay the debt, or possibly defaulting on its debt. If you are to contend with such issues, you may have to increase the firm's debt or be prepared to invest more capital in the business to ease the cash flow problem.

MARKETING CONSIDERATIONS

The previous section dealt with the internal aspects of the firm's profitability; there has been no discussion of the external determinants of these conditions. But you must be concerned with analyzing markets, customers, competition, and various other aspects of the company's operating environment.

You must carefully examine the company's current market situation. Each market segment served by the firm must be analyzed and understood. Studying maps, customer lists, traffic patterns, and other factors can help you to determine the normal market size for the business. Once the market and its various segments are understood, the composition of these segments should be determined to identify the approximate number of customers in the total market. As a buyer, you should be concerned with five key areas:

1. The company's trading area
2. Population demographics
3. The trend and size of the market
4. Recent changes in the market
5. Future market patterns

All these factors help in determining whether the firm's market area is changing, or there is a declining relevant population, or technological or other changes may be creating an obsolete operation.

This kind of information can assist you in assessing trends in the level of the business's market penetration. For example, if its market share has been increasing, then perhaps you should anticipate further growth. But if the business's market penetration has been declining or static, you should be aware that something could be wrong with the operation. It may be that the business is nearing the end of its life cycle. A shrewd seller, aware that the operation is approaching a natural decline, may be bailing out.

At the same time, a business that is not presently being marketed very well may represent a significant opportunity with the right management. John and Elisa Tait bought a store, Elements of Nature, that was little more than a museum gift boutique (Entrepreneurs in Action #16). Sales were often as low as $50 per day. During the first five years, they turned the business around so that in-store sales grew to as much as $4,000 on some days and developed a thriving Web-based business as well, attracting orders from all over the world. The business has become so successful the Taits have expanded to Calgary, where they can pursue not only new business opportunities but more personal interests and their new store, The Discovery Hut, continues to be a huge success. (www.discoveryhut.com)

Competition facing the business must also be evaluated and understood. First and foremost, you should make sure that the present owner will not remain in competition with you. Very often an owner will dispose of a business only to open up a similar operation. If the business is largely based on the personality and contacts of the owner, you may be hard-pressed to maintain the necessary rapport with customers, suppliers, and financial sources. A legal agreement may help ensure that the vendor will not go on to compete with you.

Another aspect of assessing competition is to look at that presently faced by the firm. You should be aware of the business's major competitors and what trends can be foreseen in the nature of their activity. Most of this information can be obtained either from direct observation or by talking with other people in the business.

Other aspects of the environment also should not be overlooked. You must be tuned in to developments in the economy, changes in technology, government policy and regulations, and trends in society at large that can affect your business situation. Your banker or other professionals may be able to tell you what the experts are saying about such variables. Both national and regional economic factors must be studied to develop accurate projections as to the size of the market opportunity available to the business.

HUMAN FACTORS

When a business is being purchased, personnel must be considered equal in importance to financial and marketing factors, because usually it is desirable to retain certain key people to provide some continuity. As a prospective buyer, you should assess the value of the company's personnel and try to become acquainted with the attitudes of the present employees. For example, will key employees continue to work for the firm under your management? If these key people are likely to leave, you must anticipate the consequences.

Both the quality and the quantity of trained personnel must be evaluated. The skill level of the employees has some bearing on the sale value of the business. Highly trained staff, for example, can increase the seller's bargaining power. On the other hand, inefficient and poorly trained staff may permit you to negotiate a lower purchase price because of the long-term expense involved in retraining or hiring additional employees.

OTHER CONCERNS

In assessing a business to buy, you will also have to take into account a number of other factors. These include various legal considerations as well as past company policies. The legal aspects of doing business are becoming increasingly more complex and the use of a lawyer is practically a fact of business life. A lawyer can help you

Entrepreneurs in Action

Kids-stuff connoisseurs find a niche in Calgary

John and Elisa Tait weren't monkeying around when they decided to take their Winnipeg toy store's concept out west.

The owners of Elements of Nature, located adjacent to the Manitoba Children's Museum, saw both a business and personal opportunity in Calgary.

Not only would the mountain bike addicts be able to get their fix in the nearby Rockies, but the Taits felt they could fill a void in the toy store market.

"We looked at Calgary and were amazed at how few stores there were in the marketplace. We were really encouraged by some of our suppliers. They told us if we opened a store in Calgary, we'd kick butt," said John Tait in an interview.

In April, the Taits moved west and, a month later, they opened The Discovery Hut in the Chinook Centre mall. The 2,400-square-foot store has a tropical theme similar to the slightly smaller Elements of Nature and likewise comes complete with scores of toy monkeys on the walls and world-beat music on the stereo.

Tait said such a move wouldn't have been possible if it weren't for the success of Elements of Nature. When they bought the store five years ago, it was more of a museum gift boutique. Customers were scarce and sales of some of its goods, such as rocks and magnifying glasses, were even more scarce, sometimes as little as $50 per day.

Slowly, the store was transformed into an interactive, bright, upbeat destination specializing in high-quality and educational toys such as Beanie Baby plush dolls, the Thomas the Tank Engine line, Brio Trains from Sweden, Felt Kids, Lamaze toys for infants and more than 2,000 CDs, tapes and videos of children's music, featuring the likes of local stars such as Al Simmons, Fred Penner and Heather Bishop.

As quickly as Elements of Nature sales have grown — to as much as $4,000 per day — its Web site business (www.elementsofnature.com) has grown even faster.

Eilef Ausland, Elements' manager, said Web sales are consistently up more than 60 per cent year-over-year.

"This Christmas, we'll need to double our staff levels. It's going to be crazy," he said in an interview, as he thumbed through the day's Internet orders from Poland, England, California, Illinois, Ohio and Vancouver. . . .

Both Ausland and Tait agree that the biggest challenge facing a specialty toy store is carving out a niche in the face of big box retailers such as Toys R Us and Wal-Mart.

"Traditionally, we stay away from their product lines," Tait said. "Most of their products are from major suppliers and a lot of them are war-related or violent toys. We focus on toys that provide a real quality playing and learning experience for kids."

Terry Napper, manager of the Chinook Centre, said thus far The Discovery Hut has proven to be an excellent fit for the mall, which recently underwent a $300-million facelift.

"We have a lot of families that shop here. This store is bang-on for what we need. This concept would work in 70 to 80 per cent of the shopping centres in the country," he said in an interview.

"Most malls have either a Toys R Us or Zellers or Wal-Mart with a strong toy department, but very few have educational toys, which suit a lot of the public." (www.discoveryhut.com)

Source: Geoff Kirbyson, "Kids-stuff connoisseurs find a niche in Calgary," *Winnipeg Free Press*, August 20, 2001, p. B5. © *Winnipeg Free Press*. Used with permission.

Other considerations

KEY POINTS TO CONSIDER IN BUYING A BUSINESS

- Take your time and verify the information you are given before you commit yourself.
- Don't fall in love with the business before you do your homework.
- Be careful not to pay too much for goodwill.
- Buy a business within an industry you know well, with a product or service you are comfortable selling.
- Buy based on the return on investment not the price.
- Don't use all your cash for the purchase and then run into cash flow problems.
- Investigate before you buy.

Source: "Buying a Business," Saskatchewan Regional Economic and Co-operative Development (www.canadabusiness.ca/servlet/ContentServer?cid=108194275583&lang=en&pagename=CBSC_FE%2Fdisplay&c=GuideFactSheet). Accessed November 20, 2007.

in such areas as deciding on an appropriate form of legal organization; identifying real estate documents such as zoning restrictions and covenants that may put you at a disadvantage; labour laws and union regulations; complying with all licensing and permit requirements; the transferability of intangible assets such as copyrights, patents, dealerships, and franchises; and whether buying the shares or the assets of the firm is the most advantageous way of purchasing the company.

You should also have some understanding of the historical practices of the firm relating to employees, customers, and suppliers if future policies are to enhance your opportunities for business growth. An evaluation of these practices and policies will determine if you should continue with past practices or make modifications. If you fail to make this evaluation, you may eventually find yourself in a situation where you have to continue policies that are ill-advised in the long run. For example, it may be necessary to tighten credit policies or make a change in labour practices, even though this may cause a short-term loss of customers or employees.

HOW TO DETERMINE AN APPROPRIATE PRICE TO PAY FOR A BUSINESS

Buying a business is a serious matter involving a substantial financial and personal investment. A business bought at the wrong price, or at the wrong time, can cost you and your family much more than just the dollars you have invested and lost. After you have thoroughly investigated a business opportunity according to the factors in the previous section, weighed the wealth of information you have gathered, and decided that your expectations have been suitably fulfilled, a price must be agreed upon with the seller.

Valuing a business is a very complex procedure, so it is impossible to do it justice here. Any explanation short of an entire book is probably insufficient. The process takes into account many variables and requires that you make a number of assumptions. Determining an appropriate price to pay for a business is a very technical process. If you are trying to make this determination on your own, you should either have a sound knowledge of general accounting principles or use the services of a professional accountant or business valuation expert who has taken formal training and is accredited by the Canadian Association of Business Valuators.

Setting the purchase price for a going concern typically involves two separate kinds of evaluations:

1. **Balance sheet methods** — evaluation of the firm's tangible net assets
2. **Earnings-based methods** — evaluation of the firm's expected future earnings

The balance sheet methods are generally less reliant on estimates and forecasts than the earnings-based methods; however, it should be remembered that balance sheet methods totally ignore the future earnings capability of the business.

BALANCE SHEET METHODS

This approach calls for making some evaluation of the assets of the business. It is used most often when the business being valued generates its earnings primarily from its assets, as with retail stores and manufacturing companies.

There are a number of balance sheet methods of evaluation, including *book value, modified or adjusted book value*, and *liquidation value*. Each has its proper application, but the most useful is the adjusted book value method.

Modified Book Value

If the company has a balance sheet, the quickest means of determining a valuation figure is to look at its net worth as indicated there. You simply take the total assets as shown in the financial statement and subtract total liabilities to get the *net book value*. The advantage of this method is that for most firms the numbers are readily available.

Its drawbacks, however, are numerous. The company's accounting practices will have a big impact on its book value. Similarly, book value does not necessarily reflect the fair market value of the assets or the liabilities. For example, buildings and equipment shown on the balance sheet may be depreciated below their actual market value, or land may have appreciated above its original cost. These differences will not be reflected on the company's balance sheet. Despite these drawbacks, however, net book value may be useful in establishing a reference point when considering the asset valuation of a business. This approach is illustrated in section I of Figure 4.3 on the basis of the balance sheet for The Campbell Company presented in Figure 4.1, and shows a value of $50,000.

Adjusted Book Value

The adjusted book value method is the most useful balance sheet method. It is simply the book value adjusted for differences between the stated book value and the fair market value of the business's fixed assets

---

FIGURE 4.3   **APPLICATION OF BALANCE SHEET METHODS**

BUSINESS VALUATION — THE CAMPBELL CO.
BALANCE SHEET METHODS

	(000s)
I. NET BOOK VALUE	
Total stockholders' equity*	$ 50
Net Book Value	**$ 50**
II. MODIFIED BOOK VALUE	
Net book value	$ 50
Plus:	
Excess of appraised market value of building and equipment over book value	25
Value of patent not on books	10
Modified Book Value	**$ 85**
III. LIQUIDATION VALUE	
Net book value	$ 50
Plus:	
Excess of appraised liquidation value of fixed assets over book value	9
Less:	
Deficit of appraised liquidation value of inventory over book value	(5)
Deficit due to liquidation of accounts receivable	(3)
Costs of liquidation and taxes due upon liquidation	(8)
Liquidation Value	**$ 43**

---

*Item E from Figure 4.1.

and liabilities. Adjustments are most frequently made to the book values of the following items on the balance sheet:

- Accounts receivable — often adjusted downward to reflect the fact that some receivables may be uncollectable.
- Inventory — usually adjusted downward, since some of it may be dated or stale and difficult to sell off at prices sufficient to cover its cost.
- Real estate — often adjusted upward since it has commonly appreciated in value since being acquired by the business.
- Furniture, fixtures, and equipment — adjusted upward if they are relatively new and have been depreciated below their market value or adjusted downward if they are older and worn out or technologically obsolete.

This refinement of the plain book value approach still has a number of drawbacks, but it does give a more accurate representation of the value of the company's assets at current market value than book value does. The application of this method is illustrated in section II of Figure 4.3, and shows a value of $85,000.

Liquidation Value

A third approach is to go beyond the books of the company to get a more detailed evaluation of specific assets. Generally this involves determining the *liquidation value* of the assets or how much the seller could get for the business or any part of it if it were suddenly thrown onto the market. This approach is ordinarily a highly conservative evaluation and, as such, is frequently useful in determining the lowest valuation in a range of values to be considered. The liquidation value approach is presented in section III of Figure 4.3, and shows a value of $43,000. Note that the liquidation value of the firm's fixed assets may be considerably less than their appraised market value, largely due to the distressed nature of their disposition.

INCOME STATEMENT METHODS

Although a balance sheet method is often the approach to valuing a business that can be prepared most easily, it is more common to use an income statement method, particularly for service-type businesses. In most cases a going concern is much more than just the sum of its physical assets. Income statement methods are more concerned with the profits or cash flow produced by the assets of the business rather than the assets themselves.

While the cost of reproducing or liquidating the business assets can be closely determined, the cost of duplicating the firm's experience, management, technical know-how, and reputation is not so easily determined. These intangible factors will be reflected in the firm's past and expected future earnings.

To study past earnings trends, it is important to select a time period that is true and representative. A period of five years is generally considered to be an appropriate length of time to observe an earnings trend; however, economic cycles and other factors must be taken into consideration.

Once earnings have been determined, various approaches can be used to determine an appropriate price. One approach is a simple *capitalization of an average of past profits or capitalization of earnings*. In this method, the profits for a selected period of years are adjusted for unusual items and an appropriate capitalization rate is applied to the average profit level derived. (See Figure 4.4, and section I of Figure 4.6.)

A variation on this method is to weight the earnings of prior years to give greater emphasis to more recent profit levels (for example, the most recent year is given a weight of 5, the previous year 4, the next previous year 3, and so on).

The major advantage of this approach is that it is easy to use. However, the selection of an appropriate capitalization rate or multiple to apply to past or expected future earnings is not a simple, straightforward process. For illustrative purposes we have selected a desired rate of return of 16 per cent, or approximately six times the earnings shown in Figure 4.6.

The rate that can be earned on secure investments usually serves as the "base" rate or minimum capitalization rate that would be used. The chosen capitalization rate is really an assessment of the risk you perceive to be related to the business in comparison to the risk related to obtaining the "base" rate. It is an indication of the rate of return you are prepared to accept for assuming that risk in relation to the rates of return you could earn from other, more secure investments such as bonds or guaranteed income certificates.

FIGURE 4.4   **EXAMPLE OF SUMMARY OF EARNINGS SHEET**

THE CAMPBELL CO.
SUMMARY OF EARNINGS FOR PAST FOUR YEARS

Year	Earnings After Taxes (000s)
200Y	$13.5
201Y–1	12.1
201Y–2	10.8
201Y–3	7.2
201Y–4	4.6

The selection of a capitalization rate can have a large impact on your evaluation of a business. If, for example, your desired rate of return is increased from 16 per cent to 20 per cent in Figure 4.6, the estimated value of The Campbell Co. based on capitalization of its past earnings would be reduced from $60,000 to $48,000. The estimated values using discounted future earnings and discounted cash flow would be similarly reduced if we were to use a 20 per cent rather than a 16 per cent expected rate of return.

The *discounted future earnings* approach requires estimating after-tax earnings for a number of years in the future as well as determining an appropriate rate of return for the investor. Each future year's earnings are then discounted by the desired rate of return. A higher discount rate might be considered in this case since the estimates are based on projections of future earnings rather than historical results and may be very subjective in nature. In addition, since net earnings, after tax, are used as the basis for the projection, the discount rate used should be net of tax as well. The sum of these discounted values is the estimated present value of the company (Figure 4.5 and section II of Figure 4.6).

The advantage of this approach is that future earnings potential becomes the principal investment criterion, taking into account the time value of money. The principal disadvantage is that in many situations, future earnings cannot be projected with any real accuracy because of the uncertainties of the operating environment and the marketplace.

The *discounted cash flow* approach is the valuation method most commonly used for smaller, privately held businesses. It is essentially the same as the discounted future earnings approach, except that future anticipated cash flows rather then earnings are used to determine the valuation, as can be seen in section III of Figure 4.6.

FIGURE 4.5   **EXAMPLE OF PROJECTED INCOME SHEET**

THE CAMPBELL CO.
PROJECTED FIVE-YEAR EARNINGS AND CASH FLOW

Year	Projected Earnings After Taxes (000s)	Projected Cash Flow (000s)
201Y+1	$14.0	$16.9
201Y+2	16.8	21.1
201Y+3	20.2	26.4
201Y+4	24.2	33.0
201Y+5	29.0	41.2

Assumptions:
1. Earnings are expected to grow at a rate of 20% per year.
2. Cash flow is expected to grow at a rate of 25% per year.

FIGURE 4.6   INCOME STATEMENT METHODS

BUSINESS VALUATION — THE CAMPBELL CO.
EARNINGS METHODS

I. CAPITALIZATION OF EARNINGS

	Average Earnings Over Past Five Years (Figures 4.2 and 4.4) (000s)
201Y–4	$ 4.6
201Y–3	7.2
201Y–2	10.8
201Y–1	12.1
201Y	13.5
	Total $48.2 in the previous 5 years

Average Earnings = $9.6
Divided By: Investors' desired rate of return = 16%*

Value of Company Based on Capitalization of Past Earnings = 9.6 x 100/16 = $60.0

II. DISCOUNTED FUTURE EARNINGS

	Projected After-Tax Earnings (Figure 4.5) (000s)	x	Present Value Factor Assuming 16% Return	=	Present Value of After-Tax Earnings (000s)
201Y+1	$ 14.0		0.862		$12.1
201Y+2	16.8		0.743		12.5
201Y+3	20.2		0.641		13.0
201Y+4	24.2		0.552		13.4
201Y+5	29.0		0.476		13.8
	Total $104.2				Total $64.8

Value of Company Based on Discounted Future Earnings = $64.8

III. DISCOUNTED CASH FLOW

	Projected Cash Flow (Figure 4.5) (000s)	x	Present Value Factor Assuming 16% Return	=	Present Value of Cash Flow (000s)
201Y+1	$ 16.9		0.862		$14.6
201Y+2	21.1		0.743		15.7
201Y+3	26.4		0.641		16.9
201Y+4	33.0		0.552		18.2
201Y+5	41.2		0.476		19.6
	Total $138.6				$85.0

Value of Company Based on Discounted Cash Flow = $85.0

*The actual rate of return to use depends upon your cost of capital, as well as the perceived risk inherent in the investment.

The difference between earnings and cash flow is that cash flow includes a number of non-recurring and non-cash items that may be reflected in the income statement such as:

- The net profit or loss of the business.
- Any salary paid to the owner in excess of what a comparable manager might be paid.
- Any perks or discretionary benefits paid to the owner, such as a car allowance, travel and entertainment expenses, personal insurance.
- Interest payments unless they will be assumed by the buyer.
- Any non-recurring expenses such as legal or other fees.
- Non-cash expenses such as depreciation and amortization.

Like the discounted future earnings approach, this method of valuation also depends on highly uncertain estimates and assumptions. Many people feel, however, that this method typically provides the most reasonable estimate of a company's value. Both of these approaches require detailed year-to-year forecasts that can result in data that have the illusion of precision, but in fact may be quite speculative and unreliable.

Each of these evaluation methods is illustrated in Figure 4.6 for the case of Campbell. The following assumptions are reflected in these calculations:

1. Future earnings are estimated with new management in place.
2. Earnings are expected to grow at a rate of 20 per cent per year.
3. The income tax rate, including federal and state or provincial income taxes, is 20 per cent.
4. Your desired return on investment is 16 per cent.

As illustrated in Figure 4.7, the values of The Campbell Company vary widely according to the valuation method used. The actual value of the company will depend on which method is most appropriate for the circumstances. For example, the seller will argue that the valuation method yielding the highest value — modified book value or discounted cash flow — is the most appropriate one. However, you would argue that the one reflecting the lowest value for the business — liquidation value — is probably the most appropriate. The price actually agreed on will result from extensive negotiation between you and the prospective seller, and will involve considering not only these formal evaluation methods but a host of other business and personal considerations as well.

RULE-OF-THUMB APPROACHES

In some situations, especially the purchase of service businesses, certain rules of thumb have been developed to serve as useful guides for the valuation of a business. They typically rely on the idea of a "price multiplier." One common rule of thumb in firms where there are substantial assets is to add up:

(the fair market value of the company's fixed assets) +
(the owner's cost of current inventory) +
(approximately 90 per cent of what appear to be good accounts receivable) +
(a percentage of the company's net income before taxes as goodwill) =
Approximate Value of the Business

FIGURE 4.7	CAMPBELL CO. VALUATIONS ACCORDING TO DIFFERENT METHODS

Method	Estimated Value (000s)
Net book value (Figure 4.3, I)	$50.0
Modified book value (Figure 4.3, II)	85.0
Liquidation value (Figure 4.3, III)	43.0
Capitalization of earnings (Figure 4.6, I)	60.0
Discounted future earnings (Figure 4.6, II)	64.8
Discounted cash flow (Figure 4.6, III)	85.0

TABLE **4.2**   # RULES OF THUMB FOR VALUING A SMALL BUSINESS

CAUTION: These rule of thumb valuations are only appropriate for average companies in the industries below. Fast growing, unusually risky, declining or unusually low risk companies would not be appropriate valued using these methods.

Type of Business	"Rule of Thumb" Valuation
Accounting Firms	100–125% of annual revenues
Auto Dealers	2–3 years net income + tangible assets
Auto Parts	4–5 times monthly sales plus inventory
Beauty Salon	15–25% of net profit +$2,500 per station
Book Stores	15% of annual sales + inventory
Camp Grounds (with real estate)	8 times annual net profit
Coffee Shops	40–45% of annual sales + inventory
Courier Services	70% of annual sales
Day Care Centers	2–3 times annual cash flow
Dental Practices	60–70% of annual revenues
Distributors	25–50% of annual gross sales
Dry Cleaners	70–100% of annual sales
Employment & Personnel Agencies	50–100% of annual revenues
Engineering Practices	40% of annual revenues
Florists	34% of annual sales + inventory
Fast Food Restaurants	40–50 per cent of annual gross sales
Food/Gourmet Shops	20% of annual sales + inventory
Furniture & Appliance Stores	15–25% of annual sales + inventory
Hotels	2 to 3 times annual gross sales
Gas Stations	15–25% of annual sales + equip/inventory
Gift & Card Shops	32–40% of annual sales + inventory
Grocery Stores	11–18% of annual sales + inventory
Insurance Agencies	100–125% of annual commissions
Janitorial & Landscape Contractors	40–50% of annual sales
Law Practices	40%–100% of annual fees
Liquor Stores	25% of annual sales + inventory
Manufacturing	40–50% of annual gross sales
Marinas (with real estate)	8–10 times annual net profit
Motels	$20,000 per room
Property Management Companies	50–100% of annual revenues
Pharmacies	Total daily sales times 80-120, plus inventory
Publishers (books)	2–3 times gross annual sales
Restaurants (non-franchised)	30–45% of annual sales
Retail	25–50 per cent of annual gross sales, + inventory
Sporting Goods stores	30% of annual sales + inventory
Taverns	55% of annual sales
Travel Agencies	40–60% of annual commissions
Trucking Companies	$2 thousand to $5 thousand per driver
Veterinary Practices	60–125% of annual revenues

Source: "30 Second on Less Business Valuation" Business Valuation for Busy People, (www.communityfutures.com/cms/fileadmin/files/cfdc/pdf/30 SecValuation.pdf), accessed May 11, 2010.

In companies where there are relatively few tangible assets, another rule of thumb is to calculate the selling price as a percentage of the net or gross annual receipts of the business. This method is illustrated in Table 4.2 for various types of businesses.

One word of advice, however. Many valuation professionals discourage the use of such rule-of-thumb formulas. They contend that the formulas don't address many of the factors that impact a business's actual value and rely on a "one size fits all" approach when no two businesses are ever actually alike. These rule-of-thumb formulas do, however, give you an easy way to at least get a ballpark figure on what a business might be worth. But keep in mind that using one of these rules of thumb does not mean that the balance sheet and the income statement for the business can be ignored. These rules are merely a starting point for business valuation and must be reviewed in the context of the other business factors discussed earlier in this section.

WHAT TO BUY — ASSETS OR SHARES?

The acquisition of a business may be structured under one of two basic formats:

1. You can purchase the seller's stock or shares in the business.
2. You can purchase part or all of the business's assets.

Although these alternatives are treated somewhat the same for financial reporting purposes, the tax consequences can differ significantly. A major consideration in the purchase or sale of a business may be the effect on the tax liability of both the buyer and the seller. The "best" form of a particular transaction will depend on the facts and circumstances of each case. Since the tax implications of acquiring or disposing of a business can be very complex, and a poorly structured transaction can be disastrous for both parties, it is suggested that you seek competent tax advice from your accountant or lawyer regarding this matter. Another factor to consider in deciding whether to buy assets or shares is "contingent liabilities." If assets are acquired, in most instances the buyer takes no responsibility for any contingencies that may arise subsequent to the sale such as lawsuits, environmental liabilities, or tax reassessments.

Other considerations

A CASE STUDY — THE BROWN CO.

On Dave Brown's 65th birthday, he decided to sell his business, The Brown Co., a manufacturer and importer of specialty leather products. Dave had worked hard all his life, and now he wanted time to travel. But he didn't know where to start in setting a price for his business. His lawyer suggested he contact a valuation firm to find out what his business was worth.

The valuation expert, George Smith, asked Brown to describe his business and its strengths and weaknesses. He also asked for such items as balance sheets, cash flow statements, and income statements for the past five years.

The Brown Co.'s Profile

The Brown Co., while somewhat cyclical, had a history of consistent profitability. The past year had provided an income of roughly $100,000 before taxes. Brown pays himself an annual salary of $100,000.

The Brown Co. has a stable and diverse customer base as well as an excellent reputation for quality service and product delivery. Its exclusive contracts with certain key suppliers also provide The Brown Co. with a significant competitive advantage over its rivals.

WHAT'S A BUSINESS WORTH?

Valuation Approaches

After considering all the information Brown provided and making his own investigation, Smith considered the two classic approaches to determining a value for the business:

THE INCOME APPROACH This method capitalizes or discounts the company's expected earnings stream. One of the best approaches is discounted cash flow analysis, which estimates the present value of the future stream of net cash flows expected to be generated by the business. The net cash flows are forecast for an appropriate period and then discounted to present value using a discount rate that reflects the risks of the business.

THE ASSET APPROACH This method considered the value or replacement cost of the company's assets as an indication of what a prudent investor would pay for this opportunity.

Using the Approaches

Smith used the discounted cash flow approach to provide what he thought was a realistic assessment of the business's expected selling price. He did not employ the

continued

What's a Business Worth?—continued

asset approach because he felt a going concern business like The Brown Co. has significant "goodwill" value, such as brand equity or established customer relationships, which are very difficult to account for using the asset method.

To determine a value for The Brown Co., Smith first estimated the present value of future net cash flows. Cash flow forecasts require analysis of all variables influencing revenues, expenses, and capital investment. While projections of future operating results can sometimes be difficult to forecast reliably, The Brown Co. had a history of stable sales and profitability, both growing at an annual rate of about 3 per cent. Smith therefore chose the most recent 12 months' results as his base-year forecast.

Computing Cash Flow

To obtain an accurate basis for his forecast, Smith first adjusted the income statement. As shown in Table 4.3, he added back into the net profit the difference between Brown's salary of $100,000 and a more typical manager's salary of $50,000 to run such a business. He also added back interest expenses because existing financing arrangements typically don't affect the value of a company unless they are going to be assumed by the buyer.

He then subtracted taxes at The Brown's Co.'s average effective federal and provincial tax rate of 20 per cent and calculated the company's after-tax operating profitability.

Smith next added back depreciation expense, a non-cash expense of $25,000. He then subtracted the average annual capital expenditures, estimated at $35,000, and the $5,000 average increase in working capital, such as accounts receivable, needed to finance The Brown Co.'s revenue growth.

Brown was a mechanical engineer by training and had collected a quantity of machinery not really needed in the business's operations. So, Smith had these hard assets appraised by an external firm that specialized in that business, with a resulting value of $50,000. He then added the appraised value of this excess machinery, which could be sold separately, to the total value of The Brown Co.'s operations.

Return on Investment

Would you buy a business if you could make as much simply by investing your money? Of course not; the risk in owning a business is much greater. So, Smith considered the fact that buyers expect to receive a higher return on the business than on more passive investments such as certificates of deposit and real estate. The valuation expert defines the rate at which cash flows were discounted as a competitive rate of return for The Brown Co. given its inherent risk factors. Smith also examined the rates of return of comparable publicly held companies. Based on this analysis, Smith con-

TABLE 4.3

THE BROWN CO. BASE-YEAR ADJUSTMENTS AND VALUATION

Income before taxes	$100,000
Excess salary	50,000
Interest on financing	25,000
Adjusted pretax income	175,000
Taxes at 20%	(35,000)
Adjusted profit after tax	140,000
Plus depreciation	25,000
Less working capital invest.	(5,000)
Less capital expenditures	(35,000)
Total adjusted base-year free cash flow	$125,000
Present value of discounted cash flow	$750,000
Plus excess machinery	50,000
Total value of The Brown Co.	$800,000

cluded 16 per cent was a fair cost of capital to use to discount The Brown Co.'s after-tax net cash flow.

The discounted cash flow valuation conclusion for The Brown Co. was approximately $800,000, consisting of $750,000 for the company's operations and $50,000 as the value of the excess machinery.

Happy Endings

Brown was pleasantly surprised by the final valuation. But, as Smith told him, a valuation is one thing, but the actual selling price can be quite another. He suggested that Brown ask $850,000 for the business including the extra equipment but to be prepared to accept less, or possibly assist the buyer with some financing. Brown agreed, and at Smith's suggestion also offered to stay on for a few months after the sale to ensure a smooth management transition.

What was the actual price? After about nine months, The Brown Co. was sold for $820,000. The price was slightly greater than the valuation number due to the favourable terms Brown gave the buyer. He agreed to accept $300,000 in cash, provided a promissory note to the buyer for another $300,000 at 7 per cent and the remainder was the buyer's assumption of The Brown Co.'s outstanding $220,000 of long-term debt and accrued expenses.

Source: Adapted from "What's My Company Worth? A Case Study — 'Colombo Company,'" CBIZ Valuation Group LLC, (www.cbiz.com/valuationgroup/page-print.asp?pid=1583), accessed May 11, 2010.

In some cases there may not be any choice. If the company is a sole proprietorship, for example, there are no shares, only assets and liabilities accumulated in the course of doing business that belong to the proprietor personally. So when acquiring the company, you and the owner must decide which of these assets and liabilities are to be transferred and which are to stay with the present owner. You may feel that some of the assets are not really essential to carry on the business and the seller may desire to keep something — often the real estate, which you may be able to lease rather than buy from him. This may be one way of reducing the cost of the business to you. These are matters that would have to be discussed in detail between you and the prospective seller.

FINANCING THE PURCHASE

Personal Equity

Any number of sources of financing can be used to purchase a business. Because you are buying something that already exists and has a track record, you may find this financing easier to obtain than if you were starting a business from scratch. However, the place to begin is with your own personal equity. In most transactions, anywhere from 20 to 50 per cent of the money needed to purchase a business comes from the buyer and his or her family and close friends. The notion of buying a business by means of a highly leveraged transaction with a minimum amount of up-front cash is not a reality for most buyers.

Seller Financing

If you do not have access to enough cash to make the purchase you might consider asking the seller to finance part of the purchase. This is very common in the sale of many small businesses. The seller's willingness to participate will be influenced by his or her own requirements, such as tax considerations or cash needs. For example, the seller might carry a promissory note for part of the purchase price, or you might lease rather than buy a portion of the facilities, equipment, or other assets. Another option is that you may be able to get the seller to agree to tie repayments to the actual performance of the business after the sale. Terms offered by sellers are usually more flexible and often more favourable than those available from a third-party lender like a bank. In addition, there may be some real advantages to the sellers since many of these options will provide them with a steady source of revenue instead of a lump sum payment, so they don't immediately face a tax liability on any capital gains realized from selling the business.

Third Parties

Banks and other lending institutions may provide a loan to assist in the purchase of a business, although the rate of rejection tends to be quite high on these transactions. When a bank will consider financing an acquisition, its focus tends to be on the physical assets associated with the transaction. The bank might, for example, provide financing for up to 50 to 75 per cent of the value of any real estate, 75 to 90 per cent for any new equipment acquisitions, or 50 per cent of any inventory. The only other assets that might be attractive are the accounts receivable, which it may finance to 50 or 60 per cent as well.

With any of these financing options, buyers must be open to creative solutions. They must also be prepared to take some risks. There is no sure thing, even though the business may appear to have had a long and successful operating history.

A WORD OF WARNING

As you have seen, there are a lot of things you need to worry about in buying an existing business, including undisclosed debts, overstated earnings, poor employee relations, overvalued inventory, and potential lawsuits. Therefore, you should have a good accountant and an attorney on your team for all but the simplest business acquisitions. The lawyer can either represent you in the actual negotiations or just serve as your coach, and can also act as your trustee in handling the exchange of money. It a good idea, if possible, to retain a lawyer who is very familiar with the tax aspects of business transfers, as this can often save you a lot of money. In addition, if you are buying a business for more than the value of its tangible assets, you should consider consulting with a professional business appraiser who has some experience in valuing businesses in the same industry.

FYI / FOR YOUR INFORMATION

A Comprehensive Guide to Buying a Business in Canada a comprehensive guide that explains the process, from finding a business and deciding what type of business is best for you, to determining the value of the business, negotiating with the seller, making sure your legal bases are covered, and closing the deal. (www.canadaone.com/tools/buy_a_biz/index.html)

Buying a Business: The Safer Alternative buying an established business may offer significant advantages worth considering if you want to own your own business. (entrepreneurs.about.com/od/buyingabusiness/a/buyingabusiness_2.htm)

Buying a Business An overview of the pros and cons and the key questions you need to ask yourself about buying a business. (www.canadabusiness.ca/eng/125/140/)

What's Your Business Worth? A calculator that creates a possible market value for your business. Enter your cash flow information for the next four years, your cost of capital and your expected growth rate. It will then determine the Net Present Value (NPV) of your company today. (v1.theglobeandmail.com/v5/content/calculator-smallbiz/calculate/? what=BusinessValuation)

Financing the Business Acquisition A discussion of where to get the money to finance the acquisition of a business (from a US perspective). (www.businessbookpress.com/articles/article144.htm)

STRIKING A DEAL

When the negotiations to acquire a business actually begin, you will discover that the value you may have assigned to the business during your assessment process serves as a useful benchmark to begin the negotiations but it is not likely to be the final purchase price. At this point, a number of intangibles may enter the process, and depending on the factors that motivate each party to the deal, the final purchase price may be higher or lower than the price you calculated during the valuation process. At the end of the day, a good deal is one where both parties are satisfied with the price and other terms of the deal.

The question is: How can you negotiate this type of "win–win" scenario? Here are a few things to consider:

1. As a buyer, you must know the highest amount you are willing to pay for the business before negotiations start.

2. Avoid confrontational language that will offend the other party and shut negotiations down; stick to calm, factual reasoning and arguments as you negotiate back and forth.

3. When entering negotiations, it is important to understand that intangible assets can drive up the price of a business. Sellers typically want to allocate as much to goodwill as possible so they will be better off for tax purposes, while you may want to minimize the amount allocated to goodwill and maximize the amount allocated to tangible assets, which depreciate at a faster rate.

4. As the buyer, if you are firm on one point such as the purchase price or the allocation of goodwill, then you should look for other areas where you can be flexible, like vendor financing, in order to facilitate the closing of the deal.

5. If the deal isn't working, always be willing to walk away.[1]

---

1. M. Collins and J. King, *A Comprehensive Guide to Buying a Business in Canada*, CanadaOne Toolkit (www.canadaone.com/tools/buy_a_biz/section3e.html), accessed May 12, 2010.

TAKING OVER A FAMILY BUSINESS

Another route to entrepreneurship for you may be taking over or joining a family business, perhaps a firm founded by your parents or grandparents. In fact, many family leaders actively strive to continue the family involvement in their businesses over several generations. This is a situation that has some unique opportunities and risks.

Family businesses are characterized by having two or more members of your family who may already control, are directly involved in, or own the majority of a business. It is estimated that roughly 80 per cent of all businesses in North America are family businesses. What distinguishes these firms from non-family businesses is:

1. The interrelationship between family members interacting with each other and interacting with the business.
2. The complex issue of succession planning.

As illustrated in Figure 4.8, a family business can be thought of as an integrated system with three different subsystems, each with its own boundaries that separate it from the other subsystems. These three overlapping perspectives must be integrated to facilitate effective functioning of the entire system, and a change in one subsystem has ramifications for both of the other subsystems. This is further complicated by the fact that the major subsystems — family and business — are fundamentally different.

For example, if we think for a moment about the values of a typical family, they would include such things as unconditional acceptance of each member, permanent relationships, and a nurturing environment intended to foster the well-being of the entire group. This is basically an emotion-based system, as shown in Table 4.4. On the other hand, a business system tends to be goal- and task-focused, and all about making money. It values qualities like competence, productivity, and performance, and tends to be task-based in its orientation. So, at a very basic level, these two subsystems have widely divergent goals and values. What makes a family business so challenging is that family members have to find a way to make these two differing subsystems co-exist, so that family members not only work effectively together but do so in the best interests of the business.

This situation can become further complicated when the third subsystem — ownership — is factored into the equation. The ownership group may include both family and non-family members who may or may not also be actively involved in managing the business. In addition, these individuals can have totally different experiences and expectations of the system that need to be factored in.

FIGURE 4.8   A SYSTEMS VIEW OF FAMILY BUSINESS

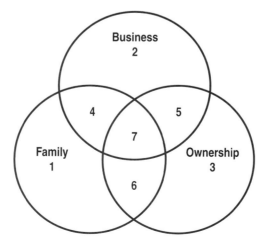

Source: M. Voeller, L. Fairburn, and W. Thompson, *Exit Right: A Guided Tour of Succession Planning for Families-In-Business Together* (Toronto: Summit Run Inc., 2000), p. 15.

| TABLE 4.4 | MAJOR DIFFERENCES BETWEEN A BUSINESS SYSTEM AND A FAMILY SYSTEM |

BUSINESS SYSTEM

Task-based system
Mission: To produce goods/services profitably
Competency prevails
Acceptance is based on performance
Relationships are temporary and contractual
Power: Based on authority and influence

FAMILY SYSTEM

Emotion-based system
Mission: To nurture offspring into competent adults
Equality rules
Acceptance is unconditional
Relationships are permanent
Power: Based on generational stage/birth order

Source: Adapted from M. Voeller, L. Fairburn, and W. Thompson, *Exit Right: A Guided Tour of Succession Planning for Families-In-Business Together* (Toronto: Summit Run Inc., 2000), p. 14.

Figure 4.8 also depicts the interaction of these three subsystems to create seven possible sets of circumstances in which you might find yourself in relation to a family-owned enterprise:

1. A family member who neither works in the business nor is a shareholder.
2. A non-family member who works in the business but is not a shareholder.
3. A non-family shareholder who does not work in the business.
4. A family member who just works in the business.
5. A non-family shareholder who works in the business.
6. A family member who is a shareholder but doesn't work in the business.
7. A family member who owns shares and works in the business.

Individuals in different circumstances will have totally different experiences and expectations for the business as a whole, yet all of them are in a position to significantly impact the ongoing success of the enterprise. These different needs and expectations need to be taken into account in managing the business.

THE QUESTION OF SUCCESSION

It is generally conceded that the most important issue facing most family businesses is the question of succession. Death or retirement of the founders or principals of all businesses is inevitable, yet most family firms lack any kind of clear succession plan. A recent report by the Canadian Federation of Independent Business (CFIB) indicated that four out of ten current small- and medium-sized business owners intend to exit their businesses within five years, largely due to retirement, with that number increasing to seven of ten within ten years.[2] This means there are thousands of Canadian businesses in transition and millions of jobs are likely to be impacted. The interesting part of this report is the lack of any formal process on the part of most SME owners to provide for this transition. The CFIB survey, for example, found that only a third of these owners were currently planning for their future succession, and of those, the majority had made only informal, unwritten plans that had not even been communicated to the intended successor. There are three main reasons for this omission:

1. The owners are often too busy keeping their business alive and operating to plan for their own departure.
2. The owners don't have any confidence in the ability of their children or the relatives who might replace them to continue to run the business.
3. The owners do not see the perpetuation of their business in the family as a major concern.

This lack of a succession plan can create difficulties for a number of people, including family members, bankers, employees, managers, lawyers, spouses, and friends. Planning with foresight for succession can create a much more favourable transition than trying to implement these changes after the fact.

2. "Two Million Jobs in Play as Small Business Succession Issue Looms," News Release, Canadian Federation of Independent Business, June 13, 2005. (www.cfib.ca/mcentre/mwire/releases/nat061305_e.asp)

Planning a Successful Transition

A number of important issues must be considered in developing a successful succession plan, including:

1. **Understanding the context for the transition** Several key aspects that contribute to a successful succession plan include the timing, the type of business, the hopes and desires of the principal owner, and environmental considerations.

TIMING

The earlier the owner starts to plan for a successor, the better the chance of getting the right person. Otherwise death, illness, or other issues can create a major problem for the business if a contingency plan is not in place.

TYPE OF BUSINESS

Some owners may be easy to replace. With others it may be a lot more difficult. Situations that require a high level of technical expertise or where the business has been built on the principal owner's personal network of connections may make transition difficult. However, finding someone to run a business that requires minimal knowledge or experience may not be very difficult.

THE HOPES AND DESIRES OF THE PRINCIPAL OWNER

Family business succession includes the transfer of ethics, values, and traditions, as well as transfer of the actual business. A successor is typically expected to share these standards and continue adherence to them in the business.

BUSINESS ENVIRONMENT CONSIDERATIONS

The business environment usually changes over time and often an accompanying change is needed at the top to address these changing circumstances. It is critical to ensure that the successor and the environment have the "right fit" if a change in leadership is to be effective.

2. **Identifying the Qualities Needed in a Successor** Successful successors may need to possess a number of qualities or characteristics. Some of the more common of these characteristics include:

- Knowledge of the business or the ability to acquire that knowledge within an acceptable time frame
- Honesty and the basic capacity to operate the business successfully
- Good health
- Energy and perceptiveness
- A genuine enthusiasm for the business
- A personality compatible with the requirements of the business
- A high level of perseverance
- Stability, maturity, and aggressiveness
- Problem-solving skills and resourcefulness
- The ability to plan and organize
- The ability to help other people to develop
- A general agreement with the owner's basic philosophy about the business[3]

If it is difficult to identify an individual with all these traits, emphasis should be placed on selecting a successor with the capacity to develop most of these characteristics within a reasonable time frame.

---

3. R.M. Hodgetts and D.F. Kuratko, *Effective Small Business Management*, 6th ed., The Dryden Press Series in Entrepreneurship (Orlando, FL: Harcourt Brace College Publishers, 1997), p. 65.

3. **Implementing the succession plan** A number of important steps can be followed in the successful implementation of a succession plan, including:

GROOMING AN HEIR

In some cases the heir apparent to take over the business may be obvious or the principal owner may pick a successor and let it generally be known in order to be able to openly help that person to develop. In others, the owner may hesitate to actually announce a choice. While one family member may appear to have the inside track, there may be a number of other possibilities and no one knows for sure who will get the job. Even if the successor has been chosen, it is not uncommon for the owner to have difficulty delegating the authority needed to effectively help that person develop the skills required to take over the business.

FAMILY ACCEPTANCE OF THE PLAN

Whatever succession plan is developed requires the general acceptance of the rest of the family. A detailed discussion with all family members about their expected duties, obligations, and responsibilities is imperative to the success of the plan. All those who will be most affected by the plan need to be included, so that hopefully the plan will gain their general acceptance and support.

A "family council" may be effective for this purpose — a formal, periodic meeting where family members share information, discuss issues, and make decisions about matters that affect them as a group. The family council should include all family members, regardless of their roles in the business, and usually also involves those who may not have a direct involvement in the business but who are nevertheless impacted by its direction and success.[4] It can be a valuable tool for enhancing family relationships and improving communication about the business.

THE USE OF OUTSIDE ASSISTANCE

Developing a succession plan and running a family business in general is a complex task involving complicated financial matters, buy–sell agreements and other legal issues, the resolution of conflict among family members, and a lot of other specialized tasks that are best handled by outside consultants and advisors. These may include expert consultants such as accountants, lawyers, financial planners, industrial psychologists, and others who have a specialized field of knowledge that can be useful for resolving a particular kind of problem.

This phase might also include "process" consultants or facilitators who help the family members to see the entire picture and move toward their broader-based goals in a coordinated way. For example, most experts recommend using a facilitator skilled in dealing with family dynamics and conflict, in conjunction with family council meetings.

The description of the succession plan outlined for Harry Rosen (Entrepreneurs in Action #17) illustrates one case of how it can be done in such a way that the probable successors gain the necessary experience to run the business, and learn the skills to be effective leaders. If Larry Rosen can follow the plan initiated by his father with his sons in turn, the business may well make a successful transition to the third generation of Rosens as well.

HOW CAN YOU PREPARE FOR RUNNING THE FAMILY BUSINESS?

If you are involved in a family business, you can't start too soon to prepare yourself for your future role in that business. Five important steps in this preparation:

- **Tell others of your interest in being involved in the family business** Don't keep your aspirations secret. Announce your goals to others and look to them for assistance, advice, and support in helping you achieve them. It is especially important that your intentions be made clear to the principal stakeholders in the business such as parents, siblings, and employees.

- **Take responsibility for your personal development** This might include an informal apprenticeship in the business, perhaps starting with summer and part-time jobs. You should also consider an appropriate educational program, perhaps taking a diploma or degree in business or a related field so that you understand the general parameters of operating a company.

---

4. M. Voeller, L. Fairburn, and W. Thompson, *Exit Right: A Guided Tour of Succession Planning for Families-In-Business Together,* (Toronto: Summit Run Inc., 2000), p. 33.

Entrepreneurs in Action

Keys to the family shop

Succession planning in family-owned and run businesses can be fraught with pitfalls, including sibling rivalries among the next generation, the potential loss of key employees who don't have the royal jelly for the top job as well as the financial complications inherent in passing an enterprise from one generation to the next.

Most are not as smooth as the well thought out transition at Harry Rosen. Although he worked summers in the family business, for a time it seemed highly unlikely Larry Rosen would take the reins of his father's famous retail operation.

While Harry Rosen was methodically expanding his company from its Toronto base, his eldest son was acquiring a university degree, capped by an MBA and law degree that led him into practising law.

A year into his legal career, the younger Rosen was lured back to the family business. "I was practising law and my father was starting to roll the company out nationally," recalls Larry Rosen, who was 27 at the time. "I just felt such pride in what he was doing in running a national organization that I sat down with him and said, ' have to be part of this.'"

Although no doubt delighted in the sudden interest, his father reacted cautiously and, ultimately, wisely to the unexpected overture. "He said if I was going to participate in a senior way, I had to go through a certain amount of learning," Larry Rosen says.

Rather than being handed the keys to the executive washroom, he left his legal position and joined another menswear retailer, Tip Top Tailors, which was part of the now-defunct Dylex Ltd. clothing empire.

Larry Rosen spent a year with the popular-priced Tip Top chain before returning to an opening in Harry Rosen's buying group, a role he filled for about three years. He was then summoned by his father and his partner and president, the late Bob Humphrey. "They said, 'That is not enough, we want you to have experience running areas of our business from an operations point of view.'" Larry Rosen next worked as a regional director, running a number of stores for a few years, then moved to head office to run marketing and special projects before being appointed pres-

ident and chief operating officer in 1997. He was named chief executive in 2000 when Bob Humphrey died.

"The lesson I learnt was I didn't walk in here and become a senior person, I had to go through a whole bunch of positions," Larry Rosen says.

Today, he describes his family company as a "poster boy" of well-thought-out succession planning and, as chairman and chief executive of the retailer, he regularly speaks on the topic to business groups. "There was a plan, a plan that was put in place to help me learn as much about the business and to develop me as much as possible to become a leader". . . .

At Harry Rosen, with 54 years of operation under its belt and successfully into its second generation, there is some talk about the third generation. "Who knows, I have three boys," said Larry Rosen. "Right now I'm just doing the same thing that my Dad did with me, I'm encouraging them to get the best education they can and who knows where their heads will be in a few years. . . . Maybe I'll have the opportunity to do as good a job with them as my Dad did with me."

Source: Paul Brent, *Financial Post,* Monday, March 12, 2007. (www.harryrosen.com)

Other considerations

THE ENDURING TRAITS OF SUCCESSFUL FAMILY FIRMS

Many people argue against family members working together in a business, yet numerous business dynasties have been created by family firms. One famous business consultant, David Bork, recommends recognizing some of the "enduring traits" that successful family firms have exhibited over the years:

1. Shared values about people, work, and money
2. Shared power by respecting one another's talents and abilities
3. Traditions that set them apart from other families
4. Willingness to learn and grow and openness to new ideas
5. Engaging together in other activities besides business to maintain relationships
6. Genuine caring for other family members
7. Mutual respect and trust for other family members
8. Assisting and supporting one another through times of grief, loss, pain, and shame
9. Respect for one another's privacy
10. Well-defined interpersonal boundaries to avoid conflict between family members

Source: S. Nelton, "Ten Keys to Success in Family Business," *Nation's Business*, April 1991, pp. 44–45.

- **Gain experience outside the family business** Working for another firm outside the family enterprise, even in another industry, can be an effective way of gaining valuable experience and building your credibility as a manager or the boss in your own business. It can also be a useful learning experience, as you have an opportunity to see different management styles, observe different operating techniques, and solve different problems — valuable skills that you can bring back to the family business. It is also an opportunity to obtain accountability training by holding positions that teach responsibility and provide important opportunities for decision making.

- **Build relationships** Build contacts with individuals who are part of the family business's current network, including customers, suppliers, lawyers, bankers, and other professional advisors. These connections are often made in community-service settings and social situations such as sporting events, at a golf club, or in similar circumstances. You might also start building up your own network through school alumni and membership in the Chamber of Commerce, service clubs, professional associations, and other organizations.

- **Avoid family feuds** Work *with* other members of the family, not against them. Learn to blend family traditions and values with your future business goals. This will help pave the way for a smooth transition when a clear takeover plan is in place.

FYI FOR YOUR INFORMATION

CAFE The Canadian Association of Family Enterprise (CAFE), is a not-for-profit national organization dedicated to promoting the well-being and understanding of families in business. There are CAFE chapters in most major business regions from British Columbia to Nova Scotia. CAFE offers an outsider's perspective and an insider's understanding of family businesses. Its objective is to educate, inform, and encourage its members in areas of unique interest to family businesses, through a program of activities that provide sources of information and professional advice. (www.cafenational.org)

CHECKLIST FOR A BUSINESS ACQUISITION

Should you start a new business or buy an existing one? At this point in your deliberations, this is the critical question. The material in the Business Acquisition Questionnaire, Figure 4.9, will aid you in making this choice.

If, after answering the questions in Part A, you decide to enter an established business rather than to start one of your own, then you should proceed to the questions in Part B. You may want to reproduce these pages and answer the same questions for several businesses you have in mind. Go through the questionnaire and answer the questions concerning each business as conscientiously as you can.

FIGURE 4.9	BUSINESS ACQUISITION QUESTIONNAIRE

PART A

Before deciding whether you will purchase an established business, you need to give consideration to the positive and negative features of this alternative. You should rate each point in the questionnaire as you perceive its significance and importance to you.

1. How would you define the nature of the business in which you are interested?

_____

_____

_____

2. How important are each of the following factors to you in electing to buy an established business? Indicate the importance of each factor to you on a scale ranging from 0 (not important at all) to 10 (extremely important):

a. Having a business with a proven performance record in sales, reliability, service, and profits _____

b. Avoiding the problems associated with assembling the composite resources — including location, building, equipment, material, and people _____

c. Avoiding the necessity of selecting and training a new workforce _____

d. Having an established product line/service _____

e. Avoiding production problems typically associated with the start-up of a new business _____

f. Having an established channel of distribution to market your product/service _____

g. Having a basic accounting and control system already in place _____

h. Avoiding the difficulty of having to work out the "bugs" that commonly develop in the initial operation of a new business _____

i. Having established relationships with suppliers and financial institutions _____

j. Being able to acquire the assets of the business for less than their replacement value _____

Total _____

3. In checking back over the points covered in question 2, the closer your total score on all items is to 100, the more purchasing an established business is likely to be of interest to you as a means of going into business for yourself.

continued

Business Acquisition Questionnaire — continued

PART B

The following is a set of considerations to be assessed in evaluating an established business. Your responses, information from the present owner, and other information concerning the status of the business should guide you to a comfortable decision as to whether this business is for you.

1. **Why Is the Business for Sale?**

_____

_____

_____

_____

2. **Financial Factors**

   a. Recent sales trend:

   _____ Increasing substantially

   _____ Increasing marginally

   _____ Relatively stable

   _____ Decreasing marginally

   _____ Decreasing substantially

   b. Recent trend in net profit:

   _____ Increasing substantially

   _____ Increasing marginally

   _____ Relatively stable

   _____ Decreasing marginally

   _____ Decreasing substantially

   c. Are the financial statements audited?

   Yes _____ No _____

   d. Apparent validity of financial statements:

   Accurate _____ Overstated _____ Understated _____

   Check the following:
   - Relationship of book value of fixed assets to market price or replacement cost
   - Average age of accounts receivable and percentage over 90 days
   - Bad debts written off in the past 6 months, 12 months

   e. Ratio analysis:

		This Company		
	Industry Standard	Year To Date	Last Year	Two Years Ago
Current ratio	_____	_____	_____	_____
Quick ratio	_____	_____	_____	_____
Debt-to-net-worth ratio	_____	_____	_____	_____
Gross-profit-to-sales ratio	_____	_____	_____	_____
Net-income-to-sales ratio	_____	_____	_____	_____
Return on assets	_____	_____	_____	_____

3. **Tangible Assets**

    a.   Are the land and buildings adequate for the business?

        Yes _____ No _____

    b.   Is the location acceptable?

        Yes _____ No _____

    c.   Is the machinery and equipment worn and out of date?

        Yes _____ No _____

    d.   How does it compare with the latest available?

_____

_____

_____

    e.   What is the maintenance status of the plant and equipment?

        Excellent _____ Good _____ Fair _____ Poor _____

    f.   Is the plant of sufficient size and design to meet your current and projected requirements?

        Yes _____ No _____

    g.   Does the plant appear to be well laid out for the efficient use of people, machines, and material?

        Yes _____ No _____

    h.   What is the approximate value of the company's inventory?

        Raw material $ _____

        Work-in-process $ _____

        Finished goods $ _____

           Total   **$** _____

    i.   Does the inventory contain a high proportion of obsolete or "dead" stock?

        Yes _____ No _____

4. **Intangible Assets**

    a.   Does the company name or any of its trade names have any value?

        Yes _____ No _____

    b.   What kind of reputation does the business have with its customers?

        Positive _____ Neutral _____ Negative _____

    c.   What kind of reputation does the business have with its suppliers?

        Positive _____ Neutral _____ Negative _____

    d.   Are any franchise, licensing, or other rights part of the business?

        Yes _____ No _____

        Are they included in the deal?

        Yes _____ No _____

    e.   Are any patents, copyrights, or trademarks part of the business?

        Yes _____ No _____

        Are they included in the deal?

        Yes _____ No _____

continued

Business Acquisition Questionnaire — continued

5. Marketing Factors

Is the market for the firm's product/service:

_____ Increasing?

_____ Stable?

_____ Declining?   If *declining*, this is principally attributable to:

_____	a. Decreasing demand due to lower popularity
_____	b. A changing neighbourhood
_____	c. A declining target population
_____	d. Technological change
_____	e. Lack of effort by present owner
_____	f. Other factors

6. Human Factors

a.   Is the present owner in good health?

Yes _____ No _____

b.   Does the present owner plan to establish a new business or acquire another business that would compete with yours?

Yes _____ No _____ Uncertain _____

What are the intentions of the present owner?

_____

_____

_____

c.   How efficient are current personnel?

i.   What is the rate of labour turnover?   _____ %

ii.   What is the rate of absenteeism?   _____ %

iii. What proportion of production is completed without rejects?   _____ %

iv.   Can you accurately determine the cost of producing an individual unit of the product or service?
Yes _____ No _____

v.   How has this changed in the past year?
Increased _____ Stayed the same _____ Decreased _____

d.   Has a union recently won an election to serve as a bargaining agent for the company's employees?

Yes _____ No _____

e.   Will most of the key employees continue to work for the firm under your management?

Yes _____ No _____

f.   Will you have to incur considerable costs in retraining or hiring additional employees?

Yes _____ No _____

7. Other Considerations

a.   Are there any zoning restrictions or caveats on the property that may put you at a competitive disadvantage?

Yes_____ No _____

b.   Can you satisfy all the federal and provincial licensing and permit requirements?

Yes _____ No _____

c.   Have you considered what would be the most advantageous way of purchasing the company?

Buy shares _____ Buy assets _____ Don't know _____

d.   Have you had a lawyer and an accountant review the material you received from the vendor and any other information you may have regarding the business?

Lawyer   Yes _____ No _____

Accountant   Yes _____ No _____

8. Your Evaluation of the Business

What have you determined to be the approximate value of the business based on the following valuation approaches?

a.   Net book value $ _____

b.   Modified book value $ _____

c.   Liquidation value $ _____

d.   Capitalization of past earnings $ _____

e.   Discounted future earnings $ _____

f.   Discounted cash flow $ _____

The areas covered by this checklist are not meant to be exhaustive; they are presented merely to guide and stimulate your own thinking about buying an existing business. The more information you can compile to assist you in making this decision the better.

Considering a Franchise

In addition to exploring the possibilities of starting your own business or buying an existing one, you may want to investigate the opportunities presented by *franchising*. Canada is said to be the franchise capital of the world: This sector is estimated to employ 1 million people and register sales of $100 billion a year, or almost 50 per cent of total retail sales in the country. Over 1,200 franchisors have nearly 76,000 outlets, giving Canada more franchised units per capita than any other place on the planet.[1]

Franchising allows you to go into business for yourself and at the same time be part of a larger organization. This reduces your chances of failure, because of the support that the established company can provide. If this appears to be an attractive situation, then a franchise may be the answer for you. Let's look at what this means in the context of starting a business of your own.

AN INTRODUCTION TO FRANCHISING

Franchising has often been referred to as an industry or a business. However, it is neither. It can best be described as *a method of doing business* — a means of marketing a product and/or service that has been adopted and used by a wide variety of industries and businesses.

WHAT IS FRANCHISING?

There is no single, simple definition of franchising. For example, Statistics Canada defines it as **a system of distribution in which one enterprise (the franchisor) grants to another (the franchisee) the right or privilege to merchandise a product or service.** The International Franchise Association, the major trade association in the field, defines it as **a continuing relationship in which the franchisor provides a licensed privilege to do business, plus assistance in organizing, training, merchandising, and management in return for consideration from the franchisee.** These are just two of the many definitions that have been offered.

Regardless of the formal definition, however, it is best to think of franchising as a legal and commercial relationship between the owner of a trademark, trade name, or advertising symbol and an individual or group of people seeking the right to use that identification in a business. A franchisee generally sells goods and services supplied by the franchisor or that meet the franchisor's quality standards. Franchising is based on mutual trust and a legal relationship between the two parties. The franchisor provides business expertise, such as a proven product or service offering, an operating system, a marketing plan, site location, training, and financial controls, that otherwise would not be available to the franchisee. The franchisee brings to the franchise operation the motivation, entrepreneurial spirit, and often the money to make the franchise a success.

Virtually all franchise arrangements contain the following elements:

1. A continuing relationship between two parties
2. A legal contract that describes the responsibilities and obligations of each party
3. Tangible and intangible assets (such as services, trademarks, and expertise) provided by the franchisor for a fee
4. The operation of the business by the franchisee under the franchisor's trade name and managerial guidance

---

1. M. Johne, "Got Guts and a Good Amount of Capital," *The Globe and Mail, Report on a Small Business*, Oct. 18, 2006, p. 82.

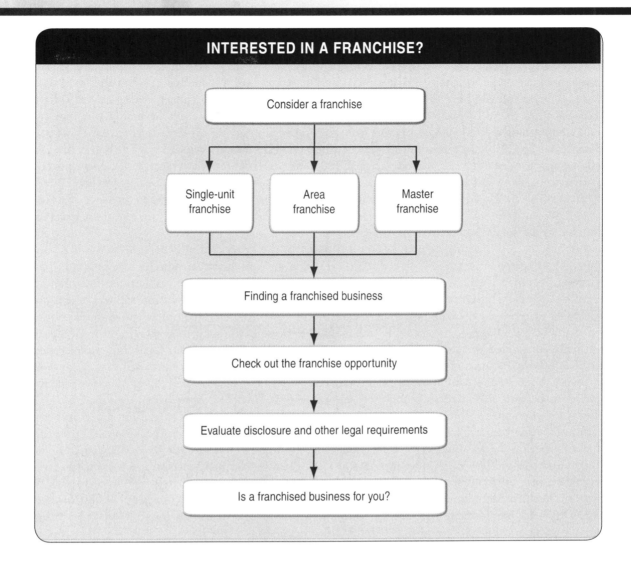

INTERESTED IN A FRANCHISE?

- Consider a franchise
  - Single-unit franchise
  - Area franchise
  - Master franchise
- Finding a franchised business
- Check out the franchise opportunity
- Evaluate disclosure and other legal requirements
- Is a franchised business for you?

Franchise arrangements can be subdivided into two broad classes:

1. **Product distribution arrangements,** in which the dealer is to some degree, but not entirely, identified with the manufacturer/supplier
2. **Entire-business-format franchising,** in which there is complete identification of the dealer with the supplier

In a *product distribution arrangement*, the franchised dealer concentrates on one company's product line, and to some extent identifies his or her business with that company. Typical of this type of franchise are automobile and truck dealers, gasoline service stations, and soft drink bottlers.

Entire-business-format franchising is characterized by an ongoing business relationship between franchisor and franchisee that includes not only the product, service, and trademark, but the entire business format — a marketing strategy and plan, operating manuals and standards, quality control, and continuing two-way communications. Restaurants, personal and business services, rental services, real estate services, and many other businesses fall into this category.

Entire-business-format franchising has been primarily responsible for most of the growth of franchising since 1950. Most of our comments will relate to this form of franchising.

ADVANTAGES OF FRANCHISING

As has been pointed out, franchising is one way for you (the franchisee) to go into business for yourself, yet at the same time be part of a chain, with the support of an established company (the franchisor) behind you. This can enable you to compete with other chains through the use of a well-known trademark or trade name. In addition, the franchisor may provide you with assistance in such areas as site selection, equipment purchasing, national advertising, bookkeeping, the acquisition of supplies and materials, business counselling, and employee training.

As a franchisee you will have the opportunity to buy into an established concept with reduced risk of failure. Statistics show that a typical franchisee has an 80 per cent chance of success. Several factors may explain this result. First, your risk is reduced because you are supposedly buying a successful concept. This package includes proven and profitable product or service lines, professionally developed advertising, a known and generally recognized brand name, the standardized design or construction of a typical outlet, and a proven and market-tested operating system. Second, you are often provided with training for your new job and continuing management support. You have the ongoing assistance of a franchisor who can afford to hire specialists in such areas as cost accounting, marketing and sales, and research and development. These are important assets usually not available to the small, independent businessperson.

As a franchisee you may also be able to take advantage of the lower cost of large-scale, centralized buying. You may be able to purchase supplies at reduced cost, since the franchisor can purchase in bulk and pass the savings along. You may also have access to financing and credit arrangements that would not otherwise be available to an independent business. Banks and other lending institutions are usually more willing to lend money to a franchisee who has the backing of a large, successful franchisor than to a completely independent business.

For example, J-P Despault and his wife were looking to do something on their own in terms of a business. They initially considered opening a Japanese restaurant, since his wife was from Japan but, upon reflection, decided that maybe the town of Bancroft wasn't ready for anything that exotic. Further investigation and discussions with about 20 companies, mostly food franchisors, led Despault to Pizza Pizza. As part of the process of applying to become a Pizza Pizza franchisee, he was provided with a comprehensive information package providing a lot of detailed information about the company. He was also required to submit a personal application form, providing the company with a lot of information about himself and his background. After submitting this information, he was invited for a personal interview and asked to submit a $30,000 franchise fee and enter a comprehensive 12-week training program at Pizza Pizza University. Acceptance as a franchisee was still conditional on his performance in the training program.

After successfully completing the training, Mr. Despault still had to find another $90,000 to meet the company's financial requirements. He and his wife took out a loan against their house. With everything now in place, Despault and his wife could move ahead with the opening of their actual store. The doors opened in November 2006, and initial sales exceeded expectations, so their life as franchisees seems to be off to an excellent start (Entrepreneurs in Action #18).

Similarly, when Cameron Neufeld and Ben Hopper were looking around to start a business, they came across the 1-800-GOT-JUNK franchise and discovered it didn't have much of a presence in the Winnipeg market (Entrepreneurs in Action #19). After doing some research, they discovered that not only was 1-800-GOT-JUNK not very well known, but no one else was providing junk removal either. They believed there was likely to be considerable demand for such a service, so went to the company's head office in Vancouver to meet with management to explore their franchise option. Mr. Neufeld and Mr. Hopper became 1-800-GOT-JUNK franchisees and started with one truck and no employees. Within six months they added a second truck, and then a third, as well as seven employees. Initial revenues exceeded their targets and they appear to be well on their way to achieving their plan for seven trucks, 25 employees and $1 million in revenue.

DISADVANTAGES OF FRANCHISING

While franchising has a considerable number of advantages, there are also several disadvantages that you should be aware of. One of the principal complaints is the degree of control that franchisors exert over their franchisees. While you will be an independent businessperson, in effect you do not have complete autonomy and must operate within the operating system as defined by the franchisor. You are usually in a subordinate position to the franchisor and must abide by the often extremely rigid terms and conditions of the franchise agreement. All franchise contracts give the franchisor either an open right to terminate the contract or the right to terminate upon breach of the agreement. As a result, you may find yourself in a weak bargaining position.

18

Entrepreneurs in Action

Pizza Pizza franchise

J-P Despault's food of choice as a university student was pizza. It was cheap, filled him up and, best of all, always available. "There was this tiny little mom and pop pizza shop near the university," he says. "I ate their pizza every day. I practically used to live out of there."

Not much has changed for Mr. Despault. Today, he owns his own pizza shop — a Pizza Pizza franchise in Bancroft, Ont. But before he took the entrepreneurial route, Mr. Despault moved to Japan in 2000, where he taught ESL. By 2006 he and his wife, whom he married in Japan, were ready for a change. "My wife wanted to give Canada a try," he said. "And we knew we wanted do something on our own in terms of business."

Initially Mr. Despault and Ms. Toshiko toyed with the idea of opening their own Japanese restaurant. "But we weren't sure a small town like Bancroft would be ready for that," he says. He began to investigate franchise opportunities by taking stock of which franchises were already operating in the city and which weren't. "I discovered that there hadn't been a Pizza Pizza in the town for two years," he says. The previous Pizza Pizza franchisee sold the business and although the chain had bought property to open a new location, they had yet to find the right franchisee.

In the summer of 2006 he began the process of applying to be a Pizza Pizza franchisee. The first step was wading through a thick information package brimming with details on the company history, its role in the franchisee's business and current company stats. Mr. Despault also had to sign documents such as a non-disclosure agreement and complete a personal application that asked for information on his background, credit history and even his likes and dislikes.

About a month after sending in all the paperwork, Mr. Despault had an interview with a Pizza Pizza sales rep. "He asked me a lot of questions about Bancroft and the area demographics, which I was ready for," he says. Once he had proven he understood the market, Mr. Despault was ready to move on to the next stage: Pizza Pizza University. Franchisees enter the 12-week training program with no guarantees that they'll actually be approved in the end. In addition to hitting the Pizza Pizza books, Mr. Despault had to fork over a $30,000 franchise fee (which he would get back if he didn't pass all the training tests).

In August, Mr. Despault relocated to Etobicoke for the first four-week segment of his training, which was entirely classroom-based. Among the topics covered were guest services, robbery prevention and Pizza Pizza's trademark recipes.

The next four weeks were a combination of classroom work and in-shop work. Mr. Despault spent part of each week doing everything a store manager would normally do: inventory counts, opening and closing, training staff, cleaning, ordering supplies, "and tons of cooking."

In late September, Mr. Despault started the last leg of PPU. He and his wife (who wasn't a formal Pizza Pizza franchisee) commuted an hour and a half each way from Bancroft to Belleville daily, spending 50 hours a week in a Pizza Pizza store there.

By the end of the 12 weeks, Mr. Despault had aced PPU. All that was left before he was formally approved was finding the rest of the money to cover Pizza Pizza's fees. He and his wife took out a loan against their house and used it to make a deposit payment against the cost of the business. Pizza Pizza requires a 30 per cent deposit, which in Mr. Despault's case amounted to $90,000. (The remainder of the $300,000 would be paid in instalments over the course of five to seven years).

Financials and training in place, Mr. Despault could finally turn his attention to the actual store, 2600 square feet of space located between Bancroft's residential and commercial areas. Pizza Pizza had taken care of all the details in terms of design, sourcing equipment and hiring contractors. They gave Mr. Despault the chance to okay the store layout, but otherwise, it was a done deal.

Next up was hiring staff, which, once again, Pizza Pizza assisted with. Mr. Despault got more than 65 applications and he interviewed every single candidate, hiring about 15 staff for the store opening in November.

Before opening his doors for business (a date that was pushed back three times because of construction delays), Mr. Despault had to train all the new hires. "We took five hours a day every day of the week to train staff," he says.

On November 13, 2006, Mr. Despault opened the doors to his very own pizza shop. "We got crushed," he says. "We did double the sales we expected to do. Our

continued

Entrepreneurs in Action #18 — continued

lobby has a capacity for 35, but we had about 150 in there every day," he says. In addition to the staff and himself, Mr. Despault had four extra sets of helping hands from Pizza Pizza HQ. . . .

The company takes care of both local and national advertising for a fee of six per cent of revenues. They also develop new recipes.

Aside from the guidance Mr. Despault gets from Pizza Pizza, he credits his store's success with the familiarity their brand offers. "J-P's pizza shop would never have survived," he says. "We get a lot of tourists in this town and they know the product name and what's behind it," he says. "They don't know the mom and pop's diner down the street, but they do know Pizza Pizza." (The chain, which has been around since 1967, now has 501 locations across Canada.)

HOW HE DID IT

J-P Despault and his wife, Toshiko Kojima, were ready to leave Japan and return to Mr. Despault's native Canada last year. After considering the business options in their new town, Bancroft, Ont., they settled on a Pizza Pizza franchise. Today, Mr. Despault manages a staff of 25 and churns out about 1,200 slices and 700 pizzas a week.

- Franchise fee: $30,000
- Cost of business: $300,000 (30 per cent up front, balance paid weekly over five to seven years; equipment includes four ovens, a walk-in fridge and freezer and three pop coolers)
- Initial inventory: $13,000

TOTAL START-UP COSTS: $343,000

- Rent: $2125 (a relatively low rate because of his rural location, says Mr. Despault)
- Staff: $24,000 (four full-time, 20 part-time)
- Monthly inventory: $10,000
- Royalties: $650 (percentage of revenues)
- Advertising: $975 (percentage of revenues)
- Renovation fund: $162 (percentage of revenues towards future store enhancements)
- Utilities: $550 (phone, electricity, water and gas)

TOTAL MONTHLY EXPENSES: $38,462

Number of $9.99 medium Hawaiian pizzas he needs to sell a day to break even: 128

(www.pizzapizza.com)

Source: Rasha Mourtada, *Globe and Mail Update*, February 27, 2007.

19

Entrepreneurs in Action

Got guts, and a good amount of capital?

Never mind that it was a dark January morning in Winnipeg and that their feet, encased in steel-toe boots, were frozen numb. Cameron Neufeld and Ben Hopper — cousins, best friends and business partners — put on their curly blue wigs, whipped out the company banner and began doing the 1-800-GOT-JUNK "wave" on the side of a busy road.

"It's a fun way to market outside the box," said Mr. Hopper who, together with Mr. Neufeld, bought a franchise two years ago from 1-800-GOT-JUNK, a Vancouver-based company that makes money by hauling away people's junk and charging them for the service. "You go out on a street where there's heavy traffic, put on a big blue wig and then you run around and wave at the passing cars."

Mr. Hopper and Mr. Neufeld are among tens of thousands of Canadians who have chosen to "get into business for yourself but not by yourself" by becoming franchisees — owners of business units that operate as part of a system set by a franchisor, the company that owns the system. . . .

When Mr. Hopper and Mr. Neufeld began thinking about buying a franchise, 1-800-GOT-JUNK had about 140 franchises across Canada and the United States. But in Winnipeg, where the cousins were looking to set up shop, not very many had heard of the company, recalls Mr. Neufeld.

"There was no market presence at all in Winnipeg," he says. "So that really presented a challenge."

continued

Entrepreneurs in Action #19 — continued

Their family and friends weren't much help, either. Both men's parents were convinced the business would flop in Winnipeg. The more encouraging friends thought a junk removal franchise was a "neat concept" but one unlikely to provide the men with a good income.

Undaunted, the men researched the junk removal industry in Winnipeg and found that it barely existed.

The pair travelled to the "Junktion" — 1-800-GOT-JUNK's head office in Vancouver — where they met with the CEO and management team and asked and answered dozens of questions. "One of my questions was, 'Tell me about the franchises that failed,' and they told me about every one of them," Mr. Neufeld says.

At the same time, the cousins had to convince the people at 1-800-GOT-JUNK that they had what it took to be successful franchisees.

Mr. Hopper says he believes his background in sales and marketing — he worked as an inside representative for Manitoba Telecom Services Inc. — and Mr. Neufeld's experience running a golf course, where he hired and managed several people, made them attractive to the "Junktion" team.

But while it helps to have business and management experience, it's more important that franchisees fit into the culture of the company, says Brian Scudamore, CEO and founder of 1-800-GOT-JUNK.

"What we're looking for is not so much experience because our systems are so strong, but a good cultural fit," he says. "When we're assessing prospective franchisees, the questions we're asking are, 'Are they energetic? Are they enthusiastic, goal-oriented?'"

"And can they follow a system," Scudamore asks. While running a successful franchise does require an entrepreneurial spirit, highly independent types who like things done their way will probably find the franchise model too restrictive, he says.

Mr. Neufeld says he was sold on the company as soon as he walked into the Junktion.

With $50,000 each to invest — they were told they needed at least $70,000 — Mr. Neufeld and Mr. Hopper became 1-800-GOT-JUNK franchisees. They started with three franchise territories that had a combined population of about 750,000 people.

They had one truck and no employees. "It was recommended to us that we stay on the truck at least in the beginning," Mr. Neufeld says. "It was the best thing we did — we got to know the job before we hired people to do it."

Mr. Neufeld and Mr. Hopper leased a second truck within six months of buying their franchise and added a third truck by the end of the year. They also hired seven full-time employees.

Today, Mr. Neufeld and Mr. Hopper have four trucks on the road and eight full-time employees.

1-800-GOT-JUNK expects its franchisees to make at least $100,000 in revenue in their first year of business. Mr. Neufeld and Mr. Hopper made $320,000 in their first year, surpassing their target of $240,000. This year they say they are on track to hit their goal of $500,000.

The plan, Mr. Neufeld says, is to have seven trucks, 25 employees and $1-million in revenue by the end of 2008. Once they reach this level, they'll start looking at ways to increase their profits.

In the meantime, they've made sure there's always a pair of blue wigs — one for each driver — in each truck, along with a 1-800-GOT-JUNK banner. (www. 1800gotjunk.com)

Source: Marjo Johne, *The Globe and Mail,* Wednesday, October 18, 2006. *Report on Small Business,* p. E8.

Franchisees also have certain reporting obligations to the franchisor and may be subject to frequent inspection and constant supervision. To fit comfortably into such an arrangement, you must accept the necessity of such controls. These restrictions, however, may be unacceptable to some individuals. You must seriously assess your personal suitability for the role of a franchisee.

Another disadvantage of franchising is that the cost of the services provided to you by the franchisor is based on your total sales revenue. These costs can amount to 10 per cent or more of your total revenue or an even larger share of your profits. A related complaint is that the markup franchisors may add to the products you must buy from them can increase your operating costs, particularly if equally good products could be purchased elsewhere at lower prices. While you might initially feel that your operating costs are likely to be lower as a result of the franchisor's central purchasing program, it may not become apparent until later that you are actually paying a huge markup on the material, equipment, and supplies you acquire.

Acquiring a franchise is not necessarily a licence to print money. Besides an initial franchise fee, you will probably also have to make periodic royalty payments and advertising contributions based on a percentage of your gross revenues. Even with these expenditures, you still run the risk of not achieving the expected sales, and thus the profit that the franchisor stated was possible.

It should also be remembered that the benefits available through franchising have not always materialized. Franchisors have not always supplied the services they promised or truthfully disclosed the amount of time and effort the franchisee would have to commit to the franchise. Termination policies of many franchisors have given franchisees little or no security in many cases.

TYPES OF FRANCHISES

FRANCHISE FORMATS

There are three major ways a franchise can be formatted:

1. **Single-unit franchise** This is the most popular and simplest format. In it, the franchisor grants you the right to establish and operate a business at a single location. This has been the most popular means of franchise expansion and the method by which many independent entrepreneurs have become involved in franchise distribution.

2. **Area franchise** This format involves a franchisor's granting you the right to establish more than one outlet within a specified territory. This territory can be as large as an entire province or state, or even a country, or it can be as small as part of a city. To assure that this territory is adequately serviced, the franchisor will usually require the construction and operation of a specific number of outlets within a period of time. Area franchising may be a means of achieving certain economies of scale, and perhaps a lower average franchise cost. On the other hand, it requires a larger total capital outlay for plant and equipment. Area franchisees with a large number of outlets can sometimes acquire greater financial strength than their franchisors. This has happened in a number of instances in the fast-food industry.

3. **Master franchise** In this format, a franchisor grants you (the master franchisee) the right, not only to operate an outlet in a specific territory, but also to sell subfranchises to others within that same territory. Granting master franchises is the fastest way for a franchisor to expand, but it is also very complex and results in a division of fees and royalties between the franchisor and subfranchisor. A master franchisee may not need as much initial capital as an area franchisee, but he or she must learn not only how to open and operate a franchise business but also how to sell franchises.

RANGE OF AVAILABLE FRANCHISES

To give you an idea of the scope of franchising, the Franchise Canada Directory 2010 of the Canadian Franchise Association (www.cfa.ca) provides information on over 1100 Canadian listings in 51 different product/service categories. The range of possibilities available to a prospective franchisee includes opportunities in the following areas and more:

- Accounting/tax services
- Automotive & truck services
- Beauty/cosmetic supplies
- Business consultants/services/training
- Commercial — janitorial services
- Computer/internet sales & services
- Consumer buying services
- Educational products & services
- Environmental products & services
- Food — baked goods/coffee/donuts
- Food — meal assembly
- Food — quick service restaurants
- Furniture/upholstery repair
- Hair and nail salons/spas

- Health & fitness/nutrition
- Home — inspection services
- Home — maid/cleaning services
- Home based businesses
- Lawn & garden supplies/services
- Pets — sales/supplies/services
- Printing/copying/shipping
- Real estate
- Seniors/home care & services
- Sports/recreation/entertainment
- Travel
- Water treatment
- Wine making

TABLE 5.1	TOP 10 FRANCHISE ORGANIZATIONS FOR 2010*					

			Number of Outlets		
Company	Description	Web Site	Franchised Total	Franchised Canada	Corporately Owned
1. Subway	Submarine sandwich restaurant chain	www.subway.com	31,425	2,436	0
2. McDonald's	Hamburger, chicken, salads	www.mcdonalds.com	25,801	1,070	6,357
3. 7-Eleven Inc.	Convenience store chain	www.7-eleven.com	35,141	0	462
4. Hampton Inn	Midprice hotels	www.hamptoninn1.hilton.com/	1,636	28	31
5. Supercuts	Hair salon	www.supercuts.com	1,027	1	1,116
6. H & R Block	Tax preparation service	www.hrblock.com	4,502	418	8,512
7. Dunkin' Donuts	Coffee, donuts, baked goods	www.dunkindonuts.com	8,924	55	0
8. Jani-King	Commercial cleaning	www.janiking.com	13,046	712	21
9. Servpro	Insurance, disaster restoration	www.servpro.com	1,478	0	0
10. ampm Mini Market	Convenience store and gas station	www.ampm.com	2,956	0	95

*Entrepreneur, "2010 Franchise 500," January 2010. The evaluation is based on such factors as financial strength and stability, growth rate, size of the system, number of years in business, length of time franchising, start-up costs, litigation, percentage of terminations, and whether the company provides financing. (www.entrepreneur.com)

At the individual franchisor level, the top 10 franchise organizations in North America in 2010, based on an evaluation by *Entrepreneur* magazine, are shown in Table 5.1.

Within this broad spectrum of available opportunities, the most popular areas have been fast food (take-out/sit-in), food retail (candy, coffee, yogurt, etc.), automotive products and services, and business-related/communication services.

CANADIAN LEGISLATION AND DISCLOSURE REQUIREMENTS

Many U.S. states have laws and regulations governing franchise companies, but the same is not true of Canada. Only Alberta, Ontario, Prince Edward Island, and New Brunswick have legislation specifically related to franchise disclosure, although other provinces are expected to soon adopt similar legislation. The legislation in all four provinces is quite similar in that it requires franchisors (with some exceptions) to provide prospective franchisees with a disclosure document containing a lot of information that otherwise would be very difficult for the prospective franchisee to obtain. This information includes:

- the business background of the directors and officers of the franchisor
- details of any litigation against the franchisor
- details of bankruptcy, insolvency, or criminal proceedings against the franchisor or its directors
- the names and addresses of existing and former franchisees
- the particulars of any advertising fund expenditures
- a set of financial statements

This information must be provided to the franchisee at least 14 days before signing any franchise agreement or paying any money to the franchisor. Otherwise the franchisee may have recourse to rescind the franchise agreement. For example, 3 for 1 Pizza and Wings (Canada) Inc. was found to be in violation of Ontario's franchise law by not providing a full package of disclosure information and ordered to repay $35,000 to a man who backed out of a deal. This was the second time the company was ordered to pay refunds, after a judge concluded that the company had not provided sufficient disclosure.[2] The basic principle behind the legislation is that everyone entering into a franchise arrangement should have access to all the information necessary to make an informed decision. The presumption is that both parties "act in good faith and in accordance with reasonable commercial standards."

In all other provinces, franchisors are still under no legal obligation to provide any specific information or file any material with a government agency or department. As a prospective franchisee, you are on your own for the most part. If your potential franchisor does operate in Alberta or Ontario, however, you should request a copy of the disclosure material they are obliged to provide to prospective franchisees in those provinces, although you may not be entitled to the same length of time for deliberation or legal recourse.

THE FRANCHISE AGREEMENT

Because two independent parties participate in a franchise relationship, the primary vehicle for obtaining central coordination and control over the efforts of both participants is a formal contract. This *franchise agreement* is the heart of the franchise relationship. It differs from the typical contract in that it contains restrictive clauses peculiar to franchising that limit your rights and powers in the conduct of the business. Franchisors argue that these controls are necessary to protect their trademark and to maintain a common identity for their outlets.

A franchise agreement should cover a variety of matters. There should be provisions that cover such subjects as:

- The full initial costs, and what they cover
- Use of the franchisor's trademarks by the franchisee
- Licensing fees
- Land purchase or lease requirements
- Building construction or renovation
- Equipment needs
- Initial training provided
- Starting inventory
- Promotional fees or allowances
- Use of operations manuals
- Royalties
- Other payments related to the franchisor
- Ongoing training
- Co-operative advertising fees
- Insurance requirements
- Interest charges on financing
- Requirements regarding purchasing supplies from the franchisor, and competitiveness of prices with those of other suppliers
- Restrictions that apply to competition with other franchisees
- Terms covering termination of the franchise, renewal rights, passing the franchise on to other family members, resale of the franchise, and similar topics

In considering any franchise proposition, you should pay a great deal of attention to the franchise contract. Since it is a key part of the relationship, it should be thoroughly understood. The rest of this section discusses the

2. J. Daw, "3 for 1 Pizza & Wings ordered to repay $35,000," *Toronto Star*, May 31, 2003, p. C3.

evaluation of an agreement for a single-unit franchise within a business-format franchise system. It is important to realize, however, that this is not a "typical" franchise agreement; there is really no such thing. While agreements may follow a fairly standard approach in terms of format, they do not do so in terms of content. Every agreement is specially drafted by the franchisor to reflect its particular objectives and the future of the business.

Obligations Undertaken by the Franchisor

The obligations undertaken by the franchisor may include any or all of the following:

1. To provide basic business training to you and your employees. This includes training in bookkeeping skills, staff selection, staff management, business procedures, and the systems necessary to control the operation. In addition, the franchisor may provide you with training relating to the operational aspects of the business.

2. To investigate and evaluate sites for the location of your franchise. You will be advised as to whether or not the site meets the franchisor's standards and what sort of performance might be expected at that location. In addition you may be assisted in the design and layout of your franchise operation.

3. To provide either the equipment or the specifications for any necessary equipment and furniture you require.

4. To provide promotional and advertising material to you, and some guidance and training on marketing and promotional principles.

5. The franchisor may provide you with a statement indicating the amount of opening inventory required, and may make arrangements for you to purchase inventory either from the franchisor's own purchasing department or from particular suppliers established for this purpose.

6. The franchisor may provide you with on-site assistance for the opening of your franchise outlet. Quite often the franchisor will provide a team of two to three people to assist you in getting the business off the ground.

7. The franchisor may also provide business operating manuals explaining the details of operating the franchise system and a bookkeeping/accounting system for you to follow. There may also be additional support through such things as business consultation, supervisory visits to your premises, and staff retraining.

Obligations Imposed on a Franchisee

Your obligations as a franchisee may require you to do any or all of the following:

1. Build your franchise outlet according to the plan or specifications provided by the franchisor.

2. Maintain construction and opening schedules established by the franchisor.

3. Abide by the lease commitments for your franchise outlet.

4. Observe certain minimum opening hours for your franchise.

5. Pay the franchise fees and other fees specified in the franchise agreement.

6. Follow the accounting system specified by the franchisor and promptly provide financial reports and payments of amounts due.

7. Participate in all regional or national co-operative advertising and use and display such point-of-sale or advertising material as the franchisor stipulates (this would include having all your advertising materials approved by the franchisor).

8. Maintain your premises in clean, sanitary condition and redecorate when required to do so by the franchisor.

9. Maintain the required level of business insurance coverage.

10. Permit the franchisor's staff to enter your premises to inspect and see whether the franchisor's standards are being maintained.

11. Purchase specific goods or services from the franchisor or specified suppliers.

12. Train all staff in the franchisor's method and ensure that they are neatly and appropriately dressed.

13. Obtain the franchisor's consent before assigning the franchise contract to another party.

14. Maintain adequate levels of working capital and abide by the operations manual provided by the franchisor.

These are only examples of some of the obligations you might expect to incur. There will probably also be clauses involving bankruptcy, transfer of the business, renewal of the contract, and provisions for the payment of royalties and other financial considerations.

Franchise Fees and Royalties

In most cases you will be required to pay an initial franchise fee on signing the franchise agreement. This fee generally pays for the right to use the franchisor's trade name, licences, and operating procedures; some initial training; and perhaps even assistance in site selection for your franchise outlet. The amount of the fee varies tremendously, according to the type of franchise business. For a large restaurant operation or hotel, for example, the fee may be as high as $50,000 or $60,000, but for a small service franchise (such as maid service or lawn care) it may be only $5,000 to $10,000. This fee is not all profit for the franchisor, as it must go to pay for franchisee recruitment, training, assistance with site selection, and other services normally provided to you. Some franchisors will charge a separate training fee, but this is usually established merely to recover the cost of providing the training to you and your employees.

In addition to this initial fee, ongoing fees may also be provided for in the franchise agreement. These will generally consist of royalties payable for ongoing rights and privileges granted by the franchisor. Royalties are usually calculated as a percentage of the gross sales, not profits, generated by your franchise. They may be paid either weekly, monthly, or quarterly, and represent the main profit centre for most franchisors. These royalties must continue to be paid even though the franchise may be losing money. For a fast-food franchise, typical royalties range from 3 per cent to 8 per cent. For some service franchises, the royalty may run from 10 to 20 per cent or even higher.

While some franchisees come to resent having to continue to pay ongoing royalties to their franchisor, this payment may be preferable to the franchisor charging a higher initial fee to the franchisee. Ongoing royalty payments at least imply a continuing commitment to the success of the franchise by the franchisor, to the ultimate benefit of both parties.

As well as royalty fees, many franchise agreements require you to contribute a proportion of your business's gross revenues to a regional or national co-operative advertising fund. This contribution may be an additional 2 to 4 per cent of gross sales. These payments are used to develop and distribute advertising material and to run regional and national advertising campaigns. These are typically not a source of profit for the franchisor.

The administration of these advertising funds has often been the subject of considerable concern to franchisees and one of the areas of greatest dispute between franchisors and franchisees. The advertising fund should be maintained as a separate trust account by the franchisor and not intermixed with its general operating revenues. The purpose of this fund should be specified in the franchise agreement. In addition, the agreement should also state how and by whom the fund will be administered.

In addition to requiring you to support a regional or national advertising program, a franchisor may require you to support your own local advertising. Typically you must spend a specific amount on a periodic basis, calculated either on the basis of a percentage of gross sales or in terms of a fixed amount. Local advertising devised by you will normally require the prior approval of the franchisor.

In some cases the franchisor also provides you with special services such as bookkeeping, accounting, and management consulting services, which are billed on a fee-for-service basis. Before acquiring a franchise you should be sure that you understand all the fees that will be payable, including any extra fees that may not be mentioned in the franchise agreement.

Purchase of Products and Supplies

A key element in the success of many franchise organizations is the sameness of each of the franchise outlets. Therefore, franchisors will work to ensure the maintenance of a certain quality of product or service and to make sure that uniform standards are employed throughout their system. Consequently, many franchisors, in an attempt to exercise complete control over their operation, require you to purchase products and services from them or from designated sources. In some cases the approved suppliers may include affiliates of the franchisor. You may also be able to purchase items from other sources of supply, provided the franchisor has approved each of those sources in advance.

If the franchisor exerts tight control over such supplies, you should try to ensure beforehand that supplies are going to be readily available when required, that they are sold to you at fair market value and on reasonable terms, and that you have the ability to choose alternative sources for any non-proprietary items if the franchisor or the designated supplier is unable to provide them to you when required.

Many franchisors earn a profit from providing supplies to their franchisees. Often, however, because franchisors exercise enormous buying power they can supply goods and services at prices and under terms that are better than those you could negotiate for yourself. You should shop around to compare prices for comparable merchandise. If the prices being charged by the franchisor are out of line, this added cost can dramatically affect your business's future earnings.

Volume rebates are often paid to franchisors by suppliers of particular products. Rather than pocket the money themselves or distribute it back to their franchisees, some franchisors will contribute this to the advertising fund. As a potential franchisee you should ask how these rebates will be handled, as a considerable amount of money may be involved.

Leased Premises

Many franchise operations require the use of physical facilities such as land and buildings. When these premises are leased rather than owned by the franchisee, there are a number of ways in which this lease arrangement can be set up:

1. The franchisor may own the land and/or buildings and lease it to you.
2. You may lease the land and/or building directly from a third party.
3. You may own the property, sell it to the franchisor, and lease it back under a sale leaseback agreement.
4. A third party may own the property and lease it to the franchisor, who then sublets it to you.

The franchise agreement should spell out who is responsible, you or the franchisor, for negotiating the lease, equipping the premises, and paying the related costs. If a lease is involved, its terms and renewal clauses should be stated and should correspond with the terms of the franchise. You must be careful not to have a 20-year lease on a building and only a 5-year franchise agreement, or vice versa.

Franchisors generally want to maintain control of the franchise premises. Accordingly they will often own or lease the property on which the franchise business is located, and then sublet these premises to you. In other situations the franchisor may assign a lease to you subject to a conditional reassignment of the lease back to the franchisor on termination of the franchise for any reason.

With respect to other leasehold improvements, you may also be required to purchase or lease from the franchisor (or from suppliers designated by the franchisor) certain fixtures, furnishings, equipment, and signs that the franchisor has approved as meeting its specifications and standards.

Territorial Protection

In many cases the franchise agreement provision with respect to your territory and protection of that territory may be subject to considerable negotiation prior to inclusion in the agreement. You will generally want to have the franchisor agree not to operate or grant a franchise to operate another franchised outlet too close to your operation. This restriction may be confined to a designated territory, or may be confined to a predetermined geographic radius from your premises.

Franchisors, on the other hand, like to see exclusive territorial protection kept to a minimum. As a result, some franchisors may restrict the protection provided to you to a grant of first refusal to acquire an additional franchise within your territory, or may subject you to a performance quota in terms of a prescribed number of outlet openings in order to maintain exclusivity within your territory. Another approach taken by some franchisors is to limit exclusivity to a formula based on population, with the result that when the population within your territory exceeds a certain number, the franchisor may either itself operate, or grant a franchise to operate, an additional outlet in the territory.

Some questions you might like to have answered in the franchise agreement are as follows:

1. Exactly what are the geographic boundaries of your territory, and are they marked on a map as part of the contract?
2. Do you have a choice of other territories?
3. What direct competition is there in your territory, and how many more franchises does the franchisor expect to sell in that area within the next five years?

4. If the territory is an exclusive one, what are the guarantees of this exclusivity?

5. Even with these guarantees, will you be permitted to open another franchise in the same territory?

6. Can your territory be reduced at any time by the franchisor?

7. Has the franchisor prepared a market survey of your territory? (If so, ask for a copy of it and study it.)

8. Has the specific site for the franchise within the territory been decided on? (If not, how and when will this be done?)

Training and Operating Assistance

Virtually every franchise agreement deals with the question of training the franchisee. Training programs may involve training schools, field experience, training manuals, or on-location training.

The franchise agreement should have some provision for an initial training program for you, and should specify the duration and location of this training and who is responsible for your related transportation, accommodation, and living expenses. This initial training is generally provided for you and the managers of your franchise business. The franchisor will usually require you and your managers to complete the training program successfully prior to the opening of your franchise business. If for some reason you should fail to complete the training program, the franchisor often reserves the right to terminate the agreement and refund all fees, less any costs incurred.

Many franchise agreements also provide for start-up advisory training at the franchise premises prior to or during the opening of the business. This typically involves a program lasting a specified number of days. The agreement should indicate who is expected to bear the cost for such start-up training, including who will be responsible for the payment of travel, meals, accommodation, and other expenses of the franchisor's supervisory personnel.

The franchise agreement may also make reference to periodic refresher training. It should specify whether attendance at such programs is optional or mandatory. If it is mandatory, you should ensure that a specified maximum number of such programs is indicated for each year of the franchise agreement. The duration and location of these programs should also be specified.

Most franchisors want tight control over the day-to-day operations of the franchise, and accordingly they provide extensive operating assistance to their franchisees. This assistance is often in the form of a copyrighted operations manual that spells out, procedure by procedure, how you are expected to run the business. The manual will include such information as the franchisor's policies and procedures, and cover such details as the hours you must remain open, record-keeping methods and procedures, procedures for hiring and training employees, and, in a restaurant franchise, such matters as recipes, portion sizes, food storage and handling procedures, and menu mix and prices. The franchise agreement may also indicate that operating assistance will be provided in relation to:

1. The selection of inventory for your franchise business

2. Inspections and evaluation of your performance

3. Periodic advice with respect to hiring personnel, implementing advertising and promotional programs, and evaluating improvements in the franchise system

4. Purchasing goods, supplies, and services

5. Bookkeeping and accounting services

6. Hiring and training of employees

7. Formulation and implementation of advertising and promotional programs

8. Financial advice and consultation

9. Such additional assistance as you may require from time to time

Contract Duration, Renewal, and Termination

The duration of your franchise agreement may be as short as one year or as long as 40 to 50 years. However, the majority of franchise contracts run from 10 to 20 years. Most agreements also contain some provision for renewal of the contract. Be sure you understand these renewal provisions and what the terms, conditions, and costs of renewal will be. Renewal provisions commonly contain requirements for the payment of additional fees and upgrading of the franchise facilities to standards required by the franchisor at that time. The cost of upgrading is usually borne by the franchisee.

You should be aware, however, that not all agreements necessarily contain provisions for their renewal at the expiration of the initial term. Some agreements merely expire at the end of this term, and the rights revert to the franchisor.

The part of the franchise agreement usually considered most offensive by many prospective franchisees are those sections relating to termination of the agreement. Franchisors typically wish to develop a detailed list of conditions in which you might be considered in default of the agreement. *Events of default* typically fall into two categories: (1) critical or material events that would allow for termination of the agreement without notice by the franchisor and (2) events about which you would first be given written notice, with an opportunity to correct the situation.

Most franchise agreements also allow the franchisor the right, on termination or expiration, to purchase from you all inventory, supplies, equipment, furnishings, leasehold improvements, and fixtures used in connection with the franchise business. The method of calculating the purchase price of such items is entirely negotiable by the parties prior to the execution of the franchise agreement. This has been another area of considerable disagreement between franchisors and franchisees.

When renewing franchise agreements, many franchisors do not require the payment of an additional fee, but they may require franchisees to pay the current, and usually higher, royalty fees and advertising contributions. These increases, of course, reduce your income. In addition, the franchisor may require you to make substantial leasehold improvements, update signage, and make other renovations to your outlet to conform to current franchise system standards. These capital expenditures can be expensive, so it should be clear from the beginning what improvements might be required on renewal.

Selling or Transferring Your Franchise

With respect to the transfer or sale of your franchise, most franchise agreements indicate that you are granted rights under the agreement based on the franchisor's investigation of your qualifications. These rights are typically considered to be personal to you as a franchisee. The contract will usually state that transfers of ownership are prohibited without the approval of the franchisor, but you should attempt to have the franchisor agree that such consent will not be unreasonably withheld.

For self-protection, you should be sure that the agreement contains provisions for the transfer of the franchise to your spouse or an adult child on your death. Also, it should be possible to transfer the franchise to a corporation that is 100 per cent owned by you and has been set up solely to operate the franchise. These transfers should be possible without the payment of additional fees.

Most franchisors, however, require transfer of your franchise to an external party who meets their normal criteria of technical competence, capital, and character.

Another common provision is for the franchisor to have a *right of first refusal* — the option to purchase your franchise in the event that you receive an offer from an independent third party to acquire your rights. In such a situation you may be required to first offer such rights back to the franchisor under the same terms and conditions offered by the independent third party. If the franchisor declines to acquire your rights within a specified period of time after receipt of your notice of such an offer, you can proceed to complete the sale or transfer to the third-party purchaser.

One problem with this right of first refusal is the response time the franchisor has to exercise this right. In some agreements the allowable period is several months, during which the third-party buyer is left on hold. In your original agreement, you should try to negotiate for a more reasonable period of 15 to 30 days for the exercise of this right of first refusal.

By anticipating these and other problems during the initial negotiations, you may be able to avoid future difficulties and enhance the marketability of your franchise.

Some Examples

As mentioned above, the specific terms included in a franchise agreement can vary substantially from situation to situation. For example, under the terms of the Enviro Masters Lawn Care (www.enviromasters.com) franchise agreement for its organic and environmentally considerate lawn care service franchise, franchisees pay $25,000 to $40,000 for an initial franchise fee plus a monthly royalty of 5 per cent of gross sales and 2 per cent of gross sales for the corporate advertising program. The minimum total investment required to get into the business is $30,000, with a total average investment of around $40,000. For this fee the franchisee receives the use of the company's trademark and trade names. The company also provides training, marketing support, and field training in turf management and similar areas.

In contrast, franchisees of Quizno's Classic Subs (www.quiznos.com) can expect to make a total investment of around $250,000 to open a typical outlet. This includes the company's standard franchise fee of $25,000. In addition, franchisees will need further funds for deposits of various types and money for working capital. Royalties amount to 7 per cent of gross sales paid monthly, and the advertising contribution is a further 4 per cent (1 per cent for national advertising and 3 per cent for expenditures in the local market). Of this amount, franchisees should have at least $90,000 in unencumbered cash. The rest may be financed through one of the national banks' franchise programs with the assistance of the company. Franchisees receive 4 weeks of intensive initial training, assistance in site selection and lease negotiations, pre-opening and ongoing operational support, and national, local, and grand opening store marketing programs.

The Keg Steakhouse and Bar (www.kegsteakhouse.com) bills itself as Canada's leading steakhouse. A typical new, stand-alone Keg restaurant requires an investment of over $2.5 million to build the facility and cover the necessary start-up costs. This includes the franchise fee of $50,000. Franchisees also pay a royalty of 5 per cent of their gross sales each month and contribute 2.5 per cent to a corporate advertising fund. This enables them to use the "Keg" brand name on their restaurant and the company provides them with training and other support before they open their location, and ongoing support in accounting, marketing, menu development, personnel management, and financial planning.

A sampling of some other popular franchisors indicating their initial franchise or dealership fee, royalty rate, required advertising contribution, and their approximate total average investment to open a typical outlet is shown in Table 5.2.

TABLE 5.2   A SAMPLING OF CANADIAN FRANCHISORS

Franchisor	Number of Owned Units in Canada	Number of Franchisees/ Dealers in Canada	Initial Fee	Royalty	Advertising Program	Approximate Investment Required	Web Site
Boston Pizza	3	330	$69,000	7%	2.5%	$500–800,000	www.bostonpizza.com
Dollar Thrifty Rent-a-Car	54	66	$5–50,000	8%	—	$50–300,000	www.thrifty.com
Great Canadian Dollar Store	—	120	$19,880	4%	—	$200–350,000	www.dollarstores.com
Molly Maid Int.	—	165	$14,000	6%	—	$35–40,000	www.mollymaid.com
Dairy Queen Canada	—	574	$30–45,000	4%	5–6%	$300,000 +	www.dairyqueen.com
We Care Home Health Services	18	29	$40,000	5%	2%	$125–150,000	www.wecare.ca
McDonald's Restaurants of Canada	338	1,083	$45,000	17% includes rent, services fee and advertising		$400,000+	www.mcdonalds.com
Midas Muffler Shop	8	186	$30,000	5%	5%	$300–400,000	www.midas.com
Domino's Pizza	20	265	$25,000	5.5%	4%	$250–300,000	www.dominos.com
Second Cup Coffee Co.	—	360	$40,000	9%	3%	$280–400,000	www.secondcup.com
Tim Hortons	102	2,800	$50,000	4.5%	4%	$430–480,000	www.timhortons.com
Kwik Kopy Printing	—	69	$29,500	6%	3%	$225–250,000	www.kwikkopy.ca
1–800-Got-Junk	1	31	$12,000	—	—	$70–110,000	www.1800gotjunk.com

Source: Adapted from the *Franchise Canada Directory 2010*, Canadian Franchise Association. (www.cfa.ca)

BUYING A FRANCHISE

FINDING A FRANCHISE BUSINESS

Perhaps the most common source of preliminary information regarding available franchises is newspaper advertisements. Major business newspapers such as the *National Post* and *The Globe and Mail* all have special sections devoted to franchise advertisements. The "Business" or "Business Opportunities" section of the classified advertisements in your local newspaper can also be an important place to look for prospective franchise situations. Business journals and trade magazines may also contain ads for many franchise organizations. Recommendations from friends, trade shows and seminars, and business opportunity shows often held in our larger cities can also be excellent means of contacting franchisors.

Another important source of information is franchise directories, which list franchisors' names and addresses along with information on the type of franchise offered, the costs involved, and other useful information. One helpful directory is the Franchise Canada magazine Directory published annually by the Canadian Franchise Association. (www.cfa.ca/Publications_Research/FranchiseCanada/directory.aspx)

CHECKING OUT THE FRANCHISE OPPORTUNITY

After sifting through the various choices available, most prospective franchisees narrow their selection down to one or two possibilities. The next step is requesting a promotional kit from each of these franchisors. Normally this kit contains basic information about the company — its philosophy, a brief history, a listing of the number of outlets, where they do business, and so on. Most kits also contain an *application form* requesting your name and address, information about your past business experience, the value of your net assets, and other data; for the process to continue with the franchisor, you must complete it in detail. The form may have any one of a number of titles:

- Confidential Information Form
- Personal History
- Confidential Application
- Franchise Application
- Pre-Interview Form
- Qualification Report
- Credit Application
- Application for Interview Form
- Request for Interview

Other considerations

OUT OF THE ORDINARY FRANCHISE OPPORTUNITIES

If fast food, oil changes, and lawn care are not your idea of an exciting business, here are some examples of new, imaginative, and unique franchise opportunities that threaten to put an entirely new face on the industry:

- **Flamingo a Friend** Place plastic animals — flamingos, cows, pigs, etc. in yards for special events like birthdays, anniversaries, graduation, etc. (www.flamingoafriend.com)
- **It's Just Lunch** Dating service for busy professionals (www.itsjustlunch.com)
- **Pointts** Defense services for people facing charges for traffic violations (www.pointts.com)
- **Crock A Doodle** A paint your own pottery franchise (www.crockadoodle.com)
- **Jupiter** A national franchise specializing in water pipes, hand pipes, vaporizers, scales, grinders, papers and other hemp-related products (www.jupitergrass.com)
- **Nerd Force** on site tech support at your home or office (www.nerdforce.ca)

Regardless of which of these titles is used, they are all different ways of describing the same thing and request much the same information. For example, you may be asked for:

1. Personal data such as your name, address, telephone number, age, health and physical impairments, marital status, number of dependants, and the names of any fraternal, business, or civic organizations to which you might belong.

2. Business data such as your present business, your position, the name and address of your employer, how long you have been involved in this business, your present annual salary, and any previous business history you may have, and the name and address of your bank.

3. Professional references from your bank manager, for example, and any other references you may care to provide.

4. Financial data such as your average annual income for the past five years and a total declaration of your current assets and liabilities to establish your net worth.

5. Additional data that relate to your particular interest in the franchise.

The application form normally requires you to provide a deposit, typically in the range of $2,000 to $5,000. In most cases the form will state that this deposit will be credited toward the initial franchise fee without interest or deduction if the transaction proceeds. However, you should make sure that if you are turned down, all or most of this deposit will be refunded, especially if it is a large amount of money and the franchise is new and unproven.

If your application is approved, the franchisor will interview you to determine your suitability as a franchisee. The focus of this interview will be on assessing your capability according to various objective criteria that have been established by the franchisor. Every franchisor has its own established criteria based on previous experience with various kinds of people. For example, many franchisors will not consider absentee owners and refuse to grant franchises strictly for investment purposes. They feel that the success of their system rests on the motivation created by individually owned and managed outlets.

The personal characteristics desired by the franchisor will vary with the type of business. For example, a different level of education is necessary to operate a management consulting service than is needed to operate a carpet cleaning firm. Research on these selection criteria indicates that many franchisors tend to rank them in the following order:

1. Credit and financial standing
2. Personal ability to manage the operation
3. Previous work experience
4. Personality
5. Health
6. Educational background

While other factors may also be considered by particular franchisors, these criteria tend to dominate the selection process.

This interview is also an opportunity for you to raise questions about the franchisor's financial stability, trademark protection policy, the ongoing services provided to franchisees, information regarding any financial packages that may have been arranged with particular banks, the names and addresses of current franchisees, and any other questions that may occur to you. This is an opportunity for you and the franchisor to assess each other and see if you can work together on a long-term basis.

At this interview, the franchisor will also provide you with a copy of the franchise agreement. At this point, you must evaluate all the available information with the help of an accountant, your bank manager, and a lawyer to ensure that you feel comfortable with the franchisor and that you are happy your investment is secure. If you have any remaining questions or doubts, now is the time to resolve them. Then, if you are still not completely sure in your own mind that you wish to proceed, you should ask for a refund of your deposit.

Well-established and popular franchisors are unlikely to change their arrangements or legal documentation very much in response to a prospective franchisee's requests. They have successful systems in which many would-be franchisees would like to participate. For them, it's a seller's market.

If one of these franchisors accepts you as a franchisee, you may have to make up your mind very quickly. It is important to be decisive. If you are comfortable with the franchisor and the franchise agreement, you should be ready to sign. If not, you should ask for a refund and pursue other opportunities.

Some franchisors will expect you to sign the contract right away. Others wait until they have found a suitable location for your outlet, usually within a predetermined period of time. In some cases, it can take weeks, perhaps even months, for a suitable site to be found or a lease negotiated before you actually sign. It should also be remembered that popular franchisors often have long waiting lists of prospective franchisees, so that one or more years can pass before you will be in business.

FRANCHISE FINANCING

One of the first steps in evaluating any franchise opportunity is to determine the total cost of getting into the business. This could include the initial franchise fee, equipment costs, start-up inventories and expenses, and initial working capital requirements. This total commitment can be substantial. A study released by the International Franchise Association in the United States indicated the following median values for the minimum and maximum range within an industry for starting a franchised outlet by industry category. These figures are in U.S. dollars and do not include the cost of real estate.[3]

- Baked Goods $210,000 – $395,000
- Business Services $51,000 – $84,000
- Fast Food $178,000 – $2,900,000
- Lodging $4,109,000 – $6,485,000
- Real Estate $31,000 – $98,000
- Restaurant $423,000 – $920,000
- Service Businesses $65,000 – $136,000
- Sports & Recreation $4,400 – $340,000
- Travel $67,000 – $135,000

Other considerations

WHAT DOES IT COST TO OPEN A FRANCHISE?

The estimated costs to open a Joey's Only Seafood Restaurants/Tennessee Jack's Rotisserie Chicken 'N' Ribs are (based on approximately 2,200 square feet, in Canadian dollars):

Franchise fee	$25,000
Opening promotion fee	$3,000–$5,000
Leasehold improvements	$125,000–$150,000
Smallwares	$9,000–$12,000
Furniture, fixtures, and kitchen equipment	$115,000–$130,000
Miscellaneous	$5,000–$13,000
Food and supplies	$10,000–$14,000
Training and pre-opening expenses	$4,500–$11,000
Deposits	$4,000–$10,000
Total Estimated Cost to Open	**$337,000–$437,000**

Source: Joey's Only (www.joeys-only.com/franchising/startup_costs.html) accessed May 13, 2010.

---

3. "The Profile of Franchising 2006: Series II – Initial Investment," International Franchise Association Educational Foundation, Inc., Washington, D.C. September 2006.

Other considerations

ADVICE WHEN CONSIDERING A FRANCHISE OPTION

- Do your own research, and take your time.
- Don't be afraid to cold-call current franchisees (especially those in other provinces) and ask them all kinds of questions.
- Try to talk to former franchisees whose business went under. The more reputable franchisors may help you with names and numbers.
- Talk to knowledgeable people in the franchising sector to get the latest word on the organization you're thinking of joining, and what it's like to work with.
- Have an experienced franchise lawyer review your contract.
- If you still want to jump into the world of franchising, assume that nothing will ever again work the way you are used to. The best you can hope for is to reduce the number of "omigawd" surprises you are going to have to face.

Source: M. Stern, "Franchise Fairy Tales," *Canadian Business*, June 23, 2003, p. 30.

You must also determine how much of this amount must be put up as an initial investment and what kind of terms might be arranged for handling the balance. Most franchisors expect the franchisee to put up 30 to 50 per cent of the total franchise package cost as an initial investment. You must ask yourself whether you have enough unencumbered capital to cover this amount.

Financing of the remainder can sometimes be done through the franchisor, or the franchisor may have previously arranged a standardized financing package for prospective franchisees through one of the major banks or trust companies. Subway, the successful submarine sandwich franchise, offers its new franchisees financing via an in-house equipment leasing program. Compucentre also has arranged an in-house financing program for franchisees in conjunction with a couple of the major banks. These programs may be somewhat more expensive for the franchisee than arranging an independent bank loan, but they can be more convenient.

The initial investment required for a restaurant, for example, can be substantial. A typical quick service restaurant like Pizza Pizza has an initial franchise fee of $30,000 and an average total investment of $100,000 to $200,000. The cost of a full-service restaurant such as Swiss Chalet Chicken & Ribs includes a franchise fee of $60,000 and a total investment ranging from $1.5 million to $1.7 million. In these cases, equipment and leasehold improvements tend to make up the largest component of the total cost.

In the retail sector, the size of the total investment will vary depending on the nature and location of the outlet. For example, a furniture store like The Brick Warehouse will require a franchise fee of $40,000 and an average total investment of $500 thousand to $1 million, with the franchisee having to come up with $400,000 to $700,000 as their initial start-up capital. An electronics store like The Source has a franchise fee of $15,000 and a total investment ranging from $75,000 to $200,000. The Wine Kitz winemaking franchise has an initial fee of $20,000 and a total required investment of $120,000 to $150,000. Much of this investment is typically in inventory.

The investment required for a service franchise is usually much lower. Many service franchises can be established for a total investment of less than $50,000. For example, Jani-King Canada, the world's largest commercial cleaning franchise, offers its franchises for a fee as low as $10,000 with a nominal additional amount of financing for equipment, supplies, and initial working capital. A residential cleaning and maid service franchise like Molly Maid can be established for a franchise fee of $14,000 plus $5,000 to $10,000 in working capital. At the other extreme, opening a franchised hotel or motel may involve a total investment of several million dollars, although the initial amount of money required may be much less, since the land and buildings for the hotel or motel can often be externally financed.

FRANCHISE YOUR BUSINESS

If you have a successful business and are looking to expand you might consider franchising as one alternative to enable you to do so. As a growth strategy, franchising can provide you with the ability to improve your market share by increasing your number of points for distributing your product or service. You can grow and expand your business faster than through internal company growth and with minimal capital since the initial investment for the additional business unit is provided by the franchisee.

Advantages of Franchising

Franchising can provide you with a number of other significant advantages such as:

Capital Since franchisees use their own capital you have no investment at the unit level so can leverage off the assets of these franchisees.

Return on Investment Because you have a smaller investment in the overall business, your ROI should be significantly higher.

Speed of Growth Establishing franchises can enable you to grow much faster without increasing your investment or adding more employees.

Reduced Role in Day-to-Day Operations As a franchisor you are primarily concerned with the overall operating performance of your franchisees, reducing the scope of your involvement in day-to-day management of the business.

Highly Motivated Management Franchisees are typically more highly motivated than hired managers since the business is their own.

Quality Control Franchisees generally keep their units in better operational condition than hired managers and, as part of the local community, are better able to promote the business locally.

Long-term Management Franchisees are more unlikely to leave in the short-term so you can realize a better return from investment in long-term training and development.

Unit Performance Franchised outlets typically outperform company outlets in terms of sales volume.

Lean Organizational Structure Through franchising you can grow your organization without necessarily adding a lot of overhead.

Brand Building Since you are able to grow your organization without adding a lot of investment and overhead, you are able to expand your market presence more rapidly and effectively than possible thought internal organizational growth.

Advertising Franchisees will typically contribute to a common advertising and promotional fund which can be used to promote your brand under your direction.[4]

Is Your Business Franchisable?

However, while these advantages may appear to be very attractive it is important to recognize that all businesses may not necessarily lend them to a franchise development strategy. In order to franchise your business, you must have a successful business concept that can be readily replicated in other locations. An appropriate first step in the decision to franchise is an examination of the question of whether or not your business concept is actually "franchisable." Any organization seriously considering franchising should undertake this analysis before going ahead an implementing a franchise strategy. The iFranchise Group, a U.S. consulting firm that specializes in assisting firms in developing and implementing franchise programs has identified a number of criteria that assess the readiness of a company for franchising and the likelihood that it will be successful as a franchisor. These include:

Credibility To sell franchises, a company must first be credible in the eyes of its prospective franchisees. Credibility can be reflected in a number of ways: organization size, number of units, years in operation, success of the prototype unit, publicity, consumer awareness of the brand, or strength of management.

Differentiation In addition to credibility, a franchise organization must be adequately differentiated from its competitors. This can come in the form of a differentiated product or service, a lower investment cost, a unique marketing strategy, or different target markets.

---

4   "Advantages of Franchising", The iFranchise Group Inc. (www.ifranchisegroup.com//index.cfm?Container_Id=334&Container_Top_Level_ ID=258&view_only=1), accessed May 17, 2010.

Transferability of knowledge The organization must have the ability to teach its operating system to others. To franchise, a business must generally be able to thoroughly educate a prospective franchisee in a relatively short period of time. Generally speaking, if a business is so complex that it cannot be taught to a franchisee in three months, a company will have difficulty franchising.

Adaptability The business concept must be able to be adapted from one market to another. Some concepts do not travel well over large geographic areas because of regional variations in consumer tastes or preferences. Others are constrained by varying provincial laws or regulations. Still other concepts work only because they are in a very unique location or because of the unique abilities or talents of the individual behind the concept.

Refined and successful prototype operations A refined and successful prototype is necessary to demonstrate that the system is proven and works, and is generally instrumental for the training of franchisees. The prototype also acts as a testing ground for new products, new services, marketing techniques, merchandising, and operational efficiencies.

Well documented systems All successful businesses have systems. But in order to be franchisable, these systems must be documented in a manner that communicates them effectively to franchisees. Generally speaking, a franchisor will need to document its policies, procedures, systems, forms, and business practices in a comprehensive and user-friendly operations manual.

Affordability Affordability must reflect a prospective franchisee's ability to pay for the franchise in question. For example, a franchise with a $100,000 start-up cost that targets prospects with clerical experience might be affordable to any number of people whereas a multi-million dollar hotel franchise might not.

Return on Investment This is the real acid test of franchisability. A franchised business must, of course, be profitable. But more than that, a franchised business must allow enough profit after paying your royalty and other costs for the franchisees to earn an adequate return on their investment of time and money.

Market trends and conditions While not an indicator of franchisability as much as a general indicator of the success of any business, these trends are key to long-term planning. Is the market growing or consolidating? How will that affect your business in the future? What impact will the Internet have? Will the franchisee's products and services remain relevant in the years ahead? What are other franchised and non-franchised competitors doing? And how will the competitive environment affect your franchisee's likelihood of long-term success?

Capital While franchising is a low-cost means of expanding a business, it is not a "no cost" means of expansion. You will need the capital and resources necessary to implement a successful franchise program. The resources required to initially implement a franchise program will vary depending on the scope of the program. If you are looking to sell just one or two franchised units, the necessary legal documentation may be completed at costs as low as $15,000. If, however, you are seeking more aggressive expansion, start-up costs can run to $100,000 or more. And once the costs of printing, marketing, and hiring additional personnel are added to the mix, you may require a budget of $250,000 or more to reach your expansion goals.

Commitment to relationships Successful franchisors focus on building long-term relationships with their franchisees that are mutually rewarding. Unfortunately, not all franchise organizations understand the link that exists between relationships and profits. Strong franchisee relationships enable the franchisor to sell franchises more effectively, introduce needed changes into the system more easily, and motivate franchisees and their managers to provide a consistent level of products and services to their customers.

Strength of management Finally, the single most important aspect contributing to the success of any franchise program is the strength of its management. Often, new franchisors will try to take everything on themselves. In addition to absorbing several new jobs for which they have little to no time, you will need to exhibit expertise in fields in which you may have little or no experience like marketing, lead handling, franchise sales, advertising fund management, personnel training, and overseeing the management of several organizational units.[5]

How to Proceed

If you make the decision to franchise the next step is to outline a *business plan* detailing your expected growth and strategy for the next five years. You will probably need to raise some additional money and hire some people with new capabilities who will have to be integrated into your existing organization structure.

---

5 "12 Criteria of Franchisability", The iFranchise Group Inc., (/www.ifranchisegroup.com//index.cfm?Container_Id=287&Container_Top_Level_ ID=258&view_only=1), accessed May 17, 2010.

You will also need to develop a detailed *operations manual* for your franchisees. This manual will serve as a sales tool demonstrating to prospective franchisees that your have developed, tested and refined your basic operating system so that it can be readily implemented in other locations and successfully transferred to other operators. This manual will serve as a sales tool, as a training guide for new franchisees, as reference guide for current franchisees and as a quality control devise for the entire chain.

You also need to develop *training programs* to induct new franchisees into your system, and also familiarize franchisee's employees and corporate employees with the system.

To be legally entitled to sell franchises in most jurisdictions now you will need a comprehensive *franchise agreement* as described earlier in this Stage and a *Franchise Disclosure Document* meeting the legal requirements of all the individual jurisdictions in which you plan to sell franchises.

Finally you will need to sell franchises. This will require a specific marketing plan and related materials to get your message successfully across to targeted franchise prospects.

As you can see from the above discussion, franchising can be an excellent strategy for growing your business but is also a very specific and complicated concept with lots of issues and potential pitfalls. Therefore it is important to have the expert support of professionals who specialize in franchising if you should decide to proceed with franchising your business. These franchise support services can include:

Franchise consultants who can lead you through the franchise process in a step-by-step basis.

Legal counsel who can advise you of the legal requirements as well as assist you in developing your franchise agreement and necessary disclosure documents.

Accountants who can help you develop a financial model for your business that includes cash flow projections, your royalty structure, etc. that may be required for your disclosure documents.

Marketing consultants who can assist in preparing your marketing plan, promotional materials, operations manual and other documents that will be necessary for convincing potential investors they should become part of your franchise organization.

Should you decide to move in the franchise direction one final thing you need to appreciate is that your role in the business will change dramatically. You will go from being deeply involved in running the operational side of your business to being the CEO of a franchise company. This means you will have to redirect your time more to marketing activities trying to generate interest among prospective franchisees, attending public speaking events to familiarize the market with your franchise and oversee new business owners trying to build a profitable business in various markets across the country.

Holly Bond, for example, is a mother, entrepreneur and self-described fitness freak. (Entrepreneurs in Action #20) She is also the founder of Bulldog Interactive Fitness, an interactive fitness facility designed

Entrepreneurs in Action

From Fat to Fit

UNDER-18-YEAR-OLDS REPRESENT A US$2-BILLION OPPORTUNITY IN THE GLOBAL FITNESS MARKET

Holly Bond is a mother, entrepreneur and self-described "avid fitness freak." Two years ago, she concluded that her 14-year-old son was overweight, and it had nothing to do with the food in the house. "He wasn't active. He would just play Xbox with his friends in his room, and they were no longer going outside," she says.

Then it occurred to her: why not combine her son's love of gaming with her own daily fitness regimen? She went looking for a high-tech solution, but found no specialized equipment on the market, and few personal trainers working with youth. Bond sensed a gap and decided to capitalize on the opportunity. It was a chance to make a career change by doing, as she puts it, "something that matters."

continued

Entrepreneurs in Action #20 — continued

Bond and her husband, James, researched the global fitness-club industry for more than a year.

The Bonds held clandestine focus groups in their basement, composed of their son's friends and hockey teammates. James, who worked in youth marketing at Coca-Cola, peppered the kids with questions about the latest fashions, sports, video games and fitness trends. They also purchased a prototype of an exercise bike they found at a trade show that could be hooked up to their son's PlayStation, and invited their teenage neighbours for a test drive. ("They went bananas for it," she says.)

With startup costs of roughly $180,000, the high-concept gym opened its doors in February 2005. Based on how much they needed to earn per square foot per hour to be profitable, the Bonds decided to charge $44 a month per child to use the facility and its programs. They chose a bulldog as their name and logo because it looked like a fitter version of their dog, a pug named Lily. Bulldog's Dartmouth gym now has more than 300 members — not quite break-even territory but getting close.

The demographic basis for the business is clear. Over the past 25 years, the proportion of overweight or obese kids has ballooned. There are more fat kids, and fatter kids, than ever before, giving Bulldog a potential market of 1.2 million overweight or obese children in Canada alone.

Parents can't rely on gym classes at schools to address the obesity epidemic, either. Only two provinces have mandated a daily minimum amount of physical activity for primary school children.

Given the ever-expanding market and relative lack of gym classes, a private high-tech workout facility tailor-made for a generation of chunky video-game-addicted teenagers sounds like, as one franchisee put it, "a winning combination." Niche fitness franchises, especially ones like Curves, the U.S.-based chain of women-only gyms, have proven that demographic-specific fitness services can tap a market that larger gyms aren't accessing. And the so-called "soccer mom tax credit" allows families to deduct $500 per child for the cost of athletic activities, presents another marketing possibility —Bulldog franchisees offer a federal tax credit with every gym membership.

The response from franchisees has been enthusiastic. After an item on Bulldog ran on CTV News one weekend, Bond received more than a hundred franchise requests. A Toronto location is the third franchise. Two

HOLLY BOND IN ACTION AT THE TORONTO LOCATION OF BULLDOG INTERACTIVE FITNESS

more Canadian store-fronts are on track to open before the end of the year, in Thornhill and London, Ont., and another four — in Guelph, Ont., Calgary, St. John's, Nfld., and the first U.S. location, in Wisconsin, are scheduled for early 2007. Out of roughly 150 formal franchise applications, Bond says she is considering about 25 of them.

"It was always our intention to franchise," says Bond, "but we thought we'd do be doing that later, maybe in three or four years, once we had a few of our own open." With requests streaming in, plus a $200,000 loan from a group of angel investors in Halifax to bankroll the franchising process, the Bonds decided to mover their plans forward. "People know that there's a problem with child obesity," Bond says. "So we said, 'Let's go for it.'"

The interest is clearly there, although the Bonds will have to see how the major metropolitan locations do to find out whether the business will scale up successfully. Choosing the right franchisees is crucial, since the core of the business is not only physically training the members, but emotionally supporting overweight kids who are often bullying victims at school. (www.bulldoginteractivefitness.com)

Source: Graham Scott, *Canadian Business*, Sept. 25–Oct.8, 2006, p.100-101.

specifically for young people from age 3 to their late teens. Holly and her husband opened the first Bulldog in Dartmouth, N.S. after considerable research, an initial investment of $180,000 and a strong belief they were on the right track to providing at least a partial solution to the growing problem of child obesity. They had always planned to franchise the Bulldog concept down the road if it seemed viable but after receiving a very enthusiastic response and over 100 requests from prospective franchises shortly after they opened, moved up their plans. They received a $200,000 loan from a local angel investor to bankroll the franchising process and went for it. Very quickly new locations were opened in southern Ontario and the company has several others scheduled for Alberta, New Brunswick, Nfld., and potentially even the U.S.

FUTURE TRENDS IN FRANCHISING

A number of trends have emerged in the past few years that will positively impact franchising opportunities, and they are likely to continue. Among the most important are:

1. **Increasing emphasis on senior care** As North America ages with the maturing of the baby boomers, it is predicted that eldercare will replace child care as the number-one social issue. As they age, many seniors want to stay in their own homes, so any business that will provide them with companionship, extra help around the house, or assistance in performing their daily activities, such as personal care and meal preparation, is likely to succeed.

2. **Child care and education** Increasingly, people want their children to have fun, become better educated, or get other forms of enrichment or special attention, and they are prepared to pay for it.

3. **Technical support** With the continual dependence of people and businesses on increasingly complex technology, advice is often needed on what to buy and what not to buy, how to handle repairs and upgrades, as well as solutions for various technological problems.

4. **Pet care** More and more, pets are being considered part of the family and companies are springing up to provide a range of services, such as boarding facilities, cleaning and grooming, pet training, and feeding and general care services.

5. **Home improvements** Consumers are increasingly spending more on their dwellings, which has created an explosion of franchisors providing a broad range of services, such as general building services, kitchen remodelling, handyman services, interior decorating and painting, and electrical and plumbing services.

6. **Fitness** Fitness and obesity have received considerable coverage in the media, fuelling consumer interest in improved diet and exercise regimes. Gyms and fitness centres have been at the centre of this trend, particularly facilities that have emphasized women-only services.

7. **Restaurants** Restaurants of all types are expected to continue to be a very popular sector of franchising. Concepts such as Asian and healthy fast food, specialty ice cream, and neighbourhood coffeehouses continue to grow.

FYI FOR YOUR INFORMATION

For more information on franchising you might check out the following sources:

Canadian Franchise Association The national voice of the franchise industry in Canada. (www.cfa.ca)

International Franchise Association A membership organization of franchisors, franchisees, and suppliers dedicated to providing members and guests with a one-stop shopping experience for franchise information. Check out their "Consumer Guide to Buying a Franchise". (www.franchise.org/franchiseesecondary.aspx?amp;langtype=1033&id=10002)

Franchise Conxions A Canadian-based franchise and small-business consulting firm that offers a wide range of services to the franchise industry. (www.franchise-conxions.com)

FranNet, The Franchise Connection An international consulting firm that provides education and support to individuals who are interested in exploring self-employment as a career option through franchised business ownership (www.frannet.com)

Canadian Franchise Opportunities An online directory of franchises and franchise business services. (canada.franchiseopportunities.com)

EVALUATING A FRANCHISE — A CHECKLIST

The checklist shown in Figure 5.1 can serve as an effective tool for you to use in evaluating a franchise opportunity. When reading through the questions, you will notice that some of them require you to do a little homework before you can reasonably respond. For example, you and/or your lawyer will have to review the franchise agreement to assess the acceptability of the various clauses and conditions. You will also have to give some thought to how much capital you personally have and where you might raise additional financing.

Some questions call for further research. Ask the franchisor for the names and addresses of a number of current franchisees. Select a sample of them and contact them to discuss their views of the franchisor and the franchise agreement. Make certain your interview takes place without the franchisor or his or her representative present. Check the length of time that the franchisee has operated in that particular location in comparison to the length of time that franchise has been in existence. If there is a difference, try to determine what happened to the earlier franchisee(s). If you have been provided with pro forma financial statements or other information by the franchisor indicating the level of sales and financial performance you might expect, ask these franchisees to confirm that these statements are reasonably close to reality. In addition, what you may feel you require in terms of training, advertising and promotion support, and ongoing operating assistance may be a function of the type of franchise you are evaluating.

Make a copy of this checklist for each franchise you intend to evaluate. By using a similar outline to assess each opportunity, it will be much easier for you to compare them.

FIGURE 5.1	**CHECKLIST FOR EVALUATING A FRANCHISE**

THE FRANCHISOR

1. What is the name and address of the franchise company?

   Name _____

   Address _____

   _____

2. The franchise company is: Public _____ Private _____

3. What is the name and address of the parent company (if different from that of the franchise company)?

   Name _____

   Address _____

   _____

4. The parent company is: Public _____ Private _____

5. On what date was the company founded and when was the first franchise awarded?

   Company founded _____ First franchise awarded _____

6. How many outlets does the franchise currently have in operation or under construction?

   a. Of these outlets, how many are franchised and how many are company-owned?

      Franchised _____ Company-owned _____

   b. How many franchises have failed?

   c. How many of these failures have been within the past two years?

   d. Why did these franchises fail?

      Franchisor's reasons _____

      _____

      _____

Franchisee's reasons _____
_____
_____

7. How many new outlets does the franchisor plan to open within the next 12 months? Where will they open?

How many _____ Where _____
_____

8. a. Who are the key principals in the day-to-day operation of the franchisor's business?

Name	Title	Background
_____	_____	_____
_____	_____	_____
_____	_____	_____
_____	_____	_____

b. Who are the directors of the company, other than those individuals named above?

Name	Title	Background
_____	_____	_____
_____	_____	_____
_____	_____	_____
_____	_____	_____

c. Who are the consultants to the company?

Name	Title	Background
_____	_____	_____
_____	_____	_____
_____	_____	_____
_____	_____	_____

THE FRANCHISE

1. Fill in the following data on each of several present franchisees.

Franchise 1
Owner _____
Address _____
_____
Telephone _____
Date started _____

Franchise 2
Owner _____
Address _____
_____
Telephone _____
Date started _____

Franchise 3
Owner _____
Address _____
_____
Telephone _____
Date started _____

continued

Checklist for Evaluating a Franchise — continued

2. Has a franchise ever been awarded in your area?   Yes _____   No _____

   a.   If Yes, and it is *still in operation*, provide details.

   Owner _____

   Address _____

   _____

   Telephone _____

   Date started _____

   b.   If Yes, and it is *no longer in operation*, provide details.

   Person involved _____

   Address _____

   Date opened _____

   Date closed _____

   Reason for failure _____

3. Is the product or service offered by the franchise:

   a.   Part of a growing market?   Yes _____   No _____

   b.   Needed in your area?   Yes _____   No _____

   c.   Of interest to you?   Yes _____   No _____

   d.   Safe for the consumer?   Yes _____   No _____

   e.   Protected by a guarantee or warranty?   Yes _____   No _____

   f.   Associated with a well-known trademark or personality? Yes _____   No _____

   g.   Accompanied by a trademark that is adequately protected? Yes _____   No _____

4. Will you be acquiring:

   a.   A single-unit franchise?   _____

   b.   An area franchise?   _____

   c.   A master franchise?   _____

5. The franchise is: Exclusive _____   Non-exclusive _____

6. What facilities will be required and will you have to own or lease?

   a.   Business can be operated out of home?   Yes _____   No _____

   b.   Facilities required:

	Yes	*No*	*Own*	*Lease*
Office	_____	_____	_____	_____
Retail outlet	_____	_____	_____	_____
Manufacturing facility	_____	_____	_____	_____
Warehouse	_____	_____	_____	_____
Other (specify)	_____	_____	_____	_____

7. Who will be responsible for:

	Franchisor	*Franchisee*
a. Location feasibility study?	_____	_____
b. Facility design and layout?	_____	_____
c. Construction?	_____	_____
d. Furnishing?	_____	_____
e. Arranging financing?	_____	_____

FRANCHISE COSTS

1. Is a forecast of expected income and expenses provided?   Yes _____   No _____

    a. If Yes, is it:

        i. Based on actual franchisee operations?   _____

        ii. Based on a franchisor-owned outlet?   _____

        iii. Based strictly on estimated performance?   _____

    b. If Yes, does the forecast:

        i. Relate directly to your market area?   Yes _____   No _____

        ii. Satisfy your personal goals?   Yes _____   No _____

        iii. Provide for an acceptable return on investment?   Yes _____   No _____

        iv. Provide for an adequate level of promotion and personal expenses?   Yes _____   No _____

2. How much money will it require to get started in the business? Itemize.

Item	Amount
a. Franchise fee	$ _____
b. Franchisor-provided services	_____
c. Supplies and opening inventory	_____
d. Real estate	_____
e. Machinery and equipment	_____
f. Furniture and fixtures	_____
g. Opening expenses	_____
h. Other	_____
Total Initial Investment	$ _____ (A)

3. How much other money will be required:

    a. To defray operating losses for first few months of operation? $ _____ (B)

    b. To cover your personal expenses for the first year of operation? $ _____ (C)

4. Total financial requirements (A + B + C = D) $ _____ (D)

5. How much of these total financial requirements do you personally have available? $ _____ (E)

6. If the franchisor provides any financial assistance:

    a. How much? $ _____ (F)

    b. What does this represent as a percentage of your total estimated costs?   _____ %

    c. What is the interest rate on this financing?   _____ %

    d. When does the money have to be paid back?   _____

7. Where will you be able to obtain the rest of the required funds?
Specify sources from the following list:

    a. Banks, credit unions, or other financial institutions $ _____

    b. Finance companies   _____

    c. Friends, relatives, and neighbours   _____

    d. Other private sources   _____

    e. Leasing arrangements   _____

    f. Suppliers' credit   _____

    g. Government assistance programs   _____

    h. Other (specify) $ _____

    Total $ _____ (G)

continued

Checklist for Evaluating a Franchise — continued

8. Total funds available from all sources (E + F + G = H)
   Grand Total $ _____ **(H)**

9. How do the funds available compare with your total estimated
   requirements? (D – H) $ _____

THE FRANCHISE AGREEMENT

1. Have you obtained a copy of the franchise agreement?   Yes _____   No _____

2. Have you given a copy to your lawyer and accountant to review?

Lawyer   Yes _____   No _____

Accountant   Yes _____   No _____

3. Does the agreement contain clauses that relate to the following areas and activities and are the
   specified terms and conditions acceptable or unacceptable to you?

		Yes	*No*	*Acceptable*	*Unacceptable*
				If Yes	
a.	Franchise fee	_____	_____	_____	_____
b.	Commissions and royalties	_____	_____	_____	_____
c.	Purchase of products and supplies	_____	_____	_____	_____
d.	Lease of premises	_____	_____	_____	_____
e.	Territorial protection	_____	_____	_____	_____
f.	Training assistance	_____	_____	_____	_____
g.	Termination	_____	_____	_____	_____
h.	Renewal	_____	_____	_____	_____
i.	Selling and transferring	_____	_____	_____	_____
j.	Advertising and promotion	_____	_____	_____	_____
k.	Operating assistance	_____	_____	_____	_____
l.	Trademark protection	_____	_____	_____	_____

RUNNING YOUR FRANCHISE OPERATION

1. Does the franchisor provide you with an initial formal training program?   Yes _____   No _____

If Yes: a.   How long does it last?   _____ days

b.   Is cost included in the franchise fee?   Yes _____   No _____   Partially _____

If No or Partially, specify how much you will have to pay for:

   i.   Training course $ _____

   ii.   Training materials   _____

   iii.   Transportation   _____

   iv.   Room and board   _____

   v.   Other   _____

      Total Costs $ _____

c.   Does the training course cover any of the following subjects?

   i.   Franchise operations   Yes _____   No _____

   ii.   Sales   Yes _____   No _____

   iii.   Financial management   Yes _____   No _____

   iv.   Advertising and promotion   Yes _____   No _____

v.	Personnel management	Yes _____	No _____
vi.	Manufacturing methods	Yes _____	No _____
vii.	Maintenance	Yes _____	No _____
viii.	Operations	Yes _____	No _____
ix.	Employee training	Yes _____	No _____
x.	Other (specify) _____		
	_____	Yes _____	No _____

2. How do you train your initial staff?

   a. Is the training program provided by the franchisor?   Yes _____   No _____

   b. Does the franchisor make a staff member available from head office to assist you?

   Yes _____   No _____

   c. What materials are included in the staff training program?

   _____

   _____

   _____

3. Is there any requirement for you to participate in a continuing training program?

   Yes _____   No _____

   If Yes:

   a. Who pays the cost of this program?   Franchisee _____   Franchisor _____

   b. If you have to pay for this continuing training, how much does it cost? $ _____

4. Is the product or service of the franchise normally sold by any of the following means?

   a. In customer's home — by appointment   Yes _____   No _____
   b. In customer's home — by cold-calling   Yes _____   No _____
   c. By telephone   Yes _____   No _____
   d. In a store or other place of business   Yes _____   No _____
   e. At customer's business — by appointment   Yes _____   No _____
   f. At customer's business — by cold-calling   Yes _____   No _____
   g. By direct mail   Yes _____   No _____
   h. Other (specify)   Yes _____   No _____

5. How do you get sales leads and customers?

   a. Provided by franchisor   Yes _____   No _____
   b. Self-generated   Yes _____   No _____
   c. Through advertising   Yes _____   No _____
   d. By direct mail   Yes _____   No _____
   e. By telephone   Yes _____   No _____
   f. Through trade shows   Yes _____   No _____
   g. Other _____   Yes _____   No _____

6. Give a brief profile of the types of customers you feel are the best prospects for the products or services offered by the franchise.

   _____

   _____

   _____

continued

Checklist for Evaluating a Franchise — continued

7. a. What is the national advertising budget of the franchisor? $ _____

    b. How is this budget distributed among the primary advertising media?

TV	% _____
Radio	_____
Newspaper	_____
Outdoor	_____
Magazines	_____
Direct mail	_____
Other (specify)	_____
Total	**100%**

8. What kind of advertising and promotion support is available from the franchisor for the local franchisee?

	Yes	*No*	*If Yes, Cost*
a. Prepackaged local advertising program	_____	_____	$ _____
b. Co-operative advertising program	_____	_____	$ _____
c. Grand-opening package	_____	_____	$ _____

9. Do you need the services of an advertising agency?   Yes _____   No _____

10. a. Who are your principal competitors? Name them in order of importance.

    1. _____

    2. _____

    3. _____

    b. Describe what you know about each and how each compares with your franchise.

Competitor 1

Owner _____

Address _____

Description _____

Competitor 2

Owner _____

Address _____

Description _____

Competitor 3

Owner _____

Address _____

Description _____

_____

_____

11. What operating assistance is available from the franchisor if you should need it?

    a. Finance and accounting   Yes _____   No _____

    b. Advertising and promotion   Yes _____   No _____

    c. Research and development   Yes _____   No _____

    d. Sales   Yes _____   No _____

    e. Real estate   Yes _____   No _____

    f. Construction   Yes _____   No _____

    g. Personnel and training   Yes _____   No _____

    h. Manufacturing and operations Yes _____   No _____

    i. Purchasing   Yes _____   No _____

    j. Other (specify)   Yes _____   No _____

12. Does the franchisor have a field supervisor assigned to work with a number of franchises?

Yes _____   No _____

If Yes: a. How many franchises is she/he assigned to?

              b. Who would be assigned to your franchise?

Name _____

Address _____

_____

Telephone _____

Organizing Your Business

One of the key issues you must resolve when starting your new venture is the legal form of organization the business should adopt. Making that decision means you should consider such factors as:

1. The complexity and expense associated with organizing and operating your business in one way or another
2. The extent of your personal liability
3. Your need to obtain start-up capital and operating funds from other sources
4. The extent to which you want ownership, control, and management of your business to be shared with others (if at all)
5. The distribution of your business's profits and losses
6. The extent of government regulation you are willing to accept
7. Tax considerations and implications
8. The need to involve other principals in your venture

The most prevalent forms your business might take are:

- An individual or sole proprietorship
- A partnership (general partnership or limited partnership)
- A corporation

INDIVIDUAL OR SOLE PROPRIETORSHIP

The *individual* or *sole proprietorship* is the oldest and simplest form of business organization. As owner or proprietor you have complete control over the conduct and management of your business. You alone are accountable for all business activities and their consequences. You control the business's profits and are liable for its debts. You and the business are one and the same. The sole proprietorship is the most common form of organization for small businesses, particularly in the early stages of their development.

ADVANTAGES OF SOLE PROPRIETORSHIP

- **Simple and inexpensive to start** A sole proprietorship is simple and inexpensive both to create and dissolve. It can be brought into existence with a minimum of legal formalities and terminated just as readily. Start-up costs are minimal — usually they are confined to registering your business name with the appropriate authorities and obtaining the necessary licences.

- **Individual control over operations** As a sole proprietor you own 100% of your business. You are literally your own boss. If the business is not successful, you are free to dissolve it. And if the business does well, you can have a strong sense of accomplishment.

- **All profits to the owner** If the business is successful you will reap the benefits of your efforts. No one will share in the profits of the business. You work for yourself and determine your own destiny.

- **Tax simplicity** As a sole proprietor you declare your business on your personal tax return rather than having to file a separate form. If part of your home or your car is used for business purposes you may be able to write some of these expenses off against the business income. In addition, if your business should incur a loss during its early stages, that loss is deductible from any other income you may have as well.

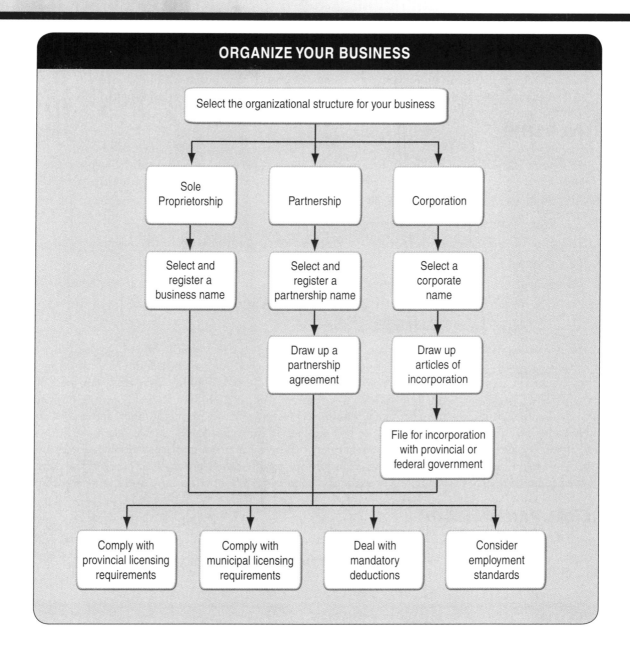

ORGANIZE YOUR BUSINESS

Select the organizational structure for your business

- Sole Proprietorship
  - Select and register a business name
- Partnership
  - Select and register a partnership name
    - Draw up a partnership agreement
- Corporation
  - Select a corporate name
    - Draw up articles of incorporation
      - File for incorporation with provincial or federal government

- Comply with provincial licensing requirements
- Comply with municipal licensing requirements
- Deal with mandatory deductions
- Consider employment standards

DISADVANTAGES OF SOLE PROPRIETORSHIP

- **Unlimited liability** Since the business and the proprietor are not recognized as being separate by law, you can be held personally liable for all the debts of your business. That means you may have to satisfy business debts with personal assets such as your house and car if the business is unable to meet its obligations. You may be able to protect some personal assets by putting them in your spouse's name before starting your venture but there is no real guarantee against domestic breakdown.

- **Higher tax rate** Any profits generated by a sole proprietorship are taxed at your higher personal tax rate, rather than at the more favourable small-business tax rate.

- **More difficult to obtain equity financing** Unlimited liability obviously limits the capital base of the business unless substantial security is available. It is not uncommon for sole proprietors to obtain the bulk of their initial funding by "maxing out" personal credit cards or by pledging their homes, cottages, or other personal assets as collateral for a loan.

- **Limited resources and opportunity** A sole proprietorship usually holds limited opportunity and incentive for employees, as it is not a form of ownership conducive to growth. One person can only do so much and may not have all the skills and knowledge necessary to run all phases of the business. Employees may have to be hired to perform these tasks. The life of the business in a proprietorship is limited to the life of the proprietor. If you should die, become ill, or encounter serious personal problems, your business is immediately affected, and unless other provisions are made, your business will die with you. This could lead to a forced sale of the business's assets by your beneficiaries, perhaps at a substantial loss.

PARTNERSHIP

A *partnership* is an association of two or more individuals carrying on a business for profit. The *principals* (partners) should jointly prepare a written partnership agreement outlining the following issues in terms that are clearly understood and mutually acceptable to all of them:

1. The rights and responsibilities of each partner
2. The amount and nature of the partners' respective capital contributions to the business
3. The division of the business' profits and losses
4. The management responsibilities of each partner involved in the operation of the business
5. Provision for termination, retirement, disability, or death of a partner
6. Means for dissolving or liquidating the partnership

Some of the potential problems that can occur in a partnership are illustrated in the case of Debie Rothenberger (Entrepreneurs in Action #21). She and a long-time friend launched their picture framing business in 2003. Three years later the partner wanted to leave the business, but the pair couldn't agree on a fair price for the partner's interest. The partners ended up in a very acrimonious dispute and had to divide up the business and its assets. Rothenberger had to start over again with a new business name, phone number, and so on, and the two old friends wound up no longer speaking to one another. In hindsight it is clear that one major issue in the partners' attempt to deal with this situation was that they had no mechanism in place to resolve serious disagreements between them. Such a process or agreement would have made things much easier on everyone concerned and enabled them to resolve their differences without jeopardizing the entire business and their friendship.

GENERAL PARTNERSHIP

A *general partnership* is similar to a sole proprietorship except that responsibility for the business rests with two or more people, the partners. In a general partnership all the partners are liable for the obligations of the partnership and share in both profits and losses according to the terms of their partnership agreement.

21

Entrepreneurs in action

Lesson learned: Put breakup rules in writing

It's advice entrepreneur Debie Rothenberger wishes she had taken. When Rothenberger and a long-time friend and co-worker launched a new picture framing business in 2003, their business adviser urged them to draw up a partnership agreement. Among other things, it would spell out how they would handle if it one later decided to leave the business.

"We went, 'yeah, yeah, we'll get around to it,'" Rothenberger said in an interview. "But then things got going for us and we never got around to it."

This July, that oversight came back to haunt them when Rothenberger's partner decided to leave and they couldn't agree upon a fair price for her share of the business. They ended up having to dissolve the

continued

Entrepreneurs in Action #21 — continued

partnership and the business, divide up what few assets there were, and Rothenberger essentially had to start over with a new business name and new telephone number. Not surprisingly, the two also are no longer speaking to one another.

Rothenberger agreed to talk about the experience in hopes of preventing other entrepreneurs from making the same mistake.

Winnipeg lawyer Reeh (pronounced Ray) Taylor, senior counsel for Taylor McCaffrey LLP and director of the University of Manitoba's Small Business Law Clinic, said it's surprising how many business partners don't bother drawing up a partnership agreement. They think because they're friends, they don't need one.

"But they do need a partnership agreement to cover a whole mess of things," he said. "If they don't have it all down in writing, then I would say chances are 90 to 10 there will be a little blood on the sand before they're through."

Rothenberger agreed that being friends can lull you into a false sense of security.

"You think, 'I would never do that!' But it does get ugly. The last week of our partnership was like a divorce. It does get personal."

She said another reason she and her business partner didn't draw up a partnership agreement was because they had no idea what it should include.

"If we would have known what to put in . . . maybe it would have made a difference."

Because a partnership agreement is a legal document, Taylor recommends partners hire a lawyer to help draw up their agreement. Otherwise they risk using unclear language or omitting something important, which could lead to costly litigation down the road if the partnership ends for one reason or another.

But while they should have a lawyer draw up the final document, that doesn't mean the partners can't do some of the homework themselves by writing down the things they would like included in the agreement, Taylor said.

Here are some of the issues he suggests be addressed in such an agreement.

- How much money is each partner expected to invest in the company?

- What happens if the business later requires additional working capital and only one of the partners has more money to invest. Does he lend some money to the other partner, and if so, on what terms?

- What are the roles and duties of each partner in the company's day-to-day operations?

- What kind of business will be carried on and what happens if one of the partners later wants to diversify into other areas? Taylor said there should be a

PHOTO OF DEBIE ROTHENBERGER BY GEORGE DOUKLIAS.

clause stipulating that all of the partners must agree to it before such a move can be made.

- What happens if one of the partners becomes permanently disabled and no longer able to perform his or her regular duties? And how will you define the term "permanently disabled" as it relates to your business?

- What happens if one of the partners dies or wants to leave the business? And what formula do you use to determine a fair value for his or her share of the company if the remaining partner wants to buy that share and continue operating the business?

- If one partner does buy out the other, should the payment be in one lump sum or can it be made in installments?

- What happens if one partner becomes bankrupt or is caught stealing from the company? Does the other partner have the right to buy out that partner's share of the company, and at a discounted price? If so, how much of a discount?

There are likely other things you or your lawyer will likely want to include, but the important thing is to make sure you have a proper agreement in place, Taylor said.

"If you've got all of these things written down, that's one major headache out of the way," he said.

Source: Murray McNeill, *Winnipeg Free Press,* September 2, 2006.
murray.mcneill@freepress.mb.ca

SHERMAN'S LAGOON

©Jim Toomey, King Features Syndicate.

Advantages of a General Partnership

- **Pooling of financial resources and talents** The partnership is useful for bringing together two or more people who can combine their skills, abilities, and resources effectively. Management of the business is shared among the principals.

- **Simplicity and ease of organization** A partnership, like a sole proprietorship, is easy and inexpensive to establish and is subject to a minimum amount of regulation.

- **Increased ability to obtain capital** The combined financial resources of all the partners can be used to raise additional capital for the business. Income from the partnership is taxed as part of the personal income of each of the partners.

- **Potential for growth** A partnership has a higher potential for growth than a proprietorship, since a valuable employee may be offered a partnership to dissuade him or her from leaving the firm. Growth, however, is still quite restricted compared to that possible with a limited company.

Disadvantages of a General Partnership

- **Unlimited liability** Partners are personally liable for all the debts and obligations of their business and for any negligence on the part of any of them occurring in the conduct of the business. This is similar to the situation with a sole proprietorship, except that the partners are liable both as a group and individually — not only for their own actions (severally) but also for the actions of all others in the partnership (jointly).

- **Divided authority** There is less control for an individual entrepreneur in a partnership with divided authority. There may be possible conflicts among partners that can be difficult to resolve and could affect the conduct of the business.

LIMITED PARTNERSHIP

In a *limited partnership*, the partners' share in the liability of the business *is limited to the extent of their contribution to the capital of the business*. In such a partnership, however, there must also be one or more general partners, that is, partners with *unlimited liability*.

The limited partners may not participate in the day-to-day management of the business of the partnership or they risk losing their limited-liability status. Also, a limited partner is entitled to interest on his or her capital of no more than 5 per cent per year and some agreed-on share of the profits. Limited partners have one major power — the ability to remove the general partner(s).

Advantages of a Limited Partnership

- **Limited liability** If properly established and registered, the liability of the limited partners is restricted to the extent of their investment. Thus, you may find it easier to recruit investors.

Other considerations

CONTENTS OF A TYPICAL PARTNERSHIP AGREEMENT

1. Names of the partners
2. Name of the business
3. Term of the partnership agreement
4. Extent of each of the partners' interest in the partnership and the capital each has contributed to the partnership
5. The financial records and banking arrangements of the partnership
6. A description of the capital accounts and salary and draw arrangements of each of the partners
7. An outline of each partner's responsibilities for the management of the business and what each can or cannot do without the approval of other partners
8. Partners' responsibilities to work within the business and their ability to assign their interest in the business to others
9. Procedures for the termination or dissolution of the partnership
10. Procedures for the resolution of any disputes among the partners
11. Insurance coverage to be carried by the partnership
12. Any process for amending the agreement

Disadvantages of a Limited Partnership

- **Centralized management** In a limited partnership only a small subgroup of the owners — the general partners — have decision-making authority and can participate in the management of the business.

- **Difficulty in changing ownership** It is generally difficult to change ownership in a partnership, since the partnership must be dissolved and reconstituted every time a partner dies or wants to retire. So it is important that the procedure for dealing with this issue be laid out in a partnership agreement.

LIMITED LIABILITY PARTNERSHIP

A limited liability partnership (LLP) is typically only available to groups of professionals like lawyers, accountants and doctors to enable them to limit the liability between partners. These agreements are governed by provincial legislation so the regulations vary from province to province. In Ontario, for example, only lawyers, and some designated accountants may form an LLP.

CORPORATION

The *corporation* is the most formal and complex of the various forms of business organization. A firm that is *incorporated* is a separate legal entity from its owners — that is, legally, it is regarded as a "person" with a separate, continuous life. As a legal person, a corporation has rights and duties of its own: It can own property and other assets, it can sue or be sued, and it files its own tax return. Ownership of a corporation is recognized through the purchase of *shares*, or *stock*, which can be held by as few as one or as many as thousands of *shareholders*.

As in the case of a partnership, it is a good idea for the shareholders of a corporation to have a shareholders' agreement to protect their interests in case of friction or other conflicts that might arise among the principals. This agreement should be developed prior to the incorporation of the business and should deal with many of the same issues typically included in a partnership agreement. An overview of such an agreement is included in the Other considerations feature on page 165.

A business need not be large to be incorporated. A sole proprietorship regularly earning in excess of $40,000 to $50,000 of taxable income annually probably should be incorporated.

Recent legislative changes in Ontario, Alberta, British Columbia, and other provinces now permit many groups of regulated professionals to enjoy the benefits of incorporation. These groups include lawyers, doctors, chartered accountants, dental hygienists, engineers, and management consultants. These professionals can now incorporate their practices in professional corporations. Some of the benefits of doing so are discussed in the FYI feature, "Incorporation and the Professional Practice."

Not-for-Profit organizations may also incorporate as *Corporations without Share Capital*. The organization does not necessarily have to be a charity. It may be an industry association, a social organization or other non-profit entity. The difference is that there are no 'owners' and it doesn't pay dividends. Any 'profits' are retained by the corporation and used to support the purposes of the organization. Doing so enables them to operate under some kind of formal structure. Incorporation may enable them to apply for financial support from government, foundations and other organizations, make them eligible for charitable status, enable them to hold title to property and land and limit the personal liability of their members.

Occasionally you may see references to other corporate forms such as S Corporations or a Limited Liability Company (LLC). These are U.S. corporate structures not applicable to Canadian registered companies and the terms can not be used in this country.

ADVANTAGES OF A CORPORATION

- **Limited liability** The owner or shareholder of a corporation is liable only for the amount he or she paid or owes for the shares, except where statutory provisions may create personal liability for the directors or officers of the company for outstanding wages, taxes, or similar obligations. In case of bankruptcy, creditors are not able to sue shareholders for outstanding debts of the business.

- **Continuity of the business even if the owner dies** Since it is an entity under the law, a corporation is not affected by the death or withdrawal of any shareholder. The shares of its stock can be sold or transferred to other individuals without difficulty. This ease of transfer allows for perpetual succession of the corporation, which is not the case with a sole proprietorship or partnership.

- **Easier to raise capital** Incorporation makes it easier to raise capital, which is done by selling stock. In addition, corporations with some history and a track record can negotiate more effectively with outside sources of financing than either a proprietorship or a partnership.

- **Employee benefits** A corporation has a better opportunity to provide benefits to employees and stockholders in a variety of ways such as salaries, dividends, and profit-sharing plans.

- **Tax advantages** Being an independent entity in the eyes of the law, a corporation receives different tax treatment than either a proprietorship or a partnership, and is taxed separately on its business profits. This may provide you with some opportunity for tax deferral, income-splitting, or the reduction of your actual tax costs through the deductibility of certain personal fringe benefits.

DISADVANTAGES OF A CORPORATION

- **Cost** Corporations are more expensive to start and operate. Initially, incorporation can cost in excess of $1,000 in legal and regulatory fees. In addition, a lawyer may charge upward of $300 per year to maintain the registered office and keep the *corporate book*, i.e., the record of annual meetings, directors' meetings, etc.

- **Legal formalities** A corporation is subject to more numerous and complicated regulatory requirements than a proprietorship or partnership. Corporations must typically file annual reports, hold annual meetings, and file federal and provincial tax returns. This can be expensive and time-consuming for a small-business person, and may require the ongoing services of an accountant and a lawyer.

- **Inability to flow losses through** It is not uncommon for a new business to incur substantial start-up costs and operating losses during its first few years. These losses are "locked in" — a corporation must accumulate them for its own use in future years, and cannot use them to offset income a shareholder may have from other sources. If your business never becomes very profitable, it is conceivable that its losses could never be used to reduce your tax liability.

Other considerations

CONTENTS OF A TYPICAL SHAREHOLDER AGREEMENT

1. The structure of the company and how equity is divided among shareholders
2. Parties to the agreement
3. Officers and directors of the company and their responsibilities
4. Right of first refusal and pre-emptive rights to acquire new shares or those of another shareholder
5. Buy-out provisions for voluntary or involuntary withdrawal of shareholders
6. Option to purchase on death or disability of a shareholder
7. Restrictions on the transfer of shares
8. Any management contracts or key person agreements
9. Any ongoing shareholder financial obligations
10. Provisions for termination of the agreement
11. A mechanism for ongoing valuation of the business and the shares

This is in contrast to a proprietorship or partnership, whose early losses would "flow through" to the owners of the business, to be deducted on their personal income tax returns in the year the losses were incurred. Therefore, it may be more beneficial financially not to incorporate, so you can offset other income for tax purposes. This can improve your overall cash flow when your business is just getting started, and cash flow is most critical. You can always decide to incorporate later without any tax consequences.

- **Guarantee** Lenders often require a personal guarantee. This largely negates the advantage of limited liability.

No matter what form of organization you decide to establish things don't always work out as originally planned. Wovenfare International, for example, was set up as a corporation but had many of the elements of a partnership. Jodi Maxwell and Michelle Shaw Williams teamed up with Cecilia de la Rocha and Justine Brown to create an online meal planning service for families too busy to plan diverse and nutritious meals on their own. Together they fine tuned the concept of selling subscribers customized meal plans and set about developing their Web site and building their database of recipes on which to base the meal plans targeted toward a January, 2007 launch date.

After working for six months and overcoming numerous issues Wovenfare was launched on time but then the women had to turn their attention to actually running the business. Some envisioned the company as a part-time business that could fit around their family schedules. Others were already engaged full-time. Running the day-to-day affairs of the company wasn't nearly as exciting as the pre-launch activities and no one had ever really decided who would do what once the company was operational. They all thought they should be the boss. In July, the partnership dissolved as Brown and de la Rocha bought out the two original founders in a relatively amicable parting of the ways. (Entrepreneurs in Action #22)

CO-OPERATIVES

A fourth but far less common form of organization for a business is that of a *co-operative*. Co-operatives blend the characteristics of traditional businesses and non-profit organizations. The differences between them include:

- Co-operatives are incorporated to provide a service to their members for the purpose of meeting certain common economic, social, or cultural needs of the members, as opposed to making a profit. Shares in a co-op do not appreciate in value and don't serve as an investment.

- Surplus earnings of a co-op are distributed to the members according to the extent of their patronage rather than as dividends associated with shares.

- In a co-op each member has only one vote, regardless of the number of shares that member holds, unlike the situation in a corporation, where each share carries a vote.

Entrepreneurs in action

The best-laid plans

It started as such a simple idea: create an online meal-planning service for families too busy to plan diverse and nutritious meals of their own. It's the sort of creative yet earnest idea you might expect from four Calgary businesswomen who wanted to stay home for their kids but also keep their hand in business.

But in the year since its launch, Wovenfare International Inc, has taken on a life of its own: under-performing in some measures, but hinting at unexpected opportunities. Although the business is still teething, conflict over its future has already split up the founding foursome. But the two remaining founders are determined to make Wovenfare synonymous with healthy meal planning and are confident it can become a $10-million firm that will more than make up for their hard work and heartbreak.

Jodi Maxwell and Michelle Shaw Williams, two 30-something parents who worked in process management at Calgary telecom companies, decided to save families from the banality that is SpaghettiOs by launching a Web-based service offering healthy weekly meal plans, with detailed recipes anyone can follow.

To round out their skill set, they teamed up with Cecilia de la Rocha, a professional engineer with marketing experience, and Justine Brown, a Web designer who's also a passionate amateur chef. Together, they fine-tuned the idea of selling subscribers customized meal plans that reflect their lifestyles. They also decided the site should generate weekly grocery lists to ensure the required ingredients — slivered almonds, basmati rice, goat cheese — are in the cupboard when needed.

With Maxwell as president, Shaw Williams overseeing operations, de la Rocha taking on marketing and Brown running Web development, the four launched Wovenfare.com — "Weaving healthy meals into everyday life."

Working towards a launch date of January 2007, the four founders set about developing Wovenfare's intellectual property. With the capital provided from all four shareholders totalling in the low six figures, Wovenfare couldn't hope to pay for that content up front. So it offered a publicity-plus-royalty offer: the rights holders receive prominent credit for every recipe

they contribute, and a small fee for every recipe of theirs that appears on a paid-up meal plan.

Wovenfare acquired the rights to more than 5,000 recipes, including recipes from The Best of Bridge.

That turned out to be the easy part. The recipes had to be input by hand. The technology ate up the lion's share of their capital. "We had no idea how complicated it is to get a recipe into a database," says de la Rocha.

While Maxwell and Shaw Williams had envisioned Wovenfare as a part-time business that would fit around their family schedules, de la Rocha and Brown were working full 40-hour weeks prior to launch.

After focusing on launch day for six months, the partners found it raised more problems than it solved.

Once the excitement of the launch had passed, the partners had to contend with the mundane day-to-day as well as planning for the future, both of which created tensions in the group. "We were aligned in development, and at launch," says de la Rocha. But not when it came to deciding who would do what next.

"We had the Web site, but we hadn't built the company yet."

By late spring, registrations sagged as Canadians started thinking about barbecuing, not meal planning. Fortunately, working out of their homes without staff or pay gave the founders a low-overhead company. But they couldn't agree on how to fix things.

Brown and de la Rocha lobbied for change. "It was resistance to changing that was the hub of the misalignment."

continued

Entrepreneurs in Action #22 — continued

"We're four headstrong women," says Maxwell. "We came to realize that with four women wanting to be the boss, ultimately something had to give." In July, the partnership dissolved as Brown and de la Rocha bought out the two original founders. The settlement was "reasonable," says Maxwell. "It was hard to give up on the dream, but it was the decision that made the most sense for the business."

Wovenfare now faces a classic dot-com dilemma. Opportunities abound, but it has only two people to chase them. To help themselves prioritize, Brown and de la Rocha work on an 80/20 system: they try to spend at least 20% of their time working *on* the business rather than *in* the business. They're also hoping to raise at least $500,000 for a U.S. marketing campaign from a "smart investor" who can contribute expertise, resources or contacts as well. But first, they realize they have to boost traffic and revenue, which takes up the other 80% of their time. "Sometimes it's really easy to get overwhelmed by it all," says de la Rocha. "We just have to display a certain amount of patience." (www.wovenfare.com)

Source: Rick Spence

Co-operatives exist worldwide and range in size from small businesses to large organizations. Virtually any business has the potential to be a co-operative organization, as long as its principal purpose is to meet the needs of its members.

Examples of co-ops include such retail co-operatives as Mountain Equipment Co-op and Red River Co-op, agricultural co-ops such as the Saskatchewan Wheat Pool and Granny's Poultry Co-op in Manitoba, and any number of housing co-operatives that have been established across the country.

ADVANTAGES OF A CO-OPERATIVE

- Owned and controlled by the members
- Form of control is democratic — one member, one vote
- Limited liability
- Any earnings surplus is distributed to the members according to their use of the services of the co-op

DISADVANTAGES OF A CO-OPERATIVE

- Typically a long decision making process
- Possibility of conflict among members
- Less incentive for members to invest additional capital
- Extensive record keeping required due to the number of members

GETTING INTO BUSINESS

REGISTRATION AND INCORPORATION — MAKING IT LEGAL

For a sole proprietorship, no formal, legal *registration* is required as long as the business is operated just under your own name. However, if a specific business name like "Regal Dry Cleaners" or "Excel Construction" is used, or if more than one owner is implied by the use of "and Associates" or "and Sons" in conjunction with your name, your business must be logged with the Registrar of Companies or the Corporations Branch of the province in which the business is located. Registration is a relatively simple and inexpensive process that you can probably take care of yourself. Partnerships must be registered in a similar fashion.

Incorporation is a more complicated and considerably more expensive process that usually requires the services of a lawyer. If your business activities will initially be confined to a single province, you need incorporate only as a provincial company. Should your business plans include expansion to other provinces, however, you will be required to register in each province in which you wish to do business as an extra-provincial company, or register as a federally incorporated company.

Companies can be classified as either private or public. *Public companies* are those like Alcan and Great-West Life, which trade their shares on one of the country's public stock exchanges. They typically employ professional managers, external directors, and a number of shareholders who are the owners of the business.

FYI / FOR YOUR INFORMATION

INCORPORATION AND THE PROFESSIONAL PRACTICE

Ottawa lawyer Ted Mann jumped at the chance to incorporate his practice.

"I incorporated in June 2002, for two reasons: It allowed me to take advantage of the small-business deduction, which means I pay less tax on the money used to run the business — filing cabinets, letterhead — and incorporation affords some protection against supplier liability," Mr. Mann says.

Lawyers are just one of the many groups of regulated professionals now able to take advantage of amendments to the Ontario Business Corporations Act that allow them to incorporate their practices into professional corporations. The legislation is similar to that previously enacted in Alberta and British Columbia.

The list of other professions also benefiting from the Ontario amendments includes chartered accountants, dental hygienists and real estate agents. They join the ranks of such professions as software engineers and management consultants who had earlier won the ability to incorporate.

"Many professionals — lawyers, accountants, for example — found it unfair when they were doing work for small businesses and saw the advantages they were not able to access," Mr. Mann says. "It's a great relief."

Although the Ontario legislation was passed in January 2002, many of the associations governing regulated professionals have only recently put in place the programs needed to incorporate, explaining each governing body's exact rules and regulations.

Since the Ontario College of Physicians and Surgeons put its program in place in November of last year, for example, it has fielded about 750 inquiries about the process and issued close to 100 of the certificates needed to incorporate, a college spokeswoman says. The college currently has 20,000 practising members.

While some professional associations have not yet been promoting the concept, it's bound to take off in a changing workplace, where the number of "Me, Inc." small businesses is growing, predicts Toronto accountant George Wall. He is president of Wall & Associates and founder of CA4IP, a national association of independent accounting firms focused on independent professionals.

"Response has been slow," Mr. Wall says. "I don't believe people are aware of the changes and many professionals are slow to change." However, he expects many more individuals to go through the process, which takes about two days and costs about $800 in Ontario, because it can result in significant benefits to the independent professional.

Perhaps the most significant impact is that of lower taxes, because earnings can be retained within the corporation, Mr. Wall explains. Whereas the top tax rate in Ontario is about 46 per cent, the corporate tax rate on what is now the first $225,000 of income (raised from $200,000 in the last federal budget) earned by a small Canadian-controlled corporation in Ontario is about 20 per cent.

To demonstrate, he compares an employee earning $150,000 to someone who has incorporated. After a $14,000 RRSP contribution, the employee would pay $50,200 in taxes. The scenario would be radically different, however, should that person own a corporation earning $150,000 with expenses of $40,000. If he paid himself and his wife $35,000 each, and they each made RRSP contributions of $5,000, their total personal tax would be $13,200. The remaining $40,000 in the corporation would be taxed at 19.2 per cent, resulting in about another $7,600. All told, the tax savings in the second scenario would come close to $30,000, Mr. Wall notes.

"Incorporating offers the flexibility to get family involved," and the resulting income-splitting can reduce taxable income, he adds. And since a corporation can exist after death or retirement, it can provide pension and/or survivor benefits.

Another plus is the ability to borrow money from the corporation for a house or a car, either paid out as dividends or reinvested in the corporation, he adds.

A corporation can also act as a long-term investment or pension fund; the first $500,000 increase in the value of a private corporation is exempted from capital gains at the time of sale, Mr. Wall says.

Incorporation also limits the owner's liability, protecting personal assets from being seized should there be a problem with the business, Mr. Wall says, adding that incorporation does not protect against professional misconduct, such as malpractice charges.

If independent professionals are slow off the mark to take advantage of the opportunity to incorporate, it goes with the territory, he adds. "Ninety per cent of them work in their business versus on their business," Mr. Wall says.

Source: Catherine Mulroney, "Filings seen rising as awareness of rules spreads," *The Globe and Mail* (globeandmail.com, *Small Business Guide*), April 14, 2003.

Private companies, on the other hand, tend to have only one shareholder, or at most a small number of shareholders. There is some restriction on the transfer of their shares in their *articles of incorporation*, and their shares cannot be offered for sale to the public. A private corporation is sometimes called an *incorporated partnership*, because it usually consists of one, two, or three people who are personal friends, business associates, or family members, each of whom may play two or three roles, serving, for example, as an officer, director, and a shareholder of the company all at the same time.

PairoWoodies Publishing, highlighted in Entrepreneurs in Action #23, is a good example of an incorporated partnership. Ian Scott first met Wendy Woudstra through the Internet. He was an experienced entrepreneur who knew something about marketing but had almost no computer skills, while she had a technical background and experience at building Web sites. Both work in the business and have quite different roles and responsibilities but have had to learn to be flexible and willing to cover for each other when required. Oh, and how did they happen to acquire the unusual name? It turns out that Ian and Wendy both had the same nickname when they were kids — Woody. Ian came up with the name when they were discussing possible business names. While at first they were hesitant to use the name, it has paid off for them. No one ever forgets it.

If you choose to incorporate, a private corporation is probably the type you will establish.

CHOOSING A NAME

Like people, all businesses must have a name. The simplest procedure is to name the business after yourself — Harry Brown's Printing, for example. In most provinces this type of name does not require formal registration for a sole proprietorship, but it does have disadvantages. For example, you might have people phoning you at home at all hours if you and your business's name are the same. In addition, your personal reputation may be tarnished if you experience some financial problems and are forced into receivership or bankruptcy. And if you ever sell your business, your name would go with it, and the new owner's actions could reflect negatively on your reputation.

For businesses to be registered or incorporated, the most important consideration in selecting a name is that it be acceptable to the Registrar of Companies in your province. All provinces require that a search be conducted of proposed names. Any name that is similar to a name already registered will be rejected to avoid public confusion. It is not uncommon to have to submit several names before one is finally approved. To avoid this problem, some individuals use a series of numbers rather than letters for the name of their corporation. On acceptance, the name is typically reserved for your exclusive use for 90 days, so that you can proceed with your registration or the filing of your articles of incorporation.

The best approach is usually to choose a distinctive name for the firm that *accurately describes* the type of business you plan to carry on. That is, a name like "Speedy Courier Service" or "Super-Clean Automobile Washing" is probably much better than one like "Universal Enterprises" or "General Distributing." A good way to check out names is to go through the Yellow Pages or local business directories and get some idea of the range of names currently in use in your business area and perhaps some inspiration for a brilliant new possibility.

Examples of some of the more clever and quirky names developed by Canadian entrepreneurs are illustrated in Entrepreneurs in Action #24.

SHERMAN'S LAGOON

©Jim Toomey, King Features Syndicate.

23

Entrepreneurs in Action

The Evolution of PairoWoodies

"Do what you can, with what you have, right where you are."

Ian Scott took these words of Theodore Roosevelt to heart and decided to start his fourth business, PairoWoodies Publishing, which began as a Web site design business, and has evolved into a full-service provider of Internet solutions for small- and medium-sized businesses and organizations.

It was definitely not the best of times for Ian to be starting a Web-based business. When the idea for PairoWoodies came to him, he had almost no computer skills and was deeply in debt due to the recent breakdown of his marriage.

So why would Ian decide to start an Internet-related business?

Ian was already an experienced entrepreneur. He had started his first business while he was in college, although he says that at that time "running a business was all a mystery to me." However, he persevered, and eventually started a part-time fishing tackle business. . . .

It was while operating Wishbone Custom Rods that Ian first become involved with the Internet. He hired Steve Henry to create a Web site for his business, and was impressed by the new business and inquiries the site generated. . . .

When Ian's marriage ended and his house had to be sold, he no longer had the space to build custom rods. He shut down Wishbone and started surfing the Internet, looking for business ideas.

Ian found lots of business ideas on the Internet— but he realized that he needed more skills. He made a deal with Wendy Woudstra, whom he met through the Internet. He would get her more clients to build Web sites for if she would teach him HTML.

Ian started calling on his acquaintances, and "almost immediately, we had enough interest that I had to learn HTML pretty swiftly in order to assist Wendy in getting the work done!" Ian and Wendy decided to form a partnership, even though they lived 2000 miles away from each other at that time.

While many partnerships fail, Ian and Wendy's has flourished. If you're a partner, as Ian points out, you have to learn to be flexible, learn how to clearly explain your vision to your partner, and be able to define your own roles. At the same time, you need to be willing to cover for each other when need be.

On the other hand, establishing a partnership with someone who has the skills you don't can be extremely helpful in getting to where you want to be, faster. Ian says that his and Wendy's different strengths really complement each other's well. "I simply could not have developed the business without her, and I think there are many things I offer to the partnership that Wendy needed to get her business going."

As PairoWoodies Publishing grew, Ian and Wendy decided that it would be in the best interests of the business if they lived closer to one another. They both moved to Toronto. . . .

When Ian and Wendy first started PairoWoodies Publishing, they realized that the key to independence was owning their own servers. Ian had kept in touch with Steve Henry. Ian and Wendy purchased an interest in Steve's ISP, providing them with the speedy, high bandwidth Internet connection they needed to grow faster without depending on some other company's services, and the ability to provide services tailored for individual businesses. . . .

PairoWoodies Publishing is now located in "downtown" Orangeville. They have three full-time employees and one part-time employee. They also contract out parts of projects when they need to. It took about three years for the business to grow to a point where Ian could leave his job and work full-time in the business, but that goal, too, has been realized.

Ian says, "When you really want something, and believe that it can be achieved, it is amazing the serendipitous events that take place!"

(www.pairowoodies.com)

Source: About (sbinfocanada.about.com/library/weekly/aa043001b.htm), accessed March 22, 2007.

Entrepreneurs in Action

What's in a name?
Businesses figure clever = success

Vancouver — Doggie Style has nothing to do with sex, but is a grooming salon for dogs in Calgary.

Death by Chocolate is not the morbid fantasy of chocoholics, but a dessert bar in Vancouver and Edmonton. Clip Art is not a computer program, it's a hair stylist in Halifax.

They're just a few of the quirky names of Canadian businesses aimed at drawing in customers and maybe drawing out smiles.

Barb Prueckel was looking for a fun, catchy name for her Calgary dog-grooming business when she came up with Doggie Style. She said the name is a big draw.

"We get tons of comments about it, mostly people find it very, very humorous. I've only had two people in the past six years that have had an issue with it," she said.

"Nobody ever forgets it and everyone knows where we are. We've had people pull into the parking lot and taken pictures of the front of the salon."

Cute names abound in the pet-grooming business. Winnipeg has Brush Puppies, Calgary has Wags to Whiskers and Edmonton has Little Arfn' Annie and Laundromutt.

There's also Kit 'n Kapoodles in Victoria, Fetching Style in Winnipeg, Ruff Cuts in Ottawa and Happy Tails in Vancouver.

Dale Griffen, a University of B.C. marketing and consumer expert, says the chief attractions of cute names are recognition and emotion.

"In the neighbourhood business — the dog groomer, the neighbourhood restaurant — where it's more of a relationship, a one-to-one, you want to catch people's attention and in most of these cases you want to give them a sense of fun, a sense of emotional connection," he said.

The Death by Chocolate dessert bar originated in Auckland, New Zealand, in 1991 and was brought to Canada by Vancouver businessman Shakil Adam, who says people are intrigued by the name.

"They want to know more so they walk into the store or they go to the website. Once in a while we'll have somebody who isn't thrilled with the name for superstitious reasons, but on an overall basis I think the name is a positive one simply because it generates a lot of excitement," Adam said in an interview.

While Death by Chocolate and Toronto's 2 Die 4 Sandwich Dessert Bar will perk up the tastebuds of some people, the names of these restaurants could stir other passions: The Amorous Oyster, Oh Darling! and the Kinki Japanese Seafood Place (all in Vancouver), the Sensual Café in Toronto and Hot For You in Calgary.

THEY'RE JUST HAVING PUN
Some unique names for Canadian business includes the following:

Restaurants:
- Sushi Q, Calgary and Vancouver
- It's a Crock, Winnipeg
- Fiasco, Halifax
- Hey Good Looking, Toronto

Coffee Bars:
- Get Grounded, Calgary
- Daily Grind, Vancouver
- Grabbajabba, various cities

Hair stylists:
- Hair Kanada, Winnipeg
- Hair France, Vancouver
- E'clips, Winnipeg, Vancouver
- Gerri's In-Hair-Itance, Edmonton

Dog Groomers:
- PetAgree, Toronto
- The Wizard of Pawz, Ottawa
- Can Nap Inn, Halifax
- Indogneat-O, Winnipeg
- Canadian Press

Restaurant names can also include, well, names. For example: My Other Brother Darrell's in Halifax, What About Bob's in Calgary, and Fred's Not Here in Toronto.

A caffeine rush may be responsible for a rash of unique names for coffee bars.

There's Bean Around the World in Vancouver and Victoria, Coffee Cats in Calgary, Cuppa Café in Halifax and Thanks A Latte in Ottawa.

continued

Entrepreneurs in Action #24 — continued

There are several variations on ground coffee, such as Alternative Grounds (Toronto), Grounds for Coffee (Vancouver) and Higher Ground (Calgary).

Getting back to dogs — if they can have fun names for grooming salons, why not humans?

Vancouver has Hair to Dye For, there's Hair-Em and Hairitage, both in St. John's, and Split NZ in Victoria.

One theme is repeated in several places: Sheer Madness in Toronto, Shear Chaos in Vancouver, and Shear Delight in Regina.

Griffen says cute names aren't always a good idea.

"The down side is they're not great at building trust, that is, giving the signals that this is reputable long-term business that you want with a big-ticket item," he said.

"But they're great for catching people's attention and they have that emotional feel-good quality that can be valuable."

Source: David Lang, *Winnipeg Free Press*, Tuesday, June 15, 2004.

Names that are likely to be rejected and should be avoided are those that:

1. Imply any connection with or approval of the Royal Family, such as names that include the word "Imperial" or "Royal"

2. Imply approval or sponsorship of the business by some unit of government, such as names containing "Parliamentary," "Premier's," or "Legislative"

3. Might be interpreted as obscene or not really descriptive of the nature of the firm's business

4. Are similar to or contractions of the names of companies already in business, even though they may be in a different field, such as "IBM Tailors" or "Chrysler Electronics"

The firm's name can become one of your most valuable assets if your business is successful, as has happened in the case of companies like McDonald's and Holiday Inn. Don't go for the first name that comes to mind. Think it over very carefully.

OBTAINING A BUSINESS LICENCE

You may require a municipal as well as a provincial licence to operate your business. Your need for the former depends on the location and nature of your business; requirements for the latter depend solely on the nature of your business.

Municipal

Not all types of businesses require a municipal licence. Every municipality regulates businesses established within its boundaries and sets its own licensing requirements and fees. In Winnipeg, for example, 114 types of businesses and occupations require a licence. In general, these are amusement operations or ones that may affect public health and safety. The licensing fees can be as high as several thousand dollars, but in most cases the fees are quite nominal — a few dollars.

In addition, all businesses — whether or not they require a licence — must conform to local zoning regulations and bylaw requirements. In fact, zoning approval is usually a prerequisite to licence approval. Companies operating in their own facilities in most cities must also pay a business tax, assessed as a percentage of the rental value of their business facilities.

Provincial

Various provincial authorities also require a licence or permit. In Ontario, for example, all establishments providing accommodation to the public, such as hotels, motels, lodges, tourist resorts, and campgrounds, must be licensed by the province. Businesses planning to serve liquor, operate long-haul cartage and transport operations, process food products, produce optical lenses, or manufacture upholstered furniture or stuffed toys may also require licensing. You should check with the local authorities to determine the types of licences and permits your business might require or consult with BizPal (www.bizpal.ca), an online project of Industry Canada and some of the provinces to simplify the business permit and licensing process for entrepreneurs and others.

Other considerations   HOW TO NAME YOUR BUSINESS

One of the first, and most vital, steps every new business takes is the selection of a name.

Choosing the name of your business wisely will have much to do with its subsequent success. That's because people will make critical decisions simply based on your business name.

It is true that people make snap decisions about other people based on simple 7-second first impressions. After those first few moments, it gets pretty hard to change someone's mind about that person later.

In the same way, people make snap decisions about your business based on first impressions. The first thing many people see is your name. With a good name, you will warrant further scrutiny. But if you choose a name poorly, the consequences can be disastrous.

An early note of caution is needed here. In cases where the business is already established, be careful about changing the name. You may lose the equity which has already been built and established. However, if you need to come up with a new company name, here are some guidelines to help you.

REFLECT YOUR TARGET NICHE

First, your business name should clearly reach your target audience. Is your offer or claim understandable? Two good name selections are the 7-11 and Hot 'N' Now stores. Your name should also fit your logo and slogan. In addition, clarity about your desired geographical service area helps people understand your business. All-City Shoe Repair tells me that they will fix shoes anywhere in my community. That's pretty clear!

However, don't use any geographical descriptions if that could ever become a limiting factor. For example, would a company called Eastside Bookkeeping ever do work for someone located downtown? In addition, geographical names tend to get overused. To see what I mean, go to the white pages of your phone book and see how many business names start with the name of your city or state.

CLARIFY WHAT YOUR BUSINESS DOES

Your business name should let the customer know what you do. Although Aaacme Services, Inc. may be listed first in your section of the Yellow Pages, a business card given to a new acquaintance doesn't tell the receiver what your business does. If a person can't remember why they have your card, they will quickly discard it. Two good names are Jiffy Lube and Fast Signs. And if you can attract your customers properly in the first place, they'll probably never even notice that they passed three of your competitors on their way to see you.

KEEP THE NAME SIMPLE

Keep your business name short and easy to say, spell and remember. Avoid tongue twisters like Watson, Smith, Howiczak, Elton and Elton. Imagine the poor secretary who has to write down a message from that company!

Also avoid acronyms or names using initials unless they will mean something to your typical customer. If IBM had been started using that name instead of International Business Machines, it is doubtful that they would have been as successful. Letters mean little or nothing to your customer, and as a result, are quickly forgotten. IBM didn't begin using that name until the marketplace had already bestowed the shortened name on them.

KEEP THE NAME FLEXIBLE

Don't let your name restrict you to a field that you may grow out of. Make the name expandable. As an example, Canned Software Company may sound good at first, but what happens if you ever decide to get into the computer hardware business? Or what if Mr. Smith ever leaves or sells Smith Watch Company. If it fails, what does that do to his reputation?

AVOID TRENDY NAMES

It seems that every few years, some new naming trend makes the rounds. How many times have you seen some type of name using Something-a-Rama or Something 'R' Us? After these fads run their course, you will be left with a stale and outdated name, and that's probably what most people will think of your company too!

AVOID AMATEURISH OR SILLY NAMES

Names like Bambi's Secretarial Service typically will not generate the confidence of your potential customers. If I were looking for a professional service, I'd be much more inclined to call ASAP Secretarial Services. For the same

continued

Land Use and Zoning

You should check with the local municipal authorities to ensure that your business conforms to zoning and building regulations.

MANDATORY DEDUCTIONS AND TAXES

If your business has a payroll you will be required to make regular deductions from employees' paycheques for income tax, employment insurance (EI), and the Canada Pension Plan (CPP). These deductions must be remitted to the Canada Revenue Agency every month.

In addition, you may also be required to pay an assessment to your provincial Workers' Compensation Board. The size of your payment will be based on the nature of your business and its risk classification as well as the estimated size of your annual payroll. These funds are used to meet medical, salary, and rehabilitation costs of any of your employees who may be injured on the job.

Depending on the size of your venture, you may also be responsible for remitting taxes of various kinds to either the provincial or the federal government. All provinces, except Alberta, apply a retail sales tax to almost all products and services sold to the ultimate consumer. Exceptions in some provinces include food, books, children's clothing, and medicine. The size and the application of these taxes varies from province to province, but if your business sells to final consumers you must obtain a permit and are responsible for collecting this tax and remitting it to the government on a regular basis.

Federal taxes largely fall into the categories of the Goods and Services Tax and income tax. A number of provinces have integrated their provincial sales tax with the federal government's Goods and Services Tax (GST) to create a Harmonized Sales Tax (HST). The GST/HST is levied on virtually all products and services sold in Canada. There are some minor exceptions for certain types of products. If your taxable revenues do not exceed $30,000 you do not have to register for the GST or HST, but you can still choose to register voluntarily even if your revenues are below this level. You should check and see whether these taxes apply in your business. If so, you will be required to obtain a Business Number (BN) and remit any taxes collected on a regular basis.

How income tax is collected depends on the form of organization of your business. Sole proprietorships and partnerships file income tax returns as individuals and the same regulations apply. Federal and provincial taxes are paid together and only one personal income tax form is required annually for both, although payments may have to be remitted quarterly on the basis of your estimated annual earnings.

A corporation is treated as a separate entity for income tax purposes and taxed individually. The rules, tax rates, and regulations that apply to corporations are very complex and quite different from those that apply to individuals. You should obtain professional advice or contact the local tax authorities to determine your obligations under the Income Tax Act and to keep the amount of tax you have to pay to a minimum.

FYI / FOR YOUR INFORMATION

A Guide to Setting Up Your Business in Canada Canada Business provides you with a wide range of information on government services, programs and regulations relevant to existing and potential business entrepreneurs. They deliver their services through an organized network of service centres across Canada, one in each province and territory. Select your province or territory and this Web site will provide you with information on each of the following topics:

- Starting a Business
- Growth and Innovation
- Grants and Finances
- Taxes and GST
- Regulations, Licenses and Permits
- Export, Import and Foreign Investment
- Business Planning
- Management and Operations

- Market Research and Statistics
- Marketing and Sales
- Selling to Governments
- Copyright and Intellectual Property
- Environment and Business
- Exiting Your Business
- Hiring and Managing Staff

(www.canadabusiness.ca/eng)

Canadaone This Web site provides links for each province and territory to the forms, information, and phone numbers you may need to get things up and running, Just click on your province or territory and you are on your way. (www.canadaone.com/tools/provincial_links.html)

EMPLOYMENT STANDARDS

All provinces have standards for employment and occupational health and safety that must be adhered to by all businesses within their jurisdiction. These requirements deal with such matters as:

1. Hours of work
2. Minimum wages
3. Statutory holidays
4. Overtime pay
5. Equal pay for equal work
6. Termination of employment
7. Severance pay
8. Working conditions
9. Health and safety concerns

You should contact the office of your provincial Ministry of Labour or its equivalent and request a copy of the *Employment Standards Act* in effect in your province, as well as a copy of the *Guide to the Act*. This will provide you with specific information on all of these topics, or you can use the services of an accountant or lawyer.

RISK MANAGEMENT

Starting a new business involves taking risks. The time and money you spend getting your new venture off the ground could prove to be a wise investment if the business is successful and makes a lot of money, or it could be an expensive flop. Every decision you made along the way carries a risk, and only time will tell whether you made the correct choice or not.

It's not helpful to spend all your time worrying about problems — worrying doesn't help, and sometimes a quick decision now can be better than a good decision later. But at the same time, you cannot afford to be too bullish — ignoring risks completely is very dangerous.

Instead, you need to take a balanced approach between these two extremes. You need to think carefully about every potential problem your business might face and determine whether you can take any action to mitigate it. This calm appraisal and considered assessment is known as **risk management.**

Some common threats to new firms include:

- The entry of new unexpected competition
- Increased cost of labour, supplies or raw materials
- Changes to the economic landscape like a recession, increased interest rates, higher taxes, currency fluctuations and inflation
- Catastrophic events or so-called acts of God like fire, flood and similar events or the sudden death of a partner
- Criminal acts such as shoplifting, burglary or embezzlement by employees

In addition to these things, you probably have some unique and more specific threats that you can identify that relate to your particular business. You need to look systematically at all these possible risks and prioritize them. Identify those that would be most damaging to your business if they occurred and those with the highest probability of occurring.

Once you have identified a problem, there are three broad approaches you can take to managing it:

- You can **reduce** it by taking some defensive action and possibly reducing its impact. This could include deciding to avoid taking an action entirely that you have determined to be too risky.
- You can **transfer** it or shift the risk to another party, for example by outsourcing the work or by obtaining insurance
- You can **retain** it, accepting it as a possible cost of doing business and budgeting for it accordingly

Of course, each of these categories encompasses a range of techniques. The specific action you need to take will depend on the risk you are dealing with, but a useful first step is to decide whether you intend to reduce, transfer or retain it.

One of the most common means of shifting at least some of the risk associated with the occurrence of a major catastrophe is through insurance. With insurance you pay a relatively small amount in premium rather than run the risk of not protecting yourself against the possibility of a much larger financial loss.

Your business may include a number of valuable assets such as computers, product inventory, machinery and equipment, vehicles, documents, and even yourself, among other things. Therefore, unexpected events like fire, flood, or the death of your partner are some of the hazards you have to protect yourself against. For example, you need to ask yourself:

- What would happen if the contents of your business premises were destroyed by fire?
- What if there was a break-in and your equipment was stolen?
- What if an employee or a client was badly hurt on your premises?
- What if you or your partner passed away unexpectedly?

Would your business be able to absorb the costs associated with these events and still be able to continue? After weighing the risks against the costs, you may decide that you need some protection if your business is likely to survive. This can be done through the use of insurance.

There are a number of different types of insurance you should consider obtaining for your business. You should discuss your situation with your insurance agent to arrange an appropriate program.

1. **General liability insurance** covers your liability to customers injured on your premises, or injured off your premises by a product you have sold to them.
2. **Business premises insurance** will protect your business premises and equipment from loss due to fire, theft, and other perils.
3. **Business-use vehicle insurance** must be obtained for cars and other vehicles used in the conduct of your business.
4. **Business interruption or loss-of-income insurance** will enable you to continue to pay the bills if your business should be closed down by damage due to fire, flood, or other catastrophe.
5. **Disability or accident and sickness insurance** can continue to provide you with a source of income if you should become seriously sick or disabled and unable to continue to run your business for a period of time.

6. **Key-person insurance** can protect your business against the death of its key personnel. It is life insurance purchased by the business with the business being the sole beneficiary.

7. **Credit insurance** protects you from extraordinary bad debt losses due to a customer going out of business.

8. **Surety and fidelity bonds** protect you from the failure of another firm or individual to fulfill its contractual obligations.

9. **Partnership insurance** can protect you against suits arising from actions taken by other partners in your business.

10. **Workers' Compensation** provides compensation for your employees in case of illness or injuries related to their employment.

Even with insurance, things can be tough. Jay Jennings opened his new trendy clothing store for twentysomething snowboarders and six weeks later a fire ruined all his clothing stock, causing him to miss the key Christmas selling season. Over the summer, local road construction made it very difficult for customers to find and access his store, and a leaky roof damaged some of his inventory and store fixtures. Just as he was gearing up for the next Christmas, thieves broke into his store and stole some of his inventory and computer equipment. And then, just as he was getting things up and running again, a second break-in occurred, causing $100,000 in damage to his merchandise and equipment. Despite having insurance for most of these disasters and submitting three claims to his insurance companies, Jay admits he is at the end of his rope and running out of money (Entrepreneurs in Action #25).

An insurance program won't protect you from *all* the risks associated with running your business, but it will provide you with some financial protection against unpredictable occurrence in several areas that could threaten the survival of your venture.

Your lease may or may not contain a penalty clause limiting your exposure should you breach the lease. A penalty of three months' rent is common in many situations, although the landlord will want you or the directors of an incorporated business to sign personal guarantees for the amount of the penalty.

Other considerations   STARTING A NEW BUSINESS

1. **Plan for success** A business plan will help you think through a number of important aspects of your new business.

2. **Select the form of business** that is right for you.

3. **Register your business** The process and requirements vary from province to province.

4. **Do you need a business licence?** Check with your municipality to find out.

5. **Do you meet zoning and local bylaw requirements?** You'll need to check your local bylaws to find out.

6. **Register for provincial taxes and local permits, if they apply.** Depending on the type of business you are in, you may need to collect provincial sales tax and apply for a vendor licence or other permits.

7. **GST, PST, HST basics** The two main taxes that businesses collect are the Goods and Services Tax (GST) and retail or provincial sales tax (PST). Several provinces combine the two taxes into a single tax known as the harmonized sales tax (HST). Check out the situation in your province or territory.

8. **Research and purchase business insurance** Running a business carries some risks. There are many types of insurance that offer protection.

9. **Understand HR issues and responsibilities** If you will be hiring staff, you'll need to understand your obligations in three principal areas:
   • Payroll obligations regarding the remission of taxes
   • Local labour laws
   • Workers' Compensation Board (WCB) requirements

10. **Keep necessary records** When you run a business, you are required to keep permanent books and records for a specified period of time.

Source: CanadaOne (www.canadaone.com/ezine/oct03/checklist.html), accessed March 22, 2007.

Entrepreneurs in Action

Disasters sending store downhill

FIRE, WATER, BREAK-INS BATTER RETAILER'S DREAM

While most retailers are counting up their biggest receipts of the year, Jay Jennings is counting losses.

He wonders how his dream of owning a trendy clothing store for twentysomething snowboarders has turned into a nightmare.

"I'm dying here," said Jennings, 30, surveying what stock he had left after the second robbery at NBS Apparel in just over three weeks.

It's been a tough haul for the young retailer. In September 2003 he realized a 10-year dream by opening his own shop.

Then came a succession of disasters.

"We've had everything under the sun happen — from fires to floods to construction, and now break-ins," Jennings said.

In October last year, just six weeks after his grand opening, a fire ruined all his clothing stock. He was closed for nearly two months while repairs were made and he rebuilt his inventory.

By the time he reopened, Jennings said he'd lost whatever momentum might have carried him through the Christmas season.

Over the summer, ongoing construction and repairs made it hard for customers to find the store, and rain kept leaking through the roof and the front window, damaging his inventory, flooring and fixtures.

Then thieves struck just as Jennings was gearing up for the Christmas season.

The first break-in occurred Nov. 12. Jennings says the thieves took inventory and computer equipment.

He had just got things up and running again when the second break-in happened on Sunday night.

Jennings says the store has lost about $100,000 in merchandise, equipment and damage. He's made three insurance claims and is with his second insurance company.

PHOTO BY WAYNE GLOWACKI/WINNIPEG FREE PRESS

"We're running on fumes," he said. "Everything's been coming out of my own personal savings, (my) credit cards. You can only squeeze so much."

The store will be closed until at least Wednesday and Jennings says the season is mostly a writeoff. "With what I have left on the floor, it's going to be very hard to make a sale."

Jennings says he wants to stay in business. He pursued this dream for a decade, working on his business plan, taking courses, getting his financing together. But he's got a family to support and can't take much more.

He likens his situation to a game of jenga, where participants try to pull building blocks out of a tower without knocking it down.

"Someone keeps pulling out of our jenga stack," he says. "One more pull and we're done."
(www.nbsapparel.com)

Source: Kerry Campbell, *Winnipeg Free Press*, Tuesday, December 7, 2004, p. B3.

CONLUSION

CONCLUSION

There is no pat answer to the question of the legal form of organization you should adopt. A lot will depend on such issues as the expected size and growth rate of your new venture, your desire to limit your personal liability, whether you plan to start the business on a part-time or a full-time basis, whether you expect to lose or make money from a tax point of view during your first one or two years of operation, your need for other skills or additional capital, and so forth. Take a look at Figure 6.1, which summarizes many of the important differences between the various forms of organization available to you and may help you make your decision.

One word of caution: If you are considering any type of *partnership* arrangement, be extremely careful. In hard reality, partners should fulfill at least one of two major needs for you: They should provide either needed *money* or needed *skills*. If you allow any other factors to overshadow these two essential criteria, you may be taking an unnecessary risk.

One of the primary reasons new venture teams often fail is ill-advised partnerships. Partnerships entered into principally for reasons of friendship, shared ideas, or similar factors can create considerable stress for both the partnership and the individuals involved. It has often been said that a partner should be chosen with as much care as you would choose a spouse. However, in contemporary society, perhaps even greater care should be exercised, since a partnership may be even more difficult to dissolve than a marriage. An unhappy partnership can dissolve your business much faster than you can dissolve the partnership.

TABLE **6.1**   WHICH FORM OF BUSINESS ORGANIZATION IS BEST FOR YOU?

This figure summarizes many of the important differences between the various forms of business available to you. Review each of the alternatives on the dimensions indicated and select which one best fits with your particular circumstances. This may vary from characteristic to characteristic since there are pros and cons of each form. Once you have reviewed all dimensions, you should be able to select the organizational form that appears to be the best overall for your particular situation.

Form of Organization	(a) Initial Requirements and Costs	(b) Liability of Owners	(c) Control	(d) Taxes	(e) Transfer of Ownership	(f) Continuity	(g) Ability to Raise Money
(1) Sole Proprietorship	Minimum requirements; perhaps only registration of your business name	Unlimited liability	Absolute control over operations	Income from business taxed as personal income	May transfer ownership of assets	Business ceases to exist when owner quits or dies	Limited to what the owner can personally secure
(2) General Partnership	Easy and inexpensive to establish	Each partner is personally liable for all debts of the partnership	Requires majority vote of all general partners	Income from business is taxed as personal income of the partners	Requires agreement of all partners	Dissolved on withdrawal or death of partner unless specified in partnership agreement	Combined resources of all the partners can be used to raise capital
(3) Limited Partnership	Moderate requirements; should be registered provincially	Liability limited to the extent of their individual investment	May not participate in the day-to-day management of the business	Same as for general partners	May sell interest in the company	Same as general partnership	Limited liability may make it easier to raise capital but can be complicated
(4) Corporation	Most expensive; usually requires a lawyer to file Articles of Incorporation	Liability limited to investment in company	Control rests with shareholders	Corporation taxed on its income and shareholders taxed on dividends received	Easily transferred by selling shares of stock	Not affected by the death or withdrawal of any shareholder	The most attractive form for raising capital

Which form best meets your needs on each dimension (select one)?

(a) _____ (b) _____ (c) _____ (d) _____ (e) _____ (f) _____ (g) _____

Which form of organization do you feel best meets your overall needs? _____

Conducting a Feasibility Study

Part 1:
Technical and Market Assessment

So far, we have considered and evaluated your new venture primarily from a conceptual point of view. That is, we have concentrated on the following questions:

1. What product/service businesses would you be interested in pursuing?

2. How attractive are these venture ideas?

3. What options should you consider in getting into a business of your own?

Now, in Stage Six, a step-by-step process will be presented to help you transform your *chosen* venture concept from the idea stage to the marketplace. This is accomplished by means of a *feasibility study* to determine the probability of your product or service idea successfully getting off the ground by subjecting it to solid analysis and evaluation. You must put your ideas through this type of evaluation to discover whether they contain any fatal flaws that are likely to impact their viability. Sometimes people get all excited about the prospects of a new business without thoroughly researching and evaluating its potential. Some time later they may discover that while the idea was good, the market was too small, the profit margins too narrow, the competition too tough, the financing insufficient, or there are other reasons that cause the business to fail. If the individuals involved had thoroughly researched their idea and conducted a feasibility study before starting, many of these failed businesses would never have been started in the first place.

A feasibility study is the first comprehensive plan you need in contemplating any new venture. It proves both to yourself and others that your new venture concept can become a profitable reality. If the feasibility study indicates that the business idea has potential, then you can proceed to write a business plan. A typical feasibility study considers the following areas:

1. The concept for your venture

2. An assessment of your market

3. The technical feasibility of your idea

4. The supply situation

5. Cost–profit analysis

6. Your plans for future action

The first four of these topics will be discussed in this Stage; the last two will be addressed in Stage Eight. Much of the same information can be incorporated into your subsequent business plan (see Stage Eleven) if it appears that your venture warrants commercial development.

The contents of a typical feasibility study are outlined in Figure 7.1 on page 183. You can use this guide to assist you in evaluating the feasibility of your new venture idea.

YOUR VENTURE CONCEPT

It is critical that you be able to clearly and concisely explain, verbally, the principal concept underlying your venture — what sets it apart from other businesses of similar character. This is what is sometimes called your

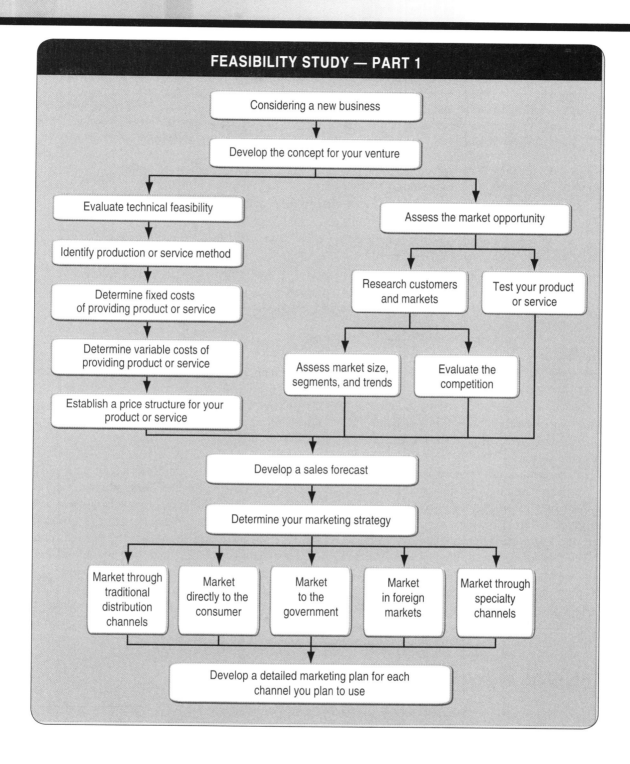

FEASIBILITY STUDY — PART 1

Considering a new business
↓
Develop the concept for your venture

Evaluate technical feasibility
↓
Identify production or service method
↓
Determine fixed costs of providing product or service
↓
Determine variable costs of providing product or service
↓
Establish a price structure for your product or service

Assess the market opportunity

Research customers and markets

Test your product or service

Assess market size, segments, and trends

Evaluate the competition

Develop a sales forecast
↓
Determine your marketing strategy

Market through traditional distribution channels

Market directly to the consumer

Market to the government

Market in foreign markets

Market through specialty channels

Develop a detailed marketing plan for each channel you plan to use

"elevator pitch" — a conversation that begins when the elevator door closes and ends when the door opens at your floor. That means you have only a few seconds to capture your listener's interest, so you had better be able to explain your concept quickly, completely, and confidently. If you have difficulty explaining to other people precisely what your business proposes to do, it is a clear sign that your concept still needs development and refinement.

An idea is not yet a concept, only the beginning of one. A fully developed concept includes not only some notion as to the product or service the business plans to provide, but also a description of the proposed pricing strategy, promotional program, and distribution plans. It will also consider such aspects of the business as what

---

Other considers — DEVELOP YOUR ELEVATOR PITCH

The idea of an "elevator pitch" is that you are alone with a prospective customer or investor for the length of a typical elevator ride, say 30 to 60 seconds, and wish to communicate the key aspects of your business concept to that person during that time. The idea is to stimulate sufficient interest on the part of the listener within that brief period of time to open the door to a more in-depth dialogue or a "tell me more" kind of conversation. Your pitch should be carefully prepared and written out. You want to practice it until you have mastered the material and can deliver it in a comfortable, conversational style. It should not appear memorized. You want to sell your prospective customer/investor on your idea and generate some enthusiasm to know more about it.

Your pitch should contain the following elements:

- Start with a "hook," something about your concept or idea that people will remember and that will stick with them.
- Focus on the market and describe what your product or service actually does for the customer.
- Explain how your firm is different from other firms that are in the same or similar business and why you have some sort of competitive advantage.
- Outline the current situation of your business. If it is a start-up, state clearly what you are looking for — financing, distributors, partners. If you are already in business, say where people can buy your product or service.

To see some examples of elevator pitches, check out www.youtube.com.

---

is unique or proprietary about your product or service idea, any innovative technology involved in its production or sale, and the principal benefits it is expected to deliver to customers.

Developing a good description of your concept can be difficult. Many concepts are too broad and general, not clearly communicating the really distinctive elements of the venture — for example, "a retail sporting goods outlet" or "a tool and equipment rental store." Other concepts may use words like "better service," — "higher quality," "new," "improved," or "precision machined," which are either ambiguous or likely to have different meanings for different people. It is much better to have a detailed, clear, definitive statement — for example, "a retail outlet providing top-of-the-line hunting and fishing equipment and supplies for the serious outdoors person" or "a tool and equipment rental business for the professional, commercial, and residential building contractor." Such descriptions are easier to visualize and allow the uninformed to really understand what it is you propose to do.

Your business concept is not necessarily etched in stone. It may need to change and evolve over time as you come to better understand the needs of the marketplace and the economics of the business. Sharpening and refining of your concept is normal and to be expected.

TECHNICAL FEASIBILITY

You should keep in mind that not all businesses are started on the basis of new or original ideas. Many, in fact, merely attempt to copy successful ventures. To simplify matters, all product and service ideas can be placed along a continuum according to their degree of innovativeness or may be placed into one of the following categories:

1. **New invention** This is something created for the first time through a high degree of innovation, creativity, and experimentation. Examples include fibre optics, hydrogen-fuelled vehicles, bionic prostheses for replacement arms and legs, WiMax and other wireless technologies, and radio frequency identification systems.

2. **Highly innovative** This term means that the product is somewhat new and as yet not widely known or used. Examples are MP3 players, smart phones, wide-ranging consumer products incorporating GPS technology, and non-invasive testing techniques for various kinds of cancer.

FIGURE 7.1   **A TYPICAL FEASIBILITY STUDY**

Feasibility Study Contents

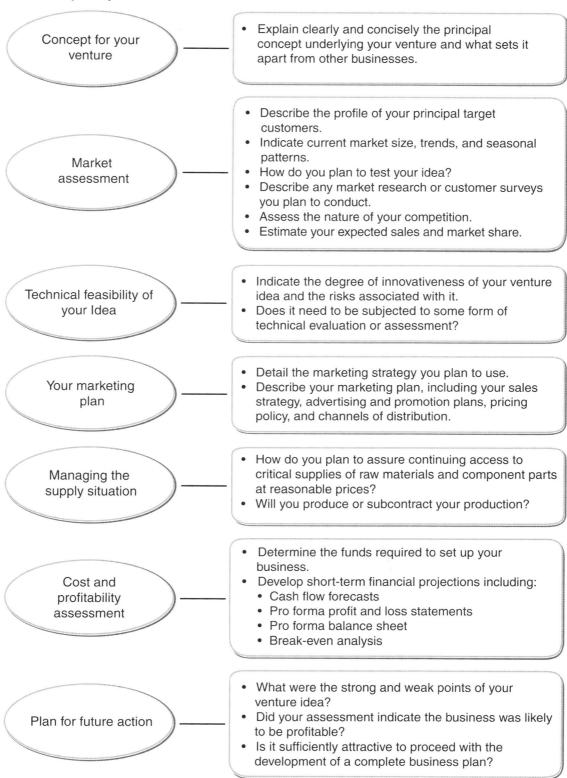

Concept for your venture
- Explain clearly and concisely the principal concept underlying your venture and what sets it apart from other businesses.

Market assessment
- Describe the profile of your principal target customers.
- Indicate current market size, trends, and seasonal patterns.
- How do you plan to test your idea?
- Describe any market research or customer surveys you plan to conduct.
- Assess the nature of your competition.
- Estimate your expected sales and market share.

Technical feasibility of your Idea
- Indicate the degree of innovativeness of your venture idea and the risks associated with it.
- Does it need to be subjected to some form of technical evaluation or assessment?

Your marketing plan
- Detail the marketing strategy you plan to use.
- Describe your marketing plan, including your sales strategy, advertising and promotion plans, pricing policy, and channels of distribution.

Managing the supply situation
- How do you plan to assure continuing access to critical supplies of raw materials and component parts at reasonable prices?
- Will you produce or subcontract your production?

Cost and profitability assessment
- Determine the funds required to set up your business.
- Develop short-term financial projections including:
  - Cash flow forecasts
  - Pro forma profit and loss statements
  - Pro forma balance sheet
  - Break-even analysis

Plan for future action
- What were the strong and weak points of your venture idea?
- Did your assessment indicate the business was likely to be profitable?
- Is it sufficiently attractive to proceed with the development of a complete business plan?

3. **Moderately innovative** This refers to a product that is a significant modification of an existing product or service or combines different areas of technology, methods, or processes. Examples include microprocessors used to control various automobile systems or single-person cars. The term could also refer to such ideas as the redesign of bicycles to make them easier to ride by handicapped or physically disabled people, thus developing a new market.

4. **Slightly innovative** This term means that a small, yet significant, modification is made to an established product or service, as in larger-scale or more exotic recreational water slides or amusement parks.

5. **"Copycatting"** This is simply imitating someone else's business idea.

The degree of innovation inherent in a business idea has strong implications for the risk, difficulty in evaluation, and profit potential of the venture. *Risk* refers to the probability of the product or service's failing in the marketplace. *Evaluation* is the ability to determine its worth or significance. *Profit potential* is the level of return or compensation that you might expect for assuming the risks associated with investing in this business.

In general, the following relationships hold:

1. New inventions are extremely risky and difficult to evaluate, but if they are accepted in the marketplace they can provide enormous profits.

2. For moderately innovative and slightly innovative ideas, the risks are lower and evaluation is less difficult, but profit potential tends to be more limited.

3. In the "copycat" category, risks are often very high and profit potential tends to be quite low. Such businesses usually show no growth, or very slow growth, and there is little opportunity for profit beyond basic wages.

Every new product must also be subject to some form of evaluation to ensure that the benefits intended for prospective customers can indeed be delivered. In developing a working prototype or an operating model of a product with this criterion in mind, some of the most important technical requirements to consider include the:

- Functional design of the product and the attractiveness of its appearance
- Flexibility of the product in permitting ready modification of its external features to meet customer requirements or competitive pressures
- Durability of the materials from which the product is made
- Expected product reliability under normal operating circumstances
- Safety of the product under normal operating conditions
- Expected rate of obsolescence
- Ease and cost of maintenance
- Ease and cost of processing or manufacture
- Ease of handling and use by the customer

If a product doesn't fare well on some of these requirements, it should be reworked until it does.

One key approach for testing a new product is to subject it to the toughest conditions that might be experienced during actual use. In addition to this kind of test there may be standard engineering tests to which the product will have to be subjected to receive Canadian Standards Association (CSA) (www.csa.ca) or Underwriters Laboratory (UL) (www.ul.com) certification. You might also undertake an evaluation of alternative materials from which the product could be made. Further assistance in conducting a technical evaluation may be available from various agencies of your provincial government as well as some colleges and universities and the Canadian Innovation Centre (www.innovationcentre.ca).

MARKET ASSESSMENT

Assessing the potential market for your concept is a critical part of any feasibility study. At the very least, you need to demonstrate that a market does in fact exist, or there is not much point in developing a full-scale business plan. In some cases the potential market may be large and obvious; in others, considerable research and investigation may be required to demonstrate if there is likely to be any significant level of demand. It is essential to determine that a sufficiently large market exists to make the concept financially viable.

WHO IS YOUR CUSTOMER?

To tailor your marketing program to the needs of your market, you must have a very clear idea of who your customers are likely to be. To do this you will need to gather some information in the marketplace. The more information you have about your target market, the better you will be able to develop a successful marketing plan.

Types of Markets

The first thing to recognize is that the term "market" does not refer to only a single type of possible customer. A number of different types of markets exist, such as:

1. **The consumer market** Individual users of products and services such as you and me

2. **The institutional market** Organizations such as hospitals, personal care homes, schools, universities, and similar types of institutions

3. **The industrial market** Other firms and businesses in your community and across the country

4. **The government market** Various agencies and departments of the municipal, provincial, and federal governments

5. **The international market** Markets similar to the above examples outside the national boundaries of the country

What Is Your Market?

Very few businesses initially operate in all of these markets. Most analyze the possibilities available to them in each situation to determine which offers the best potential. This involves asking such broad questions as:

1. Who is your customer?

2. How big is the market?

3. Where is it located geographically?

4. How fast is it growing?

5. What organizations and/or individuals are most likely to buy this kind of product or service?

6. Why do they buy it?

7. Where and how do they buy it?

8. How often do they buy it?

9. What are their principal requirements in selecting a product or service of this type?

To determine which of these markets is likely to represent the best opportunity for you, you need to understand just what your product or service has to offer to a group of people or businesses. To do this, you need to understand the primary features of your product or service offering and the benefits it can provide. A *feature*, for example, is some characteristic of a product or service that is part of its basic make-up, while a *benefit* is what motivates people to actually buy it. If an automobile has air bags or anti-lock brakes, they are features of the car, but the benefit they provide to the consumer is increased safety. By knowing what your product or service has to offer in terms of features and what will make customers buy it, you can begin to determine characteristics that may be common across the members of your potential market. This kind of assessment will serve to identify some broad areas of opportunity for you.

Failure to understand your customer, however, can be terminal. Ralph Giancola thought he had a surefire winner (Entrepreneurs in Action #26). No one else in Quebec was offering a service to hockey players that would clean their smelly gear. The market was untapped. He installed his industrial-strength cleaning equipment at a high-traffic rink in Montreal and offered his service to local players at $40 a wash. He figured he would be making money in no time. However, the business didn't materialize as he expected. It was never able to generate sufficient revenue to cover the monthly expenses, and things didn't improve even when he dropped his price to $20.

Entrepreneurs in Action

He shoots, he misses

After watching a Discovery Channel program about Esporta Wash Systems, Ralph Giancola came up with a business plan that he was sure would be a winner. Esporta, based in Kelowna, B.C., sold an industrial-strength cleaning system that worked on firefighter equipment, football pads and hockey gear. It was once the official cleaner for Hockey Canada and was even endorsed by the Great One's dad, Walter Gretzky.

Giancola was already running a commercial cleaning business (with seven employees) in hockey-obsessed Montreal, and he'd been inside enough rank dressing rooms to know that most recreational players aren't all that diligent when it comes to cleaning their equipment. "It seemed to us that nobody was washing hockey gear in Quebec," says 36-year-old Giancola. "The market was untapped."

He and a partner drafted a plan to install an Esporta machine at a high-traffic rink and offer the equipment cleaning services to players. They took their idea to TD Bank, which gave them a $100,000 small business loan; $75,000 of that went to buying the system, plus supplies like mesh bags, cage inserts, stain removers and a special hockey-glove dryer. In November, 2004, NETS Inc. (Nettoyeur Equipment Travail Sport) rented a storefront at a rink in the Montreal borough of Pierrefond that draws about 5,000 players and fans a week during peak season. At $40 a wash, Giancola figured NETS would be making money in no time. With Giancola and his partner splitting shifts, their monthly costs — including rent, loan payments and a phone line — ran to about $3,000. To supplement their clientele, NETS would also cut deals with two other rinks and a local sports store that would act as drop-off points for dirty gear.

It took just a few months for Giancola to see where they'd gone wrong. Some players didn't want to leave expensive equipment with NETS; others didn't want to come back after four hours to pick it up. Hockey parents thought it was too expensive — why spend 40 bucks cleaning gear that wouldn't even fit the kid next season? Then there were the guys who simply spritzed their gear with Febreze after each game — if that. "You can't change the way people think," says Giancola. "If someone hasn't washed their equipment in 20 years, why would they wash it now?"

"There was no way this business could make money," he says, "unless we had another three or four years, plus tens of thousands of dollars we could throw into marketing to change the way people think about cleaning their gear." He admits he didn't do enough interviews with hockey parents and players to gauge interest before starting up.

By March, 2006, the company was out of commission. Giancola sold the Esporta system back to the company for $17,000. Because the $100,000 bank loan had been guaranteed through a provincial small-business program, Giancola only had to repay 25%. But he and his partner had racked up $55,000 on a line of credit, which they're still trying to pay back.

Source: Craig Silverman, *The Globe and Mail, Report on Small Business*, January 30, 2007.

So what went wrong? Ralph gradually came to realize that some players didn't want to leave their expensive hockey equipment with the business; others didn't want to have to come back after four hours to pick it up. Many parents thought it was too expensive just to clean equipment their kids were going to outgrow in any case, and some players just didn't think cleaning their equipment was all that important. As Giancola says, "You just can't change the way people think. If someone hasn't washed their equipment in 20 years, why would they wash it now?" In March 2006 the company closed its doors. Some basic research and talking to a few prospective customers to determine whether there was a need for his service before jumping in might have helped Ralph avoid this financial disaster.

SEGMENT YOUR MARKET

It is natural to want to target as many people and groups as possible with your business offering. However, in most circumstances it is not very practical to do so. For example, you are not likely to have the promotional budget to be able to communicate effectively with many different groups at once. Even if you had a large enough promotional budget, your promotional message would not likely talk directly to any one group, thus having much less impact. So, in addition to doing the broad analysis described above, you also need to question whether within these major market types there are groups of potential customers with different preferences, requirements, and purchasing practices, or that are concerned about different benefits. For example, toddlers, teenagers, businesspeople, and older adults all have quite different clothing needs although all are members of the consumer market. Retailers, designers, and manufacturers must take these different needs into account when developing and marketing their product lines. Each of these groups should be considered a separate *target market*. This process of breaking down large, heterogeneous consumer or industrial markets into more homogeneous groups is known as *market segmentation*. Most markets can be segmented on the basis of a number of variables:

1. **Geographic location** such as part of a city or town, county, province, region, or country. If you are selling farm equipment, geographic location is obviously a major factor in segmenting your target markets since your customers will be located in particular rural areas. Climate is a commonly used geographic segmentation variable that affects industries such as sporting equipment, lawn and garden equipment, snowblowers and snowmobiles, and heating and air-conditioning equipment. If this is a factor in your business, you need to identify the geographic area where your market is located and identify the specific boundaries within which you will do business.

2. **Demographic description** such as age, gender, marital status, family size, race, religion, education level, income, and occupation. Non-consumer markets might be classified on the basis of their total purchases or sales, number of employees, or type of organizational activity. Choose those demographic characteristics of your target market that relate to their interest, need, and ability to purchase your product or service. For example, a market for luxury condominiums would include professional married couples approximately 35 to 55 years old with incomes of more than $100,000 and either no children or grown children.

3. **Psychographic or sociological factors** such as lifestyle, status, timing and means of purchasing, and reasons for buying products or services similar to yours. The desire for status or enhanced appearance, the pursuit of fun and excitement, or the desire to be socially responsible and environmentally conscious are all examples of these kinds of variables. Many products — like a variety of extreme sports such as skydiving and bungee jumping, organically grown foods, and environmentally friendly insect control methods — would appeal or not appeal to different people largely on the basis of these types of factors.

Research Your Market

WHAT IS MARKET RESEARCH?

Market research can be defined as the gathering, processing, reporting, and interpretation of market information. Small businesses typically conduct less market research than larger ones, but it is essential that all businesses engage in this process to some degree to prepare a realistic marketing plan. The market research process involves four basic steps:

1. Define the need for information
2. Search for secondary data
3. Gather primary data
4. Interpret the information

We will discuss each of these steps as they relate to obtaining the information you will require to put together your market assessment.

Define the Need for Information

Before you take the time to gather any data, you need to first decide how you are going to use the information and what you need to demonstrate or show with the information. For example, do you need to:

- Estimate the total expected size of the market for your product or service and the nature and extent of any trends in expected demand?
- Determine the expected level of demand for your product or service?
- Provide a description of who you feel will be your primary customer?
- Outline how your customers are expected to buy your product or service and with what frequency?
- Understand the nature and extent of the competition you may face in the marketplace?

Search for Secondary Data

The easiest place to start to try to answer these questions is by searching through available sources of secondary data. Secondary data comprise information that others have put together relating to your industry and/or your customers. Using secondary data is usually considerably less expensive than gathering new information so you should exhaust all readily available sources of secondary information before moving on to gather new data of your own.

Secondary data can come from a tremendous variety of sources. Often they may not exist in the exact form you require but by combining data from a number of secondary sources you may be able to compile the information you require, and at much lower cost than going out and gathering your own information.

SOURCES OF SECONDARY MARKET INFORMATION

There are a number of sources you might consult to get a handle on the approximate size of the market you are considering entering. Some of these sources are Statistics Canada publications; various industry reports, trade journals, and investment journals; and financial statements of your leading competitors. You must be careful to make some provision for error in your estimate of market size. Most of the information sources you will consult will not be able to provide complete up-to-date figures, and forecasts of future sales are always subject to error. One key source of demographic data on the Canadian market is Statistics Canada and their various publications. Their *Market Research Handbook* is an annual publication that provides extensive demographic and economic data on the Canadian marketplace. This includes population statistics, surveys of consumer expenditures, housing and household characteristics, and similar information. It is available for purchase or can be downloaded for free from (www.statcan.gc.ca/bsolc/olc-cel/olc-cel?catno=63-224-XWE&lang=eng). In addition, a wealth of other information is available from Statistics Canada. For example, they break the country up into 36 Census Metropolitan Areas (CMAs). For each CMA there are a series of referenced maps providing an index for which it is possible to get a tract number for almost any neighbourhood in the country. From this tract number you can get a detailed breakdown of the number of people and their characteristics within a single local neighbourhood or for a combination of tracts comprising a region of a city or for the entire metropolitan area. This data can be a valuable resource, providing a wide variety of information on a large number of geographic markets. The major drawback, however, is that it is largely derived from census data and may be a little stale. This should not be surprising, given the constantly changing tastes of consumers and ongoing technological advancement.

Following are listings of some of the more popular sources of market information. Much of this material is available at your local public, college, or university library.

INDUSTRY AND TRADE ASSOCIATIONS In most situations the best place to start is with the industry or trade associations for the industry in which your business will compete. For example, if you were thinking of starting a retail sporting goods store, you could find a lot of data on the industry and other useful information available from a number of industry associations, depending on your particular emphasis. Some examples are:

- Bicycle Trade Association of Canada (www.btac.org)
- Canadian Sporting Goods Association (www.csga.ca)
- Association of Pool and Spa Professionals (www.nspi.org)
- National Sporting Goods Association (www.nsga.org)
- SGMA International (www.sgma.com)

Similarly, a lot of useful information related to establishing a business to grow and distribute a variety of organic fruits and vegetables could be obtained from the following organizations, among others:

- Canadian Organic Growers (www.cog.ca)
- Certified Organics Association of British Columbia (www.certifiedorganic.bc.ca)
- Organic Producers Association of Manitoba (www.opam.mb.ca)
- Organic Crop Improvement Association (www.ocia.org)
- The National Organic Program (www.ams.usda.gov/nop/indexIE.htm)

Virtually all of these organizations have Web sites where you may be able to access market studies, cost-of-doing business reports, industry fact sheets, and other statistical data that can help you research the potential market for your business.

TRADE PUBLICATIONS Just to give you an idea of the number and diversity of the trade publications produced in Canada, take a minute to review Table 7.1 on page 191. It is by no means a listing of all trade-oriented publications, merely a sampling of the range of material available to you. Depending on the nature of your new venture, any one or more of innumerable publications could represent a source of market-related information or a means for you to communicate with potential customers.

GENERAL PUBLICATIONS In addition to trade publications there are numerous general publications that can be extremely useful in compiling relevant market data. Some of the more important of these are listed in Table 7.6 on page 221. In addition to all these publications, other sources that you should look to for information include:

1. Your local Chamber of Commerce
2. Your city or municipal government
3. Local or regional development corporations
4. District school board offices
5. Provincial government offices
6. Downtown business associations
7. Shopping centre developers
8. Advertising agencies
9. Newspapers, and radio and television stations
10. Competitors
11. Sales representatives and trade suppliers
12. Similar businesses in another location
13. Other business associates

CANADA BUSINESS SERVICES FOR ENTREPRENEURS

One prospective source of market information that should not be overlooked is Canada Business Services for Entrepreneurs (www.CanadaBusiness.ca). In addition to accessing a wealth of information on their main site, you can also link directly to the Canada Business Service Centre (CBSC) in your own province or territory. The CBSCs are a collaborative effort of the federal, provincial, and territorial governments, designed to provide businesses and entrepreneurs with a single point of access to a wide range of useful information relating to government services, programs, and regulations that might impact their businesses. Each CBSC offers a broad range of products and services, as well as access to general information tailored to meet the needs of its specific clients. These include:

- Availability of services on the Web, by toll-free telephone, by e-mail, and in person
- Access to databases and other material containing information on the services and programs of the participating departments and various community organizations
- Info-Guides and Fact Sheets that provide descriptions of services and programs that relate to a particular topic (e.g., exporting, E-business, franchising, business start-up, financing)

SOURCES OF SECONDARY MARKET INFORMATION:

Market Research Handbook To download a free copy of the annual publication with extensive demographic and economic data on the Canadian marketplace, go to www.statcan.gc.ca/bsolc/olc-cel/olc-cel?catno=63-224-XWE&lang=eng

Canada Business Market Research and Statistics A comprehensive listing of key market research resources. (www.canadabusiness.ca/eng/88/)

Statistics Canada Census Data is available from the most recent census of the Canadian population at (www12.statcan.ca/census-recensement/index-eng.cfm)

Canadian Industry Statistics An analysis of data on number of establishments, gross domestic product, and labour productivity for most industry sectors in the Canadian economy at (www.ic.gc.ca/eic/site/cis-sic.nsf/eng/Home)

CANSIM Statistics Canada's principal socio-economic database, containing detailed information on a whole variety of subjects (cansim2.statcan.gc.ca/)

Agri-Food Trade Service A list of Web sites for all Canadian trade associations having to do with food and agricultural products can be found at www4.agr.gc.ca/AAFC-AAC/display-afficher.do?id=1171041784063&lang=eng

AllYouCanRead.com A comprehensive listing of most trade magazines available in Canada, with links to their Web sites is at www.allyoucanread.com/index.asp?idCat=1146

Canada Business A collaborative effort of federal, provincial, and private sector organizations to provide businesspeople with a one-stop shopping experience for all their information needs to help them do a better job of their businesses. Sites are found in the principal communities within each province and territory at canadabusiness.ca

- Other business services, which could include interactive software for business planning, videos, business directories, how-to manuals, CD-ROM library search capability, and access to external databases

CBSCs are located in one major urban centre in each province and territory, with two in Alberta, and have partnership arrangements with local groups in most other communities as a way to provide regional access to their services.

THE INTERNET

Another place where you may be able to find a good deal of information about any idea you plan to pursue is the Internet. Not everything is available on the Internet yet, but with a little practice even new users can skim the Net's millions of Web pages and thousands of newsgroups for topics of general interest or to help find precise pieces of specific data.

The job of culling information from the millions of Web pages has been simplified by the development of a variety of search tools that enable the user to rapidly search through directories or the nooks and crannies of the Web itself to create indexes of information related to a particular topic.

Search engines are sites that contain the contents of millions of pages of information from throughout the Web, and are used to find pages containing specific words or phrases. Google (www.google.ca) and Bing (www.bing.com) are among the most popular. These search engines send out software agents or "spiders" that explore the entire Internet instead of just the Web pages that have been indexed for the directory. The problem with this approach, however, is that some of these search engines are not very discriminating. Sorting through the thousands of matches that may result from any search can be a real chore.

TABLE **7.1**	SOME CANADIAN TRADE PUBLICATIONS

Aerospace & Defence Technology	Canadian Mining Journal	Industrial Distributor News
Applied Arts	Canadian Music Trade	Industrial Product Ideas
Architecture Concept	Canadian Oil & Gas Handbook	Jobber News
Atlantic Fisherman	Canadian Pharmaceutical Journal	Lighting Magazine
Aviation Trade	Canadian Pool & Spa Marketing	Luggage, Leathergoods & Accessories
Bakers Journal	Canadian Premiums & Incentives	L'Automobile
Bath & Kitchen Marketer	Canadian Security	Machinery & Equipment MRO
Benefits Canada	Canadian Vending	Masthead
Boating Business	Computer Dealer News	Medicine North America
Bodyshop	Construction Canada	Modern Purchasing
Building Renovation	Cosmetics	Motel/Hotel Lodging
Business to Business Marketing	Dental Practice Management	Office Equipment & Methods
CAD/CAM & Robotics	Design Engineering	Plant Engineering & Maintenance
Canadian Apparel Manufacturer	Eastern Trucker	Plastics Business
Canadian Beverage Review	Electrical Equipment News	Quill and Quire
Canadian Building Owner & Property	Farm Equipment Quarterly	Sanitation Canada
Manager	Fleur Design	Service Station & Garage Management
Canadian Doctor	Floor Covering News	Shopping Centre Canada
Canadian Food & Drug	Food in Canada	Software Report
Canadian Forest Industries	Food & Drug Packaging News	Sports Business
Canadian Funeral News	Footwear Forum	The Bottom Line
Canadian Grocer	Fur Trade Journal	The Business and Professional Woman
Canadian Hairdresser	Gardenland	The Western Investor
Canadian Heavy Equipment Guide	Gifts and Tablewares	Trade Asia Magazine
Canadian Hotel & Restaurant	Greenhouse Canada	Transportation Business
Canadian Industry Shows & Exhibitions	Group Travel	Visual Communications
Canadian Jeweller	Hardware Merchandising	Water & Pollution Control
Canadian Machinery & Metalworking	Health Care	Woodworking

In addition to the basic search engines, there are a number of other search tools you should consider as well. These include:

- **All-in-one or "parallel" search engines** such as MetaCrawler (www.metacrawler.com), Dogpile (www.dogpile.com), or Ask (www.ask.com). These search engines simultaneously submit your search request to several other search engines and combine the results into one report.

- **Specialized search engines** such as About.com (www.about.com) and Search.com (www.search.com), which will provide you with access to hundreds of other specialized search engines, and Canada Business (www.canadabusiness.ca), the Government of Canada Web site that provides access to almost everything you need to know about starting and running a business in Canada.

- **Search accelerators** such as Copernic 2001 (www.copernic.com), WebFerret (www.ferretsoft.com), and BrightPlanet's DeepHarvester (www.brightplanet.com/solutions/deep-web-harvest/). These programs simultaneously query several search engines for the words or phrases you are searching for and summarize the results in a simple, easy-to-read format. Most of these accelerators are sold as separate programs to be installed on your computer.

- **Subject guides** can be an excellent source of information about a particular topic since someone who has a lot of knowledge about a subject has usually prepared the index. There are literally thousands of subject guides that contain links to a number of other Web sites. Many of them can be found by searching in directories like Yahoo! or Google. Some of the best ones for information relevant to small business include the Web sites of the Canadian Youth Business Foundation (CYBF) (www.cybf.ca), Canadian Business Online (www.canadianbusiness.com/entrepreneur/index.jsp), and the Kauffman

Foundation Entrepreneurship Web site (www.entrepreneurship.org/). These guides can be excellent starting points to begin your search for more specific information.

- **Commercial research databases** such as ProQuest (www.proquest.com), and Northern Light (www. northernlight.com). These databases contain information from newspapers, magazines, journals, and other hard-to-find information sources and make it available for a fee. This can be a flat fee per month, a per document charge, or a combination of a monthly/annual fee and a per document charge.

Most search engines provide basic instructions as to how to initiate a search as part of their home page. For a beginner, it all starts with you entering a "query." A "query" consists of one or more keywords — a company name, a city or country, or any other topic likely to appear either in the title or the body of a Web page. Most search programs employ Boolean logic, expanding or limiting a search by including "and," "but," and "or" as part of the search process. The more precise your query, the better. For example, if you are interested in a topic like antique automobiles, typing in "antique automobiles" instead of just "automobiles" will direct you to information regarding older cars, although you may also get sites for antique dealers in general and other related subjects.

There are a number of fundamental problems you need to be aware of in gathering research information off the Net. First, the quality of some of the information may be of questionable value or use. There is a lot of useless information online since literally anyone can create a Web site. Second, the information you come across may be misleading. Since anyone can set up a Web site and publish information, fraud and misrepresentation have become real problems. Third, the information may be out of date. There is no assurance that information on the Web is the most recent or reflects current research or theory.

To use the Web for research purposes it is essential that you take the time to learn how to do it effectively. Most of us simply do not take the time to learn this skill. We simply connect to the Internet, call up our favourite search engine, plug in a couple of key words, and do a search. Then we begin browsing through the results and start to surf many of the sites that come up. We then give up some time later, very frustrated and without having found much relevant information.

Professional researchers, on the other hand, think carefully about the information they are looking for. They plan a specific search strategy and decide which search terms might be the most effective in finding the information they are searching for. It is only then that they log onto the Internet to conduct a preliminary search. Based on what they find, they will try some other terms and use other search engines, continually refining their search as they go. Eventually they are likely to find just what they are looking for.

As you can see, the first approach is entirely hit and miss while the other involves some careful thought and planning and is likely to be much more effective.

Gather Primary Data

Doing your own research — called primary research — may be the best way to get the most current and useful information regarding your potential market. A number of techniques can be used to obtain primary data. These can be classified into two basic research approaches: observational methods and questioning methods.

OBSERVATIONAL METHODS This is the gathering of primary data by observing people and their actions in particular situations. It may entail such approaches as observing the behaviour of shoppers in a store as they go about purchasing a range of different products, or counting traffic flows through a mall or past a particular location, or observing patterns in traffic flows around a store or other facility.

QUESTIONING METHODS These include both the use of surveys and experimentation that involves contact with respondents. Survey research involves the systematic collection of data from a sample of respondents to better understand or explain some aspect of their behaviour. This data collection can occur by personal contact, through the mail, by telephone, or on the Internet. In addition, the information may be gathered from people individually as in an individual interview or in a group such as a focus group.

Survey research is the most widely used method of primary data collection. Its principal advantages are its relatively low cost and flexibility. It can be used to obtain many different kinds of information in a wide variety of situations.

However, there are also some problems associated with survey research. Constructing a good survey is not necessarily an easy thing to do. Sometimes people are unable or unwilling to answer survey questions, so the response rate is not always as high as you might like to see. In addition, a number of technical issues relating to survey research, such as appropriate sample size, reliability, validity, and statistical significance, need to be considered as well. These issues go beyond the scope of this book but definitely need to be considered when gathering any primary data. Before rushing out to conduct a survey, however, it is a good idea to formulate a systematic research design that addresses the following issues:

Problem statement	1. What is the decision you have to make?
	2. What information will assist you in making that decision?
Questionnaire design	1. Precisely what information do you want to collect in the interviews?
	2. What interview questions will get you that response from respondents?
	3. How should those questions be phrased?
	4. How are you going to contact prospective respondents?
Sampling procedure	1. Who should your respondents be?
	2. How many respondents should you use?

Data analysis   How will you tabulate, summarize, and analyze your data?

There are also some general guidelines you can follow to help you design effective questionnaires:

- Pre-test the survey on a small group of people to ensure that respondents clearly understand your questions.
- Make certain you are actually asking the right questions to get the information you need.
- Decide how you intend to use the information you will obtain when designing the questionnaire.
- Keep your survey concise and readily understandable.
- Ask direct questions that relate specifically to the topic in which you are interested.
- If you are providing respondents with a finite range of possible answers (as with a Likert-type scale), try to provide a maximum of five possible responses.
- Make sure your questions can be answered easily by your respondents.
- Don't offend anyone.
- Don't mislead respondents about the purpose of your survey.
- Don't answer the questions for them by prompting them for answers.
- Give respondents sufficient time to provide an appropriate response.
- Don't bias their responses by personally reacting to any answers, either positively or negatively.
- Ask all personal information at the end of the survey so the respondent is not discouraged from replying.
- Always be courteous; remember they are doing you a favour.

An example of a relatively simple survey developed by a woman who wanted to open a fitness centre and offer one-on-one training is illustrated in the Other considerations box on page 194.

MARKET-TESTING YOUR IDEA

In addition to obtaining information from prospective customers, there are also a number of primary research methods you can use to gauge likely market reaction to your particular concept or idea. These techniques are more subjective and cannot be analyzed statistically. However, most of them provide instant feedback. Usually one opinion leads to another so that overall you will receive some interesting and useful information. These techniques include prototype development, obtaining opinions from prospective distributors, comparing your idea directly with competitors' offerings, conducting in-store tests, and demonstrating at trade shows.

DEVELOPING A PROTOTYPE A *prototype* is a working model of your product. If you are considering selling a product that, when mass-produced, could cost you $5 per unit to manufacture, prototypes may cost you hundreds of dollars each. However, this could be an inexpensive investment, because with just one prototype you can get photographs, make up a brochure or flyer, show the idea to prospective buyers, and put out publicity releases. You don't need a thousand or 10 thousand units at this stage.

Other considerations   FITNESS CENTRE QUESTIONNAIRE

1. Do you exercise regularly?   YES ___   NO ___

   If NO, please go to Part A.

   If YES, please go to Part B.

PART A. PLEASE CHECK YOUR REASONS FOR NOT EXERCISING:

___ Lack of time   ___ Lack of motivation   ___ Cost

___ No convenient fitness centres   ___ Medical reasons

___ Other. Please specify _____

PART B. CHECK THE TYPE OF EXERCISE YOU DO:

___ Aerobic   ___ Nautilus   ___ Free weights   ___ Yoga

___ Pilates   ___ Tai Chi   ___ Running   ___ Swimming

___ Other. Please specify _____

2. Are you: ___ Male   ___ Female

3. What is your age group?

   ___ Under 25   ___ 26–35   ___ 36–50   ___ Over 50

4. Where do you normally exercise?

   ___ At home   ___ Fitness centre

   ___ Other. Please specify _____

5. How far do you live from (location of proposed centre)?

   ___ Nearby   ___ 5–10 kms   ___ over 10 kms

6. Do you think your community needs a new fitness centre?   YES ___ NO ___

7. Would you be interested in one-on-one training?   YES ___ NO ___

8. Do you have any comments or suggestions about the need for a fitness centre in your community?

Source: Adapted from "How to Prepare a Market Analysis," Edward Lowe Foundation, *Entrepreneurial Edge* (edge.lowe.org).

Even though you are interested in producing only a few units at this point, it is still important to get manufacturing prices from a number of (around five) different suppliers. You should find out how much it will cost to produce various quantities of the product (1,000 units, 5,000 units, 10,000 units) and what the terms, conditions, and costs of the production process would be. Once you have this information you will be able to approach buyers and intelligently and confidently discuss all aspects of the product.

OBTAINING OPINIONS FROM PROSPECTIVE DISTRIBUTORS A second way to test your product idea is to ask a professional buyer's personal opinion. For example, most major chain stores are organized into departments, each department having its own buyer. After arranging to see the buyer representing the product area in which you are interested, arm yourself with the cost information you received from potential suppliers. Remember, a buyer is a very astute person. He or she has seen thousands of items before yours, and in most cases will be able to tell you if products resembling yours have ever been on the market, how well they sold, what their flaws were, etc. You can get a tremendous amount of free information from a buyer, so it is advisable to solicit his or her independent opinion before you become too involved with your product.

COMPARING WITH COMPETITORS' PRODUCTS Most of us have only limited exposure to the vast array of products available in the marketplace and so could end up spending a lot of money producing a "new" product that is already being marketed by someone else. Test your product idea by comparing it with other products already on the market, before you invest your money.

ONE-STORE TEST Another way to test your product is to run a one-store test. This can be done by arranging with a store owner or manager to put a dozen units of your product on display. The purpose of this test is to learn what the public thinks about your product. You can often get the store owner's cooperation, because the store doesn't have to put any money up front to purchase your product. However, problems can be associated with such tests. If you are very friendly with the owner, he or she may affect the results of the test in your product's favour by putting it in a preferred location or by personally promoting it to store customers. You should request that your product be treated like any other, because you are looking for unbiased information.

Also, you should keep in mind that one store does not constitute a market; the one store in which you test may not be representative of the marketplace in general. Nevertheless, the one-store test is a good way to gather information on your product.

TRADE SHOWS Another excellent way to test your product idea is at a trade show. It makes no difference what your field is — there is a trade show involving it. At a trade show you will have your product on display and you can get immediate feedback from sophisticated and knowledgeable buyers — people who know what will sell and what will not. There are approximately 15,000 trade shows in Canada and the United States every year, covering every imaginable product area, so there is bound to be one that could serve as a reasonable test site for you.

CONDUCTING A CUSTOMER SURVEY

A critical factor in successfully launching a new venture is understanding who your customers are and what needs your product or service might satisfy. It is important to consider that not all potential customers are alike or have similar needs for a given product. For example, some people buy a toothpaste primarily to prevent cavities, while others want a toothpaste that promotes whiter teeth, fresher breath, or "sex appeal," or has been designed specifically for smokers or denture wearers. You have to determine which of these segments (i.e., cavity prevention, whiter teeth, etc.) your product or service can best satisfy.

As previously mentioned, most major markets can be broken down into more homogeneous groups or *segments* on the basis of a number of different types of variables. In developing a plan for your proposed business venture you must consider who your potential customers are and how they might be classified, as in the toothpaste example, into somewhat more homogeneous market segments. You should be clear in your own mind just which of these segments your venture is attempting to serve. A product or service that is sharply focused to satisfy the needs and wants of a specifically defined customer group is typically far more successful than one that tries to compromise and cut across the widely divergent requirements of many customer types. Small businesses are often in a position to search for "holes" in the market representing the requirements of particular customer types that larger companies are unwilling or unable to satisfy. Figure 7.2 on page 223 provides a framework you can complete to develop a market profile of your prospective customer.

To be successful, you should seek a *competitive advantage* over other firms — look for something especially desirable from the customer's perspective, something that sets you apart and gives you an edge. This may be the quality of your product, the speed of your service, the diversity of your product line, the effectiveness of your promotion, your personality, your location, the distinctiveness of your offering, or perhaps even your price.

To accomplish all this may require some basic market research. This might be thought of as one of the first steps in testing your product or service idea with potential customers.

Since you will want to provide as good a description of your offering as possible (preferably via a prototype), personal, face-to-face interviews are the best method for gathering the information. Figure 7.3 on page 224 provides an outline for a survey you might conduct. It would be wise to interview at least 30 to 40 potential customers to help ensure that the responses you receive are probably representative of the marketplace in general. This approach can be used effectively for either consumer or industrial products/services.

This customer survey will provide you with important information that will allow you to further develop and fine-tune your marketing strategy. For example, if you discover that the most customers will pay for your product is $10 and you had planned on charging $12, you will have to reconsider your pricing strategy. Similarly, if customers prefer to purchase products like yours by mail, you will have to keep that in mind as you set up a distribution system. The responses to each of the questions posed in the survey should be analyzed and their impact on areas of marketing strategy noted. These will be brought together later in your preliminary marketing plan.

Interpret the Information

Once this secondary and primary data have been gathered, they must be analyzed and translated into usable information. The research needs to aid you in making management decisions related to such issues as:

- Who should be your target customer?
- What product or service should you be selling?
- What is the total size of your potential market and how can it be broken down?
- Who are your competitors and what are their strengths and weaknesses?
- What is your estimated sales forecast?
- Where should you locate your business?
- How should you promote, price, and distribute your product?

Some conclusions based on the analysis of this data may be obvious. Others may be more difficult to decipher or you may feel the data you need to answer the question are just not available. Nonetheless market research can provide you with some of the information you need to be more proactive and help you decide what you should be doing in the future rather than just relying on what has happened in the past.

Failure to employ some of these basic techniques to try to assess consumer response and the expected level of market demand for your business concept can be an expensive lesson. Brian Stoner and his wife, Mari Okazaki, thought they had a million dollar business idea with their maternity mattress. After five years and numerous prototypes they thought they had sufficiently refined the product, and with the encouragement of family and friends launched Mari's Maternity Mattress as a business (Entrepreneurs in Action #27). Their first year sales forecast was to sell 250 units for expected revenue of $57,000. After six months of being in business they had only sold seven. At that pace they expected they might sell 25 for the year. What went wrong? Was their price too high, not enough advertising, the product didn't perform as expected or just what was the issue?

It soon became apparent that the couple really didn't understand their customer. Almost none of their sales were to their primary target market of pregnant women. Rather, a few massage therapists bought the product. Feedback from the market was that pregnant women were really only uncomfortable a month or so before their due date so were not prepared to spend money on a special mattress for such a short period of time. As a childbirth instructor commented, 'most people just wait it out.' Fortunately the pair operate their business out of their home and have not invested a lot of money in the business. They can try to improve their marketing plan and hopefully turn the situation around before they run out of funds.

Other considerations ▸ DO-IT-YOURSELF MARKET RESEARCH

Here are some things you should keep in mind when doing your own market research.

1. In conducting a survey, your information will be only as good as your sample. To be useful, your sample group needs to be relevant to and representative of your target population.
2. Design your survey or questionnaire carefully. Make sure it's focused specifically on the information you need to know.
3. Keep your survey or questionnaire as short as possible, preferably a single page.
4. Always provide some opportunity for the respondent to provide detailed answers.
5. Work out how you intend to record the information and analyze the data as you are developing the questionnaire.
6. Before you administer the survey, establish the criteria that you will use to make decisions based on the information obtained from the survey.
7. Remember, market research is needed at all stages of a business's life to keep you in touch with your customers and their needs and desires.

Source: ©J. Susan Ward, 2001 (sbinfocanada.about.com); licensed to About.com, Inc. (www.about.com). Used by permission. All rights reserved.

27

Entrepreneurs in Action

Mari's Maternity Mattress: Labouring for lift-off

In the family-oriented city of Chilliwack, B.C., 100 km east of Vancouver, Brian Stoner could be the best husband in town. When his wife, Mari Okazaki, was pregnant with their first child in 2001 and having trouble sleeping, he made her more comfortable by cutting a hole in a slab of four-inch-thick polyurethane foam — allowing Mari to sleep on her front or lie down while he gave her a pain-relieving back massage. "I just wanted to make sure she was as comfortable as she could be," says Stoner. The first time Mari slept on the mattress, "She fell asleep and didn't move for the whole night," he says. "When she spent the next four months sleeping on it, I thought this was a million-dollar business idea."

Wisely, the couple didn't rush into business. "I was listening to the small voice inside my head saying, 'It's not going to work out, you're going to lose money'," says Stoner. But friends, family and even Mari's obstetrician urged them to commercialize the product. Five years, two more children and many prototypes later, Okazaki and Stoner launched Mari's Maternity Mattress (MMM) last September. Then they sat back to watch the orders pour in.

They're still waiting. As of mid-March, after nearly six months in business, MMM had sold only seven mattress sets, at about $229 apiece.

"I guess I was just naïve, expecting to get inquiries as soon as we put up the Web site," says Stoner. "That's not what happened. We realize now that people have to see it, try it and understand it before they'll buy it."

Stoner and Okazaki aren't the first entrepreneurs to found a business on the Field of Dreams premise, "If you build it, they will come." But their attempt to commercialize their invention provides a classic case study of the perils of building a company around a single product. And it lends credence to the cynical calculation that having a rock-solid idea for a business is only 10% of the battle; everything else is execution.

The pair have done many things right. Stoner refined the idea through two more pregnancies, settling on a combination of two foam sheets about 80 inches long and four inches thick. After much trial and error, he learned to cut smooth, conical holes with a reciprocating saw—one for the stomach, two for the breasts. When a pregnant woman has trouble sleeping, she can start using the first mattress, with three holes custom-cut to fit her measurements. In her sixth month or so, when her stomach protrudes beyond the four-inch

depth, she can add the second mattress, with a single hole, which holds her stomach. Both mattresses slip inside a washable cotton cover that holds them together and provides additional support for dangly body parts. Once the baby is born, says Stoner, you can put the cut-outs back into the mattress and use it as a guest bed.

Before launching their home-based business, Stoner and Okazaki visited spas and massage centres up and down the Fraser Valley, offering to lend them mattresses for trial use. They bet that once a pregnant woman laid down on their maternity mattress, she would feel so comfortable that she'd immediately want to buy one. So far no pregnant woman has ordered anything. The first seven sales were all to massage therapists.

The couple's business plan states that if they target couples earning more than $40,000 a year and grab just a small fraction of the market, they could sell 7,167 units a year in Canada, and as many as 140,000 in the U.S.

At the current pace, they might sell 25. They sold nothing in September or October, two mattresses in November and none in December. Sales have picked up a bit since, but not to the prime target: pregnant women. "It's been tougher than I expected," says Stoner. "We need to educate the person at the same time as we do the sale."

Is Stoner's price too high? He says he chose the $229 price tag by tripling his cost of materials (about $60) and then tacking on a little extra, because marketers he consulted said that a price point below $200 would "cheapen the product's image."

"I think the reason people aren't buying our product has nothing to do with the price," says Stoner. "I haven't heard that the product is too expensive. I'm hearing that 'I've only got a month to go' [before the due date], or that 'I've already spent $500 on pillows.'"

Childbirth instructor Stephanie Ondrack wasn't surprised that sales have been slow. "I doubt many people would want to buy something like this," she says. "It's only in the late stages when you get really uncomfortable. Most people just wait it out."

Stoner, who says he'll be happy if the business sells 12 mattresses a month a year from now, is pragmatic. "We don't have the skills to take it where I think it can go," he says. "It's going to take a lot of time and some smart marketing to get it to the point where someone else can market it internationally." He's willing to sell the firm or license the product, but he knows either of those outcomes is still years away.

ESTIMATING TOTAL MARKET SIZE AND TRENDS

A large part of market assessment is determining the volume of *unit sales* or *dollar revenue* that might flow from a market and what proportion of this you might expect to capture. At first glance "unit sales" seems to mean simply how many potential customers there are in the market for your product/service. However, this would overlook the possibility that some customers may buy more than one unit of the product/service. Estimates of total market size must take these *repeat purchases* into account. Total demand is determined by multiplying the number of customers who will buy by the average number of units each might be expected to purchase. To determine the total market size in dollars, simply multiply this total number of units by the average selling price.

Figure 7.4 on page 225 provides a form you can complete to estimate the approximate total market size (past, present, and future) and the expected trends for your product/service type.

The Nature of your Competition

Unless your product or service is a "new to the world" innovation, which is unlikely, it will have to compete with other products or services that perform a similar function.

WHO ARE YOUR COMPETITORS?

In the customer survey, your respondents probably identified the names of a number of firms that offer products or services designed to serve the same function or meet the same customer need as yours. Some will be considered *direct competitors* because they offer products or services that are very similar to yours. Others could be thought of as *indirect competitors* because they offer a substitute for your product or service or combine your product with something else they provide. In addition to those mentioned by your respondents, you should seek out other potential competition by watching newspapers and magazines for ads, checking out the Yellow Pages, talking to people who live or work in the area of your business, and searching on the Internet. Identifying the competition in this way will give you some idea of just how crowded your market is and who appear to be the principal players in customers' minds at the present time.

HOW DO THEY COMPETE?

Once you have identified who you feel are your principal direct and indirect competitors, you need to ask specific and detailed questions regarding this competition. The answers will help you gain a better understanding of the level of sales and market share you could achieve, the kind of strategy you might pursue, and the type of marketing program (pricing, promotion, distribution) you might employ. The kind of information you need to gather for the top three or four competitors in your business will relate to such issues as:

- Their estimated sales and market positions
- How they are viewed by consumers and what consumers think of their products or services
- How their products/services compare to what you are planning
- Their apparent strengths and weaknesses
- The key elements of their marketing strategy in terms of
  - Pricing
  - Promotion
  - Distribution/Location

Figure 7.5 (p. 225) provides a form to help you organize your assessment of each of these competitors. Fill out a copy of this form for each major competitor you have identified. You should be on the lookout for areas where you can gain a sustainable competitive advantage and carve out a market for yourself. For example, can you provide the best quality, the lowest cost, a higher level of service, or be the most innovative?

WHERE WILL YOU GET THE INFORMATION?

Naturally your competitors will probably not co-operate by providing you with this information directly. Sources that can be useful in obtaining this information include:

- Secondary sources such as patent and trademark filings, general business and trade publications, trade associations, annual reports for public companies, and Web sites, chat rooms, and blogs on the Internet.

- Primary sources such as talking to prospective customers and suppliers, attending trade shows, and buying or trying competitors' products to assess their quality and features in order to benchmark them against what you have planned, and touring the facilities of their businesss if possible.

Using the information you have gathered, you can summarize the results in a *competitive profile matrix* similar to the one illustrated in Figure 7.6 (p. 227), to see how your plans compare with the competition on each of the dimensions listed in the matrix. This will enable you to compare your firm's strengths with those of the competition and start thinking of ways to utilize those strengths and exploit your competitors' weak areas.

One approach that might be helpful in enabling you to get a better understanding of your relative competitive situation is to perform a formal SWOT (Strengths, Weaknesses, Opportunities and Threats) analysis. This analysis helps you to see how your strengths stack up against your competitors' weaknesses and suggests ways to take advantage of opportunities out in the marketplace.

In carrying out a SWOT analysis to determine how you rate against a competitor, consider the following points:

Strengths

What are your business' strong points? They should be considered both from your own and your customers' points of view. Be realistic in your assessment and consider such issues as:

- What distinct advantages does your company offer?
- What do they like about your product or service?
- Why do your customers say they enjoy doing business with you?
- Is there anything you currently offer that can not be copied by a competitor, now or in the future?

Weaknesses

Evaluate your company's weaknesses not only from your perspective, but also from the perspective of your customers and competitors. It's sometimes difficult to think about and discuss your weaknesses, but it is best to be realistic now and face any unpleasant truths as soon as possible. For example:

- What does your company do now that has room for improvement?
- What do your customers dislike about your product or service relative to the competition?
- What does your company do poorly?
- What do your competitors do better than you?
- Do competitors have a particular market or segment locked up?

Opportunities

Next consider the areas in your market that offer room to grow. Opportunities can come from changes in technology and markets on both a broad and narrow scale; changes in government policy related to your industry; changes in social patterns, demographics or consumer lifestyle. Are any special events scheduled to take place such as the Vancouver Olympics or local events such as the closing of a competitor's store near you that may create a unique opportunity at the moment? Think about such issues as:

- What and where are the interesting opportunities in your marketplace?
- What are the important trends occurring in your local area as well as across the country which could positively impact your business?
- What do you anticipate happening in the future that may represent an opportunity?

Threats

Although we don't like to think about them, we all face threats in our businesses. Many times they're out of our control, such as the recent downturn in the economy, a shift in market demographics, or perhaps a new Walmart or other major competitor opening in your local area. It is critical to think about and be prepared for such events.

- What are the current obstacles that your business faces?
- What is your competition doing that could negatively impact your business' growth?

- Are the required specifications or government regulations relating to your products or services changing?
- Is changing technology threatening your position in the market?
- Do you have financial problems that could keep you from being able to effectively compete?

The primary purpose of a SWOT analysis is to give you a vehicle to compare your internal factors in terms of strengths and weaknesses with specific external factors to help identify areas of potential opportunity for you. The matching process can be facilitated by the construction of a SWOT matrix, constructed by creating a table showing the strengths, weaknesses, opportunities and threats that you've just identified and evaluating the inter-relationships among them as shown in Figure 7.7.

You can use the matrix to methodically compare each relevant pair of factors to generate logical matches. The four SWOT cells enable you to make comparisons of opportunities with your strengths (O/S), threats with your strengths (T/S), opportunities with your weaknesses (O/W) and threats with your weaknesses (T/W). Analyzing each of the four SWOT cells of the matrix should yield a variety of matches that will help you generate some possible strategic alternatives. For example, if an opportunity exists in the marketplace for a firm that can provide faster and more reliable service but your business is only comparable to the competition on this dimension (i.e., customer service is not one of your strengths), then you will quickly see when you do the O/S match that you must focus on improving this aspect of your business if you hope to capitalize on this market opportunity.

There are four basic categories of matches for which strategic alternatives can be considered:

- S/O matches show the company's strengths and opportunities. Essentially, the company should attempt to use its strengths to exploit these opportunities.
- S/T matches show the company's strengths in light of major threats from competitors. The company should use its strengths to avoid or defuse such threats.
- W/O matches illustrate the company's weaknesses coupled with major opportunities. The company might try to overcome its weaknesses to take advantage of such opportunities.
- W/T matches show the company's weaknesses against existing market threats. Essentially, the company must attempt to minimize its weaknesses and avoid threats. These strategy options are generally defensive.[1]

YOUR COMPETITIVE STRATEGY

Once you have completed your SWOT analysis you can then think about developing a strategic plan for dealing with your competitiors and other market forces. Although there are many areas where you might obtain an edge over the competition the primary means are through:

1. **Cost Advantage:** having a significantly lower cost, so you can charge lower prices while still achieving reasonable profit margins. These lower costs may arise from maintaining a lower variable cost per unit sold, having a lower level of marketing expenses, or having a lower level of overhead or operating expenses. Businesses focused on a niche market often have lower overhead and lower marketing costs.

2. **Differentiation Advantage:** having a meaningful difference between your products and those of the competition, which creates a higher level of perceived customer benefits. This could be in terms of the physical characteristics of the product itself, the range or level of services provided, or the image and reputation of your business. A business with a meaningful differential advantage can often charge higher prices and generate higher unit profits.

   For example, the first thing Janet Waldon and Bernard Gauvreau did when they decided to set up a florist business in Edmonton was to buy a map of the city, research all 108 other flower shops they were able to identify as possible competitors, and plot their locations on the map. They also recognized that some big-box retailers and supermarkets sold flowers as well, and had a tremendous advantage in terms of volume, selection, and price. They quickly realized that they would not be able to compete directly with these stores and that they had to find a different way. Their solution was to go high-end and open a very artistic, open-concept store, where all the work was done in front of the customer in a gallery-like setting, using exotic and unusual flowers instead of the typical florist fare. The rest of their strategy in terms of location, décor, promotion, and so on, was all directed toward reinforcing this difference and setting themselves apart from the other flower shops in the city. Ultra Violet Floral Studio seems to have been able to do this successfully, based on the market's response to their business (Entrepreneurs in Action #28).

3. **Marketing Advantage:** undertaking a marketing effort that dominates the competition in terms of distribution, sales coverage, or weight and type of promotion. You might choose to focus on a specific region, or a particular channel of distribution that you can dominate. Such businesses can often attract new customers more easily and maintain their presence with existing ones.

4. **Focus on a Market Niche:** by identifying a position in the market that has been overlooked, neglected or abandoned by one or more of your competitors. This can be particularly effective for smaller firms trying to escape direct competition with larger companies with more resources while trying to build their own competitive advantage. This niche could be a particular customer segment with very particular needs or requirements, limiting sales to a single geographic location or concentrating your efforts on a single, specialized product or service offering.

Considering these issues, and your position relative to other firms, can enable you to begin to envision an ideal strategy for building a competitive edge for your business.

SHERMAN'S LAGOON

© Jim Toomey, King Features Syndicate.

DEVELOPING A SALES FORECAST

Sales forecasting is the process of organizing and analyzing all the information you have gathered in a way that makes it possible to estimate what your expected sales are likely to be. Your sales forecast will probably be one of the most difficult and yet the single most important business prediction you ever make. If you get it wrong, the error can lead to plenty of unsold inventory and problems generating sufficient cash to keep the business going or to a number of disappointed customers.

But how do you get it right? One way is to consider the following formula:

Sales Forecast = Total Estimated Market Size × Estimated Growth Rate
× Market Share Target

Estimating Market Size

Fairly accurate market data are available from trade associations and other secondary sources for certain industries. However, companies in many other industries have to operate without any concrete information concerning the total size of the market for their products or services. Nonetheless, information on market size is vital to develop a meaningful marketing plan.

Entrepreneurs in Action

Florist

One of the first things Janet Waldon and Bernard Gauvreau did after they'd decided to set up their own flower shop was go out and buy a map of Edmonton. Then they compiled a list of every florist in the city — at the time, there were 108 of them — and put a pin on the location of each one. "We're probably the only people on the planet who actually made a pin board," says Waldon. But their project helped them identify which neighbourhoods were underserved. "We really did our research," she says.

Working together wasn't a new thing for Waldon and Gauvreau. They'd met four years earlier, when Gauvreau became Waldon's ice-dancing coach. Soon they began travelling together for workshops and skating events around Western Canada and the United States. "On all these trips, we realized that we were drawn to the same things," says Waldon. "We were always attracted to visually artistic things, and we kept finding ourselves in flower shops."

Waldon and Gauvreau had had a few casual conversations about opening their own shop one day, but nothing concrete. Then they spotted a florist in Seattle that broke all the rules: It didn't have a cooler, it was only about 100 square feet, and it had nothing but flowers and vases. "I remember standing there looking through the window at this place," says Waldon, "and it was an 'aha!' moment because it allowed us to think, Wow, we could really do this — and do something different."

Almost six months later, they opened Ultra Violet Floral Studio, inspired by the artistic approach of that Seattle shop.

With 108 rivals in the city — and with big-box retailers and grocery stores selling flowers — Waldon and Gauvreau knew they needed an edge. "Grocery stores can buy in such enormous volume and ship so quickly from their own growers that they do have a huge impact on some of the smaller florists," says Waldon. "The only way we could survive was to not even try to compete with them." Instead they went high-end, creating an open-concept store where all the designing would be done in front of the customer, in a gallery-like setting, using exotic and unusual flowers.

"We needed a location that would allow us to create a work space in the middle of the room," says Waldon. After about three months, they found just the spot in Edmonton's Inglewood neighbourhood, a 970-square-foot space that got their interior designer's stamp of approval. With a business plan complete and financing in place (personal assets plus a $20,000 bank loan), they were all set to start renovations. But just as they were about to sign an agreement with a contractor, Edmonton was hit with a monster hailstorm. "All of a sudden this contractor had more business than he knew what to do with," says Waldon. He bowed out of the florist project in favour of more lucrative work. "We had already signed our lease and felt pressure to get this thing up and running," she says. "And every contractor in Edmonton was booked."

Luckily their friends and family stepped in. For eight weeks straight, 30 relatives, friends and even friends of friends — including a few skilled tradespeople and a contractor — worked 'round the clock to finish the reno.

Just six weeks behind schedule, Waldon and Gauvreau were ready to open. Before filling their cooler with exotic flowers, they invested $4,000 in branding — everything from business cards to stickers to delivery slips. Plus, they got going on designing a Web site, something that would attract significant traffic once it was up and running.

The pair opened their doors with $4,500 worth of flowers and $10,000 worth of ribbon, vases and other supplies. They'd hoped to do more marketing before opening, but because they'd spent so much time managing the reno, they ended up relying on word of mouth, signage and a small letter board they put on the sidewalk that said, "Ultra Violet Floral Studio. We're different."

Nearly two years later, Gauvreau leads the way with the floral designing, while Waldon does the number crunching.

Ultra Violet got a clear sign they're on the right track in May, when they were invited to create a bouquet for Queen Elizabeth, who was visiting the Royal Alberta Museum. "It was unbelievable that as a new florist we were asked to do this," says Waldon. "It just felt amazing."

Source: Rasha Mourtada, *Globe and Mail Update*, July 5, 2006.

It is especially important when introducing new products that you have a good estimate of the size of the total market, but this is exactly the situation for which obtaining an accurate forecast is most difficult. For example, suppose that you were considering setting up a distribution business to sell garbage bags and shopping bags made from recycled plastic (polyethylene) in Halifax. To estimate the total potential market that might be available you would need to know the total demand for such products in the four Atlantic provinces, if that was how you had geographically defined you market. In addition, you would also be interested in determining the size of the various segments of the market. Three obvious segments that should be considered might be: (1) garbage bags for household use sold by retail stores; (2) heavy-duty garbage bags sold in bulk for commercial and industrial use; (3) printed plastic shopping bags for independent retail stores and chains. You may not wish to compete in the entire market but decide to focus on the needs of one particular segment, such as printed shopping bags for chain stores.

It is usually much easier to determine market data for established products. Data on total market sales may already exist or they can be developed using either a *top-down* or a *bottom-up* approach.

TOP-DOWN APPROACH

The top-down approach utilizes published data on statistics such as total market size and weights them by an index that may be some factor such as the percentage of the population within your designated geographic area. For example, our distributor of plastic bags needs an estimate of the total size of the potential market for these bags in Atlantic Canada. Since the four Atlantic provinces account for approximately 10 per cent of the total Canadian population, a rough estimate of the size of the plastic bag market in that region would be 10 per cent of the total Canadian market. Data concerning the entire Canadian market may be available from sources such as Statistics Canada or from trade associations or other industry sources. One word of caution, however, in using this approach: This estimate of the total market for plastic bags in the Atlantic provinces is accurate only if usage patterns of plastic bags are the same in that region of Canada as they are in the country as a whole.

BOTTOM-UP APPROACH

The bottom-up approach involves aggregating information from the customer level to the total market level. Information on past or current purchase or usage of a product or service may be collected from a sample of customers by a mail or telephone survey or through personal interviews. For frequently purchased consumer products, like plastic garbage bags, for example, the survey may simply ask how much of the product is used either by individuals or the entire household during an average week or month. These individual or household statistics are then aggregated based on population or household statistics that are available from Statistics Canada and other sources to develop an estimate of the total size of the potential market. An overview of both these approaches is illustrated in the following Other considerations box.[2]

For your business plan, these sales estimates for your first year of operation should be monthly, while the estimates for subsequent years can be quarterly. A serious miscalculation many aspiring entrepreneurs make is to assume that because their new product or service appeals to them, other consumers will buy it as well. It is important to be aware of this tendency. This type of thinking is often reflected in what is known as the "2 per cent syndrome." This syndrome follows a line of reasoning such as, "The total market for a product is $100 million. If my firm can pick up just 2 per cent of this market, it will have sales of $2 million per year."

There are, however, two things wrong with this line of reasoning. The first is that it may be extremely difficult for you to capture 2 per cent of this market unless your business has a unique competitive advantage. The second is that a 2 per cent market share may still be unprofitable, since competing firms with greater market share may benefit from *economies of scale* — lower unit cost due to mass production — and other cost advantages unavailable to your firm.

---

2. Adapted from J.G. Barnes, *Research for Marketing Decision Making* (Toronto: McGraw-Hill Ryerson Ltd., 1991), pp. 84–94.

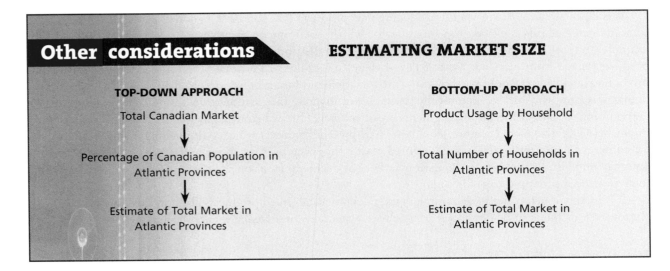

ESTIMATING MARKET SIZE

Other considerations

TOP-DOWN APPROACH

Total Canadian Market

↓

Percentage of Canadian Population in Atlantic Provinces

↓

Estimate of Total Market in Atlantic Provinces

BOTTOM-UP APPROACH

Product Usage by Household

↓

Total Number of Households in Atlantic Provinces

↓

Estimate of Total Market in Atlantic Provinces

A number of external factors can affect your sales, including:

- seasonal changes
- holidays
- special events
- political activities and events
- general economic conditions
- weather
- fashion trends and cycles
- population shifts
- changes in the retail mix

In addition, a number of internal factors must be considered, such as:

- level of your promotional effort
- your ability to manage inventory levels effectively
- the distribution channels you decide to use
- your price level relative to the competition
- any labour and personnel problems you might encounter

It is impossible to predict all these situations but you should try to take them into account in developing your sales forecast.

One approach to gaining some insight into your business's potential market is to follow the example laid out in Figure 7.8 on page 228. Refer to the *market profile* you developed in Figure 7.2. How do you feel your prospective customers would decide whether or not to buy your offering? This estimate should also consider the likely frequency and volume of a typical customer's purchases over a certain period of time.

In implementing this process, you should think about how prospective customers will likely hear about the opportunity to buy your product/service, whether from a salesperson, from an advertisement, or through a chain of intermediaries. Estimates can then be made of how many of the people you have described are good prospects and, consequently, what your total sales volume might be. This can be an "armchair" procedure involving the use of some library references or personal knowledge of similar businesses. The estimate of market potential developed using this method can be quite crude; however, it is important that you think your way through such a process and not sidestep it in favour of simply hoping a market exists for you.

Selecting a Location

It is often said that the three most important factors in the success of any retail business are "location, location, and location." Every new business faces the problem of where to locate its facilities. This problem is much more critical to retailers than to other types of businesses. Much of their business typically comes from people who are walking or driving by. As a consequence, a customer's decision to shop or not shop at a particular store may depend on such factors as what side of the street you are on, ease of access and egress, availability of parking, or similar concerns. This means that in determining the best location for your business you will have to concern yourself with a variety of issues.

1. **Zoning regulations** Zoning bylaws govern the kind of activities that can be carried on in any given area. Classifications vary from locality to locality, but many municipalities categorize activities as residential, commercial office, commercial retail, institutional, and industrial. When considering a location, make certain the business activities you plan to pursue are permitted under the zoning restrictions for that area.

2. **Municipal licences and taxes** Businesses must typically buy a municipal business licence. In the city of Winnipeg, for example, more than 115 types of businesses require a licence, which costs from $15 to over $2,000. In general, businesses in some amusement fields or that affect public health and safety require a licence.

   Businesses, like homeowners, must usually pay a business tax — a tax assessed as a percentage of the rental value of the premises or on the basis of a standard assessment per square foot of space utilized. These requirements vary from municipality to municipality.

3. **Municipal services** You should make sure that municipal services such as police and fire protection, adequate sewer and water supplies, public transit facilities, and an adequate road network are available to meet your business's requirements.

4. **Other considerations** Other things to consider are such site-specific issues as:

   - cost
   - the volume and timing of traffic past the location
   - the nature of the location, whether on a downtown street, in a strip mall, or in an enclosed mall
   - the nature of the area surrounding your location and its compatibility with your business
   - the kind and relative location of surrounding businesses
   - the volume of customer traffic generated by these other firms and the proportion that might "spin off" to your store
   - the growth potential of the area or community
   - the number and location of curb cuts and turnoffs

Figure 7.9 on page 229 provides a rating form you can use to help choose the most favourable location for a retail business.

Most of these same location factors also apply to service businesses, although perhaps not to the same degree. If your service business requires you to visit prospective customers at home or place of business, a central location providing easy access to all parts of your market area may be preferred.

Location has a quite different meaning for manufacturing firms. Manufacturers are principally concerned about locating their plant where their operations will be most efficient. This means considering such issues as:

- General proximity to primary market areas
- Access to required raw materials and supplies
- Availability of a suitable labour force
- Accessibility and relative cost of transportation and storage facilities
- Availability and relative cost of power, water, and fuel supplies
- Financial incentives and other inducements available from municipal, provincial, or federal government agencies

The importance of each of these factors in the location decision will depend on the nature of your manufacturing business and your own preferences and requirements.

Buying or Leasing Facilities

Many new businesses already own or decide to purchase the land and building in which their ventures or the machinery and equipment they will require to operate are located. With today's extremely high costs, however, this may not be a wise decision. The majority of new firms are not principally in the business of speculating in real estate and should not acquire their own property. During their early stages most businesses tend to be short of cash and many have failed because they had their capital tied up in land and buildings when it could have been more effectively used to provide needed working capital for the business itself. In addition, a business that owns its own building may be more difficult to sell at a later date, since a smaller number of potential buyers will have enough capital to buy both the business and the property. While building your own facility enables you to more carefully tailor the property to the specific requirements of your business, it tends to be a much more costly alternative.

If you are planning to rent or lease your facilities it is a good idea to have your lawyer review the terms and conditions of the agreement. You will want to ensure satisfactory arrangements in such matters as:

1. **The duration of the agreement** A business lease can last a year, three years, five years, or any other mutually agreed-on term. A short-term lease may be preferable if your situation is likely to change soon. However, the lease conditions can be a valuable asset of your business, and a short-term lease may reduce the sale value of your business (if you ever sell it) because of loss of the goodwill associated with maintaining your present location. The ideal lease arrangement should enable you to stay in the location for some time, in case your venture is successful, but give you the flexibility to move after a reasonable period of time if it doesn't work out.

   You also need to consider the terms and conditions for renewing the lease. Are there provisions for automatic renewal? Is there a maximum to any rent increase applied on renewal of your lease?

2. **The rent** Rental costs for commercial property are commonly stated in terms of the annual cost per square foot of floor space. For example, a 1,500-square-foot location rented for $8 per square foot will cost $12,000 per year, or $1,000 per month. This may be a *net lease*, in which you pay a single monthly fee that is all-inclusive (rent, utilities, maintenance costs, property taxes, etc.), or a "net-net-net" or *triple net lease*, in which you pay a base rent plus a share of all the other expenses incurred by the landlord in operating the building. In the latter situation your operating costs may fluctuate each year because of changing tax, maintenance, insurance, and other costs.

   In retail shopping malls, *participating* (or *percentage*) *leases* are common. Instead of a fixed monthly rent, the landlord receives some percentage of your sales or net profit. There are several types of participating leases. You may pay either a percentage of the total monthly sales of your business, a base rent plus some percentage of your gross sales, or a percentage of your net profit before interest and taxes. Shopping centre leases can be quite complex documents, so be certain to check with your accountant and lawyer before committing yourself.

3. **The ownership of any additions or improvements you might make to the facilities** Under the terms of most leases, all improvements and fixtures that you add to the premises are considered as belonging to the landlord. They immediately become part of the building and cannot be removed without his or her consent. If you need to install expensive fixtures to launch your business, you should try right up front to negotiate permission to remove specific items.

4. **Any restrictions on the use of the property** Most leases specify the kind of business activity you can carry on in the location. Before signing, you should think not only about the activities you now plan to engage in, but also about those you might wish to engage in in the future. Many leases also contain a non-competition clause to protect you from competitive firms coming into the premises and taking away your business.

5. **Whether you are permitted to sublet some or all of the property to a third party** This is commonly permitted, but only with the prior written consent of the landlord, and it is subject to any use restrictions and non-competition clauses in your agreement.

   A closely related issue is your ability to assign any remaining time left on your lease to another party. If you decide to sell your business, this can be an attractive part of the package. In some cases, assignment of the lease is not permitted; in others, an assignment may be acceptable with the prior written consent of the landlord, which may then not be unreasonably withheld.

6. **The nature of any default and penalty clauses** The lease will spell out the situations that constitute a breach of its conditions and the recourse available to the landlord. Obvious grounds for default include failure on your part to pay the rent, the bankruptcy of your business, violation of the use conditions or non-competition clauses, and so on. Should you default on the lease, the landlord may be able to claim accelerated rent for the time remaining on the lease. For example, if you were to move out two years before your lease expires, the landlord may claim the full two years' rent. In this situation, however, the landlord legally must try to limit his or her damages by renting out your space to another party as soon as possible.

Your lease may or may not contain a *penalty clause* limiting your exposure should you breach the lease. A penalty of three months' rent is common in many situations, although the landlord will want you or the directors of an incorporated business to sign personal guarantees for the amount of the penalty.

Home-Based Businesses

For many kinds of businesses, working out of the home has become a very popular and attractive option. Beautymark Corp., for example, is a small, home-based business that relies entirely on the Internet for its sales (Entrepreneurs in Action #29). Cindy Goble started the company after being a stay-at-home mom for 10 years. She wanted to get back into business but still spend as much time as she could with her kids. Starting a business that only sold its products online gave her the capacity to do both. Although she didn't know very much about the Internet, she bought a couple of books and hired a Web designer to develop a Web site for her and teach her how to operate it. That was enough to get her business launched. After some early struggles Cindy gradually added more lines to her original brand of skin cream and learned how to increase the profile of her business on the Web so that she could generate more traffic at her site. Now her business is starting to get some traction and beginning to take off.

There are a number of advantages to running your business out of your home, the most obvious of which is the cost.

Not only can you save on the rent for your business premises by operating in this manner, but the Canada Revenue Agency will also let you write off part of your home expenses for income tax purposes. Possible write-offs are utility costs, mortgage interest, municipal taxes, and other expenses related to maintaining that part of your premises used for your business. You can also save on the cost and time of travelling to and from work every day, and you have greater flexibility in planning and organizing your work and personal life. In addition, a home-based business may have a number of other benefits such as letting you wear more comfortable clothes and giving you more time to look after and be with your family. There are, however, a number of disadvantages.

1. It takes a lot of self-discipline to sustain a regular work schedule and resist distractions from family, friends, television, and other sources. You may find that there are too many interruptions to work effectively, that you tend to mix work with family life too much, or become distracted by household chores. Conversely, you may find it very difficult to get away from your work when you would like to, since it is so close at hand, and you may have trouble quitting after a full day.

2. Suppliers and prospective customers may not take you as seriously. You may have to rent a post office box or make other arrangements to give the appearance of operating from a more conventional commercial location.

3. The space available in your home may not be appropriate for your business, and you may not have access to facilities and equipment such as computers and fax machines that you need to conduct your business effectively.

4. If your house is in a typical residential area, operating a business from your home will probably contravene local zoning bylaws.

   It is true that most municipal governments have become reasonably flexible in this regard and do not go looking for violations; they will, however, respond to complaints from immediate neighbours and others in the vicinity. It is a good idea to check with these people before starting any kind of visible business activity from your home. Activities that may lead to complaints are posting a large sign on the front lawn; constant noise; a steady stream of customers, suppliers, or others in and out of your home; or the clutter of parked vehicles in your yard or on the street.

Entrepreneurs in Action

Sweet smell of success

Not that long ago, Cindy Goble could barely send an e-mail. Today, she spends a good part of her day peddling perfume and beauty products on the Internet, as the owner of Web-based retailer Beautymark Corp.

She'd spent the past 10 years as a stay-at-home mom in London, Ont., and she'd been itching to get into business. "I was yearning for some kind of presence in the business world," she says. But she was determined to still spend as much time as she could with her two kids.

Then a friend told her about a skin-care product that was only available in the United States. "I thought, why not try to sell this cream — which was remarkable for stretch marks and also on wrinkles — in Canada?" After speaking with the manufacturer, Goble decided that the best way to land a Canadian distribution deal was by going online. "I didn't know the first thing about the Web," says the 43-year-old, "so I was very uncomfortable at first."

She holed up at the family cottage with a stack of books on how to operate an online business. "I read and highlighted and took notes," she says. Then she hired a Web designer to create a site and teach her to run it. "It's very easy to operate, so I can add and delete products myself," says Goble. "That put me at ease." The designer also set her up to accept payments through PayPal, so she didn't need to be able to handle secure credit card transactions on her site (though she does take credit card payment by phone). To keep shipping simple, Goble restricted sales to within Canada and U.S., using Canada Post for domestic shipments and UPS for those headed south of the border.

Beautymark Corp. launched in November. But a few months later, having only served a handful of customers, Goble knew two things had to happen for her business to work: she needed to find a way to stand out online, and she had to expand her product offering beyond skin care. "I would go for weeks without any sales," she says. "I began to realize that my site was nowhere to be found in the millions of Web sites out there."

In the spring, Goble (with her husband's help) began to submit her site to online directories like Yahoo and Best of the Web. The more directories that listed Goble's site, the more likely it was that Beautymark would appear in an online search. Then, to boost her product offering, she bought the inventory from a perfume retailer who specialized in hard-to-find scents and was looking to shut down her shop. Goble updated the Beautymark site just a few weeks before Christmas and held an open house for the perfume store's existing customers in her living room. "It was a big hit," she says.

Now, when Goble sumbitted her site to all those online directories, she could add much broader keywords like "perfume," "fragrance" and "hard-to-find scents."

It worked. Goble went from fewer than 20 customers in September, to 100-plus that December. A year later, her business continues to grow. She now has more than 200 perfumes (more than 500 bottles at any given time) and stacks of coordinating boxes, tissue and bags stored in her basement. "The longer you have your Web site and the more directories you submit to, the more your business will grow. It's a snowball effect."

Goble's new products are doing so well (she has added a line of bath and beauty products to her inventory), she dropped the skin scream that started it all — it wasn't doing much to boost her sales. Now she's planning to move to a bigger home, so she can set up a permanent showroom and hold open houses. "I don't pay rent, I had no construction costs, and it's a one-employee business," she says. "My costs are very low, which made starting my own business more attainable." Plus, she's home every day when her kids get home from school. (www.beautymarkcorp.com)

Source: Rasha Mourtada, *Globe and Mail Update*, December 19, 2006.

In the end, operating a home-based business is really a very personal decision. From a practical perspective, you can probably do what you want, as long as no one complains. However, this mode of operation is not suitable for all types of businesses, and for many people may not be a comfortable decision. Some of the best current opportunities are described in the following FYI box.

FYI FOR YOUR INFORMATION

TOP 10 HOME BUSINESS OPPORTUNITIES

1. Home Renovation Services: As the population ages, more and more people will be investing in renovations to make their homes more livable and enable them to stay where they are.

2. Pet-Based Products: Is there anything indulgent pet owners won't buy for their pets? Seems the sky's the limit.

3. Catering Services: Nourishing, appealing, and healthy food, not just delivered, but served.

4. Cleaning Services: If you are good, and comfortable with the thought of running a crew, the demand for domestic cleaning services will only increase.

5. Fall Prevention Products: The development and/or distribution of products related to helping seniors prevent falls.

6. Wedding Consultant/Planner Services: People are always getting married, which means continuous opportunities for these services.

7. Dietary Consulting Services: People are increasingly concerned about eating healthy and are prepared to pay for personalized dietary planning and advice.

8. In-Home Beauty Services: There is increasing demand for services that make people feel younger and better, and a growing desire to have these services delivered to the home or office.

9. Sewing and Alteration Services: Sewing is becoming a lost art, but not everyone is the regulation size, so the demand for other people to provide these services will only increase.

10. Life/Business Coaching: Coaching has been hot for some time, but this new industry will continue to grow.

Source: S. Ward, "Top 10 Home Business Opportunities" in *About: Small Business Canada*, (sbininfocnada.about.com/cs/homebusiness/a/homebizopp_2.htm), accessed May 21, 2010.

FLESHING OUT YOUR MARKETING PROGRAM

The purpose of this section is to bring together what you have learned about the total market potential for your product or service, customer attitudes toward your particular offering, and the nature of the competitive environment you will be facing. The goal is to put down on paper a preliminary marketing strategy or plan for your new venture concept. This involves making some decisions regarding what you feel is an appropriate *marketing mix* for your business. Put simply, the principal ingredients of your marketing program that must be blended together to form your overall strategy can be grouped under the following headings:

1. Product or service offering
2. Pricing program
3. Promotional plans
4. Method of distribution

Product or Service Offering

The product area involves the planning and development of the product or service you are planning to offer in the marketplace. This involves defining the breadth and depth of your offering, the length of your line, how it will be packaged and branded, the variety of colours and other product features, and the range of complementary services (delivery, repair, warranties, and so forth) that will be made available to the customer.

Pricing Program

Your pricing strategy involves establishing the right base price for your offering so that it is appealing to customers and profitable to you. This base price may be adjusted to meet the needs of particular situations, such as to

TABLE 7.2	PRICE MARKUP CHAIN	Per Bottle	Markup
Direct factory costs		$1.00	
Indirect factory costs		0.50	
Total factory cost		$1.50	
Manufacturer's markup		0.50	25%
Manufacturer's selling price		$2.00	
Jobber's markup		0.50	20%
Jobber's selling price		$2.50	
Service station markup		2.50	50%
Service station selling price		$5.00	

encourage early acceptance of your offering during its introductory stages; to meet aggressive or — exceptional competition; to provide for trade, functional, seasonal, and other discounts; or to introduce your product/service into new market situations.

A number of approaches can be used to determine a base price for your planned market offering. These include *cost-based pricing*, *value-based pricing*, and *competition-based pricing*.

COST-BASED PRICING

One of the most commonly used strategies by retailers and small manufacturers is *cost-based pricing or markup pricing*. The cost of your product or service is determined and used as the base, and then a markup is added to determine what your selling price should be. *Markups* are generally expressed as a percentage of the selling price — for example, a product costing $2.50 and selling for $5 has a 50 per cent markup.

To illustrate, let's assume you've come up with a new formula for an automobile engine treatment that will be sold through auto parts jobbers to service stations for use in consumers' cars. Table 7.2 illustrates what the price markup chain for this product might look like.

As you can see, in this illustration a product with a factory cost of $1.50 has a retail selling price of $5 to the final consumer. The markup percentages shown here are merely examples of a typical situation, but in most wholesale and retail businesses, standard markups tend to prevail in different industry sectors. Food products and other staple items usually have a low unit cost and high inventory turnover, so the markups tend to be fairly low, 15 to 25 per cent; products such as jewellery and highly advertised specialty products typically have higher markups, perhaps as much as 50 or 60 per cent or even more.

This type of markup pricing is simple and easy to apply and can be very successful if all competitors have similar costs of doing business and use similar percentages. On the other hand, this approach does not take into account variations in the demand for the product that may occur with a different final price. For example, how much more or less of the engine treatment would be sold at a price of $4 or $6 rather than the $5 price determined by the standard markup chain?

Most manufacturers do not employ markup pricing in the same way that many wholesalers and retailers do. However, if you plan to manufacture a product that will be sold through wholesalers and various types of retail outlets, it is important for you to know the markups these distributors will likely apply to your product. For instance, in the above example if the manufacturer of the engine treatment thinks $5 is the right retail price, he or she can work backwards and determine that it must be able to sell profitably to the jobbers for $2 to succeed. If that is not possible, perhaps the overall marketing strategy for the product should be reconsidered.

VALUE-BASED PRICING

Instead of using costs, more and more companies are basing their prices on their estimate of the market's perceived value of their market offering. This is particularly true in determining the most appropriate price to charge in a service business. This perceived value is the overall value the customer places on a product or service.

The process begins by analyzing customer needs and value perceptions. This may involve much more than just the basic product or service itself and include other features such as availability, image, delivery, after-sales service, warranty considerations, and other issues. With this approach the price is set by determining the price that people are willing to pay while making sure that you can still cover all your costs.

The way businesses are able to price more effectively on "value" is by differentiating themselves in some way from the competition. This differentiation can be based on any number of factors such as promotion and advertising, availability, or the addition of value-added services. People are prepared to pay more for products produced by name designers such as Bill Blass, Calvin Klein, or Tommy Hilfiger, for example, than they are for similar items produced by others. Similarly a computer store that provides emergency service to customers on a 24/7 basis might be able to charge more for its computers or extended warranty package than an outlet that is open only from 9:00 a.m. to 6:00 p.m. five days a week.

COMPETITION-BASED PRICING

In some situations consumers base their judgements of a product's or service's value on the prices that competitors charge for similar offerings. You might decide to base your price largely on competitors' prices with less attention to your own costs or expected demand. For example, you might decide to charge the same, more, or less than your principal competitors. Some of this may depend on the image you are trying to achieve in the marketplace. If you want to create an image of a bargain or discount operation such as Dollar Store Plus or Ultracuts, for example, then your prices should be consistent with that image. Similarly, if you are trying to establish an image of a luxury operation such as Holt Renfrew or an exclusive hair salon, people may be prepared to pay more and your prices should be consistent with that position. Your target market might not be attracted to a cheaper product or service.

In addition to establishing a base price for your product or service line, you may permit some customers to pay less than this amount in certain circumstances or provide them with a discount. The principal types of discounts are quantity discounts, cash discounts, and seasonal discounts. *Quantity discounts* are commonly provided to customers who buy more than some minimum quantity or dollar value of products or services from you. This discount may be based either on the quantity or value of each individual order (non-cumulative) or on the total value of their purchases over a certain period of time, such as a month (cumulative).

Cash discounts are based on the typical terms of trade within an industry and permit customers to deduct a certain percentage amount from the net cost of their purchases if payment is made in cash at the time of purchase or full payment is made within a specified number of days. Different types of businesses have their own customary cash discounts. For example, a typical discount is expressed as "2/10 net 30." In this situation, a customer who is invoiced on October 1 for an outstanding bill of $2,000 need pay only $1,960 if payment is made before October 10. This is a 2 per cent cash discount for making payment within the 10 days. Otherwise the full face value of the invoice ($2,000) is due by October 31, or 30 days after the invoice date.

Seasonal discounts of 10 per cent, 15 per cent, 20 per cent, or more on your normal base price may be offered to your customers if their purchases are made during your slow or off-season. This gives you a method of moving inventories that you may otherwise have to carry over to the following year or of providing your dealers, agents, and other distributors with some incentive to stock up on your products well in advance of the prime selling season.

Promotional Plans

The budget that you allocate for the promotion of your new venture must be distributed across the following activities:

1. Advertising
2. Personal selling
3. Sales promotion
4. Public relations

Each of these activities differs along a number of important dimensions, such as their cost to reach a member of the target audience and the degree of interaction that can take place with that audience. Table 7.3 summarizes how these activities compare on a number of different criteria.

TABLE **7.3**	A COMPARISON OF VARIOUS PROMOTIONAL ACTIVITIES			
	Advertising	**Sales Promotion**	**Public Relations**	**Personal Selling**
Cost per Audience Member	Low	Low	Very Low	Very High
Focus on Target Markets	Poor to Good	Good	Moderate	Very Good
Ability to Deliver a Complicated Message	Poor to Good	Poor	Poor to Good	Very Good
Interchange with Audience	None	None	Low to Moderate	Very Good
Credibility	Low	Low	High	Moderate to High

Source: Adapted from Gerald E. Hills, "Market Opportunities and Marketing," in William D. Bygrave, *The Portable MBA in Entrepreneurship*, 2nd ed. (Hoboken, NJ: John Wiley & Sons, Inc., 1999). This material is used by permission of John Wiley & Sons Inc.

The distribution of your expenditures should be made to obtain the maximum results for your particular circumstances. It is impossible to generalize about the optimum distribution of your dollars to each of these activities. Different businesses use quite different combinations. Some companies put most of their money into hiring a sales force and their sales promotion program; others put most of their budget into a media advertising campaign. The proper combination for you will depend on a careful study of the relative costs and effectiveness of each of these types of promotion and the unique requirements of your business.

We often think of promotion as being directed strictly toward our final prospective customer, and in fact the largest share of most promotional activity is channelled in that direction. However, promotion can also be used to influence your dealers, your distributors, and other members of your distribution channel. This may persuade them to adopt your offering more rapidly and broaden the breadth of your distribution coverage.

ADVERTISING

Advertising is one of the principal means you have of informing potential customers about the availability and special features of your product or service. Properly conceived messages presented in the appropriate media can greatly stimulate demand for your business and its offerings. A wide range of advertising media is available to carry your messages, of which the most important are those listed in Table 7.4. Which of these media you should choose for your advertising program will depend on the consumers you are trying to reach, the size of the budget you have available, the nature of your product or service, and the particular message you hope to communicate.

SHERMAN'S LAGOON

© Jim Toomey, King Features Syndicate.

| **TABLE 7.4** | **THE MOST COMMON ADVERTISING MEDIA** |

1. **MAGAZINES**
   a. Consumer magazines
   b. Trade or business publications
   c. Farm publications
   d. Professional magazines

2. **NEWSPAPERS**
   a. Daily newspapers
   b. Weekly newspapers
   c. Shopping guides
   d. Special-interest newspapers

3. **TELEVISION**
   a. Local TV
   b. Network TV
   c. Special-interest cable TV

4. **RADIO**
   a. Local stations
   b. Network radio

5. **DIRECTORY**
   a. Yellow Pages
   b. Community
   c. Special-interest

6. **DIRECT MAIL ADVERTISING**
   a. Letters
   b. Catalogues

7. **OUTDOOR ADVERTISING**
   a. Billboards
   b. Posters

8. **TRANSPORTATION ADVERTISING**
   a. Interior car cards
   b. Station posters
   c. Exterior cards on vehicles

9. **POINT-OF-PURCHASE DISPLAYS**

10. **ADVERTISING NOVELTIES AND SPECIALTIES**

11. **THE INTERNET**

ADVERTISING ON THE INTERNET One form of advertising that is rapidly increasing in popularity is the use of the Internet. The World Wide Web is open for business and small firms, particularly retail businesses, are jumping aboard in ever-increasing numbers. Before joining this throng, however, you should consider whether a Web presence will really serve your business interests. If so, you need to formulate a clear strategy or plan, rather than just developing another Web page to join the millions that already exist on the Net.

Martin and Andrea Swinton (Entrepreneurs in Action #30), for example, have used the Web very successfully to develop their antique business in Toronto. They didn't just throw up a Web site and hope for the best. Their initial approach was to experiment by listing a number of items on eBay to test the response of the electronic marketplace to their overall business idea. A positive response there led them to develop their own Web site to demonstrate some of the merchandise they had available in their store, as well as link up to their items for auction on eBay. Their site complements the more traditional advertising and promotion they have done, such as sending out press releases, developing effective window displays, hosting neighbourhood street parties, and appearing on local television, and has enabled them to reach antique collectors all over the world.

If you decide to proceed with implementing a Web site, remember that the Web is not a passive delivery system like most other media but is an active system where the user expects to participate in the experience. Your virtual storefront must be genuinely interesting and the interactivity of the Web should be used to your advantage to attract and hold the ongoing interest of your target consumers.

Opening a successful Web site is not as complicated as it may appear, but it can be expensive to do the job right. You can do it yourself or enlist the expertise of a multimedia production house. Production costs depend entirely on the size and interactivity of your site, running anywhere from $500 on the cheap to $100,000 for a full-blown corporate site. Maintenance costs are minimal but materials and other aspects of the site's operation should be updated regularly, such as once a month.

Once your page is developed, it is important that you get a domain name and file a registration request. You will also want a reliable Web server to house your site. Try to get as many links leading to your site as possible by listing with directories, hotlinks, and so on where consumers will be able to find you quite easily. You might also give some consideration to joining a shopping centre on the Web or a 'Cybermall' such as The Best Cybermall Around (www.bcybermall.com) or Nuthin Better Cybermall (www.nuthinbetter.com)

Entrepreneurs in Action

Take-A-Boo Emporium

Take-A-Boo Emporium is an eclectic antique store in Toronto, Ontario, owned and operated by Martin and Andrea Swinton, a husband-and-wife team.

Martin and Andrea have successfully operated their antique store for four and a half years now, and are justly proud that they're not only still in business, but growing. As Andrea says, "Retail is a tough business. Several retailers have come and gone in our neighbourhood within the time that we've been open.". . .

RISING TO THE CHALLENGE OF BUSINESS PROMOTION

While many people think that finding antiques is the hardest part of Andrea and Martin's business, it isn't. Finding inventory is easy, as Andrea and Martin buy from a network of other antique dealers, do estate sales, and do consignment.

The hardest part of starting Take-A-Boo was finding customers. Like many small businesses, Take-A-Boo Emporium had no advertising budget when it opened (and still doesn't). Andrea and Martin have both spent many hours promoting the business. Rising to the challenge of business promotion means exploring a variety of promotion ideas and constantly searching for new business promotion opportunities.

Andrea regularly sends out press releases to home decor magazines, newspaper editors, and television producers. These efforts have paid off with mentions in local community newspapers. For instance, a June window display that included wedding photos of local residents was featured in a local newspaper.

"It was a nice way to tie in the community and generate awareness at the same time," Andrea says.

Take-A-Boo Emporium's second anniversary street party was another promotion idea that was a big hit with local customers and helped raise the business's profile in the community. The party included bubble-blowing for the kids and free caricatures for customers.

The company's promotion efforts on local television have also been very successful, bringing customers to the store and building credibility. Martin has appeared as an antiques expert on *Toronto Living* and appears regularly on the Rogers Community Television program *Daytime*. When he appeared on *Breakfast Television* on Citytv, two customers who called in to the shop

while Martin was on the air bought items from Take-A-Boo Emporium. Now there's great customer response!

Andrea has also often discussed story ideas with *The Globe and Mail,* the *National Post,* and a variety of home magazines. While nothing national has panned out yet, Andrea is hopeful. "Making the contact is the first part. Generating publicity takes time. The seed planted today will blossom next spring into a story.". . . .

FROM eBAY TO WEB SITE

One phase of Take-A-Boo Emporium's continued growth is its Web site.

Take-A-Boo Emporium sells unique, one-of-a-kind items. Andrea describes their store as "a return to an old-style shopping experience. From Arts & Crafts furniture to Tibetan and Chinese artifacts, to French washstands, Take-A-Boo Emporium has something for everyone.

"However, the chance of a collector of Chinese antiquities, for instance, walking in off the street and buying something is very small. The company needed a way to reach those collectors (and buyers) of such unique items. The Internet was an obvious marketing vehicle for selling antiques."

Instead of immediately throwing up a Web site and hoping for the best, though, Andrea and Martin decided to test the electronic marketplace first, using eBay to test their business idea. At the end of 2000, they posted six items on eBay, and sold four of them.

These positive eBay results led to developing their own Web site, so they could link to their eBay auctions and hopefully generate more business for the retail antique store. "Our Web site," Andrea says, "has made the world our marketplace.". . . .

Andrea and Martin have successfully met the retailing challenge of selling antiques, combining their expertise with ongoing marketing efforts to meet their goals.

"Our business philosophy is to provide antiques at a fair price," Andrea says. "We're in the antique-selling business, not the antique-storing business. We price things to move." (takeaboo.wordpress.com)

PERSONAL SELLING

Personal selling involves direct, face-to-face contact with your prospective customer. A personal sales person's primary function is usually more concerned with obtaining orders than informing your customers about the nature of your offering, as in the case of advertising. Other types of salespeople are principally involved in providing support to different components of your business or filling routine orders rather than more persuasive kinds of selling. The basic steps involved in the selling process are as follows:

1. **Prospecting and qualifying** Identifying prospective customers
2. **The sales approach** The initial contact with the prospective customer
3. **Presentation** The actual sales message presented to a prospective customer
4. **Demonstration** of the capabilities and features or most important characteristics of the product or service being sold
5. **Handling any objections or concerns** the prospective customer may have regarding your offering
6. **Closing the sale** Asking the prospective customer for the order
7. **Post-sales activities** Follow up to determine if customers are satisfied with their purchase and to pursue any additional possible sales

SALES PROMOTION

Sales promotion includes a broad range of promotional activities other than advertising and personal selling that stimulate consumer or dealer interest in your offering. While advertising and personal selling tend to be ongoing activities, most sales promotion is sporadic or irregular in nature. Sales promotion includes activities related to:

1. Free product samples
2. Discount coupons
3. Contests
4. Special deals and premiums
5. Gifts
6. Special exhibits and displays
7. Participation in trade shows
8. Off-price specials
9. Floats in parades and similar events

As you can see, sales promotion consists of a long list of what are typically non-recurring activities. They are intended to make your advertising and personal selling effort more effective and may be very intimately involved with them. For example, your advertising may be used to promote a consumer contest, or certain special deals and incentives may be offered to your salespeople to encourage them to increase their sales to your dealers or final consumers. These activities can be an effective way for businesses with a small budget and some imagination to reach potential sales prospects and develop a considerable volume of business.

PUBLIC RELATIONS

Public relations relates to your business's general communications and relationships with its various interest groups such as your employees, stockholders, the government, and society at large, as well as your customers. It is concerned primarily with such issues as the image of you and your business within the community rather than trying to sell any particular product or service. Publicity releases, product introduction notices, news items, appearances on radio and television, and similar activities are all part of your public relations program.

METHOD OF DISTRIBUTION

Your channel of distribution is the path your product or service takes to market. Physical products typically follow one or more complex paths in getting from the point at which they are produced to the hands of their final consumer. These paths involve the use of several different kinds of wholesalers and retailers who perform a variety of functions that are essential to making this flow of products reasonably efficient. These functions include buying, selling, transporting, storing, financing, and risk-taking.

Distribution channels consist of channel members that are independent firms that facilitate this flow of merchandise. There are many different kinds, and they have quite different names, but the functions they perform may not be that dramatically different. For example, wholesalers are generally classified according to whether they actually take title or ownership of the products they handle (*merchant wholesalers*) or not (*agents*). Merchant wholesalers are further classified as *full-service, limited-function, drop shippers, truck wholesalers*, and *rack jobbers*. Agents are commonly referred to as *brokers, manufacturer's agents, selling agents, food* or *drug brokers*, etc. For small manufacturers, all of these types of wholesalers, alone or in combination, represent possible paths for getting their product to market.

Retailers, too, cover a very broad spectrum, starting with the large department stores that carry a broad product selection and provide an extensive range of customer services; through specialty stores such as electronics, men's clothing, and furniture stores; on down to discount department stores, grocery stores, drug stores, catalogue retailers, and convenience stores. All represent possible members that could be included in your channel of distribution.

In addition to opportunities for marketing your products or services in conjunction with these traditional and conventional distribution channel members, you should not overlook more unconventional possibilities for reaching your potential customers. For example, over the past few years we have seen tremendous growth of various forms of non-store retailing, including:

1. Mail-order catalogues
2. Direct response advertising on television and in newspapers and magazines
3. Direct selling door to door
4. Party plan or home demonstration party selling
5. Direct-mail solicitations
6. Vending machines
7. Trade shows
8. Fairs and exhibitions
9. The Internet

DEVELOPING A PRELIMINARY MARKETING PLAN

Figure 7.10 on page 231 presents a framework to help you prepare a preliminary marketing plan for the product or service idea behind your prospective venture. It will guide you through the process and indicate the kind of information you will need to do a thorough job. It will get you thinking about the size and nature of the market opportunity that may exist for your concept or idea. It will also focus your thoughts on the marketing program you will require to take advantage of the opportunity and achieve your personal goals. The marketing plan is a key part of your feasibility study and your subsequent business plan. Much of the work you do here can be incorporated into your business plan.

Keep in mind, however, that marketing plans are not static documents. Businesses normally have to reformulate their marketing strategy several times over their active life. Economic conditions change, additional competitors come onto the scene, and customer's interests and requirements change. Consequently, the business must plan marketing programs appropriate to each stage in its development. For example, Scott and Bruce identified five stages in the growth of a typical small business: inception, survival, growth, expansion and maturity.[3] The basic features of each stage are different and the objectives of the business's marketing plan will vary as well. Table 7.5 provides an overview of some of the basic features of each stage and how the firm's marketing efforts may need to be modified to address the principal issues typical of each stage.

Take the case of Bobby Pasternak and Geoff Tait, for example (Entrepreneurs in Action #31). They established Quagmire Golf to market their line of bold-patterned, hip and youthful golf fashions to appeal to a younger market than the traditional clothing lines favoured by older golfers. By hitting the road and personally calling on individual golf shops they were able to place their clothing in a number of shops across the country.

---

3. M. Scott and R. Bruce, "Five Stages of Growth in Small Business," *Long-Range Planning*, June 1987, pp. 45–52.

31

Entrepreneurs in Action

It's in the follow-through

It wasn't exactly a five-star steak house, but for Bobby Pasternak and Geoff Tait, dinner with a new friend at a Keg in downtown Toronto at the end of July was proof that any business, even their upstart golf clothing company, has to be prepared for the unexpected.

In this case, Tait and Pasternak, founders of Toronto-based Quagmire Golf, were toasting their sudden good fortune with RBC Canadian Open champion Chez Reavie. In a stroke of luck, Quagmire had inked a sponsorship deal with the PGA Tour rookie at the start of this year. The little-known Reavie made few headlines heading into the Open. But then, wearing Quagmire's hip and youthful golf fashions, he surprised everyone, holding off conservatively attired fairway stars like Mike Weir to win Canada's biggest golf tournament. In an afternoon, Quagmire shed its start-up status and was being heralded as a Next Big Thing. Just as fast, Tait and Pasternak were dealing with a new business problem — how to build on their opportunity so that their fame wouldn't be fleeting.

The first step? Tait and Pasternak hired a U.S. public-relations firm that specializes in golf-related business to spread their story as widely as possible. Next, they went on a hiring spree, expanding their sales staff to 12 reps from one, including six in the U.S. They also leveraged their new-found celebrity to ink important deals, including a test-market program with Golf Town, Canada's largest golf retailer, that's put Quagmire products in 15 of the chain's 39 stores, and a marketing deal with Molson Canada Inc. attached to its Coors Light brand. Finally, they've been hiring staff to handle the routine duties — bookkeeping and answering the phones — that they had previously done themselves.

Tait and Pasternak came up with the idea for Quagmire back in 2004 while working at a youth golf camp in Florida. They noticed that the kids at the camp eschewed traditional clothing lines favoured by older golfers, preferring instead clothes more typically associated with surfer dudes and skater boys. They launched Quagmire the following year, putting together $6,000 they had in savings to hire a designer and register a

company name. Then they hit the road to hustle their bold-patterned fashions. "Everyone said 'no' to us at the start. The banks said 'no.' The golf shops said 'no.'" Pasternak recalls. But the duo nevertheless managed to place their clothing in 12 shops, generating $72,000 in revenue in that first year of business.

Sales have been doubling annually since then. Now, with Reavie as celebrity endorser, they are heading towards the seven figures. "We have credibility and people know us. It is a question of what we can do," Tait says.

These days, that involves acting like the heads of a rapidly maturing company. Tait and Pasternak, for instance, no longer travel from golf club to golf club to pitch their clothing to pro shops. Regional sales reps are doing that job so that Quagmire's founders — who continue to present themselves as the face of the company — can focus on national retail, attend major trade shows and develop the strategic aspects of the business. "We need to take off 20 hats and only wear two. We need to oversee the company, and not run its operations," Tait says. "We can't be plugging in orders at 2 o'clock in the morning. It is about taking Quagmire to where we know it can go."
(www.quagmiregolf.com)

At the beginning of 2008 they had the good fortune of signing little-known PGA tour rookie Chez Reavie to a sponsorship deal to wear their clothes. Later that season Chez won Canada's biggest golf tournament, the RBC Canadian Open and things changed overnight for Quagmire. All of a sudden they were in the news and had to come up with a new marketing plan to take advantage of the situation. Instead of calling on golf pro shops

TABLE 7.5	A MODEL FOR SMALL BUSINESS GROWTH				
	Stage 1 **Inception**	**Stage 2** **Survival**	**Stage 3** **Growth**	**Stage 4** **Expansion**	**Stage 5** **Maturity**
Key Issue	Obtaining customers	Increasing competition	Expansion into new products or markets	Greater external emphasis	Finding growth opportunities
Product and Market Research	None	Little	Some new product development	New product development, market research	Production innovation
Product Market	Single basic product line	Single product line and market but greater scale	Broader but limited product line, single market	Extended range of products, broader markets	Contained product lines, multiple markets
Emphasis of Marketing Plan	Limited channels of distribution, cost-plus pricing, heavy sales promotion	Reach expanding markets, broader channels of distribution	Emphasis on cost-efficiency, penetration pricing, build market awareness and distribution	Greater focus on customer needs and adapting the marketing plan (including promotion) to meet those needs	Major investment in the marketing effort, phase out weak products, cut prices, focus on profitable niches

Source: M. Scott and R. Bruce, "Five Stage of Growth in Small Business," *Long-Range Planning*, June 1987, pp. 45–52.

themselves, they hired a number of regional sales reps to do the job. They also contacted a professional public-relations firm to spread the word about their new line of clothes and were able to sign promotional deals with national firms like Golf Town and Molson Canada to broaden their distribution and create more market awareness. These moves seen to be paying off as sales now approach seven figures and the game has changed for the boys as the company becomes more mature.

MANAGING THE SUPPLY SITUATION

A key factor in the success of any new venture is some assurance of continuing access to critical supplies of raw material and component parts at reasonable prices. Many new businesses have floundered due to changing supply situations that impacted their ability to provide products of acceptable quality or that drastically increased their costs of production. These conditions are seldom correctable and tend to be terminal for the smaller firm. It is critical that you investigate the range of possible sources for these key elements well in advance of starting your venture.

Assessing your supply situation requires an understanding of the manufacturing cycle for your product or service and an in-depth appreciation of the market for equipment, materials, and parts. One strategy being followed by more and more smaller firms is to subcontract their production requirements instead of making their own products. This strategy has a number of significant advantages:

- Your business can use the subcontractor's money instead of having to raise the funds to build your own production facilities.
- You can take advantage of the expertise and technical knowledge possessed by the subcontractor without having to develop it yourself.

- Using a subcontractor may enable you to bring your business on stream more rapidly. There is no need to delay while your production facilities are being built and broken in.

- You can concentrate your time on developing a market for your products and running your business rather than on trying to produce a satisfactory product.

- You may be able to benefit from the reputation and credibility of the subcontractor; having your products produced by a firm with an established reputation will rub off on your business.

- A reliable subcontractor can also keep you up to date with technical advances in that field so that your products don't become obsolete.

- Perhaps the most important advantage of using a subcontractor is that it establishes your costs of production in advance, reducing the uncertainty and unpredictability of setting up your own facilities. A firm, fixed-price contract from a reliable subcontractor nails down one of your most important costs of doing business and facilitates your entire planning process.

As you can see, there are a number of strong advantages to subcontracting certain aspects of your operations, but that does not necessarily mean this strategy should be employed in all situations. There are a number of disadvantages that should be considered as well:

- The cost of having a job done by a subcontractor may not be as low as if you did the work yourself. Subcontractors may have antiquated equipment; high-cost, unionized labour; or other problems to deal with that make their operations very expensive. Subcontractors also factor in some margin of profit for themselves into a job. The end result may be a total production cost that would make it very difficult for you to successfully compete.

- Your business may be jeopardized if the subcontractor fails to meet commitments to you or divulges critical trade secrets about your product or process.

In any case, sometimes a suitable subcontractor is just not available. If you want your product produced, you may have no alternative but to do it yourself.

Regardless of the approach you decide to take, to cover your supply situation there are a number of key factors that have to be considered. These include:

- Delivered cost (total cost including transportation, etc.)
- Quality
- Delivery schedules
- Service level

All have to be at an acceptable level for you to have confidence that your supply situation is under reasonable control.

FYI FOR YOUR INFORMATION

The following are some helpful Web sites for developing your marketing plan:

Guidelines for Taking Your Idea to Market A case study of the approach used by chip maker Nazomi Communications to bring their new Java accelerator chip successfully from conception to launch. (www.design-reuse.com/articles/3073/guidelines-for-taking-your-idea-to-market.html)

About: Small Business: Canada A series of articles dealing with marketing strategies relating to a number of aspects of your marketing program such as advertising, networking, business promotion, Internet marketing, market research, trade shows, personal selling and marketing plans. (sbinfocanada.about.com/od/marketing/Marketing.htm)

continued

For your information — *Continued*

Canadian Business Online Articles on a variety of marketing-related issues and topics from the archives of Canadian Business and PROFIT magazines. (www.canadianbusiness.com/entrepreneur/sales_marketing/index.jsp)

Market Research A guide to help you learn the basics of market research for your business. (www.canadabusiness.ca/eng/88/)

The Business Link — Where to Find the Market Information You Need A listing of some of the key market research resources you need to help identify your target market, assess your competition and develop your marketing plan. (www.canadabusiness.ab.ca/index.php/marketing/454-market-research-where-to-find-the-market-information-you-need)

Advertising A series of guides to help you plan your advertising budget, select media, prepare ads, and determine the results of your advertising expenditures. (www.canadabusiness.ca/eng/search/results/search&keywords=Advertising/)

Marketing Basic A Web-based program sponsored by Canada Business that discusses such issues as identifying your customer, finding the right product, determining your price, forecasting your sales, and advertising and promotion. (www.canadabusiness.ca/eng/guide/full/1467/)

e-Business Factsheets: Marketing A series of guides for conducting e-business dealing with topics such as marketing your Web site, marketing on the Internet, marketing with newsgroups, and viral and e-Mail marketing. (www.ic.gc.ca/eic/site/ee-ef.nsf/eng/ee00750.html)

Business Information by Industrial Sector A comprehensive overview of Canadian business information by industry sector. (www.ic.gc.ca/eic/site/ic1.nsf/eng/h_00066.html)

Canadian Statistics A business resource of online statistics for, and publications about various business sectors, plus other information. (www.statcan.gc.ca/start-debut-eng.html)

Canadian Economic and Market Research/Statistics A statistical overview of current Canadian economic conditions and a number of industry and trade-related statistics. (www.ic.gc.ca/eic/site/ic1.nsf/eng/h_00072.html?OpenDocument&)

Corporate Information Canada Information on world securities markets, including company profiles from 55 countries worldwide. (corporateinformation.com)

Home-Based Business Home business ideas, home business opportunities, home business resources, advice for starting a home business or to help you work at home — everything you need to run a successful home-based business. (sbinfocanada.about.com/od/homebusiness/Home_Business.htm)

Start and Run Your Own Business The inspiration and information you can use to start and run a profitable small and home-based business. (www.lifemedia.ca/homebiz)

Exporting Everything you need to know to take advantage of international trade and compete in a global marketplace with your goods and services. (www.canadabusiness.ca/eng/105/165/)

The Step-By-Step Guide to Exporting The *Step-by-Step Guide to Exporting* is intended to help you learn about the world marketplace and how your company can do business there. (www.tradecommissioner.gc.ca/eng/StepENGPDF.pdf)

Customized Market Research Reports for International Trade Over 600 detailed industry sector analysis reports for countries all over the world. (www.tradecommissioner.gc.ca/eng/market-report-access.jsp)

| TABLE **7.6** | OTHER PUBLISHED SOURCES OF MARKET INFORMATION |

GENERAL

Gale Directory of Publications and Broadcast Media
    Gale Research, Inc.
    (www.gale.com)
The Standard Periodical Directory
    Oxbridge Communications Inc.
    (www.oxbridge.com)

Ulrich's Periodicals Directory
    Serials Solutions
    (www.ulrichsweb.com)

Indexes to books and magazine articles on a wide variety of business, industrial, and economic topics:

Bibliographic Index: A Cumulative
Bibliography of Bibliographies
    H.W. Wilson Co.
    (www.hwwilson.com/sales/printindexes.com)

Business Periodicals Index
    H.W. Wilson Co.
    (www.hwwilson.com/sales/printindexes.com)

Canadian Business and Current Affairs
    ProQuest LLC
    (www.proquest.com/en-US/catalogs/
    databases/detail/cbca.shtml)

A detailed listing of source books, periodicals, directories, handbooks, and other sources of information on a variety of business topics:

Encyclopedia of Business Information Sources
    Thomson Gale
    (www.gale.com)

Directories of business-oriented databases:

Gale Directory of Databases
    Thomson Gale
    (www.gale.com)

INDUSTRY AND MARKET INFORMATION

Data on income, population, expenditures, etc., by major market area prepared annually:

Survey of Buying Power
    Nielsen Claritas
    (www.surveyofbuyingpower.com/sbponline/about-us/index.jsp)

Information on population size and growth, income, expenditures, prices, and similar data by market area:

Market Research Handbook
    Statistics Canada
    (www.statcan.gc.ca/bsolc/olc-cel/olc-cel?lang=eng&catno=63-224X)

COMPANY INFORMATION

Detailed information on most major corporations:

FP Infomart
    CanWest Interactive Inc.
    (www.fpinfomart.ca)

Moody's Manuals and Investors Services
    Moody's Investor Services
    (www.moodys.com)

Globeinvestor.com
    CTV Globemedia Publishing Inc.
    (www.globeinvestor.com)

continued

Table 7.6 — continued

Listings of Canadian manufacturers by location and product category:

Fraser's Canadian Industrial Directory
(www.frasers.com/public/home.jsf#)

Scott's Directories
- *Ontario Manufacturers Directory*
- *Quebec Industrial Directory*
- *Greater Toronto Business Directory*
- *Greater Montreal and Laval Business Directory*
- *Atlantic Industrial Directory*
- *Western Industrial Directory*

(www.scottsdirectories.com/)

MARKETING INFORMATION

Listings of rates and other information on radio, television, consumer magazines, trade magazines, direct mail, and newspapers:

Canadian Advertising Rates & Data (CARD)
Rogers Media Publishing
(www.cardmedia.com)

SRDS Media Solutions — U.S. Publications
(www.srds.com)
SRDS Publications:
- *Canadian Advertising Rates & Data*
- *Business Media Advertising Source*
- *Consumer Media Advertising Source*
- *Newspaper Advertising Source*
- *Out-of-Home Advertising Source*
- *Direct Marketing List Source*
- *TV & Cable Source*
- *Radio Advertising Source*
- *Interactive Advertising Source*
- *International Media Guides*

A listing of agents and firms representing manufacturers of all types:

Manufacturer's Agents National Association Directory of Members
Manufacturer's Agents National Association
(www.manaonline.org)

Comprehensive listings of U.S. and Canadian meetings, conventions, trade shows, and expositions:

Meetings Canada
Rogers Media Inc.
(www.meetingscanada.com/public/home.jsf)

Trade Shows Worldwide
Thomson Gale
(www.gale.com)

A comprehensive listing of mail-order firms:

Directory of Mail-order Catalogs
Grey House Publishing
(www.greyhouse.com)

A comprehensive listing of all trade and professional associations in Canada:

Associations Canada
Grey House Publishing
(www.greyhouse.com)

| FIGURE **7.2** | DEVELOPING A MARKET OR CUSTOMER PROFILE |

1. Define your target customers in terms of geography, demographic characteristics, or other factors.

2. How many of these target customers are in your trading or relevant market area?

3. What are the principal features and benefits that these customers consider in the purchase of a product/service like yours?

4. What psychographic or sociological factors are likely to distinguish your target customers and be important in the purchase of a product/service like yours?

5. Why will they buy your product rather than your competitors'?

| FIGURE 7.3 | OUTLINE FOR A CUSTOMER SURVEY |

Name of Customer _____

1. NATURE OF THE CUSTOMER'S BUSINESS OR ROLE

_____
_____
_____

2. CUSTOMER'S REACTION TO YOUR PRODUCT OR SERVICE

a. What advantages/benefits does the customer see?

_____
_____
_____

b. What disadvantages does the customer see?

_____
_____
_____

c. What questions does the customer raise?

_____
_____
_____

3. SPECIFIC NEEDS AND USES

What needs and uses does the customer have for a product/service such as yours?

_____
_____
_____

4. SELLING PRICE, SERVICE, AND SUPPORT

a. What do you believe would be an acceptable selling price?

_____
_____

b. What level of service and support would the customer expect?

_____
_____
_____

c. What other terms would the customer expect?

_____
_____
_____

5. CURRENT PURCHASING PRACTICES

Where does the customer currently buy this type of product or service (retailer, wholesaler, direct mail, broker, etc.)?

_____
_____
_____

6. NAME OF COMPETITIVE FIRMS
What competing firms' products and services is the customer currently using?

_____
_____
_____

| **FIGURE 7.4** | **FORM FOR ESTIMATING MARKET SIZE** |

ESTIMATED TOTAL MARKET SIZE

1. DESCRIPTION OF PRINCIPAL MARKET

_____
_____

	Per Cent Change			
	201A–201B	201B–201C	201C–201D	201D–201E
Estimated total sales in units _____	_____	_____	_____	_____
Estimated total sales in $000 _____	_____	_____	_____	_____

2. OVERVIEW OF MAJOR SEGMENTS

a.   Description of segment: _____

	Per Cent Change			
	201A–201B	201B–201C	201C–201D	201D–201E
Estimated sales in units _____	_____	_____	_____	_____
Estimated sales in $000 _____	_____	_____	_____	_____

b.   Description of segment: _____

	Per Cent Change			
	201A–201B	201B–201C	201C–201D	201D–201E
Estimated sales in units _____	_____	_____	_____	_____
Estimated sales in $000 _____	_____	_____	_____	_____

| **FIGURE 7.5** | **FORM FOR ANALYZING YOUR COMPETITORS** |

Name of Competitor _____   **Estimated Sales $** _____

1. MARKET POSITION

a.   What is their market share? _____

b.   Have their sales been growing? Stable? Declining? _____

c.   How successful has the company been overall? _____
_____

2. WHAT ARE THEIR MAJOR STRENGTHS AND WEAKNESSES?

a.   What are their major strengths? _____
_____

continued

Form For Analyzing Your Competitors — continued

    b.   What are their major weaknesses? _____

_____

_____

3. PRODUCT OR SERVICE

    a.   How does the company's product or service differ from others available in the marketplace?

_____

_____

    b.   Do they offer a broad or narrow product line? _____

_____

    c.   What characteristics do they emphasize? _____

_____

4. PRICE

    a.   What is their average selling price? _____

    b.   What is their estimated gross margin? _____

    c.   What type of discounts do they offer? _____

    d.   Do they emphasize a low or high selling price? _____

5. PROMOTION

    a.   How much do they spend on advertising and trade promotion? _____

_____

    b.   How well-known is their product (brand recognition)? _____

    c.   In what media do they advertise? _____

_____

    d.   What other types of promotion do they use? _____

_____

    e.   How many salespeople do they have? _____

6. DISTRIBUTION/LOCATION

    a.   What type of distributors do they use (brokers, own sales force, manufacturer's agents, or other)?

_____

_____

_____

    b.   Where are they located? _____

    c.   Is location an important factor in this industry? _____

7. OVERALL MARKETING STRATEGY

    a.   Does the company try to cater to any particular segment in the market? _____

_____

    b.   Does the company offer any unique product or service features that make it different from its competitors?

_____

_____

    c.   Does it appear to be competing primarily on the basis of quality or price? _____

_____

    d.   What do you think is the principal factor that accounts for the success of this firm? _____

_____

_____

FIGURE **7.6**	FORM FOR ANALYZING YOUR COMPETITORS

Factor	Your Business	Competitor 1	Competitor 2	Competitor 3
Market Position 1. What is their current market share? 2. Has it been growing or declining? To what extent?				
Strengths 3. What are their major strengths?				
Weaknesses 4. What are their principal weaknesses?				
Target Market 5. Who appears to be their principal target market?				
Product or Service 6. How does the company's product or service differ from others? 7. Can the difference be readily replicated?				
Price 8. What is their average selling price? 9. What are their margins?				
Promotion 10. How many salespeople do they have? 11. How much do they spend on advertising and promotion? 12. Identify the primary media they use.				
Distribution 13. What type of distribution system do they utilize to reach their market? 14. Is distribution an important part of their overall strategy?				
Marketing Strategy 15. How would you summarize their overall marketing strategy?				

FIGURE 7.7 **EXAMPLE OF A BASIC SWOT MATRIX**

SWOT Matrix	Opportunities	Threats
	1.	1.
	2.	2.
	3.	3.
Strengths	**O/S Matches**	**T/S Matches**
1.	O1 and S2	T2 and S2
2.	O3 and S3	T2 and S1
3.		
Weaknesses	**O/W Matches**	**T/W Matches**
1.	O1 and W1	None
2.		
3.		

FIGURE 7.8　　**DEVELOPING A SALES FORECAST**

1. Provide a summary overview of typical individuals, companies, and organizations that are likely prospects for your product/service offering as described in the market profile you prepared in Figure 7.2 (p. 223). Ask yourself such questions as: How old would these customers be? Where do they live? What types of activities would they participate in? What primary benefits are they looking for in my product or service? Think of as many relevant questions as possible.

_____
_____
_____
_____
_____

2. How many of the prospective customers you have described as good prospects are in your trading area?

_____
_____
_____

3. Describe how you feel these prospective customers would go about deciding whether to purchase your product/service rather than a competitor's offering. Would these potential customers be principally concerned with price, convenience, quality, or some other factor?

_____
_____
_____
_____

4. How often would prospective buyers purchase your product or service? Daily? Weekly? Monthly? Other? Where would they look for it or expect to buy it? What kind of seasonal or other patterns are likely to influence sales? How will holidays or other special events affect sales patterns within a month? A year?

_____
_____
_____
_____

5. How much (in dollars and/or units) would a typical customer purchase on each buying occasion?

   _____

   _____

6. How would your customers likely hear about your product/service offering? Through newspapers? TV or radio advertisements? Word of mouth? Salespeople? Intermediaries? Other?

   _____

   _____

   _____

7. From the above information, estimate your expected annual sales in terms of *dollars* and/or *number of units* by month for the first three years of operation of your business.

	1st Year	2nd Year	3rd Year
January	_____	_____	_____
February	_____	_____	_____
March	_____	_____	_____
April	_____	_____	_____
May	_____	_____	_____
June	_____	_____	_____
July	_____	_____	_____
August	_____	_____	_____
September	_____	_____	_____
October	_____	_____	_____
November	_____	_____	_____
December	_____	_____	_____

FIGURE 7.9   RATING FORM FOR SELECTING A RETAIL LOCATION

FACTOR A: PRIMARY ACCEPTANCE OR REJECTION FACTORS
(RATE YES OR NO)

	Location No.			
	1	2	3	4
1. Will municipal zoning allow the proposed business?	____	____	____	____
2. Does this site meet the minimum operating needs of the proposed business?	____	____	____	____
3. Do existing buildings meet minimum initial needs?	____	____	____	____
4. Is the rent for this location within your proposed operating budget?	____	____	____	____
5. Is the rent for this location, with or without buildings, reasonable?	____	____	____	____

One "No" answer may be sufficient reason not to proceed with further investigation unless some modification can be achieved.

FACTOR B: SITE EVALUATION
(USE PERCENTAGE SCALE 0 TO 100)

	Location No.			
	1	2	3	4
6. How does this location compare with the best possible location available?	____	____	____	____
7. What rating would you give the present buildings on the site?	____	____	____	____

continued

Rating Form For Selecting A Retail Location — continued

	Location No.			
	1	2	3	4
8. How would you rate the overall environment of this location with the best environment existing within your trading area?	____	____	____	____
9. How would you rate the availability of parking for vehicles?	____	____	____	____
10. How would you rate the nature and quantity of combined foot and vehicle traffic passing your location?	____	____	____	____
11. What is the improvement potential of this location?	____	____	____	____
Total	____	____	____	____

FACTOR C: TREND ANALYSIS
(COMPARE THE ANSWER FOR EACH LOCATION AND RANK EACH BY NUMBER FROM AMONG THOSE REVIEWED — i.e., 1st, 2nd, 3rd, or 4th)

	Location No.			
	1	2	3	4
12. Has the location shown improvement through the years?	____	____	____	____
13. Is the owner and/or landlord progressive and co-operative?	____	____	____	____
14. What major patterns of change are affecting this location?	____	____	____	____
a. Streets: Speed limits, paving	____	____	____	____
b. Shopping centres	____	____	____	____
c. Zoning	____	____	____	____
d. Financial investment	____	____	____	____
e. Dynamic leadership and action	____	____	____	____
f. Type of shopper or other potential customer	____	____	____	____
15. What businesses have occupied this location over the past 10 years?	____	____	____	____
16. Have the businesses identified in question 15 (above) been successful?	____	____	____	____
17. Why is this location available now?	____	____	____	____
18. Are a number of other suitable locations available?	____	____	____	____

FACTOR D: PRICE–VALUE DETERMINATION

	Location No.			
	1	2	3	4
19. What is the asking rent for each location?	____	____	____	____
20. What is the estimated cost of required leasehold improvements?	____	____	____	____
21. What numerical total for each site is developed for questions 6 through 11?	____	____	____	____
22. Is there a "No" answer to any of questions 1 through 5?	____	____	____	____
23. Do the answers to questions 12 through 18 develop a pattern that is:				
a. Highly favourable?	____	____	____	____
b. Average?	____	____	____	____
c. Fair?	____	____	____	____
d. Questionable?	____	____	____	____
e. Not acceptable?	____	____	____	____

Rank each location according to numerical totals and preferences as to subjective Factors C and D.

Adapted from M. Archer and J. White, *Starting and Managing Your Own Small Business* (Toronto: Macmillan Company of Canada, 1978), 38–40. Reproduced by permission.

FIGURE 7.10

A FRAMEWORK FOR DEVELOPING A PRELIMINARY MARKETING PLAN

1. DEFINE YOUR GOALS

You need to start this process by defining two sets of goals:

- Personal goals
- Business goals

a. Your personal goals need to be defined first. You want to be certain that the business you are considering is compatible with the attainment of your personal goals.

Your Personal Goals

How much money do you want, or need, to earn? _____

_____

_____

What sort of lifestyle is desirable for you and your family? _____

_____

_____

How will your business reflect you and your values? _____

_____

_____

What are your risk parameters? What is your tolerance for risk? _____

_____

_____

What do you want to achieve in five years? _____

_____

_____

b. Your business goals need to be defined next. These are general statements of business intentions that you are aiming to accomplish, results that your business is committed to achieving over time. You can define your business goals by using such terms as "becoming the leading firm in this industry within this market" or "being the lowest cost or most efficient or most widely recognized business of its type within this area." Goals may also be more modestly defined such as to build "a business large enough to provide an income stream that will enable me to quit my current job."

Your Business Goals

How big do you want your business to be? _____

_____

_____

_____

What general goals would you like your business to achieve? _____

_____

_____

_____

2. WHAT DO YOU PLAN TO SELL?

You have given some thought to the concept or idea you would like to investigate as a prospective business opportunity. Now you need to translate that notion into a clear definition of your business and a description of the broad range of products and services you plan to offer. If you are able to explain clearly and succinctly what products or services you plan to sell, to whom, and why you think they will buy from you, you are well

continued

on the way to developing an effective marketing plan. Generally describe your proposed product/service offerings and whom you see as being your principal target market for each offering or your whole line. If you have many products/services, try to bundle them together into no more than five categories. You can always expand the list later — but for now, keep it simple.

Product/Service Offering

	Product/Service	*Primary Target Markets*
1.	_____	_____
2.	_____	_____
3.	_____	_____
4.	_____	_____
5.	_____	_____

3. **ESTABLISH PRELIMINARY SALES ESTIMATES**

   For each of the products/services in your line, estimate what you feel your sales could be if everything went perfectly after you started up your business. What would your sales be if everything went wrong? What figure in between these two estimates do you think represents the most likely case?

Preliminary Sales Estimates

Sales Goals for Each Product/Service

	Worst Case	*Most Likely Case*	*Best Case*
1.	$ _____	$ _____	$ _____
2.	$ _____	$ _____	$ _____
3.	$ _____	$ _____	$ _____
4.	$ _____	$ _____	$ _____
5.	$ _____	$ _____	$ _____

Comments:

_____

_____

_____

_____

_____

4. **ESTIMATE TOTAL MARKET SIZE AND TRENDS**

   A major component of market opportunity analysis and developing a marketing plan is determining the overall volume of unit sales, or dollar revenue, that may flow from a market. When analyzing market potential and size, it is important to refer only to that portion of the market you will be serving. For example, if you are planning to deal only with customers in Edmonton, or part of Edmonton, it does not make sense to include Calgary, Regina, or Toronto in your assessment of market size. On the other hand, if you hope to sell your product regionally or nationally, then those are the relevant market areas to be considered.

   In addition to this broad analysis, you might also investigate whether, within this major market area, there are groups of potential buyers with different preferences, requirements, or purchasing practices. This process of breaking down large heterogeneous markets into more homogeneous groups is known as *market segmentation*, as discussed in this Stage.

   Most markets can be segmented on the basis of a number of variables:

   - geographic location (such as a part of a city or town, county, province, region, or country)
   - demographic characteristics (such as age, gender, income, occupation, marital status, race, religion, or education). Institutional, industrial, and government markets can be classified on the basis of their Standard Industrial Classification category, their total purchases or sales, number of employees, or the nature of their organizational activity
   - a variety of sociological factors (such as lifestyle, user status, usage rate, timing and means of purchasing, and/or reasons for buying products similar to yours)

You can use the following templates to estimate approximate total market size (past, present, and future) and expected trends in terms of sales for your product or service type. You should do this for both the principal market and the market segments that may pertain to your product/service offering.

To obtain the information needed to complete this worksheet, there are a number of sources you may wish to consult. These have been mentioned earlier in this Stage, but include:

- trade publications, trade shows, and the trade associations for the industry in which your business will compete
- your local Chamber of Commerce or municipal office
- any local or regional economic development corporations or school board offices
- business resource centres and other agencies of your provincial government
- your Canada Business Services Centre of Industry Canada
- downtown business associations
- advertising agencies, local newspapers, radio and television stations
- your future competitors and prospective customers
- similar businesses in other locations
- prospective suppliers and their sales representatives
- commercial suppliers of industry studies and market research reports
- the Internet

Estimated Market Size — Principal Market

Description of Principal Market

_____

_____

_____

_____

_____

	Two Years Ago	Last Year	This Year	Next Year	Two Years From Now
Sales in units	_____	_____	_____	_____	_____
Sales in $000	_____	_____	_____	_____	_____

Overview of Market Segments

Describe each major segment and the principal product or service to be offered. Then, complete market size estimates for each segment.

	Description of Segment	Principal Product/ Service Benefits
1.	_____	_____
2.	_____	_____
3.	_____	_____
4.	_____	_____
5.	_____	_____

	Two Years Ago	Last Year	This Year	Next Year	Two Years From Now
Sales in units	_____	_____	_____	_____	_____
Sales in $000	_____	_____	_____	_____	_____

	Description of Segment	Principal Product/ Service Benefits
1.	_____	_____
2.	_____	_____

continued

A Framework For Developing A Preliminary Marketing Plan — continued

3. _____   _____
4. _____   _____
5. _____   _____

	Two Years Ago	Last Year	This Year	Next Year	Two Years From Now
Sales in units	_____	_____	_____	_____	_____
Sales in $000	_____	_____	_____	_____	_____

Description of Segment	Principal Product/ Service Benefits
1. _____	_____
2. _____	_____
3. _____	_____
4. _____	_____
5. _____	_____

	Two Years Ago	Last Year	This Year	Next Year	Two Years From Now
Sales in units	_____	_____	_____	_____	_____
Sales in $000	_____	_____	_____	_____	_____

Description of Segment	Principal Product/ Service Benefits
1. _____	_____
2. _____	_____
3. _____	_____
4. _____	_____
5. _____	_____

	Two Years Ago	Last Year	This Year	Next Year	Two Years From Now
Sales in units	_____	_____	_____	_____	_____
Sales in $000	_____	_____	_____	_____	_____

5. ANALYZE YOUR COMPETITION

Unless your product is a "new to the world" innovation, it will have to compete with other products and services that perform a similar function. You have probably identified a number of other firms that offer products and services designed to meet the same customer need as yours. It is important you have a thorough understanding of each of these firms and the way it conducts its business. To obtain this perspective, fill in a copy of this worksheet for each major competitor you have identified. This will enable you to get a better understanding of the sales and market share you might achieve, and the nature of the marketing program you could employ, to obtain a comparative advantage.

These competitors will likely not co-operate in providing you with this information directly. You may have to rely on articles in newspapers and the trade press, corporate annual reports, trade association reports and publications, and your own personal investigation to get all the information you require.

Form for Analyzing Your Competitors

Competitor Name: _____

Estimated Market Share (%): _____

1. PRODUCT OR SERVICE

     a. How does the company's product or service   _____

        differ from other products and services in   _____

        the marketplace?   _____

b. Does it offer a broad or narrow product line? _____

c. Does it emphasize quality? _____

2. *PRICE*

   a. What is its average selling price? _____

   b. What is its profit margin? _____

   c. What type of discounts does it offer? _____

   d. Does it emphasize a low selling price? _____

3. *PROMOTION*

   a. How much does it spend on advertising and trade promotion? _____

   b. How well known is it (brand recognition)? _____

   c. Through which media does it advertise? _____

   d. What other types of promotion does it use? _____

   e. How many salespeople does it have? _____

4. *DISTRIBUTION LOCATION*

   a. What type of distribution intermediaries does it use (brokers, company sales force, direct to wholesaler, etc.)? _____

   b. Where is it located? _____

   c. Is location very important in this industry? _____

5. *MARKETING STRATEGY*

   a. Does the company cater to any particular segment of the market? _____

   b. Does the company offer some unique product or service that makes it different from other competitors? _____

   c. Does it offer a particularly low price? _____

   d. What is the principal factor that accounts for the success of this firm? _____

6. *MARKET POSITION*

   a. What is its market share? _____

   b. Have its sales been growing? Stable? Declining? _____

   c. How successful is it? _____

7. *MAJOR STRENGTHS AND WEAKNESSES*

   a. What are its major strengths? _____

   b. What are its major weaknesses? _____

6. **DEFINE A BUDGET**

Before spelling out the details of your tentative marketing program, you need to have some idea of the resources needed to implement it. This entails developing some sort of budget indicating what you feel is required to achieve your sales and profit goals, and how these expenditures should be distributed across the range of marketing activities. This worksheet provides a starting point for you to estimate the marketing expenditures you will have to make during your first year to get your business successfully off the ground.

continued

A Framework For Developing A Preliminary Marketing Plan — continued

This is not an exhaustive list. Use it as a starting point. Your company will use some of these categories plus others peculiar to your marketing needs.

Tentative Marketing Budget

1. Selling (direct costs)

    Sales salaries and commissions: $ _____

    Travel & entertainment $ _____

2. Selling (indirect costs)

    Training $ _____

    Marketing research $ _____

    Subscriptions and dues $ _____

3. Advertising $ _____

4. Sales promotion other than advertising $ _____

5. Public relations $ _____

6. Marketing administration $ _____

7. Other items $ _____

7. **FLESH OUT YOUR MARKETING PROGRAM**

    You are now in a position to bring together everything you have learned about the total market potential for your product or service, customer attitudes toward your offering, and the nature of the competitive environment you will be facing. The goal is to put down on paper a preliminary marketing strategy, or plan, for your new venture concept. This involves making decisions regarding what you feel is an appropriate marketing mix for your business. The principal ingredients that must be blended together to form your overall strategy can be grouped together under the headings of:

    - Product or service offering
    - Pricing program
    - Promotional plans
    - Distribution strategy

    This worksheet provides an outline to help you to lay out your marketing plans and programs.

Outline for a Preliminary Marketing Plan

YOUR CONCEPT

Describe the principal concept underlying your product or service idea.

_____
_____
_____
_____
_____

What is unique or distinctive about your idea? How does it differ from similar concepts already being employed in the marketplace?

_____
_____
_____
_____
_____

Who will be the primary customers for your concept and what are the principal benefits your concept will deliver to them?

_____
_____

How innovative is your concept? How would you categorize it along the continuum from "copycatting" to being an entirely new invention?

_____

_____

_____

_____

_____

Is your idea technically feasible? Have you built a working model or prototype? Will you have to obtain Canadian Standards Association (CSA) approval or other permissions before the concept can be marketed?

_____

_____

_____

_____

_____

PRODUCTS AND SERVICES

What products or services will you sell? Be specific.

_____

_____

_____

_____

_____

What additional customer services (delivery, repair, warranties, etc.) will you offer?

_____

_____

_____

_____

_____

What is unique about your total product or service offering?

_____

_____

_____

_____

_____

CUSTOMERS

Who are your target customers?

_____

_____

_____

continued

A Framework For Developing A Preliminary Marketing Plan — continued

_____

_____

How many target customers are in your trading area?

_____

_____

_____

_____

_____

Why will they buy your product?

_____

_____

_____

_____

_____

COMPETITION

Who are your principal competitors? What is their market position? Have their sales been growing? Stable? Declining?

_____

_____

_____

_____

_____

How does your concept differ from each of these other products or services?

_____

_____

_____

_____

_____

LOCATION

What location have you selected for your business?

_____

_____

_____

_____

_____

Why did you choose that location?

_____

_____

_____

_____

_____

PRICING

Describe your pricing strategy.

_____
_____
_____
_____
_____

Complete the following table of markups from manufacturer to final customer:

Cost to manufacture	(A)	_____
Manufacturer's markup	(B)	_____
Manufacturer's selling price	(C = A + B)	_____
Agent's commission (if applicable)	(D)	_____
Wholesaler's cost	(E = C + D)	_____
Wholesaler's markup	(F)	_____
Wholesaler's selling price	(G = E + F)	_____
Retailer's markup	(H)	_____
Retailer's selling price	(I = G + H)	_____

How do your planned price levels compare to your competitors'?

_____
_____
_____
_____
_____

PROMOTION

What will be your primary promotional message to potential customers?

_____
_____
_____
_____

What will be your promotion budget?

_____
_____
_____
_____

What media will you use for your advertising program?

_____
_____
_____
_____
_____

continued

A Framework For Developing A Preliminary Marketing Plan — continued

Will you have a co-operative advertising program? Describe it.

_____

_____

_____

_____

_____

Describe your trade promotion program.

_____

_____

_____

_____

Describe any publicity, public relations, or sales promotion program you will have.

_____

_____

_____

_____

_____

DISTRIBUTION

How do you plan to distribute your product? Direct to the consumer? Through traditional distribution channels? Through specialty channels such as exhibitions, mail order, or trade shows?

_____

_____

_____

_____

Will you employ your own sales force or rely on the services of agents or brokers? How many?

_____

_____

_____

_____

_____

Once you have completed this series of worksheets, you will have a better understanding of the likely market opportunity for your concept or idea, and you will have thought through the process of determining how you feel it can be most effectively marketed. This is an essential step in deciding whether the concept really does represent a worthwhile opportunity that ought to be aggressively pursued or whether it should be abandoned. This is also a key part of your business plan. Most of this information represents the foundation on which the business plan is built and can be directly transferred to that document.

Conducting a Feasibility Study

Part 2: Cost and Profitability Assessment

In addition to determining the size and nature of the market for your new venture idea, it is also important to consider the financial components of your business. The costs associated with operating your business may include labour, materials, rent, machinery, and so on. Collecting potential sales and cost information should put you in a better position to make reasonably accurate financial forecasts that can be used not only as a check on the advisability of proceeding with the venture but also for raising capital, if required. As an example, Bill Buckwold wants to evaluate the financial feasibility of opening a Tough Guys Sporting Goods store, and sets out to do a comprehensive analysis of its expected viability.

DETERMINE YOUR START-UP FINANCIAL REQUIREMENTS

The process of financial analysis begins with an estimate of the funds required to set up the business. The start-up financial requirements can be broken down into two components:

1. **One-time expenditures** that must be made before the business can open its doors. These include both *capital expenditures* for the purchase or lease of furniture, fixtures, equipment, and the purchase of beginning inventory or supplies and *soft costs* relating to such items as utility deposits and fees, pre-opening advertising and promotion expenses, and other prepaid expenses. In the case of a retail or manufacturing business, these requirements can be considerable, while a service business may not require a very large initial expenditure to get started. Remember, what we are trying to determine here is the amount of *cash* that will be needed to get the business launched. For example, a piece of required equipment may cost $20,000, but if the seller is prepared to take a deposit of $5,000 and finance the rest or if the business will be leasing the equipment for $500 per month rather then buying it outright, only the out-of-pocket cash cost needs to be factored in and not the total cost of the item. The estimated one-time financial requirements for the start-up of Tough Guys Sporting Goods is illustrated in Figure 8.1 on page 244.

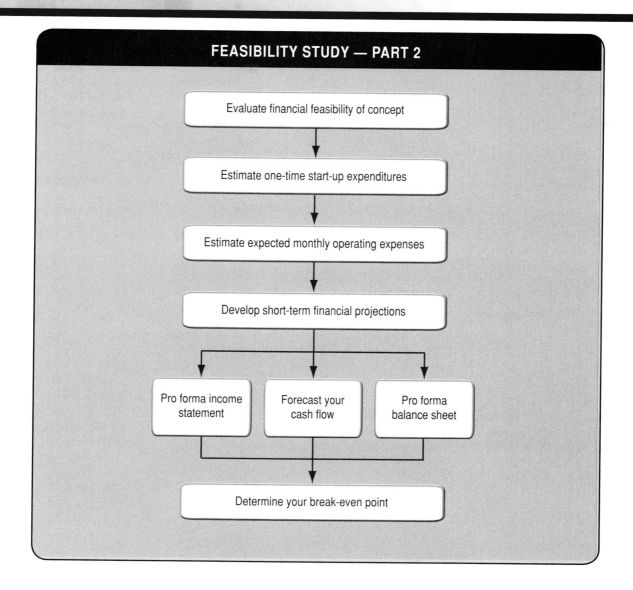

FEASIBILITY STUDY — PART 2

- Evaluate financial feasibility of concept
- Estimate one-time start-up expenditures
- Estimate expected monthly operating expenses
- Develop short-term financial projections
  - Pro forma income statement
  - Forecast your cash flow
  - Pro forma balance sheet
- Determine your break-even point

2. **Operating expenses** such as payments for Bill's and his employees' wages, rent, operating supplies, telephone, and postage, promotion, and other ongoing expenses that must be incurred until the business begins to show a profit. Many new businesses take several months or even years before they operate "in the black." Sufficient funds must be available to cover a minimum of two to three months' operations and provide a cash reserve for emergency situations. One way to determine just how much cash might be required is to review the cash flow statement to see how long it takes before the business reaches a positive cash flow situation. If, for example, it is not until the sixth month after opening the doors, Bill will need enough cash to cover the expected losses up to that time plus some additional cash as a safety factor. The estimated funds required to cover these initial operating expenses for Tough Guys is also illustrated in Figure 8.1.

Note that a sporting goods store, like many retail businesses, is a relatively capital-intensive business to start. The bulk of the money is required to finance the initial inventory Bill will need to stock the store, while most of the remaining one-time funds go to decorating and providing the necessary fixtures for the store. In addition, he should have approximately $52,000 available to cover his estimated monthly expenses until the business starts generating a positive cash flow. He does not necessarily have to have the entire cash requirements available strictly from his own resources; $100,000 to $150,000 may be sufficient. Suppliers may be prepared to grant

FIGURE **8.1**	ESTIMATED START-UP REQUIREMENTS FOR A SPORTING GOODS STORE

ESTIMATED MONTHLY EXPENSES

Item	Column 1 Bill's Estimate of Monthly Expenses Based on Sales of $800,000 Per Year	Column 2 Number of Months of Cash Required to Cover Expenses*	Column 3 Estimated Cash Required To Start Business (Column 1 × Column 2)*
Salary of Owner-Manager	$3,400	2	$6,800
All Other Salaries and Wages	$6,000	3	$18,000
Rent	$3,200	3	$9,600
Advertising	$1,000	3	$3,000
Delivery Expense/Transportation	$100	3	$300
Supplies	$0	3	$0
Telephone, Fax, Internet Service	$100	3	$300
Other Utilities	$580	3	$1,740
Insurance	$500	3	$1,500
Taxes Including Employment Insurance	$0	4	$0
Interest	$250	3	$750
Maintenance	$750	3	$2,250
Legal and Other Professional Fees	$700	3	$2,100
Miscellaneous	$1,800	3	$5,400
Total Cash Requirements for Monthly Recurring Expenses: (A)			**$51,740**

START-UP COSTS YOU ONLY HAVE TO PAY ONCE

	Cash Required to Start Business
Capital Costs	
Fixtures and Equipment	$40,000
Decorating and Remodelling	$10,000
Installation of Fixtures and Equipment	$5,600
Starting Inventory	$220,000
Soft Costs	
Deposits with Public Utility	$2,000
Legal and Other Professional Fees	$1,500
Licences and Permits	$1,000
Advertising and Promotion for Opening	$1,000
Accounts Receivable	$8,000
Cash	$5,000
Miscellaneous	$5,000
Total One-time Cash Requirements: (B)	**$299,100**
Total Estimated Cash Required to Start Business: (A) + (B)	**$350,850**

*These figures may be typical for one kind of business. You will have to decide how many months to allow for your business to offset expected shortages of cash flow.

him credit terms so that he does not necessarily have to pay for some of the stock for 30 or 60 days. Or the bank may be prepared to extend him a term loan or line of credit that he can draw on to meet some of his working capital requirements as they arise.

Insufficient financing is a major cause of new business failure, so Bill should be certain he has sufficient financing to cover both his estimated one-time and his initial operating expenses.

DEVELOP SHORT-TERM FINANCIAL PROJECTIONS

PRO FORMA INCOME STATEMENT

Bill's next step is to develop a projected operating statement, or *pro forma income statement*. This involves estimating the initial profit or loss expected by the business. Simply put, the basic formula to calculate profit and loss is:

Revenue – Expenses = Net Profit before Taxes

This means he will have to estimate the total expected revenue and expenses for at least the first year of operation of his business.

An income statement then measures the company's sales and expenses during a specified period of time — usually a month or a year. Its function is to total all sources of revenue for the business and subtract all expenses related to generating that revenue. It shows a company's financial performance over a period of time, and the heading of the income statement should always indicate the time period that is being examined (i.e., for the month ending, for the year ending, etc.).

The information Bill must be able to provide to construct a pro forma income statement includes:

1. The predicted sales volume for the period for which he is making the forecast or his projected *Net Sales*
2. How much it is expected to cost to produce or purchase the products he will sell or his projected *Cost of Goods Sold*
3. His *Fixed Operating Expenses* such as rent, utilities, insurance premiums, and interest costs
4. His controllable or *Variable Operating Expenses* such as advertising and promotion expenses, wages and salaries, and delivery expenses
5. His expected *Net Operating Profit or Loss*

Net Sales is the total sales plus any transportation costs he expects to make during the month or year being examined *minus* any cash discounts, trade discounts, or expected returns.

Cost of Goods Sold is often called *Cost of Sales*. For retail and wholesale businesses it is the total price paid for the products Bill expects to sell during the period for which he is developing the forecast. It is just the price of the goods. It does not include selling and other expenses. These are shown elsewhere on the income statement.

For most service and professional businesses, there will be no cost of goods sold. These businesses receive their income from fees, commissions, and royalties, so they do not typically have inventories of physical products. Their costs to provide these services are included in the fixed and variable operating expense sections of the statement.

Most small retail and wholesale businesses determine their cost of goods sold by:

- Determining the value of their inventory at the beginning of the period being projected
- Adding the value of any products purchased during the period, and then
- Subtracting the value of any inventory left at the end of the period

This calculation will provide a value for the amount of inventory actually sold during the period for which the projection is being developed. Net sales minus cost of goods sold yields Bill's expected *Gross Margin* or *Gross Profit*.

Fixed Expenses are operating expenses or overhead that he must pay regardless of his expected level of sales. These include expenses such as rent, telephone, insurance premiums, business taxes and licences, and interest, as well as some provision for depreciation on any capital assets used in the business.

Variable Expenses are those that are expected to rise and fall in proportion to Bill's sales. These include most of his selling expenses such as sales salaries and commissions, travel costs, advertising and promotion, delivery and vehicle expenses, and similar costs.

Net Operating Profit or Loss is the difference between his gross margin and his fixed and variable operating expenses. This is his expected net profit or loss before any consideration of federal or provincial income taxes.

The creation of a pro forma income statement is an important event for a small business. It provides a summary of many of the important activities of the company and provides valuable information to both the prospective owner and to others who may be looking to lend money or potentially invest in a business.

One means Bill might use to develop a pro forma income statement for his business is to follow the *desired income approach* suggested by Szonyi and Steinhoff.[1] This approach enables him to develop financial projections on the basis of the actual operating performance of firms similar to the business he is contemplating. It also suggests that his business should provide him with not only a return for the time he will spend running the business but also a return on the personal funds he has to invest to launch the business. For example, instead of starting a business, he could keep his present job or obtain another one and earn a salary working for someone else. He could also invest his money in common stocks, bonds, guaranteed income certificates, or other investments, where it would yield some kind of return. Both possibilities should be kept in mind for comparison purposes when determining the expected minimum level of acceptable profit performance of your new venture.

To illustrate this approach, assume Bill has determined that he would like to have a salary of $40,000 per year from the business, plus $15,000 as a reasonable return on the investment he will have to make in the business. These represent his desired income and return levels. By referring to Dun & Bradstreet Canada key business ratio information, Robert Morris Associates annual industry statement studies, or the Industry Canada SME Benchmarking Tool profiles he can obtain comprehensive financial data on sporting goods stores as well as dozens of other different lines of business.

Combining the information about his desired income and return goals with some of this published data will enable him to develop a pro forma income statement highlighting the level of operations he will have to reach to achieve his goals. The additional information he requires is:

- **The average inventory turnover for this type of business** is the number of times a typical firm's inventory is sold each year. If the business carries an inventory of $25,000 and its overall net revenue is $150,000, inventory turnover is six times per year.

- **The average gross margin** is the difference between the firm's net sales and cost of goods sold, expressed as a percentage. For example, if the business's net sales are $200,000 while cost of goods sold totals $140,000, its gross margin is $60,000 or 30 per cent of sales.

- **Net profit** as a percentage of sales is relatively self-explanatory. It can be determined either before or after the application of any federal or provincial taxes. In the case of Industry Canada's SME Benchmarking Tool profiles, it is shown before the application of any taxes.

Developing the Statement

With this data and an estimate of his desired salary and return levels, Bill can construct a pro forma income statement for a sporting goods store. For example, checking the 2006 Industry Canada SME Benchmarking Tool profile for a typical performing store in NAISC Classification code 45111 — Sporting Goods Stores[2] could provide us with the following information:

Inventory turnover	3.6 times per year
Gross margin	34.7% of sales
Net profit as a percentage of sales	1.8%

Figure 8.2 illustrates how this data, along with the information about Bill's desired salary and return, can be used to develop a pro forma income statement. This statement indicates the minimum level of sales his business will have to generate to provide him with his desired salary and level of profitability. Sales above this level will probably provide a higher level of profits, while lower sales will likely mean he will not make as much money as he had hoped. It is assumed in this evaluation that his business will be operated as efficiently as, and in a similar manner to, other sporting goods stores across the country.

All the figures in this statement have been computed from our ratio data and our stated desired salary and return on investment. For example:

1. Our $15,000 desired profit is inserted on line (E).
2. Profits for a typical retail sporting goods store are very slim, at only 1.8 per cent of sales. To determine the sales level required to provide our desired level of profitability, we divide $15,000 by 0.018 to obtain our estimate of the required level of $833,333 for net sales on line (A).

---

1. A. J. Szonyi and D. Steinhoff, *Small Business Management Fundamentals*, 3rd Canadian ed. (Toronto: McGraw-Hill Ryerson, 1988), pp. 58–65.
2. (/www.ic.gc.ca/app/sbp/prfpls/prfl/rprtStp/sv.do;jsessionid=0000Tf6S7XB-NRZfkAejTgFRBAk:1247mpv0c), accessed May 25, 2010

FIGURE **8.2**	SAMPLE PRO FORMA INCOME STATEMENT

TOUGH GUYS SPORTING GOODS PRO FORMA INCOME STATEMENT
For the year ending (date)

Net Sales		$833,333 **(A)**
Less: Cost of goods sold		
Beginning Inventory	$220,000	
Plus: Net purchases	555,647	
Goods available for sale	$775,647	
Less: Ending Inventory	231,481	
Cost of goods sold		544,166 **(B)**
Gross margin		$289,167 **(C)**
Operating Expenses		274,167 **(D)**
Net Profit (Loss) before Income Tax		**$15,000 (E)**

3. Our statistics indicate that sporting goods stores typically have an average gross margin of 34.7 per cent of net sales. In our situation this would provide a gross margin estimate of $289,167 on line (C).

4. The difference between our estimated net sales and gross margin has to provide for our cost of goods sold. In this example our cost of goods sold will be $833,333 − $289,167 = $544,166 on line (B).

5. Sporting goods stores have a relatively low level of inventory turnover in comparison with other types of retail business. A typical retail firm will turn over its inventory from six to seven times per year, while our statistics indicate a turnover ratio of only 3.6 times for a sporting goods store. This means we need to have more money tied up in inventory to support our estimated level of net sales than most other retailers. Our projected average inventory level can be determined by dividing our net sales revenue by the inventory turnover rate or $833,333/3.6 = $231,481.

6. The difference between our expected gross margin and the net operating profit (before taxes) necessary to provide our desired income level represents our total operating expenses in line (D). In this case $289,167 − $15,000 = $274,167 should be available to cover such expenses as Bill's salary and those of his employees, rent, insurance, promotion, interest, and similar expenses. Note that his expected salary of $40,000 has to be included in this amount.

This pro forma statement shows Bill the level of sales, investment in inventory, and similar information he needs to know to generate the level of income he feels he needs to obtain from the business.

The statement constructed in Figure 8.2 is based on the distinct financial characteristics of a small retail sporting goods business and relates only to that situation. A pro forma income statement for a store in another line of business could look very different due to variations in inventory turnover, gross margin percentage, and other factors reflecting the different character of that business.

This is even more true if we are considering the start-up of a service business or a manufacturing company. Service firms, like drycleaners and management consultants, typically do not carry an inventory of goods for resale and so do not have a "cost of goods sold" section on their income statement. Manufacturing companies, on the other hand, may have several types of inventory — raw materials, work in process, and finished goods. Appropriate levels for all three types of inventories should be determined and reflected in the projected income statement. The statement also tries to determine the value of raw materials and components, direct labour, factory overhead, and other inputs required to manufacture a product suitable for sale. This "cost of goods manufactured" replaces the cost of goods sold component on the pro forma statement.

Determining Reasonable Operating Expenses

So far, our pro forma income statement has lumped all Bill's business's projected operating expenses together under a single heading. For example, Figure 8.2 shows the overall, estimated operating expenses to be $274,167. This means that all operating expenses must be covered by this amount if he is to achieve his desired level of profitability.

The same statistical sources used to obtain the data for the overall pro forma statement can be used to obtain a breakdown of the typical operating expenses for his type of business. For example, the SME Benchmarking Tool provides data on the operating results of sporting goods stores. It indicates the following breakdown of operating expenses as a percentage of sales for the average incorporated firm:

Labour and commissions	15.1%
Amortization and depreciation	1.2%
Repairs and maintenance	0.6%
Utilities and telephone	1.1%
Rent	4.6%
Interest and bank charges	0.8%
Professional fees	1.3%
Advertising and promotion	2.2%
Delivery, shipping, and warehouse expenses	0.2%
Insurance	0.6%
Other expenses	5.5%

These expenses total approximately 33.2 per cent of sales. If we translate these percentages to our pro forma income statement, Bill can obtain an approximation of the detailed breakdown of his operating expenses in dollar terms. His finalized pro forma income statement would look like Figure 8.3 on page 249.

This complete pro forma statement can now serve as part of your plan for outlining the requirements of your proposed new business venture or as a guide or schedule to monitor the ongoing performance of your new business during its early stages.

A typical pro forma statement that you can use for projecting the first-year operating performance of your new business is illustrated in Figure 8.7, Outline for a Feasibility Study, on page 262.

FORECAST YOUR CASH FLOW

Your next step is to bring closer to reality the operating profit or loss Bill has projected by developing a cash flow forecast. It traces the expected flow of funds into and out of his business over some period of time. Cash flow is the lifeblood of any business. Therefore, this cash flow analysis is the most important document you will compile in assessing the financial feasibility of your business idea and also enables you to control the financial affairs of your business. It is quite a complex financial statement, so you will need to have some basic understanding of general accounting concepts to prepare it properly. As illustrated in Entrepreneurs in Action #32, failure to plan adequately for future cash requirements is one of the principal reasons small businesses fail. While Robert Bobbett and his two brothers-in-law had developed what seemed to be an excellent idea from a technological perspective, they grossly overestimated the ongoing revenue their business model for the TeePod scoring system could generate for their company. Over five years the company burned through over $3 million of their and other investors' money and eventually ended up in bankruptcy.

Even the best of plans, however, can go awry. Nico and Karri Schuermans thought they had everything under control for the opening of their Chambar restaurant in Vancouver (Entrepreneurs in Action #33 on p. 251). They estimated they needed $400,000 to open the doors. They even developed a detailed business plan, laying out how much money they needed to get started, how much to subsequently run the place, and even how much cash they needed to keep in reserve. Unfortunately things didn't work out quite as they had planned. A couple of investors they were counting on backed out, costs were higher than expected, and a change to the original concept meant higher expenses. But by counting on friends and doing a lot of the work themselves, they were able to pull it off. Upon reflection, Karri suggests that, unlike them, anyone looking to open a restaurant business have at least six months' worth of expected cash requirements available before they start. An accurate cash flow forecast can be your best means of ensuring continued financial solvency and the survival of your business.

Cash flow statements are similar to but differ from income statements in a number of ways. Cash flow is exactly as the name implies. The statement measures only the flow of cash into and out of the business. Non-cash accounting entries that may show up on an income statement such as depreciation, amortization, and asset transfers are ignored in forecasting the cash flow statement. Similarly, expenses that have been incurred but not yet paid and income that has been earned but not yet received are not included in the cash flow statement either.

| FIGURE **8.3** | **SAMPLE COMPLETED PRO FORMA INCOME STATEMENT WITH BREAKDOWN OF OPERATING EXPENSES** |

TOUGH GUYS SPORTING GOODS PRO FORMA INCOME STATEMENT
For the Year (date)

1. Gross Sales	$833,333
2. Less: Cash Discounts	0
A. NET SALES	**833,333**
Cost of Goods Sold:	
3. Beginning Inventory	$220,000
4. Plus: Net Purchases	555,647
5. Total Available for Sale	$775,647
6. Less: Ending Inventory	231,481
B. COST OF GOODS SOLD	**$544,166**
C. GROSS MARGIN	**$289,167**
Less: Variable Expenses	
7. Owner's Salary	40,000
8. Employees' Wages and Salaries	85,133
9. Supplies and Postage	0
10. Advertising and Promotion	18,330
11. Delivery Expense	1,670
12. Bad Debt Expense	0
13. Travel	0
14. Legal and Accounting Fees	10,830
15. Vehicle Expense	0
16. Miscellaneous Expenses	45,833
D. TOTAL VARIABLE EXPENSES	**$201,796**
Less: Fixed Expenses	
17. Rent	38,333
18. Repairs and Maintenance	5,000
19. Utilities (Heat, Light, Power)	8,170
20. Telephone	1,000
21. Taxes and Licences	0
22. Depreciation	10,000
23. Interest	6,667
24. Insurance	5,000
25. Other Fixed Expenses	0
E. TOTAL FIXED EXPENSES	**$ 74,170**
F. TOTAL OPERATING EXPENSES	**$274,167***
G. NET OPERATING PROFIT (LOSS)	**$ 15,000**

* Numbers may not match operating expense percentages exactly due to rounding.

The need for a cash flow analysis originates from the reality that in most businesses there is a time discrepancy between when your expenditures are incurred and when the cash is actually realized from the sale of the products or services you provide. This analysis is particularly important at the start-up stage, when businesses typically have lower revenues and higher expenditures. In fact, it is not uncommon for a new start-up to incur expenses requiring the outlay of cash several months prior to actually opening its doors. This outflow of cash should be taken into account in preparing the initial pro forma cash flow forecast.

Entrepreneurs in Action

Hit the Green

A BANKRUPT GOLF-TECHNOLOGY FIRM SEEKS THE PATH TO RESURRECTION

Golf is known as a game uniquely suited to people in business. Perhaps that's because the two disciplines share similar requirements for success: a solid strategy, calculated risk and precise execution.

Robert Bobbett has learned this lesson the hard way — in both pursuits. Although he describes himself as a "duffer" lucky to shoot 100, Toronto-bred Bobbett used to love golf, and in 2000 he combined his passion with his knowledge of technology to tee up a venture, called 4everSports. Founded in Cape Breton, N.S., with his two brothers-in-law, 4everSports sold a product dubbed the TeePod, a high-tech system that linked the Internet to the links. Touch-screen kiosks located next to each tee box allowed players to score their rounds and later track them online, as well as get detailed information on the hole and order food and drinks from the clubhouse. The system even used solar power and a wireless network to connect to a central server.

Today, however, 4everSports has been bankrupt for more than a year, and Bobbett hasn't picked up a putter since the day his business went under. "We were in the process of raising capital, and we weren't successful in raising enough before we ran out of money," he says. In its five fledgling years, the company burned through $3.2 million that it had raised through the personal investment of its principals, their friends and family, and grants from two regional government funding agencies. "There are a fair number of people who at the end of the day lost money in this, myself and partners included," says Bobbett. "But that was a risk we all took when we went into it."

Business, like golf, can humble the best of us. And as entrepreneurial tech stories go, 4everSports is not unique. Inventing a new product and turning it into a thriving concern is as tough as qualifying to play on the PGA tour. But Bobbett still holds out hope that even if his golf game is beyond saving, his company can be revived. But how can he turn this failed venture into a success?

Bobbett's assessment of what went wrong has little to do with technology. In fact, the TeePod system continues to operate at the Lingan Golf & Country Club in Sydney, N.S., the semi-public course where it was first prototyped, in 2001. "A lot of our members use it all the time. It's like a running leaderboard throughout the day," says Lingan's head pro, Chris Bunting. "We have probably 700 members, and I would think at least half of them use it on a regular basis, for sure."

But just like in golf, even the most advanced equipment won't get you very far without the right strategy. 4everSports' real problem? It couldn't find the right revenue model to work in the hyper-competitive golf industry. Initially, Bobbett's plan was to cover the cost of installing the TeePod System, and the course would charge golfers an extra $2 a round to pay 4everSports. The golf club would benefit from new sales opportunities (the screens could display local ads), a fresh way to attract more tournaments with the system's scoring tabulation features, and it could drive increased food and beverage sales.

But Bobbett found the industry too price sensitive for the surcharge. "The courses are always cutting their prices in an effort to get people to play," he says. "That's their idea of marketing: a fire sale on tee times." Golf courses viewed $2 per round as a cost they would have to absorb. At an average of 30,000 rounds per year, it added up to an additional $60,000 annually — and for an unproven concept at that. "We had a technology that worked," says Bobbett, "but a revenue model that didn't."

Source: Andrew Wahl, *Canadian Business*, September 10, 2006, pp. 73–74.

In a typical small business, sales revenue and expenses vary throughout the year. Your cash flow forecast tries to predict all the funds that you will receive and disburse within a certain period of time — e.g., a month, quarter, or year — and the resulting surplus or deficit. It allows you to estimate the total amount of cash you actually expect to receive each period and the actual bills that have to be paid. At times your cash inflows will exceed your outflows; at other times your cash outflows will exceed your inflows. Knowing your expected position

33

Entrepreneurs in Action

Chambar Restaurant

Nico and Karri Schuermans spent four frenzied months getting ready to open their restaurant in downtown Vancouver. By the time they threw open their doors in late 2004, they were flat broke. "We had $11 left in the bank a month into operating," says Karri, part of the husband-and-wife team behind Chambar. It's a modern twist on classic Belgian cuisine that has quickly grown into one of Vancouver's most talked-about hot spots. The mix of high-end elegance and mid-range prices proved popular enough to turn a profit in just five months.

But things weren't always so rosy for Chambar. Karri says she and Nico estimated they'd need $400,000 to get the doors open. They developed a detailed business plan that laid out how much money they'd need to get started, how much they'd need to actually run the place and how much cash to keep in reserve. But they weren't prepared for a few nasty snags. For one thing, two of their investors pulled out: One bailed during construction, taking $200,000 out of the project and halting work for two weeks; the other reneged on $100,000 of a $150,000 pledge two weeks before opening. The couple managed to come up with another $200,000, though they opened $100,000 short of their plan. They paid for kitchen equipment with cash flow, in instalments.

Costs ran over, too, because the couple decided to rent a heritage building, which meant construction regulations were more stringent. They couldn't touch the exterior of the building, for example, so they had to cut a 1.2-metre hole through three floors to accommodate some of their kitchen equipment. Although they did a lot of the work themselves — Karri's dad handled the carpentry — the couple still had to hire pros for a few jobs, like refinishing the floors.

Nico, who had previously worked in two Belgian restaurants — each with three Michelin stars — would have been happy cooking for an intimate crowd of 30 to 40 people, but Karri wouldn't agree to the venture unless they could make money. Eventually they settled on 120 seats.

One month in, construction and equipment costs had hit $500,000. They realized they needed "more flatware, more cutlery, more everything," Karri says. Rather than buy used refrigerators and other equipment, the couple opted to go new, adding 20% to their budget. "We decided it was better that way," she says. "We couldn't risk having food go off."

But Karri's business background paid off (she spent nine years as a marketing director in various industries). She and Nico signed a 10-year lease, with a right of first refusal for another five, thereby keeping the rental costs on their 2,800 square feet well below the recommended 11% of total costs. Thanks to word of mouth and a warm reception from locals, the restaurant did as much business in six months as they'd expected to do in a year.

Maintaining that goodwill requires spending money. Restaurant food costs are generally about 30% of the menu price, but costs at Chambar run about 4% higher because the duo place an emphasis on fresh ingredients — they use only seasonal vegetables and fish, and seafood from a sustainable harvesting program in Vancouver. While food costs of 34% are the average for some of their menu staples like lamb and other dishes make little or no money. The $15 foie gras, for example, is on the menu not because it's profitable but because it attracts affluent customers who have a taste for the delicacy.

Based on her experience at Chambar, Karri recommends any prospective restaurant owner bank at least six months' worth of cash flow before opening their doors. "You have to leave some breathing room," she says. "The stress can be unbelievable." And one more thing: "Don't sign a lease or start construction until you have the money in the bank."
(www.chambar.com)

Source: Omar el Akkad, *The Globe and Mail, Report on Small Business,* June 20, 2006.

and cash balance will enable you to plan your cash requirements and negotiate a line of credit with your bank or arrange other external financing.

Your completed cash flow forecast will clearly show to the bank loans officer what additional working capital, if any, your business may need and demonstrate that there will be sufficient cash on hand to make the interest payments on a line of credit or a term loan for purchasing additional machinery or equipment or expanding the business.

There are three sections to a typical cash flow statement:

1. Operating activities
2. Investment activities
3. Financing activities

These three sections work together to show the expected net change in cash that will occur in the business over a particular period of time. Cash inflows into the business are *added* on the statement while outflows are *subtracted* to determine total net cash flow.

Cash Flow from Operating Activities

Cash flow from operating activities is probably the most complicated section to develop. It is important to distinguish between sales revenue and cash receipts in most businesses. They are typically not the same unless all the business's sales are for cash. Revenues are determined at the time a sale is made. Cash receipts, on the other hand are not recorded until the money actually flows into the business. This may not be for a month or two in the case of sales made on credit, which would be reflected in your *accounts receivable*. Similarly expenses are incurred when materials, labour, and other items are purchased and used, but payments for these items may not be made until sometime later when the cheques are actually issued. These deferred payments would be reflected in your *accounts payable*.

In addition, your net cash flow will typically be different from your net profit. Net cash flow is the difference between your cash inflows and cash outflows. Net profit is the difference between your expected sales revenue and expenses. One reason for this difference is the uneven timing of cash receipts and disbursements mentioned above. Another is that some items on the income statement such as depreciation are non-cash expenses. They represent a charge against the business's income for the use of fixed assets owned by the firm but don't involve a direct outlay of cash.

Cash flow from operating activities can be determined from the following formula:

(+) **Cash received from customers**
(+) **Any other operating cash receipts**
  (=) **Total Cash Receipts from Operations (A)**
(−) **Cash paid to suppliers**
(−) **Cash paid to employees**
(−) **Interest paid**
(−) **Taxes paid**
(−) **Other cash payments for expenses**
  (=) **Total Cash Payments from Operations (B)**
  Total Net Cash Provided by Operations = (A) − (B)

Cash Flow from Investment Activities

Cash flow from investment activities includes changes to your expected cash position owing to the purchase or sale of any assets owned by the business. This might include land and buildings, vehicles, equipment, securities, or anything else the business may have sold or acquired that resulted in the receipt or outlay of cash.

Cash flow from investment activities can be determined from the following formula:

(+) **Cash proceeds from the sale of assets**
(−) **Cash disbursements for the purchase of property or equipment**
  (=) **Total Net Cash Provided by Investment**

Cash Flow from Financing Activities

Financing activities on a cash flow statement reflect cash received from borrowing money, issuing stock, or other cash contributions to the business as well as any payments made on loans, dividends paid to shareholders, or other similar payments.

Cash flow from financing activities can be determined from the following formula:

(+) **Cash received from bank and other loans**
(+) **Proceeds from issuing stock**
(+) **Capital contributions by owners**
    (=) **Total Cash Received from Financing (A)**
(−) **Repayment of principal on loans**
(−) **Dividends paid to shareholders**
(−) **Cash withdrawals by owners**
(−) **Other funds removed from the business**
    (=) **Total Cash Payments for Financing (B)**
    Total Net Cash Provided by Financing (A) − (B)

DEVELOPING YOUR CASH FLOW STATEMENT

Estimate Your Revenues

In most small businesses, not all sales are for cash. It is normal practice to accept credit cards or to extend terms to many customers. As a result, the revenue from a sale may not be realized until 30 days, 60 days, or even longer after the actual sale is made. In developing your cash flow forecast you must take into account such factors as:

- Your ratio of cash to credit card or credit sales
- Your normal terms of trade for credit customers
- The paying habits of your customers
- Proceeds from the sale of any auxiliary items or other assets of the business

Sales should be entered on the cash flow forecast only when the money has actually been received in payment.

Determine Your Expenditures

To estimate your cash outflow you must consider:

- How promptly you will be required to pay for your material and supplies. It is not uncommon that a new business will have to pay for its inventory and supplies up front on a cash on delivery (COD) basis until it establishes a reputation for meeting its financial commitments. Then it may be able to obtain more favourable credit terms from its trade suppliers. These terms of trade should be reflected in the cash flow forecast. For example, if you have to pay your suppliers' invoices right away, the cash payouts would be reflected in the cash flow forecast during the same month in which the purchases were made. However, if you have to pay your suppliers' invoices within 30 days, the cash payouts for July's purchases will not be shown until August. In some cases, even longer-term trade credit can be negotiated, and then cash outlays may not be shown for two or even three months after the purchase has been received and invoiced.
- How you will pay your employees' wages and salaries (weekly, biweekly, or monthly).
- When you must pay your rent, utility bills, and other expenses. For example, your rent, telephone, utilities, and other occupancy costs are normally paid every month. Other expenses like insurance and licence fees may be estimated as monthly expenses but not treated that way for cash flow purposes. Your insurance premium of $5,000 annually may have to be paid in five instalments: $1,000 in each of January, March, May, July, and September. That is how it must be entered on the cash flow worksheet. Your maintenance expenses may have to be paid as they are incurred, and would be reflected as part of your estimated expenses for that month. Other expenses, such as licence fees and club memberships, might be in the form of an annual fee paid in a particular month of each year, and would be shown when the actual expenditure is expected to be made.
- The interest and principal payments that you must make each month on any outstanding loans.
- Your plans for increasing your inventory requirements or acquiring additional assets.

Reconciling Your Cash Revenues and Cash Expenditures

To illustrate, let us continue to consider the situation of Tough Guys Sporting Goods. Tough Guys plans to open its doors at the beginning of the new year. Its owner wants to develop a monthly cash flow forecast for the expected first year of operation of the business and has made the following forecasts (see Figure 8.4):

- Total sales for the year are projected to be $833,333 with a strong seasonal pattern peaking in June and July.

- Of the store's monthly sales, 60 per cent are cash sales and 40 per cent are credit card sales for which the cash is received in the following month.

- Inventory is purchased one month in advance of when it is likely to be sold. It is paid for in the month it is sold. Purchases equal 65 per cent of projected sales for the next month.

- Cash expenses have been estimated for such items as the owner's salary and employees' wages and salaries, advertising and promotion expenses, delivery expense, rent, utilities, taxes and licences, insurance, and other expenses.

- The store's beginning cash balance is $10,000 and $5,000 is the minimum cash balance that should be available at the beginning of every month.

- The store has negotiated a line of credit with the bank at an interest rate of 10 per cent annually but the interest due has to be paid monthly. This line of credit can be drawn on in order to ensure the business has its $5,000 minimum cash balance available each month up to a limit of $80,000, and will be paid down as surplus cash becomes available.

At the end of each month it shows the cash balance that is available to be carried over to the next month's operations. To this it adds the total of the next month's cash receipts and subtracts the total of the next month's cash expenditures to determine the adjusted balance to be carried forward to the following month. In summary form this relationship can be demonstrated by the following formula:

Forecasted Cash Flow in Month (x) = Cash Balance Carried Over from Month (x − 1) + Expected Cash Inflow in Month (x) − Estimated Cash Expenditures in Month (x)

As you can see, cumulative cash surpluses or shortfalls are clearly evident well in advance of their actual occurrence. Knowing this information in advance can assist you in scheduling your initial capital expenditures, monitoring your accounts receivable, and avoiding temporary cash shortages, and can enable you to plan your short-term cash requirements well in advance. Tough Guys, for example, does not achieve a positive cash flow until July. The business will be forced to draw on its line of credit in January, February, March, April, May, and June to make certain it will have the necessary minimum cash balance available to continue to run the business. Preparing a pro forma cash flow forecast enabled Bill to anticipate these needs and avoid the possibility of any nasty surprises.

A typical cash flow forecast that you can use to project your anticipated cash surplus or shortfall at the end of each month of the first year of operation of your business is illustrated in Figure 8.7, Outline for a Feasibility Study, on page 262.

PRO FORMA BALANCE SHEET

One more financial statement should also be developed — *a pro forma balance sheet*. A balance sheet provides a snapshot of your business's health at a point in time. It tells you the value of your business at any point by forecasting what your business will own (*assets*) and what it will owe to other people, companies, and financial institutions (*liabilities*) to determine its *equity or net worth*. The basic formula of the balance sheet is:

Assets = Liabilities + Net Worth

The first section of the balance sheet deals with assets. *Current assets* would include an estimate of your expected average accounts receivable, start-up inventory requirements, available cash, and similar items. *Fixed assets* are typically items like buildings, furniture, fixtures, machinery and equipment, automobiles, and other capital items that you will need to operate your business. Except for land, fixed assets typically are used up over a period of years, and therefore must be gradually *depreciated* in value.

FIGURE 8.4   PRO FORMA CASH FLOW FORECAST FOR TOUGH GUYS SPORTING GOODS

12-MONTH CASH FLOW PROJECTIONS

Minimum Cash Balance Required = $5,000

	January	February	March	April	May	June	July	August	September	October	November	December	Year 1 TOTAL
Cash Flow From Operations (during month)													
1. Cash Sales	17,136	25,412	33,385	43,350	48,333	55,808	62,285	55,309	43,350	39,364	36,375	43,350	503,459
2. Payments for Credit Sales	0	16,942	22,257	28,900	32,222	37,205	41,523	36,873	28,900	26,243	24,250	28,900	324,215
3. Investment Income	0	0	0	0	0	0	0	0	0	0	0	0	0
4. Other Cash Income	0	0	0	0	0	0	0	0	0	0	0	0	0
A. TOTAL CASH FLOW ON HAND	$17,136	$42,354	$55,641	$72,251	$80,555	$93,013	$103,809	$92,182	$72,251	$65,607	$60,624	$72,251	$827,674
Less Expenses Paid (during month)													
5. Inventory or New Material	−31,461	−39,427	−47,838	−54,146	−61,611	−62,767	−53,305	−44,053	−40,268	−41,319	−38,165	−21,571	−535,929
6. Owner's Salary	−3,325	−3,325	−3,325	−3,325	−3,325	−3,325	−3,325	−3,325	−3,325	−3,325	−3,325	−3,325	−39,900
7. Employee's Wages and Salaries	−5,146	−7,198	−9,405	−11,411	−12,916	−14,697	−14,973	−12,716	−10,509	−9,606	−9,857	−6,546	−124,980
8. Supplies and Postage	0	0	0	0	0	0	0	0	0	0	0	0	0
9. Advertising and Promotion	−750	−1,049	−1,370	−1,663	−1,882	−2,141	−2,181	−1,853	−1,531	−1,400	−1,436	−954	−18,209
10. Delivery Expense	−68	−95	−125	−151	−171	−195	−198	−168	−139	−127	−131	−87	−1,655
11. Travel	0	0	0	0	0	0	0	0	0	0	0	0	0
12. Legal and Accounting Fees	−3,000	−700	−700	−700	−700	−700	−700	−700	−700	−700	−700	−700	−10,700
13. Vehicle Expense	0	0	0	0	0	0	0	0	0	0	0	0	0
14. Maintenance Expense	0	−1,500	0	0	−1,000	0	−1,300	0	−300	0	−900	0	−5,000
15. Rent	−3,200	−3,200	−3,200	−3,200	−3,200	−3,200	−3,200	−3,200	−3,200	−3,200	−3,200	−3,200	−38,400
16. Utilities	−580	−580	−580	−580	−580	−580	−580	−580	−580	−580	−580	−580	−6,960
17. Telephone	−100	−100	−100	−100	−100	−100	−100	−100	−100	−100	−100	−100	−1,200
18. Taxes and Licences	0	0	0	0	0	0	0	0	0	0	0	0	0
19. Interest Payments	0	−240	−372	−500	−560	−648	−656	−520	−356	−304	−292	−304	−4,752
20. Insurance	−1,000	0	−1,000	0	−1,000	0	−1,000	0	−1,000	0	0	0	−5,000
21. Other Cash Expenses	−1,874	−2,622	−3,426	−4,156	−4,705	−5,353	−5,454	−4,632	−3,828	−3,499	−3,590	−2,384	−45,522
B. TOTAL EXPENDITURES	($50,504)	($60,035)	($71,440)	($79,932)	($91,749)	($93,706)	($86,972)	($71,846)	($65,835)	($64,159)	($62,275)	($39,751)	($838,206)
Capital													
Purchase of Fixed Assets	0	0	0	0	0	0	0	0	0	0	0	0	0
Sale of Fixed Assets	0	0	0	0	0	0	0	0	0	0	0	0	0
C. CHANGE IN CASH FROM PURCHASE OR SALE OF ASSETS	$0	$0	$0	$0	$0	$0	$0	$0	$0	$0	$0	$0	$0
Financing													
Payment of Principal of Loan	0	0	0	0	0	0	−17,000	−20,500	−6,500	−1,500	0	−31,200	−76,700
Inflow of Cash from Bank Loan	30,000	16,500	16,000	7,500	11,000	1,000	0	0	0	0	1,500	0	83,500
Issuance of Equity Positions	0	0	0	0	0	0	0	0	0	0	0	0	0
Repurchase of Outstanding Equity	0	0	0	0	0	0	0	0	0	0	0	0	0
D. CHANGE IN CASH FROM FINANCING	$30,000	$16,500	$16,000	$7,500	$11,000	$1,000	($17,000)	($20,500)	($6,500)	($1,500)	$1,500	($31,200)	$6,800
E. INCREASE (DECREASE) IN CASH	($3,368)	($1,181)	$201	($182)	($194)	$306	($163)	($164)	($84)	($52)	($151)	$1,300	($3,732)
F. CASH AT BEGINNING OF PERIOD	$10,000	$6,632	$5,450	$5,652	$5,470	$5,276	$5,582	$5,419	$5,255	$5,171	$5,119	$4,968	$10,000
G. CASH AT END OF PERIOD	$6,632	$5,450	$5,652	$5,470	$5,276	$5,582	$5,419	$5,255	$5,171	$5,119	$4,968	$6,268	$6,268
MEET MINIMUM CASH BALANCE	ACCEPTABLE	ACCEPTABLE	ACCEPTABLE	ACCEPTABLE	ACCEPTABLE	ACCEPTABLE	ACCEPTABLE	ACCEPTABLE	ACCEPTABLE	ACCEPTABLE	FINANCE	ACCEPTABLE	ACCEPTABLE

The second part of a balance sheet lists liabilities. *Current liabilities* are debts you expect to incur that will fall due in less than 12 months. These usually include bills from your suppliers for the supplies and raw materials you will need for your initial inventory, short-term loans from banks and other financial institutions, any portion of your long-term debt that must be repaid during your initial year of operation, and so on. *Long-term liabilities* include any outstanding mortgages on land and buildings, notes on machinery and equipment, personal loans that you, your partners, and other stockholders may have made to the business, and any other outstanding loans of a long-term nature.

Net worth represents the value of your investment and equity in the business. Net worth can be composed of the total capital invested in the business by you and any other inside or outside investors plus any profits that have been generated by the business that have been retained within the company rather than being paid out in dividends or other means or minus any losses that may have accumulated in the business.

A typical pro forma balance sheet is illustrated in Figure 8.5.

How to Analyze Your Pro Forma Statements

Once you have created a pro forma income statement, cash flow statement, and balance sheet for your business there are some easy calculations you can perform that will give you a better understanding of your company. You can calculate a number of *financial ratios* that can help you manage your business and make knowledgeable decisions related to some key questions such as:

- Does the business have the capacity to meet its short-term financial obligations?
- Is the business producing adequate operating profits based on the level of assets it employs?
- Are the owners receiving an acceptable return on their investment?

A ratio shows the relationship between two numbers. It describes the relative size of the two numbers as they relate to one another, and so eliminates the problem of trying to compare things on different scales.

Financial ratios can be used to compare the financial performance of two businesses of different size or to compare the performance of a company with others in the same business or the industry average. This application was previously discussed in Stage 4 relative to analyzing the financial position of a business you might be looking to buy. Financial ratios can also be used to compare your business's performance from one time period to another, and that is the application we will look at here.

Financial ratios can be categorized into three common groups to analyze different aspects of your business:

1. **Liquidity ratios** help you understand your business's ability to meet its short-term obligations and continue to maintain its normal operations. The more liquid assets you have the better, because they can be readily converted into cash.

2. **Profitability ratios** tell you how well you measure up in creating financial value in your business. The money you have invested in the venture could just as easily have been invested in other things, such as real estate, bonds, and other securities, so you need to know whether your business can generate the kind of returns that justify the risks involved.

3. **Leverage ratios** measure the level of debt the business has and its ability to pay back this debt over a long period of time.

Examples of some of the more commonly used ratios of each type are illustrated in the Other considerations box below.

DETERMINE YOUR BREAK-EVEN POINT

As your preliminary financial forecasts begin to clarify the size of the potential opportunity you are investigating, there is one other key question to explore: What sales volume will be required for your business to break even? This *break-even* point indicates the level of operation of the business at which your total costs equal your total revenue. The break-even point is important because it indicates when your business begins to make a profit. If your sales level is less than the break-even point, your business will suffer a loss.

FIGURE **8.5**	**SAMPLE PRO FORMA BALANCE SHEET**

TOUGH GUYS SPORTING GOODS BALANCE SHEET
End of Year 1

ASSETS
Current Assets:

1. Cash		6,300
2. Accounts Receivable		28,900
3. Inventory		231,000
4. Other Current Assets		30,500

A. TOTAL CURRENT ASSETS   **$296,700**

Fixed Assets:

5. Land and Buildings	0	
less depreciation	0	0
6. Furniture and Fixtures	46,000	
less depreciation	2,300	43,700
7. Equipment	0	
less depreciation	0	0
8. Trucks and Automobiles	0	
less depreciation	0	0
9. Other Fixed Assets	34,000	
less depreciation	3,000	31,000

B. TOTAL FIXED ASSETS   **$74,700**

C. TOTAL ASSETS (C = A + B)   **$371,400**

LIABILITIES
Current Liabilities (due within 12 months):

10. Accounts Payable		150,000
11. Bank Loans/Other Loans		30,000
12. Taxes Owed		0

D. TOTAL CURRENT LIABILITIES   **$180,000**

Long-Term Liabilities:

13. Notes Payable (due after one year)	140,000	
14. Other Long-Term Liabilities	35,400	

E. TOTAL LONG-TERM LIABILITIES   **$175,400**

F. TOTAL LIABILITIES (F = D + E)   **$355,400**

Net Worth (Capital):

15. Share Capital		
Common Shares		1,000
Preferred Shares		0
16. Retained Earnings		15,000

G. TOTAL NET WORTH (G = C − F)   **$ 16,000**

H. TOTAL LIABILITIES AND NET WORTH (H = F + G)   **$371,400**

*Numbers may not match exactly due to rounding.

The break-even point is affected by several factors, including your fixed and variable costs and your selling price. *Fixed costs* are those that remain constant regardless of your level of sales or production. *Variable costs* vary directly with the amount of business you do. For example, your rent is a fixed cost, because it remains the same regardless of your level of sales. Your cost of goods sold, however, is variable, because the amount you spend is directly related to how much you sell. Fixed costs typically include insurance, licences and permits, property taxes, rent, and similar expenses. Variable costs include supplies, salaries and wages, raw material, utilities, and delivery expenses. Variable costs are usually determined on a per-unit or per-dollar of sales basis.

The break-even point can be determined algebraically. The basic formula is:

$$\text{Break-Even Point (Units)} = \frac{\text{Total Fixed Costs}}{\text{Contribution Margin per Unit}}$$

where:

Contribution Margin per Unit = Selling Price per Unit − Variable Cost per Unit

and the *contribution margin* ratio can be determined by:

Contribution Margin Ratio = Contribution Margin per Unit Divided by the Selling Price per Unit

Algebraically that relationship can be expressed as:

$$\text{Contribution Margin Ratio} = \frac{1 - \text{Average Variable Cost per Unit}}{\text{Selling Price per Unit}}$$

Understanding this relationship enables us to also calculate the break-even point in dollars. The basic formula for this determination is:

$$\text{Break-Even Point (Dollars)} = \frac{\text{Total Fixed Costs}}{\dfrac{1 - \text{Average Variable Cost}}{\text{Selling Price per Unit}}}$$

$$= \frac{\text{Total Fixed Costs}}{\text{Contribution Margin per Unit}}$$

Other considerations   EXAMPLES OF KEY FINANCIAL RATIOS

LIQUIDITY RATIOS

1. Current Ratio = Current Assets/Current Liabilities
2. Quick Ratio = (Current Assets − Inventories)/Current Liabilities

PROFITABILITY RATIOS

1. Gross Margin Ratio = Gross Profit Margin/Net Sales
2. Net Profit Ratio = Net Profit before Taxes/Net Sales
3. Return on Assets = Net Profit before Taxes/Total Assets
4. Return on Owner Investment = Net Profit before Taxes/Net Worth

LEVERAGE RATIOS

1. Times Interest Earned Ratio = Net Income before Interest and Taxes/Interest Expense
2. Debt-to-Equity Ratio = Long-Term Liabilities/Net Worth

FYI / FOR YOUR INFORMATION

For further information on preparing pro forma financial statements to evaluate the financial feasibility of your new venture idea you might check out some of the following Web sites:

CCH Business Owner's Toolkit — Managing Your Business Finances An outline of the basic concepts of financial management as they apply to small-business owners. Includes such topics as basic bookkeeping, credit management, managing your cash flow, and the evaluation of larger investments in facilities and capital equipment. (www.toolkit.com/small_business_guide/sbg.aspx?nid=P06_0100)

Business Development Bank of Canada (BDC) Ratio Calculators A ratio calculator that will compute the result of some of the most commonly used ratios for financial analysis. Brief explanations provided. (www.bdc.ca/en/business_tools/calculators/overview.htm?cookie_test=2)

Planning Guides: Manage Your Business and Watch It Grow. (Regions Financial Corp.) A comprehensive series of planning guides including Creating a Profit and Loss statement, Managing Your Cash Flow and Preparing a Balance Sheet that provide step-by-step instructions for the situations you may face when growing your business. (www.regions.com/small_business/planning_guides.rf)

Financing Your Business (Projecting — Acquiring and Managing Your Finances) An overview of the information you will need to obtain financing for your business. The process begins by your estimating financial needs based on projected financial statements. These statements along with a sound business plan, enable you to best determine where to seek financing — from within the business itself or from an outside lender. (/www.canadabusiness.mb.ca/home_page/contact_us/business_financing/financing_your_business_projecting_acquiring_and_managing_your_finances/)

Industry Canada's SME Benchmarking Tool (formerly Performance Plus) offers industry-specific income statement and balance sheet data for small- and medium-sized businesses. SME Benchmarking Tool allows you to:

- Estimate the operating costs for your new business;
- View financial performance averages in your industry;
- Enter your own financial data to see how your business measures up to comparably sized firms.

(www.ic.gc.ca/eic/site/pp-pp.nsf/eng/home)

Or alternatively if we are looking at the global situation for a business:

$$\text{Break-Even Point (Dollars)} = \frac{\text{Total Fixed Costs}}{1 - \dfrac{\text{Total Variable Cost}}{\text{Total Net Sales}}}$$

The following example may help illustrate the break-even concept. Suppose that the financial statements for Gino's Pizzeria, a pizza delivery outlet, indicate that the business's fixed costs every month for rent, utilities, interest expense, insurance, and similar items are roughly $3,600 per month. In addition, Gino has determined that his variable costs for making a typical large pizza are as follows:

Dough	$1.40
Tomato sauce	0.35
Cheese	0.75
Toppings	0.75
Delivery box	0.25
Delivery cost	0.50
Total Cost	$4.00

Rather than take a regular salary, Gino has decided to take any net income the business might generate as his income. In addition, Gino's sells a typical large pizza for $10.00.

From this information you can see that after the $4.00 in variable costs have been covered, each pizza sold can contribute $6.00 toward covering the fixed costs of Gino's business. This is called his *contribution margin*. His contribution margin per unit can then be expressed as follows:

$$\text{Contribution Margin per Unit} = \text{Selling Price} - \text{Total Variable Cost}$$
$$= \$10.00 - \$4.00$$
$$= \$6.00 \text{ per pizza}$$

But how many pizzas will Gino have to sell every month in order to break even? This can be determined as follows:

$$\frac{\text{Total Fixed Costs}}{\text{Contribution Margin per Unit}} = \text{Break-Even Volume (Units)}$$

Or, in this case:

$$\frac{\$3,600}{\$6.00} = 600 \text{ pizzas per month}$$

Therefore, Gino must sell a minimum of 600 pizzas every month or roughly 20 pizzas a day to cover his fixed costs of doing business. Even at that level of operation, he does not earn any income for himself. It is only after his sales exceed this level that the business starts to generate sufficient revenue to provide him with some compensation for his time and effort and give him a return on the money he has invested in the business. For example, if Gino should sell 800 pizzas one month, that would generate an income of $1,200 for him as a return on his time and money. On the other hand, if he sells only 500 pizzas his business would incur a loss of $600.

To determine the volume of sales that Gino will have to achieve each month to reach his break-even point we can use the formula:

$$\frac{\text{Total Fixed Costs}}{\text{Contribution Margin Ratio}} = \text{Break-Even Point (Dollars)}$$

Or, in this case:

$$\frac{\$3,600}{.6} = \$6,000 \text{ in sales per month}$$

Therefore, Gino must sell a minimum of 600 pizzas or generate at least $6,000 in sales every month to cover his fixed costs of doing business.

As part of this exercise, Gino might ask himself, "What would happen if I raised my price to $11.00 for a large pizza? How would that affect my break-even point?"

Re-doing the calculation shows the following:
His Contribution Margin per pizza has now increased by $1.00 as follows:

$$\text{Contribution Margin per unit} = \text{Selling Price} - \text{Total Variable Cost}$$
$$= \$11.00 - \$4.00$$
$$= \$7.00 \text{ per pizza}$$

$$\text{Or a new break-even of } \frac{\$3,600}{\$7.00} = 514 \text{ pizzas}$$

So Gino would only have to sell slightly more than 500 pizzas a month if his customers would be prepared to pay an extra dollar each. That is an assessment he would have to make based upon his knowledge of his customers, the competition, and his general understanding of local market conditions.

Similarly Gino might wonder if he should consider relocating to a new facility that has become available across the street. It has more parking for pick-up orders and higher traffic flows than where he is now, but would increase his rent by $500/month. A similar assessment indicates that would raise his

Total Fixed Costs to $4,100, assuming everything else stays the same, and would raise his break-even point as follows:

$$\text{Break-Even Point} = \frac{\text{Total Fixed Costs}}{\text{Contribution Margin per Unit}}$$

$$= \frac{\$4,100}{\$6.00} = 683 \text{ pizzas}$$

Or almost 15% more pizzas per month than he needs to sell at his present location.

Based on his experience, Gino can now judge whether those options are changes he ought to seriously consider. Going through this type of evaluation can help him assess the implications of a range of different strategic options on the overall financial performance of his business.

Relating this notion to Tough Guys Sporting Goods store, we can also determine the volume of sales Bill would require to break even. If we assume all the operating expenses indicated in Figure 8.3 are fixed at least in the short term, including such items as salaries and wages, as well as advertising and promotion expenditures, the financial statement can be summarized as follows:

Projected sales	$833,333
Projected fixed expenses	$275,966
Projected variable expenses	$544,166
(basically the cost of goods sold)	

$$\text{Total sales needed to break even} = \text{Fixed Expenses} \div \frac{1 - \text{Variable Expenses}}{\text{Sales}}$$

$$= \$275,966 \div \frac{1 - \$544,166}{\$833,333}$$

$$= \$275,966 \div (1 - 0.652)$$

$$= \$275,966 \div 0.348$$

$$= \mathbf{\$793,000}$$

Therefore the store needs to sell at least $793,000 worth of merchandise its first year to break even based on our estimate of its projected fixed costs and its average gross margin percentage and other variable costs. This concept is illustrated graphically in Figure 8.6.

The value of break-even analysis is that it can be used to determine whether some planned course of action — for example, starting a new business, opening a new store, or adding a new item to your product line — has a chance of being profitable. Once you have estimated the break-even point for the action, you are in a better position to assess whether such a sales volume can be achieved and how long it will take to reach it.

It is essential that you determine the break-even level of operation for your business before you proceed very far with its implementation. Bankers and other financial people will expect to see this information as part of the financial documentation for your venture. In addition, if it appears that the break-even volume is not achievable, the business idea is probably destined to fail and should be abandoned before any money is invested.

CONDUCT A COMPREHENSIVE FEASIBILITY STUDY

Figure 8.7 provides a detailed framework that you can use to conduct a comprehensive feasibility assessment of your own new venture idea. Much of the information you have compiled in completing the worksheets in Stage Seven can be incorporated into Figure 8.7 to facilitate your feasibility assessment. When you have completed this evaluation, you need to give some thought to where you go from here. Does the business look sufficiently viable to proceed with the development of a comprehensive business plan? Have you identified all the potential flaws and pitfalls that might negatively impact your business? What role do you expect to play

FIGURE **8.6**

FIGURE 8.6   GRAPHICAL REPRESENTATION OF THE BREAK-EVEN POINT FOR TOUGH GUYS SPORTING GOODS

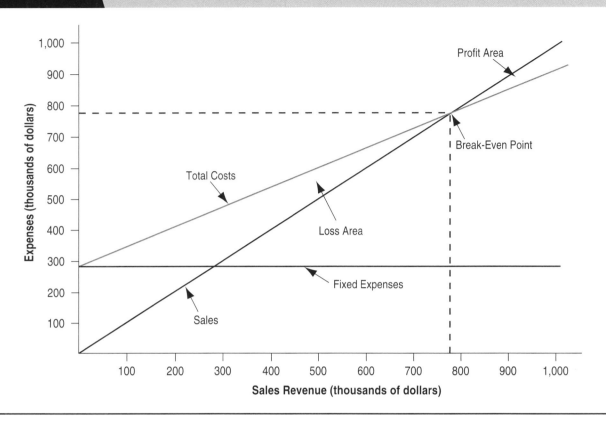

in the growth of the venture? Do you plan to produce and market the concept yourself, or do you hope to sell or license the idea to someone else? How much external money do you need and where do you think you can obtain it? These are the kinds of issues that need to be carefully considered and resolved before you will be in a position to move forward.

In most cases, the next stage is to write a complete *business plan*. This, however, requires a major commitment of time, effort, and money. Make sure your feasibility study indicates that your concept is clearly viable and that a reasonable profit can be expected.

And don't be too disappointed if your feasibility assessment indicates that your concept is not likely to be profitable. Think of all the time and money you have saved by not going forward with the implementation of a business that has a low probability of succeeding. That's why a preliminary assessment is so essential.

FIGURE 8.7   OUTLINE FOR A FEASIBILITY STUDY

YOUR CONCEPT

1. Describe the principal concept underlying your product or service idea.

_____

_____

_____

_____

2. What is unique or distinctive about your idea? How does it differ from similar concepts already in the marketplace?

_____

_____

_____

_____

3. Who will be the primary customers of your concept and what are the principal benefits your concept will deliver to them?

_____

_____

_____

_____

4. How innovative is your concept? How would you categorize it along the continuum from "copycatting" to being an entirely new invention?

_____

_____

_____

5. Is your idea technically feasible? Have you built a working model or prototype? Will you have to obtain Canadian Standards Association (CSA) approval or other permissions before the concept can be marketed?

_____

_____

_____

_____

PRELIMINARY MARKETING PLAN

Products and Services

1. What products or services will you sell? (Be specific.)

_____

_____

_____

_____

_____

2. What additional customer services (delivery, repair, warranties, etc.) will you offer?

_____

_____

_____

_____

_____

continued

Outline for A Feasibility Study — continued

3. What is unique about your total product or service offering?

_____
_____
_____
_____

Customers

1. Who are your target customers?

_____
_____
_____
_____
_____

2. How many target customers are in your trading area?

_____
_____
_____
_____

3. Why will they buy your product?

_____
_____
_____
_____

Competition

1. Who are your principal competitors? What is their market position? Have their sales been growing? Stable? Declining?

a. _____
_____

b. _____
_____

c. _____
_____

d. _____
_____

2. How does your concept differ from each of these other products or services?

_____
_____
_____
_____

Location

1. What location have you selected for your business?

   _____

   _____

   _____

   _____

2. Why did you choose that location?

   _____

   _____

   _____

   _____

   _____

Pricing

1. Describe your pricing strategy.

   _____

   _____

   _____

   _____

   _____

2. Complete the following chain of markups from manufacturer to final customer:

Cost to manufacture	_____	(A)
Manufacturer's markup	_____	(B)
Manufacturer's selling price (C = A + B)	_____	(C)
Agent's commission (if applicable)	_____	(D)
Wholesaler's cost (E = C + D)	_____	(E)
Wholesaler's markup	_____	(F)
Wholesaler's selling price (G = E + F)	_____	(G)
Retailer's markup	_____	(H)
Retailer's selling price (I = G + H)	_____	(I)

3. How do your planned price levels compare to your competitors'?

   _____

   _____

   _____

   _____

   _____

Promotion

1. What will be your primary promotional message to potential customers?

   _____

   _____

continued

Outline for A Feasibility Study — continued

_____

_____

_____

2. What will be your promotion budget?

_____

_____

_____

_____

_____

3. What media will you use for your advertising program?

_____

_____

_____

_____

_____

4. Will you have a co-operative advertising program? Describe it.

_____

_____

_____

_____

_____

5. Describe your trade promotion program.

_____

_____

_____

_____

_____

6. Describe any publicity, public relations, or sales promotion programs you will have.

_____

_____

_____

_____

_____

Distribution

1. How do you plan to distribute your product? Direct to the consumer? Through traditional distribution channels? Through specialty channels such as exhibitions, mail order, or trade shows?

_____

_____

_____

_____

_____

2. Will you employ your own sales force or rely on the services of agents or brokers? How many?

_____

_____

_____

_____

_____

_____

_____

THE SUPPLY SITUATION

1. What raw materials or component parts will you require to produce your product or service? What volume of these materials will you require? Who will be your major source of supply? Do you have alternative supply arrangements or other sources that can meet your requirements?

_____

_____

_____

_____

2. What will be the cost of these materials and components? Are prices guaranteed for any length of time? Are volume or quantity discounts available? What credit terms will your suppliers make available to you?

_____

_____

_____

3. Describe your manufacturing requirements. Will you manufacture the product yourself or use subcontractors? What will it cost to establish your own manufacturing facility?

_____

_____

_____

4. If you are planning to use subcontractors, what alternatives are available? What are their capabilities and comparative costs? Will you have to incur any other costs — e.g., for moulds, etc.? Do any of these contractors provide additional services?

_____

_____

_____

continued

Outline for A Feasibility Study — continued

COST/PROFITABILITY ANALYSIS

1. What do you estimate your costs would be and the funds required to successfully launch your business?

    a. Complete the following chart to determine your estimated start-up costs.

ESTIMATED MONTHLY EXPENSES

Item	Column 1 Your Estimate of Monthly Expenses Based on Sales of $ _____ Per Year	Column 2 Number of Months of Cash Required to Cover Expenses	Column 3 Estimated Cash Required to Start Business (Column 1 x 2)*
Salary of Owner-Manager	$0	2	$0
All Other Salaries and Wages	$0	3	$0
Rent	$0	3	$0
Advertising	$0	3	$0
Delivery Expense/Transportation	$0	3	$0
Supplies	$0	3	$0
Telephone, Fax, Internet Service	$0	3	$0
Other Utilities	$0	3	$0
Insurance	$0	3	$0
Taxes Including Employment Insurance	$0	4	$0
Interest	$0	3	$0
Maintenance	$0	3	$0
Legal and Other Professional Fees	$0	3	$0
Miscellaneous	$0	3	$0
Total Cash Requirements for Monthly Recurring Expenses: (A)			**$0**

*These figures may be typical for one kind of business. You may have to decide how many months to allow for your business to offset expected shortages of cash flow. This may be determined from your cash flow statement.

START-UP COSTS YOU HAVE TO PAY ONLY ONCE

	Cash Required to Start Business
Capital Costs	
Fixtures and Equipment	$0
Decorating and Remodelling	$0
Installation of Fixtures and Equipment	$0
Starting Inventory	$0
Soft Costs	
Deposits with Utilities	$0
Legal and Other Professional Fees	$0
Licences and Permits	$0
Advertising and Promotion for Opening	$0
Accounts Payable	$0
Cash	$0
Miscellaneous	$0
Total One-Time Cash Requirements: (B)	**$0**
TOTAL ESTIMATED CASH REQUIRED TO START BUSINESS: (A) + (B)	**$0**

    b. Do you have this much money available or have some ideas as to where you might be able to obtain it?

2. What do you estimate your sales will be, by product or service category, for your first 12 months? What will it cost you to produce those products or provide that service? What do you estimate your gross margin will be for each product or service? How does this compare with the norm for your industry? What operating expenses for such items as rent, travel, advertising, insurance, and utilities do you expect to incur? What profit do you estimate your business will show for its first 12 months?

   Complete the pro forma income statement on page 270 for your first year of operation.

3. How are your sales and expenses expected to vary throughout the year? What proportion of your sales will be for cash? On credit? What credit terms, if any, will you provide to your customers? What credit terms do you expect to receive from your suppliers? What other expenses will you have to pay on a regular, ongoing basis?

   a. Complete the table on page 271 to estimate your cash flow surplus or deficit for each month of your first year in business.
   b. Can you arrange for more favourable terms from your suppliers, accelerate the collection of your outstanding accounts receivable, negotiate a line of credit with your bank, or take other action to enable your business to continue to operate if cash flow is insufficient?

4. What do you estimate your total fixed costs will be for your first year of operation? What did you estimate your average gross margin to be as a percentage of your total sales in preparing your pro forma income statement in question 2? (This amount is also known as your contribution margin per dollar of sales.)

   Compute your break-even level of sales using the following formula:

   $$\text{Break-Even Point (\$ sales)} = \frac{\text{Total Fixed Costs}}{\text{Contribution Margin per \$ of Sales}}$$

   When do you expect to attain this level of sales? During your first year of business? Your second year? Your third year?

PLANS FOR FUTURE ACTION

1. According to your feasibility study, what were the strong points and weak points of your new venture idea? Can the weak points and potential problems be successfully overcome?

   _____

   _____

   _____

   _____

2. Does the feasibility assessment indicate that the business is likely to be profitable? Does it look sufficiently attractive that you should write a comprehensive business plan? What other information do you have to obtain, or what additional research do you have to do to develop this plan?

   _____

   _____

   _____

   _____

3. If you decide not to proceed with the development of a business plan, indicate the reasons why.

   _____

   _____

   _____

   _____

PRO FORMA INCOME STATEMENT
FOR THE PERIOD ENDING (DATE) _____

	Month 1	Month 2	Month 3	Month 4	Month 5	Month 6	Month 7	Month 8	Month 9	Month 10	Month 11	Month 12	TOTAL
1. Gross Sales													
Products													
Services													
2. Less: Cash Discounts													
A. NET SALES	$	$	$	$	$	$	$	$	$	$	$	$	$
Cost of Goods Sold:													
3. Beginning Inventory													
4. Plus: Net Purchases													
5. Total Available for Sale													
6. Less: Ending Inventory													
B. COST OF GOODS SOLD	$	$	$	$	$	$	$	$	$	$	$	$	$
C. GROSS MARGIN	$	$	$	$	$	$	$	$	$	$	$	$	$
Less: Variable Expenses*													
7. Owner's Salary													
8. Employees' Wages and Salaries													
9. Supplies and Postage													
10. Advertising and Promotion													
11. Delivery Expense													
12. Bad Debt Expense													
13. Travel													
14. Legal and Accounting Fees													
15. Vehicle Expense													
16. Maintenance Expense													
17. Miscellaneous Expenses													
D. TOTAL VARIABLE EXPENSES	$	$	$	$	$	$	$	$	$	$	$	$	$
Less: Fixed Expenses*													
18. Rent													
19. Utilities (Heat, Light, Power)													
20. Telephone													
21. Taxes and Licences													
22. Depreciation													
23. Interest													
24. Insurance													
25. Other Fixed Expenses													
E. TOTAL FIXED EXPENSES	$	$	$	$	$	$	$	$	$	$	$	$	$
F. TOTAL OPERATING EXPENSES	$	$	$	$	$	$	$	$	$	$	$	$	$
G. NET OPERATING PROFIT (LOSS)	$	$	$	$	$	$	$	$	$	$	$	$	$
H. INCOME TAXES (estimated)													
I. NET PROFIT (LOSS) AFTER INCOME TAX	$	$	$	$	$	$	$	$	$	$	$	$	$

*Expenses and other payments should be entered as negative (–) numbers.

TWELVE-MONTH CASH FLOW PROJECTIONS

	Month 1	Month 2	Month 3	Month 4	Month 5	Month 6	Month 7	Month 8	Month 9	Month 10	Month 11	Month 12	TOTAL
Cash Flow from Operations (during month)													
1. Cash Sales													
2. Payments for Credit Sales													
3. Investment Income													
4. Other Cash Income													
A. TOTAL CASH ON HAND	$	$	$	$	$	$	$	$	$	$	$	$	$
Less Expenses Paid (during month)[1]													
5. Inventory or New Material													
6. Owners' Salaries													
7. Employees' Wages and Salaries													
8. Supplies and Postage													
9. Advertising and Promotion													
10. Delivery Expense													
11. Travel													
12. Legal and Accounting Fees													
13. Vehicle Expense													
14. Maintenance Expense													
15. Rent													
16. Utilities													
17. Telephone													
18. Taxes and Licences													
19. Interest Payments													
20. Insurance													
21. Other Cash Expenses													
B. TOTAL EXPENDITURES	$	$	$	$	$	$	$	$	$	$	$	$	$
Purchase of Fixed Assets													
Sale of Fixed Assets													
C. CHANGE IN CASH FROM PURCHASE OR SALE OF ASSETS	$	$	$	$	$	$	$	$	$	$	$	$	$
Financing													
Payment of Principal of Loan													
Inflow of Cash from Bank Loan													
Issuance of Equity Positions													
Repurchase of Outstanding Equity													
D. CHANGE IN CASH FROM FINANCING	$	$	$	$	$	$	$	$	$	$	$	$	$
E. INCREASE (DECREASE) IN CASH ($E = A - B \pm C \pm D$)	$	$	$	$	$	$	$	$	$	$	$	$	$
F. CASH AT BEGINNING OF PERIOD	$	$	$	$	$	$	$	$	$	$	$	$	$
G. CASH AT END OF PERIOD ($G = F \pm E$)	$	$	$	$	$	$	$	$	$	$	$	$[2]	$
MEET MINIMUM CASH BALANCE	ACCEPTABLE	ACCEPTABLE	ACCEPTABLE	ACCEPTABLE	ACCEPTABLE	ACCEPTABLE	ACCEPTABLE	ACCEPTABLE	ACCEPTABLE	ACCEPTABLE	ACCEPTABLE	ACCEPTABLE	ACCEPTABLE

1. Expenses and other payments should be entered as negative (–) numbers.
2. This entry should be the same amount as for the beginning of the year. All other rows will be the total for the entire year.

Protecting Your Idea

Many entrepreneurs are also inventors. One of the primary problems faced by these inventor/entrepreneurs is how to protect the idea, invention, concept, system, design, name, or symbol that they feel may be the key to their business success. These ideas, inventions, etc. are commonly referred to as "intellectual property". Legislators have long recognized that society should provide some protection for the creators of this "intellectual property." The laws they have developed provide a form of limited monopoly to the creators of intellectual property in return for their disclosure of the details of the property to the public. You may not realize it but your business may be creating valuable intellectual property assets that should be protected.

Intellectual property is broken down into five components under the law:

1. **Patents** cover inventions or improvements to an existing invention.
2. **Trademarks** are words, symbols or designs used to distinguish a product or service.
3. **Copyrights** provide protection for artistic, dramatic, musical and literary creations.
4. **Industrial designs** are the visual features, such as shape, configuration and pattern, applied to a finished article.
5. **Integrated circuit topographies** are the three-dimensional electronic circuit designs used in technology.

Protection of your intellectual property can be expensive. While government costs may range from only a small fee for registration of a copyright to several hundred dollars for registration of a patent, many of the procedures can be quite complex and require you to obtain the services of a registered patent agent. This can increase the total cost of obtaining a patent by several thousand dollars, depending on the complexity of the application. Therefore, it is important that you understand the advantages and disadvantages provided by this protection, and its likely impact on the success and financial viability of your business.

APPLYING FOR A PATENT

A *patent* is a government grant that gives you the right to take legal action, if necessary, against other individuals who without your consent make, use, or sell the invention covered by your patent during the time the patent is in force. Patents are granted for 20 years from the date on which the application was first filed and are not renewable. On expiration of its patent, a patented device falls into the *public domain* — anyone may make, use, or sell the invention.

To be patentable, your device must meet three basic criteria:

1. Have "absolute novelty." The invention must be new (first in the world).
2. Be useful. A patent cannot be obtained for something that doesn't work or has no useful function.
3. It must show inventive ingenuity and not be obvious to someone skilled in that area.

A patent may be granted for a product, a chemical composition, an apparatus or machine, or a process. You *cannot* patent a scientific principle, an abstract theorem, an idea, a method of doing business, a computer program, or a medical treatment.

A patent may be applied for only by the legal owner(s) of an invention. You cannot apply for a patent for an invention you may have seen in another country even though that invention may never have been patented, described, or offered for sale in Canada.

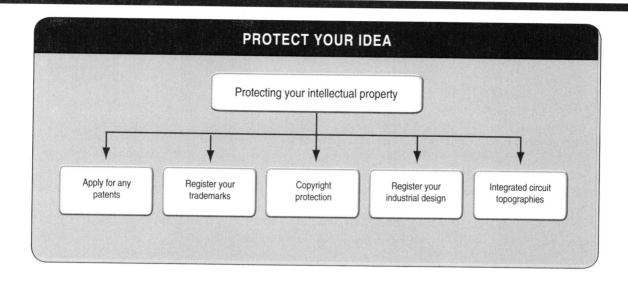

PROTECT YOUR IDEA

Protecting your intellectual property

- Apply for any patents
- Register your trademarks
- Copyright protection
- Register your industrial design
- Integrated circuit topographies

Patents are now awarded to the *first inventor to file an application* with the Patent Office of the Canadian Intellectual Property Office (CIPO). This means you should file as soon as possible after completing your invention (though not prematurely if certain key elements or features of your idea would be missing from your application). It is also important that you not advertise or display or publish information on your invention too soon, as this may jeopardize your ability to obtain a valid patent later on. There is a one-year grace period for disclosure by an applicant but it is suggested that the following rule of thumb be adopted: *Your application for a patent should be filed before your product is offered for public sale, shown at a trade show, or otherwise made public.*

HOW TO APPLY

If your idea is patentable and you wish to obtain patent protection, you should take the following steps:

1. **Find a patent agent** The preparation and prosecution (assessment) of patent applications is quite complex. You should consult a patent agent trained in this specialized practice and registered to represent inventors before the Patent Office of the CIPO. Though hiring such an agent is not mandatory, it is highly recommended. The Patent Office can provide you with a list of registered agents but will not recommend any particular one to you. Several may also be listed in your local telephone directory, but make certain they are registered with the Patent Office.

2. **Conduct a preliminary search** The first step your agent will recommend is a preliminary search of existing patents to see if anything similar to your idea has already been patented, in which case you may conclude the process immediately. This can save you a lot of time and money that might otherwise be spent pursuing a futile application. The database search can be conducted in person by visiting the CIPO Patent Office or on the CIPO Web site. The online database has descriptions and drawings of patents issued in Canada since 1920.

3. **Prepare a patent application** A patent application consists of an abstract, a specification, and drawings.

   An *abstract* is a brief summary of the material in the specification. The *specification* is a document that contains (1) a complete description of the invention and its purpose and (2) *claims*, which are an explicit statement of what your invention is and the boundaries of the patent protection you are seeking. *Drawings* must be included whenever the invention can be described pictorially. Typically, all inventions except chemical compositions and some processes can be described by means of drawings.

4. **File your application** Filing your application means submitting it along with a petition asking the Commissioner of Patents to grant you a patent. In Canada, filing must be done within one year of any use or public disclosure of the invention.

If your application is accepted, you will be required to pay an annual maintenance fee to keep it in effect for the 20-year period. Independent inventors and small businesses whose gross annual revenues are less than $2 million pay lower maintenance fees than businesses classified as "other than small." Fees range from zero in the first year to $225 in years 15 to 19 of the patent's life for these small entities.

5. **Request examination** Your application will not automatically be examined simply because you have filed it. You must formally request examination and submit the appropriate fee. This request can be made any time within five years of your filing date.

   Filing an application and not requesting examination can be a cheap and effective way of obtaining some protection for your invention without necessarily incurring all the costs of obtaining a patent. For example, let's assume you want to protect your idea but don't wish to spend all the money required to obtain a patent until you have assessed the financial feasibility of your invention. Filing an application establishes your rights to the invention and publication of the application by the Patent Office informs other people of your claim to the product or process. If someone infringes on your invention after your application is published, you have five years to decide whether to pursue the grant of a patent and seek retroactive compensation.

   Requesting an examination, however, is no guarantee that a patent will be granted. And if it is not, you will have no grounds to claim damages for infringement on your idea.

   The CIPO Patent Office receives over 35,000 applications a year, mostly from U.S. inventors and companies. As a result, the examination process can be very slow, commonly taking two to three years to complete.

6. **If necessary, file amendment letters** When you request an examination, the patent examiner will assess your claims and either approve or reject your application. If your application is rejected, you can respond by filing an *amendment letter* with the Commissioner of Patents. The letter will be studied by the examiner. If the patent is not then granted, there may be a request for further amendments. This process will continue until either the patent is granted, your application is withdrawn, or your application is rejected.

PROTECTION PROVIDED BY YOUR PATENT

As you can see, the patenting process is complex, costly, and time-consuming. If you have a patent application in process and are concerned that someone else may attempt to patent your invention, you may use the label "Patent Pending" or "Patent Applied For" to inform the public that your application for a patent has been filed. This, however, has no legal significance and does not mean that a patent will necessarily be granted. Of course, it is illegal to use this term if in fact no application is on file.

If your patent application is granted, the onus will be entirely on you to protect your rights under the patent, because the Patent Office has no authority to prosecute for patent infringement. If infringement occurs, you may (1) bring legal action to compel the offender to account for any profits made, (2) seek an injunction

Other considerations   BENEFITS OF A PATENT SEARCH

If you are a small businessperson a patent search can help you:

- Identify trends and developments in a particular field of technology
- Discover new products that you may be able to license from the patentee or use without needing a licence
- Find information that keeps you from duplicating the research
- Identify unproductive areas of inquiry by reading about the current state of the art
- Keep track of the work of a particular individual or company by seeing what patents they have been granted
- Find a solution to a technical problem you may have
- Gain new ideas for further research in a particular field

Source: "Summary of benefits of a patent search" — adapted and reproduced as "Other considerations: Benefits of a Patent Search." Reproduced with the permission of the Minister of Public Works and Government Services Canada, 2002.

to prevent further use of your patent, or (3) obtain a court order for the destruction of any materials produced that infringe on your rights. This, however, can be a very expensive and time-consuming process, which may prohibit a small business from enforcing its rights.

A patent granted in Canada or the United States provides you with no protection outside the country in which it was originally granted. To obtain protection in other countries, you must register your patent in each country within the time limit permitted by law (typically one year from your initial application). You can apply for a foreign patent either from within Canada via the Canadian Patent Office, or directly through the patent office of the country or countries concerned. Under the terms of the Patent Cooperation Treaty, it is possible to file for a patent in as many as 43 countries, including the United States, Japan, and most of Europe, by completing a single, standardized application that can be filed in Canada. Ask your patent agent about these procedures before you decide to file in another country.

You should realize that holding a patent on a worthy idea does not necessarily mean commercial success. For example, Mich Delaquis and Fred Coakes (Entrepreneurs in Action #34) developed a set of state-of-the-art, self-draining cookware. They secured patents in the United States and Canada for the locking mechanism on the lid of their pots and invested virtually all of their savings and a good portion of their families' and friends' savings in developing the concept. Even though they managed to interest a number of people in demonstrating their product, they were looking to raise another $100,000 to get the cookware sets produced in Hong Kong.

The partners managed to overcome that hurdle and raised the funds to get their pots produced abroad and had some success marketing them on live shopping channels in Canada and the U.S. and at trade shows. However, their efforts to market their EasyStrain line in conventional stores and on the Web never really panned out. Their research subsequently determined that consumers were not prepared to buy cookware over the Internet. Even a substantial price reduction was not sufficient to generate many sales and the pair were still a long way from making a profit. In fact, they never did actually turn the corner.

An invention succeeds by acceptance in the marketplace. Your patent may be perfectly valid and properly related to your invention but commercially worthless. Thousands of patents are issued each year that fall into this category. A patent does not necessarily contribute to the economic success of an invention. In some high-technology fields, for example, innovations can become obsolete long before a patent is issued, effectively making the patent worthless.

Holding a patent may improve your profitability by keeping similar products off the market, giving you an edge. But there is no guarantee you will be able to prevent all competition. In fact, disclosing your idea in a patent might open the way for a competitor to steal your concept and introduce an imitation or "knock-off" of your product. Litigation, if it becomes necessary, can require considerable financial resources, and the outcome is by no means assured. A high percentage of patent infringements challenged in court result in decisions unfavourable to the patent holder.

However, there are many instances where patenting a product concept or idea has led to commercial success. Hermann Fruhm (Entrepreneurs in Action #35) has watched sales of his Megapro multi-bit screwdriver soar to over $40 million over the last 10 years and he has yet to take his invention to the retail consumer market. Not bad for a guy who started as a keyboard player in a rock band.

Even more impressive has been the market performance of Ron Foxcroft's pea-less whistle, the Fox 40, illustrated in Entrepreneurs in Action #36. Foxcroft developed the whistle after his regular whistle failed to blow while he was refereeing a key basketball game during a pre-Olympic tournament in Brazil. To date his company has sold almost 100 million whistles in 126 countries around the world. However, it has also spent $750,000 registering dozens of patents and trademarks in an effort to protect Foxcroft's invention, and in 2001 was involved in 11 infringement cases against other firms who are either making a cheaper version of the Fox 40, selling an identical product under another name, or are just passing a cheaper imitation off as a genuine Fox 40 whistle.

Canadians particular fascination with cookware lids and multi-bit screwdrivers continues to evolve. Mac-and-cheese connoisseur Geoff Eisfeld recently came up with a simple way of keeping the gooey concoction from sticking to the pot. His solution — a rotating handle on top of a glass lid with removable paddles sticking into the pot below. The paddles make it effortless to continually stir the ingredients in the pot. The lid also has a swivel opening which allows for tasting of the mixture or the addition of other ingredients. The product is now only at the prototype stage but Geoff is preparing to file a patent and is looking for investors to help commercialize his idea.[1]

---

1. Jane Bao, "Cookware Lids", The Next Great Canadian Idea, Canadian Business, Sept. 28, 2008, p. 53

34

Entrepreneurs in Action

Feeling the Strain

POT INVENTORS REFUSE TO GIVE UP ON A DREAM

Take two Winnipeg east-end boys who made their living in a city snowmobile plant, lock them in a basement for three years and what do you get?

For Mich Delaquis and Fred Coakes, the answer is a state-of-the-art, self-draining cookware set.

Along the way, the two men exhausted their life savings and a sizable portion of their family's and friends', were knee-deep in flawed designs, fruitlessly wore out welcome mats at city banks, and were turned away by every cookware manufacturer in North America. . . .

What Delaquis and Coakes have produced is a set of pots and pans that are self-draining and with lids that lock on tight.

The design is simple. When cooking, the straining holes are covered. When it's time to strain, you line up the arrows on the lid with a matching arrow on the handle and turn clockwise; this locks the lid and exposes the holes.

The products are heavy-duty stainless steel with a thick bottom. The larger pots and pans come with an extra handle, making straining easier. . . .

Delaquis and Coakes are your typical entrepreneurs. Delaquis is the tinkerer, Coakes the hustler and deal-maker. They saw a need and went about finding a product to fill that need.

Delaquis remembers the day three years ago when, still single and living on his own, he scalded his hand while straining a pot of pasta.

"I didn't have a strainer and I had to do it with just lifting the lid a little bit," Delaquis said. "The idea popped into my head that it would be a lot easier to do this if there was a strainer already inside the pot."

It was an idea that wouldn't go away. He went to Coakes and told him of his plan.

They went into Coakes's basement and they tinkered. First, using snips and sheet metal, they tried to make their own pots and lids.

Then they concentrated on just designing the lid.

Their first design incorporated a spinning disc and a spring mechanism under the lid.

"The first five manufacturers we showed it to said it couldn't be made," said Coakes, 28. "We had to start all over again."

Along the way, the pair took a 10-week small business course from the Canada Business Service Centre. Then they found a helpful lawyer and an accountant.

© MARC GALLANT/WINNIPEG FREE PRESS. REPRINTED WITH PERMISSION

Even when they came up with what they believed was a sure thing, they couldn't find anyone in North America to make it.

They secured patents in the United States and Canada for their locking mechanism and got the name trademarked, but 14 manufacturers turned them away.

"They either said it wouldn't work or they were too busy," Coakes said. . . .

It cost them $30,000 just to get the moulds designed.

"A year ago, I told Mich we've got to start selling some of these and stop writing all these cheques," said Coakes.

But don't ask the pair to do a commercial for the Canadian banking industry. They've put $77,000 into the project to date and they need another $100,000 to make the minimum 1,250 sets the Hong Kong manufacturer will produce on a first order. All of that has been money from their own savings and that of family and friends.

"We'd be nowhere if it wasn't for the support and help from our family and friends," Delaquis said.

"One banker had the nerve to tell me that he so admired my tenacity he was certain I'd be a millionaire one day," Coakes said. "I told him I didn't need any lip service.". . . .

It's not over for Coakes and Delaquis. They're confident they'll find the investors necessary to bring the first 500 sets to market in February. Once the sales take off, they're planning on larger pots and smaller pans.

After that, they will concentrate on direct marketing, with infomercials in the United States and trade shows. Then they'll go retail.

And Delaquis is not finished.

"I've got an idea or two for some other products."

Source: Aldo Santin, "Pot Inventors Refuse to Give Up on a Dream," © *Winnipeg Free Press*, November 20, 1998, pp. B3–B4. Reprinted with permission.

Entrepreneurs in Action

Invention Sweet Music for Ex-City Rocker

When Hermann Fruhm played keyboards with rock band Mood Jga Jga, its biggest hit was "Gimme My Money."

Now Fruhm is singing that song for real as gross sales of his Megapro "world's greatest multi-bit screwdriver" soar to $40 million.

"We're not rich yet, but we're on our way," said Fruhm, with nearly two million Megapro screwdrivers already sold worldwide and patent protection in 16 countries.

That's with sales mostly to the tradesman and industrial market. Fruhm is getting set to take his invention to the retail market, which is at least 10 times larger. . . .

"My goal, my dream — and this is no joke — is to put a Megapro into every kitchen drawer, every weekend warrior toolbox, in North America and Europe," said Fruhm.

"I had dropped my screw bits once too often," explaining how he came to build a better multi-bit screwdriver. "You know. You had to dump the screw bits into your hand, find the one you wanted, then funnel them into the hollow handle."

In fact, that prototype of the multi-bit screwdriver, originally called the Uni-driver, was patented by another Canadian, George Cluthe of Waterloo, Ontario. "For some reason, Canada is the land of multi-bit screwdrivers. Don't ask me why," said Fruhm.

The Cluthe design, patented in 1967, is the screwdriver with the orange handle and the spring-loaded cap that lifts up and swings away to the side. Screw bits rattle around inside the hollow handle.

Fruhm had moved to Vancouver in 1980 and spent the next couple of years playing piano with West Coast bands, then realized his wife, Marilyn. . . and their two young sons needed a more stable home. So he got a day job at Acklands-Granger, the tool and building material supplier for the industrial market.

In his spare time, Fruhm tinkered with Cluthe's screwdriver design.

"I started thinking about this, started making some sketches," he said. "I just had this epiphany one day."

So he got parts like Plexiglas tubing from a hobby shop, and started building the "retractable cartridge" for a multi-bit screwdriver. "After I built the prototype, I became absolutely passionate in believing this was a viable, commercial product."

He patented his 15-in-one screwdriver in 1993. At the public library, he scanned the Thomas Registry, which lists every manufacturer in the United States, and looked up screwdriver makers and found someone to build Megapro.

MELVYN KSIONZEK/WINNIPEG FREE PRESS

The retractable cartridge, located inside the screwdriver handle, is the main feature. A carousel of screw bits lifts out of the handle almost as if on a hydraulic cushion of air.

Then, when pushing the carousel back inside the handle, the cartridge makes "this wonderful clicking sound," as Fruhm puts it, as it snaps shut. That clicking sound is also patented.

There are seven double-ended bits in the 15-in-one screwdriver. The 15th bit is the socket head itself, which is a quarter-inch hex chuck, an industry standard for such things as sheet metal screws. There is also a magnetized version of Megapro.

"There is no shortage of bad multi-bit screwdrivers out there," said Fruhm. One design on the market has screw bits in slots covered by a rotating cap, but the bit falls out when turned upside down. Another design has the bits slotted into the handle. . . .

Fruhm feels lucky.

"When I was 23 years old, I wanted to be a rock 'n' roll musician. I never dreamed I would be in the hand tool business," said Fruhm, 54. "Sometimes I still pinch myself. This is crazy.". . . .
(www.megaproscrewdrivers.com)

Source: Bill Redekop, "Invention sweet music for ex-city rocker," *Winnipeg Free Press*, April 17, 2003, p. A-1.

Entrepreneurs in Action

Defensive Strategy

Summer in Indianapolis can be extremely hot, but it wasn't the temperature that had me on edge as I walked across the floor of the gymnasium to referee a Pan-American basketball game. I was clutching one of the only two operating prototypes of my new Fox 40 pea-less whistle. We had spent three-and-a-half years and $150,000 in production, and the whistle had never been heard by anyone other than our small development group. Would the new whistle work when it counted most?

The idea for a pea-less whistle came to me in 1984 after I needed a police escort out of a gymnasium in Brazil when my regular whistle failed to blow at a crucial point in a pre-Olympic basketball game. Now, as I crossed the floor for the start of the Pan-Am game, I made a mental note of where the exits, security staff and police were located — in case my new invention failed to utter a sound.

The whistle not only worked, it was so loud and clear that it startled everyone in the gym. When the games were over, I came home with orders for 20,000 Fox 40 pea-less whistles, and the funds to put my invention into full production.

Today, we have sold close to 100 million whistles in 126 countries. The Fox 40 whistle is used in almost every professional and amateur league and sports association worldwide, and we have developed variations for dog trainers, hunters, hikers, campers, rescue workers and police departments. We know the whistle works, it's accepted and it sells. Now we're fighting another battle — one that has cost us legal fees in the hundreds of thousands of dollars — with no end in sight. Fox 40, like many companies with useful new products, faces the scourge of imitators supplying cheap rip-offs. But I've learned that with some foresight and planning, any inventor can nip this problem in the bud with proper patent and trademark protection.

When you look for money for a new invention, your bank manager and potential investors always ask those same two questions: 1) Do you have a business plan, and 2) Do you have a patent? Although you need both to raise money to bring your product to market, most businesspeople never read the full business plan; even fewer understand how patents and trademarks work, or how they protect your product. For the record, patents describe exactly what your products are.

Trademarks describe who you are and what your company is all about.

Thousands of patents are filed every year. Few commercial patents ever reach the marketplace and those that do are successful only if the patent is written properly and the product marketed aggressively. Patent searches must be conducted worldwide to protect your invention from infringement by others, and also to protect you from infringing on other patents. The process is incredibly detailed and far too complicated for novices to attempt on their own. Some companies advertise that they can raise money for your invention or help get your invention to market. Get references and check them out thoroughly. Many inventors have learned very expensive lessons trying to get to market using the services of these companies.

I knew we needed help navigating the patent process. The late Chuck Shepherd, from Oakville, Ontario, was a guru in the field of developing and patenting new products and ideas. But when I first showed him my concept, he immediately declined to take on the project. He soon changed his mind, not because of the whistle itself, but because he found out I was the guy who owned Fluke Transport Group, the trucking company with the slogan, "If it's on time, it's a Fluke." He said if I could be successful with that slogan, I could probably sell a pea-less whistle.

We protected our whistle with dozens of patents. Chuck made sure that the technical description of the Fox 40 pea-less whistle was comprehensive and all encompassing. When the whistle design was complete, he took me to meet Stan Rogers of Rogers & Scott, Patent Attorneys, in Oakville. Chris Scott soon joined the team and together we filed world patents for the Fox 40 whistle.

This team prepared me to take my invention to market. They told me that having a patent wouldn't make a product successful. Success would only come from making a better whistle and marketing it more aggressively than the competition. It was simple yet sound advice.

Patents — valuable assets that can be sold or licensed if necessary — are important and are absolutely necessary if you have a product with a world market or a product that can be copied easily. But I soon learned that I also needed trademark protection. Patents have an expiry date and others can patent or introduce similar patents.

Trademarks, however, are yours and provide greater protection against new products. Products are recognized by their name, and as the product becomes more popular so does the value of the trademark. I have never had a customer call me and order two dozen of a specific patent number. They ask for two dozen black Fox 40 pea-less whistles. I needed to protect the name.

My team had prepared me for this phase of our development and had filed trademarks in all the markets where we would be doing business.

We have now spent over $750,000 on patent and trademark registrations to protect our product and our name. We are currently involved with 11 infringement cases against the Fox 40 patents or trademarks. These patent and trademark infringements usually originate from one of three sources:

1. Competition who have the capability of making a similar product

2. Companies who see that a large profit can be made by selling a similar product and have the resources to fight us in court

3. Companies who get in and out of the market fast, passing their cheap imitation off as our product

These imitators find it tougher to beat a charge of trademark infringement than one of patent infringement. Companies can argue that their pea-less whistle is different than our pea-less whistle or that their patent does not infringe on ours. But no one can say that they own the Fox 40 pea-less whistle.

Imitation may be the highest form of flattery, but fighting it without the proper protection can also be extremely costly. When all is said and done, our trademarks provide the best long-term protection for our products. My best advice is to patent for design protection and trademark for revenue protection. (www.fox40whistle.com)

Source: Ron Foxcroft, "Defensive Strategy," *PROFIT*, July 12, 2001. Reprinted with permission.

Peter Kielland, meanwhile, has developed what he considers to be a new, further improved version of the multi-bit screwdriver called the Scruzol. The Scruzol looks like most other all-in-one screwdrivers with a steel shaft and a slotted plastic handle holding extra bits but two key features give it a different twist. The Scruzol has bit sockets at each end. With a bit in one end of the shaft it's a regular screwdriver. Attach the shaft onto a drill with a bit in the socket on the other end of the handle and it's a power driving accessory. The other difference is the incorporation of a strong magnet into the body of the Scruzol which enables it to hold a screw tightly to the blade of the screwdriver for easy application while keeping the extra bits firmly in the handle but still permitting their easy removal. Mr. Kielland has already commercialized the Scruzol and demonstrated it at a new product showcase organized by Canadian Tire. They liked the Scruzol so much they ordered 15,000 of them. (www.scrusol.com)[2]

Bob Dickie of Spark Innovations Inc. has built his whole business around patentable products. He holds 80 patents for his inventions and thinks patent protection is crucial to business success these days. Dickie's first product was the FlatPlug, billed as the first innovation in electrical plug design in 75 years. The FlatPlug lies flat against the wall, unlike a conventional electrical plug that sticks out perpendicular to the wall. As a result, it doesn't waste space behind furniture and is more difficult for children to pry out. Dickie got the idea when he saw his daughter reach through her crib bars for a conventional plug. FlatPlug is protected by eight U.S. and worldwide patents. Even the package — a cardboard sleeve that keeps the extension cord and the plug in place — is patented.

Dickie has a number of strict criteria that he feels a product idea should meet in order to have commercial potential:

- **It must be 10 times better** Rather than evolutionary improvements in product design, he looks for concepts with enough of a "story" to make distribution channels take serious notice.

- **It must be patentable** "If we can't get a patent, the business is absolutely dead," says Dickie.

- **It must be a mass-production item** High-volume products have a higher turnover, reducing much of the risk of holding inventory.

- **It should be smaller than a bread box** Small items are easier to make and less costly to design, package, and transport.

2. Robert Bostelaar, "Screwdriver with a Twist Bypasses the Dragons", The Financial Post, March 22, 2010, (www.financialpost.com/small-business/story.html?id=2710081), accessed May 27, 2010.

FYI / FOR YOUR INFORMATION

THE GREATEST CANADIAN INVENTIONS

In 2007 CBC Television hosted a mini-series in which they asked Canadian to vote on which invention they considered the greatest Canadian invention. The results were as follows:

1. Insulin, Treatment for Diabetes (1921, Frederick Banting, Charles Best)
2. The Telephone (1876, Alexander Graham Bell)
3. The Light Bulb (1874, Henry Woodward, Matthew Evans)
4. Five-pin Bowling (1908, Thomas Ryan)
5. Wonderbra (1964, Louise Poirier)
6. The Artificial Pacemaker (1950, John Hopps, Wilfred Bigelow, John Callaghan)
7. The Robertson Screw (1908, Peter Robertson)
8. The Zipper (1913, Gideon Sundback)
9. The Electric Wheelchair (1952, George Klein)
10. Poutine (1957, Fernand Lachance)

Source: (www.cbc.ca/inventions/), accessed May 27, 2010.

- **It must lend itself to distribution through existing channels** Going through established market lines speeds the acceptance of a new product.
- **It should have no government involvement** Spark Innovations stays away from products that are motivated by or are dependent on government support at any level.
- **It must be useful** Dickie works only with products that have long-term, practical usefulness. No novelties, fads, or games.[3]

Commercializing Your Patent

Once you have taken steps to protect your idea, you will have to give some thought to the best way to market it and hopefully turn a profit. There are a number of possible options.

- Setting up your own business, like the individuals profiled in the Entrepreneurs in Action examples, is the option that usually comes to mind. It allows you to retain full control of your idea but also means you assume all the risk.
- Another possibility is to license the invention. With a licence you grant one or more individuals the right to manufacture and sell your innovation in exchange for royalties. The licence can apply generally or only to a specific market or geographic region, as long as you have obtained patent protection for that area.
- A third option is to sell your patent. By selling your patent you give up all rights to the idea in return for a lump sum of money. However, then you don't have to worry about whether the product becomes a commercial success.

Watch Out For Invention Scams

Many people with a new idea immediately start looking for a company that they think will buy or license their idea. Any number of companies advertise on radio, TV, or in magazines, offering to help you patent your idea and market it for you. They offer their assistance as a "one-stop" do-it-all-for-you ticket to success for your great new idea. Most of these offers are outright scams. These firms generally follow a three-step process:

1. They send you a free kit with a pre-signed *confidentiality* or *non-disclosure* agreement and some general information about the services they provide.

---

3. Adapted from Ellen Roseman, "Spark of Genius," *The Globe and Mail*, September 26, 1994.

2. Next, they offer to do a marketing evaluation of the potential for your idea. This may cost several hundred dollars.

3. They then present a package offering to patent your invention and promote your idea by submitting it to manufacturers, potential licensees, and industry in general. This time the fee can be anywhere from $3,000 to $10,000 or higher.

Only after a year or two of unfulfilled promises and zero activity do you begin to realize that you might have been scammed, but by then it is too late. It's best to avoid these kinds of operators in the first place. The truth is that commercializing a new idea is a long, complicated process that takes time, energy, knowledge, and persistence. No one can guarantee you success.

REGISTERING YOUR TRADEMARK

A *trademark* is a word, symbol, picture, design, or combination of these that distinguishes your goods and services from those of others in the marketplace. A trademark might also be thought of as a "brand name" or "identifier" that can be used to distinguish the products of your firm. For example, both the name "McDonald's" and the symbol of the golden arches are (among others) registered trademarks of the McDonald's Corporation.

To *register* a trademark means to file it with a government agency for the purpose of securing the following rights and benefits:

1. Exclusive permission to use the brand name or identifier in Canada

2. The right to sue anyone you suspect of infringing on your trademark to recover lost profits on sales made under your trade name, and for other damages and costs

3. The basis for filing an application in another country should you wish to export your product

To be registerable, a trademark must be distinctive and not so similar in appearance, sound, or concept to a trademark already registered, or pending registration, as to be confused with it. For example, the following trademarks would not be registerable: "Cleanly Canadian" for a soft drink (too close to Clearly Canadian, a fruit-flavoured mineral water); "Extendo" for a utility knife (too close to Exacto).

The value of a trademark lies in the goodwill the market attaches to it and the fact that consumers will ask for your brand with the expectation of receiving the same quality product or service as previously. Therefore, unlike a patent, a trademark should be registered only if you have some long-term plans for it that will result in an accumulation of goodwill.

It is possible for you to use a trademark without registering it. Registration is not mandatory and unregistered marks have legal status. But registration is advised for most commonly used identifiers, since it does establish immediate, obvious proof of ownership, particularly if the business is looking to expand geographically.

Failing to properly register your trademarks can sometimes lead to future problems. Robert Arthurs of the True North Clothing Company in Entrepreneurs in Action #37 learned this lesson the hard way. Despite consulting with a lawyer and a government agency, his company's failure to do appropriate due diligence and search out previous registrations of the "True North" trade name ended up costing it a lot of money in legal and other fees. In the end the company had to buy the rights to use the name from the registered owner despite assurances that the term was part of the "public domain" and available for use by anyone.

HOW TO REGISTER YOUR TRADEMARK

In Canada it is possible for you to register your trademark before you actually use it, but the mark will not be validated until it is actually put into service. Registration of a trademark involves the following steps:

1. **A search of previous and pending registrations** As with a patent, a search should be conducted to determine that your trademark does not conflict with others already in use. The search can be conducted at the CIPO Trade-marks Branch in Gatineau, Quebec, where a public inventory of all registered trademarks and pending applications is maintained. You can also conduct a search electronically at the CIPO Web site.

2. **An application to register your trademark** This involves filing an application for registration of your trademark.

Entrepreneurs in Action

The Name Game

We began like so many other young companies, merrily building our company and brand name. Many years and hundreds of thousands of dollars went into laying the groundwork for our name "True North Clothing Company." And like many other young companies, we assumed we were protected against infringing on someone else's trademark. I have since learned that you should never assume.

When we began our company, my business partner spoke with a government agency in Hull, Quebec, regarding the use of trademarks. We were informed that because the phrase "True North" is part of Canada's national anthem, it is public domain and available for anyone's use. Beyond that, without the money for extensive legal advice, we could only briefly consult a lawyer. We were assured that by doing a "poor man's trademark" — sending the designs to ourselves by registered mail and not opening them unless there was a dispute — we were effectively protecting our interest in the name.

Believing our trademark secure, we started an aggressive advertising campaign in *The Globe & Mail* mail-order section, featuring our new shirt "True North Strong & Free."

After only two days of advertising, we received by registered mail a cease-and-desist letter from lawyers representing a company in Ontario. The company claimed to own the name, and ordered us to stop using their trademark. We spent the next three years involved in faxes, phone calls and face-to-face meetings (with and without lawyers present) in an attempt to come to a peaceful resolution between the Ontario company and ourselves. But it seemed that no matter what solution was proposed, we could not reach an agreement. Our costs were rising. We even made a

[five-figure] purchase of a competitor's company and trademark as a safeguard, in case we were forced to stop using "True North" and needed another name. Our legal costs were also into five figures. It reached the point where our lawyer said, "I can't keep taking your money anymore . . . you guys just can't take these legal bills."

It was clear our competitor had much deeper pockets than we did, and we could no longer afford to fight a strict enforcement of the cease and desist order. We decided to end the dispute by purchasing the trademark from the Ontario company.

So what happened to "public domain"? To this day, nobody has been able to provide us with an answer. Even representatives of the federal government, which is responsible for trademark legislation, have been at a loss for a clear explanation. And over the years, we have received so much mixed and conflicting information from lawyers that we have yet to see one firm support advice another firm has given.

If there is a lesson here, it is that trademarks and copyright should be taken more seriously. We live in an age of corporate branding, and companies have become more vigilant than ever in protecting their trademarks. But more information regarding trademark and copyright laws is available to entrepreneurs today than was available to us, both on the Internet and in libraries across Canada. Many of these resources are absolutely free. My advice to up-and-coming companies is to check out as much material as you can locate. Because even when you think you're right, you can't always win.

Source: Robert Arthurs, "The Name Game," *Profit*, December 7, 2001. Reprinted with permission.

Once your application is received, it is published in the *Trade-marks Journal* to see if anyone opposes your registration.

Even though registering a trademark is relatively simple compared with applying for a patent, it is recommended that you consult a trademark agent who is registered with the CIPO Trade-marks Branch.

MAINTAINING AND POLICING YOUR TRADEMARK

It normally takes about a year from the date of application for a trademark to be registered. Registration is effective for 15 years, and may be renewed for a series of 15-year terms as long as the mark is still in use.

As with a patent, it is up to the owner of the trademark to police its use, since the government provides no assistance in the enforcement of trademark rights. Some firms have gone to considerable lengths in an effort to enforce what they feel are their legal rights. For example, The Brick Warehouse, an Edmonton-based national chain of furniture stores, sued Fred and Cynthia Brick of the family-owned Brick's Fine Furniture in Winnipeg to get them to stop using the name "Brick" for their store. This was despite the fact that the Brick family began operating their provincially registered Winnipeg outlet in 1969, while The Brick began operating under that name in Edmonton only in 1977 and was incorporated federally in 1987. After four years of legal battles and hundreds of thousands of dollars in legal fees, the sides finally agreed to an out-of-court settlement. Part of the agreement is that both stores will display a sign at their entrances stating that there is no association between The Brick or The Brick Warehouse and Brick's Fine Furniture.[4]

More recently, in another David vs Goliath situation, Starbucks Corp., the Seattle-based multinational coffee retailer, threatened legal action for trademark infringement against a small cafe/restaurant called HaidaBucks Cafe in Masset on the Queen Charlotte Islands, off the coast of British Columbia. Starbucks demanded that the owners of the small local cafe change its name and logo because these were creating confusion in the marketplace by being too similar to their own, even though there are no Starbucks coffee shops in Masset. The owners refused to comply and with the assistance of a high-powered Victoria law firm, the exchange of correspondence and a considerable outpouring of public support appear to have won the battle. HaidaBucks eventually received a letter from Starbucks that concluded, "Starbucks considers this matter closed."[5]

Similarly, Lululemon Athletica, a Vancouver-based clothing chain, accused Madmax Worldwide Sourcing Inc. of selling a copycat version of its popular line of "yoga-inspired" clothing in Vancouver-area Costco stores and at a number of smaller retailers. Chip Wilson, the founder of Lululemon, said he is not "hung up" on the trademark infringement but is acting only because his lawyer said that failing to protect the trademark could mean losing his rights.[6]

Interestingly, in late 2009 Lululemon[7] itself was accused of engaging in 'ambush marketing' and questionable practices. They released a line of clothing named the "Cool Sporting Event That Takes Place in British Columbia Between 2009 & 2011 Edition", an apparent reference to the 2010 Winter Olympics. The name does not infringe Canada's Olympic and Paralympic Marks Act in that it does not use the terms "Olympic(s)", "Vancouver", "2010", or any other term protected under that law but the clothing is in the national colours of Canada, the USA and Germany. Representatives from the Vancouver Olympic Organizing Committee, while acknowledging that no explicit infringement had taken place, nevertheless expressed disappointment at Lululemon's tactics.

Registration of a trademark in Canada provides no protection of your trademark in other countries. If you are involved with or contemplating exporting to any other country, you should consider registering your trademark in that country as well.

Marking Requirements

The *Trade-marks Act* does not contain any marking requirements. However, trademark owners can indicate their registration through the use of certain symbols, namely ® (registered), ™ (trademark), SM (service mark), MD (marque déposée), or MC (marque de commerce). Although the act does not require the use of these symbols, it is advisable to use them.

OBTAINING COPYRIGHT

A *copyright* gives you the right to preclude others from reproducing or copying your original published work. Materials protected by copyright include books, leaflets, periodicals and contributions to periodicals, lectures, sermons, musical or dramatic compositions, maps, works of art, photographs, drawings of a scientific or technical

---

4. R. Pederson, "Legal Battle of the Bricks Finally Ends; Sides Agree to Coexist," *Edmonton Journal,* June 20, 1992, p. F1.

5. HaidaBucks, An Indigenous Experience, Latest News (www.lanebaldwin.com/hbc/news.htm), accessed May 28, 2010.

6. P. Brieger, "When Mediation Fails, Call Your Lawyer: Yoga Clothier Files Trademark Lawsuit," *National Post,* September 25, 2003, p. FP.01.F.

7. Lululemon Athletica, (en.wikipedia.org/wiki/Lululemon_Athletica), accessed May 28, 2010.

nature, motion pictures, sound recordings, databases, and computer programs. A copyright exists for the duration of your life plus 50 years following your death.

HOW TO OBTAIN A COPYRIGHT

In Canada, there is no legal requirement that your work be registered in order to obtain copyright; it is automatically acquired on creation of an original work. Nevertheless, you may wish to apply for voluntary registration. When your work has been registered, a certificate is issued that can, if necessary, be used in court to establish your ownership of the work.

You can register a copyright by completing the required application form and sending it to CIPO's Copyright Office along with the appropriate fee. You do not need to send a copy of your work with the application but you may need to send copies to the National Library of Canada. The registration process typically takes around four weeks but may be longer if amendments are required.

Indicating Copyright

There is no requirement to mark your work under the *Copyright Act*. However, you may choose to mark it with the symbol ©, your name and the year of first publication of the work, for example, © John Doe, 2008. You may use this mark even if you have not formally registered your work with the Copyright Office.

PROTECTION PROVIDED BY COPYRIGHT

Your copyright enables you to control the copying and dissemination of your own works. This includes publishing, producing, reproducing, and performing your material. As with patents and trademarks, the responsibility for policing your copyright rests with you.

It is important to understand some of the limitations of copyright protection as well. For example, for purposes of copyright protection, the term "computer program" refers to "a set of instructions or statements, expressed, fixed, embodied or stored in any manner, that is to be used directly or indirectly in a computer in order to bring about a specific result." This means that a specific computer program such as Microsoft Excel can be protected as a literary work but not the idea of spreadsheet programs in general. In addition, any accompanying documentation for a program, such as a user's guide, is considered a separate work and must be registered separately.

Unlike patents and trademarks, a copyright in Canada provides simultaneous protection in most other countries of the world.

REGISTERING YOUR INDUSTRIAL DESIGN

An industrial design comprises the features of shape, configuration, pattern, or ornament applied to a finished article made by hand, tool, or machine. This may be, for example, the shape of a table or chair, or the shape of the ornamentation of a knife or a spoon. The design must have features that appeal to the eye and be substantially original. Registering your design gives you exclusive rights to the design and enables you to prevent others from making, importing, renting, or selling any article on which the design has been registered and to which the design or a design not substantially different has been applied. However, no prior disclosure of the design is allowed, including publication in a college or university thesis. Unlike trademark and copyright protection, you can make no legal claim of ownership and have *no legal protection against imitation unless your design has been registered*.

HOW TO REGISTER YOUR INDUSTRIAL DESIGN

You can file your own application for industrial design registration; however, it is generally recommended that you hire a patent agent to prepare and follow through on your application. An application for an industrial design must contain:

- a completed application form
- at least one photograph or drawing of the design

Your application will be examined to ensure that it is original and registerable. It cannot be the same or similar to a design already applied to a similar article of manufacture. Following this assessment the examiner will either approve the application or issue a report indicating what further information or amendments may be required. You have four months to reply to the report. This process can take up to a year, but once registered, designs are valid for 10 years from that date.

Marking Your Product

You do not have to mark your design to indicate that it has been registered but marking does give you some extra protection. The proper mark is a capital "D" inside a circle along with your name or an abbreviation of it on the article itself, its label, or its packaging. If your product is marked in this way, a court may award a remedy of some kind such as financial compensation if someone is found to be infringing on or violating your design. Otherwise the court can merely issue an injunction to forbid the other party from using your design.

PROTECTION PROVIDED BY INDUSTRIAL DESIGN REGISTRATION

As with other forms of intellectual property, you may take legal action against anyone who infringes on your design in Canada. As the proprietor of the registered design, however, you have exclusive right to use it and may sell all or some of these rights to other people or authorize them to use the design, subject to certain conditions. These rights, however, relate only to Canada. To obtain similar rights in other countries you must apply for them in each country separately.

PROTECTING INTEGRATED CIRCUIT TOPOGRAPHIES

The circuits incorporated into an integrated circuit (IC) are embodied in a three-dimensional hill-and-valley configuration called a topography. These designs are protected by the *Integrated Circuit Topography Act*. IC products, commonly called "microchips" or "semiconductor chips" are incorporated into a variety of consumer and industrial products. The protection associated with the design of a topography is entirely distinct from that of any computer program embodied in the chip. Computer programs are subject to protection under the *Copyright Act*.

WHAT PROTECTION DOES THE ACT PROVIDE?

The legislation provides exclusive rights in regard to:

- Reproduction of a protected topography or any substantial part of it
- Manufacture of an IC product incorporating the topography or any substantial part of it
- Importation or commercial exploitation of a topography, or of an IC product that embodies a protected topography or any substantial part of it
- Importation or commercial exploitation of an industrial article that incorporates an IC product that embodies a protected topography

The Act provides for a full range of civil remedies, including injunctions and exemplary damages. Protection for registered integrated circuit topographies is provided for approximately 10 years.

HOW TO PROTECT AN IC TOPOGRAPHY

To protect an IC topography you must apply to CIPO's Registrar of Topographies. Applications for "commercially exploited" topographies must be filed within two years of the date of first commercial exploitation anywhere. The application may be rejected if the topography was first exploited outside Canada. Owners must be Canadian or nationals of countries having reciprocal protection agreements with Canada.

USE OF A NON-DISCLOSURE AGREEMENT (NDA)

A *non-disclosure agreement* (NDA) allows you to share details of your intellectual property with other people whose input you may be seeking without jeopardizing the information. For example, if you have a new product idea or software program in development, but need to consult an advisor for advice on how to proceed, an appropriate NDA can ensure that the advisor doesn't share the details of your new idea with anyone else.

The NDA is a legal contract between you and the other party. You agree to disclose certain information to them for a specific purpose. They agree to not disclose that information to anyone else.

There are five important elements in a typical nondisclosure agreement:

- a definition of the 'confidential information'
- material excluded from confidential information
- the obligations of the receiving party
- the time period for which the NDA is in effect
- any miscellaneous provisions

Excluded material usually covers any information created or discovered by the receiving party prior to (or independent of) any involvement with the other party. The receiving party typically has no obligation to protect this excluded information.

You should be aware, however, that some parties routinely refuse to sign non-disclosure agreements. Many venture capital companies, some R&D companies, some manufacturers and many government departments/agencies usually refuse to sign such documents. One reason is that all government employees sign a statement pledging to treat information related to their work as confidential so see the NDA as redundant.

TRADE SECRETS

A *trade secret* is difficult to define but may consist of a formula for a chemical compound, a process of manufacturing, a means of treating or preserving materials, a pattern for a machine or other device, a list of customers, or any other secrets which are used in a business, and may give it an advantage over competitors who do not know the trade secret. The most well-known trade secrets are probably the formula for Coca Cola or how Cadbury's Chocolates gets the caramel into the Caramilk bar.

There are no government forms to file with trade secrets. You have to keep the information a secret and take reasonable measures to do so if you want trade secret protection. Trade secrets are often protected by means of a NDA. Anybody to whom a trade secret has been revealed should be asked to sign a non-disclosure agreement. This could include employees, suppliers, manufacturers, sub-contractors, and component manufacturers.

FOR MORE INFORMATION ON INTELLECTUAL PROPERTY

Further information on the protection of intellectual property can be obtained from:

Canadian Intellectual Property Office
Industry Canada
50 Victoria St., Room C-229 (in person) or Room C-114 (mail or courier)
Place du Portage, Phase 1
Gatineau, Quebec K1A 0C9
(cipo.gc.ca)
Tel: (866) 997-1936

or contact your local Canada Business Service Centre.

The deadlines for filing, the length of time for which protection is provided, and the current registration fees for several types of intellectual property are summarized in Table 9.1.

TABLE **9.1**	INFORMATION ABOUT PROTECTION OF INTELLECTUAL PROPERTY IN CANADA		

Type	Application Deadline	Period of Coverage	Government Fees for Small Entities	
Patents	File within 1 year of publication (file before publication for most other countries)	20 years from filing of application	Filing fee	$200
			Examination fee	$400
			Allowance fee (Grant)	$150
			Maintenance fee	
			Years 2, 3 & 4	$ 50
			Years 5 to 9	$100
			Years 10 to 14	$125
			Years 15 to 19	$225
Trademarks	(None)	15 years; renewable indefinitely	Filing fee	$250–300
			Registration fee	$200
Copyright	(None)	50 years plus life of author	Registration fee	$50–65
Industrial Designs	File within 12 months of publication	10 years from date of registration	Examination fee	$400 plus $10 for each page over 10 pages
			Maintenance of registration fee	$350

CONCLUSION

As we have discussed, in addition to various *tangible* assets such as land, buildings, and equipment, your business may also own certain *intangible* assets, such as patents, trademarks, and copyrights. These can be just as important as, or even more important than, your tangible assets. And like tangible assets, with the permission of their owner they can be bought, sold, licensed, or used by someone else.

Ideas that are not patentable and are not otherwise protected may be protected by contract law either by means of a written *non-disclosure* agreement or by treating them as *trade secrets*. This can be done by taking every precaution to keep valuable knowledge a secret and/or by placing specific provisions in any agreement you may have with your employees that they will neither disclose to anyone else nor use for their own purposes any trade secrets they may acquire while in your employ. The advantages of this type of protection may be even greater than those of patent protection. The success of this approach depends on your ability to control the access of outsiders to the information, as there are no *legal rights* in a trade secret. Typically, once confidential information has been publicly disclosed, it becomes very difficult to enforce any rights to it.

Arranging Financing

Quite a number of sources of financing are available to established businesses. However, there are relatively few sources of *seed capital* for ventures that are just getting off the ground and have no track record. Obtaining such capital can require persistence and determination. Usually you must submit a formal proposal to a prospective source of funding in which you outline your needs, plans for the money, the investors' expected return, and a loan repayment schedule. Many financing proposals have to be revised several times before receiving a positive response. In addition, you may have to be prepared to combine financing from several sources to raise all the funds you require.

Two kinds of funds are potentially available to you: *debt* and *equity*.

DEBT FINANCING

Debt financing is borrowing money that must be repaid in full, usually in periodic payments with interest. Three important parameters associated with debt financing are:

1. Amount of principal to be borrowed
2. Interest rate on the loan
3. Maturity date of the loan

Together these three factors determine the extent of your obligation to the creditor. Until the debt has been repaid, the provider of the loan has a legal claim against the assets and cash flows of your business. In many cases the creditor can demand payment at any time and possibly force your business into bankruptcy because of overdue payments.

The *principal* of the loan is the total amount of money you hope to borrow. This could be the difference between the amount shown on your estimate of your required start-up funding (as illustrated back in Figure 8.1 on page 244) and the sum you are personally able to provide to get your business started.

The *interest rate* is the "price" you will have to pay for the borrowed funds. In most cases it will be tied to the current *prime rate*. This is generally considered to be the rate of interest that banks charge their best customers — those with the lowest risk. For example, a bank might be prepared to offer loans to a small business for prime plus some fixed percentage, perhaps 3 or 4 per cent. The prime rate may fluctuate somewhat due to periodic decisions by the Bank of Canada, so the effective interest rate on your loan may vary somewhat as well.

The *maturity* of the loan refers to the length of time for which you will obtain the use of the funds. This should coincide with your intended use of the money. Short-term needs require short-term financing. For example, you might use a short-term loan to purchase inventory that you intend to sell within a month or two or to finance some outstanding accounts receivables. A short-term loan such as a *line of credit* typically has to be repaid within a year.

Purchasing a building or a major piece of equipment may require a long-term loan or a *term* loan. This is a loan that will be repaid over an extended period of time, typically several years. The purpose of the loan will determine the maturity period.

The primary sources of debt financing are shareholder loans provided by the owners of the business and operating loans and term loans provided by banks and other financial institutions such as trust companies, Alberta Treasury Branches, and credit unions. Providing some funds as a loan rather than as an equity investment can have some advantages for you as the owner of a small business. The interest payments made to you are income tax deductible by the business and it may be easier to withdraw the money if necessary than if it was tied up in equity.

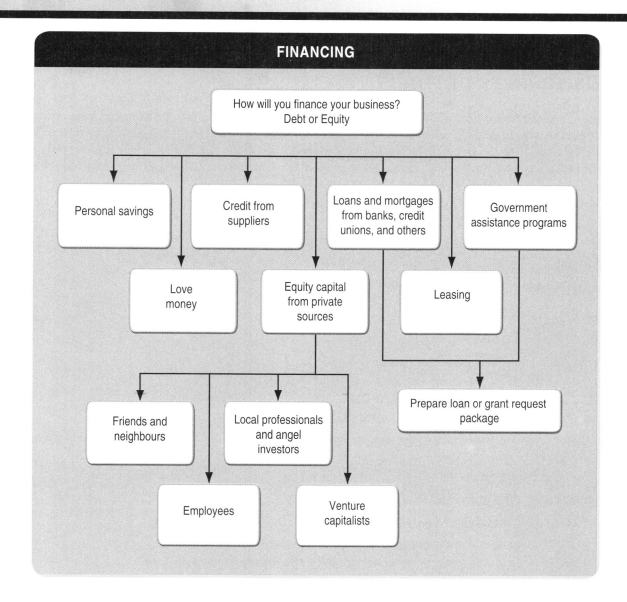

FINANCING

How will you finance your business?
Debt or Equity

- Personal savings
- Credit from suppliers
- Loans and mortgages from banks, credit unions, and others
- Government assistance programs
- Love money
- Equity capital from private sources
- Leasing
- Friends and neighbours
- Local professionals and angel investors
- Employees
- Venture capitalists
- Prepare loan or grant request package

EQUITY FINANCING

Equity funding is money supplied by yourself or investors in exchange for an ownership position in your business. Unlike debt, equity funding does not need to be repaid. Providers of equity capital forego the opportunity to receive interest and periodic repayment of the funds they have extended to your business; rather, they share in the profits their investment is expected to generate. Other than making your own personal investment, it is not easy to attract other investors to a new business. No matter how sure you are that your business will be successful, others will not necessarily share your confidence and will need to be persuaded to invest in your idea by your enthusiasm and your business plan.

In addition to providing the funds, equity investors will usually demand a voice in how your business is run. This can substantially reduce your ability to run your business as you would like. They expect to receive their return from any dividends that may be paid out periodically from the net profits of the business or, more significantly, from the increased value of the business as it grows and prospers. They expect to be able to sell all or part of their investment for a considerable profit, although the shares of a small private company may have a very limited market.

The most common sources of equity financing for start-up businesses are your own personal savings and your family and friends.

The advantages of debt versus external equity financing from your perspective as owner of the business are summarized in the following Other considerations box.

MAJOR SOURCES OF FUNDS

The major sources of funds for small business start-ups are personal funds, commercial loans and lines of credit, the use of personal credit cards for business purposes, personal loans provided to the business by the owner, and trade credit provided to the business by its suppliers. As you can see in Figure 10.1, these are the principal sources of financing for entrepreneurs of all ages, but there are some minor differences between younger and

---

Other considerations   DEBT VERSUS EQUITY

DEBT
Advantages Of Debt Financing

- It's useful for meeting a short-term deficit in cash flow.
- You do not have to give up or share control of your business.
- The term of the debt (loan) is generally limited.
- It may be acquired from a variety of lenders. You can shop around.
- The information needed to obtain a loan is generally straightforward and normally incorporated into a business plan.
- Interest paid is tax-deductible.

Disadvantages Of Debt Financing

- It can be difficult to obtain when the project is risky and its success uncertain.
- Taking on more debt than the business needs can be a burden on your cash flows.
- If the funds aren't used properly, it may be difficult for the business to repay the loan.
- If it is a "demand" loan, it can be called by the lender at any time.
- The lender may require you to provide a personal guarantee for the loan.
- Lenders will often insist on certain restrictions being put in to place. For instance, there may be a limit on how much you can draw out of the business in the form of a salary or dividends or the amount you can spend on equipment or other acquisitions without their approval.

EQUITY
Advantages Of Equity Financing

- An appropriate investor can contribute expertise, contacts, and new business as well as money.
- Equity may be the only way to fund high-risk ventures, where the cost of debt could be prohibitive.
- It can be used to fund larger projects with longer time frames.

Disadvantages Of Equity Financing

- Owner has to give up some ownership and control of the business.
- There is always the danger of incompatibility and disagreement among the investors.
- It is much more difficult to terminate the relationship if disagreements occur.

older entrepreneurs. Younger entrepreneurs are more inclined to finance their businesses through their own personal funds, as well as via other informal methods, such as their personal credit and loans from relatives and friends or "love money." Surprisingly, they also report making slightly higher use of commercial credit, in the form of loans and lines of credit. Common anecdotal stories tend to indicate that younger people have a more difficult time accessing these formal sources of funding, but from this data it seems that may not necessarily be the case. You may be able to "piece together" the combination of debt and equity funding that you require from a combination of these sources as well.

PERSONAL FUNDS

The first place to look for money to start your business is your own pocket. This may mean cleaning out your savings account and other investments, selling your second car, postponing your holiday for this year, cashing in your RRSPs, mortgaging the cottage, or any other means you may have of raising cash.

BOOTSTRAPPING

One concept actively promoted for many new entrepreneurs is the concept of "*bootstrap financing*" or *bootstrapping*. Bootstrapping is essentially looking for highly creative ways of acquiring the resources you need to get your business off the ground without "kick starting" the business with external capital by borrowing money or raising equity from traditional financing sources. It means being as frugal as possible so that your business can

FIGURE 10.1   **TOP TEN SOURCES OF FINANCING USED DURING START-UP***

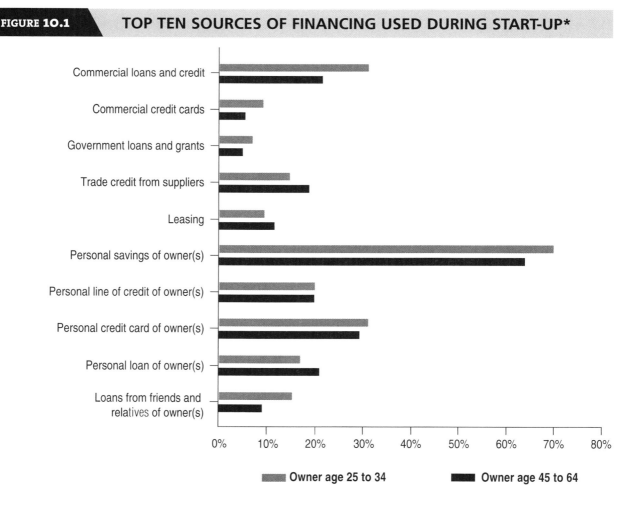

* Reported by SMEs operating in 2000, in relation to their financing experiences in starting up their business at any time between 1996 and 2000 by frequency of use.

Source: Statistics Canada, *Survey on Financing of Small and Medium Enterprises,* 2000.

get going on as little cash as possible. It is estimated that between 75 and 85 per cent of new start-ups use some form of bootstrapping to help finance themselves.[1] In some cases it may be the only way they can get the money they need to keep their new business going until the cash generated from earnings is sufficient to fund the ongoing growth of the business.

There are a number of advantages to bootstrapping. Down the road, your business may be worth more because you haven't had to raise money selling off equity positions along the way. In addition, you may be able to reduce the high interest costs on borrowed money from conventional sources. You could also find yourself in a stronger position later on to raise funds from external lenders and investors, since your business won't be saddled with a lot of debt.

Bootstrapping can take a wide variety of forms, although most of the typical techniques can be classified into specific categories, such as:

- Minimizing Your Investment
- Owner Financing
- Minimizing Your Accounts Receivable
- Delaying Payments
- Sharing Resources with Other Businesses

Some of the more common bootstrapping techniques include:

Personal Credit Cards

The credit limit extended by financial institutions on personal credit cards can provide you with ready access to a short-term loan, but usually at interest rates that are considerably higher than more conventional financing (upward of 18 to 22 per cent or more). There may be occasions, however, where other sources of working capital are not available and drawing on the personal line of credit associated with your cards may be the only source of funds available to sustain your business. This can be risky since you are personally liable for the expenditures on the card even though they may have been made for business purposes, but it may be useful if you are expecting a major payment or other injection of cash into the business within a few days.

Suppliers' Inventory Buying Plans

In some industries one way of obtaining working capital may be through supplier financing. Suppliers may be prepared to extend payment terms to 60, 90, or even 120 days for some customers. Other suppliers may offer floor plan financing or factoring options to help their dealers finance inventory purchases, usually in advance of the peak selling season. In addition, many suppliers offer discounts off the face value of their invoice (typically 2 per cent for payment within 10 days) or penalize slow-paying customers with interest charges (often 1.5 per cent a month). These programs can impact your financing requirements.

Leasing versus Buying

In competitive equipment markets, specialized leasing and finance companies will arrange for the lease of such items as expensive pieces of equipment, vehicles, copiers, and computers. Leasing, often with an option to buy rather than purchasing, can free up your scarce capital for investment in other areas of your business. While the interest rates charged on the lease contract may be somewhat higher than you might pay through the bank, the lease expenses are usually fully deductible from your taxable income. A lease contract will fix your cost of having the equipment for a specific term and may provide the flexibility to purchase the equipment at a later date at a predetermined price.

Leasehold Improvements

When locating your business in rented premises, it is usually necessary to undertake a number of leasehold improvements to make the premises appropriate to your needs. Installing new electrical outlets, adding additional

---

1. J.C. McCune (1999), "Bootstrapping: Cutting Corners and Pinching Pennies to Finance Your Business," Bankrate.com, www.bankrate.com/brm/news/biz/Cashflow_banking/19991101.asp.

partitions and walls, laying carpet, painting, installing fixtures, and similar modifications can add considerably to the cost of launching your business. Sometimes it may be possible to get the landlord of your location to assist in making these improvements, particularly if there is a lot of other space available to rent. The landlord or property manager may agree to provide a portion (an allowance of a dollar amount per square foot of space) or cover all of your leasehold improvement in return for a longer-term lease (typically three to five years). Reducing your initial expenditures in this way can reduce the start-up cash and equity you require to launch your business, even though you will be paying for these improvements in your monthly rent over the course of the lease.

Advance Payment From Customers

It may be possible to negotiate a full or partial payment from some customers in advance to help finance the costs of taking on their business. In some industries, construction for example, it is customary to receive a partial payment at certain defined stages during the course of the project rather than waiting until completion. These payments can reduce the cash needs of running your business. Any work that involves special orders or custom designs for products specifically tailored to the requirements of one customer should require a significant deposit or full payment in advance.

Jen Kluger and Suzie Orol (Entrepreneurs in Action #38) are excellent examples of young entrepreneurs who have been able to bootstrap their business successfully. They started their handmade jewellery business with very little cash and used what they had to pay for display booths at local outdoor festivals. They decided not to incur the overhead of opening their own retail store but to rely on online sales and a commission sales force to distribute their jewellery through third-party retailers. They maintain a lean operation overall with relatively few employees, do very little advertising and rely largely on public relations to make people aware of their products, keep a minimum amount of inventory and try to turn it over as quickly as possible. To date the young women have never borrowed any money for their business and are well on their way to building an international company.

Examples of other ways to bootstrap are outlined in the Other Considerations box on p. 295. Bootstrapping is not without risk, however. Many of these techniques commonly associated with bootstrapping are not recommended for everyone. Try to avoid such methods as using your personal credit cards, selling your insurance policy, cashing in your RRSP, or taking out a second mortgage on your home. We often hear stories of individuals who have successfully launched their company using such methods, but we seldom hear about those who didn't make it and the repercussions of facing a poor credit rating, personal bankruptcy, or other personal or family problems as a result of not being able to pay off the debt.

In general, however, there are a number of "rules of thumb" that can serve as a guide to effective bootstrapping.

1. Service businesses are easier to bootstrap than manufacturing businesses, since they don't require extensive machinery and equipment.
2. Keep your overhead low by working out of your home for as long as possible.
3. Run your business part-time at the beginning if you can. At least you may be able to do some consulting or other related work on the side to help generate some badly needed revenue.
4. Negotiate time rather than price. Try to get extensions for the payment of bills to 45, 60, or even 90 days, while also providing incentives for your customers to pay their bills as rapidly as possible.
5. Minimize your need for resources. Only lease or buy the machinery and equipment that is absolutely necessary and then try to find used rather than new if at all possible.

"LOVE MONEY"

Once you have scraped together everything you can from your own resources and personal savings, the next step is to talk to other people. Additional funds may come from your friends, family, and close personal relations. This is known as "love money."

Recent estimates indicate that, in fact, love money makes up more than 90 per cent of the external new business start-up capital in Canada. This personal funding is necessary because banks and other conventional sources usually will not lend money without extensive security. For example, Amanda Harburn, whose case is described in Entrepreneurs in Action #39, was able to launch her Prestige Dance Academy in Calgary only with the help of her parents, largely due to her relative lack of experience and other tangible assets.

38

Entrepreneurs in Action

No money down

Jen Kluger, 27, and her business partner, Suzie Orol, also 27, decided not to open a store, opting to sell their handmade jewellery online and through third-party retailers. To service the dozens of American stores that carry Foxy Originals, they employ eight U.S.-based sales reps, who are paid a 15% commission. "Our business model today is very similar to the one we had eight years ago," Kluger says. "We keep a nimble staff. We have minimal inventory, and we turn it around quickly."

Kluger and Orol met when they were business students at the University of Western Ontario. They discovered that they shared an interest in jewellery. Kluger had been selling her pieces to boutiques around Toronto; Orol's family worked in metal-casting, and she had drawn on this trade to design a jewellery line for teenagers. They began making necklaces and selling them on campus. Within a month, they were retailing them at local boutiques. "The idea was to make something that offered an affordable price point but was high quality," Kluger recalls.

The two women went on the road the following summer, using $900 in start-up capital to book outdoor booths at local festivals. As their customer base grew, they kept overheads low by hiring interns from Ryerson University's fashion program. After one shipment of beads failed to arrive on time, Foxy Originals switched to the decorated cast-metal pieces that are now their trademark.

There's no doubt the brand is strong. "We constantly work on PR," says Kluger, pointing to the media coverage they've scored in CosmoGIRL!, Us Weekly and many other publications. "It's one thing to have a good product, but it's another thing to have your market know about it." Besides firing off regular press releases, Kluger and Orol have raised their profile stateside by visiting the editors of major U.S. fashion magazines.

The most visible result of their hard work: Young celebrities like Paris Hilton, Sienna Miller and Tori Spelling have been photographed wearing their jewellery. Kluger and Orol delivered free samples to Hilton when she was in Toronto shooting House of Wax, and they met Spelling at the airport. "We always have jewellery on us," Kluger says with a laugh. "You never know who you're going to run into."

Kluger and Orol have never borrowed money for their business. Even more remarkable: All of their jewellery is made in Canada, at a workshop owned by Orol's parents. Although Kluger says she's happy to support the economy, there are also sound business reasons to manufacture locally. Besides ensuring quality control, it means fast turnaround for a bewildering number of product lines. "The accessories industry moves quickly, and when you're relying on overseas imports, you can run into major trouble," Kluger warns.

Its abundance of colourful bling notwithstanding, Foxy Originals is a lean operation. Head office has just seven staff, including Kluger and Orol, who still do all the jewellery design themselves. But the duo have big plans: They've secured U.K. and Australian distributors, and expect to roll out private-label collaborations with several well-known brands some time this year. (www.foxyoriginals.com)

Source: Nick Rockel, *The Globe and Mail Report on Small Business,* January 30, 2007.

FOXY ORIGINALS' JEN KLUGER (LEFT) AND SUZIE OROL (REGINA GARCIA)

Other considerations   BOOTSTRAP FINANCING TECHNIQUES

BOOTSTRAP CATEGORY	BOOTSTRAP FINANCING TECHNIQUE
Minimizing Your Investment	• Buy used machinery and equipment • Offer customer discount for cash payment • Hire temporary rather than permanent help • Negotiate favourable terms with suppliers • Apply for grants and subsidies
Owner Financing	• Run business out of your home • Employ relatives/friends at less than market salaries • Use income from other or part-time employment • Use personal credit cards for business • Withhold owner's salary if cash is tight • Have a working spouse • Sell other products/services
Minimizing Accounts Receivable	• Choose customers who pay quickly • Stop doing business with slow payers • Try to obtain advance customer payments • Charge interest on overdue accounts • Offer discount for early payment • Speed up invoicing
Delaying Payments	• Delay payments to suppliers • Delay tax payments • Lease equipment • Buy on consignment from suppliers
Sharing Resources with Others	• Share employees/equipment with other businesses • Share space with other businesses • Borrow equipment • Barter instead of buying/selling goods or services • Coordinate purchases with other businesses

Source: Adapted from J. Winborg and H. Lanstrom, "Financial Bootstrapping in Small Business: Examining Small Business Resource Acquisition Behaviour," *Journal of Business Venturing 16* (2000), p. 235–254.

The biggest risk with this source of capital is that if your new business fails and the investors lose money, it can create considerable hard feelings among family and friends. This possibility can be reduced if you lay out all the terms and conditions of the investment in advance, just as you would for any other investors. You should explain the nature of your business, your detailed implementation plans, the risks associated with the venture, and other relevant factors. In fact, it is best if you give both yourself and your investors some measure of comfort by translating your understanding into a formal, legal shareholders' agreement. If the money is provided to you as a loan, another important reason for putting it into writing is that if, for some reason, you are unable to repay the money and your investor must write it off, the amount of a properly documented loan becomes a capital loss for income tax purposes and can be offset against any capital gains, thereby providing the investor with the potential for some tax relief from the loss.

This most basic kind of financing is often not enough to get the business started, but it is important for external funding sources to see that you and your family are prepared to invest most of your personal resources in the venture. Without a strong indication of this type of individual commitment, it will be extremely difficult to raise any other money. Why should someone not directly involved in the business risk money in your business if you are not prepared to put your own assets on the line?

Entrepreneurs in Action

Youth an Obstacle to Being an Entrepreneur

Amanda Harburn is a dancer, a performer, and an artist. She is also a bookkeeper, receptionist, market analyst, manager, master negotiator, teacher, typist and an extremely experienced buffer of floors.

Just 21, Harburn is an entrepreneur — and a very successful one.

Harburn's two-year-old Prestige Dance Academy Inc. in Calgary now provides instruction to more than 200 students.

Giving her business some legs, however, required some fancy footwork.

"Everyone says, 'Yeah, yeah, yeah, we love young entrepreneurs,' but they really don't take you seriously, and they certainly don't want to give you any money," says Harburn. "It's frustrating and discouraging.". . . .

The problem is that in most cases, young entrepreneurs are inexperienced and underestimated — not to mention broke. Harburn got past that particular obstacle with some help from home.

"I ended up taking my business proposal to my parents," says Harburn. "I had looked into banks and different funding programs, but the processes were very long and complex. I probably could have eventually gotten a line of credit, but to be honest, I didn't have the patience. My most significant expenses were my lease and my renovation costs. Since I don't have any inventory, I really didn't require as much capital as some other businesses."

Unfortunately there are fewer options available for young entrepreneurs now than there were just a few years ago, says Margaret Brown, an instructor at the Bissett School of Business at Mount Royal College in Calgary.

"Most students who need only a few thousand dollars are using lines of credit. The best source of financing for young people, though, is still family and friends."

Groups like the Canadian Youth Business Foundation [CYBF] are picking up the slack in Canada, offering entrepreneurs both financial and intellectual support. (www.cybf.ca)

The CYBF is a non-profit charitable group that was founded by the CIBC, the Royal Bank, and the Canadian Youth Foundation in 1996.

"The problem is that usually the young entrepreneur doesn't have experience and they don't have any

WIL ANDRUSCHAK

collateral," says Chris Ransom, a program manager for CYBF. "In my experience, there are so few grants available that they might as well not exist, and the ones they do have are extremely niche-oriented. Approaching financial institutions can be extremely intimidating and discouraging, because often they won't even look at your business plan. Banks are conservative, and they don't like risk."

That is very unfortunate considering the potential impact that these small businesses could have on the economy.

"We do a great job of recycling money and creating business to contribute to the economy," says Vivian Woytiuk, chief executive officer of the CYBF. "Whenever you're involved in micro-lending, you're taking a chance and there will be failures, but we've seen some unbelievable successes, too."

Being an entrepreneur is also about a strong work ethic, says Harburn. While she may soon be able to hire on some more help to lighten her workload, she's not there quite yet.

"There are days when I just don't feel like cleaning the floors. But I know if I don't do it, it won't get done, and I take pride in my studio," she says. "When I drive into the parking lot and see my sign, I just say, 'Wow, its really mine,' and then I know it's worth all the long hours and movies missed with my friends. There's no better feeling in the world."
(www.prestigedance.com)

Source: Shannon Sutherland, "Youth an obstacle to being an entrepreneur," *Winnipeg Free Press*, October 20, 2003, p. F4.

BANKS, TRUST COMPANIES, CREDIT UNIONS, AND SIMILAR INSTITUTIONS

Banks and similar institutions are the most popular and widely used external source of funds for new businesses. A visit to the local banker becomes almost a mandatory part of any new venture start-up situation. Banks historically have provided debt financing in the form of self-liquidating, short-term loans to cover small businesses' peak working capital requirements, usually in the form of an *operating loan* or *line of credit*.

An operating loan extends credit to you up to a prearranged limit *on an ongoing basis*, to cover your day-to-day expenses such as accounts receivable, payroll, inventory carrying costs, office supplies, and utility bills. If you happen to be in a highly seasonal or cyclical business, for example, such a line of credit can be used to purchase additional inventory in anticipation of your peak selling period. An operating loan is intended to *supplement your basic working capital*. An operating loan can also be used to bridge unexpected cash flow interruptions and/or shortfalls. It may also give you the ability to take advantage of supplier discounts for prompt payment.

Operating loans, however, can have some restrictions. For example, your banker may prohibit you from taking retained earnings out of your company during the early stages of your business. In addition, he or she may even veto the purchase of machinery, equipment, and other fixed assets above a certain amount. These operating loans are subject to annual review and renewal by mutual agreement but can often be terminated by the lender at its option unless specific conditions have been incorporated into the loan agreement. Interest on operating loans is usually *tied to the prime rate*. That means the interest rate can change either up or down as the prime rate changes. This can be an advantage when interest rates are declining but a major issue if rates are increasing rapidly.

Banks also provide *term loans* to small businesses — loans for the purchase of an existing business or to acquire fixed assets such as machinery, vehicles, and commercial buildings, which typically must be repaid in three to ten years. The term of the loan is usually linked to the expected lifespan of the asset. Three to four years is common for a truck or computer, while the term of a loan to acquire a building could be considerably longer. Term loans typically have a fixed interest rate for the full term. Therefore your interest cost is predetermined in advance and your budgeting process is simplified. However, the loan amount tends to be limited to a percentage of the value of the asset being financed. In addition, term loans often command a one-time processing fee of half a per cent of the value of the loan.

You should realize that business bank loans, both operating and term loans, are *demand* loans so that regardless of the term, the bank can and will demand they be paid back if it feels the company is getting into trouble. While this usually occurs only when the business has real problems, there is the potential for difficulties; what the banker may perceive as a serious situation may be perceived as only a temporary difficulty by the owner of the business.

The bank may ask for your personal guarantee of business loans as well as a pledge of collateral security for the full value of the loan or more. This means that even though your business might be incorporated, your personal liability is not necessarily limited to your investment in the business; you could lose your house, car, cottage, and other personal assets if the business fails and you are unable to repay your loans to the bank.

To qualify for a loan you must have sufficient equity in your business and a strong personal credit rating. Banks do not take large risks. Their principal considerations in assessing a loan application are the safety of their depositors' money and the return they will earn on the loan. It is critical that you take these factors into account in preparing your loan proposal and try to look at your situation from the banker's point of view.

FEDERAL GOVERNMENT FINANCIAL ASSISTANCE PROGRAMS

Governments at all levels in Canada have developed a proliferation of financial assistance programs for small business. It is estimated that more than 600 programs are available from both the federal and provincial governments to help people begin a business or assist those that have already started. Many of these programs are aimed at companies in more advanced stages of their development who are looking to grow and expand, but quite a number can be utilized by firms in the start-up stage. Many of these programs offer financial assistance in the form of low-interest loans, loan guarantees, interest-free loans, or even forgivable (non-repayable) loans. Others offer incentives like wage subsidies, whereby the government will pay an employee's wage for a certain period of time. These programs are too numerous to describe in any detail, but let us briefly look at several of the more important ones.

Other considerations   ADVICE WORTH BANKING ON

One of the biggest adventures an entrepreneur can undertake is obtaining or renewing business financing — a trail that often determines the survival of many new and small businesses. Unfortunately, the application and approval process for obtaining and renewing commercial credit can be more of a nightmare than an adventure.

In my previous career, I was a branch manager with one of Canada's largest financial institutions. Since I have sat on both sides of the desk, let me share some of my thoughts and advice about seeking bank financing.

As a branch manager supervising the application and investigation process, I believed that assessing the information provided and getting to know my customers were both crucial in making lending decisions. When evaluating potential customers, I made sure not only to review personal credit histories, but I also tried to understand individuals and their personalities. I could usually determine whether I was dealing with a client who would make every effort to repay his or her debt, and I took this factor into account when making the lending decision. Many times applicants did not meet the existing lending criteria or have sufficient collateral for a loan. But if during the interview process they appeared genuine, honest, and hard-working, and if they were open about their credit history and how they planned to repay the loan, I would more then likely have approved the loan.

So far, however, as a client applying for commercial credit I have experienced this same flexibility and understanding only twice in seven years. Banks often give the impression that they support and help small business in Canada, but each year our company faces a major challenge to renew credit or obtain new financing. For the approval of commercial loans, it appears that equity, the net worth of borrowers and how much they are risking are more important to banks than the strength of the business plan, the product or the individual.

From my experience as a client, I have learned the importance of being prepared when approaching a bank for commercial financing. Here is my advice:

Provide a solid business plan with financial details of the company and its principals. Include a complete outline of the company's current and projected financial status. But remember, no matter how strong your business plan is or how good your credit history is, if you don't maintain the bulk of the risk, the bank will probably not look at your request seriously. The reality is you must not only sell yourself and your business plan, but you must also be willing to sign everything you own over to the bank.

Prepare for unforeseen financing obstacles by periodically reviewing and updating your business plan, and have strategies ready if you need to seek out new financing. Alternative financing options could include approaching smaller financial institutions such as credit unions or regional banks (which may suit smaller businesses), using the services of companies that trade accounts receivables for cash, or seeking out privately held capital companies. You might also consider finding investment funding, obtained through private placement by selling an equity position in your company, usually to friends, family, or someone willing to take an active role in the business.

Source: Ryan Magnussen (president, WDC Mackenzie Distributors Ltd., Calgary), "Advice Worth Banking On," *PROFIT* (www.profitguide.com/magazine/article.jsp?content=1027). Used with permission. Accessed August 19, 2004.

Canada Small Business Financing program

New and existing businesses with gross revenues of less than $5 million may be eligible to obtain term loans from chartered banks, caisses populaires, credit unions, or other lenders and have the loan partially guaranteed by the federal government under the Canada Small Business Financing Act. These loans are provided at a reasonable rate of interest (prime plus no more than 3 per cent for floating rate loans, or the lender's residential mortgage rate plus 3 per cent for a fixed-rate loan). In addition, lenders are required to pay a one-time loan registration fee to the government equal to 2 per cent of the amount loaned. This fee is recoverable from the borrower. These loans may be used for any number of purposes, such as the purchase or renovation of machinery and equipment and the purchase and improvement of land and buildings for business purposes. Loan proceeds may be used to finance up to 90 per cent of the cost of the asset, while the maximum value of loans a borrower may have outstanding under the CSBFA cannot exceed $500,000. For more information, contact any private sector lender or (www.ic.gc.ca/eic/site/csbfp-pfpec.nsf/eng/home).

Industrial Research Assistance Program (IRAP)

The National Research Council of Canada Industrial Research Assistance Program provides financial support to qualified small and medium-sized enterprises in Canada to help them develop technologies for competitive advantage. There are two program elements:

1. Financial support may be provided to small and medium-sized enterprises in Canada who have 500 or less full-time equivalent employees for an eligible research and development project, supporting up to 100 per cent of salary costs associated with the project, or up to 75 per cent of contractor fees.

2. The *Youth Employment Strategy* provides small and medium-sized enterprises with financial assistance to hire highly skilled post-secondary graduates. Firms can receive a financial contribution geared towards supporting a portion of the salary costs of the post-secondary graduate up to a maximum of $30,000. (www.nrc-cnrc.gc.ca/eng/services/irap/financial-assistance.html)

Community Futures and Community Business Development Corporations

Industry Canada's Community Futures Development Corporations (CFDCs) and Community Business Development Corporations (CBDCs) are a network of 269 offices across Canada that provide their communities with a variety of business development services including but not limited to the following:

BUSINESS DEVELOPMENT LOANS

- CFDCs/CBDC's each offer specific loan programs that target their community's needs, assisting entrepreneurs who may have had trouble accessing capital from traditional lenders. In some cases, these include special loans to youth entrepreneurs and entrepreneurs with disabilities.
- They can lend a maximum of $150,000 to new or existing businesses.
- Loans are fully repayable and are negotiated at competitive interest rates.

Contact your nearest CFDC/CBDC for further information or go to www.communityfuturescanada.ca for information on the entire cross-Canada network.

TECHNICAL SUPPORT

CFDCs/CBDCs provide services that include:

- Business advice, counselling, information, and referrals
- Help with business plans
- Advice on export readiness and supplier development

TRAINING

Training is available in, among other areas:

- Self-employment skills
- Marketing
- Bookkeeping
- Computer literacy

INFORMATION

CFDCs/CBDCs can provide information on relevant federal and provincial programs and services, as well as access to business libraries and business databases.

Women's Enterprise Initiative Loan Program

Western Economic Diversification, through the local Women's Enterprise Initiative in each western province, provides access to a loan fund for women entrepreneurs seeking financing for start-up or expansion of a business. To qualify, the business must have a fully completed business plan and be 51 per cent owned or controlled by a woman or women. Loans up to $150,000 are available.

For more information contact the Women's Enterprise Initiative in your province or go to (www.wd.gc.ca/eng/274.asp).

Aboriginal Business Canada

Canadian status and non-status Indians, Inuit, and Métis individuals between the ages of 18 and 35 are eligible for support with the preparation of business plans, marketing, and financing the start-up, expansion, modernization, or acquisition of a commercially viable business under Industry Canada's Aboriginal Business Canada program. The business opportunity can be in any sector. The minimum cash equity required by the applicant is equivalent to 10 per cent of eligible project costs and the contribution level can range from 30 to 75 per cent, depending on the nature of the project. These contributions are non-repayable.

For more information, contact one of the Aboriginal Business Canada offices located in each of the provinces and territories, the program's head office in Ottawa, or their Web site at (www.ainc-inac.gc.ca/ecd/ab/abc/abcnu-eng.asp).

The Self-Employment Program

The Self-Employment Program is an initiative of Human Resources and Skill Development Canada but designed and delivered by each province separately. It is intended to provide financial assistance to eligible individuals to help them create jobs for themselves by starting a business. Not everyone is eligible for the program. While the requirements may vary somewhat from province to province, basically individuals in order to qualify need to

- Be currently receiving Employment Insurance; or
- Have received Employment Insurance benefits within the past three years.

Other conditions may have to be met as well depending on the province.

The program will provide regular Employment Insurance benefits throughout the individual's benefit period or financial assistance for living expenses and other necessary expenses instead and, like the other regular benefits, the assistance doesn't have to be paid back. In addition the program typically provides entrepreneurial training and advice, one-on-one mentoring, and assistance with developing a business plan. If accepted into the program you have to commit to working full-time on starting a business of your own for close to a year. If you qualify, it can be a great opportunity to get the money to support yourself while working on starting your own business.

Business Development Bank of Canada

The Business Development Bank of Canada (BDC) is a federal Crown corporation that provides a wide range of financial, management counselling, and information services to small business through its broad network of over 100 branches across the country. Its financial services complement those of the private sector by providing funds for business projects that are not available from the commercial banks and other sources on reasonable terms. The BDC will provide term loans for the acquisition of fixed assets, working capital or operating loans, venture loans, and venture capital. Its primary focus is on small and medium-sized businesses operating in knowledge-based, growth-oriented industries and export markets.

Brian Titus, profiled in Entrepreneurs in Action #40, was able to obtain a BDC loan to help launch his successful micro-brewery in Halifax. To do so, he had to prepare a comprehensive business plan and overcome some other obstacles, but his determination and perseverance paid off as he was able to attract the capital necessary to get the business off the ground.

For further information contact one of the BDC offices located in each of the provinces and territories, the BDC head office in Montreal or at www.bdc.ca.

PROVINCIAL GOVERNMENT FINANCIAL ASSISTANCE PROGRAMS

Most of the provincial governments provide a range of grants, loans, and other forms of assistance to small business. For example, Manitoba offers the Business Start Program that provides a loan guarantee for loans up to $30,000 along with an educational component to assist new entrepreneurs in launching their business.

Entrepreneurs in Action

Tapping into Success

Before Brian Titus got his business off the ground, he made sure he did his homework.

"I spent months doing research and just learning about what was out there," says the president and general manager of Halifax-based Garrison Brewing Company Ltd., a highly successful micro-brewery that he founded.

At that time, beer was a whole new business for the naval diving officer, so he first visited other micro-breweries in Newfoundland and British Columbia to learn the ropes. "People felt comfortable sharing their knowledge with me, and it was time well spent. There's a lot of camaraderie in this industry, and I was able to gain invaluable insight," he says.

Looking back, Titus takes pride in having put together a comprehensive business plan to attract financing, including a loan from the BDC. "It took about five months to put the plan together. It was a real dream for me to start this business and I wasn't going to let it fall through," he says. His sheer determination paid off when the company immediately attracted investors and was able to purchase costly equipment to brew his darker ales using traditional brewing methods.

Titus emphasizes that the company had to overcome a few obstacles along the way. "People in Nova Scotia are traditionally domestic-beer drinkers so we first had to get our product out there and prove ourselves," he says. To get his beer selling in the same hot spots as larger breweries, the company innovated by offering its product in smaller twenty-litre kegs, which are ideal for fitting into tight places in bars. "We eliminated the need for expensive cooler systems, and once we got our

beer in the hands of consumers, we knew the company was going to take off," he adds.

© MARC GALLANT/WINNIPEG FREE PRESS. REPRINTED WITH PERMISSION.

Titus' instinct was right, because after one year in business, Garrison Brewing saw 50% growth. Five years later, the company now produces 600,000 bottles of beer a year with a minimal staff of four full-time people, and still maintains five to six per cent annual growth. "We've had to stay on our toes to keep our market share nonetheless," he says. For instance, rather than go the traditional advertising route, the company markets its products by sponsoring a local jazz festival and film festival. "Those events fit our profile very well. We sponsor sports too, but in our case, we work with squash tournaments rather than hockey or football," he says.

Now that his company is maturing, Titus has some words of wisdom to share with entrepreneurs starting up today. "In the beginning, be prepared to really focus on your goals, and don't let go of them, no matter what," he concludes.

(www.garrisonbrewing.com)

Source: Business Development Bank of Canada, *PROFIT$*, Spring 2003, p. 1.

Loan proceeds can provide funds for business registration or incorporation costs, equipment and inventory purchases, promotional costs and working capital needs. Similarly, Ontario has the Summer Company program, which provides business coaching and mentoring and awards of up to $3,000 to full-time students between the ages of 15 and 29 who want to start and run their own summer businesses. Applicants must submit a comprehensive business plan, as well as other information, and if approved they receive some business training, regular meetings with a local business mentoring group in their community, an award of up to $1,500 to help with their business start-up costs, and an additional award of $1,500 at the end of the summer upon proof of returning to school.

FYI FOR YOUR INFORMATION

For detailed information on specific federal or provincial programs, you can check the Industry Canada Web site (at www.ic.gc.ca/eic/site/ic1.nsf/eng/h_00073.html), contact your local Canada Business Service Centre, or check out one of the following publications at your local library:

Your Guide to Government Financial Assistance for Business in: (separate publication available for each province and territory) Productive Publications (www.productivepublications.ca)

Government Assistance Manual CCH Canadian Limited (www.cch.ca)

The Business Guide to Government Programs The Business Guide Incorporated (www.businessguide.net)

The list of other programs is much too extensive to provide here, but you can obtain specific information on the programs offered in your province by contacting the appropriate government department, or you can contact your local Canada Business Service Centre (www.canadabusiness.ca).

VENTURE CAPITAL

Venture capital involves equity participation in a start-up or growing business situation. Conventional venture capital companies, however, really don't offer much opportunity for firms still in the concept or idea stage. These investors are generally looking for investment situations in proven firms requiring in excess of $1 million and on which they can earn a 40 to 50 per cent annual return. While these companies will often accept high-risk situations, most new venture start-ups don't meet their primary investment criteria.

There are some exceptions to this general rule, however. During the dot-com frenzy of the late 1990s and early 2000s, the business press was full of stories of young Canadian entrepreneurs barely out of school who had received millions of dollars in venture capital financing to launch their latest Internet idea. This situation has cooled considerably. Corporate funds, pension funds, private independent venture funds, and labour-sponsored venture capital funds still have billions of dollars looking for investment opportunities, principally in the high-technology sector, but investors are being much more careful in determining where it goes.

Christopher Frey, Kisha Ferguson, and Matt Robinson are among the lucky few who have been successful in raising a significant amount of money for a somewhat more traditional business situation. (Entrepreneurs in Action #41). They were looking for a $300,000 equity infusion to help develop their adventure travel magazine, Outpost. Sometimes, however, the price can be too high. The initial offer they received to provide the funds demanded a majority stake in the business in return. Though they desperately needed the money to grow their business, they still had sufficient funds to limp along while searching out other options, so turned the offer down. In the end they connected with a Toronto venture capitalist who provided them with some bridge financing and told them how to beef up their business to make it more attractive to other investors. After 18 months they finally hooked up with another firm in the communications business that provided them with the money they needed to solidify their operations, and they learned a number of valuable lessons along the way.

There are a number of venture capital firms that may be prepared to consider smaller investments. However, keep in mind that of 100 proposals considered by a typical venture capital firm, only four or five are selected for investment purposes. Therefore, the probability of receiving any financial assistance from this source is very slim. For more information, however, check out the Canadian Venture Capital Association at www.cvca.ca.

⁴¹

Entrepreneurs in Action

In Search of Adventure Capital

It was the kind of tough call that confronts many entrepreneurs searching for capital. Christopher Frey, Kisha Ferguson, and Matt Robinson, partners in adventure travel magazine *Outpost*, badly needed the $300,000 equity infusion being dangled in front of them. The Toronto-based firm was limping along with limited money and had debts to repay. But the investor was demanding a majority stake. Would the trio have to give up control to keep their dream alive?

Frey and Ferguson had launched their quarterly magazine to chronicle Canadians' adventures in exotic locales. But their own 18-month search for capital, as they struggled to secure funding before their cash ran out, was as exciting as any trip from the pages of *Outpost* itself.

© NADIA MOLINARI

1. YOU NEED A MAP AND A COMPASS

The adventurers started with meagre rations: Frey's experience working on his university newspaper, Ferguson's editorial vision, and $60,000 from savings, family, and friends. Frey and Ferguson believed the adventure travel market — growing at an estimated 25% a year — offered a fertile source of readers and advertisers. But that wouldn't be enough. "We knew enough to start, but not enough to have a long-range plan," says Frey. "But we were quick learners, and from the very first day we started, we went about filling in the gaps in our knowledge."

One gap was filled when Matt Robinson joined *Outpost* as a third partner and advertising director. Robinson brought badly needed marketing savvy from a stint with Toronto publishing giant Maclean Hunter Ltd. To secure its future, *Outpost* needed ad revenue. To sell ads, it needed to find more readers — an expensive venture. So the trio set out to raise $300,000.

From August until October, the *Outpost* team cold-called more than 200 potential investors culled from a variety of sources, including business and publishing trade magazines. The phone calls yielded a list of some 50 interested people and companies, and the partners mailed promotional packages to them all.

2. BUILD THE VALUE IN YOUR BUSINESS

Meantime, the trio took steps to increase ad revenue, which would make *Outpost* more attractive to investors. "The advertisers are the canaries in our investment world," says Robinson. "Advertisers want value. If they come on board and are singing the praises of

the publication, you can translate that to investors as an expression of confidence in the product." The partners relaunched the magazine, doubling the print run to 25,000 copies, adding new editorial sections and more color to the magazine, and producing a media kit to sell *Outpost* to advertisers. With finances tight, they funded the improvements in part by an extended overdraft of $12,000 — guaranteed against a GIC owned by Frey's parents. The improved magazine debuted in October with $16,000 of advertising — up from $4,000 in the previous issue. Even better, for the first time several brand-name advertisers bought space. "It improved our story [to investors]," says Robinson.

On the financing front, one magazine publisher in Toronto was particularly responsive. The partners met with him six times. "The first few meetings were a reality check, coming to grips with how difficult the publishing business is," says Frey. The lessons covered both the magazine business and the gruelling requirements of venture capitalists. "It became evident that we had to evaluate every aspect of the company to reach an adequate return to investors," says Robinson. "We learned that the standard return on venture capital is 30% to 40% a year. We did our best to get our projected returns close to that amount."

Outpost was willing to give up a 30% interest for $300,000, but the publisher demanded control. The partners agonized. "We were in an onerous financial situation," says Robinson. "We weren't about to go

continued

bankrupt — we could limp along with the three of us putting the magazine out — but the money would have allowed us to repay people who had supported us. And we were sitting on this fabulous market, and we had to get the resources to take advantage of it." But, he says, "We got involved in this project because we wanted to control our destiny. You end up working for someone else and it takes some of that wonderful energy out of your sails." No deal, the trio decided.

Though Frey, Ferguson and Robinson walked away from the money, they had grown as entrepreneurs. . . .

3. LEARN FROM REJECTION

By now the partners had a 25-page business plan which, says Robinson, "was tweaked and morphed many times, not from a lack of focus on our part, but based on an educational process that was going on each time we got feedback from venture capitalists and publishers."

But fishing for investors could be discouraging. "Nothing happens 90% of the time," says Robinson. "You've got to keep your spirits up." Where they couldn't find money, the partners looked for information. "A fair number of people will sit down and listen to you, but often they're doing that just to see what ideas are out there," says Frey. "They may not have any interest at all [in investing]. Then it becomes a smart move to try to turn the meeting to your advantage by getting as much information out of them as possible."

4. ASK FOR MORE THAN YOU NEED

In the spring and summer, the partners held another important round of meetings, this time with Bob Shoniker, a Toronto venture capitalist. Shoniker asked some tough questions, including, "Do you guys really think $300,000 is enough?" Shoniker noted that it takes as much work to evaluate a $300,000 investment as a $1-million investment. "Up to that point, we had gotten by with the notion of doing as much as possible with as little as possible," says Frey. "But any investor will only invest if they think they're giving you an adequate amount of money." Before their second of three meetings with Shoniker, *Outpost* got the hint and upped the ante — to $1 million.

Shoniker didn't give *Outpost* the $1 million, but he did provide $50,000 in bridge financing. It was a lifesaver. "If the bridge capital wasn't there, we would have gone back and negotiated an agreement with the independent publisher and lost control," says Robinson.

Shoniker also challenged *Outpost* to elaborate on its idea for multimedia spin-offs. "The person who just wants to sell a print page of advertising in their publication is going to have a hard time these days," says Robinson. "We really wanted ultimately to develop a brand, with the magazine at the core." *Outpost* had been producing a 10-minute segment for a Toronto community radio station, CJRT. Now, convinced they

shouldn't hold off until the magazine was on a sound footing, the partners added plans for a syndicated radio show, Web site and TV program. *Outpost* was now presented to investors as "an integrated adventure travel communications company that publishes Canada's only adventure travel magazine."

With their new, more aggressive plan and higher revenues — up from $30,000 to $150,000 — the three partners had turned *Outpost* into a promising investment prospect. Still, the company lost $92,500, and was rapidly using up its bridge financing.

One of the companies they had approached was BHVR Communications, a Montreal media and entertainment company founded by digital video software entrepreneur Richard Szalwinski. Their approach had gone unanswered. But now *Outpost* was a substantial property with a vision. . . .

Claude Thibault, vice-president of BHVR subsidiary Normal Net, was impressed. He says BHVR went through "the usual checklist: How much money are they seeking? Where will that take them? Will they need more? What is the valuation? Is it fair? What's their business plan? Does it fit with ours? We were satisfied on all those points rapidly."

There was a discrepancy when it came to valuation. "It's impossible to value a company by any of the standard practices at that stage in its development," says Robinson. He and his two partners valued the company at $1 million; BHVR's number was $700,000. But, with everything else looking positive, BHVR agreed to pay a premium — $1 million for 47% of the company, plus the rights to use Outpost's content on its website.

5. LEVERAGE YOUR RELATIONSHIPS

On December 24, Thibault called to say they had a deal. "We gave a whoop and a holler in the office," says Robinson, "then went home and had a nice Christmas with our families."

The agreement was signed five months later. . . . On the multimedia front, they have obtained an initial commitment from a Canadian broadcaster to partially fund a pilot for a TV series. And they're looking at expanding into Australia, Europe and the United States. Outpost has launched a Web site (www.outpostmagazine.com), and when Normal Net's Web site launches shortly, Outpost's content will be there too. Robinson forecasts a loss of $130,000 for 2000, but expects to break even for the first time on the November issue. To fund its new initiatives, Outpost will need more equity, either from BHVR or outside investors. The quest for financing never ends, but at least Frey, Ferguson and Robinson are now experienced travellers. (www.outpostmagazine.com)

Source: Sheldon Gordon, "Adventure Capital," *PROFIT*, February–March 2000, pp. 45–48. Used with permission.

ANGEL INVESTORS

A new business start-up probably has a better chance of obtaining equity capital from small, private venture capitalists — often called "angels" — or provincially-supported venture capital programs. There may be doctors, dentists, lawyers, accountants, and other individuals in your community who could be approached for investment funds. Many of these people may be looking for situations where they can invest small sums (less than $50,000) with the possibility of earning a larger return than that offered by more conventional investments, and they are often prepared to invest in start-up situations.

These investors often get personally involved with the businesses they invest in, and tend to focus less on technology-oriented opportunities than most venture capitalists. They typically invest in companies that have already largely burned through the owners' own money and what they can raise from families and friends, but before they are big enough to be of any interest to a venture capitalist. The angel investor's plan is to be part of the business for three to five years and then cash in when the business is sold to an outside firm or their interest is bought out by the company itself.

A typical angel investor in Canada:

- A self-made, high income, middle-aged, well-educated male who has substantial business experience as the owner or manager of a company. They do not tend to be wealthy professionals like doctors and dentists.

- Usually prefers investing within his own locality, close to home.

- Experienced investor who does his own due diligence and is confident in his own ability to appraise investment opportunities.

- Usually opportunistic, rather than scientifically seeking out potential investment situations.

It can be difficult for a small business to find an angel investor. Most prefer to remain anonymous for fear of being overwhelmed with requests for investments. They typically operate through informal networks of friends and business associates, with few clearly defined channels to bring angels and entrepreneurs together. Some of these issues are gradually being overcome, however, as a number of communities and organizations have established programs to bring entrepreneurs and private investors together.

In 1996 the federal government started the Canadian Community Investment Plan (CCIP) as a means to improve access to risk capital for small and medium-sized firms located in smaller communities across the country. One of the more successful of these demonstration projects is Capital Connexion (www.capital-connexion.com) located in Quebec. It is a continuously updated database of proposals from entrepreneurs looking for financing, along with a list of angel investors searching for business projects in which to invest. The database is heavily oriented toward most regions of Quebec but has been expanded to include parts of other provinces such as Newfoundland, Alberta, New Brunswick, Nova Scotia, and Ontario as well. Registration of both investors and entrepreneurs on the database is free but they must be validated by a local economic development organization.

In addition, more and more private investors are getting together to form "angel networks" to work together in vetting potential deals, doing the necessary due diligence and sharing the risk with other small investors. The National Angel Organization (NAO) has become the voice of angel investors in Canada and many of the angel groups across the country are listed in the following FYI box. Many of these groups meet regularly to view investment pitches from a number of early-stage companies seeking equity investment.

Canada's chartered banks are often criticized for not providing this kind of risk capital to small business. Banks, however, are principally low-risk lenders of their depositor's money and traditionally provide debt financing. Venture capitalists and other private investors provide financing in exchange for shares or other interest in the company. Banks have neither the mandate nor the expertise to participate in this specialized market.

Jordan Banks, profiled in Entrepreneurs in Action #42, is a typical 'angel'. He had a very successful career in a couple of entrepreneurial companies like eBay and Jump TV and after leaving those firms decided to help others get started in their own business as an advisor and angel investor. Many of his investments have been made in firms where he knew the principals very well or they were operated by friends or contacts of people he knew very well. The character and integrity of the individuals behinds the businesses are very important to him in making a decision to invest. These investments give him a way to keep involved and participate in the growth and development of the business as well as provide an opportunity to make a good financial return on his investments.

Entrepreneurs in Action

Angels Step into Venture Capital Void

Canada's venture-capital industry is far from healthy, particularly if you're a start-up looking for investment to turn an idea or a prototype into a product and a business.

For entrepreneurs, there is reason for optimism as angel investors are slowly starting to emerge as an alternative source of financing. While far from abundant or easy to find, angel investors are stepping into the fray. Many of these angels are successful entrepreneurs who appreciate and understand the challenges facing new business owners looking for growth capital.

One of the more active angels these days is Jordan Banks, who spent years as general manager of eBay Canada before moving to JumpTV. After leaving JumpTV, Mr. Banks took some time off and, in the process, discovered his interest and passion for helping start-ups as an adviser and angel investor.

He says many of his investment opportunities have come through personal connections. Of the 10 companies in his portfolio, he says nine are operated by people he already knew, or people who were well known by close friends and business colleagues.

"At the end of the day, early stage investing is almost all about the people at the company and their character, integrity and work ethic," he says. "If you get that right, good things will happen. One of the ways to get it right is to have lots of points of reference on the people you are investing in through friends or colleagues."

In evaluating investment opportunities, Mr. Banks says he tries to keep the process as simple as possible by using a three-criteria process:

- He has to believe and have great confidence in the founder of the business and a proven history of showing a bias for action.

- The company needs a simple business model that he can easily understand and explain.

- The business can't require more than one more subsequent round of financing. Mr. Banks says one of the biggest perils of angel investing is getting materially diluted by institutional money in future rounds. By reducing the requirement of future rounds, he says it reduces dilution and increases the return upon exit.

Since angel investing is often a personal and financial exercise, Mr. Banks says the most important consideration between an investor and a founder is making sure both sides have the same expectations from the beginning. "In my experience, the most successful companies who have secured angel funding have mapped out the skill sets they'd ideally like or need from an investor group and then mapped the angel investors to those skills," he says.

"Getting money is the easy part; getting money that can be leveraged many times over after the initial cheque has been cut is the hard part. By setting expectations from the beginning about level of expected involvement and skill sets required, the chances for a future positive outcome are dramatically increased. Unfortunately, the flip side is also true."

Other than money, Mr. Banks says angels can also provide value to investments by attracting quality investors to the board, providing advice about structure, process and strategic priorities, making introductions, and helping attract excellent talent.

Mr. Banks says he's excited about the growing number of angels getting involved, particularly because the community is evolving from simply writing cheques to playing an active role in helping accelerate a company's growth.

Source: Mark Evans, The Globe and Mail, Report on Business, Published on Wednesday, Mar. 17, 2010 8:50AM EDT. Last updated on Friday, Mar. 19, 2010 9:24AM EDT.

FYI FOR YOUR INFORMATION

Links to Angel organizations across Canada. Many of these groups match entrepreneurs with angel investors.

ALBERTA

Alberta Deal Generator — Edmonton, AB

Venture Alberta — Edmonton & Calgary, AB

BRITISH COLUMBIA

BC Angel Forum — Vancouver, BC

Fundamental Technologies II — Coquitlam, BC

Okanagan Angel Network — Kelowna, BC

VANTEC — Vancouver Angel Technology Network — Vancouver, BC

MANITOBA

Winnipeg Angel Organization — Winnipeg, MB

NEWFOUNDLAND

Newfoundland & Labrador Angel Network — Saint Johns, Nfld

NOVA SCOTIA, NEW BRUNSWICK, PRINCE EDWARD ISLAND

First Angel Network — Halifax, NS

ONTARIO

Aprilis Ventures — Toronto, ON

Association for the Advancement of Safety Technologies — Hamilton, ON

Cleantech Angel Network — Toronto, ON

Georgian Angel Network — Collingwood, ON

Golden Horseshoe Angel Network — Oakville, ON

Golden Triangle Angelnet — Cambridge, ON

Infusion Angels — Waterloo, ON

ISCM — Innovation Synergy Centre in Markham — Markham, ON

Maple Leaf Angels — Toronto, ON

Northern Ontario Enterprise Gateway — Providence Bay, ON

Ottawa Angel Alliance — Ottawa, ON

Ottawa Capital Network — Ottawa, ON

Peterborough Region Angel Network — Peterborough, ON

Purple Angel — Ottawa, ON

Ryerson Angel Network — Toronto, ON

South western Ontario Angel Group — London, ON

York Angel Investors — Vaughn, ON

QUEBEC

Reseau Anges Quebec — Montreal, QC

SASKATCHEWAN

SAINT — Saskatchewan Angel Investor Network — Saskatoon, SK

Source: National Angel Capital Organization (www.angelinvestor.ca/Find_Angels.asp), accessed June 4, 2010.

WHAT'S ON THE TABLE?

Negotiations with private venture capital sources can be lengthy and complex. It's important to keep in mind the main issues that may be under discussion in the process. These will likely include:

- **Price** What are the business and the opportunity worth? How much will the investor pay in exchange for a position in your business? You have to have a realistic idea of the range of values you might be prepared to accept and the values an investor might be prepared to consider.

- **Control** How much of your business will the investor get for his or her investment and how much control will the investor be able to exercise over its affairs? Most private investors aren't trying to gain control of your business but they are looking to manage their risk by putting some controls in place to protect their investment. These may include:
  - Requiring prior consultation or imposing some restrictions on your ability to make financial decisions.
  - Requiring representation on your board of directors.
  - Determining the amount of equity you may have to give up based on pre-determined performance-based targets.
  - Requiring a provision giving the investors the first opportunity to participate in the future sale of equity in the business or asking for a ban on the sale of future shares without investor agreement.

- **Establishment of Performance Expectations** The investment may be laid out in stages and tied to specific achievement milestones and objectives. You and the investor need to agree on the performance measures that will be used to determine if the business is succeeding as expected in order to trigger these additional contributions or somehow change the terms of the initial deal.
- **Exit Strategy** Some of the available options by which investors might cash in their investment in your business include:
  - **Acquisition by a third party** An outright sale of the company in which the investor's shares would be sold as part of the sale of the company to a third-party acquirer. This is often viewed as the ideal route to go, especially if the buyout is for cash instead of stock.
  - **Sale of the investor's interest to a third-party investor** This can be an option, but minority interests in private companies can be very difficult to sell due to the lack of control and liquidity. Significant costs can be associated with finding new investors, and the process can consume a great deal of time and effort.
  - **Buy-back agreement** The investor's shares may be repurchased by the company. This could be in the form of a put option or a retraction clause in which the investor maintains the legal right to force you to repurchase his or her shares at an agreed and prespecified price at particular points in time.[2]
  - **Management or employee buyout** The founders and early investors can often realize a gain from the business by selling it to other partners or some of the key managers in the business in a management buyout or to a number of the employees through an employee stock ownership plan (ESOP).
  - **Debt repayment** The financing structure used could include some form of subordinated debt with specific repayment terms on exit. The debt agreement may carry conversion privileges that allow the investor to convert the debt into common shares under certain circumstances.
  - **An initial public offering (IPO)** The investor's shares would be sold when the business decides to raise additional capital through the sale of shares to the public. This exit mechanism is commonly viewed as the "holy grail" for both the company and the investor, and can be the most satisfying and financially rewarding. However, very few private firms ever actually achieve this level of success and it does come with a number of potential negative considerations. For example, going public can mean the loss of a significant portion of your ownership and leave you in a minority position. In addition, a portion of your and the investors' shares may be held in escrow, possibly for years, forcing you to remain invested in the business. It also means that by becoming "public," a lot of previously private and sensitive information must now be shared with the public.

As you can see, obtaining money from private venture capital sources might pose a number of interesting problems for you. You will probably have to give up at least partial ownership and control of your business. In addition, angel investors usually have limited resources, so additional funds may not be available if required later. Finally, as amateur investors, these people may not have the patience to wait out the situation if things don't work out as quickly as you originally planned.

The decisions you make regarding any of these issues are very important, extremely complex, and often critical to the success of your prospective deal. You should consult with a professional financial advisor before preparing any proposal for presentation in a search for private capital.

ADDITIONAL SOURCES OF FINANCING

Canadian Youth Business Foundation

The Canadian Youth Business Foundation (CYBF) (www.cybf.ca) is a national not-for-profit organization that enables young entrepreneurs (18 to 34 years old) to pursue their aspirations of building a successful business by providing them with several forms of business support and assistance. These include:

- A loan program that will provide up to $15,000 amortized over 3–5 years to cover the start-up costs of a business.

---

2. G.H. Haines Jr., J.J. Madill, and A.L. Riding, "Financing Small Business Growth: Informal Investing in Canada," *Journal of Small Business and Entrepreneurship*, Spring 2003, pp. 13–40.

Other considerations — ANGEL INVESTORS: THE DEFINITION

Angel investors are individuals who invest in businesses looking for a higher return than they would see from more traditional investments. Many are successful entrepreneurs who want to help other entrepreneurs get their business off the ground. Usually they are the bridge from the self-funded stage of the business to the point that the business needs the level of funding that a venture capitalist would offer. Funding estimates vary, but usually range from $150,000 to $1.5 million.

The term "angel" comes from the practice in the early 1900s of wealthy businessmen investing in Broadway productions. Today "angels" typically offer expertise, experience and contacts in addition to money. Less is known about angel investing than venture capital because of the individuality and privacy of the investments.

The Center for Venture Research at the University of New Hampshire, which does research on angel investments, has developed the following profile of angel investors:

- The "average" private investor is 47 years old with an annual income of $90,000, a net worth of $750,000, is college educated, has been self-employed and invests $37,000 per venture.
- Most angels invest close to home and rarely put in more than a few hundred thousand dollars.
- Informal investment appears to be the largest source of external equity capital for small businesses. Nine out of ten investments are devoted to small, mostly start-up firms with fewer than 20 employees.
- Nine out of ten investors provide personal loans or loan guarantees to the firms they invest in. On average, this increases the available capital by 57%.
- Informal investors are older, have higher incomes, and are better educated than the average citizen, yet they are not often millionaires. They are a diverse group, displaying a wide range of personal characteristics and investment behaviour.
- Seven out of ten investments are made within 50 miles of the investor's home or office.
- Investors expect an average 26% annual return at the time they invest, and they believe that about one-third of their investments are likely to result in a substantial capital loss.
- Investors accept an average of 3 deals for every 10 considered. The most common reasons given for rejecting a deal are insufficient growth potential, overpriced equity, lack of sufficient talent of the management, or lack of information about the entrepreneur or key personnel.
- There appears to be no shortage of informal capital funds. Investors included in the study would have invested almost 35% more than they did if acceptable opportunities had been available.

For the business seeking funding, the right angel investor can be the perfect first step in formal funding. It usually takes less time to meet with an angel and to receive funds, due diligence is less involved and angels usually expect a lower rate of return than a venture capitalist. The downside is finding the right balance of expert help without the angel totally taking charge of the business. Structuring the relationship carefully is an important step in the process.

- The possibility of a loan of twice the amount of the loan provided by the CYBF from the Business Development Bank of Canada (BDC)
- A mandatory mentoring orientation and mentoring program for all CYBF funded entrepreneurs
- Expansion financing of up to $10,000 that may subsequently be available to previously CYBF funded entrepreneurs.
- Access to a wide range of business resources to help young people through the start-up stage.

Karim Mitha in Entrepreneurs in Action #43 is typical of the kind of youth business funded by CYBF. Mitha and a couple of college classmates started a Web site in the Ottawa area called Specialstoday.ca to point people to restaurants around Ottawa that were offering menu specials. With the booming market for iPhone Apps they

Entrepreneurs in Action

A Taste for Apps

Karim Mitha has always been on the lookout for a good deal.

Whether it be electronics, groceries or even menu items at a restaurant, the former University of Waterloo student likes to be frugal. "Especially being a student, the bar or restaurant you went to that night was the one offering the specials," he said.

The thing was, the more Mitha looked around, the more like-minded bargain hunters he found. Mitha joined with two dormmates and started Specials Today.ca, a Web site aimed at pointing people to eateries around his home town of Ottawa that were offering menu deals.

To accompany the Web site, Mitha and his team created a free iPhone Application that taps into the device's GPS system and promotes restaurant deals based on the location of the iPhone user.

Mitha is taking advantage of the booming market for mobile applications, one of an ever-growing number of inventors in Ottawa working on their own "apps" for mobile devices. Made-in-Ottawa apps are available for everything from helping facilitate a real estate transaction, looking up OC Transpo schedules or monitoring your sleeping infant.

"There is just so much buzz around the whole app space right now," said Mitha. "We didn't know how easy it would be to make an app when we got started. It's easier than building a Web site."

With almost every major mobile technology company setting up Internet-based stores for their applications, it's easier than ever for software developers to strike it rich. Apple Inc. has its App Store, Google Inc. has the Android Market and Research in Motion has its App World. All three stores funnel millions of potential buyers through virtual doors every month.

According to researcher Garther Inc., app stores saw more than $4.2 billion U.S. in sales last year. Analysts expect those numbers to increase to $29.5 billion U.S. by 2013.

Mitha appreciates the numbers.

Thousands of people flock to his Web site monthly, more than 1,500 people have downloaded the iPhone app and more than 40 restaurants around Ottawa are paying his company to showcase their daily deals. More eateries are coming, and he's developing an app for Research in Motion's BlackBerry device.

Mitha says restaurants pay around $65 per month to be included. That price, however, can differ depending on how many specials the restaurant wants to offer. The service has been so popular that Mitha is getting requests from other markets to offer a similar service. Apps for Toronto and Vancouver are forthcoming and the three entrepreneurs — one of whom hasn't even graduated from university — has recently received a $15,000 investment from the Canadian Youth Business Foundation to help them expand their business.

Most applications are done for Apple, whose App Store accounts for 65 per cent of all mobile downloads. Last month, chief executive Steve Jobs said the App Store has sold more than three billion applications since its launch 18 months ago. For a $100 annual licensing fee, budding inventors can develop apps for the iPhone and submit them to Apple for inclusion on the App Store. If approved — some are turned down due to controversial content — the developer receives 70 per cent of all revenues.
www.specialstoday.ca

Source: Ottawa Citizen, Division of Canwest Publishing Inc., February 19, 2010.

FYI FOR YOUR INFORMATION

CANADIAN COMMUNITY INVESTMENT NETWORK CO-OP (CCINC) MEMBERS:

Community Loan Funds, Micro-Loan Funds and Peer Loan Funds

- The ACCESS Riverdale Community Loan Fund, Toronto, ON. Helps small and emerging businesses in the greater Riverdale area of Toronto to meet their need for credit by securing initial loans of up to $5,000.
- Circle of Habondia Lending Society, Slocan Valley / Nelson / Castlegar area of British Columbia. The society provides micro-loans of up to $1,000 to women.
- Compagnie F, Montreal, QC. Can provide an investment between $1,000 and $25,000 for a maximum of five years to women entrepreneurs.
- Micro-Crédit KRTB, Témiscouata, QC. Offers loans up to $15,000 that enables their clients to create, develop and sustain their independent business or cooperative organization.
- Ecotrust Canada, BC., Offers non-bank, higher-risk loans to entrepreneurs, cooperatives and non-profit groups that incorporate ecological and/or social values in their operations or that promote jobs and diversification in rural and Aboriginal communities in BC.
- The Jubilee Fund, Winnipeg, MB. Provides loan guarantees and equity investment for community economic development projects.
- Momentum, Calgary, AB. Provides character-based loans of up to $7,500 to start a business.
- The Montreal Community Loan Association (MCLA), Montreal, QC. Provide direct loans to a maximum of $ 20,000 for the start-up, consolidation or expansion of individual or social economy businesses.
- The Ottawa Community Loan Fund, Ottawa, ON. Provides short-term loans of up to $15,000 to individuals and groups with worthwhile business concepts and a solid business plan.
- Réseau Accès Crédit, l'Est du Bas-Saint-Laurent, QC.
- La Société communautaire Lavaloise d'emprunt, Laval. QC.
- The Saint John Community Loan Fund, Saint John, NB. Provides loans and other financial services to entrepreneurs who are willing to take a risk to get ahead.

Social Investors

- Canadian Alternative Investment Co-operative, Toronto, ON. Provides loans and equity investments to groups, organizations and co-operatives assisting the economic development of disadvantaged peoples or communities across Canada.
- Filaction, Quebec, QC.
- Social Capital Partners, Toronto, ON. Provides loans & equity investments to groups, organizations & co-operatives assisting the economic development of disadvantaged peoples or communities across Canada.

Co-op Funds

- Arctic Co-op Development Fund, Winnipeg, MB. Provides financing for Member Co-op projects in Canada's north.
- Tenacity Works. Provides funding to help create new and to expand existing worker-owned co-operatives in all regions of Canada.

Source: CCINC (www.communityinvestment.ca/member_list.html#alterna), accessed June 4, 2010.

decided to extend their reach and develop an Application that would point users toward these specials based on their location. More than 1,500 people have downloaded the App and over 40 restaurants have subscribed to their service and more are signing up every day. A loan from the CYBF helped them fund this development.

Canadian Community Loan Funds

Canadian Community Loan Funds are non-profit organizations who help people who can't get a loan from a conventional lending institution like a bank or credit union because they don't have the credit history or the collateral required by the traditional institution to backstop the loan. There are a number of these institutions across the country that are part of the Canadian Community Investment Network Co-op (www.community-investment.ca). A number of them have been identified in the FYI Box. While some may get a partial level of government support the majority of their funding comes from churches, service clubs and donations from local individuals and businesses.

They are independent organizations so each fund has its own lending parameters. Almost all provide loans, loan guarantees or investments to start up or expand micro businesses, small businesses, co-ops and social enterprises that support their local community as well as for other purposes. Almost all require any funding request to be backed by a solid business plan.

EVALUATING YOUR ABILITY TO SECURE FINANCING

With this extensive number of alternatives available to you as potential sources of financing, it may be useful for you to give some thought to the range of possibilities you might tap into in putting together the start-up requirements for your new venture. Figure 10.2 provides a framework for you to identify how much money you think you will need to launch your business and where you think that financing might possibly come from: your personal resources; friends, relations, and other personal contacts; lending agencies; grant programs; and other sources that may be available to you.

Financing is not a business's right. All lenders are in business to make (not lose) money. Consequently when a bank lends money it wants to ensure that it will get paid back. Johanne Dion, the CEO of Trans-HERB Inc. and one of Canada's top women entrepreneurs, says, "Banks are not there to lend you dollars. They're there to make a profit. If you don't have a good plan, if you don't do your (financial) statements every year, they'll say 'Sorry we need our money.'"[3]

When seeking a loan, it is wise to shop around for the best available terms. This includes comparing obvious features of the loan such as the interest rate but also evaluating:

- Size of transaction fees
- Prepayment policies
- Flexibility of payment terms
- Fixed or floating interest rate
- Security and personal guarantees required
- Quality of overall service provided by the institution
- Expected processing time

An important aspect of your financial condition is your ability to obtain financing. In assessing your capacity any lender will consider the 5 "C's" of Credit in deciding whether or not to extend you a loan.

Character is the general impression you make on the potential lender. The lender will form a subjective opinion as to whether or not you are of sufficiently good character to be given a loan. You must be known as a morally responsible person.

Collateral is the security you can provide the lender as a pledge for fulfillment of the obligation. It is a secondary source for repayment of the loan if your cash flow from the business in insufficient to fulfill the obligation. In real estate transactions this generally means the property or it may mean a pledge of other personal assets to assure the lender they will get their money back.

Capital is the cash and other liquid assets you personally have or are prepared to invest in the business. The more of your own money you have invested, the more likely that you will do all you can to maintain your payment obligations for any loan. In addition, the higher your net worth, the more you have as a cushion for repayment of the loan in case the business runs into financial difficulty.

Credit is the assessment of your previous performance in meeting your credit obligations. The information about your credit history is stored at the "credit bureau" and indicates how well you have paid your bills in the past. All major credit cards, auto loans, leases etc. are reported to the credit bureau. A lender will evaluate your

---

3. Kara Kuryllowicz, "Learning the Ropes," *PROFIT*, October 2001, p. 42.

FIGURE 10.2	WHERE WILL YOU GET THE MONEY?

Starting a business usually requires some money. As we have pointed out in this Stage, there are any number of sources from which this financing can be obtained. You may need to give some thought to approximately how much money you think you will need to launch your business and just where you feel you will be able to obtain it. Completing a form like the one below will give you a good estimate of roughly what your start-up financial requirements are likely to be.

How much money do you think you will need to launch your business? $ _____

Where can you get the funds?

SOURCE	POSSIBLE AMOUNT	
Personal Sources		
Cash	$ _____	
Stocks/Bonds	_____	
Mutual Funds	_____	
Term Certificates	_____	
RRSPs	_____	
Cash Value of Life Insurance	_____	
Other Investments _____	_____	
Real Estate	_____	
Vehicles	_____	
Other Assets	_____	
Credit Card Limits	_____	
Other Personal Sources	_____	
Total Available from Personal Sources		$ _____
Personal Contacts		
Family Members	$ _____	
Friends	_____	
Colleagues and Acquaintances	_____	
Partners	_____	
Other Private Investors _____	_____	
Total Available from Personal Contacts		$ _____
Lending Agencies		
Chartered Banks	$ _____	
Business Development Bank	_____	
Caisse Populaires and Credit Unions	_____	
Finance Companies	_____	
Government Agencies	_____	
Other Lending Agencies _____	_____	
Total Available from Lending Agencies		$ _____
Grant Programs		
Federal Government Programs	$ _____	
Provincial Government Programs	_____	
Municipal Programs	_____	
Other _____	_____	
Total Available from Grants		$ _____
Other Sources		
Supplier Credit	$ _____	
Customers	_____	
Others _____	_____	
Total Available from Other Sources		$ _____
TOTAL AVAILABLE FROM ALL SOURCES		$ _____

past history and your ability to maintain your obligations and try and determine how well you live within your means.

Capacity to repay the loan is probably the most critical of the five factors. The lender will want to know exactly how you intend to repay the loan. They will consider the current or expected level of income from the business and your income that may come from any other sources.

In preparing to approach a banker regarding a loan, the following are several suggestions you should keep in mind to increase your probability of getting the funds:

- Don't just drop in on your bank manager; make an appointment.
- Start your presentation by briefly describing your business and the exact reason you require a loan.
- Be prepared to answer any questions your banker may have. He or she wants to determine how well you really understand your business. If you can't answer certain questions, explain why and say when you will be able to provide the information.
- Be prepared to discuss collateral and other security you may be required to provide.
- If your business is currently operating, invite the banker to stop by to see it firsthand.
- Ask when you can expect a reply to your request. If there is a delay, inquire whether there is additional information you need to provide.

PROFIT magazine asked entrepreneurs, bankers, and financial consultants their most successful time-tested secrets for getting the best from their banker. Here are their suggestions:

- **Know what your banker is looking for** Before you set foot inside a bank, you should understand the ground rules of credit. Banks are not in the business of financing risk. Before they sign on the dotted line they need evidence you have a comprehensive plan and the management skills to successfully implement it. Ask yourself the question, "If I were a banker, would I lend money to me?" The bank needs to be reassured that you can repay your loan. The bank will also look for an existing strong base of equity investment in the company. Don't expect the bank to invest in something you wouldn't invest in yourself. To reduce its risk the bank will want some form of collateral security. In many cases, the bank will require collateral worth two or three times the amount of the loan.
- **Don't "tell" your banker, "show him"** Don't just tell your banker about the great new product you have devised. Bring it or a prototype of it along to your banker and demonstrate what makes it so great. Bring in a sample of whatever it is you plan to sell and let your banker see it, taste it, or try it firsthand.
- **Interview your banker** There are no good banks, only good bankers. Be prepared to shop around. Make certain you are dealing with the right person and the right branch for you. Visit at least three different banks before making a decision. Ask your accountant, lawyer, customers, or suppliers for a referral.
- **Passion makes perfect** The most persuasive thing entrepreneurs can do when negotiating a loan is to show how much passion they have for what they are doing. You should try to present the attitude that you are prepared to do everything possible to make the business succeed.
- **Ask for more money than you need** One of the worst mistakes you can make is to not consider your future requirements when calculating the size of the loan or the line of credit you think you will need. If you have to go back to the bank in five or six months to ask for an increase, the bank is going to be very concerned. It reflects badly on your ability to plan and you are also making extra work for the bank that could be reflected in extra charges for your loan.
- **Get your banker involved in your business** Invite your banker over, at least every six months, even if it's just for coffee. Make time to get to know your banker, to get him or her involved, and ask them for advice. Take advantage of opportunities to network with bankers and their colleagues. If the bank holds a reception, or open house, make an effort to attend.
- **Increase your credit when you don't need it** Many entrepreneurs begin looking for outside financing only when their own resources are tapped out. You should start to begin sourcing funds at least a year before you need it. Advanced planning will give you time to adequately explore all your options, meet with several banks, and ultimately work out the best deal for your business.

FYI FOR YOUR INFORMATION

For more information on obtaining financing for your new business, you could consult the following Web sites:

Canada Business
1. This site provides information on private sector associations whose members provide debt and equity financing to businesses. (www.canadabusiness.ca/eng/guide/209/)
2. Another Canada Business site that directs you to government loans, grants and other financing programs specifically tailored to your financial needs, provincial or territorial location, demographic group and the industrial classification within which your business falls. (www.canadabusiness.ca/eng/search/sof/)

Canadian Youth Business Foundation This organization is a non-profit, private-sector initiative designed to provide mentoring, business support, and loans to young Canadian entrepreneurs who are starting new businesses. (www.cybf.ca)

Canadian Bankers Association, Small Business Financing This site provides information on sources and types of small business financing. (www.cba.ca/en/consumer-information/45-small-business-services/474-small-business-financing)

Business Development Bank of Canada This site provides an overview of Business Development Bank financial products aimed at small business in general. (www.bdc.ca)

Atlantic Canada Opportunity Agency (ACOA) Programs This site provides an overview of a number of programs provided by ACOA to help Atlantic Canada entrepreneurs start new businesses or upgrade existing ones. (www.acoa.ca/English/Pages/home.aspx)

Western Economic Diversification Canada, Funding for Business A link to information about financing programs available through WD and such organizations as Community Futures, the Women Enterprise Initiative and their Growth Capital Loan program. (www.wd.gc.ca/eng/259.asp)

About Canada — Small Business, Canada Places to find the money and financial information you need to start and grow your Canadian small business, including types of financing, sources of funds, attracting investors, and financial advice from experts. (sbinfocanada.about.com/od/financing/Small_Business_Financing.htm)

Idea Cafe, Financing Your Biz This is a U.S. site but has lots of interesting information. (www.businessownersideacafe.com/financing/index.php)

America's Business Funding Directory A guide to over 4,000 business loan and venture capital sources of funding (principally in the United States). (www.businessfinance.com)

Banks You might also check the Web sites of Canada's major chartered banks.

- **Make professional introductions** Introduce your lawyer and your accountant to your banker. Make sure your accountant reviews the bank's proposal outlining the terms and conditions of your loan or line of credit.
- **If all else fails, keep looking** Finding the money to start or expand a business is hard work. Most entrepreneurs have been turned down many times for financing. The key is continuing to pursue every available means of securing the capital you need.[4]

---

4. Adapted from David Menzies, "Getting the Best From Your Bank," *PROFIT*, November, 1998, pp. 26–32. Reprinted with permission.

FIGURE 10.3	LOAN APPLICATION ASSESSMENT WORKSHEET

Assessment Factor	Poor 1	2	Good 3	4	Excellent 5
Personal credit rating	___	___	___	___	___
Capacity to pay back loan from personal assets if business fails	___	___	___	___	___
Collateral to pay back loan from personal assets if business fails	___	___	___	___	___
Character (as perceived in the community)	___	___	___	___	___
Commitment (your personal investment of time, energy, and money)	___	___	___	___	___
Clarity and completeness of your business plan	___	___	___	___	___
Viability of business concept (e.g., moderate risk)	___	___	___	___	___
Personal experience in the proposed business	___	___	___	___	___
Successful experience in your own business	___	___	___	___	___
Balanced management team available	___	___	___	___	___
Suitability of your personality to the pressures and responsibilities of the business	___	___	___	___	___

What can you do to improve the weak areas (where you have rated yourself 1 or 2)?

_____
_____
_____
_____
_____

Adapted from D. A. Gray, *The Entrepreneur's Complete Self-Assessment Guide* (Vancouver: International Self-Counsel Press Ltd., 1986), p. 123.

A financial institution may turn down your loan application for any of a number of reasons, and it is important that you ask what they are. This knowledge may help you in future attempts to secure funding. Some of the most frequent reasons why a loan application can be rejected are as follows:

1. The business idea might be considered ill-advised or just too risky.
2. You may not have offered sufficient collateral. Lenders want some assurance that they will be able to recover most or all of their money should you default on the payments.
3. The lender may feel there is insufficient financial commitment on your part.
4. You have not prepared a comprehensive and detailed business plan.
5. Your reason for requesting the loan is unclear or not acceptable to the lender. It is important that you specify the intended application of the requested funds and that this application be outlined in detail. This outline should also show your planned schedule for the repayment of the loan.
6. You do not appear confident, enthusiastic, well-informed, or realistic enough in your objectives. The lender's assessment of your character, personality, and stability are important considerations in his or her evaluation of your loan application.

The worksheet shown in Figure 10.3 will allow you to assess some of the critical factors that may affect your ability to secure external funding. It will also give you some indication of what aspects of your personal character, development of your business plan, or quality of the basic idea underlying your new venture could be improved. On the worksheet, indicate your assessment of your personal situation for each of the indicated factors as honestly as you can. How do you rate? Could some factors be improved upon? What can you do to strengthen these areas, or how might you overcome these negative factors?

One question you should consider is "How much can I possibly lose on my venture should it fail?" The losses in some types of businesses can wipe out virtually all of the funds you have invested or personally guaranteed. This tends to be true in situations like a financial planning and counselling business, travel agency, or hair salon, in which very little property or equipment is owned by the business. In other situations, such as manufacturing, construction, or real estate, there is usually an opportunity to sell the assets solely or partially owned by the business to recover at least part of your initial investment.

The way to explore this question is to consider alternative scenarios for different ways the business might fail and to estimate the liquidation value of any residual assets. To the extent that this value falls short of the initial cost of those assets less any outstanding claims, you could lose that amount of money plus the opportunity cost of the time and effort you spent in trying to develop the business.

Preparing Your Business Plan

The final stage in building a dream for a new venture of your own is developing your business plan. A business plan is a written document that describes all aspects of your business venture — your basic product or service, your prospective customers, the competition, your production and marketing methods, your management team, how the business will be financed, and all the other things necessary to implement your idea. It might be called the "game plan" of your business.

BUSINESS PLANNING — THE "BIG PICTURE"

WHY CONSIDER THE "BIG PICTURE"?

When you start your business you will find that there are many things that happen that you didn't expect, or didn't work out the way you expected. Don't worry. Your experience in this regard won't be unique. This happens to almost everyone. What is important is for you to be prepared for this to happen and ready to make adjustments. In making these changes it is important that you don't lose sight of what it is that you are really trying to do. This means that you need to keep in mind the "big picture," which is brought together in the business planning process.

THE STEPS IN THE BUSINESS PLANNING PROCESS

The business planning process focuses on the future. It enables you to relate what you wish to achieve to what your business concept or idea can deliver. It entails working your way through each of the following steps in a logical and sequential way.

1. Develop a Vision Statement

A *vision statement* focuses on the "what" of your business and should describe your idealized perception of what your business will look like under perfect conditions, if all your goals and objectives have been met. It lays out the "super goal" that you would like your business to achieve. The key components of your *vision statement* will be:

- Name of your planned business venture
- Product/service offering you plan to provide
- Target market(s) you intend to serve

Your *vision statement* should be short (a sentence or two). It should also be easy to understand and easy to remember. For example, a typical *vision statement* for a new sporting goods retailer might be:

The Hockey House plans to provide a wide range of hockey-related products and services to casual skaters, minor league hockey players, community clubs and organizations, and competitive hockey teams and players.

2. Formulate a Mission Statement

A *mission statement* focuses on the "how" of your business. It defines the purpose of your venture, outlines the reason for the existence of your business, and provides some understanding of how your business will be operated. It is, in fact, the "super strategy" of your business. The key components of your *mission statement* will describe:

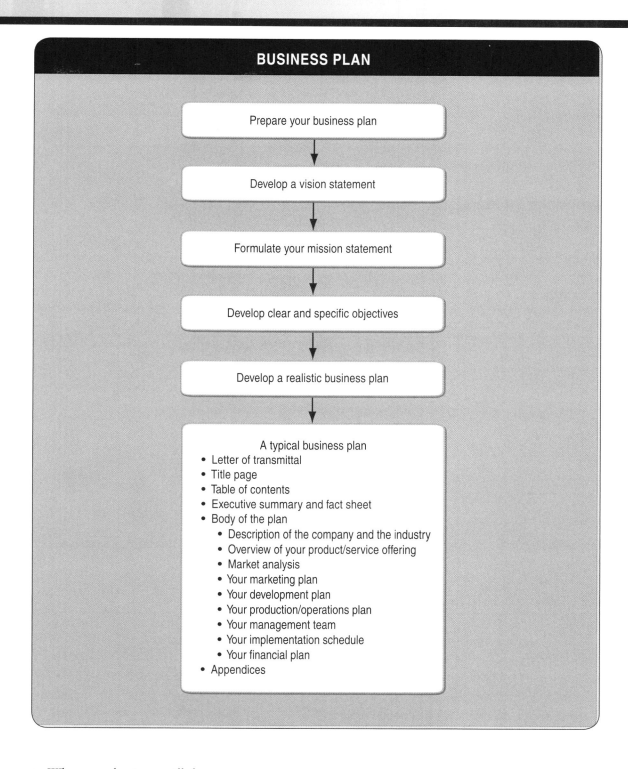

BUSINESS PLAN

Prepare your business plan

↓

Develop a vision statement

↓

Formulate your mission statement

↓

Develop clear and specific objectives

↓

Develop a realistic business plan

↓

A typical business plan
- Letter of transmittal
- Title page
- Table of contents
- Executive summary and fact sheet
- Body of the plan
  - Description of the company and the industry
  - Overview of your product/service offering
  - Market analysis
  - Your marketing plan
  - Your development plan
  - Your production/operations plan
  - Your management team
  - Your implementation schedule
  - Your financial plan
- Appendices

- What your business will do
- Its market focus, niche, or particular image
- Your planned location and the geographic market served
- How you plan to grow the business
- Your sustainable uniqueness, or what will distinguish your business from others and will continue to do so on a long-term basis

Your mission statement should be a series of short phrases that addresses each of these elements. For example, a mission statement for The Hockey House might state:

> *The Hockey House will provide a broad range of skates, sticks, pads, sweaters, and other related hockey equipment and services intended to meet the requirements of ice and in-line hockey players at all levels of ability, from beginners to semi-professional and professionals. It will also sell related supplies and equipment such as goal nets and timers, with a view to being the one-stop shop for hockey in Manitoba and northwestern Ontario. It will sell to individuals, teams, and community clubs through a retail outlet located adjacent to a major hockey complex in Winnipeg and a Web site but will also produce a four-colour catalogue and call personally on groups in communities outside the city. Our principal competitive edge will be the breadth of selection we can offer and the quality of service we plan to provide.*

3. Define the Fundamental Values By Which You Will Run Your Business

Many arguments, particularly in family businesses or partnerships, occur because the members do not share common values, even when they often assume that they do. For a new business to have a good chance of succeeding, all principals should agree on a basic set of values by which they will operate. The process of discussing and trying to achieve agreement on these values is likely to identify points of difference that should be addressed before the business is started. This process can be conducted in two steps. The first step requires you and any other principals associated with the business to define their own personal values. The second step consolidates the common values by which the business will be operated.

An example of a statement of business values might look like the following:

> *In conducting our business, we will implement our vision by conducting our affairs so that our actions provide evidence of the high value we place on:*

> ***Integrity*** *by dealing honestly with our customers, employees, suppliers, and the community*

> ***Responsibility*** *by taking into account the environment in which we do business, community views, and the common good*

> ***Profitability*** *by being conscious that an appropriate level of profit is necessary to sustain the business and allow our values to continue to be observed*

> ***Value*** *by providing quality products that are recognized as delivering value for money*

> ***Employees*** *by providing quality, equitable opportunities for development in a healthy workplace, with appropriate rewards*

4. Set Clear and Specific Objectives

Setting objectives for your business provides you with yardsticks with which to measure your ability to achieve your vision. Objectives define measurable targets whose achievement can also contribute directly to the successful accomplishment of the mission of your business. Unlike "goals," which provide a broad direction for your business, "objectives" provide you with the means to measure directly the performance of your business.

Business objectives usually relate to such issues as:

- Return on investment the business should achieve
- Desired level of market position or market share
- Projected stages of technological development
- Specific levels of financial performance

To be effective an objective should:

- Refer to a specific outcome, not an activity
- Be measurable
- Be realistic and achievable based on the actual capabilities of the business
- Contain a specific time deadline

For example, a reasonable set of objectives for The Hockey House might be:

1. *To generate $xxxx in sales by the end of year one*
2. *To achieve $yyy in after-tax profits in year one*
3. *To increase inventory turnover from x times to y times during year one*

Figure 11.2 on p. 338 near the end of this Stage outlines a framework that will enable you to develop the "big picture" for your business.

5. Make It Happen! Develop a Realistic Business Plan

Your business plan is the most important business document you will ever prepare and it is also probably the most difficult. It takes a lot of time, research, self-discipline, and commitment to complete properly and is not a lot of fun. However, regardless of whether you intend to start a small, part-time business in the basement of your home or launch a sophisticated, high-growth venture, you still need a business plan.

Your business plan is the culmination of all your self-evaluation, ideas, research, analysis, assessment, round-table discussions, bull sessions, schemes, and daydreams. It lays out the details so that everyone can see precisely where you are now, where you are going, and how you plan to get there. It presents everything about you and what you intend to do — your goals and objectives, opportunities and threats facing you, your business strengths and weaknesses, and so on. It is a comprehensive but concise disclosure of all aspects of your business venture.

How you define your business plan, however, affects your approach to writing it. If you view it as a very complex and boring task, your plan will come across that way to any reader. As a result, many business plans are dry, rambling, and highly technical because the entrepreneurs behind them see them largely as some sort of formal academic exercise.

Your business plan should be viewed as a selling document, not unlike a piece of sales literature you would distribute about your company. Except that with your business plan, rather than just promoting a particular product or service, you are selling the whole company as a package. If you are really excited about your company and the idea on which it is based, it should come through in your business plan. Your plan should convey to readers the excitement and promise that you feel about your venture.

Notice in Entrepreneurs in Action #44 the time and effort Kent Groves dedicated to the development of his business plan. He spent over a year researching the mail-order industry, studying the competition, and asking questions of people who were experts in the business. Then, with the assistance of an accountant, he wrote his "road map" to guide him through every aspect of the implementation of his business. With the plan, he was also able to win the confidence of a banker who provided him with the necessary line of credit to carry his seasonal business over its slow periods. His business plan has become a combined operations manual/corporate bible that can be continually referred to so that he knows if, in fact, the business is evolving as he had originally anticipated.

WHY DEVELOP A BUSINESS PLAN?

Your business plan can accomplish many things for you and your proposed venture. These can largely be categorized into two basic areas:

1. **For the internal evaluation of your business,** both as a checklist to see that you have covered all the important bases and as a timetable for accomplishing your stated objectives
2. **For external use** in attracting resources and obtaining support for your venture

From an internal perspective, developing a plan forces you to seriously consider the important elements of your venture and the steps you feel are necessary to get it off the ground. Your plan can be used to inform employees about the goals and direction of your business. It lets everyone know how they fit into the organization and what you expect of them. Your plan can also help you develop as a manager. It requires you to deal with problems relating to competitive conditions, promotional opportunities, and other situations that your business will encounter.

Externally, your business plan can serve as an effective sales document and is considered by many experts to be the heart of the capital-raising process. Any knowledgeable banker or prospective investor will expect you to be professional in your approach, fully prepared, and armed with a thoroughly researched, well-written business plan when seeking their support. Very little money has been raised for business ideas scribbled on the back of envelopes or on restaurant placemats, despite considerable folklore to the contrary.

Entrepreneurs in action

Business Plans: The Lies We Tell Our Bankers?

Some business people call them "the lies we tell our bankers." In this economy, however, a company looking for credit must put a lot more than creative writing in its business plan.

Kent Groves, president of catalogue retailer Maritime Trading Co. (MTC) of Falmouth, N.S., and a former Nutrilawn International manager who spent a lot of time approving franchises, knows the importance of business plans. "Some of the best plans I saw were put together by people who totally ignored them once the loan was approved. And their franchises were in trouble."

Groves took a year to research the mail-order industry, studying catalogues, trade magazines and reports, and asking questions of industry experts. Then, with an accountant, he spent six weeks writing what he calls a "road map to guide you through every aspect of your operations."

The result: a 68-page plan with 16 appendices. Groves' Rand-McNally approach to mapping business highways offers an executive summary, mission statement ("we are the leader in the direct marketing of the highest quality Maritime products in the world"), profile, industry overview, and bibliography. And he provided details on sales and marketing, operations, and financing. "It helped to have an accountant who would say, 'Those figures don't make sense,'" says Groves. "She asked the hard questions."

Most of Groves' efforts were geared to winning a line of credit — essential for a firm that makes all its money at Christmas. But the effort proved frustrating: MTC's application was rejected by Scotiabank, CIBC, and Hongkong Bank. The setback soured Groves: "The banks advertise 'We support small business.' Yeah, until you need money. What a crock!"

After moving to Nova Scotia full-time in June, Groves approached the Royal Bank in Halifax. There he met account manager Earl Covin, who got excited by his plan. "It was a breath of fresh air," says Covin. "I didn't have to do a lot of background work. It had more detail than most bankers ever expect, and it was very realistic." Once past the collateral hurdle — Groves' father helped out — the bank approved a $75,000 credit line in a day.

Beyond winning financial support, MTC's business plan has become a combined operations manual/corporate bible. Says Groves, "We continually check our expenses and they're right on track. We know where we stand." So when he saw catalogue costs coming in 25% below projections, he knew he could boost marketing spending 20%.

More importantly, revenue projections are also on budget. Another catalogue company, using one of the same mailing lists as Groves, received a 1.5% response rate — "dead on" for MTC's projections. MTC forecast an operating deficit of $49,200 at the end of September; the actual amount was $45,000. With his catalogues just hitting the market in October, Groves still expects sales to reach $100,000 by Dec. 31.

Like most road maps, MTC's business plan allows for dirt roads and detours. "When we stray," says Groves, "we know it and at what capacity we're varying. What's important is flexibility that allows you to make changes." (www.maritimetrading.com)

Source: Allan Lynch, *PROFIT* magazine. Lynch is also author of *Sweat Equity: Atlantic Canada's New Entrepreneurs* (Halifax, NS: Nimbris Publishing, 1996).

In the course of attracting external support for your venture, a number of people may have occasion to read your plan. These include bankers, suppliers, prospective customers, and potential investors. Each of them will be viewing your business from a slightly different perspective. Bankers, for example, are primarily interested in the business's fixed assets and other available collateral. They want to know if you can pay back their loan at prevailing interest rates. Venture capitalists and other private investors, on the other hand, are more interested in their expected return on investment. They tend to like innovative products and services in growth industries that promise significant returns. These differing viewpoints should be taken into account in developing your plan.

Shelley Dufault of Urban Canine definitely learned the value of having a well-formulated business plan when she went to her banker to obtain a start-up loan for the business she wanted to start with her daughter (Entrepreneurs in Action #45). The business was started largely on the basis of their observation that there were

Other considerations

ADVANTAGES OF PREPARING A BUSINESS PLAN

A business plan:

- Helps you to face reality and the facts
- Forces you to think ahead and consider the future
- Assists you in summarizing your skills and points out the strengths of others involved in your venture
- Helps you identify and define your product/service, pricing strategy, distribution strategy, and marketing and promotional strategy
- Establishes the amount of financing or outside investment you require
- Outlines the financial future of your business through projected statements such as cash flow, income and expenses, and balance sheets
- Provides you with an effective sales tool
- Inspires confidence in yourself and projects that confidence to others

Source: Dawn Braddock, "How to Write a Business Plan that Makes Good Business Sense," *Business Sense*, November 2000, pp. 16–17.

only a couple of companies offering any kind of day care service for pets, and none offering the kind of special service they wanted for their dogs. Their research, however, indicated there was a growing demand across North America for pet-related products and services as consumers with high discretionary income wanted to spend more money on pampering their pets. With no local competition, they thought they should jump into the market.

When they went looking for the money, however, their banker told them bluntly — no business plan, no loan. Dufault reluctantly spent the next three-and-a-half weeks putting together their plan. For her it was a painful experience and a lot harder than she expected it to be. But in the end, when she presented it to the banker, her loan was approved within a couple of days, largely on the strength of the plan.

HOW LONG SHOULD YOUR BUSINESS PLAN BE?

Business plans can be broadly categorized into three types: the summary business plan, the full business plan, and the operational business plan.

The Summary Business Plan

Summary business plans commonly run about 10 pages or so, considerably shorter than the 40 or so pages traditional for business plans. Summary business plans have become increasingly popular and accepted for use by early-stage businesses in applying for a bank loan, or they may be all that is required for a small, lifestyle business such as a convenience store, home-based business, graphic design company, or consulting firm. A summary business plan may also be sufficient to whet the appetite of friends, relatives, and other private investors who might subsequently receive a copy of the full plan if they are sufficiently interested.

The Full Business Plan

A full business plan similar to the one you would develop by following the samples at the end of this Stage will likely run from 10 to 40 pages. This is the traditional plan. It covers all the key subjects in enough depth to permit a full exploration of the principal issues. The full business plan is most appropriate when you are trying to raise a substantial amount of external financing or if you are looking for a partner or other major private investors.

The Operational Business Plan

The operational business plan will usually exceed 40 pages in length but is used only infrequently, such as when a business is planning to grow very rapidly and must try to anticipate a wide variety of issues. Or it might be

Entrepreneurs in action

Importance of plan can't be overstated

ENTREPRENEURS FIND LENDERS DEMAND THE DOCUMENT

One of the most common mistakes aspiring entrepreneurs make is not taking the time to develop a proper business plan for their new venture. "Of all the types of business documents, the business plan is by far the most important," says the Canada/Manitoba Business Service Centre (C/MBSC).

For the uninitiated, a business plan is a document that describes all of the different aspects of the proposed venture. It should include information about such things as the owners, the product or service they plan to offer, who their customers are, who their competition is, whether it's a growth industry, their marketing strategy, who the management team will be, and how they plan to finance their venture.

Roland Gagné, a business development officer with C/MBSC, said in an interview it never ceases to amaze him how many entrepreneurs come through the centre's doors with either no business plan or a bad business plan.

"There are huge amounts."

The Assiniboine Credit Union also sees lots of them, according to Nigel Mohammed, the institution's manager of community services. And like Gagné, Mohammed said he can't stress enough the importance of having a good business plan.

"We focus on the business plan because that puts us in a better position to gauge if the business is going to be a success," he said. "We also take into account their credit rating and their assets, but fundamentally, it comes down to the plan they have developed."

Shelley Dufault, co-owner of Urban Canine, a new doggie day care she and her daughter Jana-Rai Dufault opened last spring in Winnipeg, was one of those entrepreneurs who thought she could get away with not having a formal business plan. But she found out differently when she went to see her banker for a startup loan for their business. "He said he wanted to see a business plan," Shelley said, and his message was clear: no plan, no loan.

She reluctantly spent the next three and a half weeks painstakingly putting together a detailed plan with help from the C/MBSC.

PHOTO BY KEN GIGLIOTTI, *WINNIPEG FREE PRESS.*

"It was a lot harder than I ever thought it would be," she confessed. "It was brutal."

The C/MBSC's Gagné and the ACU's Mohammed said one of the benefits of having entrepreneurs develop a business plan for their new ventures is that it forces them to take a long, hard look at what they want to do and how they're going to do it. It also helps them to identify strengths and weaknesses in their plans, and to address issues before they become problems.

Mohammed said a good business plan also can serve as a blueprint for managing the business on an ongoing basis, and helps keep the owner focused for the longer term.

"They should go back and look at it probably on a monthly basis," he added, and also update it where needed.

Dufault said while putting their plan together was a painful experience, it was worth it.

"I have to say, it was one of my proudest moments when I got that finished," she said. "I gave it to my banker and three or four days later he called me and said, 'you got your loan, and you got it solely on the basis of the strength of your business plan... It was excellent.'"

Dufault said it taught her a valuable lesson, and one she now shares with other aspiring entrepreneurs.

"I really thought I could do it without it, but it was the most important thing I did," she added. (www.urbancanine.ca)

Source: Murray McNeill, *Winnipeg Free Press*, Monday, November 7, 2005, page B3.

Other considerations

TIPS FOR DEVELOPING YOUR BUSINESS PLAN

Here are some pointers to consider in developing your business plan:

- **Business planning involves a great deal of work** Be prepared to spend weeks — or months — completing your plan.
- **Work on sections at a time** While this undertaking may appear overwhelming at first, don't get discouraged. Break the project down into manageable chunks and work on each chunk separately.
- **Be brief but complete** Although you may have volumes of important material, aim for a plan that is brief and succinct but includes everything important to the business.
- **Focus on your intended reader** Use your plan to organize your efforts around your objectives to ensure you have all the bases covered.
- **Use layman's terms** Avoid highly technical descriptions of your products, processes, and operations.
- **A business plan is a "living" document** Update it as your knowledge grows and whenever your plans become more concrete.
- **Be realistic** Base your projections on the results gathered from your analysis. Be honest about both positive and negative findings.
- **Discuss your firm's business risks** Your credibility can be seriously undermined if existing risks and problems are discovered by readers on their own.
- **Don't make vague or unsubstantiated statements** Back up your statements with background data and market information.

Source: Adapted from *Entrepreneurial Edge*, Edward Lowe Foundation, "How to Develop and Use a Business Plan" (www.edwardlowe.org/index.elf?page=sserc&storyid=7704&function=story), accessed June 7, 2010.

---

part of an annual process where it is necessary to get into great detail about distribution, production, advertising, and other areas where it is essential for everyone involved with the organization to understand clearly everything that is going on. Traditional business plans that grow to this length should be avoided as they reflect a lack of discipline and focus.

WHO SHOULD WRITE YOUR BUSINESS PLAN?

You should write your business plan. If someone else develops the business plan for you, it becomes their plan, not yours. If you are part of a management team, each individual should contribute his or her part to the overall project.

Do not under any circumstances hire someone else to write the plan for you. This doesn't mean that you shouldn't get help from others in compiling information, obtaining licences, permits, patents, and other legal considerations, or preparing your pro forma financial statements — only that the final plan should be written by you and your team.

The people who may be assessing your plan want to know that you see the big picture as it relates to your business and understand all the functional requirements of your company, not that you can hire a good consultant. It is very difficult to defend someone else's work. If you put your business plan together yourself, you have a better understanding and feel for the business. Your business plan should be a personal expression written in your own unique style, though of course it should look professional and businesslike.

HOW LONG DOES IT TAKE?

Putting together a business plan does not happen overnight. A plan for a relatively simple, straightforward business might be completed within a few weeks, while a plan for a complex, high growth new venture could take several months.

WHAT SHOULD YOUR PLAN CONTAIN?

Your business plan is the nuts and bolts of your proposed business venture put down on paper. You will have to decide exactly what information to include, how your plan can be best organized for maximum effectiveness, and what information should be given particular emphasis. All plans, however, require a formal, structured presentation so that they are easy to read and follow and tend to avoid confusion. A number of forms and sample outlines for a business plan are available, but virtually all suggest that business plans contain the following components: (1) letter of transmittal, (2) title page, (3) table of contents, (4) executive summary and fact sheet, (5) body, and (6) appendices. The contents of a typical business plan are outlined in Figure 11.1. on p. 328. You can use this framework as a guideline to assist you in the development of the plan for your business.

SHERMAN'S LAGOON

© Jim Toomey, King Features Syndicate.

1. LETTER OF TRANSMITTAL

The letter of transmittal officially introduces your business plan to the reader. It explains your reason for writing the plan, gives the title of the plan or the name of your business, and outlines the major features of your plan that may be of interest.

2. TITLE PAGE

The title page, or cover page, of your plan provides identifying information about you and your proposed business. It should include the name, address, and telephone number of the business as well as similar information about yourself. The date the plan was finalized or submitted to the recipient should also be included on the title page.

3. TABLE OF CONTENTS

The table of contents is a list of the major headings and subheadings contained in your plan. It provides readers with a quick overview of the contents of your plan and allows them to quickly access the particular sections that may be of primary interest to them.

4. EXECUTIVE SUMMARY AND FACT SHEET

The executive summary may be the most important part of your business plan. It must capture the attention of the reader, stimulate interest, and get the reader to keep on reading the rest of your plan. In two or three pages this summary should concisely explain your business's current status; describe its products or services and their benefits to your customers; provide an overview of your venture's objectives, market prospects, and financial forecasts; and, if you are using the plan to raise external financing, indicate the amount of financing needed, how the money is to be used, and the benefits to the prospective lender or investor.

FYI FOR YOUR INFORMATION

BUSINESS PLAN OUTLINES AND TEMPLATES

Here are some examples of Web sites that have detailed instructions, outlines, or templates for developing a comprehensive business plan.

Community Business Development Corporations Online business plan is a Web-based application allowing new and aspiring entrepreneurs the ability to prepare a three year business plan online. (www.cbdc.ca/obp.php)

Canadian Youth Business Foundation The **CYBF Interactive Business Planner** is a tool designed to guide both new and experienced entrepreneurs through the process of writing a comprehensive business plan. (www.cybf.ca/entrepreneurs/interactivebusinessplanner.php)

Writing an Effective Business Plan A downloadable Business Plan Workbook that can be used as a tool for helping you put your business plan together from The Entrepreneurship Centre, Ottawa. (www.entrepreneurship.com/tools/pdf/businessPlanWorkbook.pdf)

Business Planning and Financial Forecasting A well-developed business plan guide and outline, with heavy emphasis on putting together your financial plan. (www.smallbusinessbc.ca/pdf/bpff2002.pdf)

BizPlanIt's Virtual Business Plan This unique and free online resource mirrors the major sections of a business plan, and enables you to learn the fundamentals of writing a business plan. (www.bizplanit.com/vplan.html)

Money Hunt Business Plan Template A U.S. site claiming to have the best business plan outline on the Web. (www.moneyhunt.com/mhtemplate.html)

Most Canadian banks can also provide you with basic templates and tools to help you develop your business plan.

This summary should give the essence of your plan and highlight its really significant points. In many instances the summary will either sell the reader on continuing to read the rest of the document or convince him or her to forget the whole thing; the game may be won or lost on the basis of the executive summary.

The fact sheet should appear as a separate page at the back of the executive summary. It summarizes the basic information that relates to your venture:

1. Company name
2. Company address, telephone/fax numbers, e-mail address
3. Type of business and industry
4. Form of business organization (proprietorship, partnership, or corporation)
5. Principal product or service line
6. Registered patents or trademarks
7. Number and name of founders/partners/shareholders
8. Length of time in business
9. Current and/or projected market share
10. Funds invested in the business to date and their source
11. Additional financing required
12. Proposed terms and payback period
13. Total value or net worth of the business
14. Name of business advisors (legal counsel, accountant, others)

FIGURE 11.1   A TYPICAL BUSINESS PLAN

Business Plan Contents

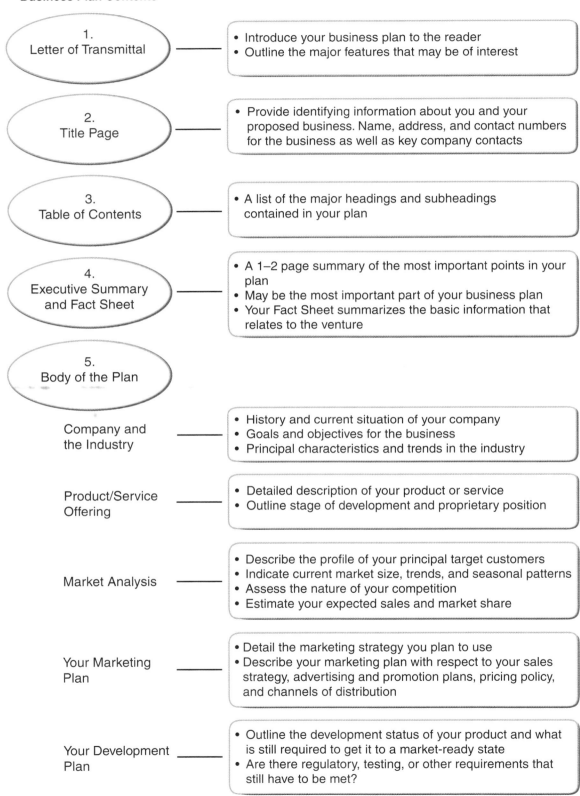

1. Letter of Transmittal
- Introduce your business plan to the reader
- Outline the major features that may be of interest

2. Title Page
- Provide identifying information about you and your proposed business. Name, address, and contact numbers for the business as well as key company contacts

3. Table of Contents
- A list of the major headings and subheadings contained in your plan

4. Executive Summary and Fact Sheet
- A 1–2 page summary of the most important points in your plan
- May be the most important part of your business plan
- Your Fact Sheet summarizes the basic information that relates to the venture

5. Body of the Plan

Company and the Industry
- History and current situation of your company
- Goals and objectives for the business
- Principal characteristics and trends in the industry

Product/Service Offering
- Detailed description of your product or service
- Outline stage of development and proprietary position

Market Analysis
- Describe the profile of your principal target customers
- Indicate current market size, trends, and seasonal patterns
- Assess the nature of your competition
- Estimate your expected sales and market share

Your Marketing Plan
- Detail the marketing strategy you plan to use
- Describe your marketing plan with respect to your sales strategy, advertising and promotion plans, pricing policy, and channels of distribution

Your Development Plan
- Outline the development status of your product and what is still required to get it to a market-ready state
- Are there regulatory, testing, or other requirements that still have to be met?

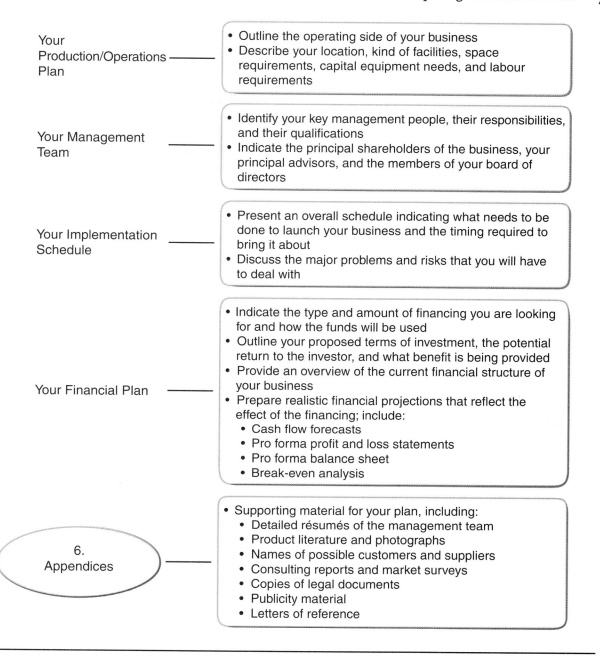

Your Production/Operations Plan
- Outline the operating side of your business
- Describe your location, kind of facilities, space requirements, capital equipment needs, and labour requirements

Your Management Team
- Identify your key management people, their responsibilities, and their qualifications
- Indicate the principal shareholders of the business, your principal advisors, and the members of your board of directors

Your Implementation Schedule
- Present an overall schedule indicating what needs to be done to launch your business and the timing required to bring it about
- Discuss the major problems and risks that you will have to deal with

Your Financial Plan
- Indicate the type and amount of financing you are looking for and how the funds will be used
- Outline your proposed terms of investment, the potential return to the investor, and what benefit is being provided
- Provide an overview of the current financial structure of your business
- Prepare realistic financial projections that reflect the effect of the financing; include:
  - Cash flow forecasts
  - Pro forma profit and loss statements
  - Pro forma balance sheet
  - Break-even analysis

6. Appendices
- Supporting material for your plan, including:
  - Detailed résumés of the management team
  - Product literature and photographs
  - Names of possible customers and suppliers
  - Consulting reports and market surveys
  - Copies of legal documents
  - Publicity material
  - Letters of reference

5. BODY OF THE PLAN

The body of your business plan is by far the longest component, because it presents the detailed story of your business proposition. It should be broken down into major divisions using headings, and each major division divided into sections using subheadings. It is probably better to have too many rather than not enough headings and subheadings.

What follows is a typical overview of the kind of material that should be included in the body of your plan.

Your Company and the Industry

Describe the start-up and background of your business and provide the reader with some context within which to fit all the information you will be providing later in your plan.

Familiarize the reader with your company; the industry within which you will be competing, your understanding of it, and where it is headed; and what opportunities you see for your business.

YOUR COMPANY

BACKGROUND Give the date your business was started, its present form of organization, its location, and pertinent historical information on the firm. Name the founders and other key people, how your key products or services were chosen and developed, and what success the business has achieved to date.

CURRENT SITUATION Discuss such issues as how you have identified your market opportunity, assessed the competition, and developed some unique factor or distinctive competence that will make your business stand out from the rest.

FUTURE PLANS Discuss your goals and ambitions for the business and your strategy for achieving them.

THE INDUSTRY

PRINCIPAL CHARACTERISTICS Describe the current status and prospects for the industry in which your business will operate. How big is the industry? What are its total sales in dollars? In units? What are typical industry standards, gross margins, seasonal patterns, and similar factors?

MAJOR PARTICIPANTS Identify the major industry participants and describe their role, market share, and other performance measures. What are their principal strengths and weaknesses and how do you feel you will be able to successfully compete in this situation?

INDUSTRY TRENDS Discuss how you feel the industry will evolve in the future. Is it growing or stable? What do you feel industry sales will be five and ten years from now? What general trends are evident and how is the industry likely to be affected by economic, social, technological, environmental, and regulatory trends?

YOUR PRODUCT/SERVICE OFFERING

DESCRIPTION Describe in detail the product or service you plan to sell, explaining any unique characteristics or particular advantages. How will features of your product or service give you some advantage over competitors?

Indicate the stage of development your product is at and whether prototypes, working models, or finished production units are available. Include photographs if possible.

PROPRIETARY POSITION Describe any patents or trademarks you may hold or have applied for, or any licensing agreements or other legal contracts that may provide some protection for your product or service. Are there any regulatory or government-approved standards or requirements your product must meet? How and when do you plan to obtain this certification?

POTENTIAL Outline your market opportunity as you see it and explain how you plan to take advantage of it. What are the key success factors in this business and how do you plan to exploit them to your advantage?

Market Analysis

This section of your plan should convince the reader that you thoroughly understand the market for your product or service, that you can deal with the competition and achieve sufficient sales to develop a viable and growing business. You should describe the total market and how you feel it can be broken down into segments. You can then indicate the segment or niche you plan to concentrate on and what share of this business you will be able to obtain.

Your analysis of the market may be based on:

1. Market studies available from private research firms and government departments and agencies
2. Statistics Canada or U.S. Census Bureau data
3. Information from trade associations and trade publications
4. Surveys or informal discussions with dealers, distributors, sales representatives, customers, or competitors

This is often one of the most difficult parts of the business plan to prepare, but it is also one of the most important. Almost all other sections of your business plan depend on the sales estimates developed from your market analysis. The outline provided in Stage 7 can help you in this process.

TARGET MARKET AND CUSTOMERS Identify who constitute your primary target markets — individual consumers, companies, health care or educational institutions, government departments, or other groups.

Examine beforehand if these target markets can be segmented or broken down into relatively homogeneous groups having common, identifiable characteristics such as geographic location, age, size, type of industry, or some other factor. Present these facts in the most logical or appropriate format.

Describe the profile of your principal target customers. Who and where are they? What are the principal bases for their purchase decisions? What are their major applications for your product? What principal benefit will they obtain from using your product rather than one of your competitors'?

Identify, if possible, some major buyers who may be prepared to make purchase commitments. If possible, get a purchase order.

MARKET SIZE AND TRENDS Estimate the size of the current total market for your product or service in both units and dollars. How are sales distributed among the various segments you identified? Are there any strong weekly, monthly, or seasonal patterns? Ensure you include answers to these questions.

Describe how the market size for each of these segments has changed over the past three to four years in units and dollars. Outline how it is expected to change over the next three to four years.

Include the major factors that have affected past market growth (e.g., socioeconomic trends, industry trends, regulatory changes, government policy, population shifts). What is likely to happen in these areas in the future?

COMPETITION Identify each of your principal competitors. Make a realistic assessment of each of these firms and its product or service offering. Compare these competing products or services on the basis of price, quality, performance, service support, warranties, and other important features.

Present your evaluation of the market share of each segment by each competitor, its relative profitability, and its sales, marketing, distribution, and production capabilities. How do you see these factors changing in the future?

ESTIMATED SALES AND MARKET SHARE Estimate the share of each segment of the market and the sales in units and dollars that you feel you will acquire for each of the next three to five years. This should be developed by month for the next year and annually for each year thereafter. This information can best be presented in tabular form. Indicate on what assumptions you have based these projections.

Your Marketing Plan

Your marketing plan outlines how your sales projections will be achieved. It details the marketing strategy you plan to use to establish your product or service in the marketplace and obtain a profitable share of the overall market. Your marketing plan should describe *what* is to be done, *when* it is to be done, *how* it is to be done, and *who* will do it insofar as your sales strategy, advertising and promotion plans, pricing policy, and channels of distribution are concerned.

PRICING Summarize the general financial characteristics of your business and the industry at large. What will be typical gross and net margins for each of the products or services you plan to sell? How do these compare with those of other firms in the industry? Provide a detailed breakdown of your estimated fixed, variable, and semivariable costs for each of your various products or services.

Discuss the prices you plan to charge for your product. How do they compare with your major competitors'? Is your gross margin sufficient to cover your transportation costs, selling costs, advertising and promotion costs, rent, depreciation, and similar expenses — and still provide some margin of profit?

Detail the markups your product will provide to the various members of your channel of distribution. How do these compare with those they receive on comparable products? Does your markup provide them with sufficient incentive to handle your product?

Indicate your normal terms of sale. Do these conform to industry norms? Do you plan to offer cash, quantity, or other discounts?

Indicate how long it will take you to break even, basing your opinion on your anticipated cost structure and planned price.

SALES AND DISTRIBUTION Indicate the methods you will use to sell and distribute your product or service. Do you plan to use your own salaried or commissioned salespeople, rely on manufacturers' agents or other wholesalers and distributors, or utilize a more non-traditional means of distributing your product such as export trading companies, direct-mail selling, mail-order houses, party plan selling, or other means of selling directly to the final consumer?

If you plan to use your own sales force, describe how large it will be and how it will be structured. Indicate how salespeople will be distributed, whom they will call on, how many calls you estimate it will take to get an order, the size of a typical order, how much you estimate a typical salesperson will sell each year, how he or she will be paid, how much he or she is likely to make in a year, and how this compares with the average for the industry.

If you plan to use distributors or wholesalers, indicate how they have been or will be selected, who they are if possible, what areas or territory they will cover, how they will be compensated, credit and collection policies, and any special policies such as exclusive rights, discounts, and cooperative advertising programs.

Indicate any plans for export sales or international marketing arrangements.

ADVERTISING AND PROMOTION Describe the program you plan to use to make consumers aware of your product or service. What consumers are you trying to reach? Do you plan to use the services of an advertising agency? What media do you plan to use — radio, television, newspapers, magazines, billboards, direct mail, coupons, brochures, trade shows? How much do you plan to spend on each medium? When? Which specific vehicles?

Outline any plans to obtain free publicity for your product or company.

SERVICE AND WARRANTY PROGRAM Indicate your service arrangements, warranty terms, and method of handling service problems. Describe how you will handle customer complaints and other problems. Will service be handled by the company, dealers and distributors, or independent service centres? How do these arrangements compare with those of your competitors?

Your Development Plan

If your product or service involves some further technical development, the planned extent of this work should be discussed in your business plan. Prospective investors, bankers, and others will want to know the nature and extent of any additional development required, how much it will cost, and how long it will take before your business has a finished, marketable product.

DEVELOPMENT STATUS Describe the current status of your product and outline what still remains to be done to make it marketable. Do you presently have only a concept, detailed drawings, a laboratory prototype, a production prototype, or a finished product? Is further engineering work required? Has the necessary tooling to produce the product been adequately developed? Are the services of an industrial designer or other specialist required to refine the product into marketable form?

COSTS Indicate how much money has been spent on product development to date and where it has been spent. Present a development budget indicating the additional funds required, how they will be spent, and the timing involved in completing the project.

PROPRIETARY ISSUES Indicate any patents or trademarks that you own, have, or for which you plan to apply. Are there any regulatory requirements to produce or market the product? Has the product undergone standardized testing through the Underwriters' Laboratory, the Canadian Standards Association, or some other agency? If not, what are your plans? Have you tested the product at all in the marketplace? What was the result?

Your Production/Operations Plan

Your production/operations plan outlines the operating side of your business. It should describe your plant location, the kind of facilities needed, space requirements, capital equipment needed, and your labour requirements.

If your plan is for a manufacturing business, you should also discuss such areas as your purchasing policy, quality control program, inventory control system, production cost breakdown, and whether you plan to manufacture all subcomponents of the product yourself or have some of them produced for you by someone else.

LOCATION Describe the planned location of your business and discuss any advantages or disadvantages of this location in terms of the cost and availability of labour; proximity to customers; access to transportation, energy supplies, or other natural resources; and zoning and other legal requirements.

Discuss the characteristics of your location in relation to market size, traffic flows, local and regional growth rates, income levels, and similar market-related factors.

FACILITIES AND EQUIPMENT Describe the property and facilities currently used or that will be required to operate your business. This should include factory and office space, selling space, storage space, property size and location, etc. Will these facilities be leased or purchased? What is the cost and timing of their acquisition?

Detail the machinery and equipment that is required for your manufacturing process. Is this highly specialized or general-purpose equipment? Is it leased or purchased? New or used? What is the cost? What will it cost for equipment set-up and facility layout? What is its expected life? Will it have any residual or scrap value?

If possible, provide a drawing of the physical layout of the plant and other facilities.

MANUFACTURING PLANS AND COSTS Develop a manufacturing cost outline that shows standard production costs at various levels of operation. Break down total costs into raw material, component parts, labour, and overhead. Indicate your raw material, work-in-process, and finished goods inventory requirements at various sales levels. How will seasonal variations in demand be handled?

Indicate your key suppliers or subcontractors for various raw materials and components. What are the lead times for these materials? Are back-up suppliers or other alternatives available?

Outline the quality control procedures you will use to minimize service problems. Do you need any other production control measures?

On the basis of this configuration of facilities and equipment, indicate your production capacity. Where can this be expanded? Do you have any plans to modify existing plant space? What is the timing and cost?

LABOUR Describe the number of employees you have or need and their qualifications. Will they be full-time or part-time? Have you developed a job description for each position? What in-house training will be required? How much will each employee be paid? What kinds of pension plan, health insurance plan, profit-sharing plan, and other fringe benefits will be required? Have you registered with the necessary government departments?

Indicate whether your employees will be union or non-union. If employees will be members of a union, describe the principal terms of their contract and when it expires.

ENVIRONMENTAL AND OTHER ISSUES Indicate any approvals that it may be necessary for you to obtain related to zoning requirements, permits, licences, health and safety requirements, environmental approvals, etc. Are there any laws or regulatory requirements unique to your business? Are there any other legal or contractual matters that should be considered?

Your Management Team

Your management team and your directors are the key to success. You should identify who your key people are; their qualifications; what they are being paid; who has overall authority; who is responsible for the various functional areas of the business such as sales, marketing, production, research and development, and financial management; and so forth.

In most small businesses there are no more than two or three really key players — including yourself. Concentrate on these individuals, indicating their education, qualifications, and past business achievements. Indicate how they will contribute to the success of the present venture. Don't hire friends, relatives, or other people for key positions who do not have the proper qualifications.

Many external investors are more concerned about the management of the business than the business itself. They invest in the people rather than the project. They will conduct a thorough and exhaustive investigation of each of your key players to determine whether they are the kind of people in which they wish to invest. This portion of your plan should instill confidence in the management of your business in the mind of the reader.

DESCRIPTION OF MANAGEMENT TEAM Outline the exact duties and responsibilities of each key member of your management team. Prepare a brief résumé of each individual indicating education, professional qualifications, employment experience, and other personal achievements. (You will include a complete, more detailed résumé for each of these individuals in an appendix to your plan.)

DIRECTORS Indicate the size and composition of your board of directors. Identify any individuals you are planning to invite to sit on your board. Include a brief statement about each member's background, indicating what he or she will bring to the company.

MANAGEMENT AND DIRECTORS' COMPENSATION List the names of all members of your management team and board of directors and the compensation they will receive in fees or salary. Initially, at least, you and your management team should be prepared to accept modest salaries, perhaps well below what you received in your previous job, if you hope to attract external investors to your business.

SHAREHOLDERS Indicate the name of each of the individual shareholders (or partners) in your business, the number of shares each owns, the percentage of ownership, and the price paid.

Describe any investors in your business other than your management team and members of your board. How many shares do they have? When were these shares acquired? What price did the investors pay?

Summarize any incentive stock option or bonus plans that you have in effect or plan to institute. Also indicate any employment contracts or agreements you may have made with members of your management team.

PROFESSIONAL ADVISORS Indicate the name and complete address of each of your professional advisors, for example your lawyer, accountant, banker, insurance broker, and management or technical consultants. Disclose any fees or retainers that may have been paid to any of these people.

Implementation Schedule and Risks Associated with the Venture

It is necessary to present an overall schedule indicating the interrelationship among the various events necessary to launch your business and the timing required to bring it about. A well-prepared schedule demonstrates to external investors that you have given proper thought to where you are going and have the ability to plan ahead. This schedule can be a very effective sales tool.

Your plan should also discuss the major problems and risks you feel you will have to deal with in developing your business.

MILESTONES Summarize the significant goals that you and your business have already reached and still hope to accomplish in the future. What still needs to be done for the business to succeed? Who is going to do these things? When will they be completed?

SCHEDULE Develop a schedule of significant events and their priority for completion. What kind of strategic planning has been done to see that things occur as necessary? Have you developed a fallback or contingency position in case things don't come off as you have planned?

RISKS AND PROBLEMS You might start by summarizing the major problems you have already had to deal with and how they were resolved. Were any particularly innovative or creative approaches used in addressing these issues?

Identify the risks your business may be faced with in the future. What are you attempting to do to avoid these? How will you deal with them if they arise? How can their impact on your business be minimized?

Summarize the downside risk. What would happen in the "worst case" scenario? What, if anything, could be salvaged from the business for your investors? Have you developed any contingency plans in case any of these risks should occur?

Your Financial Plan

Your financial plan is essential to enable a prospective investor or banker to evaluate the investment opportunity you are presenting. The plan should illustrate the current financial status of your business and represent your best estimate of its future operations. The results presented should be both realistic and attainable.

Your financial plan should also describe the type of financing you are seeking, the amount of money you are looking for, how you plan to use these funds in the business, the terms of repayment and desired interest rate, or the dividends, voting rights, and redemption considerations related to the offering of any common or preferred stock.

FUNDING REQUESTED Indicate the amount and type (debt or equity) of funding you are looking for. For what do you intend to use the money? How will it be applied in your business — to acquire property, fixtures, equipment, or inventory, or to provide working capital?

Give an overview of the current financial structure of your business. Indicate the level of investment already made in the business and where the funds came from. What effect will the additional capital have on your business in terms of ownership structure, future growth, and profitability?

Outline your proposed terms of investment. What is the payback period and potential return on investment for the lender or investor? What collateral, tax benefit, or other security is being offered?

CURRENT FINANCIAL STATEMENTS If your venture is already in operation, you should provide copies of financial statements (profit and loss statement and a balance sheet) for the current year and the previous two years.

FINANCIAL PROJECTIONS In developing your financial plan, a number of basic projections must be prepared. These should be based on realistic expectations and reflect the effect of the proposed financing. The projections should be developed on a monthly basis for the first year of operation and on a quarterly or annual basis for another two to four years. These projections should include the following statements:

1. **Profit and loss forecasts** These pro forma income statements indicate your profit expectations for the next few years of operation of your business. They should be based on realistic estimates of sales and operating costs and represent your best estimate of actual operating results.

2. **Pro forma balance sheet** Your pro forma balance sheet indicates the assets you feel will be required to support your projected level of operations and how you plan to finance these assets.

3. **Projected cash flow statements** Your cash flow forecasts are probably your most important statements, because they indicate the amount and timing of your expected cash inflows and outflows. Typically, the operating profits during the start-up of a new venture are not sufficient to finance the business's operating needs. This often means that the inflow of cash will not meet your business's cash requirements, at least on a short-term basis. These conditions must be anticipated so that you can predict cash needs and avoid insolvency.

4. **Break-even analysis** A break-even analysis indicates the level of sales and production you will require to cover all your fixed and variable costs. It is useful for you and prospective lenders and investors to know what your break-even point is and how easy or difficult it will likely be to attain.

An example of each of these statements and a discussion on how to determine the break-even point for your venture is presented in Stage Eight of this book.

6. APPENDICES

The appendices are intended to explain, support, and supplement the material in the body of your business plan. In most cases this material is attached to the back of your plan. Examples of the kind of material that might be included in an appendix are:

1. Product specifications and photographs
2. Detailed résumés of the management team
3. Lists of prospective customers
4. Names of possible suppliers
5. Job descriptions for the management team
6. Consulting reports and market surveys
7. Copies of legal documents such as leases, franchise and licensing agreements, contracts, licences, patent or trademark registrations, and articles of incorporation
8. Letters of reference
9. Relevant magazine, trade journal, and newspaper articles

Other considerations

THE SEVEN DEADLY SINS FOR BUSINESS PLANS

Less than five minutes. That's the amount of time your plan has in the hands of many potential investors before they decide to turn "thumbs up" or "thumbs down" on it. In other words, they evaluate a document that may have taken you weeks or even months to prepare in just a few moments. For this reason, it is absolutely imperative that you avoid errors that will doom your plan to the rejection pile no matter how good other sections of it may be. We term these blunders the "Seven Deadly Sins of Business Plans," and here they are for you to recognize — and avoid:

Sin #1: The plan is poorly prepared and has an unprofessional look (e.g., no cover page, a cover page without contact information, glaring typos). This carelessness triggers the following investor reaction: "I'm dealing with a group of amateurs."

Sin #2: The plan is far too slick (e.g., it is bound like a book, is printed on shiny paper, and uses flashy graphics). This leads investors to think: "What are they trying to hide behind all the glitter?"

Sin #3: The executive summary is too long and rambling — it doesn't get right to the point. This failure to be concise leads investors to think: "If they can't describe their own idea and company succinctly, I don't want to waste my time — and certainly not my money — on them."

Sin #4: It's not clear where the product is in terms of development — does it exist or not? Can it be readily manufactured? If investors have to ask these questions, they may conclude: "I can't tell whether this is real or just another pipedream; I'll pass on this one."

Sin #5: No clear answer is provided to the question: "Why would anyone ever want to buy one?" Many entrepreneurs seem to assume that their new product or service is so wonderful that it will virtually sell itself. This kind of blind faith on the part of entrepreneurs leads investors to think: "How naive can you get? Even a machine that grew hair on the heads of bald men would need a marketing plan. These are truly amateurs."

Sin #6: It gives no clear statement of the qualifications of the management team: This oversight leads investors to conclude: "They probably have no relevant experience — and may not even know what relevant experience would be!"

Sin #7: Financial projections are largely an exercise in wishful thinking: This over optimism leads potential investors to conclude: "They have no idea about what it is like to run a company, or (even worse) they think I am incredibly naïve or stupid. Pass!"

The moral is clear: keep a sharp lookout for these deadly errors, because if you commit even one, your chance of obtaining financial support and other forms of help from sophisticated investors will fade quickly.

Source: Robert A. Baron and Scott A. Shane. *Entrepreneurship: A Process Perspective.* 2nd Edition. (Thomson South-Western 2008). p. 220.

CONCLUSION

It is important that your plan make a good first impression. It should demonstrate that you have done a significant amount of thinking and work on your venture. You should ensure your material is presented to prospective investors, lenders, and others in an attractive, readable, and understandable fashion.

Figure 11.3 on p. 341 provides a checklist that you can use to assess your finished plan for completeness, clarity, and persuasiveness.

The length of your business plan should not exceed 40 double-spaced, typewritten pages, not including appendices. Each section should be broken down into appropriate and clearly identifiable headings and subheadings. Make sure your plan contains no errors in spelling, punctuation, or grammar.

Prepare a number of copies of your plan and number each one individually. Make sure each copy is appropriately bound with a good-quality cover on which the name of your business has been printed or embossed.

FYI FOR YOUR INFORMATION

SAMPLE BUSINESS PLANS

Before starting on your business plan, it may be a good idea to see what a typical plan actually looks like. There are a couple of examples included with this book, but here are some Web sites that have some sample plans as well.

CCH Business Owner's Toolkit This site provides the component elements of sample business plans for three fictitious companies to illustrate the type of information that is essential to the creation of a high-quality business plan. (www.toolkit.com/tools/bt.aspx?tid=buspln_m)

Palo Alto Software This site contains sample business plans for 500 different businesses, including a flower importer, software publisher, tennis pro shop, buffet restaurant, Internet cafe, medical equipment company, and many others. (www.paloalto.com/sample_business_plans/categories.cfm)

Business Plan Archive An educational Web site created by the University of Maryland to archive business plans and other information about companies; covers a broad range of industries, principally from the dot-com era. You must register first and can then access the plans in the archive. (www.businessplanarchive.org)

Moot Corp Competition — The Super Bowl of Business Plan Competitions A library of different business plans, each of which was a finalist in the Moot Corp competition for MBA students from all over the world. (www.businessplans.org/businessplans.html)

SmallBusinessPoint.com, Inc. A sample of business plans from existing successful profitable companies and start-ups. The business plans are available for a nominal fee. (www.smallbusinesspoint.com/sampleplans.aspx)

| FIGURE 11.2 | DEVELOPING THE "BIG PICTURE" |

1. DEVELOP YOUR VISION STATEMENT

   a. Write short phrases to describe each of the three elements in your vision statement:

   – the name of your planned venture

   – your product/service offering

   – the target market(s) you plan to serve

   b. Combine these phrases into a single sentence

   _____

   _____

   _____

   _____

   _____

2. FORMULATE YOUR MISSION STATEMENT

   a. Write short phrases to describe each of the following elements of your business:

   – what your business will do

   – its market focus, niche, or particular image

   – its planned location and geographic market served

   – how growth of the business will be achieved

   – your sustainable uniqueness or distinguishing characteristics

   b. Combine these phrases into short, linked sentences.

   _____

   _____

   _____

   _____

   _____

   _____

3. DEFINE THE FUNDAMENTAL VALUES BY WHICH YOUR BUSINESS WILL BE RUN

   Step 1 Personal Values

   Have each principal involved in the business complete the following framework for five values that they hold to be personally important.

   a. _Value:_ Express as a single word _____

   What: A brief explanation of what the word means to you. _____

   _____

   _____

   Why? Outline why it is important to you that the business operate this way. _____

   _____

   _____

   b. _Value:_ Express as a single word _____

   What: A brief explanation of what the word means to you. _____

   _____

   _____

Why? Outline why it is important to you that the business operate this way. _____

_____

_____

c. *Value:* Express as a single word _____

What: A brief explanation of what the word means to you. _____

_____

_____

Why? Outline why it is important to you that the business operate this way. _____

_____

_____

d. *Value:* Express as a single word _____

What: A brief explanation of what the word means to you. _____

_____

_____

Why? Outline why it is important to you that the business operate this way. _____

_____

_____

e. *Value:* Express as a single word _____

What: A brief explanation of what the word means to you. _____

_____

_____

Why? Outline why it is important to you that the business operate this way. _____

_____

_____

Step 2 Values by Which the Business Will Be Managed

Complete Step 2 from the information provided by each of the principals in Step 1. Include only values that were *common to all principals*. Others should be included only after discussion, negotiation, and consensus among all individuals. Since some values will differ, it is necessary for all parties to agree which will be the common values used to guide the operations of the business. This list should contain five or six values at a maximum and it is important that they be compatible with each other. Each principal will then have to decide whether he or she will be able to work in a business where, perhaps, only some or none of his or her personal values will be given expression.

a. *Value:* _____

_____

What: _____

_____

_____

_____

_____

Why? _____

_____

_____

_____

continued

Developing the "Big Picture" — continued

    b. *Value:* _____

       What: _____

       Why? _____

    c. *Value:* _____

       What: _____

       Why? _____

    d. *Value:* _____

       What: _____

       Why? _____

    e. *Value:* _____

       What: _____

       Why? _____

4. DEFINE YOUR OBJECTIVES

The business's vision will be achieved when the following objectives have been attained:

a. Objective _____

b. Objective _____

c. Objective _____

d. Objective _____

e. Objective _____

FIGURE 11.3   **CHECKLIST FOR ASSESSING YOUR BUSINESS PLAN**

After completing your business plan you should thoroughly review it. This checklist will help you to do so. Decide whether or not you think the answers you have provided are clear and complete. Evaluate the information from the standpoint of a prospective investor or lending agency and ask yourself whether you are satisfied with your responses.

	Answer Is Included (X)	Answer Is Clear (Yes/No)	Answer Is Complete (Yes/No)
1. YOUR COMPANY AND THE INDUSTRY			
a. Type of business you are planning	_____	_____	_____
b. Products or services you will sell	_____	_____	_____
c. History of the company	_____	_____	_____
d. Why does the business promise to be successful?	_____	_____	_____
e. Your future goals and objectives	_____	_____	_____
f. Description of the industry	_____	_____	_____
g. Major participants and significant trends	_____	_____	_____

General Comments

_____

_____

_____

_____

_____

_____

	Answer Is Included (X)	Answer Is Clear (Yes/No)	Answer Is Complete (Yes/No)
2. PRODUCT/SERVICE OFFERING			
a. Description of your product/service	_____	_____	_____
b. Present stage of development	_____	_____	_____
c. Patent/trademark position	_____	_____	_____
d. Other formal requirements	_____	_____	_____
e. Growth opportunities and key factors for success	_____	_____	_____

General Comments

_____

_____

_____

_____

_____

continued

Checklist for Assessing Your Business Plan — continued

	Answer Is Included (X)	Answer Is Clear (Yes/No)	Answer Is Complete (Yes/No)
3. MARKETING ANALYSIS AND PLAN			
a. Who are your target customers?			
b. What are their characteristics?			
c. How do they buy?			
d. How large is the market and its various segments?			
e. Factors affecting the market			
f. Who are your competitors? How are they doing?			
g. How much of the market will you be able to attract?			
h. What will be your principal marketing strategy?			
i. Have you detailed all aspects of your marketing plan?			
(i) Pricing			
(ii) Sales and distribution			
(iii) Advertising and promotion			

General Comments

_____

_____

_____

_____

_____

	Answer Is Included (X)	Answer Is Clear (Yes/No)	Answer Is Complete (Yes/No)
4. PRODUCTION/OPERATIONS PLAN			
a. Where will your business be located?			
b. What are the characteristics of your location?			
c. Description of machinery and equipment you will require			
d. What are your costs to produce your product?			
e. What are your inventory requirements?			
f. Who will be your principal suppliers or subcontractors?			
g. Description of your quality control procedures			
h. How many employees will you require?			
(i) What type?			
(ii) How will they be paid?			
i. Will you require any licences, permits, or other authorizations?			

General Comments

_____

_____

_____

_____

5. MANAGEMENT TEAM

   a. Who will manage your business? _____ _____ _____

   b. What are their qualifications? _____ _____ _____

   c. What is the size and composition of your
      board of directors? _____ _____ _____

   d. What are your managers and directors
      being paid? _____ _____ _____

   e. What is the ownership structure of the business? _____ _____ _____

   f. Who are your advisors and consultants? _____ _____ _____

General Comments

_____

_____

_____

_____

_____

6. FINANCIAL PLAN

   a. How much money will you need to start the
      business and sustain it for the first few months? _____ _____ _____

   b. How much money do you have now? _____ _____ _____

   c. How much more do you need? _____ _____ _____

   d. How will this additional money be used? _____ _____ _____

   e. What kind of collateral or security will
      be provided? _____ _____ _____

   f. How will this money be repaid? _____ _____ _____

   g. Provided financial statements:

      For the current year _____ _____ _____

      For the past two years _____ _____ _____

   h. Total estimated net income:

      Monthly for the first year _____ _____ _____

      Quarterly or annually for the next two to
         four years _____ _____ _____

   i. Estimated cash flow situation:

      Monthly for the first year _____ _____ _____

      Annually for the next two years _____ _____ _____

   j. What is your estimated financial position at
      the end of each of the next three to five years? _____ _____ _____

   k. What sales volume will you need to break even? _____ _____ _____

General Comments

_____

_____

_____

_____

_____

continued

Checklist for Assessing Your Business Plan — continued

7. APPENDICES

Do you need to include the following appendices?	*Yes*	*No*
a. Product photographs and specifications		
b. Résumés of your management team		
c. List of prospective customers		
d. List of possible suppliers		
e. Job descriptions for management team		
f. Consulting reports		
g. Market surveys		
h. Legal agreements and contracts		
i. Publicity articles and promotional pieces		
j. Other supporting material		

CleanAir Technologies Inc.

Breathe Healthy.
Breathe Easy.

"The Future of Mould Prevention <u>Today</u>"

Company Name:	CleanAir Technologies Inc.
Product:	WaVeS© — Wall Ventilation System
Description:	A drying system consisting of wall panels and an active dehumidification system designed to remove moisture from the surface of walls, rather than letting it evaporate into the living space air. It provides a long-term solution to mould prevention and improves the air quality in your home, thus eliminating any health risks associated with or caused by mould.
Capital Required:	$750,000
Prepared By:	Justin Umlah

TABLE OF CONTENTS

Executive Summary   2

1. Fact Sheet   3

2. Opportunity   4

3. Company information   4
   3.1 Mission statement   4
   3.2 Relationship with inventor   4
   3.3 Offices   5
   3.4 Management team   5
   3.5 Board of directors   6

4. Mould   6
   4.1 What is mould?   6
   4.2 Health risks   6

5. Current basement finishing options   7

6. Product information — WaVeS   8
   6.1 Overview   8
   6.2 How it works   8
   6.3 Advantages   9
   6.4 Components, manufacturing, and maintenance   9
   6.5 Intellectual property   9
   6.6 Future products   9
   6.7 Product pricing   9

7. Market Analysis   10
   7.1 Market potential   10
   7.2 Target market   10
   7.3 Selling strategy   10
   7.4 Marketing strategies   10

8. Operational phases   11

9. Financial Summary   12
   9.1 Financial statements summary   12
   9.2 Financing activities   12
   9.3 Harvest strategies   12
   9.4 Offering   12

FINANCIAL EXHIBITS:

Exhibit 1   Operational timeline and milestones

Exhibit 2   Projected unit sales

Exhibit 3   Pro forma monthly cash flow statement, 2009

Exhibit 4   Pro forma monthly cash flow statement, 2010

Exhibit 5   Pro forma annual cash flow statements, 2009–14

Exhibit 6   Pro forma annual income statements, 2009–14

Exhibit 7   Pro forma annual balance sheet, 2009–14

APPENDICES:

Appendix 1   Financial notes and assumptions

Appendix 2   Reference list

EXECUTIVE SUMMARY

Mould has put increasing strains on the real estate industry, the insurance industry, the court system, the medical system and construction practices. Many health and structural problems have been associated with mould and moisture problems in buildings. CleanAir Technologies has been formed to commercialize the WaVeS™ system, which consists of specially grooved wall panels and an active dehumidification system that is designed to remove moisture from interior basement walls and prevent mould at the source. Current moisture and mould prevention techniques have proven ineffective — labelled "band-aid" solutions — and there are no technologies available that provide a long-term solution to both mould and moisture build-up in homes. The WaVeS™ system takes a proactive approach to moisture and mould prevention, improves indoor air quality, and acts as insulation. Testing has shown the WaVeS™ system's effectiveness, removing 1.9 litres of moisture every three days over a two-month period.

Studies show that 40–50 per cent of homes in North America have moisture and mould problems that are serious enough to significantly increase respiratory symptoms among occupants. Mould has been cited as the cause of many problems, ranging from skin irritation to cancer, and extreme cases, including neurological and immunological damage. Mould is also an asthma trigger and has been found to increase children's asthma risk about 2.5 times. Approximately 35 million Americans suffer from allergic reactions to moulds, yet most of them do not realize that mould is the cause of their symptoms. The proliferation of mould-related claims has cost the insurance industry billions of dollars in payouts, and, at the industry's urging, has led numerous states to allow insurers to exclude mould coverage from homeowner policies. The market for mould and moisture prevention techniques in residential homes — CleanAir's target market — has reached $4.5 billion dollars, growing at an annual rate of 10 per cent; this represents approximately 500,000 homes. An improved technology that attacks mould and moisture before it becomes an issue has the potential to save the United States economy hundreds of millions of dollars annually.

CleanAir's intellectual property portfolio is strong. CleanAir currently employs the inventor of the WaVeS™ system, and has exclusive licensing rights to the technology and any future products based on the WaVeS™ system technology, including a floor technology that will be developed upon the successful launch of the WaVeS™ system.

A management team and board of directors experienced in start-up businesses, medicine, sales, housing development, logistics, and related industries leads CleanAir. With over 100 years of experience, CleanAir's team will ensure the successful market launch of the WaVeS™ system. CleanAir is positioned to introduce a product that adds value to its customers through long-term cost savings, a permanent and proactive solution to moisture reduction, and mitigating health risks attributed to mould. Sales of the WaVeS™ system will begin in the Midwestern United States and Canada by January 2010 upon completion and successful results of final testing. CleanAir plans to expand across the U.S. in subsequent stages, and third-party distributors will be used for the marketing and sales of the WaVeS™ system internationally.

CleanAir's WaVeS™ system and growth potential presents a rewarding investment opportunity. With technology development, prototype development, and initial stage testing already complete, equity financing will provide a means of financing business operations and beginning sales activities. Sales are projected at $8.5 million, $13.1 million, and $20.7 million in 2012, 2013, and 2014, respectively. The demand for CleanAir's system, combined with the strength of its intellectual property, makes CleanAir a very desirable acquisition, enhancing the exit strategy for investors.

1. FACT SHEET

Company name:	**CleanAir Technologies Inc.**

Office locations:

United States:
10560 Wayzata Boulevard
Minneapolis, Minnesota
55305
Phone: 952.555.9960
Fax: 952.555.9819

Canada:
900-330 St. Mary Avenue
Winnipeg, Manitoba
R3B 1Y6
Phone: 204.555.4724
Fax: 204.555.4640

Web site: www.CleanAir.com

General email: info@CleanAir.com

Product name: WaVeS™

Cost to manufacture: $3,750–$4,200

Average selling price: $8,250–$9,000

Funding requirements: $250,000 in Q1 of 2009
$500,000 in September 2009

Financial summary:

	Sales	Net Profit AT	Net Profit Margin AT
2010:	$ 2,610,000	$ (155,432)	
2011:	$ 4,482,000	$ 361,335	8.06%
2012:	$ 8,474,500	$ 1,326,600	15.65%
2013:	$ 13,137,600	$ 2,400,654	18.27%
2014:	$ 20,667,000	$ 4,434,546	22.46%

Management team:

CEO	Charles Smith
COO and VP Technology	Justin Umlah
CFO	Miriam Wilson
VP Sales & Marketing	Jacob Jackson
Director of Sales & Marketing	Andrew Longstreet

2. OPPORTUNITY

Over the past several years, mould has put increasing strains on the real estate industry, the insurance industry, the court system, and construction practices.

In the United States, approximately 1.5 million new homes are built each year. Newer homes and buildings are not immune to moisture; in fact, they are often more susceptible to mould. Many experts believe that the energy-efficient building techniques (e.g., vapour barriers, exterior sheathing) that have become standard in recent decades have resulted in airtight, less ventilated homes that trap moisture inside, leading to mould growth.

In addition to newer homes, research indicates that a significant portion of older homes suffer from basements that are unacceptable as living spaces due to dampness and poor air quality. Studies by Health and Welfare Canada and Harvard University have shown that between 40 and 50 per cent of homes — or 50 to 60 million homes — in North America have moisture and mould problems that are serious enough to significantly increase respiratory symptoms among occupants. People spend roughly 90 per cent of their time indoors, which leaves them more susceptible to poor indoor air quality issues related to excessive moisture or mould. What is most disturbing about mould is that it is almost impossible to know how much damage it has caused to one's health until it is too late. Approximately 35 million Americans suffer from allergic reactions to moulds, yet most of them do not realize it is mould that causes their reactions.

Mould and fungal growth can cause damage to possessions, walls, floors, and ceilings in a home or building. In extreme cases, it can compromise the structural integrity of the building as it eats away at wood and drywall, causing it to disintegrate. Remediation costs to correct mould problems are substantial and growing. On average, it costs between $15,000 and $30,000 for remediation on a 2400 sq. ft. home, reaching upwards to hundreds of thousands of dollars.

The explosion of mould-related claims has hit the insurance industry hard. According to U.S. insurance industry statistics, the insurance industry paid out $3 billion in mould-related claims in 2005, up from $1.3 billion in 2005. Roughly 10,000 mould-related lawsuits have been filed nationwide in the last three years, and over 24,000 insurance claims are still unresolved. Several claimants have received multi-million-dollar awards. At the industry's urging, 35 U.S. states have allowed insurers to exclude mould coverage from homeowner policies. In some states, insurers have introduced caps on the coverage for this type of claim, usually between $5,000 and $10,000 — all of which comes at the expense of homeowners and building owners. According to CNN Money, "insurers have spelled out more clearly that policies do not cover mould," in response to the growth of mould litigation.

The installation of the WaVeS™ system in residential homes in CleanAir's target market constitutes a $4.5 billion dollar industry, growing at an annual rate of 10 per cent; this represents approximately 500,000 homes. This is roughly the equivalent of what is being spent on current mould and moisture prevention techniques, and thus presents a large opportunity for CleanAir.

The need for improved technology in this field is reinforced by the fact that companies have tried to address this market in the past but have been unsuccessful due to problems inherent in their technologies or the method they used to address the problem (passive as opposed to active). CleanAir's WaVeS™ system, which serves as a permanent mould prevention solution, has the potential to finally satisfy this long-standing unfilled market demand.

3. COMPANY INFORMATION

3.1 MISSION STATEMENT

CleanAir will strive to improve the quality of peoples' lives and their surrounding environments and revolutionize the housing and construction industry through the continuous development of cutting-edge technologies, while creating maximum value for homeowners, contractors, homebuilders, and shareholders.

3.2 RELATIONSHIP WITH INVENTOR

The WaVeS™ system technology was developed by John Davis in 2004. CleanAir has finalized negotiations with Mr. Davis, and CleanAir now holds the patent to the technology. As compensation for the transfer of the patent, Mr. Davis received $250,000 in upfront cash, a 20 per cent equity stake, and a 2 per cent royalty on gross sales (capped at $2 million). CleanAir will employ Mr. Davis on the Research and Development side of the business, and he will continue to work to extend CleanAir's product line.

3.3 OFFICES

In addition to the office located in Winnipeg, CleanAir's main office will be located in Minneapolis, Minnesota. Minneapolis is recognized around the world as a leader in the technological arena, and is home to a strong network of companies. Location in Minneapolis provides CleanAir with recognition as well as quick access to specialized resources and support industries. This cross-border relationship also allows CleanAir's corporate structure to be set up in such a way that all available tax credits and government programs are fully utilized.

3.4 MANAGEMENT TEAM

Parts of the management team are light on credentials and experience but offer the very strong drive and entrepreneurial spirit needed for the company to succeed. This is augmented by the invaluable experience of CleanAir's CEO, board of directors and VP of Sales & Marketing.

Charles Smith, CEO: Mr. Smith has 30 years' experience in the real estate industry, including time as president of a major real estate company. He graduated from the University of Manitoba with a Bachelor of Commerce in 1969 and received the Chartered Financial Analyst designation in 1974. Mr. Smith has extensive knowledge and experience in the financial field, as Manager of the Real Estate Finance Department for Brown Securities of Canada, and has experience in mergers and acquisitions, mortgage bond underwriting, and sale of real estate equities. He has served as director or trustee for numerous companies, boards, and trusts. Mr. Smith's contacts within the property development industry will be vital in sales of the WaVeS™ system to home developers. Mr. Smith has already secured a contract with a Minneapolis developer who has agreed to install the WaVeS™ system in 350 homes per year for the next seven years.

Justin Umlah, VP Technology and COO: Mr. Umlah has held various relevant positions in recent years, including Lab Technologist and Marketing Assistant at Novra Technologies in Winnipeg, and Executive Assistant for the corporate finance department at Wellington West Capital. Mr. Umlah has experience starting up his own business, Trinity Medical Devices, Inc. — an early-stage medical device company formed to commercialize TriView™, a non-invasive technology designed to assess burn depth using near infrared spectroscopy. Through his roles and experience, Mr. Umlah has developed a large network of contacts. Mr. Umlah's engineering and business background from the University of Manitoba will provide technical vision for CleanAir as well as increased technical understanding.

Miriam Wilson, CFO: Ms. Wilson comes from a family-owned Winnipeg-based manufacturing business, and has relevant experience in the manufacturing industry. She has five years' experience working with day-to-day accounting, and three years' experience working in the financial services industry with a chartered bank. Ms. Wilson has valuable corporate fundraising experience gained through her work with various charitable and not-for-profit organizations. Her business background from the University of Manitoba combined with her finance experience will enable CleanAir to achieve financially conservative controlled growth.

Jacob Jackson, VP Sales & Marketing: Mr. Jackson has over 30 years' of sales and marketing experience in the medical industry, as well as general sales experience. He has worked as Director of International Sales and Director of North American Sales for several companies in recent years, and has been instrumental in the negotiation of strategic partnerships among suppliers. His knowledge and experience in European and Asian markets will aid CleanAir's overseas sales efforts in the future.

Andrew Longstreet, Director of Sales and Marketing: Mr. Longstreet has four years' experience as the Marketing Director of a start-up Internet pharmacy, and has extensive experience with direct mail and Internet marketing. He has also served on numerous committees as marketing director for organizations such as the Polish Combatants Association in Winnipeg. In 2007, Mr. Longstreet was named Vice President of Beta Gamma Sigma, Manitoba Chapter. His background in finance and international business will further aid in correctly allocating funds to promotional budgets and stepping up marketing efforts internationally.

3.5 BOARD OF DIRECTORS

The Board of Directors will include Mr. Smith, Mr. Umlah, Ms. Wilson, and Mr. Longstreet, in addition to the following:

Ken Thompson: Mr. Thompson has many years of experience in start-up businesses, having opened his first business at the age of 22. In 2004, Mr. Taylor created a business that reported a net income of over $4.2 million after its first year. Mr. Thompson is currently Vice President of A–1 Custom Services, and is credited with making it one of the most profitable customs brokerage operations in Canada. Mr. Thompson has attended many graduate programs in business and logistics throughout the U.S., and has earned his Professional Logisticians Certification (P. Log) from the Logistics Institute Toronto. He is a member of the Council of Supply Chain Management Professionals (CSCMP) and has been a track chair at CSCMP conferences throughout the U.S.

Steve Black: Mr. Black graduated from the University of British Columbia with a Bachelor of Law in 1995. Mr. Black is currently the Vice President of a major investment company and the President and CEO of the Conviron Group of Companies. He is also currently a board member for Precision Metalworks Inc., Canadian Manufacturers and Exporters, and a member of the advisory committee for First Class Wireless Solutions. In 1998 he was the recipient of the Manitoba Business Magazine "Best in Business" award, and in 2004 was a finalist for the E&Y Entrepreneur of the Year.

Dr. Bill Graham: Dr. Graham is a Director of the Institute for Biodiagnostics and a member of the National Research Council of Canada. Dr. Graham has many publications to his credit and is well respected in the community. He has many connections in the industry, and will be instrumental in CleanAir's research and development.

Dr. Ian Martens, M.D.: Dr. Martens is a Professor at the University of Manitoba, Department of Pediatrics and Child Health. In addition to his knowledge and experience in the field, Dr. Martens will assist in sourcing endorsements from appropriate health organizations. Dr. Martens is very highly regarded in the Canadian medical community, and currently serves with the Canadian Network for Asthma Care and the National Asthma Educator Certification Management Committee.

4. MOULD

4.1 WHAT IS MOULD?

Mould grows on substances such as wood, fabric, fibreboard, drywall, and fibrous insulation materials. Certain environmental factors (temperature, nitrogen, oxygen, etc.) are needed for indoor moulds to thrive. In order to grow, mould requires moisture and an organic source of food. Water damage that is not addressed within 24 to 72 hours may result in the growth and spreading of mould, as these conditions are conducive to mould growth.

Mould produces mycotoxins, which have metabolites, or by-products, that are toxic to humans. Also classified as neurotoxins (toxins that cause neurological damage), they most commonly reach people from the air via spores; they can spread very easily through any HVAC system. Spores, when inhaled, can begin to colonize in the sinuses and throughout the body, including the brain, lungs, and gut, after a period of time.

4.2 HEALTH RISKS

Mycotoxicosis (poisoning caused by ingestion of a mycotoxin), has reached epidemic proportions. Mould has been cited as the cause of many problems, ranging from skin irritation to cancer. The most commonly reported symptoms include: running nose, nasal congestion, nosebleeds, eye irritation, cough, congestion, fatigue, headaches, skin irritation, respiratory infections, difficulty concentrating, and others. These effects are greater for infants and children, the elderly, pregnant women, and individuals with existing medical conditions, allergies, or a compromised immune system. These symptoms are the basis for the concepts of Sick Building Syndrome (SBS) and Building-Related Illness (BRI). In 1999, the Mayo Clinic found that mould was the cause of 96 per cent of chronic sinusitis (sinus infections).

Mould is also an asthma trigger. In a recent study, household mould was found to increase children's asthma risk 2.5 times. In the United States, more than 20 million people suffer from asthma. According to the American Academy of Allergy, Asthma and Immunology, 35 million Americans suffer from reactions to mould — 12 per cent of the nation's population.

The following health problems have all been associated with mould:

- allergies
- arthritic-like aches
- asthma
- bloody noses
- chronic headaches
- coughing
- "crawly" feeling skin
- depression
- dizziness or stuffiness

- epileptic-like seizures
- equilibrium or balance loss
- fatigue
- irritation of the eyes, nose, or throat
- loss of memory
- loss of hearing
- loss of eyesight
- nausea
- upper respiratory distress

- restlessness
- runny nose
- sinus congestion
- skin rashes
- sneezing
- trouble breathing
- unexplained irritability
- flu-like symptoms

Examples of mould in homes

5. CURRENT BASEMENT FINISHING OPTIONS

Traditional methods for keeping moisture out of basements include using landscaping techniques through proper slopes, well-positioned downspouts, weeping tiles with a slope to a sump pump, and finishing interior basements using vapour barriers. Although these methods mitigate the risk of moisture, they have all proven to be ineffective in preventing mould growth within a home. A typical basement finishing option for most homes includes the installation of studs, a vapour barrier, and fibreglass insulation. Drywall is then installed to finish the walls. The WaVeS™ system is an alternative to installing studs and fibreglass insulation, and actively removes moisture from the basement walls. The current method and the WaVeS™ system have the same appearance to the homeowner once construction is finished.

6. PRODUCT INFORMATION — WAVES™

6.1 OVERVIEW

The WaVeS™ system has the ability to effectively and reliably remove moisture from within basement walls. The WaVeS™ system is the current leader in mould prevention for the following reasons:

1. Takes a proactive approach to mould prevention by removing moisture from the inside of walls, eliminating any chance of mould growth.
2. Improves indoor air quality.
3. A substitute for insulation.
4. Not visible — on the inside of walls.
5. Installed during home construction phase or when finishing basement.
6. A permanent solution.

6.2 HOW IT WORKS

The system utilizes air circulation and dehydration concepts that are common to many refrigeration and dehumidification applications. The WaVeS™ system consists of specially grooved wall panels and an active dehumidification system. The panels are firmly attached to the interior basement wall with the grooved side against the surface, yielding air passages between the panel and the surface to be dried. Ducts or headers are installed at opposite ends of the panels and use a vacuum system to draw air from one end to the other to create an even airflow over the entire grooved surface. Upper and lower plenums connect the air channels of the wall unit to the heating and dehumidification unit. Dry air circulates through the grooved panels along the walls/floors, picking up moisture. The moist air returns via the ducts to a dehumidifying unit that removes the moisture. The dry air is re-circulated back through the manifolds and panels, effectively creating a closed-loop system.

Preliminary tests have shown the WaVeS™ system's effectiveness. The system removed, on average, 1.9 litres of condensate every three days over a two-month period. Pictured are the two main components, the dryer and the wall mount panels (grooves showing are mounted towards the wall), as well as the system installed (before drywall). Once installed, the system is fully drywall-ready.

WaVeS© dehumidification unit

WaVeS© wall mount panels

Install for first testing lab

Install for second testing lab

6.3 ADVANTAGES

The WaVeS™ system offers several benefits over current methods of mould prevention. The system removes moisture from the surface of walls, rather than allowing it to evaporate into the living space air. This increases the overall air quality and comfort level in the home. The thickness of the panels replaces the need for insulation and wall studs, and allows builders to attach drywall directly to the extruded polystyrene panels, eliminating the time and expense of constructing and insulating a traditional stud wall around the interior perimeter of the basement. With no airspace between the vapour barrier and the panels, there is no potential for build-up of any moisture, eliminating any chance of mould growth. Additionally, because a low volume of air is being circulated through a closed loop system, energy expenditure is minimal. Taking a proactive approach saves money and eliminates detrimental health risks posed by moisture and mould in the home.

6.4 COMPONENTS, MANUFACTURING, AND MAINTENANCE

The WaVeS™ dehumidification unit requires several components: a drying unit, a heater, a fan, an electrostatic air filter, and a universal air damper, which are all widely available from a variety of well-known suppliers across Canada and the United States. In addition, CleanAir uses grooved 31/2" extruded polystyrene panels that act as both insulation and the passageways through which the air will travel. The extruded polystyrene panels have been produced by Owens Corning® for a number of years, and the company will produce them to CleanAir's specifications. The dehumidification unit will be manufactured by Owens Corning's OEM division.

The WaVeS™ system has been designed for manufacturability. Complicated engineering has been avoided, allowing easier assembly. Any and all defects in machinery are guaranteed for three years, and Owens Corning® will provide a lifetime warranty for the extruded polystyrene panels. High quality components and inspection upon completion will reduce maintenance costs considerably. Once the technology is installed, it will be the contractors' responsibility to determine the warranty on their work. CleanAir will address all technical problems in the unlikely event a system is not functioning correctly. Problems that cannot be solved over the phone or Internet will fall under the responsibility of a company representative who will service the unit.

6.5 INTELLECTUAL PROPERTY

CleanAir's intellectual property portfolio is **strong**. There are currently two internationally recognized patents issued or pending for the technology utilized in the WaVeS™ system, including U.S. patent protection until January 2023.

6.6 FUTURE PRODUCTS

In addition to the wall ventilation system, CleanAir will be developing a floor-based technology. Many homes are built without basements, yet still suffer from mould problems. This has been evident in areas such as southern California and Texas, which lead the nation in mould claims, and Louisiana and Oregon. The devastating effects of Hurricane Katrina have produced a significant opportunity for the installation of moisture removal systems in new homes built in the New Orleans region. The floor-based technology will use methods similar to the WaVeS™ system, as it will be an active moisture reduction method. The floor system is expected to be fully developed and ready for sales by May 2011. Ongoing research and development will produce a complete line of products to improve indoor air quality.

6.7 PRODUCT PRICING

Market research has shown that consumers are willing to pay a premium price for this product, primarily because the WaVeS™ system presents a long-term, proactive solution. Owens Corning® has agreed to manufacture the WaVeS™ dehumidification unit and the grooved panels for $4,100 for a standard 2400 sq. ft. home, decreasing to $3,600 for volume orders. CleanAir will sell the WaVeS™ system for a price ranging from $7,000 to $9,000, depending on order sizes. Traditional wall installation (fibreglass insulation, studs) costs an average of $5,000.

7. MARKET ANALYSIS

7.1 MARKET POTENTIAL

The demand for a system such as the WaVeS™ system has the potential to become an industry standard installed in every home. The proliferation of mould-related research, literature, and litigation has increased awareness of the health risks and financial implications attributed to mould. Mould problems arise primarily from high soil moisture levels and precipitation levels, but also stem from various other sources, such as hot water tanks, pipe leaks, old closets, seepage (foundation), storms, floods, and sewage backups, thus not limiting the demand for the WaVeS™ system to a specific geographical region. In the United States, there are 100 million existing homes and 1.5 million new homes built each year. Commercial properties, housing units and apartments, and government buildings further add to CleanAir's potential market. The attainable worldwide market vastly increases the market potential for the WaVeS™ system.

7.2 TARGET MARKET

CleanAir's primary market is the United States. Within the United States, CleanAir will first target locations where there will be a high demand for the WaVeS™ system, mainly those regions characterized by high soil moisture conditions and precipitation levels. These regions include the West, Midwest, and Northeast regions of the United States. The primary target market within this region includes newly built homes, with basements, selling for more than $150,000.

Targeting newly built homes would reduce the cost of installing the system, as it will bypass the need for contractors. Also, an added cost of roughly $3,000 to an average home represents an increase in the selling price of approximately one per cent, or $1.20 per sq. ft. The total number of homes built in these regions (with basements) is about 500,000 each year, increasing by 3 per cent per year. This represents a market of $4.3 billion dollars for the WaVeS™ system alone, growing to $5 billion by 2016.

CleanAir's other markets would include homes with unfinished basements, remediation, restoration, and older home renovations. The appeal of the WaVeS™ system for homes with unfinished basements is to assure a comfortable living space in the basement prior to investing in finishing the walls. In this case, the homeowner would be taking a proactive approach to permanently prevent dampness in the basement, even if such a problem has not yet been realized.

Older dwellings have a high probability of suffering from mould or moisture damage due to past construction methods. In 2007, Americans spent $200 billion on residential improvements, $103 billion of which was spent on alterations alone.

Target market share in 2010 is projected at 0.03 per cent. This is expected to grow to 0.06 per cent, 0.13 per cent, 0.22 per cent, and 0.36 per cent in 2011, 2012, 2013, and 2014, respectively. These estimates are considered to be realistic and reasonable, and CleanAir is capable of increasing production to meet a significant increase in demand on short notice.

7.3 SELLING STRATEGY

CleanAir will employ regional sales managers to ensure penetration of the U.S. market. Each regional manager will be responsible for several independent sales representatives, who will contact contractors, homebuilders, and associations via their established networks. Regional managers will earn a base salary with an additional 2 per cent commission on sales. They will be responsible for after-sales service, warranty service, and maintaining and strengthening relationships with contractors. Independent sales representatives will receive a 5 per cent commission.

Once WaVeS™ system sales become established in the U.S., CleanAir will look into licensing its technology to companies internationally to effectively and efficiently increase its global reach.

7.4 MARKETING STRATEGIES

HOUSING INDUSTRY: To successfully achieve market acceptance in the United States, it is extremely important to recognize and understand the changing U.S. housing industry. Increasing demand for better quality, increased safety, and cost savings, combined with heavy competition, are a few of the factors currently shaping the U.S. housing market. Consumers are very conservative, which increases the difficulty of gaining market acceptance and promoting and implementing a brand-new technology. This requires CleanAir to prove that its product adds value and works effectively before installation is considered. CleanAir will focus primarily on a push strategy aimed at contractors and homebuilders (the purchasers) in order to sell the WaVeS™ system, but will also incorporate pull strategies aimed at homeowners (the end consumers). The primary focus will be on the U.S. market, with additional marketing efforts dedicated to the Canadian and International markets.

INITIAL MARKET: Homebuilders and contractors will be approached first, with the goal of obtaining positive feedback and endorsements. CleanAir will utilize trade magazines, educational brochures and DVDs, and personal selling to increase awareness and demand for the WaVeS™ system. Additional techniques will include training seminars and building prototypes, to allow contractors that install the WaVeS™ system to provide additional training. Other means of disseminating information and increasing awareness include gaining acceptance from various organizations and associations, such as the Associated General Contractors of America, which is dedicated to promoting use of the latest technology. Also, CleanAir's CEO and board of directors have experience and contacts in the real estate development industry and related industries. Leveraging these relationships will allow CleanAir to demonstrate its product effectiveness and gain market acceptance.

TRADE SHOWS AND CONFERENCES: To reach homebuilders' and contractors' associations, representatives of CleanAir will attend select conferences and trade shows to demonstrate the WaVeS™ system and build awareness. A comprehensive review of these events has been undertaken. CleanAir has already received support from the Government of Manitoba to defray impending trade show event costs.

HOMEOWNERS: Given the significant impact mould has on health and its financial implications, the public is a very important influential group. Homeowners would be reached via Internet, radio, and television advertisements, in hopes of increasing awareness and creating urgency towards implementing the WaVeS™ system in homes. For example, an "ask your local contractor about the WaVeS™ system" campaign will be used, similar to the strategy used by pharmaceutical companies.

8. OPERATIONAL PHASES

PHASE 1 — PRE-MARKET: CleanAir is currently in its first phase of operations, expected to end by September 2009. CleanAir's management team and board of directors are in place, offices have been set up, and initial funding is being raised. CleanAir is in its final stage of testing of the WaVeS™ system, concluding in August 2009. Supplier relations are in the process of finalization. At the end of this phase, testing will conclude and marketing efforts of the WaVeS™ system will commence.

PHASE 2 — SELLING THE WAVES™ SYSTEM IN WESTERN CANADA AND MIDWESTERN U.S.: Marketing of the WaVeS™ system will begin in September of 2009 upon receipt of successful test results. Sales are expected to commence in January 2010; Western Canada, Minnesota, Illinois, Wisconsin, and North and South Dakota will be the initial markets targeted by CleanAir due to their similar soil moisture conditions. During this time, CleanAir will set up regional sales offices and focus on initial marketing efforts.

PHASE 3 — EXPAND THROUGHOUT THE U.S.: In May 2010, CleanAir will begin to focus marketing efforts on acquiring national homebuilders as customers, and expanding sales further west and to the Northeastern states, effectively covering roughly 50 per cent of the U.S. housing market. Development efforts of the floor-based technology will increase, and testing of this product will commence.

PHASE 4 — DEVELOPMENT OF FLOOR-BASED TECHNOLOGY, CONTINUOUS R&D, AND EXIT: By May 2011 CleanAir expects to release its floor-based technology, and marketing efforts will be substantially increased to support this product. At this point CleanAir will be established and have sufficient revenues and structure to support further sales growth. CleanAir will seek to further increase market share by exploring commercial viability and bringing manufacturing activities in-house, and expanding internationally via licensure and third-party distributors. During this phase, CleanAir will also begin exploring potential harvest strategies.

9. FINANCIAL SUMMARY

9.1 FINANCIAL STATEMENTS SUMMARY

CleanAir will incur a loss of $568,139 and $155,432 in 2009 and 2010, respectively, but will have subsequent earnings as follows:

Financial Summary:	Sales Net	Profit AT	Net Profit Margin AT
2010:	$ 2,610,000	$ (155,432)	
2011:	$ 4,482,000	$ 361,335	8.06%
2012:	$ 8,474,500	$ 1,326,600	15.65%
2013:	$ 13,137,600	$ 2,400,654	18.27%
2014:	$ 20,667,000	$ 4,434,546	22.46%

At the end of 2016, 14,719 WaVeS™ systems will have been installed. Please see the attached financial exhibits and assumptions for further analysis.

9.2 FINANCING ACTIVITIES

John Davis, the creator of the WaVeS™ system technology, has invested $220,400 in seed money for development of the WaVeS™ system technology and subsequent testing. A further $175,000 is available to CleanAir by way of grants offered by the Manitoba Business Development Fund, the Government of Manitoba's Technology Commercialization Program, and various other provincial and federal grants. This money will primarily be used to finance the final testing of the WaVeS™ system. With technology development, prototype development, and the first stage of testing already complete, additional equity investments will provide the means of financing business operations and the commencement of sales activities. CleanAir is currently seeking a $750,000 investment upon completion of milestones.

The first tranche of funding, $250,000, will be required in the second quarter of 2009 to complete the final stage of testing. Upon receipt of successful test results, $500,000 will be needed by September 2009 as a marketing investment to ramp up for sales, which are expected to begin January 2010.

CleanAir Technologies — EQUITY STRUCTURE	
STOCKHOLDER	**PERCENTAGE OF EQUITY OWNED**
John Davis	20%
Charles Smith	5%
Justin Umlah	25%
Miriam Wilson	25%
Andrew Longstreet	25%

9.3 HARVEST STRATEGIES

MERGER OR ACQUISITION: As CleanAir's sales increase, the company could likely become a target for buyout. Upon receipt of an appropriate offer, CleanAir Technologies would be available for takeover. Potential buyers would likely include companies currently in the basement finishing industry, or larger homebuilders. Acquiring CleanAir would give these companies a significant competitive advantage in their fields, making CleanAir an attractive acquisition.

9.4 OFFERING

In return for the total equity required, $750,000, CleanAir expects to relinquish 25 per cent to 40 per cent of ownership to investors. This range is based upon an expected annual rate of return of 52 per cent, or a final return after five years of 10x. CleanAir is open to discussion with interested investors regarding financing terms.

CLEANAIR TECHNOLOGY — EXHIBIT 1

OPERATIONAL TIMELINE & MILESTONES

Tasks	2009												2010				2011				2012		2013	
	1	2	3	4	5	6	7	8	9	10	11	12	Q1	Q2	Q3	Q4	Q1	Q2	Q3	Q4	Q1,2	Q3,4	Q1,2	Q3,4
	PHASE 1												PHASE 2								PHASE 3			
Established CleanAir Technologies, inc.																								
Management and technical team in place																								
U.S. patent filed Jan. 16, 2006																								
Tested prototype at Red River College																								
Protype built (November 2005)																								
Secure and receive $250,000 in equity financing																								
Assembled Board of Directors																								
Solidify supplier relationships																								
Secure $115,000 in government grants																								
Begin paying salaries, full-time effort begins																								
Secure and receive $500,000 in equity financing																								
Hire sales managers and increase advertising																								
Begin sales																								
Expand Further into Northwest USA																								
Expand Further into Northeast USA																								
Ongoing selling																								
Proceed with IPO or seek partner/buyout																								
Continually release new products																								

Legend:
- Completed Tasks
- Unfinished Tasks
- Ongoing Tasks

CLEANAIR TECHNOLOGY — EXHIBIT 2

PROJECTED UNIT SALES
January 1, 2010 to December 31, 2013

TARGET MARKETS & ESTIMATED CAPTURE

	2010	2011	2012	2013	2014	2015	2016
1. New homes in the United States target market	500,000	515,000	530,450	546,364	562,754	579,637	597,026
2. Basement renovations in the target market	500,000	500,000	500,000	500,000	500,000	500,000	500,000
3. CEO's home developments	150	150	250	250	250	200	150
Units sold into target market (1)	125	310	684	1,200	2,000	4,400	6,000
Units sold into target market (2)	15	38	63	114	240	528	720
Units sold into target market (3)	150	150	250	250	250	200	150
Total units sold	290	498	997	1,564	2,490	5,128	6,870
1. Per cent of target marget captured	0.03%	0.06%	0.13%	0.22%	0.36%	0.76%	1.00%

COMPONENT PRICE BREAKDOWN (per Average Home)

WaVeS	2010	2011	2012	2013	2014	2015	2016
Average retail price	$ 9,000	$ 9,000	$ 8,500	$ 8,400	$ 8,300	$ 8,300	$ 8,250
Total product cost	$ 4,200	$ 4,200	$ 3,900	$ 3,750	$ 3,750	$ 3,750	$ 3,750

PROJECTED UNIT SALES

2010	January	February	March	April	May	June	July	August	September	October	November	December	Total
New home	6	7	5	10	10	15	20	25	15	10	10	5	125
Basement renovation	4	8	2		3		1	2		2	3	2	15
CEO projects	15		15	15	15	15	15	15	15	15	15	15	150

2011	January	February	March	April	May	June	July	August	September	October	November	December	Total
New home	6	7	13	22	22	42	51	66	41	29	6	5	310
Basement renovation	4	8	1	2	2		2	3		8	3	5	38
CEO projects	15		15	15	15	15	15	15	15	15	15	15	150

2012	Quarter 1	Quarter 2	Quarter 3	Quarter 4	Total
New home	75	244	244	121	684
Basement renovation	22	7	12	22	63
CEO projects	15	45	45	45	150

2013	Quarter 1	Quarter 2	Quarter 3	Quarter 4	Total
New home	130	432	433	205	1,200
Basement renovation	40	12	22	40	114
CEO projects	15	45	45	45	150

Total installations at the end of 2016:

New homes	14,719
Basement renovations	1,718
CEO's developments	1,400

Notes:
Component cost reduces in 2012 and in 2013 due to increase in volume.

CLEANAIR TECHNOLOGY — EXHIBIT 3

PRO FORMA MONTHLY CASH FLOW STATEMENTS FOR START-UP PHASE
January 1, 2009 to December 31, 2009

	January	February	March	April	May	
CASH INFLOWS						
Investment Income	188	176	153	100	979	
TOTAL CASH INFLOWS	$ 188	$ 176	$ 153	$ 100	$ 979	
CASH OUTFLOWS						
Sales, Marketing & Training						
VP Sales & Marketing —	-	-	-	-	-	
Director Sales & Marketing — Andrew Longstreet						
Regional Sales Managers	-	-	-	-	-	
Office Assistants — Sales	-	-	-	-	-	
Total Payroll	-	-	-	-	-	
Payroll Taxes & Benefits	-	-	-	-	-	
Travel & Travel Expenses — Sales	-	-	-	-	1,800	
Advertising & Literature	-	-	-	-	2,500	
Trade Shows & Seminars	-	-	-	-	-	
Total Sales, Marketing & Training Expense	$ -	$ -	$ -	$ -	$ 4,300	
# of Sales & Marketing Employees	1	1	1	1	1	
Administration						
CEO —	-	-	-	-	-	
CFO — Miriam Wilson	-	-	-	-	-	
Office Assistants — Admin/Accounting	-	-	-	-	-	
Total Payroll	-	-	-	-	-	
Payroll Taxes & Benefits	-	-	-	-	-	
Travel & Travel Expenses — Admin	1,000	1,000	2,000	4,000	4,000	
Accounting/Legal Fees	-	-	4,500	4,500	3,500	
Rent, Utilities, Building Insurance	1,000	1,000	1,000	1,000	1,000	
Postage, Supplies, Phone, Internet	1,000	1,000	1,000	1,000	1,000	
Insurance	-	-	1,500	1,500	1,500	
Membership & Subscriptions	-	-	-	-	-	
Total Administration Expense	$ 3,000	$ 3,000	$ 10,000	$ 12,000	$ 11,000	
# of Administration Employees	2	2	2	2	2	
Research & Development						
COO & VP Technology — Justin Umlah	-	-	-	-	-	
Technicians	-	-	-	-	-	
Total Payroll	-	-	-	-	-	
Payroll Taxes & Benefits	-	-	-	-	-	
Product Development (contract expense)	-	-	-	-	-	
Equipment	-	-	-	-	1,000	
Travel & Travel Expenses — R&D	-	-	-	1,500	1,500	
Agency Fees — Patents, FDA, FCC, UL	-	-	-	-	-	
Total Research & Development	$ -	$ -	$ -	$ 1,500	$ 2,500	
# of R&D Employees	1	1	1	1	1	
Other						
Miscellaneous Expenses	250	250	250	250	250	
Directors and Advisors Expense	-	-	-	-	-	
Consultants	-	3,000	4,000	2,000	2,000	
Interest Payments	-	-	-	-	-	
Income Taxes	-	-	-	-	-	
Total Other	$ 250	$ 3,250	$ 4,250	$ 2,250	$ 2,250	
TOTAL CASH OUTFLOWS	$ 3,250	$ 6,250	$ 14,250	$ 15,750	$ 20,050	
FINANCING						
Government Grants	-	-	-	-	-	
Bank Line of Credit	-	-	-	-	-	
Issuance of Common Shares	-	-	-	250,000	-	
Issuance of Preferred Shares	-	-	-	-	-	
CHANGE FROM FINANCING	$ -	$ -	$ -	$ 250,000	$ -	
CASH AT BEGINNING OF PERIOD	$ 50,000	$ 46,938	$ 40,864	$ 26,767	$ 261,117	
CASH AT END OF PERIOD	$ 46,938	$ 40,864	$ 26,767	$ 261,117	$ 242,046	

	June	July	August	September	October	November	December
	908	1,039	686	421	1,971	1,628	1,283
	$ 908	$ 1,039	$ 686	$ 421	$ 1,971	$ 1,628	$ 1,283
	4,000	4,000	4,000	4,000	4,000	4,000	4,000
		3,000	3,000	3,000	3,000	3,000	3,000
	-	-	-	3,000	3,000	3,000	3,000
	3,000	3,000	3,000	3,000	3,000	3,000	3,000
	7,000	7,000	10,000	13,000	13,000	13,000	13,000
	1,120	1,120	1,600	2,080	2,080	2,080	2,080
	1,800	1,800	1,800	3,600	3,600	3,600	3,600
	2,500	2,500	2,500	28,000	28,000	28,000	15,000
	-	10,000	-	-	10,000	10,000	-
	$ 12,420	$ 22,420	$ 15,900	$ 46,680	$ 56,680	$ 56,680	$ 33,680
	2	2	2	3	3	3	3
	5,000	5,000	5,000	5,000	5,000	5,000	5,000
		4,000	4,000	4,000	4,000	4,000	4,000
	3,000	3,000	3,000	3,000	3,000	3,000	3,000
	8,000	8,000	12,000	12,000	12,000	12,000	12,000
	1,280	1,280	1,920	1,920	1,920	1,920	1,920
	4,000	4,000	4,000	4,000	4,000	4,000	4,000
	3,500	3,500	3,500	3,500	-	-	-
	1,500	1,500	1,500	1,500	1,500	1,500	1,500
	1,250	1,250	1,250	1,250	1,250	1,250	1,250
	1,500	1,500	1,500	1,500	1,500	1,500	1,500
	5,000	-					
	$ 26,030	$ 21,030	$ 25,670	$ 25,670	$ 22,170	$ 22,170	$ 22,170
	3	3	3	3	3	3	3
	5,000	5,000	5,000	5,000	5,000	5,000	5,000
	-	2,500	2,500	2,500	2,500	2,500	2,500
	5,000	7,500	7,500	7,500	7,500	7,500	7,500
	800	1,200	1,200	1,200	1,200	1,200	1,200
	15,000	15,000	-	-	-	-	-
	5,000	1,000	1,000	1,000	1,000	1,000	1,000
	1,500	1,500	1,500	1,500	1,500	1,500	1,500
	-	-	15,000	-	-	-	-
	$ 27,300	$ 26,200	$ 26,200	$ 11,200	$ 11,200	$ 11,200	$ 11,200
	1	2	2	2	2	2	2
	250	500	500	500	500	500	500
	-	-	-	-	-	-	-
	15,000	25,000	3,000	3,000	3,000	3,000	3,000
	-	-	-	-	-	-	-
	-	-	-	-	-	-	-
	$ 15,250	$ 25,500	$ 3,500	$ 3,500	$ 3,500	$ 3,500	$ 3,500
	$ 81,000	$ 91,150	$ 71,270	$ 87,050	$ 93,550	$ 93,550	$ 70,550
	115,000	-	-	-	-	-	-
	-	-	-	-	-	-	-
	-	-	-	500,000	-	-	-
	-	-	-	-	-	-	-
	$ 115,000	$ -	$ -	$ 500,000	$ -	$ -	$ -
	$ 242,046	$ 276,954	$ 182,843	$ 112,258	$ 525,629	$ 434,050	$ 342,128
	$ 276,954	$ 182,843	$ 112,258	$ 525,629	$ 434,050	$ 342,128	$ 272,861

CLEANAIR TECHNOLOGY — EXHIBIT 4

PRO FORMA MONTHLY CASH FLOW STATEMENTS FOR 2ND PHASE
January 1, 2010 to December 31, 2010

	January	February	March	April	May	
CASH INFLOWS						
Investment Income	1,023	570	213	100	115	
Revenues from New Homes	-	-	45,000	90,000	90,000	
Revenues from Basement Renovations	-	-	18,000	-	27,000	
Revenues from CEO's Projects	-	-	135,000	135,000	135,000	
TOTAL CASH INFLOWS	$ 1,023	$ 570	$ 198,213	$ 225,100	$ 252,115	
CASH OUTFLOWS						
Product Expense						
Payments to Supplier — Owens Corning	-	-	92,400	105,000	117,600	
Licensing Payments (2%)	-	-	3,960	4,500	5,040	
Sales Commissions (Regional Managers @ 2%)	-	-	3,960	4,500	5,040	
Sales Commissions (Sales Representatives @ 5%)	-	-	9,900	11,250	12,600	
Total Product Expense	$ -	$ -	$ 110,220	$ 125,250	$ 140,280	
Sales, Marketing & Training						
VP Sales & Marketing —	5,000	5,000	5,000	5,000	5,000	
Director Sales & Marketing — Andrew Longstreet	4,000	4,000	4,000	4,000	4,000	
Regional Sales Managers	4,000	4,000	4,000	4,000	4,000	
Office Assistants — Sales	3,500	3,500	3,500	3,500	3,500	
Total Payroll	**16,500**	**16,500**	**16,500**	**16,500**	**16,500**	
Payroll Taxes & Benefits	2,640	2,640	2,640	2,640	2,640	
Travel & Travel Expenses — Sales	3,000	6,000	6,000	6,000	6,000	
Advertising & Literature	10,000	15,000	15,000	15,000	15,000	
Trade Shows & Seminars	25,000	-	12,500	-	-	
Total Sales, Marketing & Training Expense	$ 57,140	$ 40,140	$ 52,640	$ 40,140	$ 40,140	
# of Sales & Marketing Employees	3	4	4	4	4	
Administration						
CEO —	6,250	6,250	6,250	6,250	6,250	
CFO — Miriam Wilson	5,000	5,000	5,000	5,000	5,000	
Office Assistants — Admin/Accounting	7,000	4,500	4,500	4,500	4,500	
Total Payroll	**18,250**	**15,750**	**15,750**	**15,750**	**15,750**	
Payroll Taxes & Benefits	2,920	2,520	2,520	2,520	2,520	
Travel & Travel Expenses — Admin	5,000	5,000	5,000	5,000	5,000	
Accounting/Legal Fees	3,200	3,200	3,200	3,200	3,200	
Rent, Utilities, Building Insurance	1,450	1,450	1,450	1,450	1,450	
Postage, Supplies, Phone, Internet	1,100	1,100	1,100	1,100	1,100	
Insurance	2,700	2,700	2,700	2,700	2,700	
Membership & Subscriptions	5,000	-	-	-	-	
Total Administration Expense	$ 39,620	$ 31,720	$ 31,720	$ 31,720	$ 31,720	
# of Administration Employees	4	4	4	4	4	
Research & Development						
COO & VP Technology — Justin Umlah	6,250	6,250	6,250	6,250	6,250	
Technicians	8,000	8,000	8,000	8,000	8,000	
Total Payroll	**14,250**	**14,250**	**14,250**	**14,250**	**14,250**	
Payroll Taxes & Benefits	2,280	2,280	2,280	2,280	2,280	
Equipment	1,500	1,500	1,500	1,500	1,500	
Travel & Travel Expenses — R&D	3,000	3,000	3,000	3,000	3,000	
Total Research & Development	$ 21,030	$ 21,030	$ 21,030	$ 21,030	$ 21,030	
# of R&D Employees	3	3	3	3	3	
Other						
Miscellaneous Expenses	1,000	1,000	1,000	1,000	1,000	
Directors and Advisors Expense	-	-	10,000	-	-	
Consultants	3,000	1,850	1,850	1,850	1,850	
Interest Payments	-	-	-	-	-	
Income Taxes	-	-	-	-	-	
Total Other	$ 4,000	$ 2,850	$ 12,850	$ 2,850	$ 2,850	
TOTAL CASH OUTFLOWS	$ 121,790	$ 95,740	$ 228,460	$ 220,990	$ 236,020	
FINANCING						
Issuance of Common Shares	-	-	-	-	-	
Issuance of Preferred Shares	-	-	-	-	-	
CHANGE FROM FINANCING	$ -	$ -	$ -	$ -	$ -	
CASH AT BEGINNING OF PERIOD	$ 272,861	$ 152,094	$ 56,925	$ 26,678	$ 30,788	
CASH AT END OF PERIOD	$ 152,094	$ 56,925	$ 26,678	$ 30,788	$ 46,884	

	June	July	August	September	October	November	December
	176	208	377	637	634	670	674
	135,000	180,000	225,000	135,000	90,000	90,000	45,000
	-	9,000	18,000	-	18,000	27,000	18,000
	135,000	135,000	135,000	135,000	135,000	135,000	135,000
	$ 270,176	$ 324,208	$ 378,377	$ 270,637	$ 243,634	$ 252,670	$ 198,674
	126,000	151,200	176,400	126,000	113,400	117,600	92,400
	5,400	6,480	7,560	5,400	4,860	5,040	3,960
	5,400	6,480	7,560	5,400	4,860	5,040	3,960
	13,500	16,200	18,900	13,500	12,150	12,600	9,900
	$ 150,300	$ 180,360	$ 210,420	$ 150,300	$ 135,270	$ 140,280	$ 110,220
	5,000	5,000	5,000	5,000	5,000	5,000	5,000
	4,000	4,000	4,000	4,000	4,000	4,000	4,000
	4,000	4,000	4,000	4,000	4,000	4,000	4,000
	3,500	3,500	3,500	3,500	3,500	3,500	3,500
	16,500	16,500	16,500	16,500	16,500	16,500	16,500
	2,640	2,640	2,640	2,640	2,640	2,640	2,640
	9,000	9,000	9,000	9,000	9,000	9,000	9,000
	15,000	15,000	15,000	15,000	15,000	15,000	15,000
	12,500	-	-	12,500	-	12,500	12,500
	$ 55,640	$ 43,140	$ 43,140	$ 55,640	$ 43,140	$ 55,640	$ 55,640
	4	4	4	4	4	4	4
	6,250	6,250	6,250	6,250	6,250	6,250	6,250
	5,000	5,000	5,000	5,000	5,000	5,000	5,000
	4,500	4,500	4,500	4,500	4,500	4,500	4,500
	15,750	15,750	15,750	15,750	15,750	15,750	15,750
	2,520	2,520	2,520	2,520	2,520	2,520	2,520
	5,000	5,000	5,000	5,000	5,000	5,000	5,000
	3,200	3,200	3,200	3,200	3,200	3,200	3,200
	1,450	1,450	1,450	1,450	1,450	1,450	1,450
	1,100	1,100	1,100	1,100	1,100	1,100	1,100
	2,700	2,700	2,700	2,700	2,700	2,700	2,700
	-	-	-	-	-	-	-
	$ 31,720	$ 31,720	$ 31,720	$ 31,720	$ 31,720	$ 31,720	$ 31,720
	4	4	4	4	4	4	4
	6,250	6,250	6,250	6,250	6,250	6,250	6,250
	8,000	8,000	8,000	8,000	8,000	8,000	8,000
	14,250	14,250	14,250	14,250	14,250	14,250	14,250
	2,280	2,280	2,280	2,280	2,280	2,280	2,280
	1,500	1,500	1,500	1,500	1,500	1,500	1,500
	3,000	3,000	3,000	3,000	3,000	3,000	3,000
	$ 21,030	$ 21,030	$ 21,030	$ 21,030	$ 21,030	$ 21,030	$ 21,030
	3	3	3	3	3	3	3
	1,000	1,000	1,000	1,000	1,000	1,000	1,000
	-	-	-	10,000	-	-	-
	1,850	1,850	1,850	1,850	1,850	1,850	1,850
	-	-	-	-	-	-	-
	$ 2,850	$ 2,850	$ 2,850	$ 2,850	$ 2,850	$ 2,850	$ 2,850
	$ 261,540	$ 279,100	$ 309,160	$ 271,540	$ 234,010	$ 251,520	$ 221,460
	-	-	-	-	-	-	-
	-	-	-	-	-	-	-
	$ -	$ -	$ -	$ -	$ -	$ -	$ -
	$ 46,884	$ 55,519	$ 100,628	$ 169,845	$ 168,942	$ 178,565	$ 179,715
	$ 55,519	$ 100,628	$ 169,845	$ 168,942	$ 178,565	$ 179,715	$ 156,929

CLEANAIR TECHNOLOGY — EXHIBIT 5

PRO FORMA ANNUAL CASH FLOW STATEMENTS
January 1, 2009 to December 31, 2014

	2009	2010	2011	2012	2013	2014
CASH INFLOWS						
Investment Income	9,531	5,398	7,062	25,066	112,164	267,680
Revenues from New Homes	-	1,125,000	2,790,000	5,814,000	10,080,000	16,600,000
Revenues from Basement Renovations	-	135,000	342,000	535,500	957,600	1,992,000
Revenues from CEO's Projects	-	1,350,000	1,350,000	2,125,000	2,100,000	2,075,000
TOTAL CASH INFLOWS	$ 9,531	$ 2,615,398	$ 4,489,062	$ 8,499,566	$13,249,764	$ 20,934,680
CASH OUTFLOWS						
Product Expense						
Payments to Supplier — Owens Corning	-	1,218,000	2,091,600	3,888,300	5,865,000	9,337,500
Licensing Payments (2%)	-	52,200	89,640	169,490	262,752	413,340
Sales Commissions (Regional Managers @ 2%)	-	52,200	89,640	169,490	262,752	413,340
Sales Commissions (Sales Representatives @ 5%)	-	130,500	224,100	423,725	656,880	1,033,350
Total Product Expense	$ -	$ 1,452,900	$ 2,494,980	$ 4,651,005	$ 7,047,384	$ 11,197,530
Sales, Marketing & Training						
VP Sales & Marketing —	28,000	60,000	84,000	95,000	120,000	120,000
Director Sales & Marketing — Andrew Longstreet	15,000	48,000	60,000	84,000	84,000	84,000
Salesmen/Trainer	12,000	48,000	75,000	110,000	130,000	150,000
Office Assistants — Sales	21,000	42,000	45,000	45,000	45,000	85,000
Total Payroll	**76,000**	**198,000**	**264,000**	**334,000**	**379,000**	**439,000**
Payroll Taxes & Benefits	12,160	31,680	42,240	53,440	60,640	70,240
Travel & Travel Expenses — Sales	21,600	90,000	157,117	160,000	200,000	200,000
Advertising & Literature	109,000	175,000	200,000	200,000	200,000	200,000
Trade Shows & Seminars	30,000	87,500	50,000	50,000	50,000	50,000
Total Sales, Marketing & Training Expense	$ 248,760	$ 582,180	$ 713,357	$ 797,440	$ 889,640	$ 959,240
# of Sales & Marketing Employees	3	4	6	8	10	12
Administration						
CEO —	35,000	75,000	100,000	120,000	140,000	140,000
CFO — Miriam Wilson	20,000	60,000	84,000	95,000	120,000	120,000
Office Assistants — Admin/Accounting	21,000	56,500	120,000	160,000	200,000	260,000
Total Payroll	**76,000**	**191,500**	**304,000**	**375,000**	**460,000**	**520,000**
Payroll Taxes & Benefits	12,160	30,640	48,640	60,000	73,600	83,200
Travel & Travel Expenses — Admin	40,000	60,000	75,000	90,000	120,000	120,000
Accounting/Legal Fees	26,500	38,400	60,000	60,000	60,000	60,000
Rent, Utilities, Building Insurance	15,500	17,400	20,000	20,000	20,000	20,000
Postage, Supplies, Phone, Internet	13,750	13,200	22,000	22,000	25,000	25,000
Insurance	15,000	32,400	50,000	50,000	50,000	50,000
Membership & Subscriptions	5,000	5,000	10,000	10,000	10,000	10,000
Total Administration Expense	$ 203,910	$ 388,540	$ 589,640	$ 687,000	$ 818,600	$ 888,200
# of Administration Employees	3	4	6	7	8	10
Research & Development						
COO & VP Technology — Justin Umlah	35,000	75,000	100,000	120,000	140,000	140,000
Technicians	15,000	96,000	90,000	90,000	90,000	90,000
Total Payroll	**50,000**	**171,000**	**100,000**	**210,000**	**230,000**	**230,000**
Payroll Taxes & Benefits	8,000	27,360	16,000	33,600	36,800	36,800
Product Development (contract expense)	30,000	-	-	-	-	-
Equipment	12,000	18,000	25,000	35,000	50,000	50,000
Travel & Travel Expenses — R&D	13,500	36,000	36,000	36,000	36,000	36,000
Agency Fees — Patents, FDA, FCC, UL	15,000	-	-	-	-	-
Total Research & Development	$ 128,500	$ 252,360	$ 177,000	$ 314,600	$ 352,800	$ 352,800
# of R&D Employees	2	3	4	4	4	4
Other						
Miscellaneous Expenses	4,500	12,000	24,000	24,000	24,000	24,000
Directors and Advisors Expense	-	20,000	40,000	40,000	40,000	40,000
Consultants	66,000	23,350	50,000	50,000	50,000	50,000
Interest Payments	-	-	-	-	-	-
Income Taxes	-	-	-	-	571,420	1,600,436
Total Other	$ 70,500	$ 55,350	$ 114,000	$ 114,000	$ 685,420	$ 1,714,436
TOTAL CASH OUTFLOWS	$ 651,670	$ 2,731,330	$ 4,088,977	$ 6,564,045	$ 9,793,844	$ 15,112,206
FINANCING						
Government Grants	115,000	-	-	-	-	-
Bank Line of Credit	-	-	-	-	-	-
Issuance of Common Shares	750,000	-	-	-	-	-
Issuance of Preferred Shares	-	-	-	-	-	-
CHANGE FROM FINANCING	$ 865,000	$ -	$ -	$ -	$ -	$ -
CASH AT BEGINNING OF PERIOD	$ 50,000	$ 272,861	$ 156,929	$ 557,014	$ 2,492,534	$ 5,948,454
CASH AT END OF PERIOD	$ 272,861	$ 156,929	$ 557,014	$ 2,492,534	$ 5,948,454	$11,770,928

CLEANAIR TECHNOLOGY — EXHIBIT 6

PRO FORMA ANNUAL INCOME STATEMENTS
January 1, 2009 to December 31, 2014

	2009	2010	2011	2012	2013	2014
SALES						
Revenues from New Homes	-	1,125,000	2,790,000	5,814,000	10,080,000	16,600,000
Revenues from Basement Renovations	-	135,000	342,000	535,500	957,600	1,992,000
Revenues from CEO's Projects	-	1,350,000	1,350,000	2,125,000	2,100,000	2,075,000
TOTAL SALES	$ -	$ 2,610,000	$ 4,482,000	$ 8,474,500	$13,137,600	$20,667,000
COST OF GOODS SOLD						
Payments to Supplier — Owens Corning	-	1,218,000	2,091,600	3,888,300	5,865,000	9,337,500
TOTAL COST OF GOODS SOLD	$ -	$ 1,218,000	$ 2,091,600	$ 3,888,300	$ 5,865,000	$ 9,337,500
VARIABLE EXPENSES						
Licensing Payments (2%)	-	52,200	89,640	169,490	262,752	413,340
Sales Commissions (Regional Managers @ 2%)	-	52,200	89,640	169,490	262,752	413,340
Sales Commissions (Sales Representatives @ 5%)	-	130,500	224,100	423,725	656,880	1,033,350
TOTAL VARIABLE EXPENSES	$ -	$ 234,900	$ 403,380	$ 762,705	$ 1,182,384	$ 1,860,030
GROSS PROFIT	$ -	$ 1,157,100	$ 1,987,020	$ 3,823,495	$ 6,090,216	$ 9,469,470
Gross Profit Margin Ratio	-	44.33%	44.33%	45.12%	46.36%	45.82%
FIXED EXPENSES						
Wages, Payroll Taxes, and Benefits	234,320	650,180	774,880	1,066,040	1,240,040	1,379,240
Travel & Travel Expenses	75,100	186,000	268,117	286,000	356,000	356,000
Advertising and Promotion	139,000	262,500	250,000	250,000	250,000	250,000
Rent, Utilities, Building Insurance	15,500	17,400	20,000	20,000	20,000	20,000
Postage, Supplies, Phone, Internet	13,750	13,200	22,000	22,000	25,000	25,000
Research & Development	30,000	-	-	-		
Accounting/Legal Fees	26,500	38,400	60,000	60,000	60,000	60,000
Insurance	15,000	32,400	50,000	50,000	50,000	50,000
Membership & Subscriptions	5,000	5,000	10,000	10,000	10,000	10,000
Agency Fees — Patents, FDA, FCC, UL	15,000	-	-	-	-	-
Directors and Advisors Expense	-	20,000	40,000	40,000	40,000	40,000
Consultants	66,000	23,350	50,000	50,000	50,000	50,000
Interest Payments	-		-	-		
Depreciation	3,000	7,500	13,750	22,500	26,250	32,000
Depreciation IP	50,000	50,000	50,000	50,000	50,000	50,000
Miscellaneous Expenses	4,500	12,000	24,000	24,000	24,000	24,000
TOTAL FIXED EXPENSES	$ 692,670	$ 1,317,930	$ 1,632,747	$ 1,950,540	$ 2,201,290	$ 2,346,240
NET OPERATING PROFIT (LOSS)	$ (692,670)	$ (160,830)	$ 354,273	$ 1,872,955	$ 3,888,926	$ 7,123,230
OTHER INCOME						
Investment Income	9,531	5,398	7,062	25,066	112,164	267,680
Government Grants	115,000	-	-	-	-	-
TOTAL OTHER INCOME	$ 124,531	$ 5,398	$ 7,062	$ 25,066	$ 112,164	$ 267,680
TOTAL TAXABLE INCOME	$ (568,139)	$ (155,432)	$ 361,335	$ 1,898,021	$ 4,001,090	$ 7,390,910
Income Taxes	-	-	144,534	759,208	1,600,436	2,956,364
Research Tax Credit	-	-	-	-		
Benefit of Loss Carryforward	-	-	144,534	187,788	-	-
NET INCOME	$ (568,139)	$ (155,432)	$ 361,335	$ 1,326,600	$ 2,400,654	$ 4,434,546
Net Profit Margin Ratio	-	-5.96%	8.06%	15.65%	18.27%	21.46%

CLEANAIR TECHNOLOGY — EXHIBIT 7

PRO FORMA ANNUAL BALANCE SHEET
January 1, 2009 to December 31, 2014

	January, 2009	End 2009	2010	2011	2012	2013	2014
CURRENT ASSETS							
Cash	50,000	272,861	156,929	557,014	2,492,534	5,948,454	11,770,928
TOTAL CURRENT ASSETS	50,000	272,861	156,929	557,014	2,492,534	5,948,454	11,770,928
FIXED ASSETS							
Equipment	-	12,000	30,000	55,000	90,000	140,000	190,000
less depreciation	-	3,000	10,500	24,250	46,750	73,000	105,000
Intellectual Property	1,000,000	1,000,000	1,000,000	1,000,000	1,000,000	1,000,000	1,000,000
less depreciation	-	50,000	100,000	150,000	200,000	250,000	300,000
TOTAL FIXED ASSETS	1,000,000	959,000	919,500	880,750	843,250	817,000	785,000
TOTAL ASSETS	$ 1,050,000	1,231,861	1,076,429	1,437,764	3,335,784	$ 6,765,454	$ 12,555,928
CURRENT LIABILITIES							
Taxes Payable	-	-	-	-	571,420	1,600,436	2,956,364
Bank Loans	-	-	-	-	-	-	-
TOTAL CURRENT LIABILITIES	-	-	-	-	571,420	1,600,436	2,956,364
LONG TERM DEBT							
Long Term Debt	-	-	-	-	-	-	-
Other Long Term Liabilities	-	-	-	-	-	-	-
TOTAL LONG TERM DEBT	-	-	-	-	-	-	-
TOTAL LIABILITIES	-	-	-	-	571,420	1,600,436	2,956,364
SHAREHOLDERS' EQUITY							
Common Shares Issued	-	750,000	750,000	750,000	750,000	750,000	750,000
Initial Equity	1,050,000	1,050,000	1,050,000	1,050,000	1,050,000	1,050,000	1,050,000
Retained Earnings	-	(568,139)	(723,571)	(362,236)	964,364	3,365,018	7,799,564
TOTAL SHAREHOLDERS' EQUITY	1,050,000	1,231,861	1,076,429	$ 1,437,764	$ 2,764,364	$ 5,165,018	9,599,564
TOTAL LIABILITIES & SHAREHOLDERS' EQUITY	$ 1,050,000	$ 1,231,861	1,076,429	$ 1,437,764	3,335,784	$ 6,765,454	$ 12,555,928

APPENDIX 1

FINANCIAL NOTES AND ASSUMPTIONS

1. All funds are expressed in U.S. dollars.
2. Taxes are based on an effective rate of 40%. Losses in previous years can be carried forward to offset profits in current years.
3. Investment income is calculated by multiplying the beginning monthly cash balance by a monthly investment rate of 0.375% (4.5% annually).
4. No salaries are paid until June 2009.
5. Payroll taxes and benefits expense is calculated at 16% of total payroll.
6. Proposals to the government of Manitoba for grants totalling $115,000 are received.
7. Sales begin January 2010. As these statements have been calculated to show the potential of WaVeS sales alone, receipts from customers and payments to suppliers have been shown to occur in the month of sale. Additional financial projections are available from CleanAir Technologies upon request.
8. Sales revenues are based on projected unit sales.
9. Commissions for regional managers calculated at 2% of sales.
10. Commissions for sales reps calculated at 5% of sales.
11. Royalties of 2% paid to the inventor on a monthly basis.
12. Directors' Fees include honorarium, travel expenses, and liability insurance.
13. Business is cyclical and peaks in August.
14. Size of an average home being built is 2400 sq. ft.

APPENDIX 2

REFERENCE LIST

1. Canadian Centre for Occupational Health and Safety.
2. Canadian Manufacturers and Exporters. November 10. <www.cme-mec.ca>.
3. CMHC Winnipeg Housing Outlook. 2008. < www.cmhc-schl.gc.ca>.
4. CNN Money, Homeowners Insurance: Use it and Lose it. June 3, 2008. <http://money.cnn.com/2008/05/26/pf/insurance/use_it_lose_it/index.htm>.
5. EnergyStar homepage. 2008. <http://www.energystar.gov/>.
6. Government of Manitoba, Public Information. November 3. <www.gov.mb.ca/emo/pubinfo/moldhome.html>.
7. Kelwin Management Consulting. Air Current Technologies Commercialization Plan. Winnipeg, 2008.
8. McNickol, Dave. Phone conversation. 16 November 2008.
9. October 28. <www.ccohs.ca/oshanswer/biol_hazards/iaq_mold.html>
10. Red River Flood. <http://en.wikipedia.org/wiki/Red_River_Flood,_1997#Recovery_and_legacy>.
11. Renovations and Décor Magazine. 2008. <www.renovationsanddecor.com>.
12. Statistics Canada. "Persons with Asthma by Sex, by Provinces." 2008.
13. Statistics Canada. 2005. <www.statscan.ca>.
14. U.S. Census Bureau, Expenditures for Residential Improvements and Repairs by Property Type. <http://www.census.gov/const/histtab2new.pdf>.
15. U.S. Environmental Protection Agency, Mold Resources. <http://www.epa.gov/iaq/molds/moldresources.html#Health%20and%20Mold>.
16. United States Postal Service. 2008. <www.usps.com>.

Lite Bites Grill

A BUSINESS PLAN BY:

Bill Benson

TABLE OF CONTENTS ....

Mission Statement	2
Company Management	2
Advisory Team	2
Executive Summary	3
Lite Bites Grill	3
Business Goals	3
The Industry	3
The Concept	4
Market Analysis	4
Target Market	4
Market Size	5
Estimated Sales and Market Share	5
Competition	5
Marketing Plan	6
Pricing	6
Advertising and Promotion	7
Management Team	8
Management Compensation	8
Shareholders	8
Advisory Team	8
Operations Plan	9
Location	9
Facilities	9
Equipment	9
Supply Chain	10
Human Resources	10
Regulatory Requirements	11
Insurance Plan	11
Implementation Schedule	12
Financial Plan	12
Funding Requested	12
Financial Projections	12
Risk Factors	13
Divestiture/Harvest Strategy	13
Financial Statements	14
Bibliography	21
Appendices	22

LITE BITES GRILL
(LBG Enterprises Inc.)

#7 – 1045 St. James Street   Phone: 204-555-1349
Winnipeg, Manitoba R3Y 2B6   Fax: 204-555-9345

(www.litebites.com)

MISSION

"To be the leading alternative to traditional fast-food restaurants, offering healthy and flavourful meals in a quick-service format."

COMPANY MANAGEMENT

Name	Position	Experience	Share
Bill Benson	President & GM	Operations Management Finance & Accounting	100%
Leonard Burgess	Restaurant Manager	Restaurant Management	

ADVISORY TEAM

Name	Position	Experience
Bonnie Vandenberg	Banker	Finance
Gordon Harlock	Accountant	Certified Management Accountant
Lorena Perlock	Dir. Of Marketing	Marketing
Ian Rollins	Lawyer	Commercial Law

EXECUTIVE SUMMARY

LITE BITES GRILL is an exciting new restaurant concept geared toward busy professionals who don't have the time to cook due to today's increasingly hectic lifestyle. The fast-food industry is experiencing explosive growth of 20 per cent per year, yet industry giants offer a very limited variety of healthful and nutritious meals. Research shows that lighter meal options are the fastest-growing menu items, and the majority of consumers take these options into consideration when determining where to eat. Furthermore, 2.5 per cent of the population can be considered vegetarian — another market segment that has been traditionally under-serviced. The LITE BITES GRILL concept is intended to fill these niche markets with a wide variety of tasty and healthful meals, including several attractive vegetarian offerings.

The typical customer is expected to be a homeowner, educated, mid- to upper-income, 25 to 54 years old, and health-conscious. Based upon this profile and factoring in the vegetarian population, the Winnipeg, Manitoba, test market is estimated to consist of 70,850 individuals, 16,942 of whom live within the vicinity of the original test restaurant location. The restaurants will be richly appointed and will possess a relaxing colour scheme consisting of muted earth tones. With an average meal price in the $6 to $9 range, first-year sales are anticipated to be $300,000, reaching $600,000 for each location within three years.

The business is led by Bill Benson, a seasoned operations manager and professional engineer, who is also nearing completion of an MBA. Bill is the sole owner of LBG, based upon his $47,000 equity investment. Day-to-day management will be handled by Leonard Burgess, who has over 20 years of industry experience, primarily with the Denny's chain. The management team is supported by an exceptional advisory group that will provide guidance in their areas of expertise.

A capital investment in equipment and leasehold improvements of $126,500 is required to launch the business. Financing has been arranged with the CIBC through the Canada Small Business Financing Act (CSBFA) program for $113,985 of this amount. The balance of the funding will come via an initial equity investment by the owner. This will provide for the necessary operating expenses as well as the portion of the capital investment not covered by the CSBFA loan. The owner estimates that up to $100,000 could be made available by refinancing his home and cashing in investments. This should provide for any contingencies as well as adequate reserve funds.

The first restaurant will open July 1, 2008, and is expected to post a healthy profit in the second year of operation. After three years, profitability is forecast to be more than double the industry average of 2.4 per cent net profit. By the end of the fifth year, the business will have three locations in operation and net profits (after tax) are forecast to be a healthy $63,200, with retained earnings reaching $100,000. A strong cash position will allow the flexibility to aggressively reduce debt to facilitate developing additional Winnipeg locations in years 3 and 5. Long term, the goal of the business is to have 20 company-owned locations across Western Canada.

LITE BITES GRILL

LITE BITES GRILL (LBG) is an incorporated business that plans the development of a chain of corporate-owned restaurants catering to busy, health-conscious professionals and vegetarians. Presently, the large fast-food outlets are under-servicing these rapidly growing market segments, with very limited product offerings. The LBG vision is to exploit this opportunity by developing a premium quick-service menu offering a wide variety of healthful and nutritious meals.

BUSINESS GOALS

The mission of the LITE BITES GRILL concept is "To be the leading alternative to traditional fast-food restaurants, offering healthy and flavourful meals in a quick-service format." Long term, the goal of the business is to have 20 company-owned locations across Western Canada.

THE INDUSTRY

North Americans spent over $120 billion on fast food in 2005 and fast-food sales are growing at a rate of more than 20 per cent per year (1). This can at least partly be attributed to today's increasingly hectic lifestyle. In 2004,

41 per cent of Canadians claimed to be short of time — a 19 per cent increase in just two years (2). A contributing factor is the return of women to the workforce, leaving them little time to shop, plan, or prepare meals as they once did. Not surprisingly, attitudinal studies reveal that Canadian consumers would like to simplify their lives — in the food realm, they do this by delegating some of the responsibility to foodservice.

It's estimated that 61 per cent of Canadian adults are either overweight or obese (3). Consequently, in choosing where to eat, consumers are taking their health into greater consideration. As evidence of this trend, a recent study by the Canadian Restaurant and Foodservices Association (CRFA) indicated that 60 per cent of fast-food customers rate the availability of healthful or nutritious foods as important in their decision of where to eat. In a further study by the CRFA, newer menu items such as veggie burgers and wrap sandwiches were "among the fastest-growing menu items in 2006." Furthermore, Canadians are eating more salads, while the popularity of French fries and hamburgers is slipping (4).

THE CONCEPT

A quick-service restaurant offering busy health-conscious consumers, including vegetarians, a healthy and flavourful alternative to traditional fast food.

The LITE BITES GRILL menu will include soups, veggie burgers, grilled chicken breast sandwiches, salmon burgers, tuna steak sandwiches, veggie pastas, Asian noodles, vegetarian chili, veggie wraps, and an assortment of fresh salads with low-fat dressings. Low-fat, multi-grain breads will be baked fresh on the premises. Several beverage options will be offered, including a juice bar. A small kids' menu will offer items like baked chicken nuggets and baked fries. Only lunch and dinner items will be offered, with hours of operation from 10:30 a.m. to 9:00 p.m.

The initial restaurant model is intended for a strip mall location, requiring approximately 2,000 square feet, with a seating capacity of 40 people. Bold signage will be employed to intrigue people from a distance. Both carry-out and dine-in options will be available and, based upon similar concepts, it's estimated that 40 per cent of sales will be taken out (5). Customers will be given a number once they've ordered and paid for their meals. Numbers will be called out as the orders are ready. For the benefit of take-out customers awaiting their orders, a small lounge area will be located next to the juice/coffee bar. The day's top news stories will be displayed in Plexiglas cases to help make the brief wait enjoyable.

In terms of physical amenities, the restaurant will be more richly appointed than typical fast-food outlets, with padded booths and chairs and wood trim throughout. Flooring will consist of low-maintenance ceramic tile. The colour scheme will consist of muted earth tones, while the décor will include baskets of fresh vegetables and fruit to convey a healthy image. High ceilings will help create an inviting open-air atmosphere within the confines of a small setting. Nutritional information (including fat grams, calories, cholesterol, etc.) will be posted so that customers can match their orders to their specific dietary needs. An open-kitchen concept will be used to allow the customers to see their food being prepared and to permit direct selection of various ingredients like spices, sauces, and dressings.

Winnipeg is an ideal test location as it's a demanding market. Evidence of the city's suitability as a test market is the fact that McDonald's uses Winnipeg to test the viability of new products. After two years of testing this model restaurant at the Polo Park location, LITE BITES GRILL will add a second and third location in years 3 and 5, respectively. Subsequently, the concept will gradually be rolled out across Western Canada with additional outlets that will remain company-owned.

MARKET ANALYSIS

TARGET MARKET

In considering the aforementioned trends, the target market for this concept is the on-the-go, health-conscious business professional. This concept will primarily appeal to adults within the range of 25 to 54 years of age, seeking tasty and healthful food on the run that's more appealing than what traditional fast food has to offer. Women are expected to comprise 60 per cent of the target market, based on prototypes of similar ventures in the United States.

A secondary, but not insignificant, market is the growing number of vegetarians who are typically poorly serviced, with limited offerings from the major fast-food chains — particularly for true vegan offerings. Vegans are strict vegetarians who refrain from eating any animal products, including all meats (beef, pork, seafood, fish, and poultry), dairy products, eggs, and honey. The number of Canadians who rarely or never eat meat is on the rise — approximately 2.5 per cent of the population can be considered vegetarian (6). This does not include people who occasionally or rarely eat meat or animal products.

Consumers want to eat healthy, but do not want to sacrifice taste. D'Lites, a vegetarian chain that grew to 86 locations throughout the United States before closing its doors, cut calories at the expense of flavour, and this led to its demise. Furthermore, consumers are finding a limited variety of healthy options available at the traditional fast-food chains. Most chains have little to offer beyond veggie burgers and salads. LITE BITES GRILL will offer a comprehensive menu of tasty and nutritious quick-service meals. All menu items will be health-oriented, so that consumers will not have to resist the temptations offered by calorie-laden menu items.

MARKET SIZE

A variety of detailed information for the target market is available in the 2006 Census data released by Statistics Canada (7). The typical customer profile for this concept is expected to be a homeowner, educated, mid- to upper-income, aged 25 to 54, and health-conscious. Using the relevant education and age demographics for the City of Winnipeg, we learn that 19.1 per cent of the individuals in our target age bracket have a university education. Assuming that the university-educated individuals within the age bracket of 25 to 54 are representative of the target market, it is estimated that this market in Winnipeg consists of 57,250 individuals. Furthermore, using this same methodology, the market in Canada for this concept is estimated to be 2,580,000.

These figures do not reflect the vegetarian component of the potential market. Using the 2.5 per cent approximation, vegetarians comprise an additional 13,600 Winnipeg customers and 607,000 Canadians. Only individuals over the age of 14 were considered in making these calculations. It was assumed that vegetarians under the age of 15 would not have much say in making decisions of where to dine, and consequently this segment of the market is not expected to comprise a significant portion of our clientele.

Thus, our total potential market size is expected to be 70,850 (57,250 + 13,600) Winnipeggers and 3,187,000 (2,580,000 + 607,000) Canadians.

ESTIMATED SALES AND MARKET SHARE

Based upon Census data (8), the typical household in the Winnipeg test market is spending $1,367.08 per year, on average, for food purchased from restaurants. It is assumed that this *household* data will apply to *individuals* in the target market, due to the higher income levels and hectic schedules that will make restaurant visits more common than at lower income levels. Based on this assumption, the 16,942 individuals in the Winnipeg target market spend a total of $23,161,069 in restaurants. This figure represents the total market potential for this concept in the market area of the test restaurant. This is expected to be a conservative estimate, as it does not include that spent by visitors to the city or commuters from surrounding areas.

O'Naturals (see "Competition" section below) appears to have achieved the highest sales success of similar concepts, with sales of $2,000 to $3,000 per day, roughly on par with a typical Burger King (9). However, based upon surveys of other restaurants, typical annual sales for a mature restaurant in this market are expected to be approximately $600,000. Using a start-up year factor of about 50 per cent, as recommended by the Canada Business Service Centre (10), the forecasted sales for the first year are $300,000. Using a "top down" approach to estimate sales (11) would yield our first-year sales forecast at an estimated market share of 1.3 per cent, which appears highly achievable.

Preliminary sales estimates are outlined in Appendix 1. Sales are expected to be relatively strong the first month due to grand opening sales promotions. The forecast tapers off for the next few months, followed by gradual growth as the business begins to establish itself.

COMPETITION

The fast-food industry is intensely competitive and the large traditional chains, with their considerable brand equity, are evolving product lines to address changes in consumer preferences. Among the primary competition:

MCDONALD'S (www.mcdonalds.com): The world's largest restaurant operator, McDonald's had a 43 per cent share of the quick-service hamburger market in 2006 — down slightly from the previous two years as

McDonald's struggled to expand its product line. Recent additions to the menu include salads, chicken burgers, veggie burgers, and a low-fat yogourt/granola snack. In 2006 McDonald's purchased a minority stake in the London, England, Pret a Manger, a 16-year-old chain specializing in fresh, handmade wraps, salads, and sandwiches that are free of additives and preservatives. The company plans to develop 20 Manhattan units by the end of the year and an additional 40 New York City shops before expanding into other markets.

BURGER KING (www.burgerking.com): Considered to have the burgers with the highest fat content in the industry, Burger King is revamping its product offerings to include a vegan-friendly veggie burger, a Chicken Whopper, and better-tasting coffee. It's not so much the vegetarian or health-conscious consumer that the chain is targeting, but rather the veto power this market segment may have over a minivan full of hungry, burger-eating family members. Market share at the number-two hamburger chain has eroded to 18.4 per cent in 2006, down from 19.6 per cent in 2004.

WENDY'S (www.wendys.com): The number-three hamburger chain, with a 13.2 per cent market share in 2006, has been boosting its market share for five consecutive years. Unlike its two larger rivals, who compete on price, Wendy's has been boosting market share without discounting core menu items. Recent additions to the menu include a popular line of salads.

SUBWAY (www.subway.com): With more than 17,000 locations in 75 countries, SUBWAY has now overtaken McDonald's as the largest restaurant chain by number of stores in the United States. SUBWAY is heavily promoting its low-fat line of subs (7 subs with 6 grams of fat or less) through its "Jared" campaign. Jared Fogle, SUBWAY's weight-loss hero, lost 245 pounds through his own diet and exercise regime, incorporating SUBWAY's "7 under 6" menu of low-fat sandwiches.

In addition to the large chains, there are many small concepts emerging, primarily in the United States, with plans to franchise out to regions that include the Canadian market. These are considered a distant threat, as the concepts are still being tested and developed in regional areas and do not have plans to aggressively pursue the Canadian market for the foreseeable future. These include:

TOPZ (www.topz.com): A Southern California concept with healthier versions of traditional fast-food fare — soy, turkey, and lean-beef burgers are on the menu, as well as baked "fries." Topz has six locations in the greater Los Angeles market. Franchising will add 10 to 12 stores in the next year, and in the longer term it plans 100 to 200 more.

O'NATURALS (www.onaturals.com): An emerging concept in the New England area of the United States that represents "family-friendly, tasty, natural, and organic fast food." Not specifically a low-fat or vegetarian concept, the company is targeting consumers with an ethical and environmental consciousness — offering meat from free-range livestock that has been raised without unnecessary chemicals and hormones. There is presently only one prototype location, in Falmouth, Maine. Plans included two new units in 2007 and three additional restaurants in 2008. From there, O'Naturals plan to roll out the concept throughout the Northeast and nationally, with the potential for several hundred locations.

HEALTHY BITES GRILL (www.hexs.com): Claims to be the United States' "first fast-food restaurant franchise to feature gourmet health food." The concept is presently being rolled out in the Fort Lauderdale, Florida, region.

MARKETING PLAN

PRICING

The pricing strategy employed will be that of a premium quick-service restaurant. Based upon similar concepts in the United States, the average meal will cost between $6 and $9. LBG will not be competing based on price, but rather will be focusing on value. The higher quality and more nutritious meals will command a higher price in the market. In support of this strategy, the focus group established for the purpose of defining this market indicated that many senior businesspeople are very conscious of their image. Consequently, there is a perception that executives would not come back to the office with a take-out bag from the typical fast-food chain because it would give the image that they have low standards. LBG's concept will appeal to a mid- to upscale market and will be priced accordingly.

A detailed breakdown of fixed and variable costs can be found in Schedule 2 (the financial statements follow the body of this business plan). Typical gross margins in this industry are approximately 70 per cent, while net margins are a slim 2.4 per cent. LBG margins are expected to be on par with the industry norm. However, after the second year of operation, net income is forecast to be more than double the industry average. Although the break-even sales volume of $318,900 is not expected to be achieved in the first year, it is anticipated the restaurant will be profitable in its second year of operation. As restaurants are a cash business, they have the significant advantage of having no potential credit issues that can negatively impact operations.

ADVERTISING AND PROMOTION

A multi-faceted promotional campaign is planned for the official launch of the concept and grand opening of the first restaurant. A complete summary of the first-year marketing budget is shown in Appendix 2. The Industry Canada SME Benchmarking Tool web site indicates that the typical company in this industry spends, on average, 3 per cent of gross sales on advertising. Based on first-year forecast sales of $300,000, this would put $9,000 into the advertising budget. However, due to the fact that this is a start-up, a 100 per cent premium will be used to bring the first-year advertising budget to $18,000. Factoring in expenses for sales promotions, personal selling, and the development of a Web site, brings the total first-year marketing budget to $25,125.

To help build brand awareness and to support general inquiries, a Web site will be developed and will go "live" approximately one month prior to the grand opening. The Web site will be established to ensure that information on the concept is readily available to the computer-savvy consumers that make up a large percentage of the target market. The site will include pictures of the restaurant, as well as a menu, complete with information on the applicable nutritional content. This nutritional information will compare and contrast with that of typical menu items at the large fast-food chains. In addition, general health and dietary facts will be provided in an interactive menu format. Patrick Doerksen, a freelance computer programmer, will develop the site for a quoted $2,500 fee plus $50 per month for updating. Other costs include $35 annually for a domain name and $20 per month for hosting services.

The promotions program will officially begin approximately one week prior to the grand opening of the restaurant. Two university marketing students will be hired to visit local businesses within the target market to conduct personal selling. Menus will be dropped off, in addition to sales promotions consisting of coupons for a free menu item. Eighty hours has been budgeted for this activity at $10 per hour. In addition, a promotional billboard will be developed and displayed approximately one week prior to the grand opening. It will be in place for a four-week period.

The marketing program will also include a comprehensive newspaper advertising campaign. This will include sponsoring a sampling campaign in conjunction with *The Winnipeg Sun*. For a nominal $1,500, the *Sun* offers a full-page wrap that is delivered with a free paper to approximately 3,000 to 4,000 homes and businesses within the target area. The wrap is issued the day of the grand opening. The front page announces the opening with the specials for that day. The second and third pages provide special coupons for the second and third days of the grand opening period. The back page of the wrap will have a ballot that can be dropped off to enter a draw for a Blu-Ray player. Thus, the wrap generates at least three days of traffic.

After the grand opening, an ongoing newspaper advertising program will be established. The campaign will stress the availability of a new alternative to traditional fast food — an alternative that offers more variety than the few bland options available from the big chains. Both *The Winnipeg Sun* and the *Winnipeg Free Press* will be utilized, as each paper targets different market segments. *The Winnipeg Sun* is number one in readership among adults 25–34, based on NADbank 2002 (13), an independent survey measuring 72 daily newspapers in 46 urban markets. The overall reach of the *Sun* is 266,400 weekly readers. Meanwhile, the *Winnipeg Free Press,* with a reach of 404,700 weekly readers, has higher readership in the 35+ category, and is more skewed to females than the *Sun*. Thus, the *Free Press* advertising will reach the mature female component of the target market. The budgeted $9,650 will include one more wrap-style campaign in the *Sun*, as well as four inserts in the *Free Press* at $2,000 each. These advertisements will be spread evenly throughout the remainder of the year.

A small radio budget of $2,500 will be established for the grand opening. Radio station BOB FM was chosen for the campaign due to its listener base being well represented by members of the target market. Radio advertising will begin on the day of the grand opening and the campaign will last for a period of three days. During the actual day of the grand opening, BOB FM will have on-air giveaways and live broadcasts on location.

MANAGEMENT TEAM

Bill Benson is the President and General Manager of the LITE BITES GRILL and will be responsible for overall operation of the business. Bill received a Bachelor of Science degree in Industrial Engineering from the University of Manitoba in 1995. He received his Professional Engineer designation in 1997 from the Association of Professional Engineers of Manitoba. Bill has held a variety of senior-level operations positions and is presently Operations Manager for Malon Plastics Inc. This position has overall P & L responsibility for the company's three divisions and includes direct and indirect supervision of 75 employees. To complement his diverse work experience, Bill has been working toward receiving a Masters of Business Administration in the part-time program at the University of Manitoba. He will graduate from the program in April 2008, at which time he plans to focus his efforts on developing and growing the LITE BITES GRILL restaurant concept. Bill has previous entrepreneurial experience, having founded and successfully run a private automobile wholesaling business for three years.

Leonard Burgess is the Restaurant Manager and will be in charge of running day-to-day operations. Leonard has 20 years' experience in the restaurant industry, working in a variety of capacities. His experience ranges from cooking and waiting tables through to managerial positions. One of his most recent achievements involved managing a Denny's restaurant for eight years in Calgary, Alberta. Leonard will assume a "hands-on" role at LITE BITES GRILL, supervising his staff as well as helping out as needed during peak demand. As Manager, he will be responsible for the hiring and training of all restaurant personnel. In addition, he will perform all purchasing of food supplies and management of the supply base. Basic accounting software will be utilized to maintain a system of bookkeeping. In this capacity, Leonard will report directly to the General Manager. A detailed resumé for Leonard, outlining his vast work experience in the food-services industry, can be found in Appendix 7.

MANAGEMENT COMPENSATION

Bill Benson will remain with his present employer for the first two years of operations. During this time, he will not draw a salary from the business, although he plans to work evenings and weekends furthering the development of the chain. As Restaurant Manager, Leonard Burgess will receive a salary of $30,000 per annum.

SHAREHOLDERS

Bill Benson will be the sole shareholder in the business, with 100 per cent ownership as a result of the $47,000 initial personal capital investment.

ADVISORY TEAM

To successfully launch and develop a new venture like this, a team of advisers has been assembled to support the management team. The team has been selected based on their relevant expertise and proven abilities.

Bonnie Vandenberg is a Financial Adviser with CIBC. LBG has consulted Bonnie regarding CIBC commercial banking for securing start-up capital. Bonnie, in conjunction with Al Taylor — CIBC's General Manager, Small Business — has helped LBG management determine the appropriate financing for the business. The CIBC will also provide financial guidance during periods of expansion. Bonnie is a Certified Financial Planner and has a Masters of Business Administration from the University of Manitoba.

Gord Harlock is the Controller of Malon Plastics Inc. and has held a variety of senior-level accounting positions over the past 20 years. Gord has several years' experience as a consultant specializing in setting up accounting systems for small businesses. He has a Bachelor of Commerce (Honors) and is a Certified Management Accountant (CMA). Gord will advise LBG in the set-up and implementation of its accounting system.

Lorena Perlock is Director of Marketing with *The Winnipeg Sun*. Lorena recently graduated with an MBA from the University of Manitoba and has extensive experience in the field of marketing. She will provide guidance to LBG in areas of marketing, advertising, and promotions.

Ian Rollins practises commercial law and is a partner in the firm Rollins & Rollins. The practice has emphases in the following areas of law: business organizations, corporate and commercial transactions, real estate, general contractual matters, and employment law. Ian's extensive academic accomplishments include a Masters degree in Law from Oxford University. He teaches the Commercial Law course at the University of Manitoba in the Asper School of Business. Ian has been retained by LBG to provide all legal advice.

OPERATIONS PLAN

LOCATION

The site chosen for the initial restaurant is at 1045 St. James Street in The Brick Plaza commercial complex. A detailed facility location and site plan are provided in Appendix 3. The site is ideally located at Ellice Avenue and St. James Street, an intersection with one of the busiest traffic counts in Winnipeg. The site offers additional benefits of superior access and egress, signage offering maximum exposure, and an excellent, well-lit parking lot with an ample supply of parking spaces.

The location is just north of the Polo Park Shopping Centre, Winnipeg's premier shopping complex. This site has all of the desirable features for this concept: (1) it is close to the downtown area, home to the employers of many business professionals, (2) it is within reasonable proximity of the mid- to upscale neighbourhoods of St. James, River Heights, Linden Woods, Tuxedo, and Whyte Ridge, and (3) the area is home to a number of large retail outlets and a major shopping centre, which is expected to ensure adequate traffic volume around the restaurant throughout all hours of the day and into the early evening. Census data for the relevant areas for the City of Winnipeg can be found in Appendix 4 (8). As indicated in the exhibit, it is estimated that 16,942 individuals who fit our target market profile reside within the vicinity of the original restaurant location.

FACILITIES

The total space available of 1,913 square feet will provide ample room for the dining area, kitchen, storage, and a small office. At present, the facility is serving as warehouse space for an adjacent business. Drywall is in place but the area is otherwise unfinished, with the exception of separate male and female handicap-accessible washrooms. The premises are zoned C-2, which is suitable for a restaurant.

The premises are available for lease at an asking rate of $12 per square foot, net. However, the listing agent felt that if the lessee developed the space, the lessor would reduce this amount to around $10 per square foot. Additional fees for common area management (CAM) amount to $4.06 per square foot. The CAM includes exterior building maintenance, real estate taxes, landscaping, and snow removal. Furthermore, a management fee of 5 per cent of net rent would be applicable. This would bring the total annual rent to $27,853, which equates to $2,321 per month. The lessor is requesting a lease of between a three- to five-year term. With the substantial investment in leasehold improvements, LBG will seek a five-year lease and will likely gain further concessions for doing so. The lessee will be expected to give a personal guarantee together with the first and last months' rent as a security deposit. All utilities and business taxes are separate.

In terms of general leasehold improvements, decorating and remodelling is estimated to be $55,000. This amount was based upon the average leasehold improvement cost for opening a SUBWAY restaurant in Canada (14).

Signex Manufacturing Inc. will provide and install a 5-foot 3 8-foot internally illuminated sign for the front entrance of the restaurant. The sign will have a white acrylic face with high-performance translucent graphics applied to the surface. Cost for the sign is $1,800. An additional fee of $155 is required for a standard City of Winnipeg permit.

EQUIPMENT

A wide variety of equipment is required to ensure the restaurant is capable of preparing the breadth of menu items to be offered. Due to the specific nature of some of the equipment and the lack of availability of good used equipment on the market, all items will be purchased new from Russell Food Equipment. All kitchen equipment will be of commercial quality, with National Sanitation Foundation (NSF) or equivalent approval. A detailed equipment listing can be found in Appendix 5. The optional dishwasher will be purchased to allow the staff to focus on cooking and service activities and to keep staffing levels to a minimum. The prices listed include delivery and setting in place. Also included is the mounting of the menu sign, the set-up of the storage shelves, and the set-up and testing of the walk-in cooler/freezer. Total cost of the equipment amounts to

$63,000. Due to the magnitude of the purchase, it is expected that a 5 per cent discount will be negotiated, reducing the total cost to $59,850. Lead time for delivery of the equipment is four to six weeks. The expected life of the equipment is approximately 10 years.

Electrical hook-up and plumbing costs are extra. Industrial Electrical Services has estimated $3,000 for electrical hook-up of the equipment, including the permit, labour, and all materials. The 200-amp service presently available on the premises was deemed sufficient to meet the electrical requirements of the installed equipment. Elmwood Plumbing and Heating has estimated $2,000 for all plumbing connections, including all materials.

Russell Food Equipment provides consultant services on a no-charge basis to its clients during new start-ups. In addition, the owner of LBG is a Registered Professional Engineer. Thus, design of the layout and the development of drawings and specifications for tendering the leasehold improvements will be performed at a minimal out-of-pocket expense.

SUPPLY CHAIN

SYSCO Food Services has been chosen to be the primary supplier for food and general supplies. SYSCO is a broadline food distributor, offering a complete line of products including produce, meats, poultry, seafood, frozen foods, paper, cleaning supplies, chemicals, dairy, and full beverage programs featuring Citavo fresh ground coffee and Sunkist premium juices. Over 9,000 items are carried at the local branch and 40,000 items are stocked by SYSCO's parent company. These are standard items and availability is not a problem. Nutritional information is available so that fat content, cholesterol, and calorie information can be passed on to LBG customers. Meats are cryogenically frozen and vacuum-packed in single-serving portions so that the entire case need not be thawed. Most menu items are available in a heat-and-serve format, minimizing the need to develop recipes from scratch.

Deliveries are offered free of charge on orders above $500 and will take place once per week. Orders can be made through a convenient Web-based system or via direct contact with a marketing associate. Specialists are on staff to assist with a wide range of matters, from nutritional information and cooking tips to kitchen design assistance.

Due to unpredictable market elements, the longest pricing contract that can be arranged is for a period of six months. Products like poultry are heavily dependent on weather conditions. Poultry is sourced locally and a hot dry stretch, for example, could lead to high death rates and significant upward price pressure. However, with SYSCO's nationwide network, items can be sourced in other regions, minimizing the impact of regional conditions. Until a credit history can be established, orders will remain C.O.D. for the first several months. However, a direct electronic funds transfer (EFT) service is offered at no charge to SYSCO customers. This system essentially provides up to one week of working capital by delaying electronic transfer of funds until the following Tuesday morning, allowing time for deposit of funds from the busy weekend period.

Additional benefits will be achieved by selecting specific brands to be utilized in the restaurant. For example, Campbell's Soups has a soup kettle program that provides some equipment, as well as slide cards and menu displays, when Campbell's Soup products are used exclusively. Similarly, a paper program is available whereby towel and paper dispensers are offered free of charge when paper products are purchased through SYSCO. Likewise, beverage equipment is provided at no charge when Citavo coffee and Sunkist juices are purchased exclusively.

Due to the size and stability of the SYSCO organization, backup suppliers are not deemed necessary. However, alternative suppliers are available if the need ever did arise. For example, To-Le-Do Foodservice distributes a full line of top-quality chilled and frozen products including beef, veal, pork, smoked meats, chicken, turkey, seafood, and fresh-cut produce.

HUMAN RESOURCES

Each LBG location will employ two full-time serving personnel and an additional four casual workers in a non-unionized environment. Serving personnel perform a range of duties, including taking customer orders, preparing meals, operating the cash register, and performing general clean-up activities. A staffing schedule can be found in Appendix 6. During peak periods, one full-time employee will be supported by two casual workers. It is also expected that the restaurant manager will assist staff during peak hours.

Employees hired must be personable and well organized. Previous restaurant experience is desired but not mandatory, as all employees will receive extensive training. To entice employees to work for LBG in this environment of low unemployment, a starting wage of $7 per hour will be paid to all casual labour. This represents a $0.50 per hour premium over the $6.50 per hour minimum wage that is typically paid in the industry. The two full-time employees will be paid a more attractive $8 per hour to help retain these key personnel.

Initial start-up training will consist of one week of "hands-on" training conducted by representatives of the foodservices supply industry and the equipment manufacturers. Likewise, ongoing training will be performed on an as-needed basis by various suppliers. New hires will receive a brief indoctrination to the company by the Manager. After indoctrination, the "buddy" system will be used for the following week by pairing up the new hire with an experienced employee.

Every effort will be made to create a fun, stimulating, and rewarding environment whereby employees feel appreciated and respected. Incentives will be provided to achieve targets in areas like customer satisfaction, workplace cleanliness, and safety. These promotions may include tickets for sporting events, T-shirts, gift certificates, and company-sponsored recreational activities. Additional benefits include vacation pay ranging from 4 per cent for new hires up to 8 per cent for employees with 10 years of tenure.

REGULATORY REQUIREMENTS

The foodservices industry is heavily regulated. Consequently, there are several permits and licences that will be obtained prior to the opening of the first restaurant:

- A Food Handling Establishment Licence (By-Law 6551/95) must be obtained from the City of Winnipeg Licence Branch. Licences are valid for one year and must be renewed annually. There is a $311 fee for each licence. To be approved, the premises must comply with applicable zoning regulations and must be examined by a Medical Health Officer and deemed to be in a fit, clean, and suitable condition.

- An Occupancy Permit must be obtained from the City of Winnipeg Zoning and Permits Branch. Five sets of detailed plans and specifications must be submitted to a Zoning Officer at the Plan Approval Office. The one-time fee of $585.85 includes the occupancy permit itself, the building permit for renovations (a variable fee, based on development costs), the fire department review fee, and the health department review fee.

- A Food Health Permit must be obtained from an Environmental Health Officer at Manitoba Conservation in order to operate a foodservice establishment. The Food Health Permit is issued upon completion of an inspection by an Environmental Health Officer and satisfactory compliance with the Food Service Establishment By-Law 5160/89. In addition, the applicant must register for the Certified Food Health Training Program. The Food Health Permit must be posted and displayed in a clearly visible location in the establishment. There is no cost for the permit itself. The premises are, however, subject to ongoing monitoring to ensure compliance.

INSURANCE PLAN

MILNCO Insurance has developed a comprehensive insurance program for LBG, with protection from a range of perils. A detailed outline of the insurance coverage can be found in Appendix 8. There are several key elements to the insurance plan. Firstly, the business premises insurance will provide coverage for loss of physical assets, including equipment, inventory, and improvements/betterments. Coverage is based on replacement cost of equipment and fixtures and actual cash value on inventory. Secondly, the $2,000,000 comprehensive general liability coverage will cover liability to customers injured on the premises or off the premises when attributed to products sold by LBG. Lastly, business interruption insurance will enable LBG to continue to pay the bills if the business were to be closed down by fire or any other insured peril. The annual premium for this package would be $1,798, with a $500 deductible applying to each loss.

IMPLEMENTATION SCHEDULE

A comprehensive implementation schedule has been developed to ensure that all phases of the venture have been adequately planned. The development of the concept has been broken down into four distinct components: preliminary phase, development phase, pre-opening phase, and growth phase.

The preliminary phase took approximately seven months to complete — the bulk of which was involved with the development of the formal business plan. The development phase will commence shortly. The first steps of this phase will be to register the business name at the Companies Office ($30 fee) and to contact the Tax Services Office to arrange for a business number, a Provincial Sales Tax (PST) number and a Goods and Services Tax (GST) number. Subsequently, the business will be incorporated and the financing will be formally secured, as previously arranged in the business plan. The development phase is expected to take three months, with the majority of the time consumed by leasehold improvements and installation of equipment. This work is expected to be completed by May 30, 2008.

The pre-opening phase is primarily involved with two elements. The first element consists of the hiring of the restaurant manager, after which the menu will be finalized. Cooking and serving personnel will be hired shortly thereafter. These employees will receive a comprehensive one-week training program to primarily become familiarized with the menu and equipment. The second element of the pre-opening phase involves the extensive grand opening advertising and promotion campaign, as outlined under the marketing plan. Lastly, the long-term growth of the restaurant is outlined in the growth phase. This involves the development of a comprehensive operations manual in addition to planned openings of the second and third locations.

FINANCIAL PLAN

FUNDING REQUESTED

The major capital costs involved in launching this concept are the fixtures and equipment, installation of the fixtures and equipment, and decorating and remodeling (leasehold improvements). These costs are $61,650, $10,000, and $55,000, respectively, for a total of $126,650. LBG will be financed through a combination of debt and an equity investment. The Canadian Imperial Bank of Commerce (CIBC) has agreed to finance a large portion of this major expenditure.

For fixtures, equipment, and installation, the CIBC will use the government-guaranteed Canada Small Business Financing Act (CSBFA) program, which allows financing up to 90 per cent of the cost. The interest rate is prime plus 2.25 per cent, which includes a 1.25 per cent administration fee paid to the federal government. Payments would be monthly for a period of seven years. Security would be via a general security agreement with a specific charge over the various pieces of equipment, the assignment of fire insurance, and a personal guarantee from the owner for 25 per cent of the loan amount. Likewise, renovation expenses also qualify for the CSBFA loan. Thus, CIBC has agreed to a loan for $113,985.

The balance of the funding will come via a $47,000 equity investment by the owner, giving him 100 per cent of the common shares in the corporation. Proceeds will fund operating expenses as well as the portion of the capital investment not covered by the CSBFA loan. The owner estimates up to $100,000 in total, including the initial investment, could be made available by refinancing his home and cashing in investments. This should provide for any contingencies as well as adequate reserve funds.

The second and third locations will be added in years 3 and 5, respectively. Growth will again be financed through the CIBC, under the same terms and conditions. For planning purposes, it is assumed that equipment and renovation costs will remain approximately the same. No further equity investment will be required on the part of the owner to finance the expansion.

FINANCIAL PROJECTIONS

Detailed financial projections have been provided in several schedules with this business plan. As indicated, LBG is expected to lose $13,264 in its first year of operations, primarily due to an aggressive promotions campaign. The $300,000 estimated first-year sales figure falls short of the break-even point of $318,900. However, operations are expected to be profitable in the second year. By year 4, profitability is forecast to be more than double the industry norm of 2.4 per cent net profit (as a percentage of sales). After five years, the business will have three locations in operation and net profits (after tax) are forecast to be a healthy $63,200, with retained earnings reaching $100,000.

As indicated in the cash flow projections in Schedule 4, the initial CIBC loan and $47,000 equity investment give the operation more than adequate cash flow. This will give the business the advantage of paying down debt more aggressively and/or possibly reducing the start-up capital required for the launch of the additional locations. Dividends will not be paid to the owner initially in order to maximize funds available for growth. The current and quick ratios provide further evidence that there should be no problem meeting financial obligations going forward. If cash is drawn down to reduce debt, it will be done under the condition that the current ratio be maintained at a minimum of 2:1.

RISK FACTORS

In undertaking any new business venture, there are many risks that must be identified and contended with. LBG has identified the key risks present in the foodservices industry as well as risks associated with this particular concept:

1. **Fire or other damage forcing closure:** LBG will limit the impact of a fire by ensuring the business has comprehensive insurance protection, including adequate business premises insurance as well as business interruption insurance.

2. **Liability for illness related to foods served**: The $2,000,000 comprehensive general liability insurance coverage will ensure the business has adequate liability coverage in the event a customer becomes injured on the premises or where an illness is attributed to products sold by LBG.

3. **Delays in construction from leasehold improvements and equipment installation**: Penalty clauses will be written into the contracts to ensure that LBG is compensated for damages resulting from delays to opening.

4. **Stagnant or inadequate sales**: If sales growth proves unacceptable and/or the concept is not well received in the marketplace, the theme will be modified accordingly, based upon further assessment of the market.

5. **Difficulties with suppliers**: This is considered to be a minor risk as there are several general suppliers to the foodservice industry so that a switch could be made if warranted.

6. **Limited experience of the owner in the foodservices industry**: This is not a major concern as LBG has an experienced advisory team, a seasoned restaurant manager, and reputable suppliers. In addition, were the situation severe enough, a consultant could be hired to guide the operation through short-term difficulties. The owner will seek out training opportunities to minimize the impact of any shortcomings.

DIVESTITURE/HARVEST STRATEGY

In the event that the LBG owner desires to exit the business, every attempt will be made to sell the business as a going concern. If a sale cannot be made, however, the assets of the business will be sold off individually. There is a market for used commercial cooking equipment and if satisfactory arrangements cannot be made locally, the equipment will be sold over the Internet. The proceeds of any such sale shall be used to pay off the debt obligations of the business and any remaining funds will be paid to the owner. Furthermore, due to the prime location(s) of the restaurant(s), subletting the premises is not expected to be difficult.

The owner does feel, however, that the concept has significant upside potential. As LBG adds locations and builds market share, it is expected to attract the attention of large national chains. LBG may become a takeover target as chains look to consolidation as a means to achieve growth targets while the market for traditional fast-food menu items stagnates. The owner would give serious consideration to selling the business if it could be sold for a substantial profit.

SCHEDULE 1   **LBG REQUIRED START-UP FUNDS**

ITEM	COLUMN 1 ESTIMATE OF MONTHLY EXPENSES BASED ON SALES OF $300,000 PER YEAR	COLUMN 2 NUMBER OF MONTHS OF CASH REQUIRED TO COVER EXPENSES*	COLUMN 3 CASH REQUIRED TO START BUSINESS (COLUMN 1 X COLUMN 2)*
Salary of Manager	$2,500	2	$5,000
All Other Salaries and Wages	$4,700	3	$14,100
Rent	$2,321	3	$6,963
Advertising	$1,500	3	$4,500
Delivery Expense/Transportation	$300	3	$900
Supplies	$100	3	$300
Telephone, Fax, Internet Service	$200	3	$600
Other Utilities	$700	3	$2,100
Insurance	$150	3	$450
Taxes Including Employment Insurance	$300	4	$1,200
Principal & Interest (Loan)	$1,734	3	$5,202
Maintenance	$450	3	$1,350
Legal and Other Professional Fees	$175	3	$525
Miscellaneous	$3,650	3	$10,950

Total Cash Requirements for Monthly Recurring Expenses: (A)   **$54,140**

START-UP COSTS THAT HAVE TO BE PAID ONLY ONCE

	CASH REQUIRED TO START BUSINESS
Capital Costs	
Fixtures and Equipment	$61,650
Decorating and Remodelling	$55,000
Installation of Fixtures and Equipment	$10,000
Starting Inventory	$7,500
Soft Costs	
Deposits with Public Utilities	$2,000
Legal and Other Professional Fees	$1,200
Licences and Permits	$1,052
Advertising and Promotion for Opening	$14,705
Accounts Receivable	$0
Cash	$5,000
Miscellaneous	$5,000

Total One-Time Cash Requirements: (B)   **$163,107**

TOTAL ESTIMATED CASH REQUIRED TO START BUSINESS: (A) + (B)   **$217,247**

SCHEDULE 2 — PRO FORMA INCOME STATEMENT FOR LITE BITES GRILL
For The Year Ending June 31, 2009

	July	August	September	October	November	December	January	February	March	April	May	June	TOTAL
1. Gross Sales	30,000	28,000	24,000	20,000	20,000	22,000	24,000	24,000	24,000	26,000	28,000	30,000	300,000
2. Less: Cash Discounts	0	0	0	0	0	0	0	0	0	0	0	0	0
A. NET SALES	$30,000	$28,000	$24,000	$20,000	$20,000	$22,000	$24,000	$24,000	$24,000	$26,000	$28,000	$30,000	$300,000
Cost of Goods Sold:													
3. Beginning Inventory	7,500	7,500	7,500	7,500	7,500	7,500	7,500	7,500	7,500	7,500	7,500	7,500	7,500
4. Plus: Net Purchases	8,940	8,344	7,152	5,960	5,960	6,556	7,152	7,152	7,152	7,748	8,344	8,940	89,400
5. Total Available for Sale	16,440	15,844	14,652	13,460	13,460	14,056	14,652	14,652	14,652	15,248	15,844	16,440	96,900
6. Less: Ending Inventory	7,500	7,500	7,500	7,500	7,500	7,500	7,500	7,500	7,500	7,500	7,500	7,500	7,500
B. COST OF GOODS SOLD	$8,940	$8,344	$7,152	$5,960	$5,960	$6,556	$7,152	$7,152	$7,152	$7,748	$8,344	$8,940	$89,400
C. GROSS MARGIN	$21,060	$19,656	$16,848	$14,040	$14,040	$15,444	$16,848	$16,848	$16,848	$18,252	$19,656	$21,060	$210,600
Less: Variable Expenses													
7. Owner's Salary	0	0	0	0	0	0	0	0	0	0	0	0	0
8. Employees' Wages and Salaries	7,200	7,200	7,200	7,200	7,200	7,200	7,200	7,200	7,200	7,200	7,200	7,200	86,400
9. Supplies and Postage	100	100	100	100	100	100	100	100	100	100	100	100	1,200
10. Advertising and Promotion	14,705	70	2,070	70	70	3,720	70	70	2,070	70	70	2,070	25,125
11. Delivery Expense	360	336	288	240	240	264	288	288	288	312	336	360	3,600
12. Bad Debt Expense	0	0	0	0	0	0	0	0	0	0	0	0	0
13. Travel	0	0	0	0	0	0	0	0	0	0	0	0	0
14. Legal and Accounting Fees	1,200	0	0	0	0	0	0	0	0	0	0	2,100	3,300
15. Vehicle Expense	0	0	0	0	0	0	0	0	0	0	0	0	0
16. Maintenance Expense	540	504	432	360	360	396	432	432	432	468	504	540	5,400
17. Miscellaneous Expenses	3,960	3,696	3,168	2,640	2,640	2,904	3,168	3,168	3,168	3,432	3,696	3,960	39,600
D. TOTAL VARIABLE EXPENSES	$28,065	$11,906	$13,258	$10,610	$10,610	$14,584	$11,258	$11,258	$13,258	$11,582	$11,906	$16,330	$164,625
Less: Fixed Expenses													
18. Rent	2,321	2,321	2,321	2,321	2,321	2,321	2,321	2,321	2,321	2,321	2,321	2,321	27,852
19. Utilities (Heat, Light, Power)	700	700	700	700	700	700	700	700	700	700	700	700	8,400
20. Telephone	200	200	200	200	200	200	200	200	200	200	200	200	2,400
21. Taxes and Licenses	1,052	0	0	0	0	0	0	0	0	0	0	0	1,052
22. Depreciation	825	825	825	825	825	825	825	825	825	825	825	825	9,900
23. Interest	702	628	689	660	676	648	662	656	628	642	615	629	7,835
24. Insurance	150	150	150	150	150	150	150	150	150	150	150	150	1,800
25. Other Fixed Expenses	0	0	0	0	0	0	0	0	0	0	0	0	0
E. TOTAL FIXED EXPENSES	$5,950	$4,824	$4,885	$4,856	$4,872	$4,844	$4,858	$4,852	$4,824	$4,838	$4,811	$4,825	$59,239
F. TOTAL OPERATING EXPENSES	$34,015	$16,730	$18,143	$15,466	$15,482	$19,428	$16,116	$16,110	$18,082	$16,420	$16,717	$21,155	$223,864
G. NET OPERATING PROFIT (LOSS)	($12,955)	$2,926	($1,295)	($1,426)	($1,442)	($3,984)	$732	$738	($1,234)	$1,832	$2,939	($95)	($13,264)
H. INCOME TAXES (estimated)													$0
I. NET PROFIT (LOSS) AFTER INCOME TAX													($13,264)

SCHEDULE 3 — PRO FORMA INCOME STATEMENT FOR LITE BITES GRILL
For The Year Ending June 31

		2009	2010	2011	2012	2013
1.	Gross Sales	300,000	400,000	900,000	1,000,000	1,300,000
2.	Less: Cash Discounts	0	0	0	0	0
A.	NET SALES	$300,000	$400,000	$900,000	$1,000,000	$1,300,000
	Cost of Goods Sold:					
3.	Beginning Inventory	7,500	7,500	7,500	15,000	5,000
4.	Plus: Net Purchases	89,400	119,200	268,200	298,000	374,400
5.	Total Available for Sale	96,900	126,700	275,700	313,000	389,400
6.	Less: Ending Inventory	7,500	7,500	15,000	15,000	22,500
B.	COST OF GOODS SOLD	$89,400	$119,200	$260,700	$298,000	$366,900
C.	GROSS MARGIN	$210,600	$280,800	$639,300	$702,000	$933,100
	Less: Variable Expenses					
7.	Owner's Salary	0	0	30,000	40,000	60,000
8.	Employee's Wages and Salaries	86,400	115,200	229,200	248,000	314,400
9.	Supplies and Postage	1,200	1,200	2,400	2,400	3,600
10.	Advertising and Promotion	25,125	12,000	43,125	30,000	55,125
11.	Delivery Expense	3,600	4,800	10,800	12,000	15,600
12.	Bad Debt Expense	0	0	0	0	0
13.	Travel	0	0	0	0	0
14.	Legal and Accounting Fees	3,300	2,800	6,300	7,000	9,100
15.	Vehicle Expense	0	0	0	0	0
16.	Maintenance Expense	5,400	7,200	16,200	18,000	23,400
17.	Miscellaneous Expenses	39,600	52,800	118,800	132,000	171,600
D.	TOTAL VARIABLE EXPENSES	$164,625	$196,000	$456,825	$489,400	$652,825
	Less: Fixed Expenses					
18.	Rent	27,852	27,852	55,704	55,704	83,556
19.	Utilities (Heat, Light, Power)	8,400	12,000	27,600	31,200	39,600
20.	Telephone	2,400	2,400	4,800	4,800	7,200
21.	Taxes and Licenses	1,052	0	1,052	0	1,052
22.	Depreciation	9,900	13,200	29,700	33,000	42,900
23.	Interest	7,835	6,885	13,654	11,579	17,139
24.	Insurance	1,800	2,400	5,400	6,000	7,800
25.	Other Fixed Expeses	0	0	0	0	0
E.	TOTAL FIXED EXPENSES	$59,239	$64,737	$137,910	$142,283	$199,247
F.	TOTAL OPERATING EXPENSES	$223,864	$260,737	$594,735	$631,683	$852,072
G.	NET OPERATING PROFIT (LOSS) (G = C – F)	($13,264)	$20,063	$44,565	$70,317	$81,028
H.	LOSS CARRIED FORWARD	N/A	($13,264)	N/A	N/A	N/A
I.	INCOME TAXES (estimated)	$0	$4,414	$9,804	$15,470	$17,826
J.	NET PROFIT (LOSS) AFTER INCOME TAX	($13,264)	$15,649	$34,761	$54,847	$63,202

SCHEDULE 4 — PRO FORMA CASH FLOW FORECAST FOR LITE BITES GRILL
12-Month Cash Flow Projections

Minimum Cash Required = 5000	July	August	September	October	November	December	January	February	March	April	May	June	2008/09 TOTAL	2009/10 TOTAL	2010/11 TOTAL
Cash Flow From Operations (during month)															
1. Cash Sales	30,000	28,000	24,000	20,000	20,000	22,000	24,000	24,000	24,000	26,000	28,000	30,000	300,000	400,000	900,000
2. Payments for Credit Sales	0	0	0	0	0	0	0	0	0	0	0	0	0	0	0
3. Investment Income	0	0	0	0	0	0	0	0	0	0	0	0	0	0	0
4. Other Cash Income	0	0	0	0	0	0	0	0	0	0	0	0	0	0	0
A. TOTAL CASH FLOW ON HAND	$30,000	$28,000	$24,000	$20,000	$20,000	$22,000	$24,000	$24,000	$24,000	$26,000	$28,000	$30,000	$300,000	$400,000	$900,000
Less Expenses Paid (during month)															
5. Inventory or New Material	-16,440	-8,344	-7,152	-5,960	-5,960	-6,556	-7,152	-7,152	-7,152	-7,748	-8,344	-8,940	-96,900	-119,200	-268,200
6. Owner's Salary	0	0	0	0	0	0	0	0	0	0	0	0	0	0	-30,000
7. Employee's Wages and Salaries	-7,200	-7,200	-7,200	-7,200	-7,200	-7,200	-7,200	-7,200	-7,200	-7,200	-7,200	-7,200	-86,400	-115,200	-229,200
8. Supplies and Postage	-100	-100	-100	-100	-100	-100	-100	-100	-100	-100	-100	-100	-1,200	-1,200	-2,400
9. Advertising and Promotion	-14,705	-70	-2,070	-70	-70	-3,720	-70	-70	-2,070	-70	-70	-2,070	-25,125	-12,000	-43,125
10. Delivery Expense	-360	-336	-288	-240	-240	-264	-288	-288	-288	-312	-336	-360	-3,600	-4,800	-10,800
11. Travel	0	0	0	0	0	0	0	0	0	0	0	0	0	0	0
12. Legal and Accounting Fees	-1,200	0	0	0	0	0	0	0	0	0	0	-2,100	-3,300	-2,800	-6,300
13. Vehicle Expense	0	0	0	0	0	0	0	0	0	0	0	0	0	0	0
14. Maintenance Expense	-540	-504	-432	-360	-360	-396	-432	-432	-432	-468	-504	-540	-5,400	-7,200	-16,200
15. Rent	-2,321	-2,321	-2,321	-2,321	-2,321	-2,321	-2,321	-2,321	-2,321	-2,321	-2,321	-2,321	-27,852	-27,852	-55,704
16. Utilities	-2,700	-700	-700	-700	-700	-700	-700	-700	-700	-700	-700	-700	-10,400	-12,000	-27,600
17. Telephone	-200	-200	-200	-200	-200	-200	-200	-200	-200	-200	-200	-200	-2,400	-2,400	-4,800
18. Taxes and Licenses	-1,052	0	0	0	0	0	0	0	0	0	0	0	-1,052	-1,052	-1,052
19. Interest Payments (CIBC Loan)	-702	-628	-689	-660	-676	-648	-662	-656	-628	-642	-615	-629	-7,835	-6,884	-13,654
20. Insurance	-150	-150	-150	-150	-150	-150	-150	-150	-150	-150	-150	-150	-1,800	-2,400	-5,400
21. Other Cash Expenses	-3,960	-3,696	-3,168	-2,640	-2,640	-2,904	-3,168	-3,168	-3,168	-3,432	-3,696	-3,960	-39,600	-52,800	-118,800
B. TOTAL EXPENDITURES	($51,630)	($24,249)	($24,470)	($20,601)	($20,617)	($25,159)	($22,443)	($22,437)	($24,409)	($23,343)	($24,236)	($29,270)	($312,864)	($366,736)	($833,235)
Capital															
Purchase of Fixed Assets	-126,650	0	0	0	0	0	0	0	0	0	0	0	-126,650	-126,650	0
Sale of Fixed Assets	0	0	0	0	0	0	0	0	0	0	0	0	0	0	0
C. CHANGE IN CASH FROM PURCHASE OR SALE OF ASSETS	($126,650)	$0	$0	$0	$0	$0	$0	$0	$0	$0	$0	$0	($126,650)	($126,650)	$0
Financing															
Payment of Principal of Loan	-1,032	-1,106	-1,046	-1,074	-1,059	-1,087	-1,072	-1,078	-1,106	-1,092	-1,119	-1,106	-12,977	-13,928	-27,970
Inflow of Cash From Bank Loan	113,985	0	0	0	0	0	0	0	0	0	0	0	113,985	113,985	0
Issuance of Equity Positions	47,000	0	0	0	0	0	0	0	0	0	0	0	47,000	0	0
Repurchase of Outstanding Equity	0	0	0	0	0	0	0	0	0	0	0	0	0	0	0
D. CHANGE IN CASH FROM FINANCING	$159,953	($1,106)	($1,046)	($1,074)	($1,059)	($1,087)	($1,072)	($1,078)	($1,106)	($1,092)	($1,119)	($1,106)	$148,008	$100,057	($27,970)
E. INCREASE (DECREASE) IN CASH	$11,673	$2,645	($1,516)	($1,675)	($1,676)	($4,246)	$485	$485	($1,515)	$1,565	$2,645	($376)	$8,494	$6,671	$38,795
F. CASH AT BEGINNING OF PERIOD	$0	$11,673	$14,318	$12,802	$11,127	$9,451	$5,205	$5,690	$6,175	$4,660	$6,225	$8,870	$0	$8,494	$15,165
G. CASH AT END OF PERIOD	$11,673	$14,318	$12,802	$11,127	$9,451	$5,205	$5,690	$6,175	$4,660	$6,225	$8,870	$8,494	$8,494	$15,165	$53,960
MEET MINIMUM CASH BALANCE	Acceptable	Acceptable	Acceptable	Acceptable	Acceptable	Acceptable	Acceptable	Acceptable	Acceptable	Acceptable	Acceptable	Acceptable	Acceptable	Acceptable	Acceptable

SCHEDULE 5 — PRO FORMA BALANCE SHEET FOR LITE BITES GRILL

	OPENING	JUNE 31/09	JUNE 31/10	JUNE 31/11
ASSETS				
Current Assets:				
1. Cash	26,835	8,494	15,165	53,960
2. Accounts Receivable	0	0	0	0
3. Inventory	7,500	7,500	7,500	15,000
4. Other Current Assets	0	2,000	2,000	2,000
A. TOTAL CURRENT ASSETS	**$34,335**	**$17,994**	**$24,665**	**$70,960**
Fixed Assets:				
5. Land and Buildings	0	0	0	0
less depreciation	0	0	0	0
6. Furniture and Fixtures	65,000	65,000	130,000	130,000
less depreciation	0	0	0	-29,700
7. Equipment	61,650	61,650	123,300	123,300
less depreciation	0	0	0	0
8. Trucks and Automobiles	0	0	0	0
less depreciation	0	0	-13,200	-13,200
9. Other Fixed Assets	0	0	0	0
less depreciation	0	-9,900	-9,900	-9,900
B. TOTAL FIXED ASSETS	**$126,650**	**$116,750**	**$230,200**	**$200,500**
C. TOTAL ASSETS	**$160,985**	**$134,744**	**$254,865**	**$271,460**
LIABILITIES				
Current Liabilities: (due within 12 months)				
10. Accounts Payable	0	0	0	0
11. Bank Loans / Other Loans	12,977	13,928	27,970	30,045
12. Taxes Owed	0	0	0	0
D. TOTAL CURRENT LIABILITIES	**$12,977**	**$13,928**	**$27,970**	**$30,045**
Long-term Liabilities:				
13. Notes Payable (due after one year)	101,008	87,080	173,095	143,050
14. Other Long-term Liabilities	0	0	0	0
E. TOTAL LONG-TERM LIABILITIES	**$101,008**	**$87,080**	**$173,095**	**$143,050**
F. TOTAL LIABILITIES	**$113,985**	**$101,008**	**$201,065**	**$173,095**
NET WORTH (Capital)				
SHARE CAPITAL				
Common Shares	47,000	47,000	33,736	53,800
Preferred Shares	0	0	0	0
RETAINED EARNINGS	0	-13,264	20,064	44,565
G. TOTAL NET WORTH	**$47,000**	**$33,736**	**$53,800**	**$98,365**
H. TOTAL LIABILITIES AND NET WORTH	**$160,985**	**$134,744**	**$254,865**	**$271,460**
	BALANCED	BALANCED	BALANCED	BALANCED

SCHEDULE 6 FINANCIAL RATIOS FOR LITE BITES GRILL

		End of Year 1	End of Year 2	End of Year 3
1. Gross Margin/Sales	= $\dfrac{\text{Gross Profit}}{\text{Net Sales}}$	$\dfrac{\$210,600}{\$300,000}$ 0.70	$\dfrac{\$280,800}{\$400,000}$ 0.70	$\dfrac{\$639,300}{\$900,000}$ 0.71
2. Current Ratio	= $\dfrac{\text{Current Assets}}{\text{Current Liabilities}}$	$\dfrac{\$17,994}{\$13,928}$ 1.29	$\dfrac{\$24,665}{\$27,970}$ 0.88	$\dfrac{\$70,960}{\$30,045}$ 2.36
3. Quick Ratio	= $\dfrac{\text{Current Assets - Inventories}}{\text{Current Liabilities}}$	$\dfrac{\$10,494}{\$13,928}$ 0.75	$\dfrac{\$17,165}{\$27,970}$ 0.61	$\dfrac{\$55,960}{\$30,045}$ 1.86
4. Net Profit/Sales	= $\dfrac{\text{Net Income (After Tax)}}{\text{Net Sales}}$	$\dfrac{(\$13,264)}{\$300,000}$ -0.04	$\dfrac{\$15,649}{\$400,000}$ 0.04	$\dfrac{\$34,761}{\$900,000}$ 0.04
5. Net Profit/Net Worth	= $\dfrac{\text{Net Profit}}{\text{Net Worth}}$	$\dfrac{(\$13,264)}{\$33,736}$ -0.39	$\dfrac{\$15,649}{\$53,800}$ 0.29	$\dfrac{\$34,761}{\$98,365}$ 0.35
6. Sales/Net Worth	= $\dfrac{\text{Net Sales}}{\text{Net Worth}}$	$\dfrac{\$300,000}{\$33,736}$ 8.89	$\dfrac{\$400,000}{\$53,800}$ 7.43	$\dfrac{\$900,000}{\$98,365}$ 9.15
7. Fixed Assets/Net Worth	= $\dfrac{\text{Fixed Assets}}{\text{Net Worth}}$	$\dfrac{\$116,750}{\$33,736}$ 3.46	$\dfrac{\$230,200}{\$53,800}$ 4.28	$\dfrac{\$200,500}{\$98,365}$ 2.04
8. Current Liabilities/Net Worth	= $\dfrac{\text{Current Liabilities}}{\text{Net Worth}}$	$\dfrac{\$13,928}{\$33,736}$ 0.41	$\dfrac{\$27,970}{\$53,800}$ 0.52	$\dfrac{\$30,045}{\$98,365}$ 0.31
9. Total Liabilities/Net Worth	= $\dfrac{\text{Total Liabilities}}{\text{Net Worth}}$	$\dfrac{\$101,008}{\$33,736}$ 2.99	$\dfrac{\$201,065}{\$53,800}$ 3.74	$\dfrac{\$173,095}{\$98,365}$ 1.76
10. Debt/Net Worth	= $\dfrac{\text{Total Outstanding Debt}}{\text{Net Worth}}$	$\dfrac{\$87,080}{\$33,736}$ 2.58	$\dfrac{\$201,065}{\$53,800}$ 3.74	$\dfrac{\$173,095}{\$98,365}$ 1.76
11. Return On Assets	= $\dfrac{\text{Net Income (After Tax)}}{\text{Total Assets}}$	$\dfrac{(\$13,264)}{\$134,744}$ -0.10	$\dfrac{\$15,649}{\$254,865}$ 0.06	$\dfrac{\$34,761}{\$271,460}$ 0.13

SCHEDULE 7   BREAK-EVEN POINT FOR FIRST YEAR

OPERATING EXPENSES

Owner's Salary	0
Employees' Wages	86,400
Supplies and Postage	1,200
Advert. and Promotion	25,125
Delivery Expense	3,600
Bad Debt Allowance	0
Travel	0
Professional Fees	3,300
Vehicle Expense	0
Maintenance Expense	5,400
Other Variable Expenses	39,600
Rent	27,852
Utilities	8,400
Telephone	2,400
Taxes & Licences	1,052
Depreciation	9,900
Interest	7,835
Insurance	1,800
Other Fixed Expenses	0
TOTAL OPERATING EXPENSES	**$223,864**

$$\text{CONTRIBUTION MARGIN} = \frac{\text{Gross Margin}}{\text{Net Sales}} = 70.20\%$$

$$\text{BREAK-EVEN POINT (\$Sales)} = \frac{\text{Total Operating Expenses}}{\text{Contribution Margin}}$$

$$\$318,894.59$$

BIBLIOGRAPHY

1. **Welcome to Health Express USA, Inc.**
   www.hexs.com/info/about.html

2. **Canadian Restaurant and Foodservices Association**
   www.crfa.ca/research/foodservicetrends/research_foodservicetrends_evolutionofmealtime.htm

3. **Fast Food Gets Healthy Too**
   www.cnn.com/2002/HEALTH/diet.fitness/09/23/healthy.fast.food.ap/

4. **Canadian Restaurant and Foodservices Association**
   www.crfa.ca/research/research_dinersoptforlighterfare.htm

5. **Burgers Go Green**
   www.chainleader.com/archive/1101/1101segments.html

6. **The Vegetarian Resource Group, Baltimore, Md.**
   www.vrg.org/nutshell/poll2000.htm

7. **Statistics Canada**
   www.statcan.ca/english/Pgdb/famil27g.htm

8. **City of Winnipeg Census Data**
   www.city.winnipeg.mb.ca/census2006/data/05-00.pdf

9. **Fast Food for Fitness Fans**
   www.inc.com/magazine/20011101/23597.html

10. **Canada Business Service Centre, Sales Forecasting for a New Business**
    www.cbsc.org/osbw/salefore.html#new

11. **Good, Walter S.** *Building a Dream: A Canadian Guide to Starting Your Own Business,* 6th edition, Toronto: McGraw-Hill Ryerson Ltd., 2005, p. 151.

12. **Industry Canada SME Benchmarking Tool**
    www.ic.gc.ca/eic/site/pp-pp.nsf/eng/home

13. **Newspaper Audience Databank**
    www.nadbank.com

14. **SUBWAY Restaurants**
    www.subway.com

APPENDICES

Appendix 1   Preliminary Sales Forecast

Appendix 2   Marketing Budget for First Year

Appendix 3   Facility Location and Site Plan

Appendix 4   Market Size of First Restaurant Location

Appendix 5   Detailed Equipment Listing

Appendix 6   Staffing Schedule

Appendix 7   Resumé: Leonard Burgess

Appendix 8   Insurance Proposal

APPENDIX 1 **PRELIMINARY SALES FORECAST**

	YEAR ONE	YEAR TWO	YEAR THREE
January	$30,000		
February	$28,000		
March	$24,000	$90,000 (Q1)	$120,000 (Q1)
April	$20,000		
May	$20,000		
June	$22,000	$90,000 (Q2)	$140,000 (Q2)
July	$24,000		
August	$24,000		
September	$24,000	$110,000 (Q3)	$160,000 (Q3)
October	$26,000		
November	$28,000		
December	$30,000	$110,000 (Q4)	$180,000 (Q4)
TOTAL	**$300,000**	**$400,000**	**$600,000**

APPENDIX 2 **MARKETING BUDGET FOR FIRST YEAR**

Selling (direct costs)

- Sales salaries for personal selling	$800	(80 hrs @ $10/hr)
- Printing menus/brochures/coupons	$250	

Advertising

- Newspaper sampling campaign	$1,500	
- Ongoing newspaper advertising	$9,650	
- Radio promotion (Grand opening)	$2,500	
- Billboard (one month)	$4,350	

Sales promotions (coupons)

Sales promotions (coupons)	$2,500	(Coupons)
	$200	(Blu-Ray player — draw)

Web site

Web site	$2,500	(Development)
	$600	(Maintenance)
	$35	(Domain name)
	$240	(Hosting)

TOTAL MARKETING BUDGET (YEAR 1)	**$25,125**	

APPENDIX 3 FACILITY LOCATION AND SITE PLAN

THE BRICK PLAZA
1045 ST. JAMES STREET
IN WINNIPEG'S MOST POWERFUL SHOPPING AREA

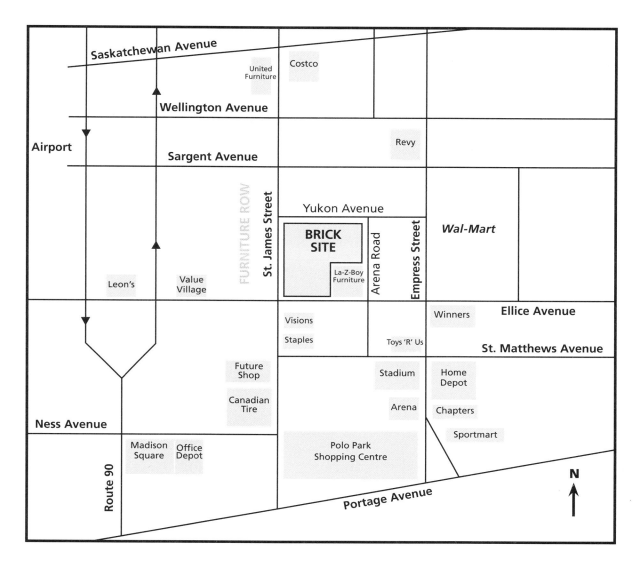

HIGH TRAFFIC:

- Ellice Avenue & St. James Street has one of the busiest traffic counts in Winnipeg
- superior access and egress

RENT: $12 sq. ft., net
ADDITIONAL RENT: $4.06 sq. ft. + Management Fees

HIGH VISIBILITY:

- signage offering maximum exposure
- excellent, well-lit parking lot

SPACE AVAILABLE:

- 1,913 sq. ft.

(Site plan on next page)

Areas and sizes are approximate. Reasonable efforts have been made to ensure that the information contained herein is accurate. All details are subject to final confirmations by all interested parties.

continued

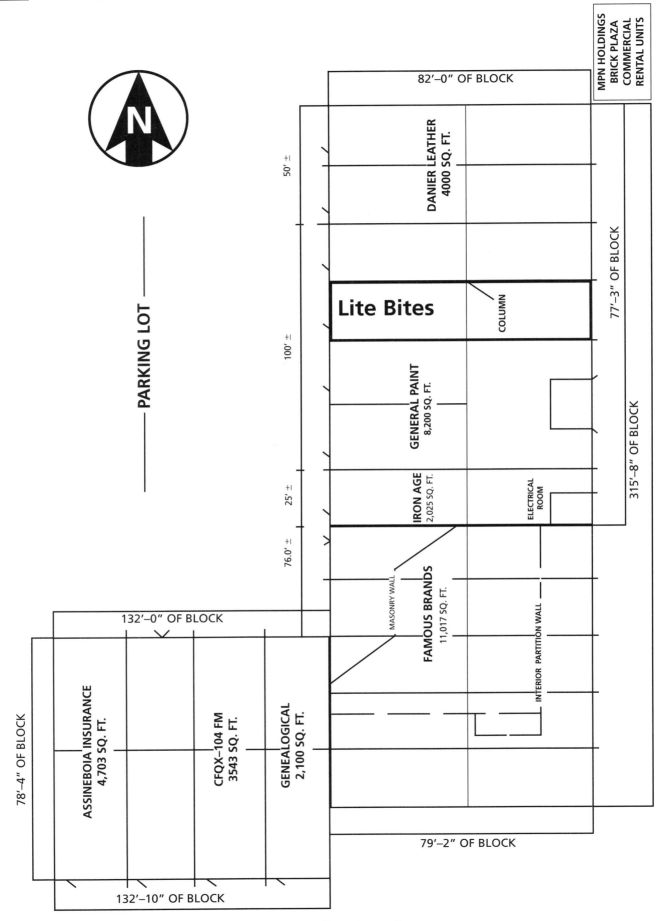

MARKET SIZE OF FIRST RESTAURANT LOCATION

	POPULATION
St. James (Age 25–54)	15,295
River Heights (Age 25–54)	17,855
Fort Garry (Age 25–54)	20,995
Fort Rouge (Age 25–54)	19,885
Total (Age 25–54)	74,030
19.1% University Educated	*14,139*
Total Population over 15 (in above areas)	112,100
Vegetarian market (2.5%)	***2,803***
TOTAL MARKET	**16,942**

APPENDIX 5 DETAILED EQUIPMENT LISTING

951 Erin Street
Winnipeg, MB R3G 2W8

RUSSELL
FOOD EQUIPMENT LTD.

To: Bill Benson   Fax: 1 page
From: Russell Food Equipment Ltd.   Date: December 18, 2007

( ) Urgent   (X) For Review   ( ) Please Comment   ( ) Please Reply   ( ) Please Recycle

Hi Bill:

I have updated your budget quote for your business plan. Please note changes made.

1) 12" Electric Slicer added.
2) Delivery and set in place includes:
    - Set up and testing of Walk-in Cooler/Freezer
    - Set up of all storage shelving
    - Mounting menu signs
3) Electrical and plumbing connections by others
    - This part of your costing will vary by building depending on what plumbing and electrical is existing.
    - When you have selected a building location we take into consideration existing electrical and plumbing supply in our overall design.

I will mail out an original quote for your presentation.

Best wishes with your proposal and have a good holiday season.

RUSSELL FOOD EQUIPMENT LTD.

951 Erin Street
Winnipeg, MB R3G 2W8

RUSSELL
FOOD EQUIPMENT LTD.

To: **Bill Benson**	**Fax: 1 page**
From: **Russell Food Equipment Ltd.**	**Date: December 16, 2007**

( ) **Urgent**   (X) **For Review**   ( ) **Please Comment**   ( ) **Please Reply**   ( ) **Please Recycle**

Hi Bill:

Further to your request for quotation we are pleased to submit the following.

1 only	3 Compartment Sink	2000.00
1 only	Undercounter Dishwasher	5000.00 optional
1 only	2 Door Reach-In Cooler	2400.00
1 only	Walk-in Cooler/Freezer Combo c/w Shelving	15,000.00
2 only	Soup Warmers	600.00
2 only	Pannini Grills	2000.00
1 only	Electric Convection Oven	7000.00
1 only	Microwave Oven	600.00
1 only	Electric Range	4400.00
1 only	Refrigerated Prep Table	4000.00
1 only	4 Slice Toaster	1000.00
1 only	Refrigerated Display Case	3500.00
1 lot	Tables and Chairs	150.00/person
1 only	12" Electric Slicer	1000.00
1 lot	Menu Signage	2000.00
1 lot	Smallwares	2000.00
1 lot	Millwork	3000.00
1 lot	Dry Storage Shelving	1000.00
1 only	Delivery and Set in Place	2000.00

Electrical and Plumbing Connections by others.

Please allow 4–6 weeks for delivery.

The above pricing is for budget purposes only, f.o.b. Winnipeg and all taxes are extra. Trusting this information will be helpful in developing your business plan. Overall equipment specified will depend on building layout, budget, and specific menu items.

Our consultant services are provided on a no-charge basis to our clients when we are handling the project. Where tendering is desirable or mandatory, we can provide drawings and specifications for equitable tendering at modest fees and have many advantages to offer over the independent consultant that we would be glad to review with you.

Food services require considerable investment. Professional planning can avoid pitfalls and give you a well-planned food facility that will go a long way toward ensuring an efficient and profitable operation.

RUSSELL FOOD EQUIPMENT LTD.

APPENDIX 6 · STAFFING SCHEDULE

Shift Time	# Employees Mon. – Fri.	# Employees Sat./Sun.	Hrs./Shift	Total hrs./week
10:30 a.m.–11:30 a.m.	1	2	1	9
11:30 a.m.–1:00 p.m.	3	3	1.5	31.5
1:00 p.m.–4:00 p.m.	1	2	3	27
4:00 p.m.–5:00 p.m.	2	2	1	14
5:00 p.m.–6:30 p.m.	3	3	1.5	31.5
6:30 p.m.–8:00 p.m.	1	2	1.5	13.5
			TOTAL:	**126.5 HRS./WEEK** (506 hrs./month)

APPENDIX 7 | RESUMÉ: LEONARD T. BURGESS

LEONARD T. BURGESS   RESUMÉ

Calgary, AB T2Z 1M3
Telephone: 555-2971

EDUCATION

1985–1990	High School Diploma: John Taylor H.S., Winnipeg, MB
1988–2000	Business Administration
	Red River Community College, Winnipeg, MB

WORK EXPERIENCE

2006–2007 — **General Manager**, *ABC Restaurant*, Calgary, AB
Responsibilities included: food & labour cost control, purchasing, maintenance, repairs, payroll, supervision, observation of sanitation standards, customer service, staff selection, computerized POS system management

1998–2006 — **Restaurant Manager**, *Denny's Restaurant*, Calgary, AB
Responsibilities included: food & labour cost control, purchasing, maintenance, repairs, payroll, supervision, observation of sanitation standards, customer service, staff selection

1993–1998 — **Head Cook**, *Boyd's Seafood Kitchen*, Calgary, AB
Responsibilities included: portion control, preparation of homemade chowders, general operation of kitchen

1992–1993 — **Installation Supervisor**, *Pacific Warehouse Ltd.* Calgary, AB
Responsibilities Included: supervising job sites and crew, ensuring timely completion of installation of industrial shelving units

1988–1992 — **Evening Supervisor,** *Jim's Fish & Chips Restaurant*, Winnipeg, MB
Responsibilities included: purchasing, customer service, balance cash out, supervision, cooking as necessary

1988–1992 — **Owner/Manager,** *Jim's Seafood Shop* (Retail Fish Market), Winnipeg, MB
Responsibilities included: purchasing, customer service, payroll, supervision, staff selection, marketing, cost control.

INTERESTS

Fishing, big game hunting, cross-country skiing, hockey, model building

References available upon request.

BILL BENSON

O/A

BENSON'S HEALTH FOOD BAR

INSURANCE PROPOSAL

MILNCO INSURANCE
200 – 207 Donald Street
Winnipeg, MB R3C 1M5

MILNCO INSURANCE

Ste. 200 – 207 Donald St., Winnipeg, MB R3C 1M5

Mr. Bill Benson
o/a Benson's Health Food Bar

PROPERTY INSURANCE

Coverage on all real and personal property of the Insured or for which they may be held responsible against the perils as set out below and in the amounts specified. Property is insured to 100% of value in recognition of the possibility of a total loss.

Equipment (including improvements and betterments)		$	125,000
Stock		$	7,500
Business Interruption – Profits Form		$	165,000
Auditors' Fees		$	5,000
Sign		$	2,000
Crime – Broad Form Money & Securities	Inside	$	2,000
	Outside	$	2,000
Comprehensive General Liability			
Limit of Insurance	Inclusive		$1,000,000
Basis of coverage – will pay those			
sums that the insured becomes legally			
obligated to pay as compensatory damages			
because of bodily injury or property damage			
to which this insurance applies.			

Includes the following:

Products/Completed Operations
Premises/Operations
Personal Injury – includes illegal trespass and wrongful eviction, libel, and slander
Employees as additional insureds
Blanket Contractual (all written contracts)
Contingent Employers
Non-Owned Automobile
Medical Payments - $2,500 per person/$25,000 per accident (to cover all reasonable medical expenses for bodily injury to any persons arising out of your operation or condition on your premises subject to the terms, conditions and exclusions of the policy wording.)

Tenants Legal Liability – *Comprehension General Liability* will not pay for damage to the portion of the building leased to you. Coverage against this contingency is provided by means of a *Tenants Fire Legal Liability* insurance. Limit - $150,000.

continued

<u>Terms & Conditions:</u>

<u>PERILS INSURED</u>: Coverage is against "All Risks of Direct Physical Damage or Loss" subject to the terms, conditions and exclusions of the policy wording.

Deductible of $500 applies to each loss

Basis of Loss Settlement – Replacement Cost on Equipment and Fixtures and Actual Cash Value on Stock.

Co-Insurance Condition – 90% (equipment and fixtures must be insured for at least 90% of the replacement cost values).

Business Interruption – Limit is based on projected sales of $300,000 plus cost of sales of approximately 33% and ordinary payroll of approximately $35,000.

Boiler & Machinery coverage covers an accident or loss to property resulting from the explosion of pressure vessels or from accidental breakdown including miscellaneous electrical apparatus, switch panels and transformers.

Limit	**$135,000**
Deductible	**$500**

Includes consequential loss to stock for an amount of $5,000 (this would cover spoilage of food due to a mechanical or electrical breakdown of the refrigerator units).

PREMIUM SCHEDULE

Equipment		$ 325
Stock		$ 20
Business Income – Profits		$ 396
Sign		$ 5
Broad Form Money & Securities		$ 100
Commercial General Liability -	**$1,000,000** Limit	$ 500
	$2,000,000 Limit	$ 650
Tenants Legal Liability		$ 52
Boiler & Machinery		$ 250

Building a Dream — Eighth Edition

STAGE ONE: WHAT IS ENTREPRENEURSHIP

www.gemconsortium.org   Global Entrepreneurship Monitor, Research, Datasets, Publications

www.ic.gc.ca/eic/site/sbrp-rppe.nsf/eng/h_rd02440.html   Key Small Business Statistics

www.hugelsteel.com   Murray Hugel's company, Huge L Steel Inc.

www.investorwords.com   The biggest, best investing glossary on the web.

www.canadabusiness.ab.ca/index.php/operations/160-failure-factors-thirteen-common-causes-of-business-failure-   Thirteen Common Causes of Business Failure by Deborah Barrie

www.sbinfocanada.about.com/   About Small Business: Canada

www.canadabusiness.ca/eng/88/1194/   Canada Business Services for Entrepreneurs and your link to the Canada Business Service Centre in your province or territory

www.ic.gc.ca/eic/site/ic1.nsf/eng/home   Industry Canada's web site

www.canadaone.ca/   Canada's small business information source

www.canadianbusiness.com/entrepreneur/index.jsp?utm_source=profitguide.com&utm_medium=referral   Link to PROFIT magazine with articles, etc. of interest to Canadian entrepreneurs

www.enterprisemag.com/Default.aspx   Website of Enterprise Magazine

www.entrepreneur.com   Entrepreneur Magazine

www.inc.com   Inc.com

STAGE TWO: EXPLORING NEW BUSINESS IDEAS AND OPPORTUNITIES

www.ezinearticles.com/?Entrepreneurs —Top-10Essential-Entrepreneurial-Traits&id=531367   Basile, H. Entrepreneurs — Top 10 Essential Entrepreneurial Traits

www.entleap.com/   The more comprehensive and detailed version of the EAO business attitudes survey. Entrepreneurial Assessment Profile

www.seppsfoods.com   Sepp's Gourmet Foods Ltd.

www.cactusclubcafe.com/   The Cactus Club Cafe — Every Customer Leaves Happy

www.econsumer.equifax.ca/index_en.html   The consumer credit reporting agency Equifax Canada Inc.

www.transunion.ca/ca/home_en.page   The consumer credit reporting agency TransUnion Canada

www.freethechildren.com/aboutus/history.php   Jeff Skoll's foundation that supports the efforts of social entrepreneurs

www.ladybugfoundation.ca/   Hannah Taylor's Ladybug Foundation to help put an end to homelessness

www.winnipegfreepress.com/local/hannah-gets-a-helping-hand-69948307.html   Cohen, e. Hannah Gets a Helping Hand

www.aimpersonnel.ca/   The AIM Group — Worldwide Provision of Recruitment and Personnel

www.tlcvision.com/   TLC Laser Eye Centres

www.canadianbusiness.com/profit_magazine/article.jsp?content=20031103_152750_3588&page=2   Vamvakas, E. Goodwill Hunting

www.loblaw.ca/en/comm_csr.html   Loblaw Targets and Achievements

www.yesmontreal.ca/yes.php?section=entrepreneurship/tools/quiz   Interactive business start-up quiz hosted by Youth Employment Services (YES) Montreal

www.canadianbusiness.com/entrepreneur/quiz/article.jsp?content=20060828_090533_5312   Home of the National Entrepreneurship Test developed by PROFIT magazine

www.bdc.ca/EN/advice_centre/tools/entrepreneurial_self_assessment/Pages/entrepreneurial_self_assessment.aspx   The Business Development Bank of Canada's entrepreneurial self-assessment questionnaire

www.bizmove.com/other/quiz.htm   The Entrepreneur Test

STAGE THREE: EXPLORING NEW IDEAS AND OPPORTUNITIES

www.gumdropsonline.com   Shanda Jerrett's retail and internet-based wet weather boutique

www.youtube.com/watch?v=zy6cHuXa8Hs   Bryan Shopka's physiotherapy clinic

www.hooplaclothing.com   Jessica Williamson's high quality, Canadian activewear clothing store

www.bioped.com   Crystal Kaufman's Bioped franchise

www.ggtelecom.ca   Yan and Sebastian Gagnon's cameras, motion detectors and receivers

www.brooklynwarehouse.ca   George Christakos' casual fine dining restaurant.

www.cybf.ca/awards/2009/entrepeneur.htm   Video submissions, profiles, and websites of the recipients of the 2009 Canadian Youth Business Foundation (CYBF) Chairman's Awards

www.cameradepartment.tv/   Camera Department which specialises in video services and equipment rentals to commercial clients

www.dessertlady.ca/   Mandy Kan, "the Dessert Lady" and her high quality bakery in the Yorkville district of Toronto

www.trackitback.com/portal/ Jason Wagner's website for his Trackitback loss recovery service identification labels and ID tags

www.theglobeandmail.com/ The Globe and Mail daily newspaper

www.theglobeandmail.com/report-on-business/your-business/ The Globe and Mail Report on Business Your Business section

http://nationalpost.com/home/index.html/ The National Post daily newspaper

https://order.wsj.com/sub/f2 The Wall Street Journal daily newspaper

www.canadianbusiness.com/entrepreneur/quiz/article.jsp?content=20060828_090533_5312 Canadian Business online magazine

www.canadianbusiness.com/entrepreneur/index.jsp?utm_source=profitguide.com&utm_medium=referral PROFIT magazine

www.financialpost.com/small-business/index.html Financial Post Small Business

www.inc.com/ INC Magazine

www.entrepreneur.com/ Entrepreneur Magazine

www.money.cnn.com/magazines/fortune/ Fortune Magazine

www.tellusaboutus.com Kirby and Tyler Gompf's customer survey company Tell Us About Us (TUAU)

www.srds.com/portal/servlet/LoginServlet Standard Rates and Data Service listing of available trade publications in the US

www.cardonline.ca or www.cardmedia.com/public/home.jsf Canadian Advertising Rates and Data listing of rates for virtually all mass media advertising vehicles available in Canada

www.inventnet.com/tradeshows.html The Inventor's Network which provides a list of the major inventor's shows held in the US

www.gale.cengage.com/about/ Gale®, part of Cengage Learning, is a world leader in e-research and educational publishing for libraries, schools and businesses. Best known for its accurate and authoritative reference content as well as its intelligent organization of full-text magazine and newspaper articles, the company creates and maintains more than 600 databases that are published online, in print, as eBooks and in microform. Publishers of Trade Shows Worldwide and Newsletters in Print.

www.tradeshowcalendar.globalsources.com/TRADE-SHOW/ALL-TRADE-SHOWS.HTM Global Sources Trade Show Centre

www.allconferences.com/ A comprehensive directory focusing on conferences, conventions, tradeshows, and work shops across a range of industries.

www.eventseye.com/ A searchable international database of 8 207 Trade Shows, Exhibitions and Conferences coming from 2 027 Fairs Organizers, with a total of 14 799 event's dates. New Trade Shows & Exhibitions are added in every month

www.flintbox.com/ An intellectual property matchmaking system linking industry, researchers, and others from over 100 countries around the world.

www.brevets-patents.ic.gc.ca/opic-cipo/cpd/eng/introduction.html The Canadian Patents Database administered by the Canadian Intellectual Property Office as a vehicle for inventors and entrepreneurs to get together.

www.canadabusiness.ca/eng/ Business services for entrepreneurs. Starting a business, growth and innovation, grants and finances, taxes & GST, human resources, importing, exporting, etc.

www.mindtools.com/index.html Leadership skills, problem solving, project planning, creative thinking, decision making. Essential skills for an excellent career.

www.notabletv.com Julian Brass' NotableTV

www.sbinfocanada.about.com/cs/bestpractices/a/aa122902a_htm Best Business Opportunities for 2010

www.cira.ca Canadian Internet Registration Authority

www.sbinfocanada.about.com/od/onlinebusiness/a/onlinebizmodels.htm Ward, s. Online Business Models, Part 1: How to Make Money Online

www.canadabusiness.ca/eng/145/148 E-Business

www.ic.gc.ca/eic/site/ee-ef.nsf/eng/home Ebiz.enable

www.ontario.ca/en/business/STEL02_039938 E-Business Info-Guide

www.canadabusiness.ca/eng/145/148/ E-Business

www.sbinfocanada.about.com/lr/starting_an_online_business/201275/4/ About.com: Small Business: Canada

www.ic.gc.ca Industry Canada Website

www.innovationcentre.ca Canadian Innovation Centre

STAGE FOUR: BUYING A BUSINESS

www.sme.ic.gc.ca SME Benchmarking Tool

www.discoveryhut.com The Discovery Hut

www.dnb.ca/default.htm Dun & Bradstreet: Financial ratios for firms.

www.rmahq.org/RMA/ Risk Management Association: Financial ratios for firms.

www.cbiz.com/valuationgroup/ CBIZ Valuation. Business valuation.

www.businessbookpress.com/articles/article144.htm Financing the Business Acquisition.

www.canadaone.com/tools/buy_a_biz/index.html A Comprehensive Guide to Buying a Business in Canada

www.entrepreneurs.about.com/od/buyingabusiness/a/buyingabusiness_2.html Buying a Business: The Safer Alternative

www.canadabusiness.ca/eng/125/140/ Buying a Business

www.v1.theglobeandmail.com/v5/content/calculator-smallbiz/calculate/?what=BusinessValuation What's Your Business Worth?

www.businessbookpress.com/articles/article144.htm Financing the Business Acquisition

www.harryrosen.com   Harry Rosen Men's Wear
www.cafenational.org   Canadian Association of Family Enterprise.
www.bdc.ca/en/advice_centre/articles/Pages/acquisition_business_evaluate.aspx   How to evaluate a proposed business acquisition.
www.canadaone.com/tools/buy_a_biz/section3e.html   A Comprehensive Guide to Buying a Business in Canada

SECTION FIVE

www.pizzapizza.ca   Pizza Pizza.
www.1800gotjunk.com/   1-800-GOT-JUNK
www.entrepreneur.com   Entrepreneur, 2010 Franchise 500
www.subway.com   Subway
www.mcdonalds.com   McDonald's
www.7-eleven.com   7-Eleven Inc.
www.hamptoninn1.hilton.com/   Hampton Inn
www.supercuts.com   Supercuts
www.hrblock.com   H & R Block
www.dunkindonuts.com   Dunkin' Donuts
www.janiking.com   Jani-King
www.servpro.com   Servpro
www.ampm.com   ampm Mini Market
www.enviromasters.com   Enviro Masters Lawn Care
www.quiznos.com/   Quizno's Classic Subs
www.kegsteakhouse.com/en/   The Keg Steakhouse and Bar
www.bostonpizza.com   Boston Pizza
www.thrifty.com   Dollar Thrifty Rent-a-Car
www.dollarstores.com   Great Canadian Dollar Store
www.mollymaid.com   Molly Maid Int.
www.dairyqueen.com   Dairy Queen Canada
www.wecare.ca   We Care Home Health Services
www.midas.com   Midas Muffler Shop
www.dominos.com   Domino's Pizza
www.secondcup.com   Second Cup Coffee Co.
www.timhortons.com   Tim Hortons
www.kwikkopy.ca   Kwick Kopy Printing
www.cfa.ca/Publications_Research/FranchiseCanada/directory.aspx   Franchise Canada Magazine Directory
www.pointts.com   Pointts Defence Services
www.flamingoafriend.com   Flamingo a Friend
www.itsjustlunch.com   It's Just Lunch
www.crockadoodle.com   Crock a Doodle
www.jupitergrass.com   Jupiter
www.nerdforce.ca   Nerd Force
www.swisschalet.ca   Swiss Chalet
www.thebrick.com   The Brick Warehouse
www.thesource.ca   The Source
www.winekitz.com   Wine Kitz
www.janiking.ca   Jani-King
www.mollymaid.ca   Molly Maid
www.cfa.ca   Canadian Franchise Association
www.joeys.ca/franchising/startup_costs.vhtml   Costs to open a Joey's Only Seafood Restaurant
www.franchise.org/franchiseesecondary.aspx?id=10002&LangType=1033   Consumer Guide to Buying a Franchise
www.iFranchisegroup.com   The iFranchise Group Franchise Consultants
www.canadabusiness.ca/eng/guide/2014/   Franchising. Investing in an already successful franchise concept may be a great choice for your new business venture.
www.frannet.com   Fran Net Franchise Experts
www.bulldoginteractivefitness.com   Bulldog Interactive Fitness
www.franchise.org/franchiseesecondary.aspx?amp;langtype=1033&id=10002   International Franchise Association
www.franchise-conxions.com   Franchise Conxions
www.canada.franchiseopportunities.com/   Canadian Franchise Opportunities

STAGE SIX: ORGANIZING YOUR BUSINESS

www.pairowoodies.com   PairoWoodies Publishing

www.bizpal.ca   BizPalbusiness permit and licensing

www.wovenfare.com   Wovenfare International Inc.

www.canadabusiness.ca/eng   A Guide to Setting up Your Business in Canada

www.canadaone.com/tools/provincial_links.html   Provincial links for starting your own business.

www.canadabusiness.ca/eng/guide/page/2550/2552/   Choosing a business structure.

www.canadaone.com/ezine/oct03/checklist.html   Starting a New Business Checklist

www.nbsapparel.com   Manitoba's only specialty retailer focused specifically on snowboard culture and lifestyle.

STAGE SEVEN: CONDUCTING A FEASIBILITY STUDY

www.Youtube.com   Elevator pitch

www.ul.com   Underwriters Laboratory certifications

www.csa.ca   Canadian Standards Association

www.innovationcentre.ca   Canadian Innovation Centre

www.statcan.gc.ca/bsolc/olc-cel/olc-cel?catno=63-224-XWE&lang=eng   Statistics Canada's Market Research Handbook

www.btac.org   Bicycle Trade Association of Canada

www.csga.ca   Canadian Sporting Goods Association

www.nspi.org   Association of Pool and Spa Professionals

www.nsga.org   National Sporting Goods Association

www.sgma.com   SGMA International

www.cog.ca   Canadian Organic Growers

www.certifiedorganic.bc.ca   Certified Organics Association of British Columbia

www.opam.mb.ca   Organic Producers Association of Manitoba

www.ocia.org   Organic Crop Improvement Association

www.ams.usda.gov/nop/indexIE.htm   The National Organic Program

www.cbsc.org/servlet/ContentServer?cid=1104766631694&pagename=CBSC_AB%2FCBSC_WebPage%2FCBSC_WebPage_Temp&c=CBSC_WebPage   The Business Link — Where to Find the Market Information You Need

www.canadabusiness.ca/eng/88/   Market Research and Statistics

www12.statcan.ca/census-recensement/index-eng.cfm   Data available from the most recent Canadian census of population.

www.ic.gc.ca/eic/site/cis-sic.nsf/eng/home   Canadian industry statistics.

www.cansim2.statcan.gc.ca/   CANSIM — Statistics Canada's principal socio-economic database.

www.ats-sea.agr.gc.ca/intro/index-eng.htm   Agri-Food Trade Service

www.allyoucanread.com/   AllYouCan Read.com

www.canadabusiness.ca/eng/   Canada Business.

www.google.ca   Google search engine.

www.bing.com   Bing search engine

www.metacrawler.com   MetaCrawler parallel search engine.

www.dogpile.com   Dogpile parallel search engine.

www.ask.com   Ask Jeeves parallel search engine.

www.about.com   About specialized search engine.

www.search.com   Search specialized search engine.

www.copernic.com   Copernic 2001 search accelerator

www.ferretsoft.com   WebFerret search accelerator

www.brightplanet.com/   BrightPlanet's DeepHarvester search accelerator.

www.cybf.ca   Canadian Youth Business Foundation subject guide.

www.northernlight.com   Northern Light commercial research database

www.canadianbusiness.com/entrepreneur/index.jsp   Canadian Business Online Entrepreneur Magazine

www.entrepreneurship.org   Kaufman Foundation Entrepreneurship Web Site

www.proquest.com   ProQuest is the leading provider of research and learning solutions to serve the needs of Canada's academic, corporate and K-12 library markets.

www.sbinfocanada.about.com   About.com Small Business Canada

www.regions.com/small_business/planning_guides.rf   Analyzing Your Competition, Regions Planning Guides

www.sbinfocanada.about.com/cs/homebusiness/a/homebizopp_2.htm   About.com: Small Business: Canada: Top 10 Home business Opportunities

www.takeaboo.wordpress.com/   Take-a-Boo Appraisals and Estate Sales

www.beautymarkcorp.com   Fine collection of discount women's and men's fragrances direct from the manufacturer including hard to find fragrances.

www.bcybermall.com   The Best Cybermall Around

www.nuthinbetter.com   Nuthin Better Cybermall

www.quagmiregolf.com   Quagmire Golf

www.design-reuse.com/articles/3073/guidelines-for-taking-your-idea-to-market.html   Design and Reuse guidelines for taking your idea to market

www.sbinfocanada.about.com/od/marketing/Marketing.htm   Small business marketing tips.

www.canadianbusiness.com/entrepreneur/sales_marketing/index.jsp   Sales and marketing for small business and entrepreneurs.

www.canadabusiness.ca/eng/88/   Guide to Market Research and Analysis

www.canadabusiness.ca/eng/88/1194/   Conducting Market Research.

www.canadabusiness.ab.ca/index.php/marketing/454-market-research-where-to-find-the-market-information-you-need   The Business Link — Where to Find the Market Information you Need

www.canadabusiness.ca/eng/search/results/search&keywords=Advertising/   Advertising

www.canadabusiness.ca/eng/guide/full/1467/   Marketing Basic

www.ic.gc.ca/eic/site/ee-ef.nsf/eng/ee00750.html   e-Business Factsheets: Marketing

www.canadabusiness.ca/eng/89/899/   Promoting and Advertising Your Business

www.canadabusiness.ca/eng/89/897/   A series of guides for dealing with marketing issues. Key marketing concepts, learn how to develop a marketing plan, and assess strategic marketing options for your company.

www.ic.gc.ca/epic/site/ic1.nsf/en/h_00066e.html   Business information by industrial sector.

www.statcan.gc.ca/start-debut-eng.html   Statistics Canada. Canada's national statistical agency.

www.ic.gc.ca/epic/site/ic1.nsf/en/h_00072e.html?OpenDocument&   Canadian Economic Statistics

www.corporateinformation.com   Corporate Information. We deliver the financial world.

www.canadabusiness.ca/eng/guide/2031/   Home Based business.

www.sbinfocanada.about.com/od/homebusiness/Home_Business.htm   Home Based Business

www.canadabusiness.ca/eng/105/165/   Exporting

www.lifemedia.ca/homebiz   Start & Run Your Own Business

www.canadabusiness.ca/eng/105/165/   Thinking of finding new markets for your products or services? Exporting is one way to increase sales and grow your business. While the rewards of exporting can be great, it is not without risks.

www.canadabusiness.ca/eng/105/165/924/   Identify countries with the most open markets and the right customers for your goods or services.

www.tradecommissioner.gc.ca/eng/StepENGPDF.pdf   The Step-by-Step Guide to Exporting

www.tradecommissioner.gc.ca/eng/market-report-access.jsp   Customised Market Research Reports for International Trade

www.tradecommissioner.gc.ca/eng/home.jsp   The Canadian Trade Commissioner Service. The Virtual Trade Commissioner. Services to help Canadians in the international marketplace.

www.gale.cengage.com/servlet/BrowseSeriesServlet?region=9&imprint=000&titleCode=DOP   Gale Directory of Public Broadcast Media. This premier media directory contains thousands of listings for radio and television stations and cable companies.

www.ulrichsweb.com   Ulrich's Periodicals Directory Serials Solutions

www.oxbridge.com   The Standard Periodical Directory

www.mediafinder.com   The Standard Periodical

www.hwwilson.com/databases/biblio.cfm   Bibliographic Index Plus

www.il.proquest.com/brand/micromedia.shtml   Canadian Business and Current Affairs

www.hwwilson.com/sales/printindexes.cfm   Business Periodicals Index

www.gale.cengage.com/servlet/ItemDetailServlet?region=9&imprint=000&titleCode=EBIS&cf=p&type=3&id=247326   Encyclopaedia of Business Information Sources identifies live, print and electronic sources of information listed under alphabetically arranged subjects — industries and business concepts and practices

www.gale.cengage.com/servlet/ItemDetailServlet?region=9&imprint=000&titleCode=GDOD&cf=p&type=3&id=242251   Indispensable for industry professionals, librarians and others seeking detailed information about electronic publishing and products, the Gale Directory of Databases profiles thousands of databases available worldwide in a variety of formats.

www.surveyofbuyingpower.com/sbponline/index.jsp   Survey of Buying Power

www.statcan.ca/bsolc/english/bsolc?catno=63-224-x   Statistics Canada Market Research Handbook

www.fpinfomart.ca   FPinfomart.ca is Canada's largest provider of news & broadcast media monitoring, financial and corporate data.

www.theglobeandmail.com/globe-investor/   CTV Globemedia Publishing Inc. Globe Investor is part of The Globe and Mail's Report on Business.

www.moodys.com/cust/default.asp   Moody's Investor Services

www.frasers.com/public/home.jsf   Frasers is a comprehensive directory and search tool, providing information on Canadian industrial wholesalers, manufacturers, distributors and their products and services. In addition, we list international companies that supply goods and services to the Canadian marketplace

www.scottsdirectories.com   Scott's Directories

www.cardmedia.com   Canadian Advertising Rates & Data

www.srds.com   SRDS Media Solutions — U.S. Publications

www.manaonline.org   Manufacturer's Agents National Association Directory of Members

www.meetingscanada.com/public/home.jsf   Meetings Canada

www.goodreads.com/book/show/5684211-catalogue-of-canadian-catalogues   Catalogue of Canadian Catalogues

www.greyhouse.com/marketing.htm   Directory of Associations in Canada

STAGE EIGHT: CONDUCTING A FEASIBILITY STUDY
PART 2: COST AND PROFITABILITY ASSESSMENT

www.sme.ic.gc.ca/epic/site/pp-pp.nsf/en/Home   Industry Canada SME Benchmarking Tool

www.chambar.com   Chambar Restaurant, Vancouver

www.toolkit.cch.com/text/P06_0100.asp   Managing Your Business Finances

www.bdc.ca/EN/advice_centre/tools/calculators/Pages/overview.aspx   BDC Benchmarking tools and ratio calculators

www.bdc.ca/en/business_tools/calculators/overview.htm?cookie_test=2   Business Development Bank of Canada (BDC) Ratio
  Calculators

www.regions.com/small_business/planning_guides.rf   Planning Guides: Manage Your Business and Watch it Grow

www.canadabusiness.mb.ca/home_page/contact_us/business_financing/financing_your_business_projecting_acquiring_and_
  managing_your_finances/   Financing Your Business (Projecting — Acquiring and Managing Your Finances)

www.ic.gc.ca/eic/site/pp-pp.nsf/eng/home   Industry Canada's SME Benchmarking Tool

www.canadabusiness.ca/eng/82/151/   Managing your finances: Resources to help you understand financial concepts and learn
  about tasks like budgeting, financial analysis and bookkeeping.

STAGE NINE: PROTECTING YOUR IDEA

www.megaproscrewdrivers.com   Seahawk Enterprises: Home of the Megapro Screwdriver

www.scruzol.com   Scruzol

www.cbc.ca/inventions   The Greatest Canadian Inventions

www.fox40whistle.com   Fox 40 International Inc.

www.lanebaldwin.com/hbc/index2.htm   Haidabucks Café

www.cipo.gc.ca   Canadian Intellectual Property Office

www.en.wikipedia.org/wiki/Lululemon_Athletica   Lululemon Athletica

STAGE TEN: ARRANGING FINANCING

www.bankrate.com   News, Tips, and Advice

www.foxyoriginals.com   Foxy Originals, a company dedicated to creating fun, funky and affordable jewelry for you to wear for
  work or play.

www.prestigedance.com   Prestige Dance Academy

www.cybf.ca   Canadian Youth Business Foundation: We help young Canadians who have a great business idea and require
  financing, mentoring and the right business resources to start a business.

www.strategis.ic.gc.ca/epic/site/csbfp-pfpec.nsf/en/Home   The Canada Small Business Financing (CSBF) Program Website

www.irap-pari.nrc-cnrc.gc.ca   National Research Council Canada

www.nrc-cnrc.gc.ca/eng/services/irap/financial-assistance.html   Industrial Research Assistance Program (IRAP)

www.wd.gc.ca/eng/274.asp   Women's Enterprise Initiative Loan Program

www.communityfutures.ca   Pan Canadian Community Futures Group

www.wd.gc.ca/eng/274.asp   Business Financing for Western Canada: Women's Enterprise Initiative Loan Program

www.ainc-inac.gc.ca/ecd/ab/index-eng.asp   Aboriginal Business Canada

www.bdc.ca   Business Development Bank of Canada

www.canadabusiness.ca   Canada Business: Service Centre

www.garrisonbrewing.com   Garrison Brewing Co.

www.ic.gc.ca/eic/site/ic1.nsf/eng/h_00073.html   Industry Canada federal and provincial programs

www.productivepublications.ca   Your guide to Government Financial Assistance for Business

www.cch.ca   Government assistance Manual

www.businessguide.net   The Business Guide to Government Programs

www.cvca.ca   Canada's Venture Capital & Private Equity Association

www.outpostmagazine.com   Outpost: Travel for Real Adventurers

www.capital-connexion.com   Carrefour Capital Connexion Network

www.angelforum.org   BC Angel Forum

www.okangels.org/   Okanagan Angel Network

www.vantec.ca/   Vancouver Angel Technology Network

www.albertadealgenerator.ca   Alberta Deal Generator

www.saint.sk.ca   Saskatchewan Angel Investor Network
www.wao.ca/Pages/Main.html   Winnipeg Angel Organization
MichaelMFranks@Yahoo.com   Active Angels
www.hedgewood.com/   Hedgewood Entrepreneurial Capital
www.techbiztoronto.com/financing.html   Toronto Organizations that Run Events: Angel Networks
www.noeg.ca/   Northern Ontario Enterprise Gateway
www.angel-investor-network.com/Ottawa-Capital-Network.html   Ottawa Capital Network Angel Investor Network
www.purple-angel.com   Purple Angel
www.angel-investor-network.com/Toronto-Angel-Group.html   Toronto Angel Group Angel Investor Network
www.fundingpost.com/angelgroup/angel-group-profile.asp?fund=60   Toronto Network of Angels
www.angelinvestmentnetwork.ca   Canadian Angel Investment Network
www.firstangelnetwork.ca   First Angel Network
http://nlangelnetwork.ca/   Newfoundland & Labrador Angel Network
www.angelinvestor.ca   National Angel Capital Organization
www.cba.ca/en/consumer-information/45-small-business-services/474-small-business-financing   Canadian Bankers Association Small Business Financing
www.businessownersideacafe.com/financing/index.php   IdeaCafe Financing Your Business
www.businessfinance.com   America's Business Financing Directory
www.canadabusiness.ca/eng/82/149/   Industry Canada Sources of Financing
www.acoa-apeca.gc.ca/english/iwantto/startabusiness/pages/gethelpfinancing.aspx   Atlantic Canada Opportunities Agency — Sources of Financing
www.sbinfocanada.about.com/od/financing/Small_Business_Financing.htm   About: Small Business: Canada: Small Business Financing
www.communityinvestment.ca   Canadian Community Investment Network Co-op
www.canadabusiness.ca/eng/guide/209/   Canada Business information on debt and equity financing
www.canadabusiness.ca/eng/search/sof/   Canada Business government loans, grants, and other financing programs
www.acoa.ca/English/Pages/home.aspx   Atlantic Canada Opportunity Agency (ACOA) Programs
www.sbinfocanada.about.com/od/financing/Small_Business_Financing.htm   About Canada — Small Business Canada
www.wd.gc.ca/eng/259.asp   Western Economic Diversification Canada, Funding for Business

STAGE ELEVEN: PREPARING YOUR BUSINESS PLAN

www.maritimetrading.com   Maritime Trading Co.
www.urbancanine.ca   Urbane Canine — Winnipeg's premiere doggy daycare
www.edwardlowe.org   Edward Lowe Foundation
www.cbdc.ca/obp.php   CBDC Online Business Plan
www.cybf.ca/entrepreneurs/interactivebusinessplanner.php   CYBF Interactive Business Planner
www.entrepreneurship.com/tools/pdf/businessPlanWorkbook.pdf   Writing an Effective Business Plan
www.smallbusinessbc.ca/pdf/bpff2002.pdf   Business Planning and Financial Forecasting
www.bizplanit.com/vplan.html   BizPlanIt's Virtual Business Plan
www.entrepreneurship.com/starting/business_tutorials.php?id=16   Business Plan Tutorial
www.smallbusinessbc.ca/pdf/businessplanning.pdf   Business Planning and Financial Forecasting A Start-up Guide
www.moneyhunt.com/mhtemplate.html   Money Hunt Business Plan Template
www.toolkit.com/tools/bt.aspx?tid=buspln_m   CCH Business Owner's Toolkit — Sample Plans
www.toolkit.cch.com/tools/buspln_m.asp   Sample Business Plan Components
www.paloalto.com/sample_business_plans/categories.cfm   Palo Alto Software sample business plans
www.paloalto.com/ps/bp/samples.cfm   Palo Alto's Business Plan Pro
www.businessplanarchive.org   Business Plan Archive
www.businessplans.org/businessplans.html   MOOT CORP® Competition "The Super Bowl of Business Plan Competition."
www.smallbusinesspoint.com/sampleplans.aspx   SmallBusinessPoint sample business plans

Glossary of Financial Terms

Accounts payable Money owed by a firm to its suppliers for goods and services purchased for the operation of the business. A current liability.

Accounts receivable Money owed to a firm by its customers for goods or services they have purchased from it. A current asset.

Amortization To pay off a debt over a stated time period, setting aside fixed sums for interest and principal at regular intervals, like a mortgage.

Angels Private individuals with capital to invest in business ventures.

Assets The resources or property rights owned by an individual or business enterprise. Tangible assets include cash, inventory, land and buildings, and intangible assets including patents and goodwill.

Bad debts Money owed to you that you no longer expect to collect.

Balance sheet An itemized statement that lists the total assets and total liabilities of a given business, to portray its net worth at a given moment in time.

Bankruptcy The financial and legal position of a person or corporation unable to pay its debts.

Break-even point The level of sales in either units or dollars at which sales revenue and costs are equal so that a business is neither making nor losing money.

Capital asset A possession, such as a machine, that can be used to make money and has a reasonably long life, usually more than a year.

Capital costs The cost involved in the acquisition of capital assets. They are "capitalized," showing up on the balance sheet and depreciated (expensed) over their useful life.

Capital gain The difference between the net cost of an asset and the net sales price, if the asset is sold at a gain.

Capital loss The difference between the net cost of an asset and the net sales price, if the asset is sold at a loss.

Capital requirement The amount of money needed to establish a business.

Capital stock The money invested in a business through founders' equity and shares bought by stockholders.

Cash discount An incentive provided by vendors of merchandise and services to speed up the collection of accounts receivable.

Cash flow The movement of cash in and out of a company. Its timing is usually projected month by month to show the net cash requirement during each period.

Cash flow forecast A schedule of expected cash receipts and disbursements (payments) highlighting expected shortages and surpluses.

Collateral Assets placed by a borrower as security for a loan.

Contribution margin The difference between variable revenue and variable cost.

Conversion In the context of securities, refers to the exchange of a convertible security such as a bond for shares in a company.

Cost of goods sold The direct costs of acquiring and/or producing an item for sale. Usually excludes any overhead or other indirect expenses.

Current assets Cash or other items that will normally be turned into cash within one year (accounts receivable, inventory, and short-term notes) and assets that will be used up in the operation of a firm within one year.

Current liabilities Amounts owed that will ordinarily be paid by a firm within one year. Such items include accounts payable, wages payable, taxes payable, the current portion of a long-term debt and interest, and dividends payable.

Current ratio Current assets divided by current liabilities. Used as an indication of liquidity to show how easily a business can meet its current debts.

Debt Money that must be paid back to someone else, usually with interest.

Debt capital Capital invested in a company that does not belong to the company's owners. Usually consists of long-term loans and preferred shares.

Debt-to-equity ratio The ratio of long-term debt to owners' equity. Measures overall profitability.

Demand loan A loan that must be repaid in full, on demand.

Depreciation A method of writing off the costs to a firm of using a fixed asset, such as machinery, buildings, trucks, and equipment, over time.

Employee stock ownership plan (ESOP) A company contributes to a trust fund that buys stock on behalf of employees.

Equity The difference between the assets and liabilities of a company, often referred to as *net worth*.

Equity capital The capital invested in a firm by its owners. The owners of the equity capital in the firm are entitled to all the assets and income of the firm after all the claims of creditors have been paid.

Escrow Property or money held by a third party until the agreed-on obligations of a contract are met.

Factor A financial institution that buys a firm's accounts receivable and collects the accounts.

Financial statements Documents that show your financial situation.

Fiscal year An accounting cycle of 12 months that could start at any point during a calendar year.

Fixed assets Those things that a firm owns and uses in its business and that it keeps for more than one year (including machinery, land, buildings, vehicles, etc.).

Fixed costs or expenses Those costs that don't vary from one period to the next and usually are not affected by the volume of business (e.g., rent, salaries, telephone, etc.).

Floor plan financing An arrangement used to finance inventory. A finance company buys the inventory, which is then held in trust for the user.

Franchise The right to sell products or services under a corporate name or trademark, usually purchased for a fee plus a royalty on sales.

Goodwill The value of customer lists, trade reputation, etc., which is assumed to go with a company and its name, particularly when trying to arrive at the sale price for the company. In accounting terms it is the amount a purchaser pays over the book value.

Gross margin or gross profit margin The difference between the volume of sales your business generates and the costs you pay out for the goods that are sold.

Income statement The financial statement that looks at a business's revenue, less expenses, to determine net income for a certain period of time. Also called *profit-and-loss statement*.

Industry ratios Financial ratios established by many companies in an industry, in an attempt to establish a norm against which to measure and compare the effectiveness of a company's management.

Initial public offering (IPO) A company's first sale of stock to the public. Securities offered in an IPO are often, but not always, those of young, small companies seeking outside equity capital and a public market for their stock. Investors purchasing stock in IPOs generally must be prepared to accept considerable risks for the possibility of large gains.

Intangible assets Assets such as trade names or patent rights that are not physical objects or sums of money.

Interest A charge for the use of money supplied by a lender.

Inventory The supply of goods, whether raw materials, parts, or finished products, owned by a firm at any one time, and its total value.

Inventory turnover The number of times the value of inventory at cost divides into the cost of goods sold in a year.

Investment capital The money set aside for starting a business. Usually this would cover such costs as inventory, equipment, pre-opening expenses, and leasehold improvements.

Lease An agreement to rent for a period of time at an agreed price.

Leverage ratios Measures of the relative value of stockholders' capitalization and creditors' obligations, and of the firm's ability to pay financing charges.

Liabilities All the debts of a business. Liabilities include short-term or current liabilities such as accounts payable, income taxes due, and the amount of long-term debt that must be paid within 12 months; long-term liabilities include long-term debts and deferred income taxes. On a balance sheet, liabilities are subtracted from assets; what remains is the shareholders' equity.

Line of credit An agreement negotiated between a borrower and a lender establishing the maximum amount of money against which the borrower may draw.

Liquid assets Cash on hand and anything that can easily and quickly be turned into cash.

Liquidation value The estimated value of a business after its operations are stopped and the assets sold and the liabilities paid off.

Liquidity A term that describes how readily a firm's assets can be converted into cash.

Liquidity ratios Ratios that measure a firm's ability to meet its short-term financial obligations on time, such as the ratio of current assets to current liabilities.

Loan guarantee The assumption of responsibility for payment of a debt or performance of some obligation if the liable party fails to perform to expectations.

Long-term liabilities Debts that will not be paid off within one year.

Management buyout (MBO) A leveraged buyout in which the acquiring group is led by the firm's management.

Markup The amount vendors add to the purchase price of a product to take into account their expenses plus profit.

Maturity For a loan, the date on which the principal is required to be repaid.

Net worth The value of a business represented by the excess of the total assets over the total amounts owing to outside creditors (total liabilities) at a given moment in time. Also referred to as *book value*.

Operating costs Expenditures arising out of current business activities; what it costs to do business — the salaries, electricity, rental, deliveries, etc., that are involved in performing the operations of a business.

Operating loan A loan intended for short-term financing, supplying cash flow support, or to cover day-to-day operating expenses.

Overhead Expenses such as rent, heat, property tax, etc., incurred to keep a business open.

Principal The face amount of debt; the amount borrowed or loaned.

Pro forma A projection or estimate. A pro forma financial statement is one that shows how the actual operations of the business will turn out if certain assumptions are realized.

Profit The excess of the selling price over all costs and expenses incurred in making the sale. Gross profit is the profit before corporate income taxes. Net profit is the final profit of the firm after all deductions have been made.

Profitability ratios Ratios that focus on how well a firm is performing. Profit margins measure performance with relation to sales. Rate-of-return ratios measure performance relative to some measure of size of the investment.

Profit-and-loss statement A financial statement listing revenue and expenses and showing the profit (or loss) for a certain period of time. Also called an *income statement.*

Profit margin The ratio of profits (generally pre-tax) to sales.

Put option The right to sell (or put) a fixed number of shares at a fixed price within a given period of time.

Quick ratio Current cash and "near" cash assets (e.g., government bonds, current receivables, but excluding inventory) compared to current liabilities (bank loans, accounts payable). The quick ratio shows how much and how quickly cash can be found if a company gets into trouble. Sometimes called the *acid test ratio.*

Retained earnings The profits that are not spent or divided among the owners but kept in the business.

Return on investment (ROI) The determination of the profit to be accrued from a capital investment.

Royalty Payment for the right to use intellectual property or natural resources.

Seed capital The first contribution by an investor toward the financing of a new business.

Stock buyback A corporation's purchase of its own outstanding stock.

Subordinated debt Debt over which other senior debt takes priority. In the event of bankruptcy, subordinated debt holders receive payment only after senior debt claims are paid in full.

Term loan A loan intended for medium-term or long-term financing to supply cash to purchase fixed assets such as land or buildings, machinery and equipment, or to renovate business premises.

Terms of sale The conditions concerning payment for a purchase.

Trade credit The credit terms offered by a manufacturer or supplier to other businesses.

Transactions fees Fees charged to cover the time and effort involved in arranging a loan or other financial package.

Turnover The number of times a year that a product is sold and reordered.

Variable expenses Costs of doing business that vary with the volume of business, such as manufacturing cost and delivery expenses.

Venture capital Funds that are invested in a business by a third party either as equity or some form of subordinated debt.

Working capital The funds available for carrying on the day-to-day operation of a business. Working capital is the excess after deduction of the current liabilities from the current assets of a firm, and indicates a company's ability to pay its short-term debts.

Index

ABI Inform, 77
Aboriginal Business Canada, 300
About Guide to Small Business: Canada, 13, 76, 219, 315
About.com, 191
abstract, 273
accident and sickness insurance, 176
accountants, 147
accounts payable, 252
accounts receivable, 100, 252
achievement, need for, 16
acquaintances, 66
acquisitions. *See* business acquisition
action orientation, 16
Adam, Shakil, 171
Adams, Rick, 30
adjusted book value, 105–106
administrative skills, 25
advance payment, 80, 293
advertising, 212, 332
    Internet, 213
Advertising guides, 220
advertising media, 213*t*
agents, 216, 273
aging population, 2
Agri-Food Trade Service, 190
AIM Personnel Services Inc., 32, 33
    Code of Ethics & Standards, 33*f*
Alcan, 167
all-in-one search engines, 191
AllConferences.com, 65
AllYouCanRead.com, 190
ambiguity, tolerance of, 17
amendment letter, 274
America's Business Funding Directory, 315
anchoring, 70
angel investors, 305, 307, 309
angel networks, 305
appendices, 335
area franchise, 132
Arthurs, Robert, 281, 282
articles of incorporation, 169
Ask, 191
Asper, Gail, 31
assessment of a business
    financial factors, 27, 94–101
    historical practices, 104
    human factors, 102–103
    key points to consider, 104
    legal concerns, 103–104
    marketing considerations, 102
    reason for the sale, 94
assets, 27
    balance sheet, in, 254
    current assets, 254
    fixed assets, 100, 254
    intangible, 100
    shares, versus, 111, 113
    tangible, 98, 100

Assiniboine Credit Union, 324
Association of Canadian Search, Employment and Staffing Services (ACSESS), 32, 33
Atlantic Canada Opportunity Agency (ACOA), 315
atmosFEAR, 70
attitude, 19
    measuring, 20
attributes of entrepreneurs, 14–19
average collection period, 96
average gross margin, 246
average inventory turnover, 246

Babson University Academy of Distinguished Entrepreneurs, 14
baby boomers, 2
balance sheet
    personal, 27–28, 46–47*f*
    pro forma, 254, 256, 257*f*, 335
    sample, 257*f*
    sample form, 46–47*f*
    simplified, 97–98*f*
    valuation methods, 104, 105–106
banks, 297, 305
Banks, Jordan, 305, 306
Beautymark Corp., 207, 208
being alive, 70
benefit, 185
Best Cybermall Around, The, 213
BHVR Communications, 304
Bilyea, Cliff G., 77
Bing, 190
BizPal, 172
BizPlanIt's Virtual Business Plan, 327
Blanchard, Kenneth, 32
blog, 75
Bobbetts, Robert, 248, 250
Bond, Holly, 147–149
book value, 105
Boolean logic, 192
bootstrapping, 291–293, 295
Bork, David, 120
bottom-up approach, 203–204
brainstorming, 66–69, 78
    four-step process, 69
    solutions, 78
Brass, Julian, 66, 67, 76
break-even analysis, 261, 335
break-even point, 256, 258–261, 262*f*
Breakey, John, 7
Brick Warehouse, The, 144, 283
Brick's Fine Furniture, 283
Brick, Fred and Cynthia, 283
BrightPlanet, 191
brochure site, 76
brokers, 92, 216
Brown, Justine, 165, 166–167
Brown, Margaret, 296
budget, personal, 28, 47–48*f*

Bulldog Interactive Fitness, 147–149
business acquisition
    advantages, 90
    assets vs. shares, 111, 113
    checklist, 121
    disadvantages, 90–92
    due diligence, need for, 101
    entry strategy, as, 90
    exit strategy, as, 308
    factors to consider, 94–104
    family business, 115–120
    financial factors, 94–102
    financing the purchase, 113
    finding the right business, 92–93
    historical practices, 104
    human factors, 102–103
    key points, 104
    legal considerations, 103–104
    marketing considerations, 102
    negotiating the deal, 114
    online resources, 114
    other factors, 103–104
    process, 91*f*
    questionnaire, 121–125
    reason for the sale, 94
    valuation of, 104–111
    warning, 113
business assistance, 27
Business Development Bank of Canada, 26, 41, 66, 300, 309, 315
    Ratio Calculators, 259
business development loans, 299
business goals, 77
business growth, model, 218*t*
Business Guide to Government Programs, 302
Business Information by Industrial Sector, 220
business interruption insurance, 176
business licence, 172, 174
Business Link, The, 220
business name, 169, 171–172, 173–174
Business Number (BN), 174
business organization
    comparison of forms, 179*t*
    co-operatives, 165, 167
    corporation, 163–165
    factors to consider, 158
    form, 179*t*
    individual proprietorship, 158–160
    need for, 8
    outline, 159*f*
    partnership, 160–163
    setting up your business, 167, 169, 172, 174–177
    sole proprietorship, 158–160
business plan
    advantages of, 323
    appendices, 335
    assessment checklist, 341–344*f*

business plan—*Cont.*
  common mistakes, 336
  described, 8, 318, 319
  feasibility assessment and, 262
  franchise, 146
  full business plan, 323
  length of, 323, 325
  operational business plan, 323, 325
  outlines and templates, 327
  purpose of, 321–323
  sample business plans, 337
  steps in developing, 318–321, 319*f*
  summary business plan, 323
  time to develop, 325
  tips, 325
  typical business plan, 328–329*f*
  writing your business plan, 325
Business Plan Archive, 337
business plan contents
  body of plan, 329–330
  development plan, 332
  executive summary and fact sheet,
    326–327
  financial plan, 334–335
  implementation schedule, 334
  letter of transmittal, 326
  management team, 333–334
  market analysis, 330–331
  marketing plan, 331–332
  production/operations plan, 332–333
  risks, 334
  table of contents, 326
  title page, 326
business planning
  big picture, 318, 338–341*f*
  developing a realistic business plan, 321
  fundamental values, 320
  mission statement, 318–320
  objectives, 320–321
  steps in process, 318–321
  vision statement, 318
Business Planning and Financial
  Forecasting, 327
business premises insurance, 176
business ratios. *See* ratio analysis
business skills
  acquisition of, 26–27
  breakdown of, 25*f*
  evaluation of, 23
  managerial skills inventory, 25,
    44–45*f*
Business Start Program, 301
Business Start-up Quiz, 41
business start-ups. *See also* setting up
    your business
  entry strategy, as, 90
  financial requirements,
    242–244, 272
  key points, 177
  myths and realities, 54*f*
  reasons for, 4*t*
  requirements, 7, 244
  sources of financing, 291*f*
  sources of ideas for, 56–70, 70*f*
  sporting goods store example, 244
  statistics, 2

business valuation. *See* valuation of a
    business
business values, statement of, 320
business-use vehicle insurance, 176
buy-back agreement, 308
buying a business. *See* business
    acquisition
Buying a Business, 114
Buying a Business: The Safer
    Alternative, 114
buying facilities, 206–207

Cactus Club Café, 23–25
Canada Business, 76, 175, 190, 191,
    220, 315
  Market Research and Statistics, 190
Canada Business Service Centre
    (CBSC), 13, 66, 189–190, 302
Canada Business Services for
    Entrepreneurs, 13, 189–190
Canada/Manitoba Business Service
    Centre (C/MBSC), 324
Canada Revenue Agency, 207
Canada Small Business Financing
    Program, 298
CanadaOne, 13, 114, 175
*Canadian Advertising Rates
    and Data*, 64
Canadian Association of Family
    Enterprise (CAFE), 120
Canadian Bankers Association, 315
Canada Business Market Research and
    Statistics, 190
Canadian Business, 64, 114
Canadian Business and Current Affairs
    (CBCA), 77
Canadian Business Online, 191, 220
Canadian Community Investment
    Network Co-op (CCINC),
    311, 312
Canadian Community Investment Plan
    (CCIP), 305
Canadian community loan funds,
    311–312
Canadian Economic and Market
    Research/Statistics, 220
Canadian Federation of Independent
    Business (CFIB), 116
Canadian Franchise Association, 132,
    141, 149
Canadian Franchise Opportunities, 149
Canadian Industry Statistics, 190
Canadian Innovation Centre,
    66, 81, 184
Canadian Intellectual Property Office,
    65, 273, 274, 281, 284, 285, 286
  See also intellectual property
Canadian Internet Registration
    Authority (CIRA), 75
Canadian Patents Database, 65
Canadian Standards Association, 184
Canadian Statistics, 220
Canadian Venture Capital Association, 302
Canadian Youth Business Foundation
    (CYBF), 54, 66, 67, 191, 296,
    308–309, 311, 315, 327

CANSIM, 190
capacity, 314
capital, 312
Capital Connection database, 305
capital expenditures, 242
capitalization of an average of past
    profits, 106
capitalization of earnings, 106
capitalization rate, 106–107
cash discounts, 211
cash flow, 100–101, 248–253
cash flow forecast. *See* cash flow
    statement
cash flow statement
  business plan, in, 335
  cash flow from financing activities,
    252–253
  cash flow from investment
    activities, 252
  cash flow from operating
    activities, 252
  described, 248–252
  expenditures, determination
    of, 253
  need for, 249
  pro forma, sample, 255*f*
  reconciliation of revenues and
    expenditures, 254
  revenues, estimate of, 253
  sections in, 252
cash on delivery (COD), 253
cashing out, 71
casual observation, 60, 62
CCH Business Owner's Toolkit,
    259, 337
Census Metropolitan Areas
    (CMAs), 188
Center for Venture Research, 309
Chambar restaurant, 248, 251
character, 312
child care and education, 149
Chinook Centre, 103
Christakos, George, 54
claims, 273
clanning, 71
closing the sale, 215
club activities, 26
Cluthe, George, 277
co-op funds, 311
co-operatives, 165, 167
Coakes, Fred, 275, 276
code of ethics, 32, 32*f*
cold calls, 92
collateral, 312
collateral security, 297
collection period, 96
commercial real estate agents, 92
commercial research databases, 192
commitment, 15, 29
Community Business Development
    Corporations (CBDCs),
    299, 327
Community Futures Development
    Corporations (CFDCs), 299
community loan funds, 311
compensation, 334

competition
    assessment of, 102
    direct, 198
    form for analyzing, 225–227f
    identifying, 198
    indirect, 198
    lack of, 80
    market research on, 198, 331
    nature of, 198–199
    sources of information on, 198–199
    SWOT analysis, 199–200
competition-based pricing, 211
competitive advantage, 195
competitive profile matrix, 199
competitive strategy, 200–201
competitors' products, 194, 198–199
comprehensive feasibility assessment,
    261–262, 262–271f
Comprehensive Guide to Buying a
    Business in Canada, A, 114
Compucentre, 144
confidential advisors, 92
confidentiality agreement, 280
conflict resolution, 18
consumer market, 185
contractor referral service, 71
contribution margin ratio, 258, 260
control, 307
conventions, 65
Copernic 2001, 191
copycatting, 184
copyright, 283–284
corporate book, 164
Corporate Information Canada, 220
corporate social responsibility, 35
corporation, 163–165
Corporations Branch, 167
corporations without share capital, 164
cost advantage, 200
cost-based pricing, 210
cost of goods sold, 245, 247
cost of sales, 245
craftspeople, 22
creative thinking, 66–69
credit, 312, 314
credit cards, 292
credit insurance, 177
credit rating, 28
credit unions, 297
Crock A Doodle, 141
current assets, 95, 254
current liabilities, 95, 256
current ratio, 95, 258
customer profile, 195, 223f
customer survey, 195, 198, 224–225f
customers, advance payment
    from, 293
Customized Market Research Reports
    for International Trade, 220
Cybermall, 213

data
    collection methods, 192–193
    competitive information, 198–199
    customer survey, 195
    market-testing your idea, 193–195
    primary, 192–195
    secondary, 188–192
de la Rocha, Cecilia, 165, 166–167
Death by Chocolate, 171
debt, 95
debt financing, 288, 290
debt repayment, 308
debt-to-equity ratio, 258
debt-to-net-worth ratio, 95
decision trees, 66
DeepHarvester, 191
default clauses, 207
Delaquis, Mich, 275, 276
deliberate search for ideas, 62, 64
demand loan, 297
demographic description, 102, 187
demonstration, 215
depreciation, 254
Département Caméra, 57
desired income approach, 246
Despault, J-P, 128, 129–130
Dessert Lady, 58, 59
determination, 15
development plan, 332
Dickie, Bob, 279
differentiation advantage, 200–201
Dion, Johanne, 312
direct competitors, 198
direct selling, 71
directories, 190, 191, 213, 221f
directors, 334
disability insurance, 176
disclosure document, 133, 147
discounted cash flow, 107–109
discounted future earnings, 107–109
discounts, 211
Discovery Hut, The, 102, 103
distribution channels, 215–216, 332
distribution system, 80
do-it-yourself market research, 196
Doggie Style, 171
Dogpile, 191
Dolan, Karen, 101
dollar revenue, 198
domain name, 75
dot-com millionaires, 3
down-aging, 71
downsizing, 2
drawings, 273
drop shippers, 216
Drucker, Peter, 10
drug brokers, 216
due diligence, 101
Dufault, Shelley, 322–323, 324
Dun & Bradstreet, 95, 246
Dun & Bradstreet Canada, 246
Dylex Ltd., 119

e-business, 74, 76
    reasons to start, 74
E-Business, 76
E-Business Factsheets, 220
E-Business Info-Guide, 76
E-Business Overview, 76
e-commerce Web site, 75
e-learning, 71

Eakins, Marty, 101
earnings-based valuation methods, 104,
    106–109, 108f
    See also income statement
eBay auction model, 75
Ebiz.enable, 76
economic values, 29
economies of scale, 203
education, 26
egonomics, 71
Eisfeld, Geoof, 275
elaboration, 53
eldercare, 73, 149
Elements of Nature, 102, 103
elevator pitch, 181, 182
employee buyout, 308
employment standards, 175
Engage.com, 66, 67
Enron, 31
Enterprise Magazine, 13
entire-business-format franchising, 127
Entrepreneur magazine, 13, 64, 133
Entrepreneur Test, 41
Entrepreneur's Creed, 20
entrepreneurial assessment
    questionnaire, 48–49f
Entrepreneurial Attitude Orientation
    (EAO), 19–21
    survey, 41–44
entrepreneurial mindset, 20
entrepreneurial opportunity, 50f, 53
entrepreneurial personality, 14
entrepreneurial potential
    assessment of, 15f
    attributes, 14–19
    business skills evaluation, 23–25
    ethical challenges, 31–33
    managerial skills inventory, 44–45f
    personal finances, assessment of, 27
    personal self-assessment, 21–22,
        48–49f
    readiness, 29
entrepreneurial process, 7–9, 9f
entrepreneurial quiz, 14, 37–40
Entrepreneurial Self-Assessment, 41
entrepreneurs
    attitude approach to describing,
        19–21
    attributes of, 14–19
    as component in entrepreneurial
        process, 7
    described, 6
    external role demands, 28–29
    not-so-learnable characteristics, 19
    roles of, 6
    top 10 characteristics, 18f
    types of, 22–23
entrepreneurship
    components of successful ventures, 8f
    ethical challenges, 31–33
    legal considerations, 32
    meaning of, 4, 6
    myths and realities, 10–12
    personal self-assessment, 21–22
    readiness for, 29
    revolution, 2–4

entrepreneurship—*Cont.*
  social, 29–30
  triggering event, 4
Entrepreneurship Centre Business Plan
  Outline, 327
entry strategies, 86–87
Enviro Masters Lawn Care, 139–140
Equifax Canada Inc., 28
equity, 254
equity financing, 289–290
Esporta Wash Systems, 186
ethics, 31–33
Ethics Check, 32
evaluation, 53, 184
evaluation of a business. *See* assessment
  of a business
evaluation of ideas, 77–81
events of default, 139
EventsEye, 65
EVEolution, 71
examination, 274
executive summary, 326–327
exit strategy, 308
Exporting, 220
external role demands, 28–29

facilities
  buying or leasing, 206–207
  equipment and, 333
fact sheet, 327
failure
  response to, 17
  small business failures, reasons for, 11*f*
family, 27
family businesses
  described, 115
  differences between business system
    and, 115, 116*t*
  grooming an heir, 118
  outside assistance, 118
  preparation for running, 118, 120
  subsystems in, 116
  succession issues, 116–118
  systems view of, 115*f*
  traits of successful family firms, 120
family council, 118
family feuds, 120
fantasy adventure, 71
fashion obsolescence, 80
Fast Times Political Dictionary, 6
favourite industries, 77
feasibility study
  break-even point, 256, 258–261
  comprehensive feasibility assessment,
    261–262, 262–271*f*
  described, 180
  market assessment. *See* market
    assessment
  marketing mix, 209–216
  part 1 flow chart, 181*f*
  part 2 flow chart, 243*f*
  preliminary marketing plan, 216–
    218, 231–240*f*
  sales forecasting, 201–208
  short-term financial projections,
    245–256

start-up financial requirements,
  242–244
supply situation, 218–219
technical feasibility, 182, 184
typical feasibility study, 183*f*
venture concept, 180–182
feature, 185
federal government financial assistance
  programs, 297–300
feedback, 16
Ferguson, Kisha, 302, 303–304
finances
  cash flow statement, 248–254
  one-time expenditures, 242
  operating expenses, 243
  personal finances, assessment of, 27
  pro forma balance sheet, 254, 256,
    257*f*, 335
  pro forma income statement, 245–
    248, 247*f*, 249*f*, 270
  short-term financial projections,
    241–254
  start-up financial requirements,
    242–244, 288
financial factors
  cash flow, 100–101
  intangible assets, value of, 100
  profit trend, 94
  ratio analysis, 95–98
  tangible assets, value of, 98, 100
financial institutions, 297
financial plan, 334–335
Financial Post Magazine, 64
financial projections
  analysis of pro forma statements, 256
  business plan, in, 335
  cash flow forecast, 248–253, 255*f*
  cash flow statement, 248–254
  financial ratios, 256, 258
  pro forma balance sheet, 254, 256,
    257*f*, 335
  pro forma income statement, 245–
    248, 247*f*, 249*f*, 270
financial ratios, 256, 258
financing
  ability to secure financing, 312,
    314–317
  additional sources, 308–309,
    311–312
  advance payment from customers, 293
  advice, 298
  angel investors, 305, 307, 309
  banks, 297
  bootstrapping, 291–292, 295
  credit unions, 297
  business acquisition, 113
  debt financing, 288, 290
  equity financing, 289–290
  federal government financial
    assistance programs, 297–300
  financial institutions, 297
  franchise acquisition, 143–144
  leasehold improvements, 292–293
  leasing versus buying, 292
  loan application assessment
    worksheet, 316*f*

love money, 293, 295
personal credit cards, 292
personal equity, 113
personal funds, 291
provincial government financial
  assistance programs, 300–302
seed capital, 288
seller financing, 113
sources of funds, 289, 290–291,
  291*f*, 313*f*
start-up financial requirements,
  242–244
suppliers' inventory buying
  plans, 292
third parties, 113
trust companies, 297
venture capital, 302, 307–308
Financing the Business Acquisition, 114
Financing Your Business, 259
Fischl, Chad, 62, 63–64
fitness, 31, 149
fixed assets, 100, 254
fixed costs, 258
fixed expenses, 245
fixed operating expenses, 245
Flamingo a Friend, 141
Flintbox, 65
food brokers, 216
force field analysis, 66
Fortune, 64
four-step process, 69
Foxcroft, Ron, 275, 278–279
Foxy Originals, 294
4everSports, 250
franchise acquisition
  application form, 141–142
  costs of opening a franchise, 143
  financing, 143–144
  finding a franchise business, 141
  franchise evaluation checklist,
    150–157
  future trends, 149
  interest in, 127*f*
  interview, 142–143
  key points to consider, 144
  out-of-the-ordinary
    opportunities, 141
  promotional kit, 141
  service franchise investment, 144
franchise agreement
  described, 134, 147
  duration of contract, 138–139
  events of default, 139
  examples, 139–140
  franchise fees and royalties, 136
  franchisee's obligations, 135–136
  franchisor's obligations, 135
  leased premises, 137
  purchase of products and supplies,
    136–137
  renewal of contract, 139
  right of first refusal, 139
  sale or transfer, 139
  termination of contract, 139
  territorial protection, 137–138
  training and operating assistance, 138

franchise arrangements
    elements of, 126
    types of, 127
Franchise Canada Directory, 132, 141
franchise consultants, 147
Franchise Conxions, 149
franchise disclosure document, 147
franchise evaluation checklist, 150–157
franchisee, 126, 135–136
franchises
    advantages of, 128, 145
    area franchise, 132
    arrangements, elements of, 126
    business plan, 146
    Canadian franchisors, sampling
        of, 140t
    characteristics of successful, 145–146
    checklist for evaluating, 150–157
    definitions of, 126
    disadvantages of, 128, 131–132
    disclosure requirements, 133–134
    entire-business-format
        franchising, 127
    formats, 132
    future trends, 149
    growth strategy, as, 144–149
    legislation, 133–134
    master franchise, 132
    operations manual, 147
    proceeding with, 146–149
    product distribution
        arrangements, 127
    range of available franchises,
        132–133
    selling, 147
    single-unit franchise, 132
    support services, 147
    top 10 franchise organizations, 133t
    training program, 147
    types of, 132–140
franchising. See franchises
franchisor, 126, 135
FranNet, 149
Free the Children, 29
freedom fighters, 22
frequent purchasing, 79
Frey, Christopher, 302, 303–304
friends, 26, 66
Fruhm, Hermann, 275, 277
full business plan, 323
full-service wholesalers, 216
Fuller, Stan, 24
funding. See financing
future
    best businesses, 72–76
    business trends, 70–76
    franchise trends, 149

Gagné, Roland, 324
Gagnon, Sebastian and Yan, 54
Garrison Brewing Company Ltd., 301
Gauvreau, Bernard, 200–201, 202
general liability insurance, 176
general partnership, 160, 162
general publications, 189
geographic location, 187

getting into business. See setting up
    your business
Giancola, Ralph, 185, 186
Global Entrepreneurship Monitor
    (GEM), 2
Global Sources Trade Show Centre, 65
Globe and Mail, The, 64
    Report on Business Magazine, 64
goals
    identification, 77
    orientation, 16
Goble, Cindy, 207, 208
Gompf, Tyler and Kirby, 62–63
Goods and Services Tax (GST), 174
goodwill, 100, 281
goodwill cycle, 33, 34
Google, 190
government agencies, 66
Government Assistance Manual, 302
government market, 185
Granny's Poultry Co-op, 167
Great-West Life, 167
greatest Canadian inventions, 280
Griffen, Dale, 171, 172
grooming an heir, 118
gross margin, 79, 245, 246
gross margin ratio, 258
gross profit, 96, 245
gross-profit-to-sales ratio, 96
group brainstorming, 66
Groves, Kent, 321, 322
guarantees, 165
Guidelines for Taking Your Idea to
    Market, 219
Guide to Setting Up Your Business In
    Canada, A, 175

HaidaBucks Cafe, 283
Harburn, Amanda, 293, 296
Harmonized Sales Tax (HST), 174
Harry Rosen, 119
Henry, Steve, 170
high-growth ventures, 56
hobbies, 59–60
Home-Based Business, 220
home-based businesses, 207–208, 209
home experiences, 27
home health service, 73
home improvements, 149
home inspection, 71
hook, 182
Hopper, Ben, 128, 130–131
Huge L Steel, 5
Hugel, Murray, 2, 4, 5, 6
human factors, 102–103
Human Resources and Skill
    Development Canada, 300
Humphrey, Bob, 119

icon toppling, 72
Idea Cafe, 315
"ideal" business model, 78–81
ideas
    brainstorming, 66–69
    concept, vs., 181–182
    conventions, 65

creative thinking, 66–69
deliberate search, 62, 64
evaluation of, 77–81
friends, 66
future, 72–74
government agencies, 66
hobbies, 59–60
"ideal" business model, 78–81
inventors' shows, 65
job experience, 56–57, 59
market-testing, 193–195
personal observation, 60, 62
product licensing information
    services, 65
protection of. See intellectual
    property
publications, 64–65
search for new ideas, 51f
sources of, 56–70, 70f
survey results, 69–70, 70f
trade shows, 65
types, 55
iFranchise Group, The, 145
Illenium Board Shop, 59
immigrants, 2
implementation schedule, 334
Inc., 13, 64
income statement
    cash flow, 109
    developing, 246–247
    pro forma, 245–248, 247f,
        249f, 270
    sample, 247f
    simplified, 98f
    valuation methods, 106–109, 108f
incorporated partnership, 169
incorporation, 163, 167–169
incubation, 53
indirect competitors, 198
individual proprietorship, 158–160
industrial design, 284–285
industrial market, 185
Industrial Research Assistance Program
    (IRAP), 299
industry associations, 188–189
Industry Canada, 13, 66, 77, 95, 98,
    172, 220
    Community Business Development
        Corporations (CBDCs), 299
    Community Futures Development
        Corporations (CFDCs), 299
    SME Benchmarking Tool, 95, 98,
        246, 248, 259
industry research, 77
industry segments, 77–78
info-site, 76
information professional, 71
initial public offering (IPO), 308
innovation, 6
innovativeness, degree of, 182, 184
insight, 53
institutional market, 185
insurance, 176–177
intangible assets, value of, 100, 287
integrated circuit topographies, 285
integrity, 18

intellectual property
components of, 272
copyright, 283–284
industrial design, 284–285
information about, 286, 287*t*
integrated circuit topographies, 285
non-disclosure agreement
(NDA), 286
patents, 272–275, 279–281
trade secrets, 286
trademarks, 281–283
Interactive Business Planner, 327
interest rate, 288
International Franchise Association,
126, 143, 149
international market, 185
Internet
advertising on, 213
business model, 75–76
business opportunities, 74
market research, 190–192
production costs, 213
search engines, 190
search tools, 191–192
invention scams, 280–281
InventNET, 65
inventors' shows, 65
inventory, 98, 100
inventory buying plans, 292
inventory turnover, 246
investment, 79
It's Just Lunch, 141

Jaffray, Richard, 23–25
Jani-King Canada, 144
Jennings, Jay, 23–25, 177, 178
Jerrett, Shanda, 54
job contacts, 92
job experience, 26, 56–57, 59
Joey's Only Seafood Restaurants, 143
Jupiter, 141

Kan, Mandy, 57–59
Kauffman Foundation
Entrepreneurship, 191–192
Kaufman, Crystal, 54
Keg Steakhouse and Bar, 140
key business ratios in Canada, 99*f*
key-person insurance, 177
Kielburger, Craig and Mark, 29
Kielland, Peter, 279
Kluger, Jen, 293, 294
Knowles, Ronald A., 77
Kojima, Toshiko, 130
KPMG, 101

Labour, 333
labour force, 79
Ladybug Foundation, 30–31
Lamontagne, Jacques, 56–57
land-use regulations, 174
Lawrence, Jeanne, 100, 101
leasehold improvements, 292–293
leasing, 292
leasing facilities, 206–207
legal counsel, 147

letter of transmittal, 326
leverage ratios, 256, 258
liabilities, 27–28, 254
licensing, 65, 172, 174, 205
lifestyle ventures, 55
limited-function wholesalers, 216
limited liability, 162, 164
limited liability partnership (LLP), 163
limited partnership, 162–163
line of credit, 288, 297
liquidation value, 106
liquidity ratios, 256, 258
loan application assessment
worksheet, 316*f*
Loblaw, 35
Corporate Social Responsibility
Report, 35, 36*f*
location
facilities, buying or leasing, 206–207
home-based businesses,
207–208, 209
manufacturers' concerns, 205
product/operations plan, 333
retail location rating form, 229–230*f*
selection considerations, 205
Loiselle, 101
Lombardi, Vince, 12
long-term expectations, 55–56
long-term liabilities, 256
loss-of-income insurance, 176
love money, 293, 295
Lululemon Athletica, 283
Lundström, Linda, 7

MacDonald, Jason, 63–64
Machat, Dr. Jeff, 34
Madmax Worldwide Sourcing Inc., 283
magazines, 64
management, 6
management buyout, 308
management consulting, 71
management team, 333–334
managerial skills inventory, 25, 44–45
mandatory deductions, 174
Manitoba Business Start Program, 300
Manitoba Wildlife Rehabilitation
Organization, 93
Mann, Ted, 168
manufacturer's agents, 216
manufacturing plans and costs, 333
Mari's Maternity Mattress (MMM),
196, 197
Maritime Trading Co. (MTC), 322
market, 79, 102
market analysis, 102, 330–331
market assessment
customer survey, 195
determining your market, 185–186
estimating total market size and
trends, 198–200, 225*f*
location selection, 205
market research, 187–193
market-testing your idea, 193–195
segment your market, 102, 187, 195
types of markets, 185
market niche, focus on, 201

market profile, 204, 223*f*
market research
Canada Business Services for
Entrepreneurs, 189–190
company information, 221–222*t*
definition of, 187
do-it-yourself market research, 196
general published sources of market
information, 221*t*
industry and market
information, 221*t*
industry and trade associations,
188–189
Internet, 190–192
interpretation of results, 196
market size, estimate of, 198–
200, 225*f*
marketing information, 221–222*t*
need for information, 188
observational methods, 192
primary data collection, 192–195
questioning methods, 192–193
sales forecast, 201, 203–208,
228–229*f*
secondary data search, 188–192
steps, 187
survey research, 195
trade and professional
associations, 222*t*
trade publications, 189, 191*t*
trends, estimate of, 198–200
Market Research, 220
Market Research Handbook, 188, 190
market segmentation, 102, 187, 195
market share, 331
market size, estimate of, 102, 198–200,
201, 203–204, 225*f*, 331
marketing advantage, 201
Marketing Basic, 220
marketing considerations, 102
marketing consultants, 147
marketing mix, 209–216
See also mix
marketing plan, 187, 216–218, 231–
240*f*, 331–332
markup pricing, 210
markups, 210
master franchise, 132
maturity of loan, 288
Maxwell, Jodi, 165, 166–167
McGowan, Ross, 66–69
measurable market, 79
merchant wholesalers, 216
MetaCrawler, 191
micro-loan funds, 311
milestones, 334
mission statement, 318–320
Mitha, Karim, 309–311
mix
described, 209
distribution channels, 215–216
pricing strategies, 209–211
product or service offering, 209
promotional plans, 211–215
modified book value, 105
Mohammed, Nigel, 324

Molly Maid, 144
money, 8
Money Hunt Business Plan Template, 327
Moot Corp Competition, 337
Morison, Scott, 23–25
mountain climbers, 22–23
Mountain Equipment Co-op, 167
municipal licences and taxes, 172, 205
municipal services, 205

Naisbitt, John, 72
name, business, 169, 171–172, 173–174
Napper, Terry, 103
National Angel Organization (NAO), 305
National Association of Retail Grocers, 95
national entrepreneurship test, 41
National Post, 64
National Red Scarf Campaign, 30
National Research Council of Canada, 299
National Retail Hardware Association, 95
Nazomi Communications, 219
NBS Apparel, 178
negotiating the deal, 114
Nerd Force, 141
net book value, 105
net cash flow, 252
net lease, 206
net operating profit or loss, 245
net profit, 96, 246
net profit ratio, 258
net-profit-to-sales ratio, 96
net sales, 245
net worth, 95, 254, 256
Nettoyeur Equipment Travail Sport (NETS) Inc., 186
Neufeld, Cameron, 128, 130–131
new invention, 182
newsletters, 64
Newsletters in Print, 64
newspapers, 64, 92
Nianiaris, Dr. Nick, 34
99 lives, 70
non-disclosure agreement (NDA), 280, 286
Northern Light, 192
not-for-profit organizations, 164
not-so-learnable characteristics, 19
Notable TV, 66, 67, 76
Nuthin Better Cybermall, 213

objections, handling of, 215
objectives, 320–321
observational methods, 60, 62, 192
oil and gas industry, 2
Okazaki, Mari, 196, 197
on-site computer service, 71
1-800-GOT-JUNK, 128, 130–131
one-store test, 195
one-time expenditures, 242
online business model, 75–76

online gaming, 71
Ontario Business Corporations Act, 168
Ontario College of Physicians and Surgeons, 168
operating expenses, 243, 247–248
operating loans, 297
operational business plan, 323, 325
operations manual, 147
opinions, obtaining from distributors, 194
opportunity
    best businesses for the future, 72–74
    comparing possible solutions with, 78–82
    described, 8
    entrepreneurial, 50f
    future opportunity areas, 70–74
    most promising opportunities, focus on, 82
    selection process, 77
    social trends, 70–71
    starting with, 16
    SWOT analysis, 199
    top 10 business opportunities, 71
    top 10 home business opportunities, 209
opportunity orientation, 16
opportunity recognition, 50–55
    model for, 52–54, 52f
organizational structure. *See* business organization
organizing your business. *See* business organization
Orol, Suzie, 293, 294
Outpost, 302, 303–304
outsourcing, 2

PairoWoodies Publishing, 169, 170
Palo Alto Software, 337
parallel search engines, 191
participating leases, 206
partnership, 160–163
    agreement, 160, 163
    general, 160, 162
    insurance, 177
    limited, 162–163
    limited liability, 163
Pasternak, Bobby, 216–218
Patent Cooperation Treaty, 275
patents, 272–275, 279–281
    agent, 273
    application, 273–274
    commercializing, 280
    criteria, 272
    invention scams and, 280–281
    protection provided, 274–275, 279–280
    search, 274
payroll deductions, 174
Peale, Norman Vincent, 32
peer loan funds, 311
Pelz, Dave, 68
penalty clauses, 207
percentage leases, 206
performance expectations, 308

Performance Plus Small-Business Profiles, 259
perishability, 80
perseverance, 15
personal credit cards, 292
personal equity, 113
personal finances
    assessment of, 27
    balance sheet, 27–28, 46–47f
    budget, 28, 47–48f
personal funds, 291
personal goals, 77
personal indulgences, 72–73
Personal Living Expenses Worksheet, 47–48f
personal network, 92–93
personal observation, 60, 62
personal responsibility, 16
personal self-assessment, 21–22
Personal Self-Assessment Questionnaire, 48–49f
personal selling, 215
personal services, 73–74
personal values, 29
pet care and pampering, 73, 149
Pizza Pizza, 128, 129–130, 144
Planning Guides: Manage Your Business and Watch It Grow, 259
pleasure revenge, 72
Plus Minus Interesting (PMI) assessment, 66
Pointts, 141
Poole, Tom, 21–22
Popcorn, Faith, 70–72
post-sale activities, 215
potential. *See* entrepreneurial potential
power, low need for, 17–18
Preferred Perch, The, 92, 93
preparation, 52
presentation, 215
Prestige Dance Academy, 293, 296
price markup chain, 210, 210t
price multiplier, 109
pricing strategies, 209–211, 307, 331
primary data, 192–195, 199
prime rate, 288, 297
principal of loan, 288
principals, 160
private companies, 169
PRK, 34
pro forma statements
    analysis of, 256
    balance sheet, 254, 256, 257f, 335
    cash flow statement, 255f
    financial ratios, 256
    income statement, 245–248, 247f, 249f, 270
    sample, 247f
problem areas, 78
problem solving, 16
problem statement, 193
product distribution arrangements, 127
product liability, 80
product licensing information services, 65
product offering, 209

production/operations plan, 332–333
professional advisors, 334
professional buyers, 194
professional corporations, 164
PROFIT magazine, 7, 13, 64, 314
profit and loss forecasts, 335
profit potential, 184
profit trend, 94
profitability ratios, 256, 258
PROFITguide, 22, 34
projected income sheet, 107*f*
promising industries, 77–78
promotional plans
    advertising, 212–213
    business plan, 332
    comparison of promotional
        activities, 212*t*
    described, 211–212
    personal selling, 215
    public relations, 215
    sales promotion, 215
proprietary right, 81, 332
propriety, 31
ProQuest, 192
prospecting, 215
prototype, 193–194
provincial government financial
        assistance programs, 300–302
provincial licences or permits, 172
Prueckel, Barb, 171
psychographic factors, 187
public companies, 167
public domain, 272, 281
public relations, 215
public relations consulting, 71
publications, 64–65, 189, 191*t*
publicity, 80
purchase price. *See* valuation of a
        business
purchasing a business. *See* business
        acquisition
put option, 308

Quagmire Golf, 216–218
qualifying, 215
quantity discounts, 211
query, 192
questioning methods, 192–193
questionnaires, 193, 194
quick ratio, 95, 258
Quizno's Classic Subs, 140

rack jobbers, 216
Rae, David, 82
Ransom, Chris, 296
ratio analysis, 95–98, 99*t*, 256
ratio calculator, 259
readiness for entrepreneurial career,
        28–29
reality orientation, 16
Reavie, Chez, 217
recognized market, 79
Red River Co-op, 167
Registrar of Companies, 167
registration, 167, 169, 281
regulation, 79

reliability, 18
rental costs, 206
repeat purchases, 198
resources, 8
restaurants, 127, 138, 144, 149
retail boutiques, 73
retailers, 216
retraction clause, 308
return on assets, 96, 258
return on owner investment, 258
right of first refusal, 139
right stuff, 14
rights, 100
rightsizing, 2
risk, 175–177, 184, 334
risk management, 175–177
Risk Management Association, 95
risk-taking and risk-sharing, 17
risk taking, 6
Robert Morris Associates, 95, 246
Robinson, Dan, 62, 63–64
Robinson, Matt, 302, 303–304
Rogers, Stan, 278
Rosen, Harry, 118, 119
Rosen, Larry, 118, 119
Rothenberger, Debie, 160–161
rule-of-thumb valuation approaches,
        109–111
Russell, Bertrand, 60

sales approach, 215
sales forecast
    bottom-up approach, 203–204
    developing, 201, 203–208,
        228–229*f*
    external factors affecting, 204
    formula for, 201
    internal factors affecting, 204
    market size, estimate of, 201, 203,
        204, 225*f*
    top-down approach, 203
sales letter e-commerce Web site, 75
sales promotion, 215
sales-to-inventory ratio, 96
sampling procedure, 193
Saskatchewan Wheat Pool, 167
Save the Children, 29
Say, Jean-Baptiste, 6
schedule, 334
Schuermans, Nico and Kerri, 248, 251
Schuster, Joe, 63–64
Scott, Ian, 169, 170
Scudamore, Brian, 131
search accelerators, 191
search engine optimization, 71
search engines, 190, 191
Search.com, 191
seasonal discounts, 211
secondary data, 188–192, 198
seed capital, 288
segment, 195
Self-Assessment Questionnaire, 48–49
self-confidence, 16
Self-Employment Program, 300
self-reliance, 16
seller financing, 113

selling agents, 216
senior care, 73, 149
service and warranty program, 332
service business Web site, 75–76
service offering, 209
setting up your business. *See also*
        business start-ups
    business licence, 172, 174
    employment standards, 175
    incorporation, 167, 169
    insurance, 176–177
    key points, 177
    land use and zoning, 174
    mandatory deductions and
        taxes, 174
    name, choosing, 169, 171–172,
        173–174
    registration, 167, 169
    risk management, 175–177
shareholder agreement, 165
shareholders, 163, 334
shares, 111, 113, 163
Shepherd, Chuck, 278
Shoniker, Bob, 304
Shopka, Bryan, 54
Short Game Golf Corporation, 68
Shutout Solutions Inc., 63–64
Simplex Problem Solving Process, 66
simplified balance sheet, 97–98*f*
single-unit franchise, 132
Skoll, Jeff, 29
small businesses
    failure, reasons for, 11*f*
    long-term expectations, 55–56
    skills required by, 25, 25*f*
small indulgences, 72
small, profitable ventures, 55–56
SmallBusinessPoint.com, Inc., 337
social entrepreneurship, 29–30
social funds, 311
social networks, 66
social responsibility, 35
social trends, 70
sociological factors, 187
soft costs, 242
sole proprietorship, 158–160
SOS (Save Our Society), 72
Source, The, 144
Spark Innovations Inc., 279
specialized search engines, 191
SpecialsToday.ca, 309–311
specification, 273
spiders, 190
stages of building your dream
        described, 3*f*
    entrepreneurial process,
        outline of, 9*f*
Standard Rate and Data Service, 64
Starbucks Corp., 283
Start and Run Your Own Business, 220
start-up. *See* business start-ups
starting a business. *See* business start-
        ups; setting up your business
Statistics Canada, 126, 188, 220
    Census, 190
status, low need for, 17–18

Steinhoff, D., 246
Step-by-Step Guide to Exporting,
    The, 220
stock, 163
Stoner, Brian, 196, 197
strategy, 8
strengths, 199
stress management, 29
subject guides, 191–192
subletting, 206
Subway, 144
success orientation, 16
succession issues, 116–118
succession plan
    business environment
        considerations, 117
    family acceptance of, 118
    grooming an heir, 118
    implementing, 118
    outside assistance for, 118
    principal owner's hopes and
        desires, 117
    reasons for omission of, 116
    successful transition, 117–118
    successor's qualities, 117
    timing, 117
    type of business, 117
Sullivan, Steve, 59–60
summary business plan, 323
summary of earnings sheet, 107*f*
Summer Company program, 301
supplier financing, 292
supply situation, 218–219
supply source, 79
surety and fidelity bonds, 177
survey research, 192–193, 195
Swinton, Martin and Andrea, 213, 214
Swiss Chalet Chicken & Ribs, 144
SWOT analysis, 199–200
SWOT matrix, 200, 228*f*
Szalwinski, Richard, 304
Szonyi, A. J., 246

table of contents, 326
Tait, Geoff, 216–218
Tait, John and Elisa, 102, 103
Take-A-Boo Emporium, 214
tangible assets, value of, 98, 100, 287
target market, 187, 331
Taylor McCaffrey LLP, 161
Taylor, Reeh, 161
taxes
    federal, 174
    Goods and Services Tax (GST), 174
    Harmonized Sales Tax (HST), 174
    Incentives, 80
    mandatory deductions for, 174
    municipal, 172, 205
    provincial, 174
    treatment, 80, 164
Taylor, Hannah, 30
team building, 18
technical feasibility, 182, 184

technical obsolescence, 80
technical support, 149
Tell Us About Us (TUAU), 62
Tennessee Jack's Rotisserie Chicken 'N'
    Ribs, 143
term loan, 288, 297
testing your product idea, 193–195
Thibault, Claude, 304
3 for 1 Pizza and Wings (Canada)
    Inc., 134
third party lenders, 113
threats, 199–200
times interest earned ratio, 258
Timmons, J.A., 53
Tip Top Tailors, 119
title page, 326
Titus, Brian, 300, 301
TLC Laser Eye Centres, 33, 34
top-down approach, 203
total demand, 198
Trackitback, 60–61
trade associations, 92, 188–189
trade publications, 64–65, 189, 191*t*
trade secrets, 286
trade shows, 65, 195
Trade Shows Worldwide, 65
Trade-Marks Act, 283
Trade-marks Journal, 282
trademarks, 281–283
    maintaining and policing, 282–283
    marking requirements, 283
    registering, 281–282
    search, 281
training, 138
training program, 147
Trans-HERB Inc., 312
TransUnion Canada, 28
trends, 94, 102, 149, 198–200, 331
triggering event, 4
triple bottom line, 35
triple net lease, 206
truck wholesalers, 216
True North Clothing Company,
    281, 282
trust companies, 297
typical feasibility study, 183*f*

UBC Research Enterprises, 65
Ultimate Fighting Championship,
    63–64
Ultra Violet Floral Studio, 201, 202
uncertainty, tolerance of, 17
Underwriters Laboratory (UL)
    certification, 184
unit sales, 198
unlimited liability, 162
Urban Canine, 322–323, 324

valuation of a business
    balance sheet methods, 104,
        105–106, 105*f*
    case study, 111–112
    earnings-based methods, 104

income statement methods, 106–
    109, 108*f*
    methods, 104–111, 109*t*
    rule-of-thumb approaches,
        109–111, 110*t*
    value-based pricing, 210–211
Vamvakas, Elias, 33, 34
Vanderzwan, Catherine, 5
variable costs, 258
variable expenses, 245
variable operating expenses, 245
venture capital, 302, 307–308
venture concept, 180–182
Venture Opportunity Screening Model
    (VOSM), 82–86
Versluis, Sherrie, 92, 93
Versper, Karl, 23
vigilante consumer, 72
vision statement, 318

Wagner, Jason, 60–61
Waldon, Janet, 200–201, 202
Wall, George, 168
Wall Street Journal, The, 64
Ward, Susan, 75
Warrilow, John, 22
weaknesses, 199
weather, 81
Web sites, 74, 75–76
WebFerret, 191
wellness trend, 72
Wellspring Worldwide LLC, 65
Western Economic Diversification
    Canada, 299–300, 315
What's Your Business Worth?, 314
wholesalers, 216
Williams, Michelle Shaw, 165,
    166–167
Williamson, Jessica, 54
Wilson, Chip, 283
Wine Kitz, The, 144
Wishbone Custom Rods, 170
Wolfe, Tom, 14
Women's Enterprise Initiative, 299–300
Workers' Compensation, 177
Workers' Compensation Board, 174
WorldCom, 31
Woudstra, Wendy, 169, 170
Wovenfare International Inc., 165,
    166–167
Woytiuk, Vivian, 296
Writing an Effective Business Plan, 327

Yahoo!, 191
Your Guide to Government Financial
    Assistance for Business, 302
Youth Employment Services
    (YES), 41
Youth Employment Strategy, 299

Zevulunov, Erez, 7
zoning regulations, 174, 205